SDL '97
TIME FOR TESTING
SDL, MSC and Trends

SDL '97
TIME FOR TESTING
SDL, MSC and Trends

Proceedings of the Eighth SDL Forum
Evry, France, 23-26 September, 1997

edited by

Ana CAVALLI
INSTITUT NATIONAL DES TELECOMMUNICATIONS
Evry, France

Amardeo SARMA
EURESCOM
Heidelberg, Germany

1997

ELSEVIER
Amsterdam • Lausanne • New York • Oxford • Shannon • Singapore • Tokyo

ELSEVIER SCIENCE PUBLISHERS B.V.
Sara Burgerhartstraat 25
P.O. Box 211, 1000 AE Amsterdam, The Netherlands

ISBN: 0 444 82816 8

This book is printed on acid-free paper.

Transferred to digital printing 2006
Printed and bound by CPI Antony Rowe, Eastbourne

INTRODUCTION

It seems quite incredible to be looking back 16 years to the First SDL Forum in 1981. Considering that SDL existed for some years before that, the coming Eighth SDL Forum may have the first participant younger than the language itself. This is quite remarkable, given that the computing environment of today is totally different from the one 16 or 20 years ago. It gives us an opportunity to reflect on the path SDL has taken and on why SDL has been successful over two decades where other languages addressing the same market have failed. The use of a graphical syntax for SDL may have seemed strange for many in the 70s or early 80s. No one had a computer with graphical facilities. Some engineers used templates to draw diagrams until late in the 80s. It almost seems as if SDL had been conceived of in the 70s for the 90s. But it is not only the graphical syntax that has been a strength of SDL. Developers of SDL have remained in close contact with the users, both within ITU and outside to make sure that it meets the needs of the customers. This goes to the credit of all those working with SDL at CCITT, now ITU, since the Question on SDL was established. It was more important to see SDL applied in reports at conferences than to hear of yet another proof of some theoretical interest. This close link to customers of SDL and to vendors developing SDL tools is one of the reasons for success that must be maintained.

Another event since the last SDL Forum is important enough to be mentioned specifically. A Common Interchange Format or "CIF" has finally been established, giving users the possibility to interchange SDL specifications without losing graphical information. This can be especially useful for people working across companies and departments using different tools, for example in projects. It is also reassuring to see that ETSI and ITU are finally making full use of the potential of SDL by using tools and checking specifications for errors. This quality aspect has long been advocated by ITU-T Study Group 10 and it is good to see that ETSI and ITU are beginning to see the benefits that a formal language can offer.

SDL now also has a permanent companion in MSC, Message Sequence Charts. Ekkart Rudolph and Jens Grabowski could hardly have known that their paper in 1989, incidentally the first paper in the Proceedings, would end up as a standard language. MSC today is a language in its own right and has its areas of application both in conjunction with SDL and independently or in combination with other techniques. MSC has strong structuring concepts to specify message sequences for large systems and can be used to develop scenarios. This is extremely helpful for test and design environments. The SDL Forum today really is the SDL and MSC Forum. This also applies to the new organisation, the SDL Forum Society (http://www.sdl-forum.org), which is responsible for disseminating information on SDL and MSC and promotes these languages. The intention of this organisation is not to take over the work done so far in ITU, but rather to use the flexibility of a small organisation to deal with promotion work and to keep in touch with users all over the world. The SDL Forum Society, led by Yair Lahav, now owns the SDL Forum Conference Series.

We hope this SDL Forum will be useful to all those attending and that they will exchange ideas and take back impulses to their home company. In these days of competition, we can hardly expect many enthusiasts to be primarily interested in promoting SDL or MSC. But if they find means to use SDL and MSC to the benefit of their company, this is all we can hope for. It is only their success with SDL and MSC that will end up being a success for SDL and MSC. And if the Forum also provides some ideas for research at universities or elsewhere, so much the better. The Eighth SDL Forum would have served its purpose.

The Eighth SDL Forum will be held in Evry, France, at the INT (Institut National des Télécommunications). It is organized by the INT with the collaboration of the CNET (Centre National d'Etudes des Telecommunications). INT is an engineering telecommunication school and one of the first involved in teaching the SDL language and in the research on test generation methods from SDL specifications. CNET is the research center of France Telecom and one the most important in Europe. SDL is largely used by their engineers in different domains such as protocol engineering and test generation methods from SDL specifications, especially in the area of ISDN systems, ATM networks, Intelligent networks and mobile communication. These contributions have helped the introduction and use of SDL technology in French industry.

Our thanks go to the authors, who produced the papers, and to the colleagues of the program committee that carefully reviewed the manuscripts and helped set up the programme. The responsible for tutorials, Daniel Vincent, and the local organising committee, Toma Macavei, Luiz Paula Lima and Marine Tabourier, our conference secretaries, Maria Guilbert and Jocelyne Vallet, have been indispensable in putting this conference together. Finally, we mention the generous sponsorship of France Telecom, Telelogic, Verilog and INT.

Ana Cavalli and Amardeo Sarma editors

TABLE OF CONTENTS

PROGRAMME COMMITTEE

Chair persons: Ana Cavalli
Amardeo Sarma

Rolv Braek
Laura Cerchio
Pierre Combes
Jan Ellsberger
Vincent Encontre
Ove Faergemand
Joachim Fischer
Oystein Haugen
Dieter Hogrefe
Yair Lahav
Lennart Mansson
Maria Manuela Marques
Birger Moeller-Pedersen
Anders Olsen
Omar Rafiq
Rick Reed
Ekkart Rudolph
Louis Verhaard
Daniel Vincent
Milan Zoric

CORRESPONDING MEMBERS

Deepinder Sidhu
Rachida Dssouli

Applications I

Designing a Multi-User Software Environment for Development and Analysis using a combination of OMT and SDL92

Carla G. N. Macário[a*], Moacir Pedroso Jr.[b] and Walter C. Borelli[c]

[ac]Department of Telematics - Faculty of Electrical and Computer Engineering, UNICAMP, P.O.Box 6101, 13081-970, Campinas SP, Brazil. (carla,borelli)@dt.fee.unicamp.br

[b]Brazilian Agricultural Research Corporation - CNPTIA/EMBRAPA, P.O.Box 604, 13083-970, Campinas SP, Brazil. pedroso@cnptia.embrapa.br

This work presents a novel approach to the development of AIDA, a software environment for the management and statistical analysis of experimental data, being developed by EMBRAPA, Brazil. This approach combines the use of an object-oriented methodology with a SDL formal description, greatly enhancing the software development process. The proposed object model and its SDL92 specification, as well as a simulation example are giving for a multi-user AIDA network configuration.

1. INTRODUCTION

The "Ambiente Integrado para Desenvolvimento e Análise" - AIDA (Integrated Environment for Development and Analysis) [2] is the result of the evolution of another similiar software system, called SW NTIA [5] and is targeted for the management and statistical analysis of experimental data generated by Brazilian Agricultural Research Corporation - EMBRAPA, which is a government owned company with 39 research units scattered all over the country, with modern laboratories and 9500 employees, 2100 of them researchers.

Agricultural research generates large quantities of data to be analyzed. Until 1986, EMBRAPA's agricultural researchers used to send their experimental data for statistical processing at EMBRAPA's mainframe, far away from the experimental fields. It was a very awkward procedure, subject to many delays and difficulties. By the same time, microcomputers began to become available at EMBRAPA research units, and it was felt that the development of a most suitable microcomputer software system for data analysis and management was in order to alleviate those problems.

The original goal to be achieved by SW NTIA was to provide a tool to the agricultural researchers and statisticians so that they could perform most of the data management and analysis they needed at their local microcomputers. Furthermore, since some of the research units were also using some sort of minicomputers running clones of the Unix(TM) operating

* On leave from CNPTIA/EMBRAPA - Campinas - SP.

system, SW NTIA was also built to be portable among many operating systems. Besides MS-DOS, versions for many Unix variations and DEC VMS operating system were also provided. Since the main statistical system in use at EMBRAPA's mainframe at that time was the Statistical Analysis Systems - SAS [9], SW NTIA was developed to resemble that system.

SW NTIA was in permanent evolution, incorporating several user's sugestions and expanding it's scope of applicability to cover areas not originally antecipated. In a sense, it is quite successful and is still in use, although it retains its original full-screen character-oriented interface. By 1995, it was becoming very clear that the users were demanding more modern interfaces, taking advantage of the power of the newer machines and the facilities of the MS Windows operating environment.

After a quick inspection, it became clear that it would not be an easy job to convert SW NTIA to an event-based architecture, needed for modern Graphic User Interfaces - GUIs. Besides that, a lot of experience had already been accumulated indicating the best route to take was indeed the development from scratch towards to a whole new system. Among others, the new system should present funcionalities such as: software tools for descriptive statistics, linear models, linear programming and graphics, and also facilities like: report generation with customization of output format, session file with a historical of the analysis done in a working session, convertion of external files to the AIDA format, basic library of statistical and mathematical functions, and a general purpose programming language. Firstly, it would be developed a version for a single user, the mono-user AIDA system, considering already that it should be evolved to a multi-user system in future versions.

Accordingly and adopting the Object Modelling Technique - OMT [8], AIDA has been proposed as a software system framework geared towards data analysis and data management, with an easy to use programming language and interface to existing data base management systems. By "framework" it is meant a software system that provides the basic architecture upon which new facilities and functionalities could be easily added.

In this way, a demonstration version of the mono-user AIDA system, which contemplates only tools for basic statistics, has been implemented for MS-Windows operating environment, and was made to run by middle of 1996 at EMBRAPA's Informatics Center for Research in Agriculture(CNPTIA/EMBRAPA).

The present paper proposes as an alternative approach to the development of a software environment such as AIDA the use of the OMT methodology in the ealier phase of system requirements definition, accompained by the strenght of a formal description such as giving by the Specification Description Language - SDL92 [3]. The combination of both methodologies greatly enhances the software development process.

Next it is presented the object model for the multi-user AIDA system followed by its SDL specification. In the last session it is given a simulation example of a multi-user AIDA network configuration using the SDT Package[1][10] showing its corresponding message sequence chart, MSC [4].

---

[1]SDT Package, version 3.02 (SDT Base, MSC Editor and Simulator): purchased by DT/FEEC/UNICAMP through a grant from the State of Sao Paulo Foundation for Research - FAPESP (Proc. 91/3660-0).

2. THE MULTI-USER AIDA OBJECT MODEL

There are two main classes in AIDA: the Analysis Environment and the Programming Language Environment. We shall be centered on the Analysis Environment, because this part of the system mainly represents the AIDA funcionalities: the statistics and mathematical analysis, plus the output formatter and the file converter.

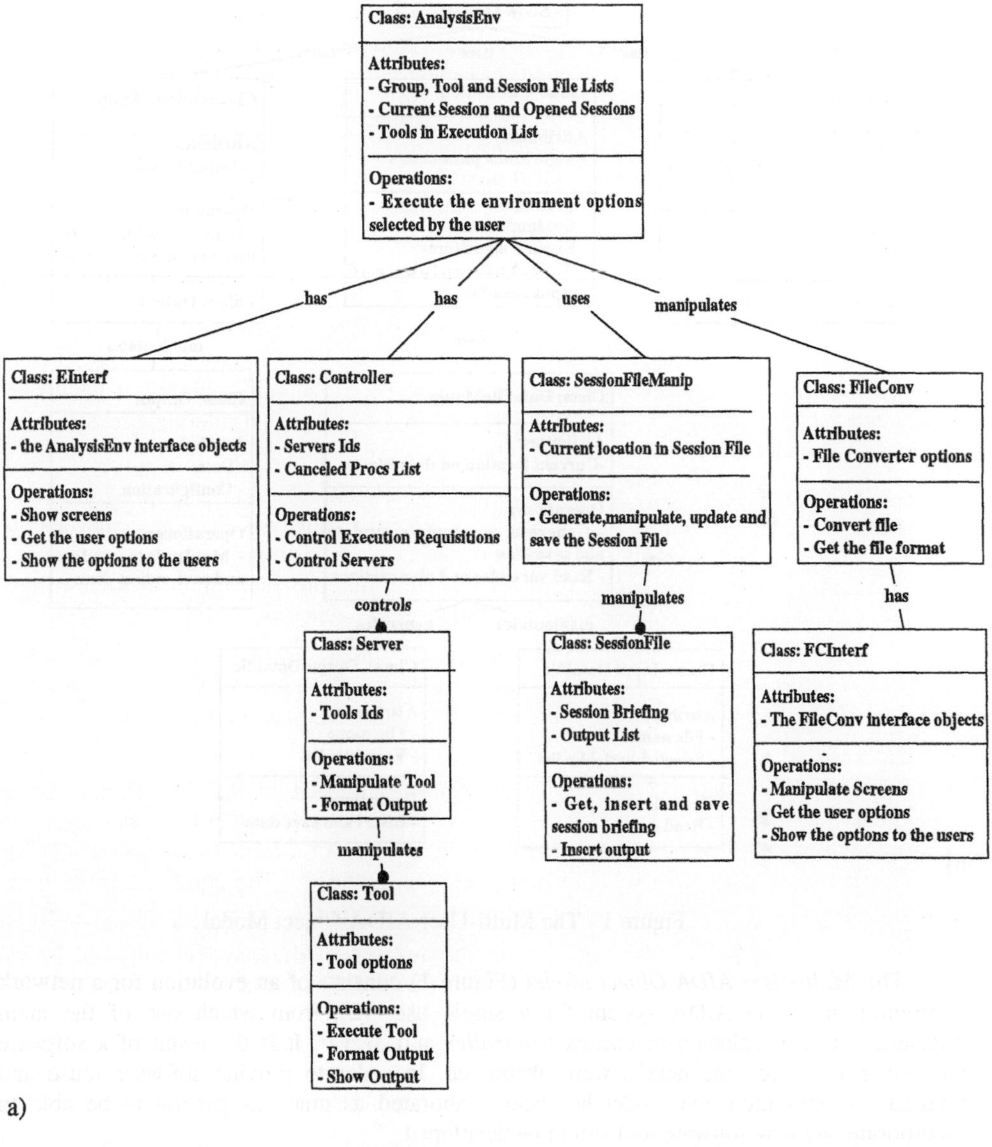

a)

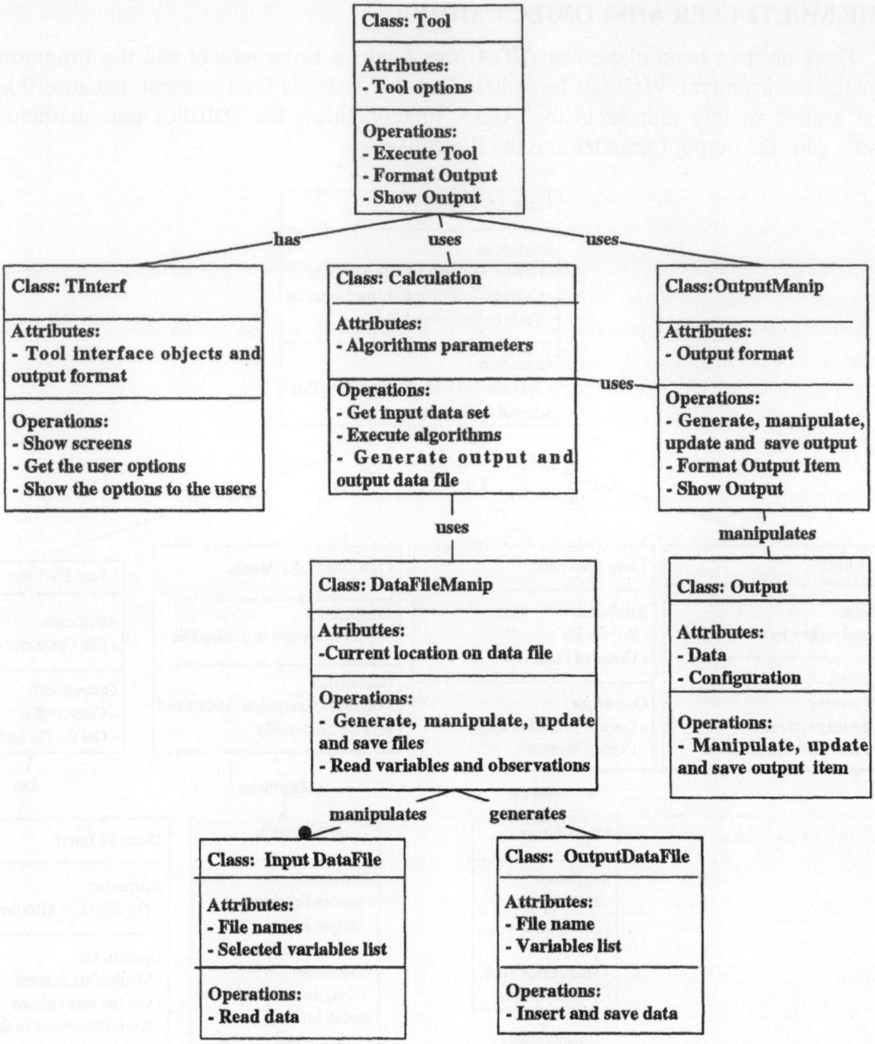

b)

Figure 1 - The Multi-User AIDA Object Model

The *Multi-User AIDA Object Model* (Figure 1) consists of an evolution for a network configuration of the AIDA system for a single user [2], from which one of the main differences is the inclusion of classes *Controller* and *Server*. It is the result of a software analysis from which the details were abstracted. In order to provide software reuse and facilitate its evolution, the model has been elaborated as much as general to be able to incorporate any new software tool still to be developed.

According to the proposed model, class *AnalysisEnv* (Figure 1 a) has some kind of association with four others classes: *EInterf*, *Controller*, *SessionFileManip* and *FileConv*. It is responsible for the manipulation of sessions and options selected by users. Class *EInterf* does the interaction between the user and the AIDA environment, and the session file manipulation is done by class *SessionFileManip*. Class *FileConv* converts external files to the AIDA format. It interacts with the users through class *FCInterf*. Class *Controller* controls the users requisitions for executing tools and formatting outputs. This class is related to class *Server*, which receives its requisitions and send them to class *Tool*.

Class *Tool* (Figure 1 b) executes each tool and formats its output. This class uses three other classes: *TInterf*, for the interaction between the user and the environment; *OutputManip*, for formatting the tool output; and *Calculation*, for executing specific algorithms and accessing data files. Class *Calculation* is related to class *OutputManip*, in order to generate the output after completing the algorithms executions. Class *DataFileManip* manipulates and generates the Input and Output Data Files, respectively.

3. THE MULTI-USER AIDA SDL MODEL

The Multi-User AIDA specification using SDL has been done in order to validate the proposed object model, for this specification language is very useful to represent the system structure and also its behaviour, using diferent levels of abstraction. Its graphics representation, called SDL-GR, does a great deal to the system understanding by heterogeneous groups enrolled in the system development [1]. Furthermore, in being a formal language, it is possible to simulate and validate the object model, using the SDT, a SDL tool for system design. The mapping from the object model to SDL92 is presented in Table 1.

OMT Classes	SDL Representation
Multi-User AIDA	System Type MultiUserAIDA, composed by block types AnalysisEnv, FileConv and Tool
AnalysisEnv	Redefined block type AnalysisEnv, composed by redefined process types AnalysisEnv and EInterf
FileConv	Block type FileConv, composed by process types FileConv and FCInterf
Tool	Redefined block type Tool, composed by process types Controller, Server, TInterf and Calculation and redefined process type Tool
Output, SessionFile, DataFile	Passive classes to be represented as Abstract Data Types -ADTs
OutputManip, SessionFileManip, DataFileManip	Classes to be represented as ADTs operations

Table 1- Mapping from OMT to SDL92

Differently from [6], the system type *MonoUserAIDA* (Figure 2) was specified using block and process types (some of them VIRTUAL), in order to evolve to the system type *MultiUserAIDA* (Figure 3), using concepts such as packages, inheritance and reuse, presented in SDL92[3]. In this way, apart from defining the new process types, i.e., *Controller* and *Server*, for the multi-user system, it was possible to reuse the entire mono-user specification, by redefining some of its block and process types.

In the mono-user version (Figure 2), there was only one user, which could execute locally a single tool *or* format a single output per time. In a different way, in the multi-user system (Figure 3), each of many users in a network concurrent fashion, is allowed to submit to more than one Server, via the Controller, several tools *and* several output formatting, at the same time, in a time-sharing basis.

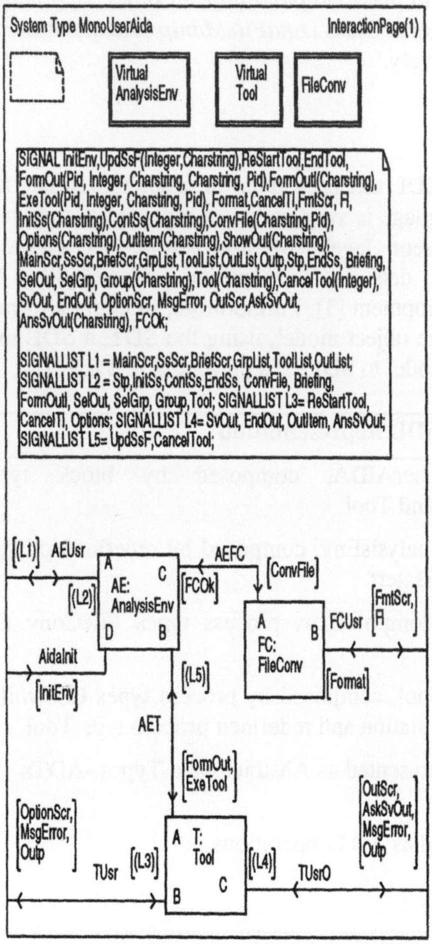

Figure 2 - System Type MonoUserAida

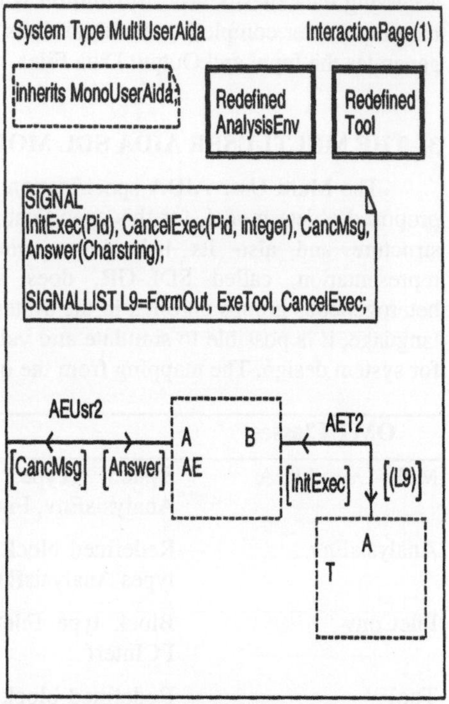

Figure 3 - System Type MultiUserAida

In this way, the multi-user AIDA system was defined inheriting the mono-user AIDA system [7], which had block types *AnalysisEnv* and *Tool* defined as VIRTUAL in order to be redefined in the multi-user system (Figure 3). The block type *FileConverter* remained without modification.

In the redefined block type *AnalysisEnv* (Figure 4) process types *AnalysisEnv* and *EInterf,* which were redefined in order to control several users, had new instances defined (*AE2* and *EI2*) to receive new signals, besides the original ones. The process *AnalysisEnv* is responsible for managing the tools execution, the file convertion, and the working sessions. It also creates instances of process *EInterf,* which represents its interface. There is one instance of process *AnalysisEnv* for each user executing the system.

In the redefined block type *Tool,* (Figure 5), process type *Tool* was redefined, to receive signals directly from process type *Server*. Process types *Controller* and *Server* were included in the multi-user system in order to manage the many users requisitions of tool executing and output formatting. While intances of process *Tool* effectively execute the users requistions, intances of process *TInterf* are responsible for the actual tool interfaces, and those of process *Calculation* for the calculation algorithms and data file accessing.

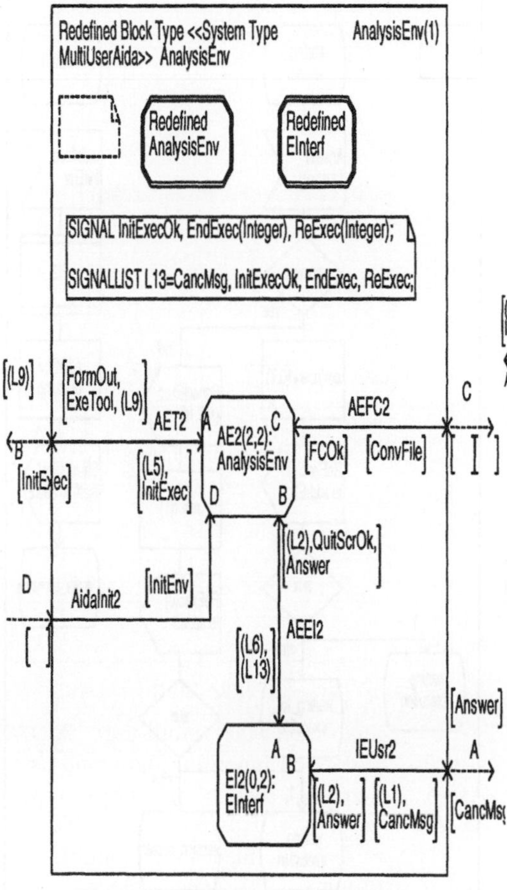

Figure 4 - Redefined Block Type AnalysisEnv

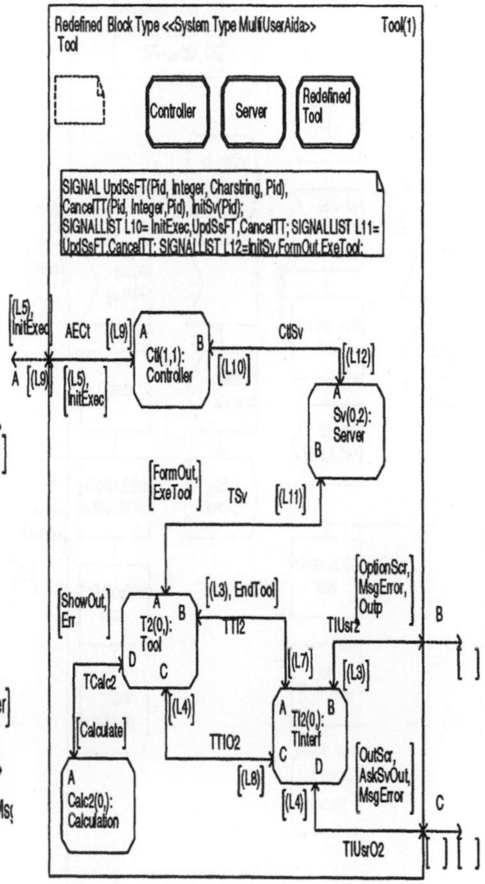

Figure 5 - Redefined Block Type Tool

The specification of processes in SDL mainly represents the messages exchange between them. Like in the object model, tasks were abstracted and represented in SDL using TASK symbols with a text describing the corresponding action, for instance: 'save output' and 'execute algorithm'.

Unlikely in the mono-user system, process *AnalysisEnv* (Figure 6) has now a timer *T*, which is set whenever each of its users makes a requisition, to indicate the maximum period of time that this process shall wait an answer of process *Controller* signalling that its requisition had been succeded. Otherwise, if no confirmation is received, the user is asked by interface process *EInterf* either to mantain or to remove its requisition from the process *Controller* queue.

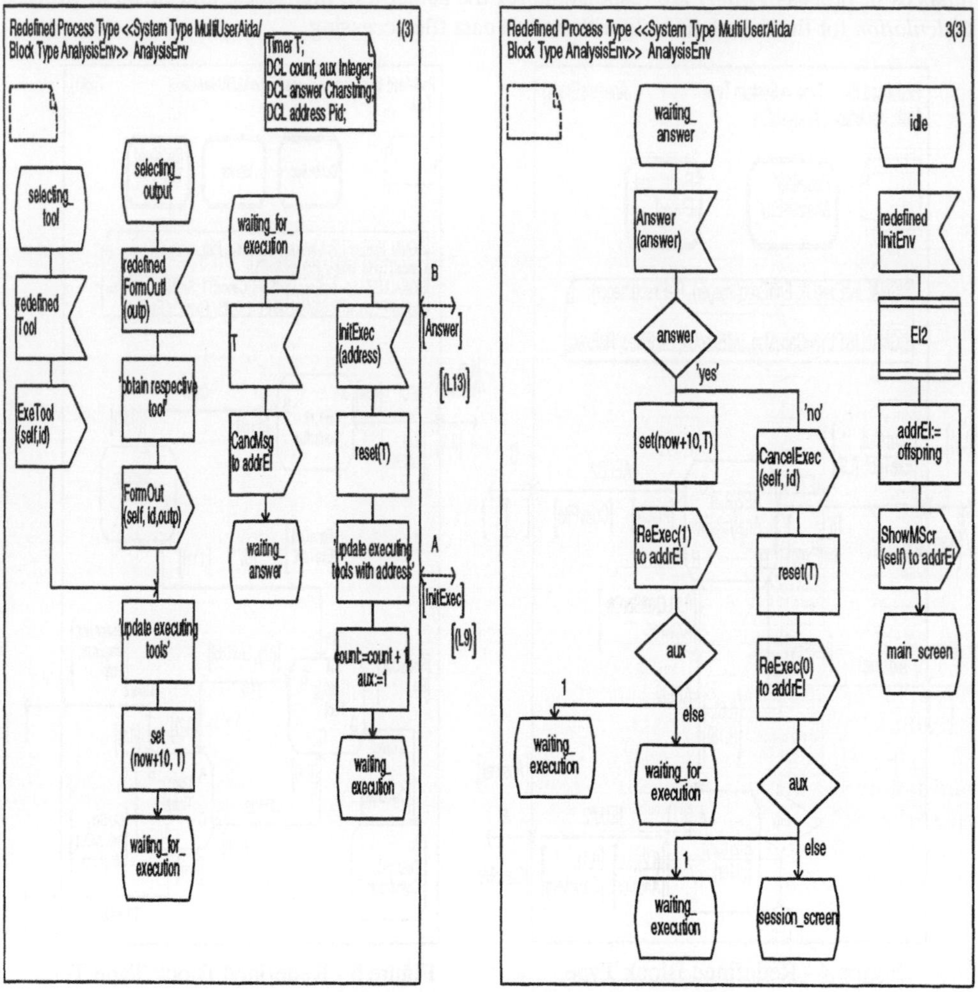

Figure 6 - Redefined Process Type AnalysisEnv (Partial)

Process types *Controller* and *Server* are given in Figure 7 and Figure 8, respectively. Suppose without any lack of generality, that each instance of process type *Server* can execute only a limited number of requisitions. Then, when there is no *Server* available, process *Controller* put in a queue (via the SAVE construction) every eventual new requisition from users.

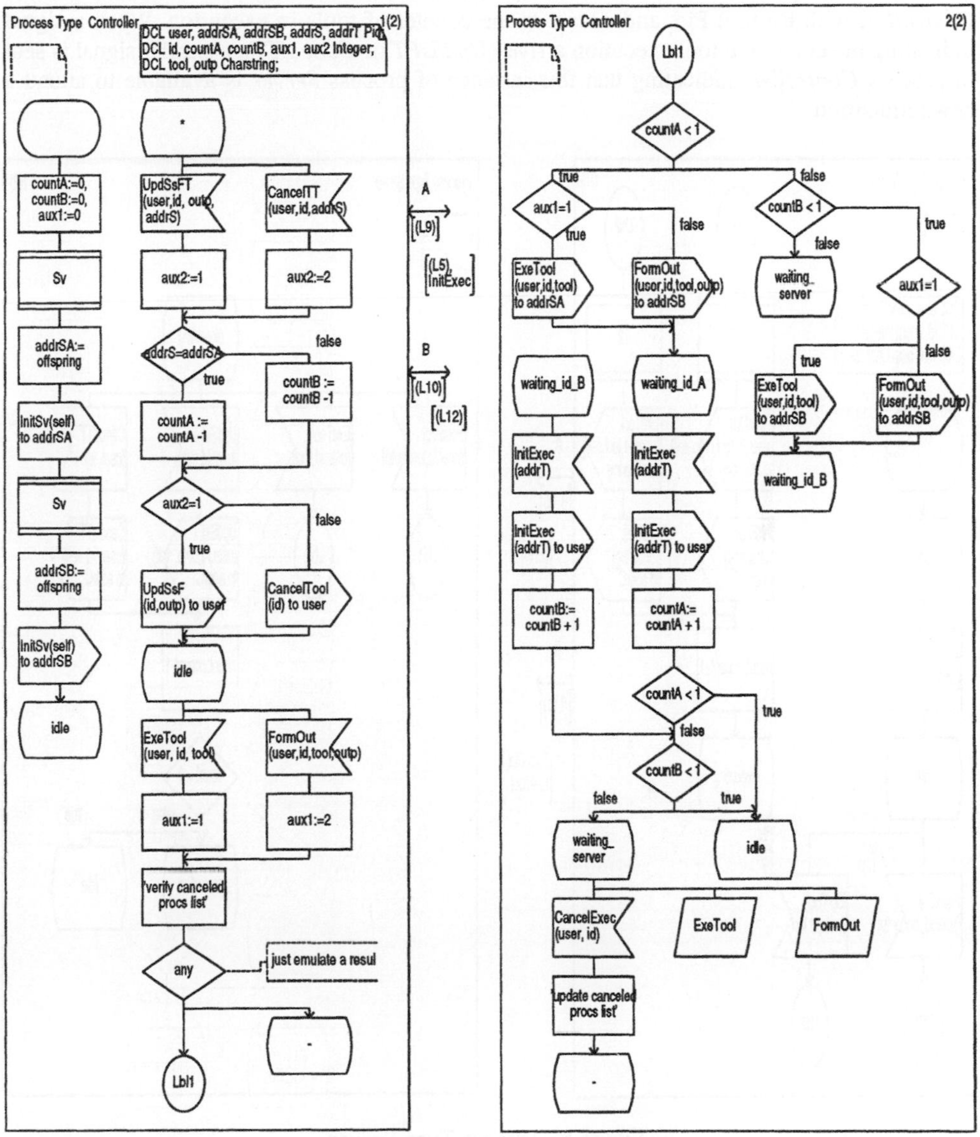

Figure 7 - Process Type Controller

On the other hand, whenever one of the *Server* instances is ready to execute a new requisition, process *Controller* gets the first signal in its queue with a FIFO policy, and send it to that *Server*.

Whenever an instance of process *Server*(Figure 8) receives a requisition, it creates an instance *T2* of process *Tool*, initializes its execution, returns signal *InitExec* to process *Controller*, with the tool Pid, and adds 1 to the counter of tools in execution. When a signal indicating the end of the tool execution arrives(*UpdSsFT* or *CancelTT*), a similar signal is sent to process *Controller*, indicating that this instance of process *Server* is available to attend a new requisition.

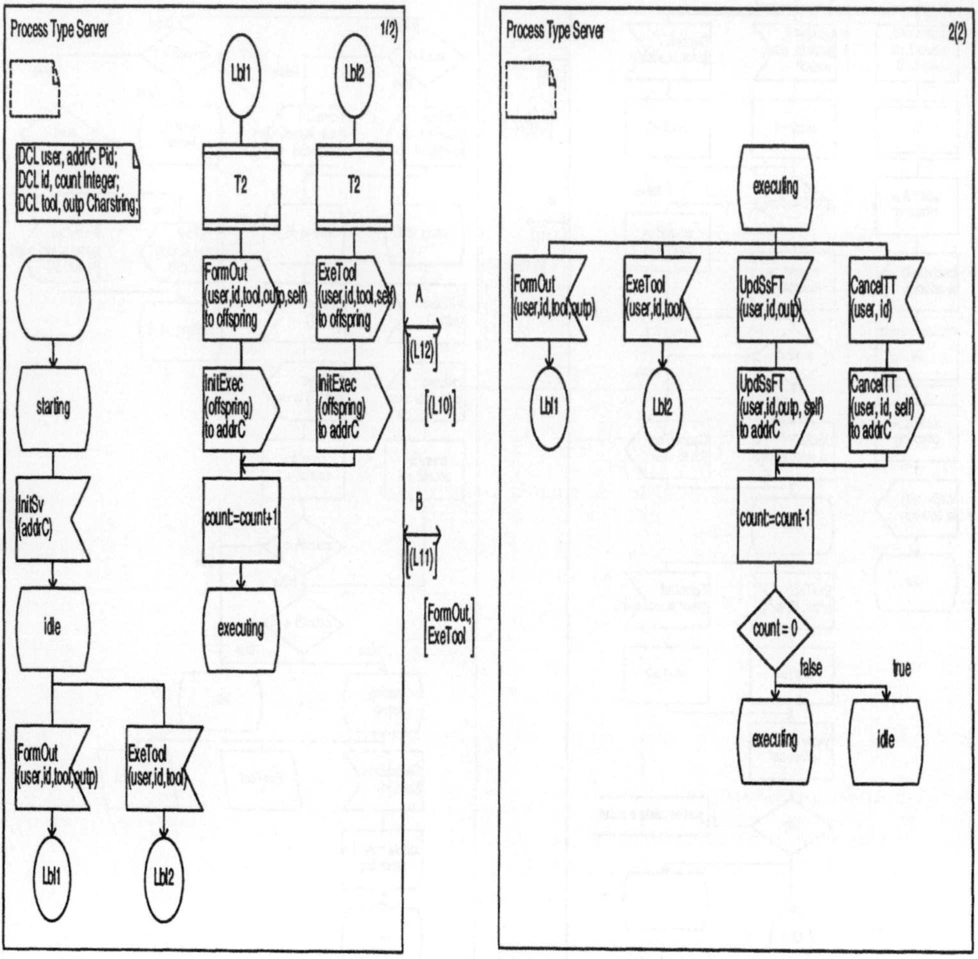

Figure 8 - Process Type Server

Process *Tool* (Figure 9) was redefined to create instances *TI2* and *Calc2* of process types *TInterf* and *Calculation,* and to include some new signals, for instance: *CancelTT* and *UpdSsFT,* with additional information on the user identification.

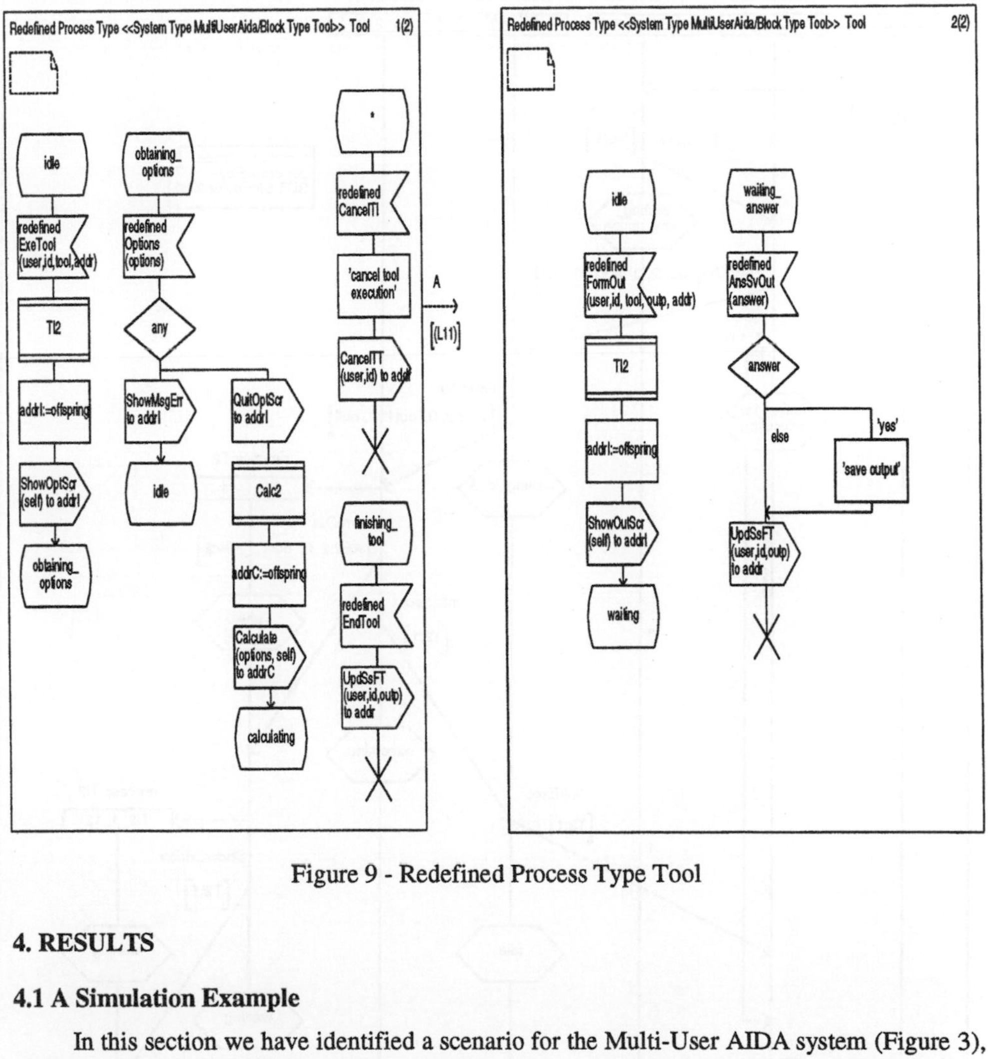

Figure 9 - Redefined Process Type Tool

4. RESULTS

4.1 A Simulation Example

In this section we have identified a scenario for the Multi-User AIDA system (Figure 3), with only two users and two servers executing, each, a maximum of one requisition per time. In the simulation example, User1 starts executing one tool and User2 formatting one output. Then, User2 tries to execute another tool simultaneously. However, as only two requisitions may be attended at the same time, the second requisition of User2 will be accepted only when one of the servers has completed its job.

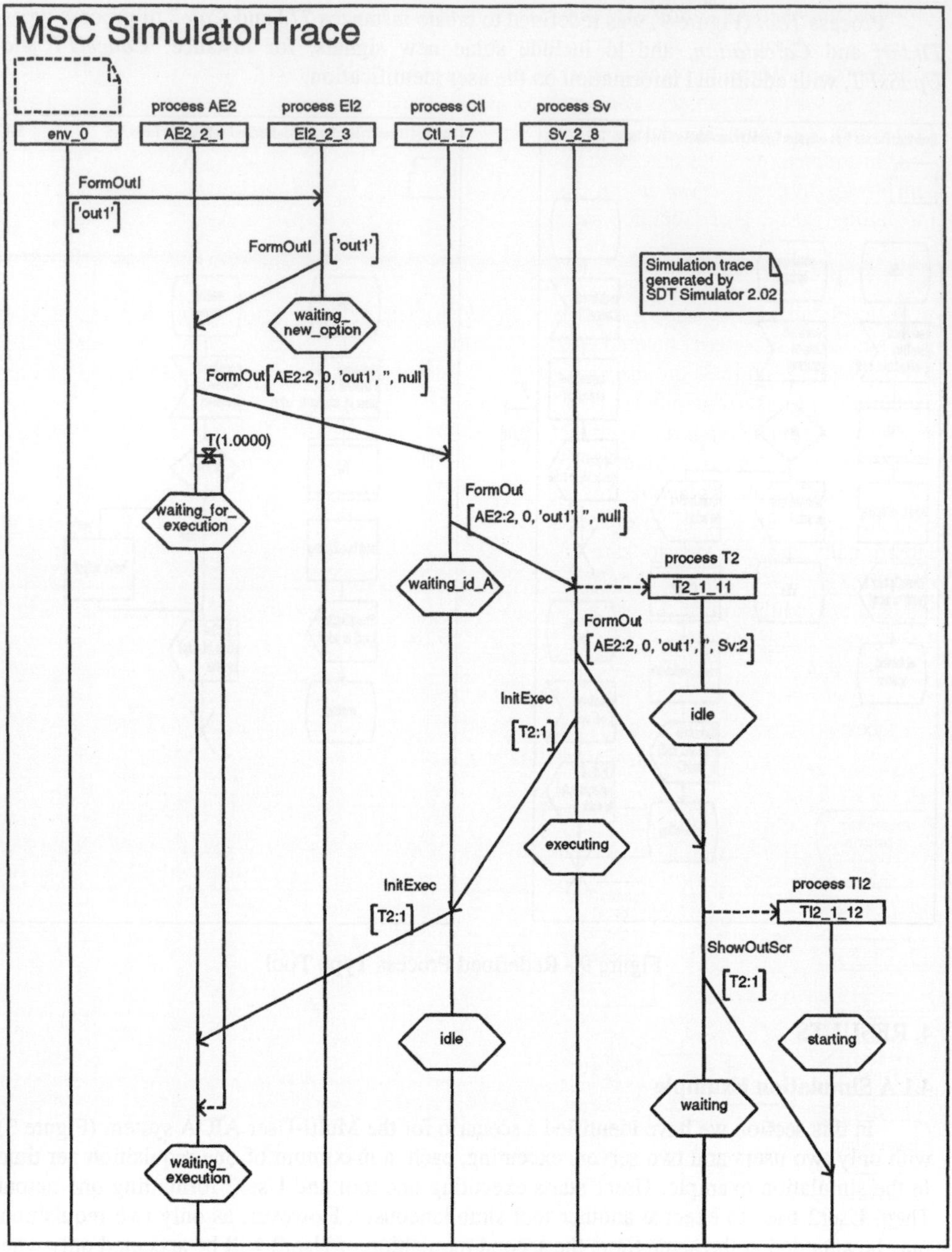

Figure 10 - Part of a Simulation Example

Part of the simulation example is represented by corresponding MSC SimulatorTrace, which is generated by the SDT Simulator 2.02[10], and is presented in Figure 10. It corresponds to the point when User2 is making its first requisition of formatting one output. A timer *T* is set up by process *AnalysisEnv* (*AE2*), the *FormOut* requisition is sent to process *Controller* (*Ctl*) and from this to process *Server* (*Sv*), which creates an instance *T2* of process *Tool* in order to execute this requisition. When an instance *T2* is created, a signal *InitEnv* is sent from process *Server* to process *Controller*, and from this to process *AnalysisEnv*, indicating that the tool execution has been started.

4.2 Identification of Errors

In Figure 11, it is shown a situation of a specification error being detected by simulation very similar to those encountered during the various simulations sessions with the Multi-User AIDA system (Figure 3). In this figure, process *Tool* is in state *obtaining_options*, receives the execution options from process *TInterf*, creates an instance *Calc2* of process *Calculation*, sends to it a signal *Calculate*, with the execution options and goes to state *calculating*, waiting for the result of the calculation algorithm. Process *Calculation* when is created, goes to state *idle*, receives signal *Calculate* from process *Tool*, executes the required calculations and, to emulate the occurrence of an eventual error by the calculating algorithm, variable ***result*** was intentionally made equal to zero. Signal *Err* is sent to process *Tool*, which is in state *calculating* and is prepared only to receive signal *ShowOut*, which alternatively would indicate the exhibition of the correct algorithm results. Hence, the simulation halts for signal *Err* is not being consumed as indicated by the asterisk "*" in the corresponding MSC SimulatorTrace.

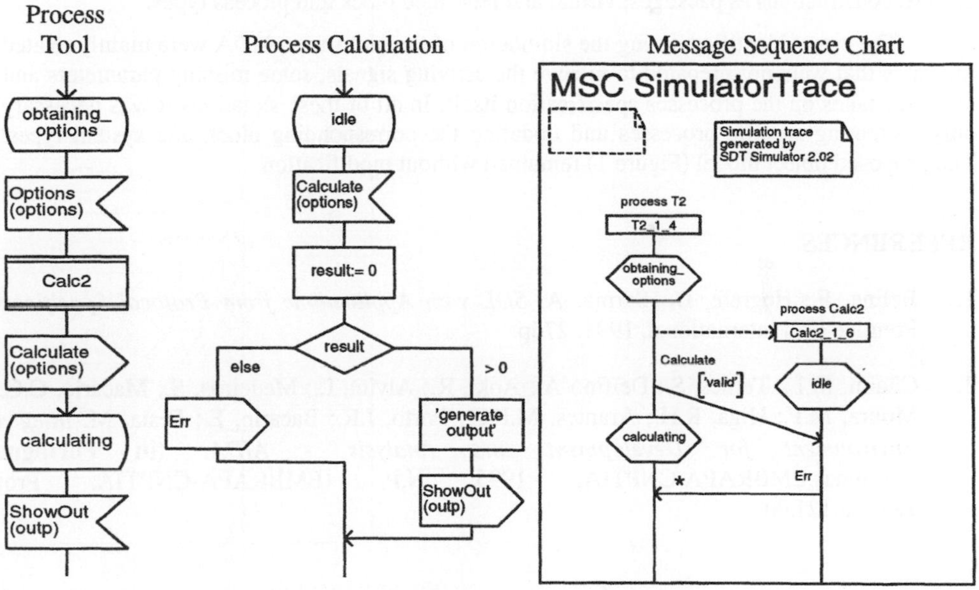

Figure 11 - Identification of an error

In order to correct this specific situation, the input signal *Err* should be added at the state *calculating* of process *Tool*. In general, whenever errors are identified, one shall return to the processes, blocks and system specifications in SDL and eventually to the object model, for the corresponding corrections and due updating.

5. CONCLUSIONS

The use of Object Modelling Technique - OMT has been shown as an excellent option in the software development process. Besides other features, it allows software reuse, some abstraction details, and provides modularity, making the evolution and maintenance activities much easier. However, as this technique does not consists itself in a formal method, its modelling might be ambiguous.

In this way, the combined use of OMT with SDL seems to be very opportune and interesting, mainly considering that SDL apart from being a formal specification language, allows a much more detailed system specification, that else would be possible with the OMT dynamic model. Moreover, a system specified using SDL is passive of code generation, simulation and formal verification of its correctness.

This work has proposed the use of this combined methodology as an alternative approach to the specification of AIDA, an "Integrated Environment for Development and Analysis" for management and statistical analysis of experimental data generated by the Brazilian Agricultural Research Corporation - EMBRAPA. From the specification with SDL92 of a mono-user AIDA system, it has been possible to efficiently evolve to the multi-user AIDA configuration using OMT concepts, such as inheritance and reuse, through the use of SDL constructions as packages, virtual and redefined block and process types.

The errors identified during the simulation of the multi-user AIDA were mainly related to: states that were not prepared to receive the arriving signals, some missing parameters and some mistakes on the processes specification itself. In all of these situations it was necessary only correcting specific processes and updating the corresponding block and system types. The proposed object model (Figure 1) remained without modification.

REFERENCES

1. Belina, F.; Hogrefe, D.; Sarma, A. *SDL with Applications from Protocol Specification*, Prentice Hall International, 1991. 275p.

2. Chaim, M.L.; Ternes, S.; Delfino A.; Aoki, R.; Alvim, L.; Medeiros, S.; Macário, C.G.N.; Moura, M.F.; Higa, R.H.; Arantes, M.P.C.; Porto, J.R.; Bacarin, E.; Festa, M. *Integrated Environment for Development and Analysis - AIDA*. **(in Portuguese)** Campinas:EMBRAPA-CNPTIA, 1995 N.P. (EMBRAPA-CNPTIA. Projeto 12.0.96.121.00).

3. ITU-T Recommendation Z.100. *CCITT Specification and Description Language (SDL)* , Helsinki, 1993.

4. ITU-T Recommendation Z.120. *Message Sequence Chart* (MSC), Helsinki 1993.

5. Macário, C.G.N.; Bonfim, W.S.; Chaim, M.L.; Antunes, J.F.G.; Ternes, S.; Aoki, R.; Alvim, L.; Pacheco, O.I.P.; Palmieri, S.; Festa, M.N.; Gaspar, D.M.; Serra, R.; Higa, R.H.; Arantes, M.P.C. *The Software Ntia Evolution.* **(in Portuguese)** Campinas: EMBRAPA-CNPTIA, 1994. N.P. (EMBRAPA-CNPTIA. Projeto 12.0.94.071.00).

6. MACÁRIO, C.G. N.; PEDROSO JÚNIOR, M.; BORELLI, W. C. *OMT+SDL: An alternative methodology for the AIDA development.* In: III INTERNATIONAL CONGRESS ON INFORMATION ENGINEERING, Buenos Aires. ICIE 96-97: Proceedings. Buenos Aires:Universidad de Buenos Aires - Faculdad de Ingenieria - Departamento de Computacion,[1997]. p.438-448.

7. Macário, C.G.N. *MSc. Thesis*, in preparation - DT/FEEC/UNICAMP, 1997.

8. Rumbaugh, J.; Blaha, M.; Premerlani, W.; Eddy,F.; Lorensen, W. *Object Oriented Modelling and Design*, Prentice Hall International, 1991. 500p.

9. SAS Institute (Cary, NC, USA). *SAS User's Guide:Basics.* Cary, 1985. 1290p.

10. Telelogic AB (Malmö, Sweden). *SDT 3.01 User's Guide: A Task-oriented Guide to SDT 3.01*, Sweden, 1995. 512p.

3. ITU-T Recommendation Z.100: CCITT Specification and Description Language (SDL) Helsinki, 1993.

4. ITU-T Recommendation Z.120: Message Sequence Chart (MSC) Helsinki 1993.

5. Madeira, C.G.N.; Bonfim, W.S.; Chaim, M.J.; Antunes, J.F.G.; Torres, S.; Abdo, R.; Alves, L.; Pedroso, O.L.; Padulla, E.; Brum, M.K.; Gaspar, D.M.; Serra, R.; Higa, R.H.; Antunes, M.P.C. *The Software Nine Evolution* (in Portuguese) Campinas: EMBRAPA-CNPTIA, 1994. NP: EMBRAPA-CNPTIA. Projeto 12.0.94.071.00.

6. MACÁRIO, C.G. N.; PEDROSO JÚNIOR, M.; BORELLI, W. C. OMT-SDL, an alternative methodology for the MDA development. In: III INTERNATIONAL CONGRESS ON INFORMATION ENGINEERING, Buenos Aires. - ICIE 96-97. Proceedings. Buenos Aires: Universidad de Buenos Aires - Facultad de Ingeniería - Departamento de Computación, 1997. p.438-448.

7. Macário, C.G.N. *M.Sc. Thesis*, in preparation - DT/FEEC/UNICAMP, 1997.

8. Rumbaugh, J.; Blaha, M.; Premerlani, W.; Eddy, F.; Lorensen, W. *Object Oriented Modelling and Design*. Prentice Hall International, 1991. 500p.

9. SAS Institute (Cary NC, USA), *SAS User's Guide: Basics*, Cary, 1985, 1290p.

10. Telelogic AB (Malmö, Sweden) *SDT 3.01 User's Guide: A Task-oriented Guide to SDT 3.0*. Sweden, 1995, 512p.

SDL '97: TIME FOR TESTING - SDL, MSC and Trends
A. Cavalli and A. Sarma (Editors)

SDL-based Modelling and Design of IN/UMTS Handover Functionality

A. Alonistioti [a], G. Nikolaidis [b], I. Modeas [b]

[a] National Centre of Scientific Research "Demokritos", Institute of Informatics and Telecommunications, 153 10 Ag. Paraskevi, Athens, Greece.

[b] University of Athens, Department of Informatics, Communication Networks Laboratory, 157 84 Athens, Greece.

ABSTRACT

In this paper a handover functional model and corresponding functionality description in SDL for the IN/UMTS concept for third generation mobile systems protocol development is presented. The model is based on ETSI NA-61301 [1] handover functional model. The main focus is on the introduction and specification of necessary Functional Entities for control and execution of the switching function for handover service provisioning. The mapping methodology of the handover IN/UMTS model, functional entities and their behaviour to SDL mechanisms is described. This results in the introduction of a generic, extendible for future requirements and faithful specification methodology, that serves as a basis for the simulation and implementation of handover protocols able to cope with various handover types and UMTS environments.

1. INTRODUCTION

For the advancement of third generation mobile communication systems, the Universal Mobile Telecommunication System (UMTS) concept was introduced [2-3]. In standardisation fora, like ETSI, progress has been made towards the specification of the model and services that would satisfy the criteria and requirements for the development of the target UMTS. Along this effort, IN architecture [4-5] has decisive impact on UMTS functions evolution.

One of the most essential and time critical mobility functions, is handover (HO). It ensures the continuity of the call while the mobile terminal is moving outside a switching control area. HO is the most time-critical feature. It may be triggered due to degradation of the radio link and consequently of the quality of the offered service, or due to network maintenance and management (e.g. re-allocation of radio resources).

For the development of the wide range of UMTS services, the formal specification of the functional model and corresponding functional entities, their behaviour and functionality in a reusable and extendible way becomes a necessity. In this paper the use of SDL [6] for the modelling and specification part was favoured due to the variety of potentials offered in terms of modelling (e.g. object orientation), behaviour specification and tool support (simulation, validation etc.), as well as its wide acceptance among the communications society. In this paper we introduce a handover functional model and handover and switching service algorithms for the extended IN/UMTS functionality, specified in SDL [7] using the SDT Tool. This results in introducing a design methodology of a reusable, impervious to development errors crop up and unambiguous protocol modules specification. The proposed model and handover switching algorithms described in SDL, serve as a generic "executable specification platform" for the implementation and simulation of handover protocols covering the various handover types in different UMTS environments. Moreover, services, functional behaviour and interaction of entities constituting the target IN/UMTS environment are flexibly developed. Simulations of the proposed handover switching algorithms have been performed and are presented here in the form of Message Sequence Charts obtained from the highly illustrative and user friendly SDT Tool Simulator environment. The methodology for the mapping of the IN/UMTS handover functional model in SDL diagrams, as well as the handover and switching functions behaviour is introduced and described in the following sections.

2. SDL-BASED IN/UMTS HANDOVER FUNCTIONAL MODEL

2.1. The IN concept

The Intelligent Network Conceptual Model, defined in Rec. Q.1211 [4-5] leads to an implementation framework for the provision of rapid and flexible introduction of new services and facilities in a service feature based environment. One of the main principles of IN is to identify a modular design for the construction, change and enhancement of service functionality, as well as implementation of service independent network platform. This results in the introduction of new features and system evolution and expansion without disrupting its overall operation. This is achieved by means of a four plane structure, describing in different levels of abstraction aspects of the various services, IN functionality in terms of independent building blocks, definition of Functional Entities (FEs) for the distributed functions and physical aspects of IN. The object-oriented approach is a beneficial means, in terms of modularity, reusability and extendibility, for the specification and implementation of services in IN architecture. SDL and its object-oriented features has been used for efforts to map the IN objects to SDL mechanisms [7] and modelling the distributed functionality of IN services [8].

Thus, a major driving force for the introduction of an IN-based architecture for the integration of fixed and mobile networks, appears to be the ability to support both fixed services and mobility service features by the same infrastructure. Application of IN concepts are a part of a trend which aims to enable a flexible introduction of new communication services and ease their evolution, based on the modularity of the network infrastructure. Such a perspective motivates research institutions and standardisation fora to build future mobile communication systems (i.e. UMTS, FPLMTS) upon IN concepts.

2.2. IN/UMTS functional model

Universal Mobile Telecommunication System (UMTS) is a mobile communications technology which will allow the provision of a wide range of sophisticated services to mobile users, such as teleservices (including voice, video and data) and other bearer capabilities. The service quality offered in fixed and mobile networks and between personal mobility and terminal mobility must be equivalent and impervious to the means of transmission (wired or wireless), the underlying radio access technology, the terminal used and location. Mobility service features will be provided via a variety of radio interfaces and the goal of UMTS is to support advanced services up to 2 Mbps. UMTS will offer mobile access facilities in various telecommunication environments, most currently being served by dedicated systems. Roaming and handovers between different zones and between zones under different ownership, probably resulting in changing tariff or service provision scheme, must be supported in the UMTS environments. For this reason UMTS must enable an individual service provider to provide services with features that are distinct from similar services from other providers, without causing limitations for roaming in other networks.

Influenced favourably by the IN concept, UMTS is likely to be IN based. Many system functions, such as location registration and handover, could potentially be implemented as IN-like services. This extension of the IN concept enables mobility functions being handled by service control functions which offer flexibility in service provisioning and tailoring. To this end, effort has been devoted in standardisation fora such as ETSI and ITU-T for the development of a basic functional model for future mobile telecommunication systems like UMTS. In order to develop suitable signalling protocols to support all the services and mobility features for UMTS, the ITU-T Rec. I.130 [9] methodology has been adopted in principle. From the service requirements and the mobility features, functional entities and their relationships could be identified, in order to construct suitable service specific functional models from the basic functional model. With this functional model, the detailed functionality of each FE can be specified, information flows between the FEs can be developed and eventually the protocol could be defined. This functional model, based on IN concept, describes the application area without specifically identifying the location of the FEs into physical network entities, in order to be applicable to many network configurations. Key system features that require specific functional model developments include call handling, user services, location updating, paging, data base access, security and, last but not least, handover.

2.3. Structure of Handover IN/UMTS Functional Model and SDL

Taking into account the aforementioned considerations regarding the UMTS development, effort has been devoted in standardisation fora for the introduction of generic and flexible system functional model, able to cope with the system and services evolution. The effort for the development of a generic IN/UMTS functional model in ETSI has resulted in the production of the IN/UMTS Framework document (ETSI NA6-61301) [1]. Based on this generic functional model, a specific functional model for handover aspects is introduced and a methodology for modelling and design UMTS functional entities using SDL mechanisms is presented. Moreover, in this paper, a specification in SDL for the identification of the functional entities and their relationships, along with message sequence charts and diagrams for the handover algorithm and corresponding Handover State Model (HSM) and Switching Bridging State Model (SBSM) are presented. The use of SDL proves a powerful means for a robust, comprehensive and flexible design that adheres to the requirement for modular and extendible system design for building services and faithful protocol development. Figure 2 shows the generic handover functional model introduced, based on the generic IN/UMTS functional model shown in Figure1 and described in detail in [1].

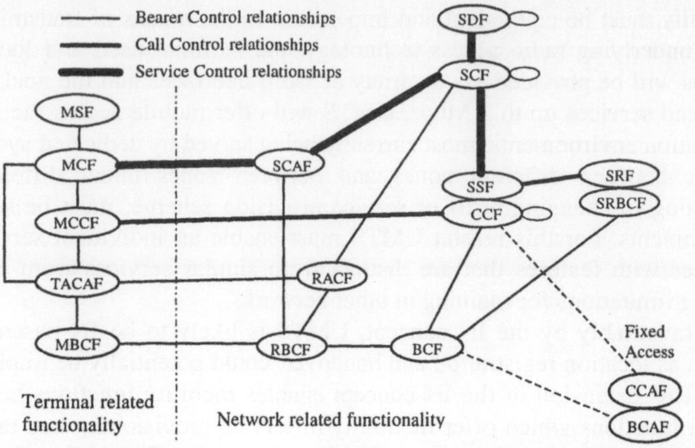

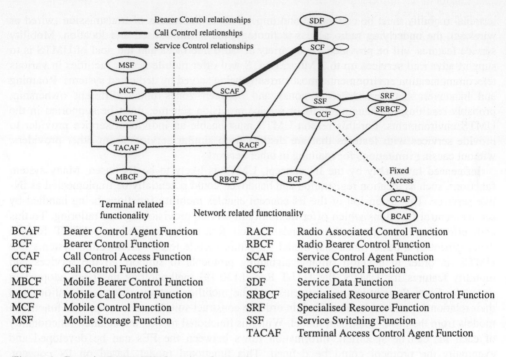

BCAF	Bearer Control Agent Function	RACF	Radio Associated Control Function
BCF	Bearer Control Function	RBCF	Radio Bearer Control Function
CCAF	Call Control Access Function	SCAF	Service Control Agent Function
CCF	Call Control Function	SCF	Service Control Function
MBCF	Mobile Bearer Control Function	SDF	Service Data Function
MCCF	Mobile Call Control Function	SRBCF	Specialised Resource Bearer Control Function
MCF	Mobile Control Function	SRF	Specialised Resource Function
MSF	Mobile Storage Function	SSF	Service Switching Function
		TACAF	Terminal Access Control Agent Function

Figure 1. Generic IN/UMTS functional model.

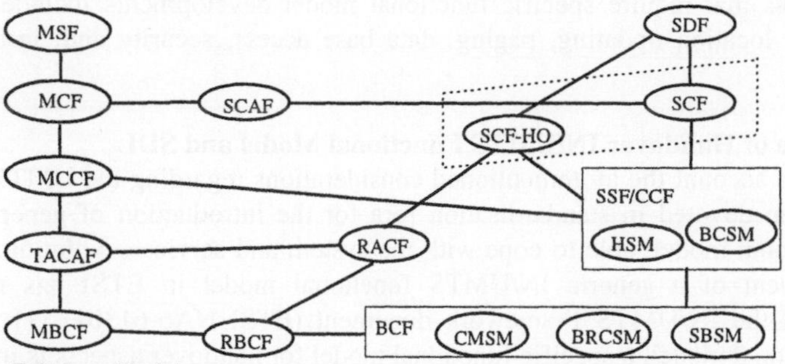

BCSM	Basic Call State Model		
BRCSM	Bearer Resource Control State Model	HSM	Handover State Model
CMSM	Combining/Multicasting State Model	SBSM	Switching Bridging State Model

Figure 2. IN/UMTS handover functional model

In the methodology proposed in this paper, the model is structured as a system (System IN_UMTS_HOFM) in SDL (Figure 3). The mapping of the handover functional entities onto SDL properties is performed by grouping the FEs in three blocks in the system level. The blocks correspond to the sets of FEs comprising the Service Control functions, Radio Associated Control functions, Call and Bearer Control functions, as defined in ETSI NA-61301 [1]. The use of block types was favoured for generality reasons, because according to the service requirements and environment, additional instances of these blocks may be necessary for the implementation of the target system structure. The relationships between the different groups of FEs and the Environment are represented by channels. All relationships with entities that are not presented in the handover functional model, but may exist in the generic IN/UMTS functional model, are implied in the interaction with the Environment.

The various *signals*, *signallists*, *parameters*, *variables* and other data or timer declarations are included in *macro Defs*. All names with the format ***_L** at channels or signalroutes correspond to signallists.

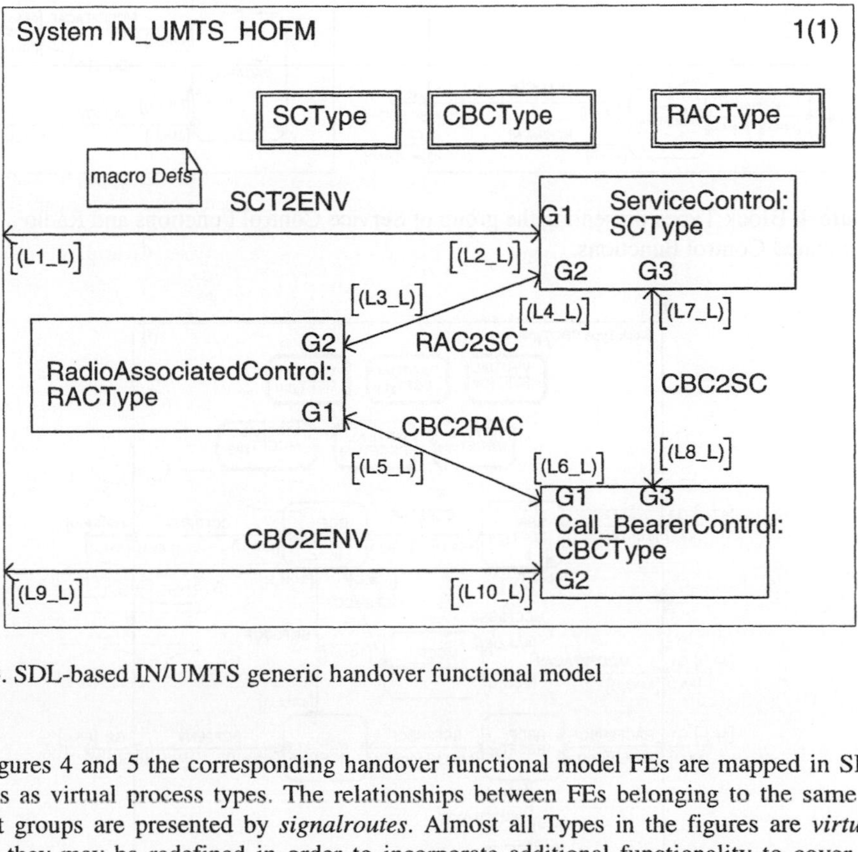

Figure 3. SDL-based IN/UMTS generic handover functional model

In Figures 4 and 5 the corresponding handover functional model FEs are mapped in SDL diagrams as virtual process types. The relationships between FEs belonging to the same or different groups are presented by *signalroutes*. Almost all Types in the figures are *virtual*, because they may be redefined in order to incorporate additional functionality to cover all services necessary for the target UMTS implementation (i.e. service management, call set-up with macrodiversity). It should be noted that the use of *virtual types* is also imposed by the design needs for *redefinition* and *specialisation* for the different UMTS environments that should be considered for the development of the target UMTS (i.e. Macro-Cell Environment,

Pico-Cell Environment etc.). For every call and corresponding handover a new instance of the FEs types is created. In this paper the Macro-Cell environment (Macro-Cell access) is assumed.

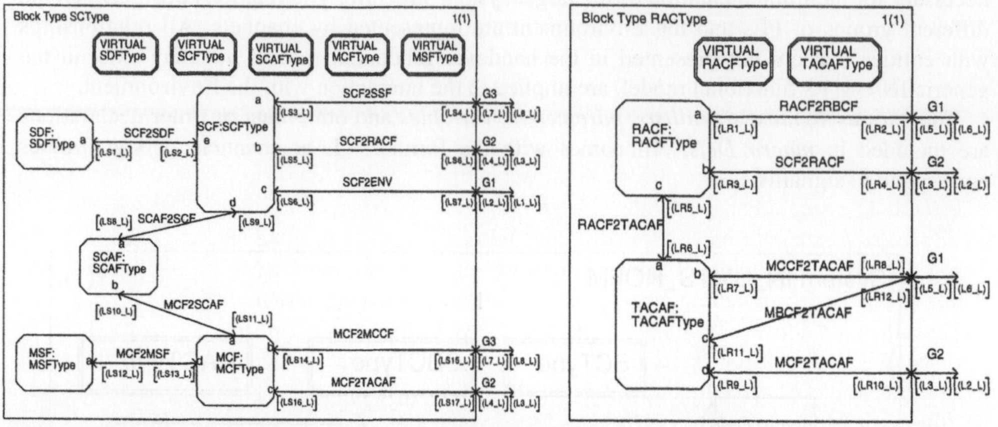

Figure 4. Block Types presenting the group of Service Control Functions and Radio Associated Control Functions.

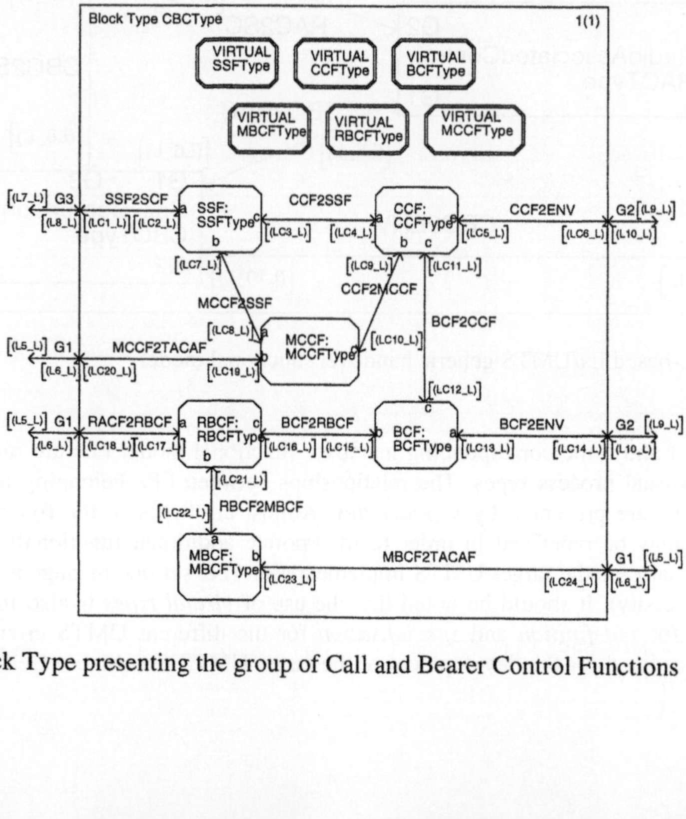

Figure 5. Block Type presenting the group of Call and Bearer Control Functions

In this paper attention is paid on handover issues and corresponding functionality, since this model is intended to provide a specification platform for the simulation and implementation of various handover switching algorithms in the UMTS environments. Therefore, the CCF and BCF FEs are described in more detail (Figure 6). The CCF Type comprises the Handover State Model (HSM) virtual service type and the Basic Call State Model (BCSM) virtual service type for fulfilling the requirement for call/connection control separation. The BCSM service type is responsible for the call control, while HSM for the handover processing which has direct impact on the bearer control.

The use of the SDL *service* property to build the overall CCF functionality was chosen, because it covers the requirement that Basic Call transitions and Handover transitions can not be performed in parallel, since they have impact on the same call.

The BCF type consists of the Combining Multicasting State Model (CMSM) for macrodiversity calls and handovers, the Bearer Resource Control State Model (BRCSM) for setting up and releasing the bearers and bearer control and the Switching Bridging State Model (SBSM) for switching bearers and handling uplink and downlink traffic buffering during call and handover. The use of *virtual services* for the mapping of the functional parts of BCF satisfies the need for extendibility and the assumption that for one call there can be no parallel transitions of these modules. The handover and switching algorithms are introduced in the following sections and the behaviour of corresponding FEs is presented formally using SDL.

The need for the use of virtual types can be identified by the following assumptions. The inclusion of other environment or service related functions, like a Transcoding State Model, depends on the service requirements of each service of each specific environment where UMTS operates. Therefore it may be present in some environments and absent in others. In the case of UMTS Pico-Cell environment, inclusion of a Transcoding Function is imposed and implemented as a redefinition of the virtual process type BCFType (Figure 7).

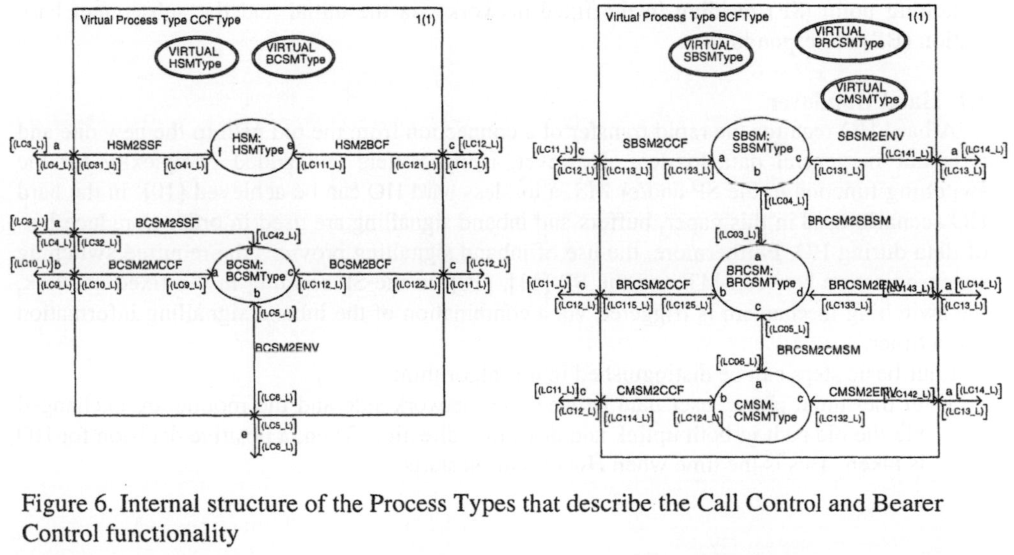

Figure 6. Internal structure of the Process Types that describe the Call Control and Bearer Control functionality

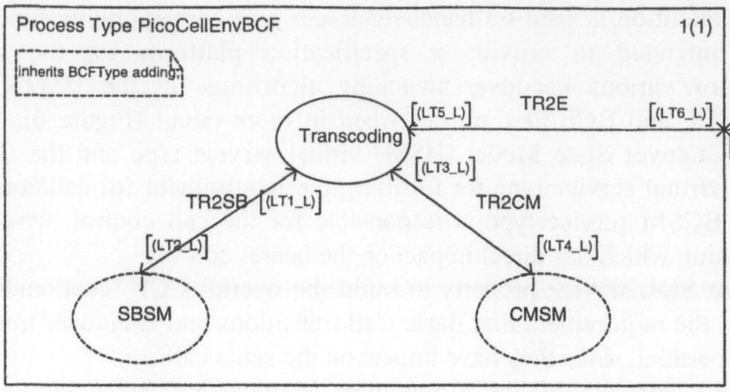

Figure 7. Redefinition of BCF type for the Pico-Cell environment modelling and specification

3. HANDOVER ALGORITHMS

Two types of HO can be identified: hard and soft. In a hard HO, only one connection is active during the HO procedure. In a soft handover, there are two active connections between the mobile terminal (MT) and the bridging point within the fixed network, at least for a short time interval.

In this paper, two algorithms for hard and soft HO are presented, in order to show the mapping onto SDL mechanisms in specifying the HO specific functional model and FEs functionality, as they are described in the previous section. These two algorithms are presented in the following paragraphs. In this presentation, as "old path" and "new path", we denote the full connection (fixed and radio links) between the mobile station (MS) and the switching point (SP) residing in the fixed network, via the initial and the subsequent base station (BS) correspondingly.

3.1. Hard Handover

A hard HO requires the rapid transfer of a connection from the old path to the new one and it is not in general data lossless. However, using buffers and added complexity for the switching function in the SP and/or MS, a lossless hard HO can be achieved [10]. In the hard HO scenario used in this paper, buffers and inband signalling are used in order to reduce loss of data during HO. Furthermore, the use of inband signalling provides the required switching synchronisation between MT and the SP [11], [10]. In the SP residing in the fixed network, the switching mechanism is triggered via a combination of the inband signalling information and a timer.

Four basic steps can be distinguished in this algorithm:

1. In the initial phase, user data between the network side and the mobile are exchanged via the old path in both uplink and downlink direction. Then, a positive decision for HO is taken. This is the time when HO execution starts.

2. SCF instructs SSF/CCF to establish all new connections required in order to support the HO.
3. When all new connections are established, switching (in both the MS and the SP) can be performed. Inband signalling information is used over the old path, indicating that there is no more data coming over it, i.e. inband signalling info is the last data transmitted over the old path. Switching is performed in BCF after having received the inband signalling information over the old path. A timer is used in this point, in order to avoid excessive period of waiting the inband signalling. This means that switching occurs when one of the two happens: either the inband signalling information is detected, or the timer expires.
4. Release of the old connections.

In this paper, we focus on the HO mechanism as it can be executed in the fixed network (SP). The MS side could be handled with the same procedure, but it is much more radio specific. The specification of this algorithm for the SP is presented in the following section.

3.2. Soft Handover without Macrodiversity

Soft HO can be implemented either using macrodiversity or not. In this paper, when we refer to a soft HO, the second case is implied, i.e. no use of macrodiversity between the MT and the SP. Even if this is not the more robust soft HO mechanism (since there is no combining of the multicasted data [10]), it is preferred here for simplicity reasons.

This algorithm is quite similar to the previous one. The main difference is in step 3. All other steps (decision for HO, establishment of new connections and release of the old ones) are identical. After setting-up the new path, all data from the SP to MS and vice-versa are multicasted over both old and new path. The start of multicasting is indicated with inband signalling. Switching occurs either when inband signalling information is detected over both the new and old path, or when a timer expires. This timer again is used in order to avoid long delays in the HO mechanism. When switching is completed, multicasting of user data is stopped. The specification of this algorithm is presented in the next section.

The main advantage of this algorithm is that it is more robust from the previous one in environments where the old radio link fades rapidly and finally fails [10].

4. SPECIFICATION

In the following paragraphs the handover and switching functionality as described in the previous section will be described using SDL mechanisms. Note that this specification is applicable to the SP in the fixed network.

4.1. Information Flows

After the set-up phase, each call is active, which means that user data are exchanged. SBSM within BCF is involved from the call set-up till the call release. Between these two events, a HO may occur. Till then, SBSM is in a "call_mode" state and it returns at this mode when a HO is completed. On the contrary, HSM is active only during HO. These two state machines will be described and specified in more details in the following section.

The information flow and signals exchange for the two algorithms described earlier is shown in Figure 8 in the form of a message sequence chart (MSC). In this chart, it is assumed

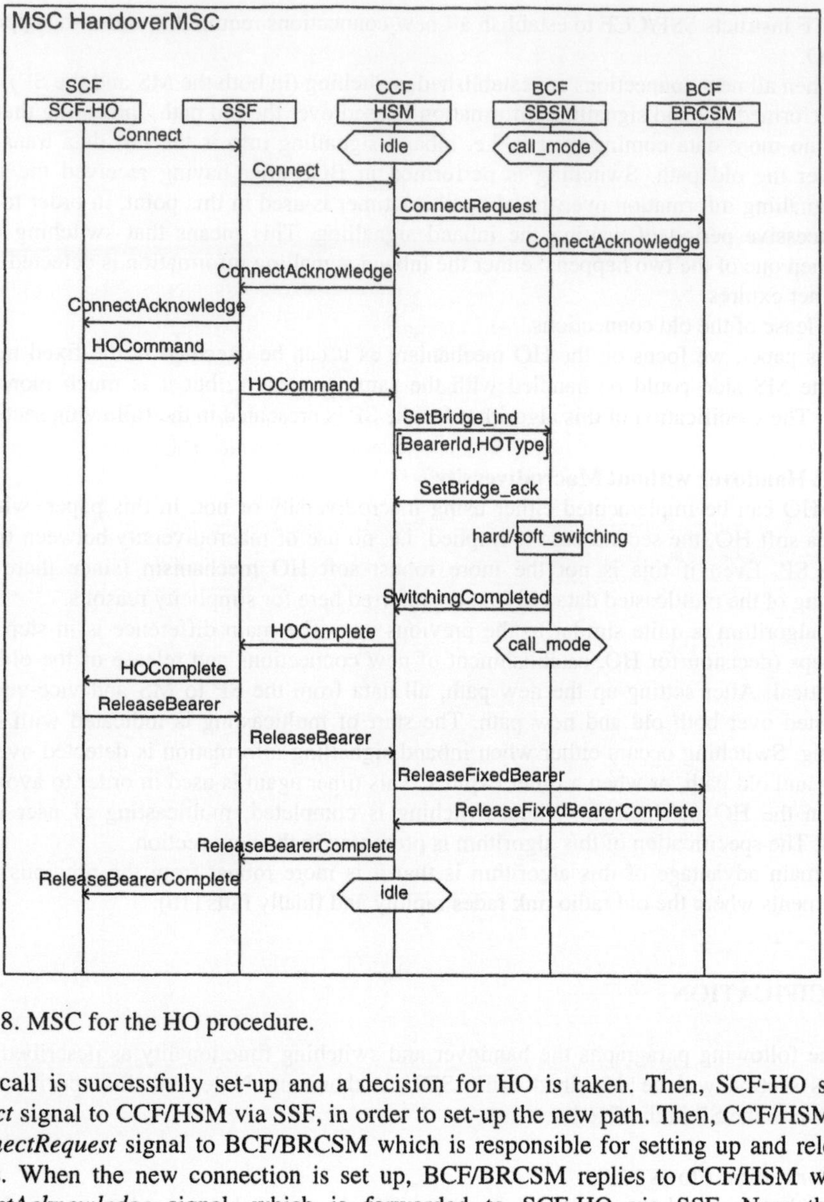

Figure 8. MSC for the HO procedure.

that a call is successfully set-up and a decision for HO is taken. Then, SCF-HO sends a *Connect* signal to CCF/HSM via SSF, in order to set-up the new path. Then, CCF/HSM sends a *ConnectRequest* signal to BCF/BRCSM which is responsible for setting up and release of bearers. When the new connection is set up, BCF/BRCSM replies to CCF/HSM with the *ConnectAcknowledge* signal, which is forwarded to SCF-HO via SSF. Now the new connection is established and SCF-HO instructs to proceed with the switching, sending the *HOCommand* message.

After receiving the *HOCommand* signal, HSM sends the *SetBridge_ind* to SBSM in order to set-up a new bridge between the two connections. SBSM responds with *SetBridge_ack* and the switching from the old connection to the new one is performed. When switching is completed, SBSM notifies HSM about it, using the *SwitchingCompleted* signal, and returns to the *call_mode* state. HSM replies to *HOCommand* signal with the *HOComplete* and now the old connection can be released. This is a analogous procedure to the setting up of the new connection. The old connection is released with interaction of SCF-HO, HSM and BRCSM. When the old connection is released, the HO is completed and the HSM returns to the *idle* state till a new HO occurs.

4.2. Description of HSM

Since HSM is initiated when a HO is in progress, the start transition of the CCF (comprising both HSM and BCSM) process is performed in BCSM. The specification of the virtual service type HSMType is depicted in Figure 9. In this diagram, three types of HO are considered, namely 'hard', 'soft', and 'md'. The first and the second corresponds to the hard and soft HO algorithms described earlier. The last one stands for the soft with macrodiversity HO case. This one is introduced in order to show that this model can be easily extended. Depending on the HO type, the appropriate procedure is called. The procedure *switching* which is called in the first two cases is shown in Figure 10.

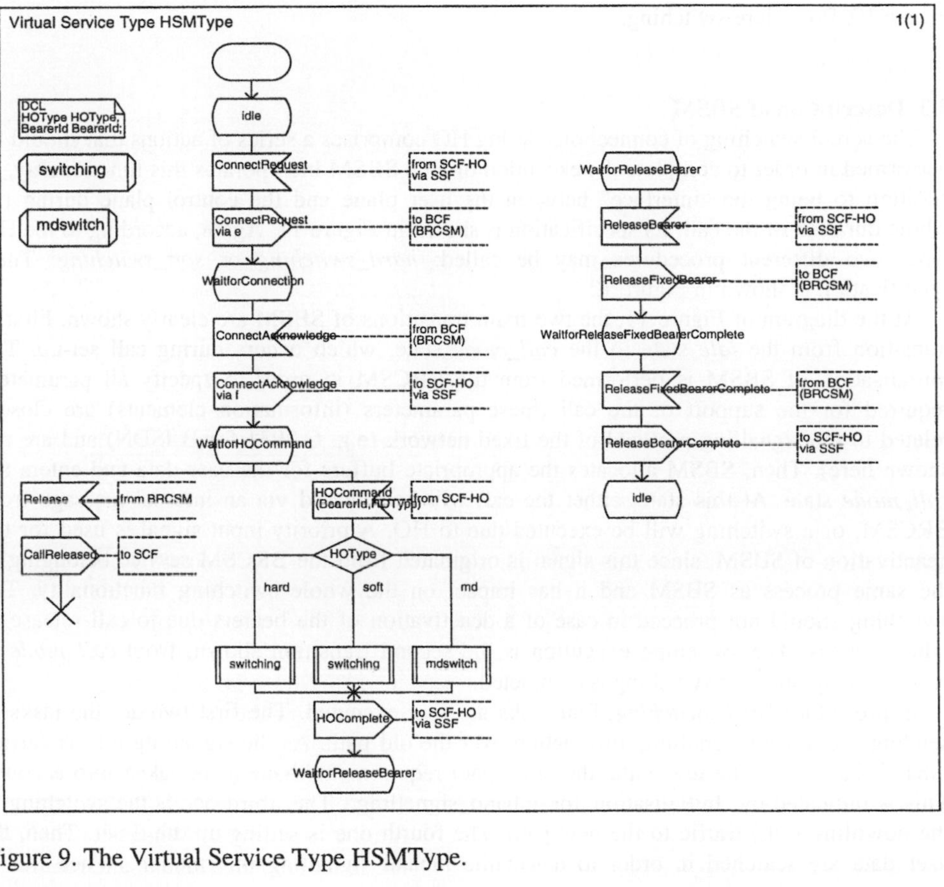

Figure 9. The Virtual Service Type HSMType.

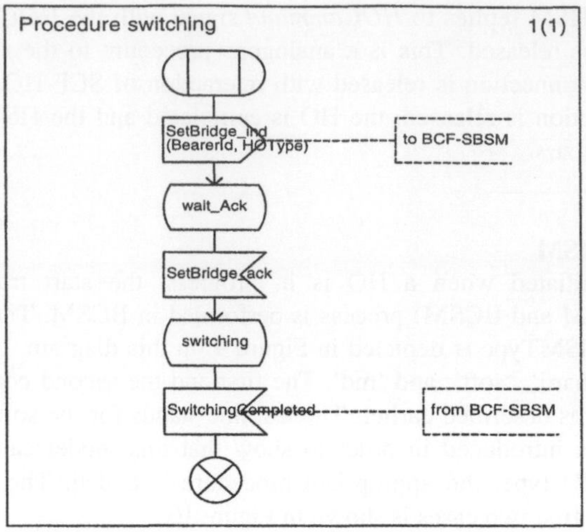

Figure 10. Procedure switching.

4.3. Description of SBSM

The actual switching of connections during HO comprises a series of actions that should be performed in order to complete the execution of HO. SBSM incorporates this functionality, in addition to being the "interface" between the user plane and the control plane during the whole duration of the call. Its specification is shown in Figure 11. Again, according to the HO type, two different procedures may be called: *hard_switching* or *soft_switching*. Their specification is shown in Figure 12.

At the diagram of Figure 11, the two main transitions of SBSM are clearly shown. First, a transition from the *idle* state to the *call_mode* state, which occurs during call set-up. The initialisation of SBSM is performed from the BRCSM in order to specify all parameters required for the support of the call (these parameters (information elements) are closely related to the signalling protocol of the fixed network (e.g. Q.2931 for B-ISDN) and are not shown here). Then, SBSM allocates the appropriate buffers for the user data and enters the *call_mode* state. At this state, either the call will be released via an internal message from BRCSM, or a switching will be executed due to HO. A priority input signal is used for the deactivation of SBSM, since this signal is originated from the BRCSM service belonging to the same process as SBSM and it has impact on the whole switching functionality. The switching should not proceed in case of a deactivation of the bearers due to call release or other reasons. The switching execution is the second transition shown, from *call_mode* to *call_mode* again, after switching is completed.

In procedure *hard_switching*, four tasks are first executed. The first two are the tasks of sending the inband signalling information over the old path. As the signalling info is carried inband, i.e. within the user data, the radio path requirements have to be taken into account. This is indicated by 'Initialisation_for_inband_signalling'. The third one is the switching of the downlink (DL) traffic to the new path. The fourth one is setting up the timer. Then, the user data are searched in order to detect the inband signalling information. When this is

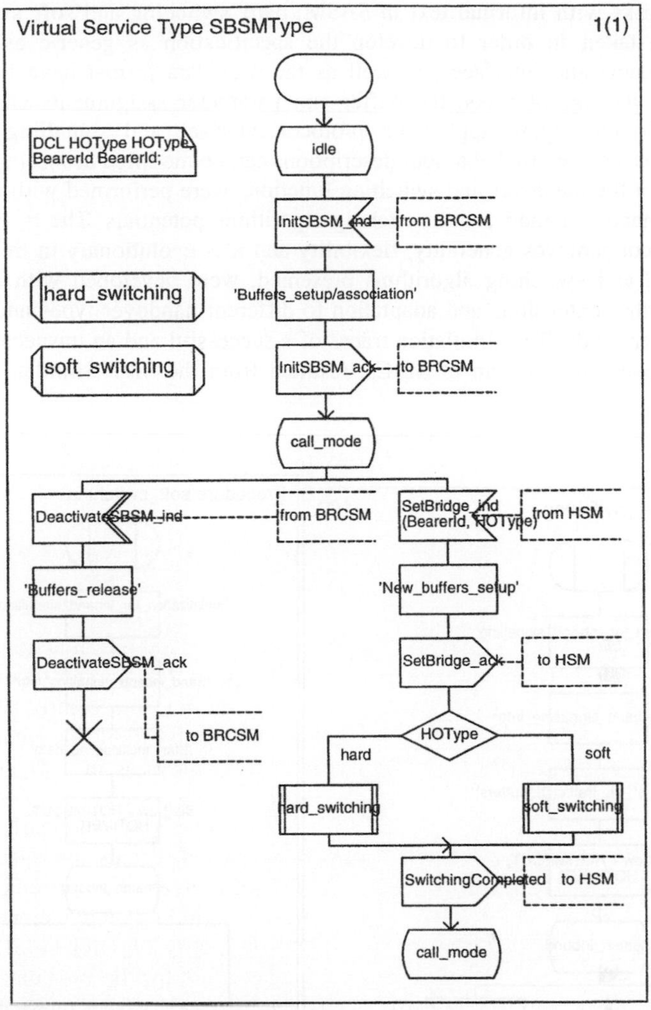

Figure 11. The Virtual Service Type SBSMType.

detected or the timer expires, switching of the uplink (UL) traffic is performed (see also [10]). The signal *InBandDetected* is an external one, originating outside the SDL system. This solution was preferred since it helps us to specify the procedure independently from the user data format.

In procedure *soft_switching*, a similar approach is followed. According to the algorithm under consideration, the inband signalling information is initially multicasted and then all the data. At the end, switching at both the uplink and downlink direction is performed and multicasting is ended.

The use of tasks with informal text in SBSM, hard_switching and soft_switching, was a design decision taken in order to develop the specification as generic as possible. The underlying protocols and interfaces, as well as the user data format have impact on these functions. With the use of tasks, the buffer and parameter assignments can be formatted according to the underlying application protocol interface and signalling protocol (e.g. Q.2931), whereas the specific behaviour descriptions can be modified accordingly.

Simulations of the handover and switching functions were performed with the intention to investigate the handover model and switching algorithms potentials. The resulting handover signalling protocol achieves generality, flexibility and it is evolutionary in the sense that the handover model and switching algorithms presented, were developed with a methodology allowing for further extensions and adaptation to different handover types and environments and to future user needs. The simulation traces of a successful and an unsuccessful switching of a hard handover, in the form of MSCs, resulted from the SDT Simulator are shown in Figure 13.

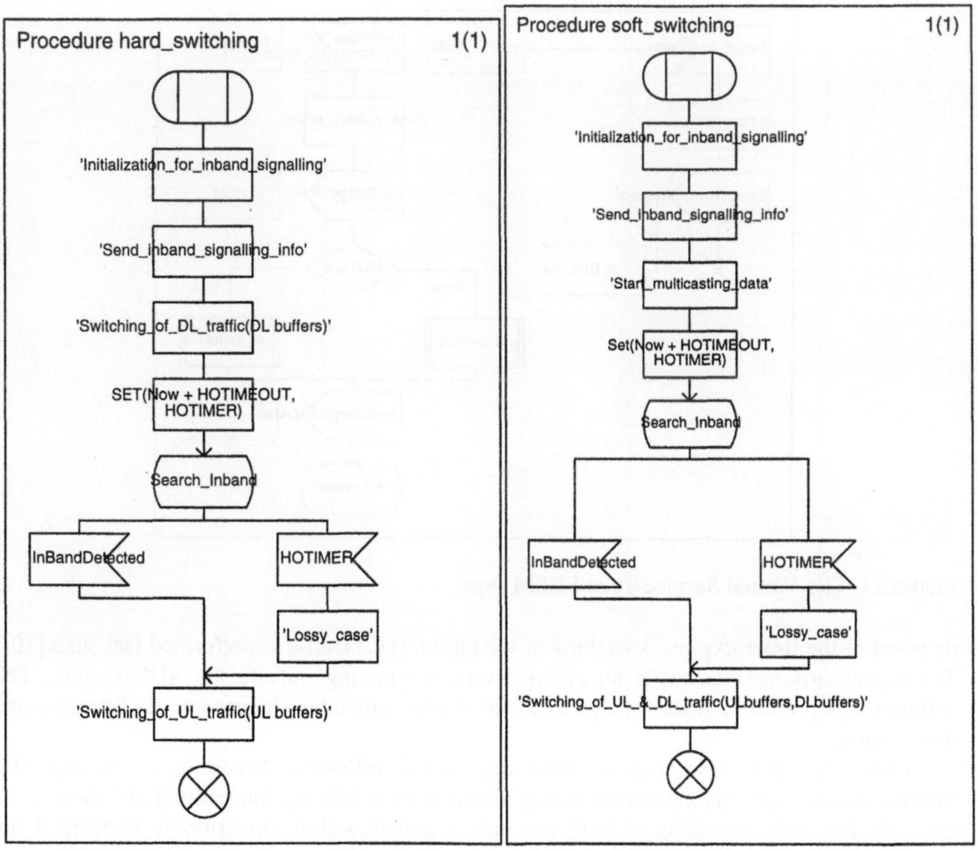

Figure 12. The procedures hard_switching and soft_switching.

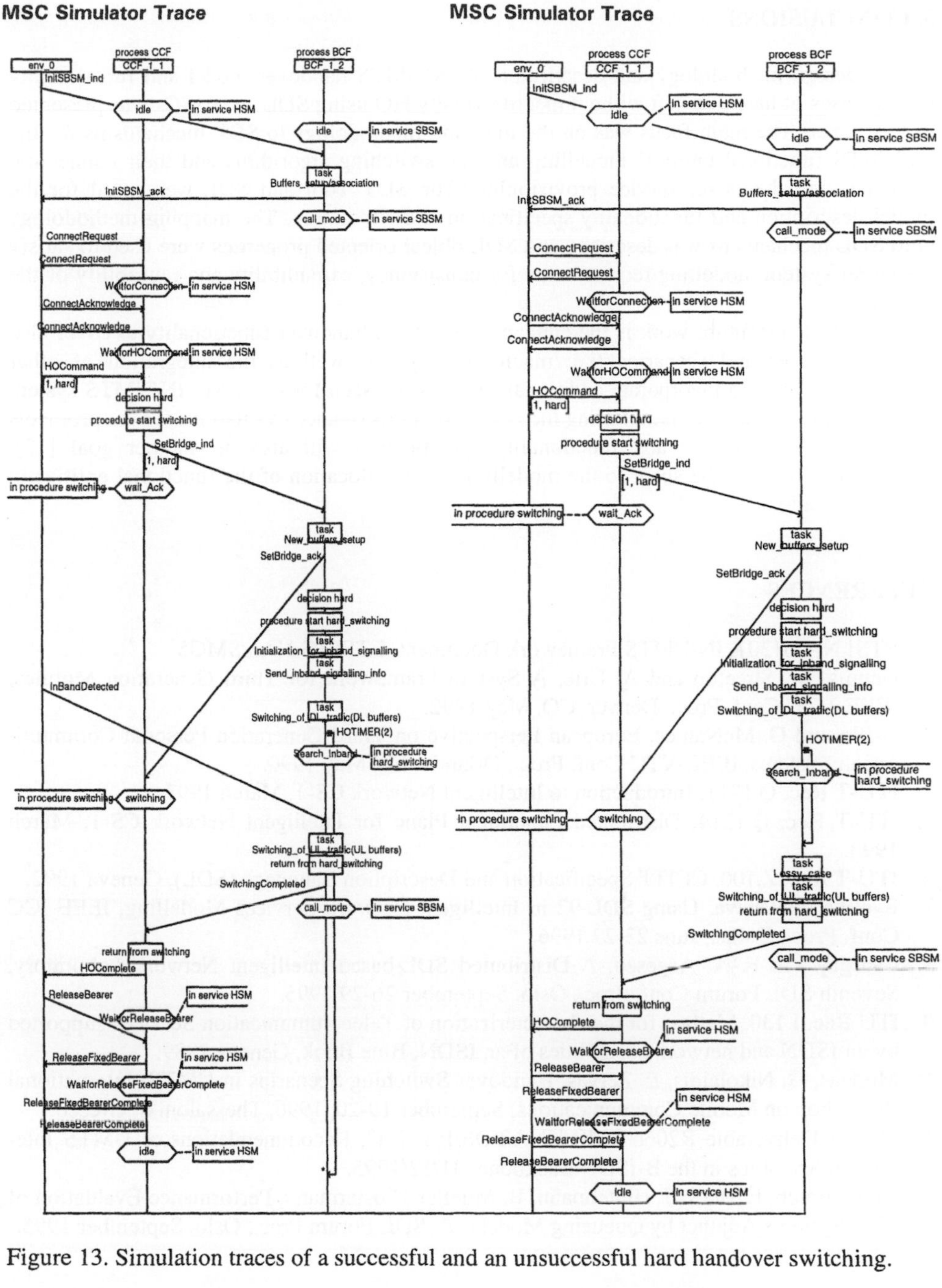

Figure 13. Simulation traces of a successful and an unsuccessful hard handover switching.

5. CONCLUSIONS

The design methodology and description of IN/UMTS handover model and functionality for the cases of hard and soft without macrodiversity HO using SDL and MSCs was presented in this paper. The main focus was on the mapping methodology to SDL mechanisms for the IN/UMTS functional entities' modelling and the switching algorithms and their connection with the main handover service provisioning. The SDT Tool and SDL were used for the model description and functionality specification and simulation. The mapping methodology onto SDL mechanisms was described and SDL object oriented properties were used to satisfy the target system modelling requirements for consistency, extendibility and reusability of the modules.

As part of our future work is the enhancement of the handover functionality to cover also other HO cases and scenarios (i.e. macrodiversity), as well as the integration of other functional entities to incorporate additional services foreseen for the target IN/UMTS system and have full system simulation using the SDT tool. Performance evaluations for the protocols derived from the model and functionality specification will also be another goal [12]. Moreover, effort will be spent to the modelling of the allocation of the functional entities to physical locations.

REFERENCES

1. ETSI NA-61301, IN/UMTS Framework Document, ETSI JG NA6/SMG5.
2. Dennis, M. Streeton and A. Urie, A System Framework for Third Generation Mobiles, IEEE-VTC Conf. Proc., Denver, CO, May 1992.
3. Grillo and G. McNamee, European Perspective on Third Generation Personal Communication Systems, IEEE-VTC Conf. Proc., Orlando, FL, May 1990.
4. ITU-T Rec. Q.1211, Introduction to Intelligent Network CS-1, March 1993.
5. ITU-T Rec. Q.1214, Distributed Functional Plane for Intelligent Network CS-1, March 1993.
6. ITU-T Rec. Z.100, CCITT Specification and Description Language (SDL), Geneva 1992.
7. Evelina Pentcheva, Using SDL-92 in Intelligent Network Services Modelling, IEEE-ICC Conf. Proc., Dallas, June 23-27 1996.
8. Csurgay and F. A. Aagesen, A Distributed SDL-based Intelligent Network Laboratory, Seventh SDL Forum Conf. Proc., Oslo, September 26-29 1995.
9. ITU Rec. I.130, Method for the characterization of Telecommunication Services supported by an ISDN and network capabilities of an ISDN, Blue Book, Geneva 1989.
10. Modeas, G. Nikolaidis, E. Zervas, Handover Switching Scenarios in UMTS, International Workshop on Mobile Communications, September 19-20, 1996, Thessaloniki, Greece.
11. MoNet Deliverable R2066/RMR/UNA2/DS/P/107/a3, Recommendations of UMTS Integration Scenarios in the B-ISDN Backbone, 31/12/1995.
12. Diefenbruch, E. Heck, J. Hintelmann, B. Mueller-Clostermann, Performance Evaluation of SDL Systems Adjunct by Queueing Models, 7th SDL Forum Proc., Oslo, September 1995.

SDL '97: TIME FOR TESTING - SDL, MSC and Trends
A. Cavalli and A. Sarma (Editors)

An SDL-based platform for the simulation of communication networks using dynamic block instantiations

Andreas Iselt and Achim Autenrieth

Technical University Munich, Institute for Communication Networks

Arcisstr. 21, D–80290 München, Germany

e–mail: iselt@lkn.e–technik.tu–muenchen.de

This paper discusses a new platform for network simulation. It combines the advantages of a functional description technique (SDL) with the advantages of graphical design entry and visualization possibilities known from network simulators. Thus it is well suited for protocol simulation and performance simulation. From basic considerations on simulation environments to the specific new platform this paper introduces the basic knowledge for network simulation with SDL. Further, a novel SDL construct for dynamic block instantiations is proposed, that simplifies this simulation platform and is also very useful for other applications.

1. Introduction

For the development of communication networks elements, as well as for the design of complete communication networks, simulations and visualizations form an essential part of the whole design process. The development of new protocols also requires simulation as a means of understanding and debugging the new mechanisms and proof the applicability to a network.

Currently a wide variety of simulation tools and techniques are used for these simulation needs. Besides traditional simulation using standard programming languages (e.g. C, FORTRAN) a lot of supporting libraries aiming to simplify simulation programming have been developed. Simulation techniques known from hardware design (e.g. VHDL or Verilog) claim to cover the whole top down simulation range from system specification to detailed implementation. They do not only require from the engineer to learn a new simulation and specification language, but also to learn a totally new programming style, that is usually used to described the concurrency of signal assignments in electronic circuits. Even though some hardware simulation tools offer graphical design entry, they are not very well adapted to protocol simulation. A more convenient way for topology entry and simulation control is offered from simulation tools especially designed for network simulation (e.g. Opnet). These tools mostly come with a library of some standard network elements (sources, multiplexers, switches) and are well suited for the simulation of real networks or networks intended to be realized. Because of this they are more related to network planning tasks. The simulation tasks regarded in this paper focus mainly on the protocol evaluation and on performance measures of novel network techniques.

Another development in the past years is the dissemination of functional description techniques (FDT) for the specification and implementation of protocols [3,4,9]. Examples are Lotos, Estelle and SDL. They offer a lot of advantages for the design and evaluation of systems:

- Well defined set of constructs for an unambiguous system description.
- Support of hierarchical structuring of systems
- Specification serves as a means of documentation
- Forms a basis for simulation, verification and implementation

SDL as a FDT further offers a graphical representation of the system design and increases the understandability. In addition to the advantages enumerated above, SDL provides some more:

- Support for top down design from high level descriptions to detailed system design
- Modularity enabling simple extendibility
- Defined interfaces
- Manifold data structures
- Timer mechanisms
- Recommended by standardization body (ITU–T Z.100)
- Already widespread use in protocol specification (e.g. Q.931 for ISDN, GSM) and industries

While FDT and SDL are state of the art for protocol development, the programming languages and simulation tools mentioned above mostly lack the ability to use functional specification techniques. Even for the more advanced network simulators the node models have to be programmed using C–code (Opnet).

This discrepancy has stimulated a development at the author's institute, to combine the advantages of specification and simulation using SDL with a visualization environment targeting the easy topology entry for networks and the interactive graphical simulation (visualization). A platform has been set up based on the SDT (SDL Design Tool, Telelogic) combined with the public domain scripting language Tcl/Tk for GUI design [5].

The following chapter gives a short overview on network simulation and its applications and targets. Next, known simulation techniques are summarized and compared. The application of SDL to network simulation is introduced and the new simulation platform is presented. Finally the main topics are summarized and an outlook is given on future applications and extensions.

2. Network simulation

2.1. General aspects, functional separation, layering

A communication network consists of network nodes, that are interconnected using links. Nodes may either be user terminals at the border of the network or network elements residing within the communication network. The links are used to transmit information between the nodes. Depending on the protocol used for the transmission, this information is partitioned in information packets (also called messages or cells) of different or equal size. For the simulation it is important to note, that the communication between nodes over links can be modelled as a flow of discrete messages.

For some purposes it is not necessary or useful to model the whole information flow, but only the part of information that concerns a single functionality. For example it is not needed to model the flow of user information, when one is just interested in the signaling mechanisms for the call control or network management. Thus it is important to analyze to what extent it is useful to implement the full functionality.

Another aspect is the layering method in communication protocols. Protocols are usually divided in several layers dealing with different aspects of the communication. The ISO–OSI layering model uses 7 layers to form a protocol stack from user interface to physical network transmission. For example in B–ISDN the packetized information transfer in the ATM layer may be mapped in a framed transmission on the next lower SDH layer. For simulation it is again important to identify the right layer for modelling the network. It would be very inefficient to simulate transmission on the physical layer (using bitwise transmission) for a simulation of ATM OAM protocols. In this case it would be better to abstract the behaviour of the lower layers using some typical properties (delay, loss) and simulate on the ATM cell layer with messages representing OAM messages or cells.

2.2. Simulation aims

In principle two types of simulation aims have to be distinguished. For protocol development the main interest is focused on the functionality of the mechanisms, whereas performance simulations deal with the performance (e.g. delays, queue length, loss) of networks. Their main properties and requirements will be discussed in more detail in the following paragraphs.

Another categorization, that is rather orthogonal to that mentioned first, regards the differences between the simulation of new protocols or network technologies (research and development) and the simulation of the application of well known techniques to an actual network topology (network planning). In this article the focus is on the first type of simulations (new protocols and techniques). These simulations require an easy and efficient technique for the description of node and link models. In contrary the network planning approach needs a large database of already described network elements, to be able to start the simulation from a quick sketch of the desired network scenario.

Performance simulation

Performance simulation aims towards the determination of performance parameters of the network or a single network element. Examples for such parameters are delay, queue length, errors or cell loss. All these measures have in common that a large number of simulation cycles are required to gather a result with acceptable statistical accuracy. Especially for the simulation of rare events (e.g. total link failures) very long simulation times are needed. Additionally it is often necessary to take into account larger networks during performance simulation.

This leads to a high number of messages flowing through the network. Strong requirements are posed to the performance of the performance simulation itself. That is the main reason why up to now most of these performance simulations are realized using standard programming languages like C or C++, that lead to a more compact and optimal code than machine generated source code.

Concerning the visualization, one may note that, during the simulation execution no dynamic visualizations are required. More important are convenient graphical entry of the simulated network topology and configuration of the network elements. After the simulation a graphical representation of the simulation results is a useful support for the evaluation. This representations may even be shown in the network's topology map. For example the load of a network link may be represented by the thickness of the line that represents the link. But also additional gauges may be placed to visualize measures.

Protocol simulation

In contrary to the performance simulation, the protocol simulation aims more towards the validation of the correct functionality of the protocols. Protocol simulation serves as a means to understand and evaluate new protocols and thus is mostly used for protocol design and implementation.

Since the focus is on the functionality and no statistical data is gathered, the simulation will be very limited regarding simulated time. Further, protocol simulations often do not take into account the flow of user data. This leads to a rather low number of messages flowing through the network. These are the reasons why the performance of the simulation does not play a premier role for protocol simulation.

A more important topic is, that with protocol simulation often a very complex functionality has to be described. So it is essential to decide for a simulation language, that offers good support for structured, hierarchical design and precise specification. As mentioned in the first chapter standardization bodies provide functional specification languages for this purpose.

It is desirable to provide a visualization already during the simulation and means for an interactive simulation control. For example single stepping or breakpoints may be used to have a closer look at details of the examined protocol. Internodal messages, as well as messages internal to a node and states of nodes should be visualized for debugging of protocol specification. Visualization may for example change colors of network nodes or links or show text giving information on messages that are transferred. Such graphical supported simulations are also very well suited for presentations.

For functional design and simulation several commercial and non–commercial tools exist. For SDL we are using SDT (Telelogic) supporting the graphical SDL specification and offering an SDL code generator to get C–code from the specification and an SDL simulator with debugging options and the possibility to generate message sequence charts from the simulation.

Combined protocol and performance simulations

In some cases it is desired to run a performance simulation after a new protocol has been designed and tested. For this purpose it is an advantageous feature to generate a performance simulation from the protocol description. This becomes even more important with the appearance of complex protocols already on the lower protocol layers of high speed networks (e.g. ABR protocol, ATM protection switching).

For example a two step approach may be chosen using SDL with the SDT toolset. Specifying and simulating first, using a visualization tool or network simulation platform as described hereafter, the functionality may be developed or proven. After the verification of the correct functionality the debugging and visualization options are switched off and a performance simulation derived from the same specification is executed.

On the one hand this technique simplifies the design and speeds up the development phase. On the other hand it makes it obsolete to reimplement the functionality using other languages. In this way it is also ensured, that no coding errors are introduced during simulation programming. A drawback is of course the slightly reduced simulation performance compared to handwritten C–simulations. Our experiences with generated code from Telelogic's SDT is that it runs approximately half as fast to nearly as fast as a C–programmed simulation using a special commercial library (CSIM [8]).

2.3. Known simulation techniques and tools

Standard programming languages (C, FORTRAN)

Standard programming languages like C, C++ or FORTRAN offer the advantage of a fast compilation and the generation of very performant machine code. For that reason they are often preferred for performance evaluations with the need for a large number of simulation cycles. To simplify the simulation programming several libraries are available, that provide routines for event oriented simulations. Examples are the C++ based object oriented simulation library CNCL from RWTH Aachen and the commercial simulation library CSIM [8]. They offer constructs like process scheduling, timers, message transfer, queues and servers. Some of these libraries also provide functions to gather statistical data from the simulation.

As already mentioned, the main disadvantage of these programming techniques is the necessity to describe the systems functionality on a very low level and to have limited support for analysis and testing of the specification. Further, they often do not provide a GUI for topology entry and visualization.

Simulation languages from other application domains (e.g. VHDL)

Simulation languages coming from other application domains may also be used for network simulations. For example hardware simulation languages (VHDL, Verilog) provide support for the simulation of concurrent processes and offer constructs to describe inter–process signal transfer. But in the same way as the standard programming languages they do not support a functional system specification. Further, they require a different description style, since they mainly focus on concurrent signal assignments in electronic circuits. Even though some hardware simulation tools offer graphical design entry, they are not very well adapted to protocol simulation.

Network simulators (e.g. Opnet)

Network simulation tools (e.g. Opnet) are targeting the simulation of communication networks in the network planning phase. They offer a bundle of models for existing network equipment and allow graphical entry of the network, that should be investigated. In principle they may also be suited for the simulation tasks addressed in this paper. For performance simulation they offer a C–based implementation of the network models and for protocol analysis the offer graphical visualization possibilities. Their main drawback is again the lack of a functional, precise specification technique. New node models have to be programmed in handwritten C–code leading to the problems already mentioned above.

3. Network simulation using SDL

As shown in the first chapter, functional description and SDL offer a lot of advantages that make it desirable to use them for network simulation, too. In [10,11] performance modelling with the use of SDL has already been described. At the author's institute a simulation environment for communication networks has been developed, that bases on SDL descriptions and further offers a GUI for topology entry and visualizations. After an overview of different simulation models this environment will be presented.

There are different possibilities to model the network in SDL. They can be categorized by the SDL type that is used to represent a network node. Following three models are presented. While the first model implements one network node as a whole SDL system, the other two approaches make use of the type concept in SDL'92 and represent node models as block types. Model 2 and 3 differ in the structuring of the network topology. While model 2 tries to be as close as possible to the real network topology, model 3 aggregates node instances of the same type to block instance sets.

Model 1: Network of SDL systems

In the first approach network nodes are modeled as SDL systems. An implementation of this approach has been used in [1] and [2]. With a simulation tool (SDT) these SDL systems (each representing one node) are implemented as separate UNIX processes. The internodal network communication is realized outside SDL also in a separate UNIX process dealing with all the links and implementing some basic link properties (delay, availability).

The SDL systems, which are representing network nodes are interconnected via a non-SDL communication process implementing the network links. Fig. 1 shows the simulation environment. It consists of a central process called SimCore, that has two main tasks. It implements the

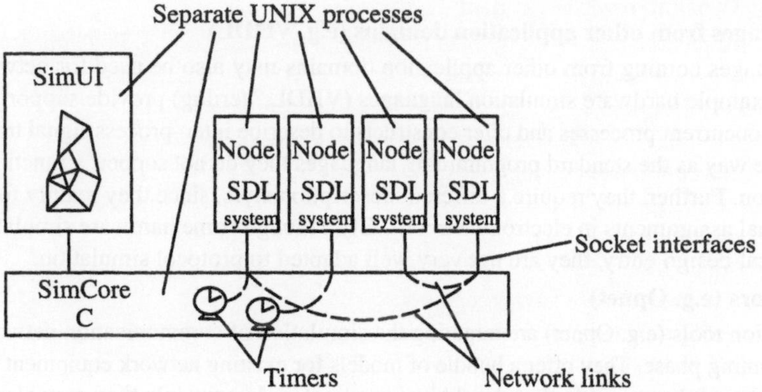

Figure 1 : Simulation model using one SDL–system per node

communication links with their delay properties and it offers global timer instances for all processes. Communication between the nodes and the simulation core is realized with UNIX TCP/IP sockets.

An advantage of this simulation model is the easy dynamic network topology configuration. New network topologies can be simulated by just executing the required number of node modelling processes and configuring the link process accordingly. Also nodes of different types may be instantiated. The number of network nodes and their types has not to be known when analyzing or compiling the node models. That is especially advantageous if the SDL tool for the code generation is not always available during simulation or the source code should be kept confidential.

Another advantage is the possibility to distribute the simulation on multiple workstations and in that way use their combined processing and storage resources for large systems. If node models are compiled for different platforms, one can even take advantage of the resources of a heterogeneous workstation environment.

But on the other hand this approach has also several drawbacks. It uses a lot of memory during simulation because every node's process requires its own simulation kernel. Additionally task switches between different processes in UNIX are more time consuming, than task switches within one UNIX process (between threads or internal to the SDL simulation kernel). The socket communication between the modules also limits the simulation speed. Further the use of several simulation kernels tied together via communication links leads to a synchronization problem. If local timers are provided in the distributed nodes these have to be synchronized. That is the reason why in the implementation [1,2] no local timer definitions in the node modelling processes have been allowed and timers have been moved to the central simulation core (SimCore). This also increases the communication needs between the node processes and the SimCore.

Message sequence charts (MSC) are a valuable tool for debugging, testing and commenting a system. They show an exemplary message sequence for the system. Some SDL simulation tools offer the opportunity to generate MSCs from simulation runs. Unfortunately these MSCs can only show messages contained in one SDL system. This means for the simulation model using SDL systems as node representations, that no inter–nodal, networkwide MSC can be generated. For protocol simulation particularly these MSCs would be very useful.

Model 2: Whole network in one SDL system

All the disadvantages mentioned above have lead to the development of a new simulation model that implements the whole communication network within one SDL system. The network nodes are modeled with SDL block types. The network links may either be mapped directly to SDL channels or may be represented using SDL processes. The latter simplifies the connection to the environment via signalroutes and channels as explained later in more detail.

Fig. 2 shows an example for the system view of this kind of simulation. Three different node models are defined as block types (NodeModel_A, NodeModel_B, NodeModel_C). These type definitions may also come from packages, forming a library of node models. The block types are instantiated according to the desired network topology and interconnected via SDL channels. For the definition of channel properties either channel substructures may be used or SDL processes (contained in additional blocks) are inserted in the links. Channel substructures raise the problem, that no communication channels can be set up to other entities than the blocks at their channel endpoints. So signal communication to a simulation manager or the environment for example could hardly be realized (fig. 3).

The use of the object oriented modelling approach enables all advantages of object orientation (e.g. reusability of code, inheritance and redefinition). A basic node block type can be specified incorporating the basic node functions common to all nodes. The different node models can afterwards be realized by inheriting the basic block type and redefining or adding the particular behaviour.

A network simulation tool should provide a graphical topology editor to enter and edit network topologies and parametrize the network elements. This information is normally stored in netlist files. From the network definition a simulation model should be generated. Using the approach of Model 2 this means that from the netlist information an SDL source file has to be generated, instantiating the desired number of nodes and inserting the necessary links (possibly with substructures). After that a new SDL analysis, code generation and compilation is required, before the simulation can be started. This leads on the one hand to long setup times for simulations and on

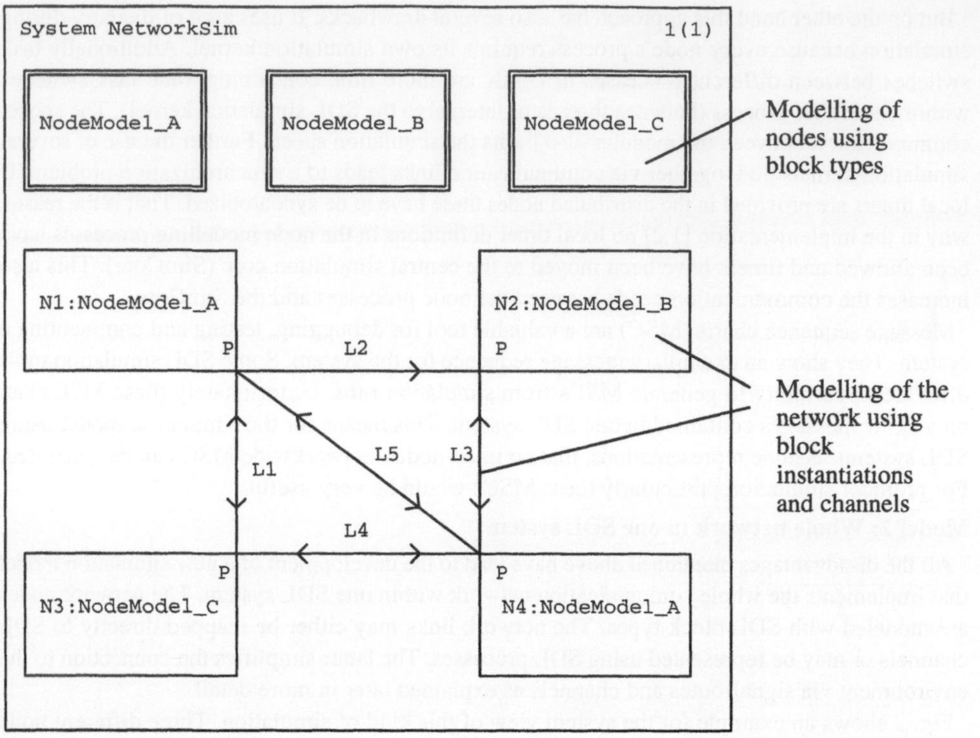

Figure 2 : Simulation model representing the simulated network in one SDL system

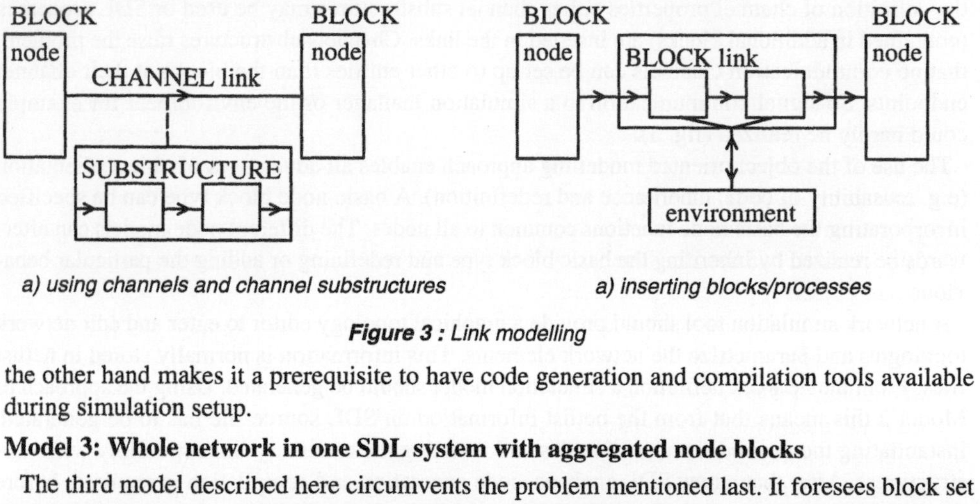

a) using channels and channel substructures *a) inserting blocks/processes*

Figure 3 : Link modelling

the other hand makes it a prerequisite to have code generation and compilation tools available during simulation setup.

Model 3: Whole network in one SDL system with aggregated node blocks

The third model described here circumvents the problem mentioned last. It foresees block set instantiations for all possible block types. Their number of instances can be given as parameters during simulation setup. So the number of blocks that are really instantiated can be given at run-

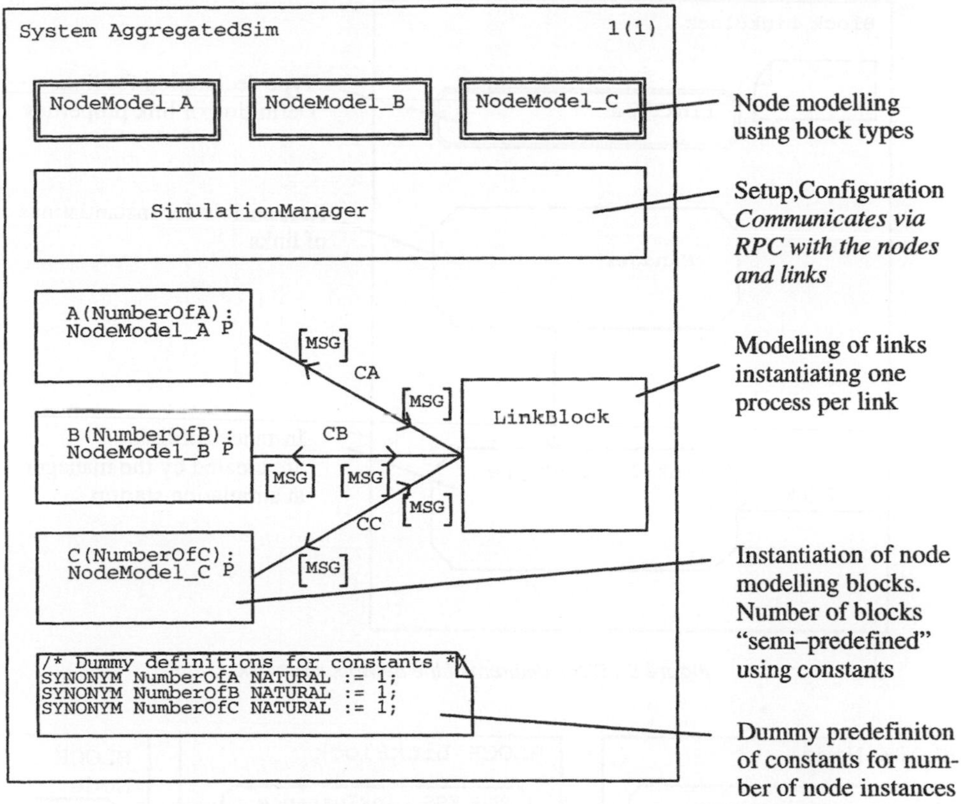

***Figure 4 :** Simulation model using "semi–dynamic" block instantiations*

time and has not to be specified in advance, during code generation or compilation. Fig. 4 shows an example for this technique.

Link implementation

The network links are all combined in one block (LinkBlock, fig. 5). When the simulation is started no links are existing. The manager process creates for each network link one process during simulation setup. The connectivity of the network nodes and the needed links may be read from a netlist file in this phase. The addressing of the link's destination is done via PID (SDL process identifier) addressing. The SimulationManager initializes the links to know their destination node's receiver process PIDs. In the same way the output ports processes in the node modelling blocks are initialized to know the PIDs of the link processes according to the desired network topology (fig. 6).

Dynamic block instantiations

As already mentioned above this simulation model is based on a new feature, the dynamic definition of the number of blocks during simulation startup. Since this is neither foreseen in the SDL specification [Z.100] nor implemented in the codegenerator (SDT), a workaround had to be provided. The block instantiations have been parameterized as shown in fig. 4 and allow a "semi–dynamic" instantiation of blocks. "Semi–dynamic" means, that the number of instances has not to

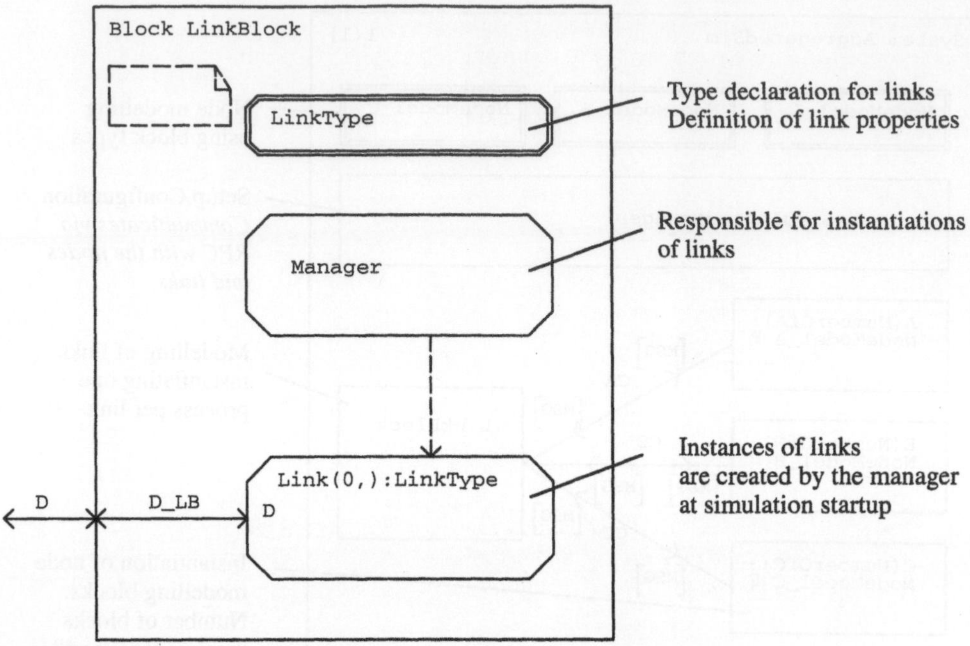

Figure 5 : *Block diagram of the network link block*

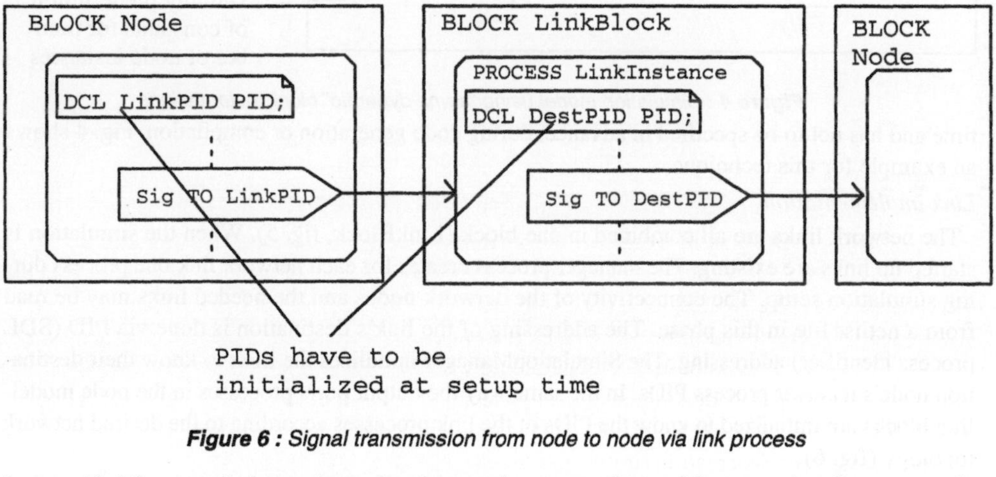

Figure 6 : *Signal transmission from node to node via link process*

be provided for compilation and may be given at the startup phase of the execution, but may not be changed later during the simulation runtime.

Normally the SDL syntax checker and the code generator require a constant number of instances to be defined already for the code generation. For this reason a dummy synonym definition has been inserted giving dummy values (e.g. 1) for the number of instances. The codegeneration generates a `#define` statement for the constant. To allow the specification of this parameter at runtime the `#define` statement is replaced by a variable definition and some code to read in the variable value from the environment (e.g. commandline arguments). Although with this workaround the number of instances has to be defined at the beginning of the simulation and cannot be changed later on, it is not necessary to recompile the system to change these values. Figure 7 shows the steps for the realization of this technique using the codegenerator from Telelogic.

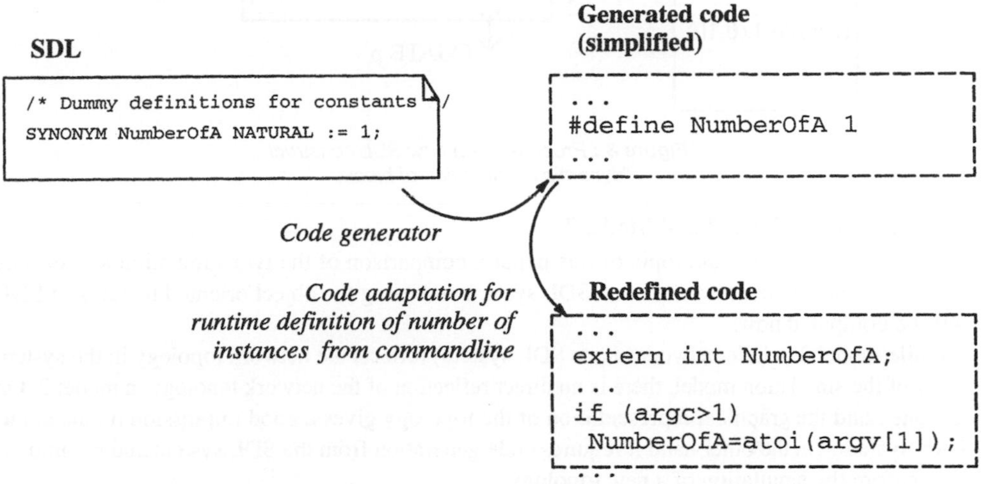

***Figure 7 :** Implementation of the "semi–dynamic" block instantiations*

Proposal of a new SDL construct

At this point a new syntax element for future SDL standards shall be proposed: Dynamic block creation (DBC). DBC should work like the dynamic process creation, but on the block level. Graphical representation could look like fig. 8. From a create command within one process a block instance may be created. To represent the creation link a new gate is introduced (CGATE) that connects the create link from within the creating block to the one outside the creating block. In case of ambiguous possibilities to generate new blocks when more than one block with the same name is present (e.g. on different hierarchy levels) these links may also be necessary to identify the desired block. The definition of the dynamically instantiated block may have parameters as known from process creation (initial and maximum number of instances).

This dynamic block creation is not only necessary for the network simulation application described in this paper. With larger systems it is often desirable to instantiate whole blocks of functionality during runtime. For example one could think of a universal network interface incorporating several protocol standards. It would be desirable to decide at runtime which protocol is to be used in the actual application. Depending on this decision only the necessary blocks are instantiated, instead of instantiating (by default) all possible blocks and only make use of some of them.

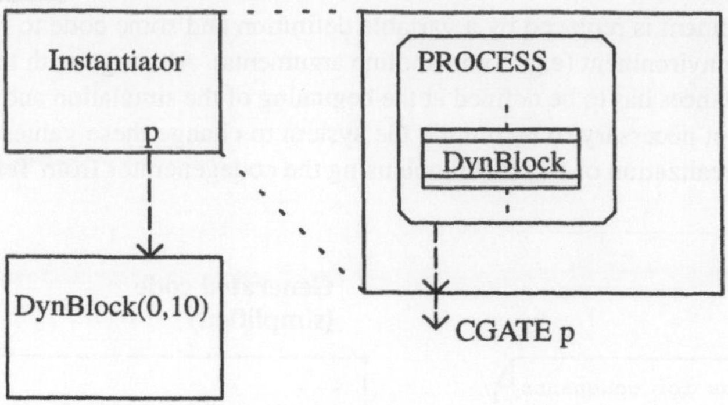

Figure 8 : *Proposal for a new SDL construct "dynamic instantiation of blocks"*

Comparison of Model 2 and Model 3

Coming back to the main topic of this paper a comparison of the two simulation approaches modelling the whole network in one SDL system and using the object oriented features of SDL will be compared now.

While model 2 (whole network in one SDL system) reflects the network topology in the system view of the simulation model, there is no direct reflection of the network topology in model 3. On the one hand the graphical representation of the topology gives a good impression on the simulated system. On the other hand it requires code generation from the SDL system and recompilation before the simulation of a new topology.

With the aggregation of nodes and links in model 3 the configuration from a netlist is very much simplified. It is only necessary to give the numbers of the different node types for the simulation at startup and to instantiate the network link processes in the SDL system. With the topology oriented model a translation of the netlist to SDL code is required. A disadvantage of model 3 is that with an increasing number of possible node types the code tends to become large, because code for every kind of node has to be integrated. Model 2 only creates code for the models really used during simulation and therefore is more compact.

4. The integrated simulation environment

4.1. Overview

At the author's institute a simulation environment for the types of network simulation mentioned in the introduction, namely protocol simulation and performance simulation, has been developed. The simulation environment is built around the SDL design tool (SDT) from Telelogic.

SDT consist of several modules that are concurrently executed on a UNIX platform. The main modules are a graphical editor for SDL/GR, a syntactical and semantical analyzer for SDL code, a codegenerator to generate C code from the specification and a simulation environment with graphical debugging options. Furthermore an MSC editor is contained, that allows to enter MSCs manually for system requirements specification and verification and also to generate MSCs automatically from simulation execution. Each module forms a single UNIX process. The modules are all interconnected via socket connections to the central communication manager POSTMASTER, which processes the routing of messages between modules.

The second part of the simulation environment is the graphical user interface for topology entry and visualizations. It is implemented using the public domain Tcl/Tk tools for GUI implementation. Fig. 9 shows the overall view of the software environment during the simulation.

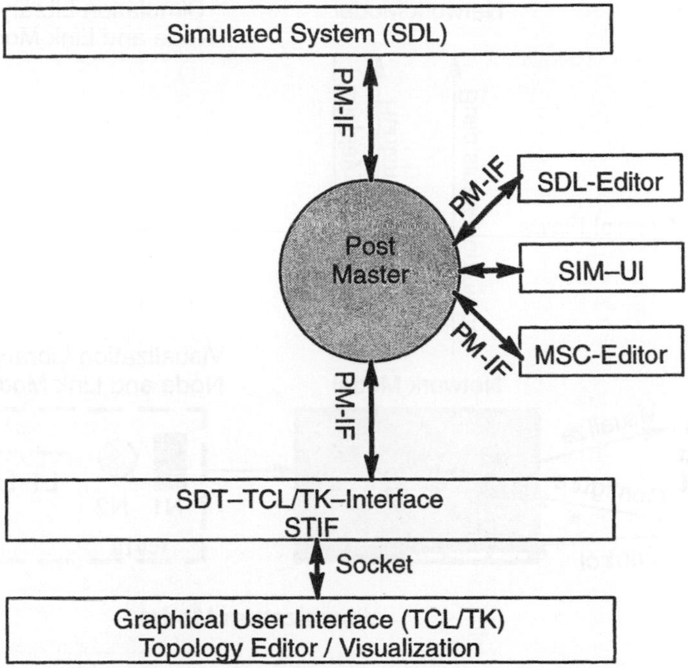

***Figure 9**: Software environment of the simulation platform*

The SDL simulation of the network is connected to the POSTMASTER via the Postmaster–Interface (PM–IF). Also connected to the POSTMASTER is the SIM–UI, allowing to control and debug the simulated system. In the SDL editor the state transitions may be displayed during the simulation. The MSC editor allows to trace the simulated messages. A new feature is the SDT–Tcl/Tk–Interface (STIF) that connects the POSTMASTER to a Tcl/Tk based GUI via socket communication.

On this simulation platform network simulations can be executed. To ease the design the GUI provides graphical, topological design entry by instantiating models of network elements. The network elements may be taken from a library. For each element in the library a simulation model and the according graphical model are stored (fig. 10).

The user may describe and configure the desired network using the elements from the visualization library. From this representation a simulation model is created. The simulation sends animation commands to the visualization model during the simulation. While the simulation is executing the user may control the simulation (e.g. single stepping, variable assignments). This control information leads to runtime interactions that are transmitted to the simulation.

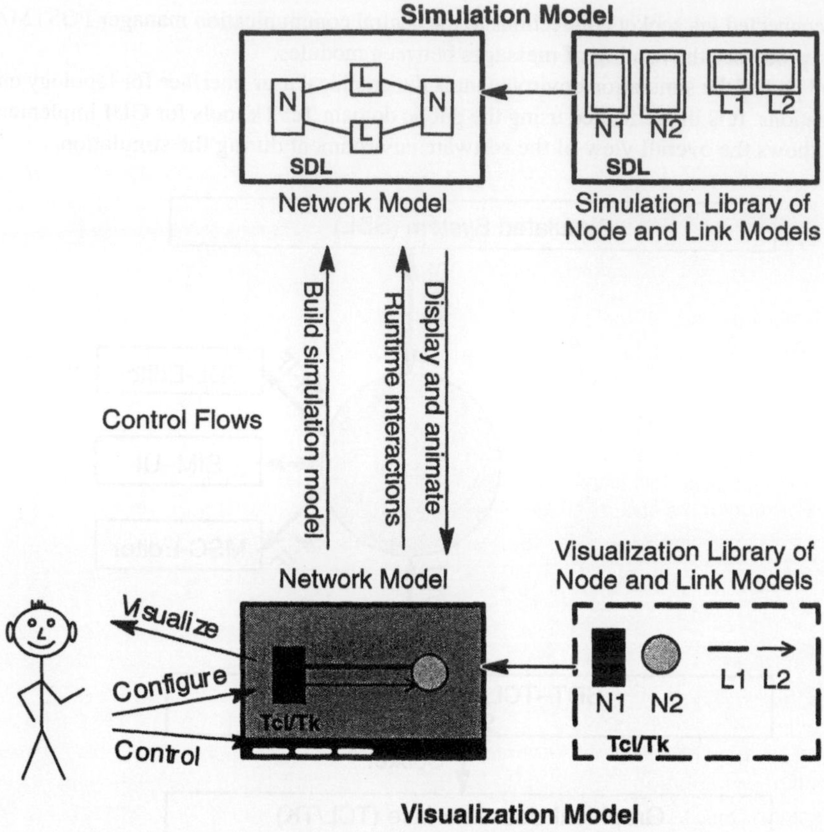

***Figure 10** : Network configuration from libraries*

4.2. Graphical interface

For a network simulation, especially for the protocol evaluation, a graphical representation of the network and of messages in the network is a very useful feature. The tasks of a graphical user interface (GUI) for network simulations may be divided in some main areas:

- Topological design entry serves as a means to easily setup network scenarios for the simulation. Advanced tools allow even an hierarchical structuring of the network.
- Animation and visualization during the simulation support the debugging and evaluation in protocol simulations.
- Presentation of simulation results is mainly used in performance simulations.

For the GUI of our network simulation tool we have chosen the public domain graphical interface design kit Tcl/Tk. It consist of an interpreter for a scripting language (Tcl=Tool command language) very similar to UNIX–shellscripts and a library of graphic functions to place standard user interface elements (e.g. buttons, listboxes) and basic graphic elements (rectangles, circles, icons). Tcl/Tk is very easy to learn (some hours of learning is sufficient to start working). The limited speed due to the interpreted execution doesn't raise a problem since during a protocol simulation the change in the graphic display is not too rapid.

For the graphical representation of nodes, rectangles or small bitmap icons are used. These graphical node elements are stored in a library. The library provides for each element in the simulation model library (SDL models) a counterpart of the graphical representation.

For visualization during simulation or to show simulation results after a performance simulation all kinds of operations may be applied to the objects (e.g. change of position, size, color, bitmap, text).

4.3. SDL simulation

The SDL simulation is realized as described in the previous chapter for model 3. For each possible type of network element a block set instantiation is provided. In that way it is not necessary to recompile for a new system topology.

The step from graphical representation to the simulator is done in the Tcl based GUI. A Tcl script analyzes the topology, that has been entered and generates a netlist, that can be read from the simulation. In the simulation a special block (SimControl) reads this file during startup and instantiates the required topological elements. Further, configuration information for network elements may also be transferred with this file. The control of the simulation can either be via the normal SDT simulator interface or via the new GUI.

4.4. Examples

Currently two example applications are being implemented using the simulation environment. The first example implements a basic ATM switch and will be used for performance simulation of the switch model in a networked environment. Among other things delay and cell loss will be measured from the simulation. An example for the protocol simulation is also currently emerging. It implements the OAM mechanisms within the ATM layer and will be extended by new mechanisms and protocols. The visualization allows to follow the message flow throughout the network and see the state of the nodes.

5. Summary

While functional description techniques are currently becoming state of the art for protocol design and implementation, the simulation of a networkwide application of the protocols has not been paid too much attention up to now. In this paper the main simulation aims (performance simulation and protocol simulation) have been identified and categorized. Following the evaluation of existing simulation techniques some approaches for the use of SDL in network simulations have been presented. The new simulation platform incorporates one of these models with a graphical user interface.

To review the advantages of the novel simulation environment the main features are summarized here:

- Functional description of network node models using the recommended description language SDL with all the advantages of FDT and SDL
- Automatic code generation for simulation and implementation
- Graphical topological network description with automated simulation configuration

- Change of network topology without codegeneration and recompilation
- Simulation control from the GUI
- Visualization of protocols for debugging and presentation
- Possibility to build libraries of network elements for simulation and visualization

Unfortunately the standard for SDL (Z.100) does not foresee the possibility of dynamic instantiation of blocks, what is a prerequisite for the proposed simulation model. A workaround has been presented to overcome the limitation and a new SDL construct has been proposed, to allow dynamic instantiation of blocks.

With all the features enumerated above, the proposed simulation environment is a valuable tool for the design and evaluation of communication networks and protocols. Future work will focus on the implementation of new simulation and visualization models for network nodes.

References

[1] B. Edmaier, *"ATM Network Design Tool"*, Technical Report, Technical University Munich – LKN, June 1995

[2] B. Edmaier, *"Pfad–Ersatzschalteverfahren mit verteilter Steuerung für ATM–Netze"*, PHD thesis, Technical University Munich – LKN 1996, ISBN 3–89675–112–3

[3] W. Kellerer, A. Iselt, R. Riek, *"Using SDL for the specification, simulation and implementation of an advanced OSI data–link protocol on an embedded microcontroller system"*, IFIP TC6/6.1 International Conference on Formal Description Techniques IX/ Protocol Specification, Testing and Verification XVI, Kaiserslautern, Germany, 8–11 October 1996

[4] A. Olsen, O. Færgemand, B. Møller–Pedersen, R. Reed, J.R.W. Smith, *"Systems engineering using SDL–92"*, Elsevier Science B.V., 1994

[5] J. Ousterhout, *"Tcl and the Tk Toolkit"*, Addison–Wesley, 1994

[6] ITU–T Z.100, *"Functional Specification and Description Language (SDL)", 1992*

[7] ITU–T Z.120, *"Message Sequence Charts (MSC)", 1992*

[8] H. Schwetman, *"CSIM Users's Guide – for use with CSIM Revision 16"*, Microelectronics and Computer Technologies Cooperation, Austin USA, June 1992

[9] R. Braek, O. Haugen, *"Engineering real time systems"*, Prentice Hall, UK, 1993

[10] M. Bütow, M. Mestern, C. Schapiro, P.S. Kritzinger, *"Performance Modelling with the Formal Specification Language SDL"*, IFIP TC6/6.1 International Conference on Formal Description Techniques IX/Protocol Specification, Testing and Verification XVI, Kaiserslautern, Germany, 8–11 October 1996

[11] M. Diefenbach, J. Hintelmann, B. Müller–Clostermann, *"The QUEST–Approach for the Performance Evaluation of SDL–Systems"*, IFIP TC6/6.1 International Conference on Formal Description Techniques IX/Protocol Specification, Testing and Verification XVI, Kaiserslautern, Germany, 8–11 October 1996

II
Performance Analysis

SDL '97: TIME FOR TESTING - SDL, MSC and Trends
A. Cavalli and A. Sarma (Editors)

SPEET — SDL Performance Evaluation Tool

Martin Steppler and Matthias Lott[1]

Abstract

This paper presents a new tool, named *SDL Performance Evaluation Tool* (SPEET)[2], for the performance analysis of formally specified systems under real–time conditions. SPEET facilitates the simulation and emulation of several formal specifications at the same time. The systems to be simulated, resp. to be emulated, can be triggered by traffic load generators and can be interconnected with transmission links which correspond to physical channels. The user can easily define probes within the formal specifications. The data of these probes generated during simulation runs, resp. emulation runs, can be statistically evaluated. SPEET provides a new *Computer Aided Software Engineering* (CASE) oriented solution for product development using formal methods.

1. INTRODUCTION

The objective of SPEET is the design and evaluation of complex, formally specified communication systems in an early phase of their development by means of simulation and emulation.

The main goal is to evaluate the capacity of formally specified systems under real–time conditions in regard to performance, required storage space, etc. Sufficient information in order to dimension the capacity of the target system is provided by statistical evaluation.

Amongst others, the real target system environment is emulated accordingly. Thus, a new solution for product developers has been created to allow early assessment of the real performance of communication systems as well as that of the required resources.

So far, the design of system soft– and hardware has only been based on the respective developer's experience. With the help of SPEET, systems can be designed using a dedicated tool with the possibility to simulate a formally specified system's implementation on a virtual hardware, to examine its behaviour under various load scenarios, and to predict its hardware requirements.

[1]Dipl.–Ing. Martin Steppler and Dipl.–Ing. Matthias Lott, Aachen University of Technology, Chair for Communication Networks, Prof. Dr.–Ing. Bernhard Walke, Kopernikusstr. 16, D–52074 Aachen, Germany. E–mail: {steppler,lott}@comnets.rwth–aachen.de. This paper is also available via WWW from http://www.comnets.rwth–aachen.de/~steppler/publications.

[2]SPEET is a spin–off of the project *"Entwicklung und Erprobung neuer Methoden und Werkzeuge zur Simulation, Analyse und Synthese komplexer Kommunikationssysteme"* (METWERK — Development of New Methods and Tools for Simulation, Analysis, and Synthesis of Complex Communication Systems), which was funded by *"Bundesministerium für Bildung, Wissenschaft, Forschung und Technologie"* (BMBF — Federal Ministry of Education, Science, Research and Technology of Germany) and developed in cooperation with S&P Media, Gadderbaumer Str. 19, D–33602 Bielefeld, Germany (WWW: http://www.sp–media.de).

In section 2, SPEET's twofold recursive cycle of product development and its interaction with other SDL CASE tools are explained. The following section 3 describes SPEET's tool components in further detail.

The implementation of an SDL specification can be stressed with the help of various traffic load generators, i. e. speech and packet data generators. Section 4 illustrates the characteristic features of these generators and demonstrates how a workload mix can easily be set up for specific implementations.

Due to SPEET's goal to assess the performance of a communications system, a realistic approach to model such a system must also include a model of the physical transmission of signals in a fixed or mobile radio network. These transmission models are explained in section 5.

Statistical performance evaluations can only be trusted, if the methods of collecting, examining and evaluating statistical data are reliable. Section 7 presents the statistical evaluation algorithms used by SPEET. This paper concludes with a summary of SPEET's features.

2. PRODUCT DEVELOPMENT AS A TWOFOLD RECURSIVE CYCLE

SPEET extends object–oriented software design methods for communication systems — these methods usually comprise the four phases system requirements analysis, system analysis, system design, and implementation — by a twofold cyclic approach of product development (see *Fig.* 1). The first recursive cycle of product development consists of the following steps:

1. The formal specification of an SDL system [8,10] is implemented by compiling automatically generated C source code under the same operating system SPEET runs on, i. e. a UNIX operating system or Windows NT (see *Fig.* 1, *arrow* 1).
2. Prior to code generation and compilation, the user can insert probes into the specification (see *sec.* 7). With the help of these probes, additional information about the simulation model itself can be gained during a simulation run of the previously compiled implementation (see *Fig.* 1, *arr.* 2).
3. This knowledge is derived from stochastic evaluation of the data generated by the user defined probes (see *Fig.* 1, *arr.* 3).
4. Therefore, the user can easily improve his system's specification and will get the best possible results (see *Fig.* 1, *arr.* 4).

In order to assess the performance of a specification's implementation on a real–time target processor system, the verification and validation of the specification does not yield sufficient information only by means of simulation. This is why SPEET provides following second recursive cycle of product development:

5. Analogously to step 1, C source code is automatically generated from an SDL specification and compiled. The difference to step 1 is that it is cross–compiled for a real–time target processor system (see *Fig.* 1, *arr.* 5), e. g. a microcontroller such as Motorola 680x0 [4], Intel 8051, etc. (see *sec.* 6).
6. Before emulating the target system, it can be designed according to the user's wishes, i. e. number and type of the processor system's components can be configured, e. g. the

amount and type of *Random Access Memory* (RAM). During and before the emulation, the user may modify the parameters of the just configured processor system, e. g. the processor's frequency or RAM access and cycle times, etc. (see *Fig.* 1, *arr.* 6).

7. Again, data generated by user defined probes results in knowledge about a specification's performance (see *Fig.* 1, *arr.* 7). Thus, reliable predictions can be made about the target system's hardware requirements, e. g. required processor speed, required storage space, etc. This knowledge not only has an impact on the design of the target system, but also on the respective specification (see *Fig.* 1, *arr.* 4).

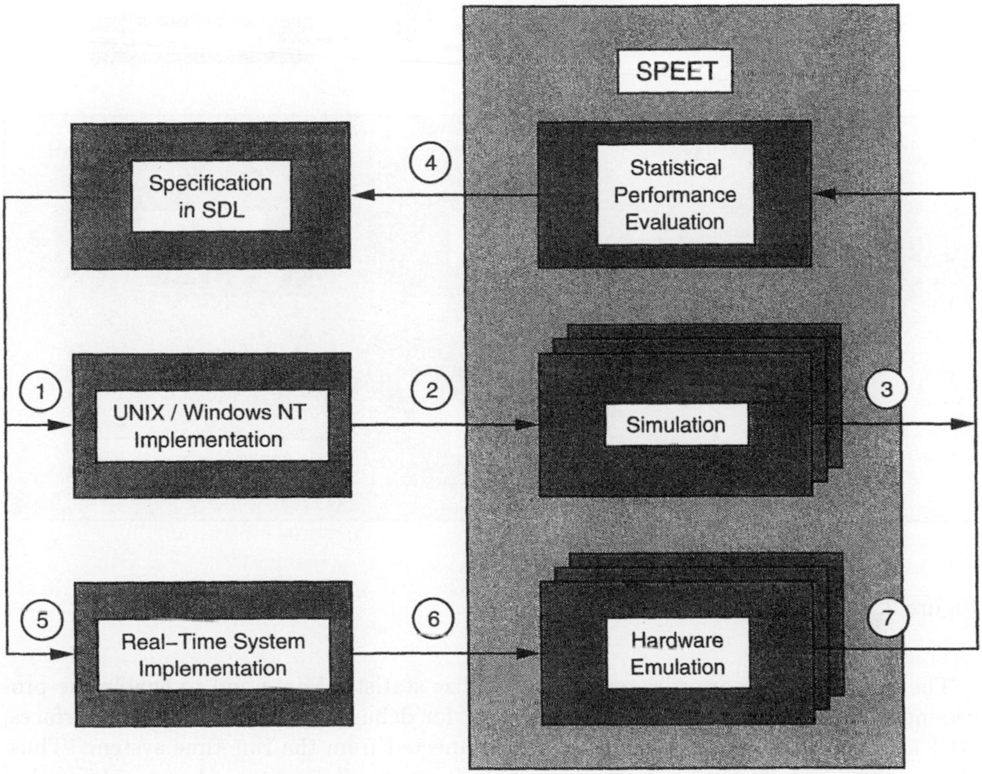

Figure 1. Product development as a twofold recursive cycle

3. SPEET TOOL COMPONENTS

The modular structure of SPEET is shown in Figure 2. The run–time system consists of one UNIX, resp. Windows NT, process. The implementations of one or more SDL systems and the traffic generators, transmission models, and hardware emulators chosen by the user are part of this process. The simulation, resp. emulation, process can be controlled via two types of interfaces: the *Command Line Interface* (CLI) and the *Graphical User Interface* (GUI).

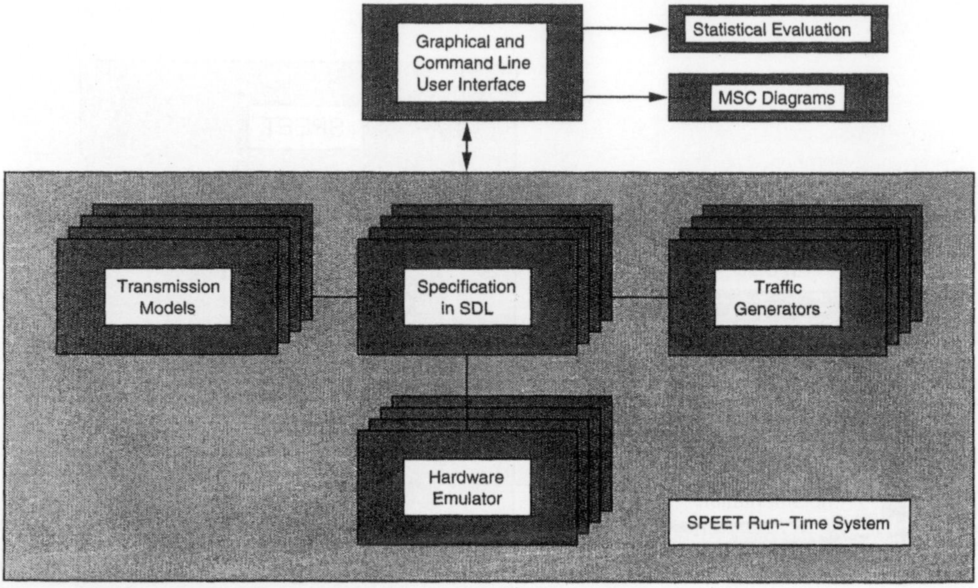

Figure 2. SPEET tool components

The latter one also provides means to visualize statistical data and to enable the processing of *Message Sequence Charts* (MSC) [7] for debugging purposes. Both interfaces, GUI and CLI, can be connected to and disconnected from the run–time system. Thus, the user connects to the run–time system during a simulation run whenever he wishes to retrieve results or to visualize statistical data and disconnects after this in order not to slow down the simulation by the communication between GUI and run–time system required for information interchange.

Figure 3 shows a typical SPEET scenario. Imagine a mobile radio communications system consisting of one base station and several mobile stations. Furthermore, suppose that *System A* and *System B* in Figure 3 correspond to the SDL specification of the mobile station's (*System A*), resp. base station's (*System B*), protocol stack.

When configuring a SPEET scenario, the user first defines the number of different SDL systems and the number of instances of each SDL system which are to be examined. For each instance or a subset of instances of an SDL system, he further can decide whether to simulate or emulate this instance. In the latter case, a target hardware processor system has to be configured (see *sec.* 6). Thus, several emulations of absolutely different processor systems and several simulations can be performed in parallel in one UNIX, resp. Windows NT, process at the same time.

Additionally, a traffic load mix can be assigned to an instance or a subset of instances of SDL systems. This traffic load mix consists of one or more traffic load generators as described in section 4.

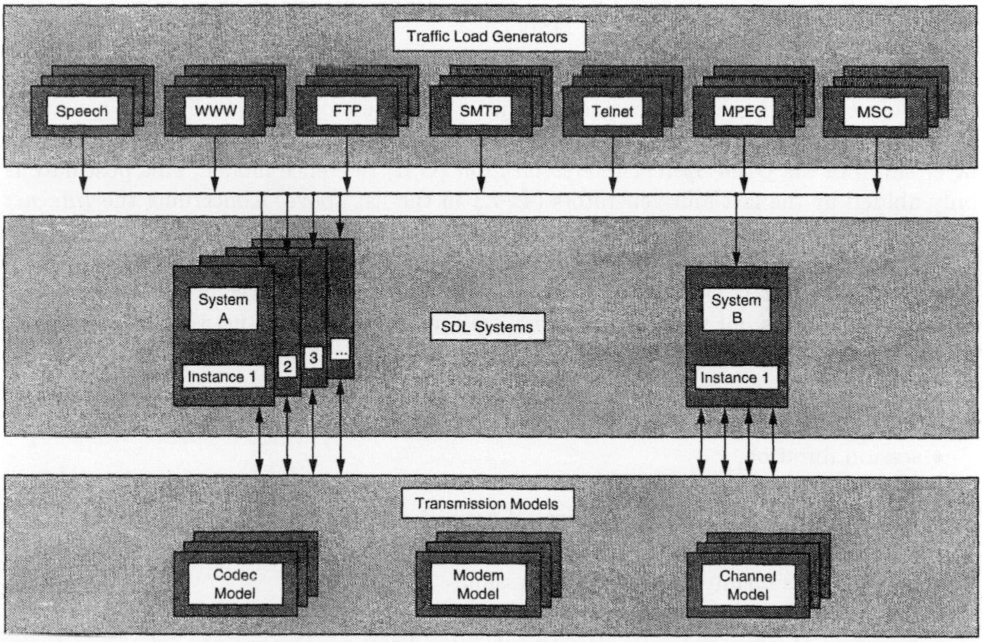

Figure 3. Typical SPEET scenario

Finally, SPEET provides means to connect instances of different SDL systems, e. g. a mobile and a base station, and to configure the characteristics of the information transporting medium, i. e. the transmission model which is composed of a model of the modulation and demodulation (modem model) used by the communication partners and a model of the physical channel (see *sec.* 5). If not specified in the protocol stacks, a channel encoder and decoder (codec model) can be made use of.

In Figure 3, for example, all mobile stations are connected to one base station. All these connections can be configured differently.

4. TRAFFIC LOAD GENERATORS

As shown in Figure 3, a traffic load mix consisting of one or more of the following seven traffic load generator types can be assigned to each instance or subsets of instances of an SDL system:

1. *World Wide Web* (WWW) [2],
2. *File Transfer Protocol* (FTP) [13],
3. *Simple Mail Transfer Protocol* (SMTP) [12],
4. Telnet [14],
5. conversational speech [3],
6. video and audio in *Moving Picture Experts Group* (MPEG) 1 and 2 format [9], and
7. load patterns with use–cases in MSC [7].

These traffic load generators have been designed to assist in the evaluation and verification of new communication protocols. This is why the model of a traffic load generator should be independent of sublayer protocols, i. e. a generator should be located above layer seven of the *Open System Interconnection* (OSI) reference model. This postulate is only abided by the last four generators (4.–7.) in the list above. Concerning the *Internet Protocol* (IP) services (1.–3.), OSI layers five to seven are also taken into account.

In general, SPEET traffic load is defined by the interarrival time and the size of a *Protocol Data Unit* (PDU) at the service border between OSI layer five and four. As a consequence of this, all traffic load generators are independent of network–oriented sublayers (OSI layer 1.–4.) and some are completely independent of all OSI layers (generators 4.–7.)[3].

The following model parameters characterize a *session* of an application:

- session duration,
- total size of transmitted data,
- distribution and duration of phases of activity and inactivity,
- number of connections per session,
- number of transmitted objects per session,
- distribution of object sizes,
- direction of transmission (bidirectional or unidirectional), and
- destination addresses of connections.

The size and interarrival time of a PDU depends on the respective type of application. SPEET discerns *OSI sublayer independent* and *OSI sublayer dependent* applications. The PDU sizes of IP oriented services such as WWW, FTP, and SMTP may vary in a wide range from some bytes to several mega bytes. PDU of the latter size need to be segmented and depend on sublayer flow control protocols.

On the other hand, OSI sublayer independent applications either depend on the user only, e. g. the speech and telnet generators, — PDU sizes of such applications are relatively small and, due to this, there is no need to segment these PDU in sublayers —, or they are

[3]The MSC load generator's independence of OSI sublayers depends on the type of signals specified in the respective MSC, i. e. signals to layer three of a protocol stack, of course, remove OSI sublayer independence.

real–time applications, e. g. the MPEG generator, which expect the respective sublayers to sustain a certain bit–rate and ignore sublayer flow control mechanisms.

The *speech generator* models talkspurts and pauses of one speaker in a conversation as proposed by BRADY [3]. The traffic load generators of IP oriented services are based on long–term measurements [1,11]. The statistical properties of MPEG video and audio traffic is modeled with the help of Markov chains, which are parameterised by analysing films, TV shows, etc. [15].

Finally, MSC with time constraints can be used to stress and test formal specifications (see *Fig.* 4).

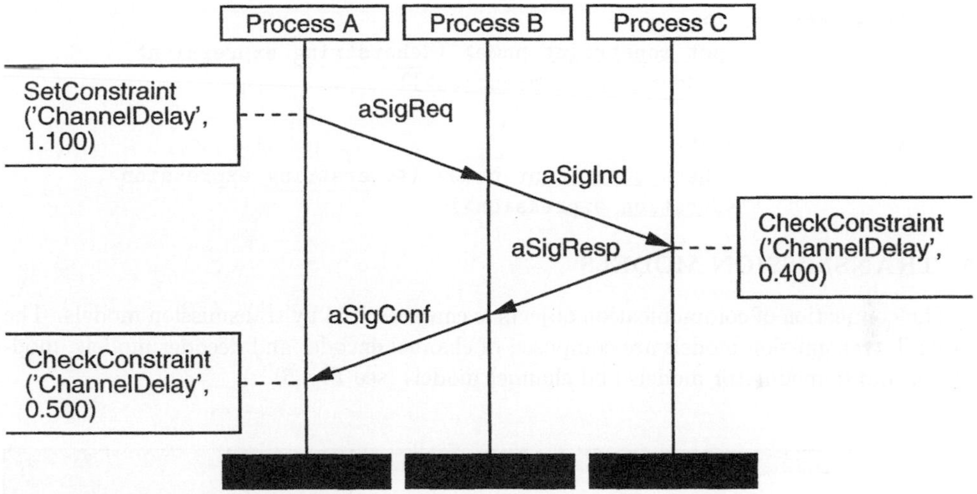

Figure 4. MSC with time constraints

A time constraint is set and checked as follows: Whenever a comment symbol containing text of the form

`SetConstraint(CharString, Duration)`

is connected to an input or output message, this defines a time constraint identified by the `CharString` parameter. The optional `Duration` parameter can be used to delay an outgoing message by a fixed time span. Then, a comment symbol containing text of the form

`CheckConstraint(CharString, Duration)`

may be used to check whether the time elapsed since the definition of the time constraint refered to by `CharString` exceeds the value of the second `Duration` parameter. A time constraint may be checked several times and at several places within an MSC diagram since its defintion. Depending on SPEET's settings the user is notified in case of time constraint violations. Of course, MSC without time constraints can be used to trigger SDL systems, too. SetConstraint always redefines preceeding definitons of the same name. The abstract syntax of the time constraint commands in *<u>B</u>ackus-<u>N</u>aur <u>F</u>orm* (BNF) is

```
<time constraint list> ::=
                  <time constraint list item>
                  {, <time constraint list item>}

<time constraint list item> ::=
                  <set time constraint>
                | <check time constraint>

<set time constraint> ::=
                  <set constraint name> (<charstring expression>
                  [, <duration expression>])

<check time constraint> ::=
                  <check constraint name> (<charstring expression>,
                  <duration expression>)
```

5. TRANSMISSION MODELS

The connection of communication objects is characterized by transmission models. The SPEET transmission models are composed of channel encoder and decoder models, modulator and demodulator models and channel models (see *Fig.* 5).

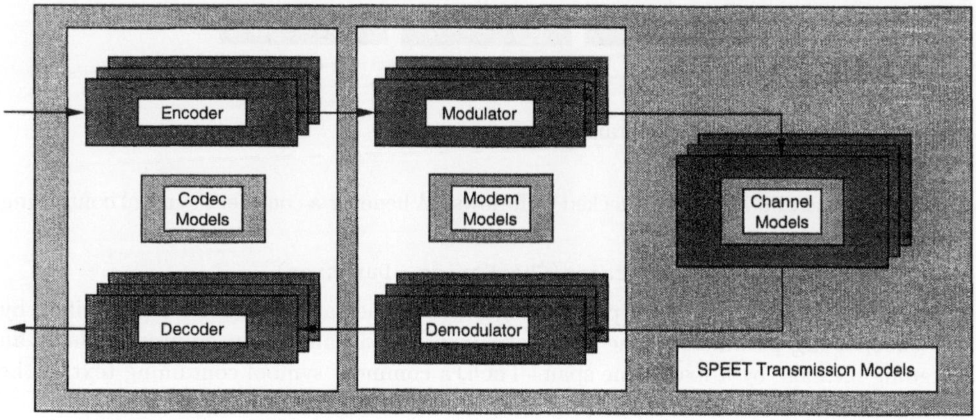

Figure 5. SPEET transmission models

To model the reduction of the error rate on the transmission links by means of *<u>F</u>orward <u>E</u>rror <u>C</u>orrection* (FEC) and error detection the appropriate algorithms are implemented in the codec models as far as this functionality is not implemented in the formally specified protocol stack.

For wired networks, the transmission model is very simple because the channel characteristic will not change during data transmission and no modulation of the carrier frequency is required in many cases. For data transfer on the radio link on the other hand, the transmitted signals have to be adapted to the channel characteristics by means of modulation. This is modeled in SPEET with the help of the modem models.

They reflect the impact of the radio channel on the modulation scheme and take into account the attenuation as well as delay spread and doppler spread. This effects the *Bit Error Ratio* (BER) which is the output of this model and is used for the performance analysis of the protocols which are under test in SPEET. The required information on the statistics of the radio channel is obtained out of the channel models which describe the radio wave propagation.

The simulation of radio wave propagation is of the utmost importance to realistic simulation of the BER. In SPEET, methods have been developed to determine the properties of radio channels which take the main physical effects into account in the form of models. They simulate various characteristics of a channel, i. e. the propagation coefficients and fading behaviour. Especially, fading has to be considered in mobile communication scenarios.

In SPEET, the rapidly changing amplitude due to multipath propagation also named short–term fading is modeled by the Rayleigh distribution. If a *Line Of Sight* (LOS) path is present, it is modeled with a Rice distribution. The slowly varying signal strength due to shadowing is called long–term fading and can be described by a log–normal distribution. Respective values for the variance of the distribution are known from measurements and are dependent on topology and morphology. The mean attenuation can be obtained by averaging the fading values over different locations at respective distances.

The mean attenuation values which are used in SPEET are based on the models of HATA–OKUMURA [6] and COST–231–WALFISCH–IKEGAMI [5]. For very small distances and LOS between transmitter and receiver free–space attenuation is assumed. Depending on the frequency, the path length, the characteristics of the propagation medium, and the antenna engineering the appropriate model is selected and the following parameters characterizing the behaviour of the time variant attenuation are chosen:

- carrier frequency,
- topology and morphology,
- antenna heights, and
- path length.

Especially for the COST–231–WALFISCH–IKEGAMI model, additional parameters are:

- heights of roofs,
- street directions,
- width of roads, and
- distance between buildings.

Finally, the COST–231–WALFISCH–IKEGAMI model also takes diffraction into account.

6. HARDWARE EMULATION

SPEET's main objective is the performance analysis of formally specified systems under real–time conditions. In order to meet this goal, SPEET provides emulation of microcontroller systems, e. g. Intel 8051, Siemens SAB801C66/67, Motorola MC680x0, etc.

When the user has chosen a subset of instances of SDL systems to be emulated as described in section 3, the target processor system can be configured. See Figure 6 for the components of an example processor system.

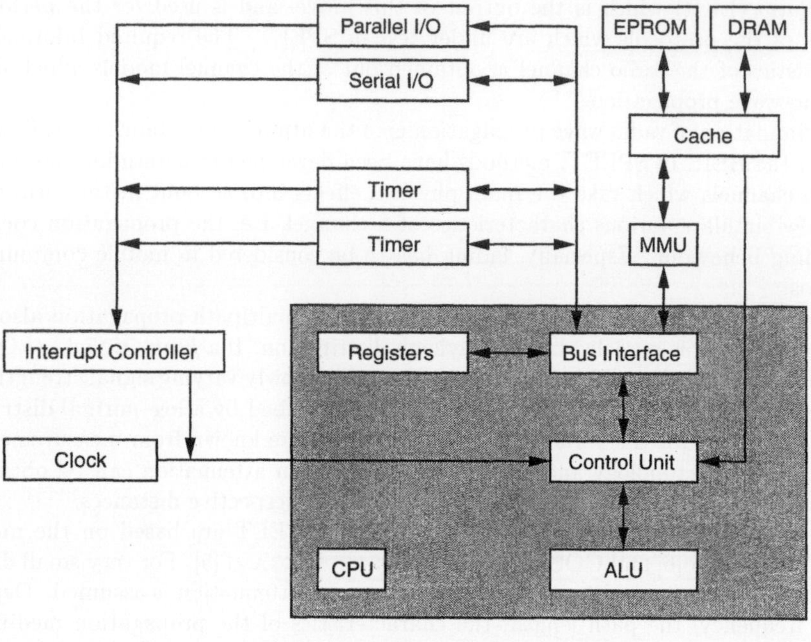

Figure 6. Components of example processor system

After having chosen a *Central Processing Unit* (CPU), other components can be added and parameterised, e. g. the type of RAM — dynamic or static — and its access and cycle time. Due to the fact that several emulations can be carried out in parallel (see *sec.* 3), the same hardware configuration may be used to perform a series of performance evaluations, e. g. the parameter "clock speed" may be varied, or different hardware configurations may be used to compare the performance of an SDL specification on different hardware platforms.

In contrast to non–software solutions, emulations with "unreal" parameters, e. g. an 8051 microcontroller with 1 GHz clock speed, are possible. Furthermore, changes to the hardware configuration, e. g. changing RAM storage space from 1 MB to 100 MB, are quickly made. These features facilitate an easier detection of bottlenecks.

The hardware emulation itself is event–driven. The number of used CPU cycles is calculated for each machine instruction which corresponds to an event. Furthermore, the instruction is executed, e. g. memory is read, registers are modified, etc. The next event, i. e. the next instruction, takes place after the required number of CPU cycles is elapsed. Each component of the processor system such as RAM chips, multiplexers, code and data caches, etc. is an event–handler. A central event–scheduler controls the emulation and dispatches events to the addressed event–handlers. For each processor system component, emulation as close to reality as possible is intended.

7. STATISTICAL EVALUATION

SCHREIBER presents in [16] a new algorithm which allows the analysis of correlated random sequences in order to gain the stationary distribution function $F(x)$. This algorithm can be used to control systematically the required number of trials of a simulation run by a formula which depends on the desired minimum value F_{min} of $F(x)$, on the prescribed upper limit d_{max} of relative error per $F(x)$ interval, and also on the measured mean value of the correlation coefficient $\bar{\varrho}(x)$. Correlated random sequences are typical for simulation runs of communications systems. Therefore, this algorithm is more appropriate for the analysis of formally specified systems than conventional evaluation methods such as batch means. Nevertheless, SPEET provides both methods, *Limited Relative Error* (LRE) and batch means.

In order to analyse the performance of a formal specification, random sequences to be evaluated should be generated by the specification itself. This is why the user should be able to insert probes into the specification, which do not interfere with the semantics of the specification. The most convenient way of inserting a probe into a specification is a new probe symbol which can be connected to normal SDL symbols just like a comment symbol, i. e. the connecting line is dashed (see *Fig.* 7). The user may specify three different SDL expressions inside this new probe symbol:

```
ProbeReal(CharString, Real)
ProbeDuration(CharString, Duration)
ProbeTime(CharString, Natural, Time)
```

Their abstract syntax in BNF is

```
<probe list> ::=
                <probe list item> {, <probe list item>}

<probe list item> ::=
                <probe real>
              | <probe duration>
              | <probe time>

<probe real> ::=
                <probe real name> (<charstring expression>,
                <real expression>)
```

```
<probe duration> ::=
              <probe duration name> (<charstring expression>,
              <duration expression>)

<probe time> ::=
              <probe time name> (<charstring expression>,
              <natural expression> [, <time expression>])
```

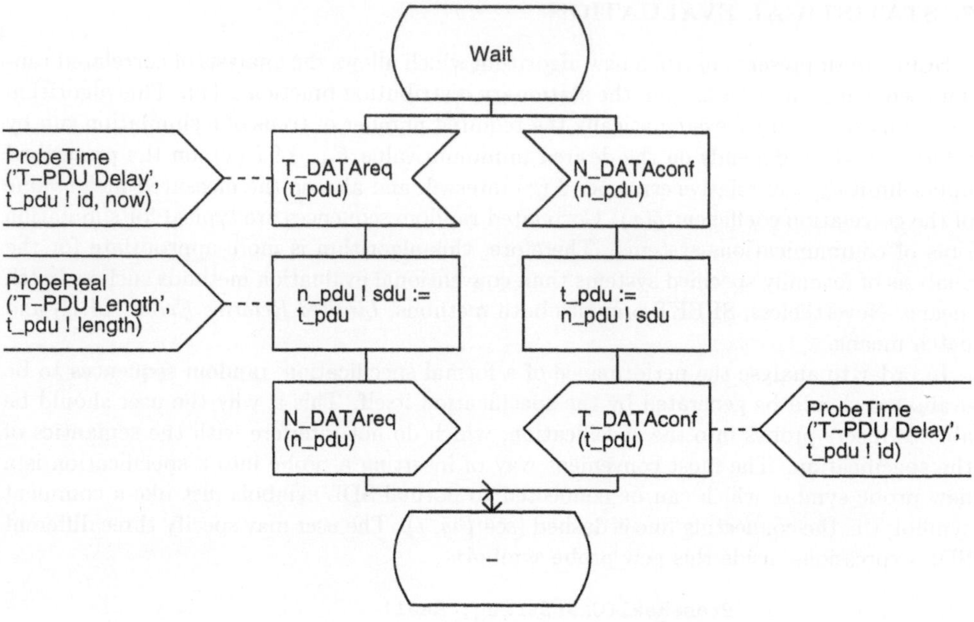

Figure 7. Example usage of the new probe symbol

SPEET's run–time system (see *Fig.* 2) interprets these probes. The meaning of their parameters is as follows: The `CharString` parameter always denotes the name of the probe. All data sent to the statistical evaluation with the help of probes, which are named the same, are considered to belong to the same set of statistical data. In case of the probes `ProbeReal` and `ProbeDuration` the second parameter is the value which is to be sent to the statistical evaluation.

On the other hand, the probe `ProbeTime` can be used to measure time spans. The natural expression denotes a measurement identifier. When the user sends the probe `ProbeTime` with the same name and identifier for the second time to the run–time system, the difference between the two time parameters is statistically evaluated and is considered to belong to the data set `<charstring expression>`. By using identifiers, several parallel measurements can be carried out at the same time. If the third parameter of the probe `ProbeTime` is left out, `now` is considered to be its default value.

See the simplified OSI network–layer protocol in Figure 7 for example usage of the new probe symbol. Whenever the signal `T_DATAreq` is received, the probe `ProbeTime('T-PDU Delay', t_pdu!id, now)` is sent to the statistical evaluation method and the measurement is started. Assume that the transport–layer PDU `t_pdu` and the network–layer PDU `n_pdu` are objects of an *Abstract Data Type* (ADT) `PDU` and that each PDU is uniquely identified by its member `id`. Furthermure, assume that the member `length` holds the length of each PDU in bit. The member `sdu` holds the *Service Data Unit* (SDU) of each PDU, i. e. the PDU of the resp. super–layer.

When the network–layer peer–entity has acknowledged the reception of `n_pdu`, the network–layer receives the signal `N_DATAconf`. The measurement of the round–trip delay started after the reception of `T_DATAreq` is now finished by sending `ProbeTime('T-PDU Delay', t_pdu!id)` to the run–time system.

The probe `ProbeReal('T-PDU Length', t_pdu!length)` is used to measure the average length of all PDU.

The end of a simulation run, resp. emulation run, is reached, when the abortion criterion of all probes is fulfiled, i. e. a sufficient number of random values has been evaluated in order to present a statistically trustworthy result. In contrast to batch means, the abortion criterion of LRE depends on the measured correlation. Nevertheless, a maximum limit of elapsed time can also be used as an abortion criterion, although trustworthy results cannot be guaranteed in this case.

8. CONCLUSIONS

Computer aided software engineering using formal methods has been extended by a new tool for the performance evaluation of formally specified systems as presented in this paper.

The CASE cycle of development does not only include object–oriented analysis using the *Object Modeling Technique* (OMT) and formal specification of this analysis' result in SDL, but from now on also the evaluation and verification of the implementation of formal specifications under real–time conditions on target hardware processor systems. For this purpose, SPEET provides

- simulation of several SDL systems in parallel,
- emulation of several SDL systems in parallel implemented for real–time hardware processor systems,
- various traffic load generators representing video, audio, speech, and packet data applications,
- models for encoding and decoding, modulation and demodulation, and physical transmission of signals, and
- statistical evaluation of data measured during simulation runs, resp. emulation runs.

Future work will concentrate on the emulation of further processor systems such as Intel 80x86 processors, on an additional MPEG 4 traffic load generator and more sophisticated transmission models for the *Super High Frequency* (SHF, 3–30 GHz) band and the *Extreme*

High Frequency (EHF, 30–300 GHz) band in regard to absorption due to oxygen and water.

REFERENCES

1. Martin F. Arlitt, Carey L. Williamson. *A Synthetic Workload Model for Internet Mosaic Traffic.* In *Proceedings of the 1995 Summer Computer Simulation Conference*, pp. 24–26, Ottawa, Canada, July 1995.
2. T. Berners-Lee, R. Fielding, H. Frystyk. *Hypertext Transfer Protocol (HTTP) 1.0.* Network Working Group, Request For Comments (RFC) 1954, May 1996. This document is also available via http://ds.internic.net/rfc/rfc1954.txt.
3. Paul T. Brady. *A Model for Generating On–Off Speech Patterns in Two-Way Conversation.* The Bell System Technical Journal, Vol. 48, No. 9, pp. 2445–2472, September 1969.
4. Barry B. Brey. *The Motorola Microprocessor Family: 68000, 68008, 68010, 68020, 68030, and 68040: Programming and Interfacing with Applications.* Series in Electronics Technology. Saunders College Publishing, 1992.
5. Commission of the European Communities. *Urban transmission loss models for mobile radio in the 900 and 1,800 MHz bands.* European Cooperation in the Field of Scientific and Technical Research, Vol. COST 231 TD (91) 73, September 1991.
6. M. Hata. *Empirical Formula for Propagation Loss in Land Mobile Radio Services.* IEEE Transactions on Vehicular Technology, Vol. VT–29, pp. 317–325, August 1980.
7. Telecommunication Standardization Sector of ITU. *Message Sequence Chart (MSC).* ITU–T Recommendation Z.120, International Telecommunication Union, March 1993.
8. Telecommunication Standardization Sector of ITU. *Specification and Description Language (SDL).* ITU–T Recommendation Z.100, International Telecommunication Union, March 1993.
9. Joan L. Mitchell, William B. Pennebaker, Chad E. Fogg, Didier J. LeGall, Hrsg. *MPEG Video Compression Standard.* Digital Multimedia Standards Series. Chapman & Hall, New York, USA, 1997.
10. Anders Olsen, Ove Færgemand, Birger Møller-Pedersen, Rick Reed, J. R. W. Smith. *Systems Engineering Using SDL–92.* Elsevier Science B. V., Amsterdam, The Netherlands, 1994.
11. Vern Paxson. *Empirically-Derived Analytic Models of Wide-Area TCP Connections.* IEEE/ACM Transactions on Networking, Vol. 2, No. 4, pp. 316–336, August 1994. This document is also available via ftp://ftp.ee.lbl.gov/papers/WAN–TCP–models.ps.Z.
12. Jonathan B. Postel. *Simple Mail Transfer Protocol.* Network Working Group, Request For Comments (RFC) 821, August 1982. This document is also available via http://ds.internic.net/rfc/rfc821.txt.
13. Jonathan B. Postel, J. Reynolds. *File Transfer Protocol (FTP).* Network Working Group, Request For Comments (RFC) 959, October 1985. This document is also available via http://ds.internic.net/rfc/rfc959.txt.
14. Jonathan B. Postel, J. Reynolds. *Telnet Protocol Specification.* Network Working Group, Request For Comments (RFC) 854, May 1983. This document is also available

via http://ds.internic.net/rfc/rfc854.txt.

15. Oliver Rose. *Simple and Efficient Models for Variable Bit Rate MPEG Video Traffic.* Technical Report 120, Institute of Computer Science, University of Würzburg, July 1995. This document is also available via http://www–info3.informatik.uni–wuerzburg.de/TR/tr120.ps.gz.
16. Friedrich Schreiber. *Effective Control of Simulation Runs by a New Evaluation Algorithm for Correlated Random Sequences.* Archiv für Elektronik und Übertragungstechnik (AEÜ), Vol. 42, No. 6, pp. 347–354, November 1988.

SDL '97: TIME FOR TESTING - SDL, MSC and Trends
A. Cavalli and A. Sarma (Editors)

Performance Analysis of TCP's Flow Control Mechanisms using Queueing SDL

Jörg Hintelmann, Reinhard Westerfeld
University of Essen, Dept. of Mathematics & Computer Science, D 45 117 Essen
{jh, rwesterf}@informatik.uni-essen.de

In this paper we use simulation models which have been derived from an extended SDL-specification to compare the performance behaviour of different TCP flow control mechanisms. We present a method and a tool that help system designers to integrate model based performance evaluation into the design of communication protocols. We illustrate this method by investigation of the throughput of a TCP connection in case of lost packets due to congestion. We show that TCP-Reno one of the most common reference implementation has good performance if only a single loss occurs, whereas TCP-Tahoe the other reference implementation is well designed to handle multiple losses from one window of data. We explore the performance benefits of adding selective acknowledgement to TCP which overcomes the performance problems of Tahoe and Reno. This study shows the application of SDL-based performance evaluation using the tool QUEST.

1. INTRODUCTION

In this paper we investigate the performance behaviour of different TCP variants, known as TCP-Reno, TCP-Tahoe and SACK-TCP. We use simulation models which have been derived automatically from extended SDL-specifications of the protocol versions under study. Since a formal specification has to be as implementation-independent as possible specification languages do not (and should not) cover performance aspects. Hence, the integration of performance evaluation techniques with the main stream of computer and communication system engineering is an important requirement. Here we contribute to this method integration process and propose a performance evaluation methodology that is based on SDL-specifications extended by queueing stations.

Our approach supports the analysis of performance behaviour during early design phases and allows protocol designers to make a careful choice of design alternatives. The main advantage of the method is, that an SDL-specification is used as the core of the performance model. This reduces time and effort for the development of early performance models and their adaption to the system under development.

In chapter 2 we present the language Queueing SDL (QSDL) as an extension to SDL and the tool QUEST that implements our approach. In chapter 3 we describe TCP-Reno and TCP-Tahoe the two most common reference implementations of TCP [7] and a third version that uses selective acknowledgement as proposed in the Internet Engineering Task Force (IETF) [6].

In chapter 4. we introduce the SDL-specification of TCP and show how to supplement descriptions of traffic sources and bounded resources like buffer sizes, processor speeds or channel bandwidths which are nessecary to obtain a performance model. Finally, in chapter 5. we present our modelling scenario, describe the experiments and show the results of our investigation.

2. THE LANGUAGE QSDL AND THE QUEST-TOOL

Here we sketch the main ideas of our approach, following the detailed informations given in [3] and [4]. The starting point of our performance evaluation is the formal description of a system using SDL. Time consuming machines that model the congestion of processes for limited resources are adjunct to an SDL-system. The machines are derived from queueing stations and provide services to their environment. The provided service may be requested or called by entities from the environment. The total time a request spends in a queueing station depends on the amount and the priority of the required service, the speed of the server and additionally the wait time suffered in the queue.

The QSDL machines offer their services to the QSDL-processes that are SDL-processes requesting for service. Now we give an overview of the graphical representation of QSDL, named QSDL/GR and then we introduce the language QSDL and sketch our tool QUEST.

2.1 Overview of QSDL

Here we introduce the extension of SDL by syntactical constructs for *load* and *machines*. The resulting specification and performance analysis language QSDL provides means for the specification of load, machines and their binding. These extensions strive for maximum structural and syntactical consistency with SDL.

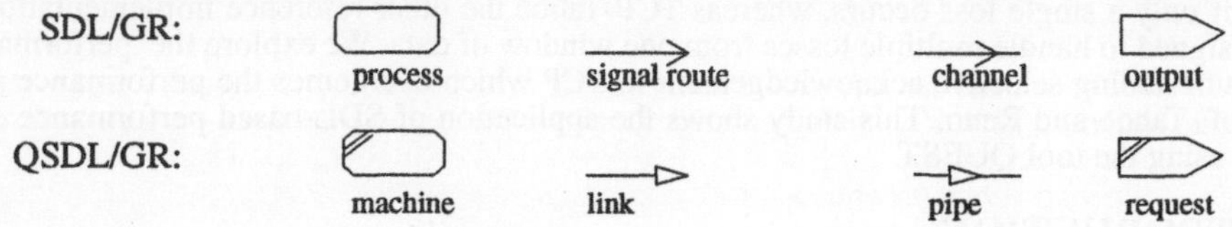

Figure 1. Elements of SDL/GR and QSDL/GR

The binding of the load to the machines is managed by a *service call* transport mechanism, which is totally independent of the signal transport mechanism of SDL. *Load* occurs in the QSDL-processes by the instantiation of time consuming *requests* that are referred for execution to adjunct machines given by queueing stations. The graphical representation of the new constructs (QSDL/GR) is displayed in figure 1. An example is given in figure 2.

QSDL-processes are bound to the machines via links and pipes. Processes and machines within the same block are only connected with a link. The processes serve as starting point and the machine as endpoint of the link. In the case that the process and the derived machine are in different blocks the binding has to carry out in two steps. First of all it is necessary to define a pipe between these blocks and links from the process to the border of the block and from the border of the block to the machine, see figure 2 , link Li3 pipe Pi1 and link Li4.

In the second step the links and pipes are interconnected. This is done in the same way as the connection of SDL-channels and signalroutes with the difference of using „*bind to*“ instead of „*connect and*“.

Note that for the purpose of workload modelling, traffic sources may be located everywhere in the system. Generally, these sources are QSDL-processes that generate signals according stochastic distributions for the signal interarrival times. In particular, the so called multi-state sources that are convenient for the modelling of on/off-sources or variable bit rate video sources may be represented straightforwardly as QSDL-processes. Since traffic sources are described as processes they may be connected to blocks by channels and signalroutes.

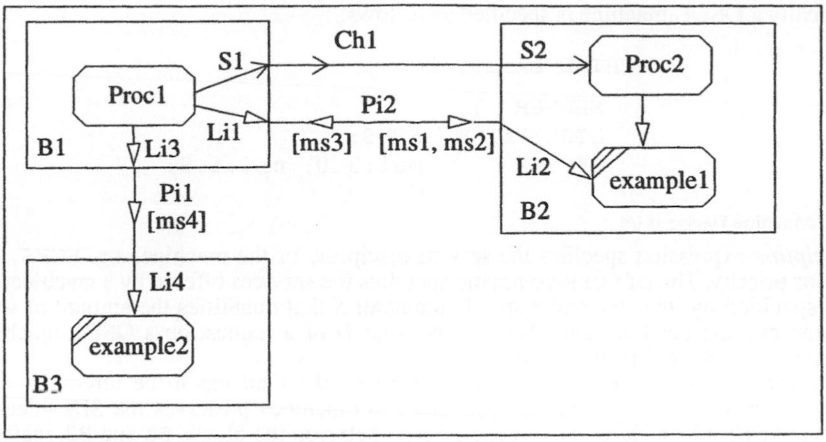

Figure 2. A System described with QSDL/GR

2.2 QSDL-Syntax for Modelling Load and Machines

In QSDL we associate temporal durations (deterministic and probabilistic) and the use of resources with certain actions. The first step concerns the declaration of all service types used in the machine specifications. QSDL-service types are declared in the same style as SDL-signals. The keyword *machineservice* marks the beginning of the declaration followed by an enumeration of the declared services e.g.:

```
machineservice ms1, ms2, ..., msn;
```

Example 1. Declaration of Machine Services

The keyword *request* followed by at least one machineservice name instantiates a time consuming request. The requests have to be routed to the serving machines. If the destination machine is unambiguously defined no further informations are necessary. Otherwise the desired machine has to be identified by adding the path information after the keyword VIA. Every request instruction requires the service amount which can be a raw value specifying the cost of request execution. Examples for amounts are the number of instructions to be executed or the number of bytes to be sent. The actual service amount is obtained by evaluating a real expression, in particular it may either be constant or random. The latter case requires a variable, whose actual value can be set by calling one of the random functions provided by appropriate predefined datatypes. A second (optional) parameter can supplement a request-instruction to specify the priority of a request. A priority is a cardinal number and has the default value 0 (lowest priority).

We now turn to the specification of machines in QSDL. A QSDL-machine is constructed like a queueing station and has the parameters: *name*, the number of servers, *service discipline*, set of *services* offered and the service-specific *speed* values.

Syntactically a QSDL-machine is specified as follows:

```
MACHINE example1;

        SERVER   1;
        DISCIPLINE  FCFS;
        OFFERS      ms1:3.0, ms2:5.0;
```

Example 2. Machine Declaration

The *discipline*-expression specifies the service discipline of the machine, e.g. `FCFS,RANDOM,PS`[1] or priority. The `offers`-command specifies the services offered by a machine. Each service is specified by its name and a speed parameter *S* that quantifies the amount of work a machine can execute per time unit. The service time *D* of a request on a QSDL-machine is given by $D = A/S$, where *A* is the service amount.

After the formal specification of load and machines, the load has to be referred unambiguously to the machines. The *binding* of requests to machines preserves the SDL-hierarchy. The following example declares a bidirectional pipe between the blocks `B1` and `B2`, which can forward the machineservice types `ms1` and `ms2` from `B1` to `B2` and `ms3` vice versa, cf figure 2.

```
pipe Pi2
        from B1 to B2 with ms1, ms2;
        from B2 to B1 with ms3;
```

Example 3. Declaration of Pipe *Pi2*

Connecting processes in block to their boundaries is done with ***links***, in figure 2 named as *Li1, ..., Li4*. For the complete QSDL-Syntax we refer to [4].

2.3 Overview of the QUEST-Tool

The transformation of the QSDL-description to an executable simulation program is performed automatically by a tool system that has been developed at the University of Essen. The tool system includes a QSDL-parser, a library named SCL which supports simulation, and a compiler for translation of QSDL-specifications to a simulator in the programming language C++. A survey of the SDL-features supported by the QSDL-parser of QUEST is given in [4].

Furthermore there are components for the evaluation and visualization of experiments by gathering statistical data as well as by *message sequence charts* (MSC) that are extended by timing informations. Also techniques for timed validation and verfication are included in the QUEST-tool[2].

3. TCP-RENO TCP-TAHOE AND SACK-TCP

TCP provides a connection oriented, reliable, byte stream service using an unreliable datagram service which is offered by IP. The main functions are:

---

1. PS denotes Processor sharing that means all customers are served in parallel with less speed
2. More Information about QUEST is available via web. URL: http://www.cs.uni-essen.de/Fachgebiete/SysMod/Forschung/QUEST/

- break down application data into TCP-segments
- when sending a segment a timer is maintained; if no acknowledgement is received the segment will be retransmitted
- duplicated IP-datagrams are discarded

Another essential function of TCP is flow control. That means a faster host is prevented to exhaust the buffers of a slower host. TCP uses a sliding window mechanism to control the data flow of connections. The window size of the usable window determines the number of segments the sender may transmit without receiving an acknowledgement. The initial window size is negotiated during connection establishing, see [7]. The negotiated initial window size for every connection does not take into account that multiple connections may slow down routers or gateways that connect different networks. To reduce congestion due to multiple connections TCP uses an algorithm called *slow start.* It operates by observing that the rate at which new packets should be injected into the network equals the rate of acknowledgements returned by the other end. The slow start algorithm maintains a variable named *cwnd,* which controls the sender's congestion window. When a new connection is established, the congestion window is initialized to the length of one segment. Each time an acknowledgement is received, the congestion window is increased by one segment (given as number of bytes). Note that *cwnd* is maintained in bytes and slow start always increments it by the segmentsize. This scheme allows to double the congestion window for each round trip yielding an exponential increase.

Of course internet routers may be overloaded and packets may get lost. Congestion avoidance is a way to deal with the problem of dropped packets. The assumptions of the algorithm is that packet lost by damage is much less than 1% and therefore lost packets are a signal of congestion somewhere in the network between sender and receiver. There are two indications of packet losses, first the expiration of retransmit timers and second the receipt of duplicated acknowledgements. Note that TCP is required to generate an immediate acknowledgement in case an out-of-order segment is received. This acknowledgement is called a duplicated ack and indicates that a segment has been received out of order and what sequence number is expected.

The congestion avoidance algorithm defines a slow start threshold size (*sstresh*) for each connection. The combined congestion avoidance and slow start algorithm operates as follows:

1. Initialize the values of *cwnd* and *ssthres*:

   $cwnd := segmentsize$ [bytes]

   $ssthresh := 65535$ [bytes]

2. When congestion occurs (indicated by timeout or by duplicated ack):

   $$ssthresh := \max(2 \cdot segmentsize, \frac{cwnd}{2})$$

   $cwnd := segmentsize$

3. When receiving new acks:

   if $cwnd > ssthresh$ then $cwnd := cwnd + \frac{1}{cwnd} + \frac{segmentsize}{8}$

   else $cwnd := cwnd + segmentsize$

There are a set of TCP implementations which differ from each other in the way they react if congestion has been detected. Here we focus on TCP-Tahoe and TCP-Reno which are the most common reference implementations and SACK-TCP that uses the selective acknowledgement option [6] to let the sender know about segments which were received and saved out of order.

3.1 TCP-Tahoe

TCP-Tahoe is similar to TCP with slow start, congestion avoidance and fast retransmit. This algorithm retransmits a segment after the receipt of 3 duplicated acks without waiting for a retransmission timer to expire. This leads to higher channel utilization and connection throughput. TCP-Tahoe assumes that every lost packet indicates buffer overflow in an intermediate node between sender and receiver. To reduce network load, this version of TCP always performs slow start whenever a loss has been indicated. The main problem of performing slow start every time a loss occurs is, that the communication path is going empty after a single pakket loss. This decreases the connection throughput, see chapter 5..

3.2 TCP-Reno

TCP-Reno retained the enhancements incorporated into Tahoe, but it modifies the fast retransmission algorithm to prevent the communication path from going empty. Reno distinguishes whether a loss is indicated by receiving the third duplicated ack or by timer expiration. In the former case the slow start algorithm is not executed, because the receipt of duplicated acks indicates that there is still data flowing between the two ends. In case the third duplicated acknowledgement has been received Reno enters the fast recovery phase. The algorithm operates as follows:

1. In case the third duplicated ack is received

   $ssthresh := \frac{cwnd}{2}$

   retransmit the missing segment

   $cwnd := ssthresh + 3 * segmentsize$

2. if another duplicated ack arrives

   $cwnd := cwnd + segmentsize$

   transmit a packet if allowed by the new value of *cwnd*

3. if the next ack arrives that acknowledges new data

   $cwnd := ssthresh$

   exit fast recovery

This algorithm is optimized for the case when a single packet is dropped from a window of data, but can suffer from performance problems when multiple packets are dropped from one window of data, see chapter 5..

3.3 SACK-TCP

To avoid the disadvantages of TCP-Reno and TCP-Tahoe the receiver must feedback more information to the sender. Using the selective acknowledgement option [6] the receiver uses the SACK option field, which containes a number of blocks, where each block represents a noncontiguous set of data that has been received and queued, to let the sender know which segments have correctly been received.

Note that a confirmation using the SACK option field is not the same as a confirmation using the normal ack field. The receiver should save all segments confirmed using SACK but in the case of buffer overflow these packets will be dropped by the receiver. So every time a retransmit timer expires the oldest not yet acknowledged segment using the ack field has to be retransmitted.

If a sender has received the third duplicated acknowledgement it enters the fast recovery phase as in TCP-Reno. During fast recovery the sender maintains a variable called ***pipe***, that represents the estimated number of packets in the pipe. The variable is incremented by one when the sender either sends a new packet or retransmits an old packet. It is decremented by one when receiving a duplicated acknowledgement with a SACK option reporting that new data has been arrived at the receiver [5] The sender only sends new or retransmitted data when the estimated number of packets is less than the value of *cwnd* which controls the congestion window. The decision whether new data or retransmit has to be sent based on a datastructure named *scoreboard*, which is maintained by the sender. New data will be send only if there are no packets missing at the receiver. Fast recovery will terminate if the sender receives an acknowledgement which contains no SACK-information. This indicates that all segments are correctly received without missing one. When a retransmitted packet is itself dropped, the SACK-implementation detects the drop with a retransmit time out. The dropped packet is transmitted again and the senders performs slow start.

The performance behaviour of the TCP variants are evaluated and presented in chapter 5..

4. FROM SDL-SPECIFICATION TO QSDL-SPECIFICATION

In this chapter we describe the system's structure and sketch the behaviour of central components. In particular, the division of the system into the parts application, communication and network is described in some depth. Note that the term application refers to the layer 6 and 7 of the OSI reference model, whereas communication refers to the layers 5 to 3 and the network includes the lower layer 1 and 2 respectively. Then we draw attention to the description of implementation dependent aspects and how to integrate these aspects into the QSDL-specification. More detailed, we describe the machines, their services, the service specific speeds and how to bind the processes to the machines.

4.1 The SDL-specification

The SDL-specification shows the structure of the system, see figure 3.

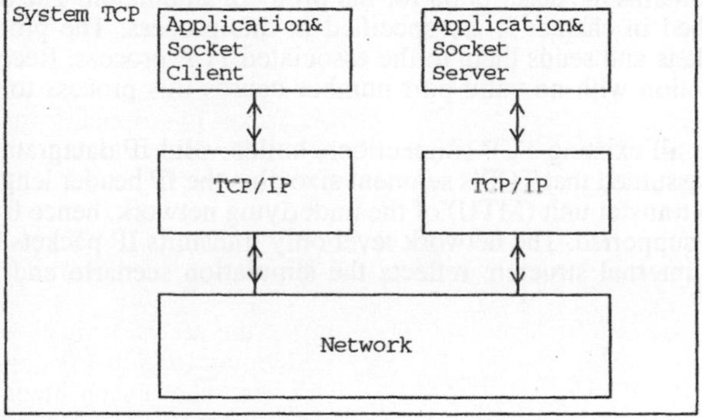

Figure 3. SDL-specification (block-level)

There are two protocol stacks including TCP/IP-layer and on the top an application level, including a socket layer, in two different variants. The blocks *Client* and *Server* build the TCP/IP's environment and describes the structure and the behaviour of certain applications. In the QSDL-specification the client contains processes which model the timed behaviour of TCP- users, see section 4.2.

The socket layer builds an interface between the TCP-protocol and the application layer. Each client has to ask for a socket before it can initiate a TCP-connection. The server processes initiate a passive open to the socket layer. As a consequence they are waiting for a connection request from the client side.

The process *ClientGenerator* creates for each connection a *Client-* or a *Server- Application* process, see figure 4. Every *ClientApplication* process tries to connect to a peer server process. The process *Source* creates application data which has to be transmitted to the server side. During connection establishing the *ClientApplication* process has to establish a socket for that connection. This is done by sending the signal socket to the process *SocketGenerator.* A socket is established if the maximum number is not reached yet. Otherwise the connection will be refused. The application data are passed to the socket which forwards them to the TCP process.

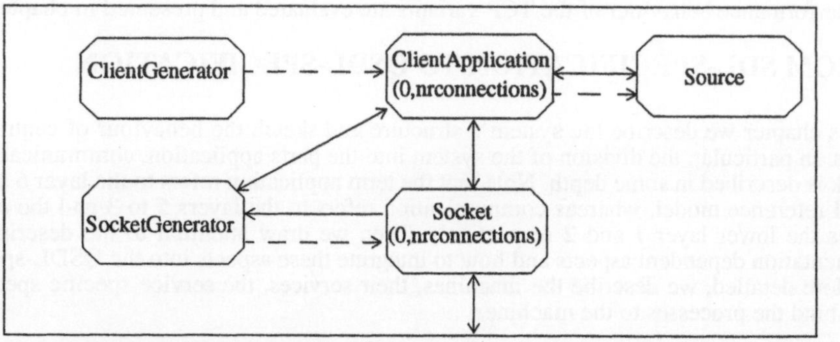

Figure 4. Processes of Application and Socket Level

The process *PortGenerator* creates the *TCP* processes, one for each connection, see figure 5. The *PortGenerator* binds the *socket* process to a *TCP* process. In our specification exist a port for every connection whereas in real implementations a port is able to support multiple connections. The process *TCP* contains the description for the protocol automaton. The different protocol mechanisms described in chapter 3. are specified in this process. The process *TCP_in* receives incoming IP packets and sends them to the associated *TCP* process. Receiving a pakket belonging to a connection with no valid port number causes this process to send a reset signal to the sender.

The process *IP* supports all existing TCP connections, builds valid IP datagrams and routes them to the receiver. It is assumed that TCP's segment size plus the IP header length is smaller than the size of maximum transfer unit (MTU) of the underlying network, hence fragmentation is not neccessary and not supported. The network level only transmits IP packets between client and server side. The internal structure reflects the simulation scenario and is described detailed in section 4.2.

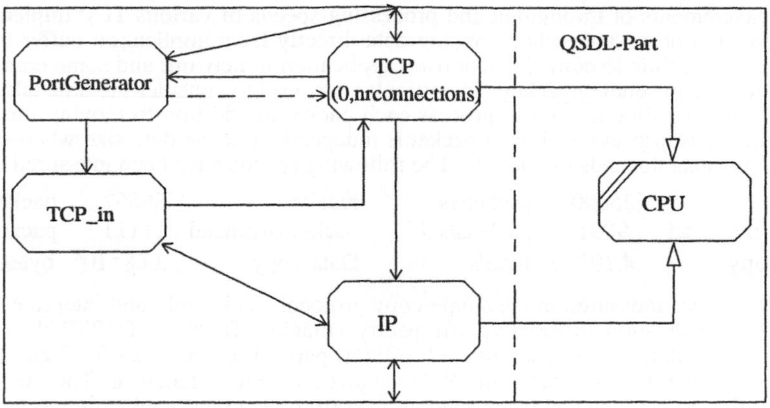

Figure 5. Processes of TCP/IP Level

4.2 The QSDL-specification

A pure SDL-specification describes the functional behaviour of the system but does not reflect the performance behaviour. To observe performance measures we have to add implementation dependent informations to the SDL-specification.

A standard implementation of TCP/IP copies data from program buffer first to kernel buffer and then from kernel buffer to the network interface, see figure 6.

The transport layer reads the data from the kernel buffer to compute checksum and header [1],[2]. Some processors are able to calculate the checksum while copying the data. This is done without reducing the copy rate. Using a new network interface allows to move the socket buffer to the network interface and to eliminate the kernel buffer. The data are copied directly from application to network interface where it is held until an acknowledgement has been received. The function of this buffer is logically identical to the socket buffer, but we can eliminate one copy function and reduce the number of system memory access. This is called a single-copy protocol stack [1].

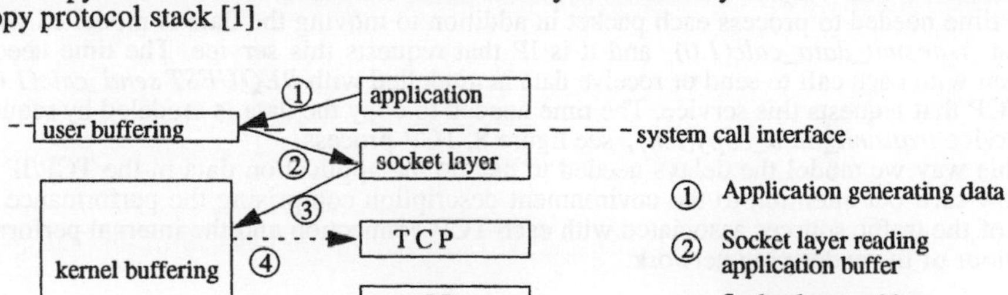

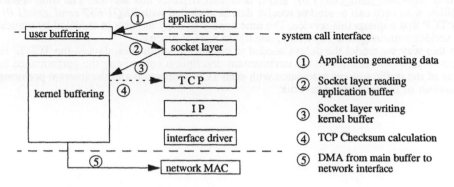

Figure 6. Data paths in a conventional protocol stack modified from [1]

In [2] measurements of throughput and processing speeds of various TCP implementations are reported. It is observable when copying data directly from application buffer to network buffer we need the time to copy the data from application to network and some computational overhead incurred in sending packets. In particular, we need to consider the time taken by each call to send and the time needed to process each packet in addition to moving the data. The time to send and to process each data packet is independent of the data size whereas the time needed to copy data depends on the size. The following speeds have been measured in [2].

send	25000	packets/s	receive	66667	packets/s
packet-overhead	9091	packets/s	packet-overhead	11111	packets/s
Data-copy	$4.19*10^8$	byte/s	Data-copy	$2.68*10^8$	byte/s

We use the values measured in the single-copy protocol stack study and integrate the results in the QSDL-specification under study. We specify a machine for every TCP/IP block which do the copy and calculation work, see figure 5 (QSDL-part). The processes TCP and IP use the machine every time TCP-segments or IP datagrams are sent or received. The machine CPU provides all the services needed when sending data from the client application to the network, see figure 7.

The machine offers their services simultaniously to all instances of TCP and IP processes. When serving more than one request at the same time the service speeds will be reduced.

```
MACHINE CPU;
  Server 1;
  DISCIPLINE PS;
  OFFER transmit_data_copy   :transmit_copy_speed,
     transmit_data_calc      :transmit_calc_speed,
       receive_data_copy     :receive_copy_speed,
       receive_data_calc     :receive_calc_speed,
       send_calc             :send_speed,
       receive_calc          :receive_speed;
ENDMACHINE;
```

Figure 7. Machine declaration (QSDL/PR)

The time needed to process each packet in addition to moving the data is modelled with the request *transmit_data_calc(1.0)* and it is IP that requests this service. The time needed in addition with each call to send or receive data is modelled with *REQUEST send_calc(1.0)* and it is TCP that requests this service. The time needed to copy the data is modeled by requesting the service *transmit_data_copy(len)*, see figure 8, TCP-process.

In this way we model the delays needed to handle the application data in the TCP/IP layer. We now turn our attention to the environment description comprising the performance behaviour of the traffic sources associated with each TCP-connection and the internal performance behaviour of the underlying network.

```
PROCESS IP (1, 1);
  PROCEDURE Deliver REFERENCED;
  PROCEDURE SendPacket REFERENCED;
  DCL  TCP_in TCP,
       ip_in IP;
  START;
NEXTSTATE WaitForInput;
  STATE WaitForInput;
INPUT tcp_packet(TCP_in);
DECISION TCP_in!da = OWN_ADDRESS;
  (TRUE) :
  (FALSE) :
  REQUEST transmit_data_calc(1.0);
  OUTPUT tcp_packet(TCP_in) VIA UpperSap;
  CALL SendPacket(TCP_in);
 ENDDECISION;
 NEXTSTATE WaitForInput;
 INPUT ip_packet(ip_in);
 Decision ip_in!dst = OWN_ADDRESS;
   (TRUE) :
     REQUEST receive_data_calc(1.0);
   (FALSE):
  ENDDECISION;
  CALL Deliver(ip_in);
  NEXTSTATE WaitForInput;
 ENDPROCESS;
```

```
Process TCP(0,connections);
  :
  :

 State established;
 INPUT send(sp, len, psh,
            urg, tout, toa);
REQUEST transmit_data_copy(len);
 REQUEST send_calc(1.0);
 CALL DataRequest
        (len, ACK_FLAG, NO_SYN_FLAG,
         urg, psh, NO_RESET_FLAG,
         NO_FIN_FLAG);

NEXTSTATE Established;
  INPUT tcp_packet(TCP_in);
 TASK pak_saved := FALSE;
REQUEST receive_calc(1.0);
CALL CheckChecksum(TCP_in, ok);
   :
   :
  NEXTSTATE -
   :
   :

  ENDPROCESS;
```

Figure 8. Procss IP and Process TCP (partial)

5. Simulation Scenario Experiments and Results

We investigate the performance behaviour of the TCP variants in an environment similar to the scenario used in [5]. The environment consists of two host which are connected via a finite-buffer droptail gateway which connects both hosts, see figure 9. The links between the sending host and the gateway has a bandwidth capacity of 8 Mbit/s and a delay of 0.1 ms, the link between gateway and receiving host has a bandwidth capacity of 0.8 Mbit/s and a delay of 100 ms.

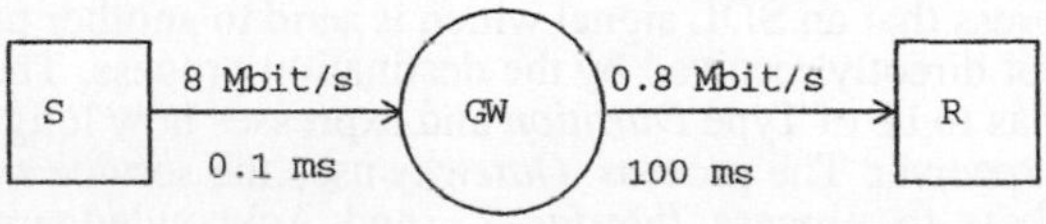

Figure 9. Simulation Scenario used in [5]

The structure and performance behaviour of this reference scenario is displayed in the internal structure of the network level of the system under study, see figure 10.

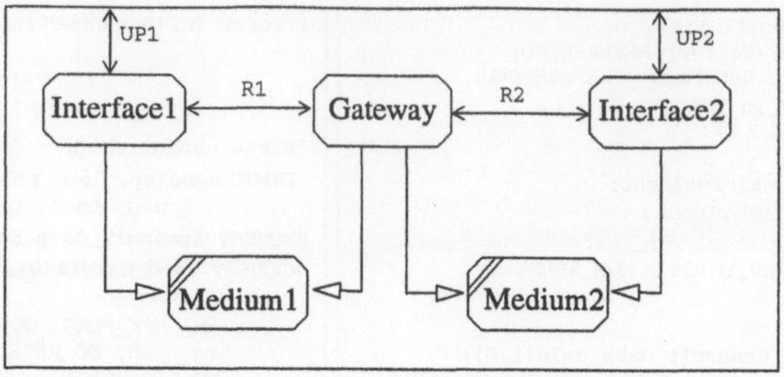

Figure 10. Processes of Network Level

There are two machines named *Medium1* and *Medium2*. The machines offer the service *transmit* to their environment and the Processes *Interface1* and *Gateway* use this service when sending IP packets. Machine *Medium1* offers this service with a speed of 0.8 Mbit/s. This models the time delay to put the packet on the cable. The delay is modeled with QSDL's delay-construct , see figure 11.

```
PROCESS Interface1;
 DCL ip_in IP;
 START;
 NEXTSTATE wait;
 STATE WAIT;
 INPUT IP_packet(ip_in);
 DECISION ip_in!dst = self;
   (TRUE) : OUTPUT IP_packet(ip_in) VIA UP1;
            NEXTSTATE Wait;
  (FALSE): REQUEST transmit(ip_in!len);
           OUTPUT IP_packet(ip_in)
                  VIA R1 DELAY Delay1;
           NEXTSTATE WAIT;
  ENDDECISION;
ENDPROCESS;
```

```
MACHINE Medium1;
    SERVER server1;
    DISCIPLINE FCFS;
    OFFERS transmit: BANDWIDTH1;
ENDMACHINE;
```

Figure 11. Process Interface1 and Machine Declaration (QSDL/PR)

QSDL allows to express that an SDL signal which is send to another process using the SDL-Output-statement is not directly received by the destination process. The expression following the keyword *DELAY* has to be of Type *Duration* and expresses how long it will take to send the signal from sender to receiver. The process *Gateway* uses the service *transmit* from *Medium2* to send IP data packets to process *Interface2* and Acknowledgements back to process *Interface1*. In this way we model both the bandwidth and the delay due to links.

The gateway between the host may drop IP-datagrams due to congestion. We assume that congestion phases are exponentially distributed. The mean time between two congestion phases have been chosen as 10 s, 20 s and 30 s. As a further parameter we increase the number of losses per congestion phase from 1 drop until 4 drops in every congestion phase, see figure 14 to figure 16.

The QUEST tool allows online model monitoring, see figure 12 and figure 13. It is observable how the different TCP variants will react in case of dropped packets from a window of data. When only one packet gets lost TCP-Tahoe starts with the slow-start-algorithm and then continoues with congestion avoidance after 3 times the round trip time (RTT), see left window of figure 12. The throughput of that connection decreases dramatically and TCP-Tahoe needs 7 times the RTT to reach the throughput as before. This effect is strengthened if the maximum window size grows.

TCP-Reno and TCP-SACK behave similar in the case of a single dropped packet. Both protocols will start with the fast recovery algorithm and then they do congestion avoidance, see the right window of figure 12. The throughput decreases from 95 packets per second to 70 packets per second and both protocols need 5 times the RTT to reach the maximum throughput as provided before.

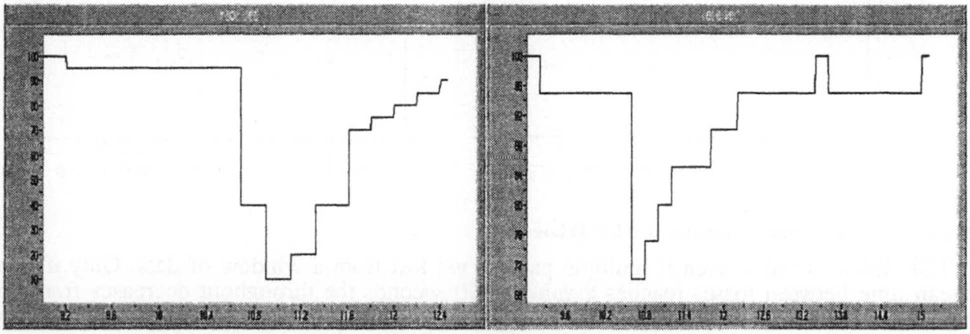

Figure 12. Performance Behaviour in Case of Packet Losses (1 Packet dropped)

When two packets get lost from a window of data, see figure 13 (Tahoe, Reno SACK from left to right), it is observable that TCP-Tahoe reacts similar to the case of a single loss. The protocol starts with slow-start and proceeds with congestion avoidance and reaches the maximum throughput after 8 times the RTT. TCP-Reno set the window size to half the value when detecting the loss. The second loss is detected because the retransmit timer expires. This causes TCP-Reno to start with slow start TCP-SACK begins with fast recovery when detecting the lost packet. The detection of the second lost packets decreases the throughput only insignificantly and the maximum throughput is reached after 6 times the RTT.

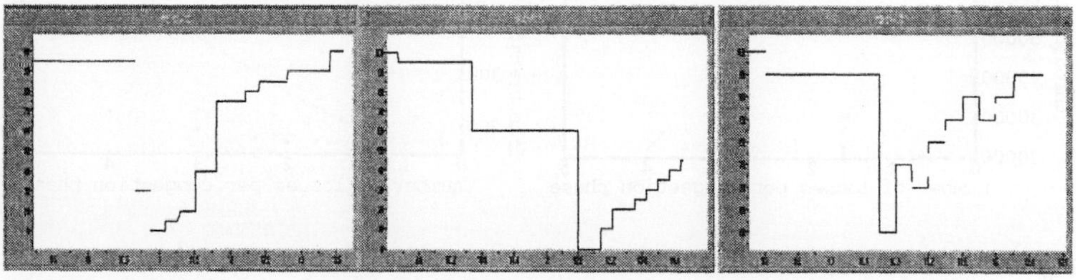

Figure 13. Performance Behaviour in Case of Packet Losses (2 Packets dropped)

Additionally to online model monitoring the tool QUEST evaluates steady state performance metrics. The results of experiment series performed with the QUEST tool sketched above are presented graphically, see figure 14 to figure 16.

We investigate the throughput of a single TCP connection from client to server when sending 15 Mbyte of user data using TCP segments of 1024 byte. The maximum window size is set to 32 Kbytes. The first dropped packet is always detected by the fast retransmit procedure after the sender receives three duplicated acks. In addition to TCP's throughput we evaluate the file transfer time to send the user data to the reveiver.

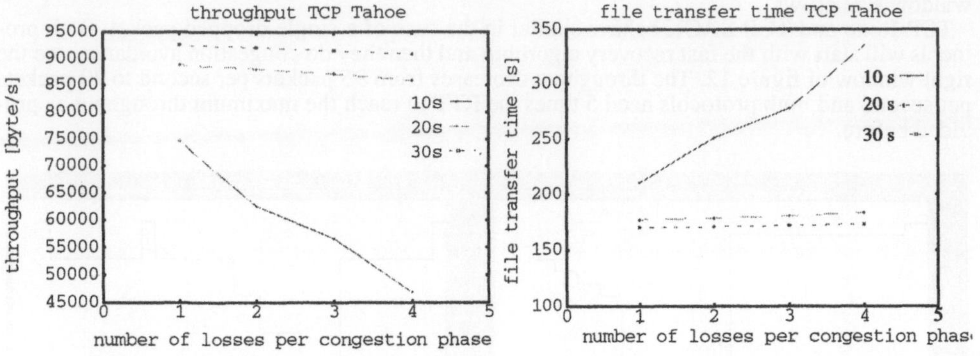

Figure 14. Steady State Measures of TCP Tahoe

TCP-Tahoe is stable even if multiple packets get lost from a window of data. Only if the mean time between losses reaches a value of 10 seconds the throughput decreases from 95 Kbytes/s down to 75 Kbytes/s when one packet is dropped and from 90 Kbytes/s down to 45 Kbytes/s when 4 packets are dropped. The file transfer time increases from 150 seconds up to 320 seconds.

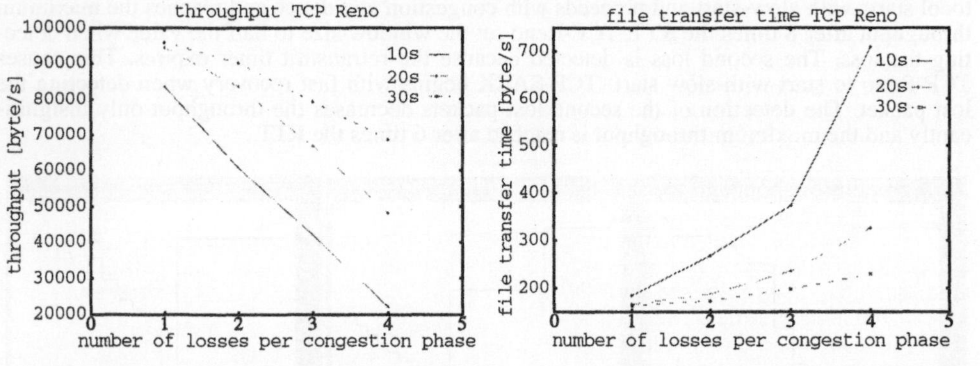

Figure 15. Steady State Measures of TCP Reno

TCP-Reno has performance problems if multiple packets get lost. The throughput decreases from 92 Kbytes/ss down to 82 Kbytes/s if only one packet is dropped, even if this will happen every 10 seconds. In case of multiple dropped packets the throughput decreases from 90 Kbytes/s down to 24 Kbytes/s (4 losses every 10 seconds). The file transfer time reaches a maximum of about 700 seconds that is twice the time TCP Tahoe needs to transmit the data from sender to receiver.

TCP-SACK has the best performance values of all investigated protocol variants. It offers a minimal throughput of about 73 Kbytes/ss. This minimum is improved to 92 Kbytes/s if the distance between losses is at least 20 seconds. The file transfer time of TCP-SACK reaches a maximum of about 220 seconds and a minimum of about 165 seconds.

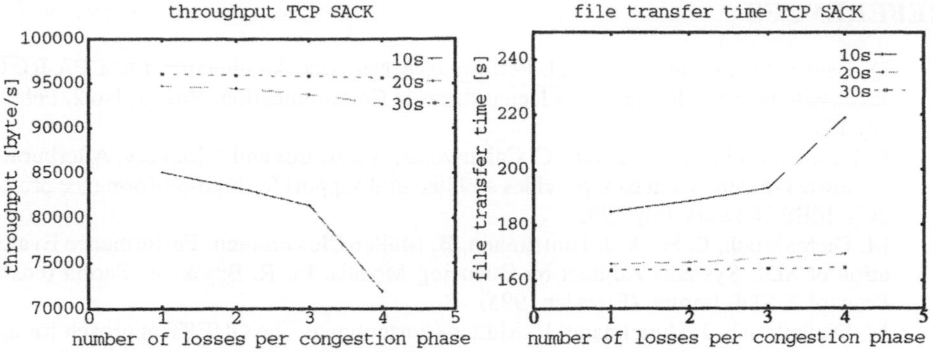

Figure 16. Steady State Measures of TCP-SACK

The results of the evaluation above shows that TCP-Tahoe has performance problems if the mean distance between lost packets is reduced or the the maximum window size is enlarged, because TCP-Tahoe always starts with slow start reducing the throughput drastically.

TCP-Reno overcomes this performance problems in case of single losses, but it has considerable problems if multiple losses occurs. The improvements implemented in TCP-SACK reduces the time needed to send user data and makes TCP more stable against losses due to congestions and therefore it should be mostly prefered.

6. CONCLUSION AND OUTLOOK

In this paper we have explored the performance restrictions imposed by the lack of selective acknowledgements in TCP and we have evaluated the performance measures of TCP-sack.We have shown that the throughput of connections using TCP-Reno may decrease from 100 percent down to 25 percent and that the file transfertime may reach a value that is twice the time TCP-Tahoe needs for the same amount of data. Another result is that neither TCP-Reno nor TCP-Tahoe have good performance in case of single *and* multiple losses. One solution to overcome these problems is to implement a selective acknowledgement mechanism. This leads to the highest throughput and the shortest file transfer times.

The results we achieved are partly the same as in the [5] . The short time behaviour, which is directly observable when running the QUEST simulator, reflects these results. The slowstart algorithm as well as congestion avoidance and the fast retransmit algorithm and their effects are observable. In addition we show the effects on long time behaviour like connection throughput or file transfer times. The results presented in [5] based on simulation models which have been made by hand. We used simulation models which have been derived directly from an SDL-specification. This reduces effort and time to develop the performance models and it makes it easier to show that the performance model and the functional model are in common. Moreover, analyses of protocols under time and resource restrictions may be done by designers themselves improving their understanding of protocol behaviour.

The proposed method allows the integration of model based performance evaluation into early design phases as well as the adaption, parametrization and tuning of existing protocols.

In the future we focus our work on multimedia systems and use the method and the QUEST-tool to design protocols which support the requirements made of multimedia applications. Especially we concentrate upon the problem of mapping, (re-) negotiation and policing quality of service parameters.

REFERENCES

[1] D. Banks, M. Prudence. A High-Performance Network Architecture for a PA-RISC Workstation. IEEE Journal on Selected Areas in Communication, Vol 11, No 2, February 1993.

[2] C. Dalton, G. Watson, D. Banks, C. Calamvokis, A Edwards and J. Lumely: Afterburner A network-independent card provides architectural support for high-performance protocols. IEEE Network July 1993.

[3] M. Diefenbruch, E. Heck, J. Hintelmann, B. Müller-Clostermann: Performance Evaluation of SDL Systems Adjunct by Queueing Models. In: R. Braek, A. Sarma (eds.); Proc. of 7. SDL Forum, (Elsevier 1995)

[4] M. Diefenbruch, J. Hintelmann, B. Müller-Clostermann: The QUEST approach for the Performance Evaluation of SDL-Systems. In: R. Gotzhein, J. Bredereke (eds.); Proc. of IFIP TC6 / 6.1 International Conference on Formal Description Techniques IX / protocol Specification, Testing and Verification XVI, (Chapman & Hall 1996)

[5] K. Fall, S. Floyd: Simulation-based Comparison of Tahoe, Reno and SACK TCP. Computer Communication Review Vol 26, July 1996 p. 5 - 21.

[6] M. Mathis, J. Mahdavi, S. Floyd and A. Romanow: TCP Selective Acknowledgement Options, RFC 2018, October 1996

[7] W. Richard Stevens: TCP/IP Illustrated, Volume 1: The protocols (Addison Wesley 1994)

Tuning Development of Distributed Real-Time Systems with SDL and MSC: Current Experience and Future Issues

R. Gerlich

BSSE System and Software Engineering, Auf dem Ruhbuehl 181, D-88090 Immenstaad, Germany
Phone: +49/7545/91.12.58, Fax: +49/7545/91.12.40, e-mail: gerlich@t-online.de

Keywords: System verification and validation, interdependence between behaviour and performance, system architecture, performance modelling, performance evaluation, exhaustive simulation, automated code generation, SDL, MSC

Abstract:

SDL provides powerful capabilities for verification[1] and validation[2] of a system's behaviour and for automated code generation. This allows to perform system validation at a higher level of abstraction and earlier in the development life cycle. However, one needs to be carefully to really gain advantage of such capabilities, especially when applying SDL to a broader class of applications which may be called "decision-making, distributed systems". Firstly, state explosion may prevent to get any benefit from exhaustive simulation or much effort is required to limit the number of states thereby loosing most of the advantages of automated testing. Secondly, the current means of SDL and of SDL tools may not be sufficient to identify all bugs of a system's specification and design. Even when exhaustive simulation does not report any error, the system may not run correctly on the target, or vice versa, the optimum practical solution may be rejected as erroneous. This paper will analyse the situation, provide with a solution for tuning of system development which is based on an additional layer, called EaSySimII, on top of the ObjectGEODE tool, and will identify future issues.

1. Introduction

Compared with other languages a major advantage of SDL and MSC is their capability to provide on an abstract and formal level the means for definition of (a) information exchange between a system's components by MSC's (Message Sequence Charts) and (b) a system's behaviour by FSM's (Finite State Machines). This allows to automate verification of information exchange and of behaviour. In consequence, verification can be performed at a higher level of abstraction and earlier in the development life cycle. This helps to save costs and to reduce risks.

---

[1] "Verification" means to check if the system is built right.

[2] "Validation" means to confirm that the right system is built. Hence, validation refers to all system properties, while verification may only refer to some properties.

Due to these advantages SDL was selected during the project OMBSIM [1] which was exeecuted for the European Space Agency ESA/ESTEC in order to define an alternative system life cycle [2,3,4,5]. As it was already known by previous activities [6] that consideration of performance impacts is a "must" for system validation the SDL tool ObjectGEODE [7] was complemented by performance analysis and simulation capabilities provided by the SES/workbench tool [8]. The resulting tool environment was called "EaSySim" (Early System Validation Simulation" environment). This environment has been improved significantly in mean time by BSSE and a completely new implementation "EaSySim II" [9] is now available which overcomes all the weakness of the first environment and provides new capabilities for system validation. It is based on ObjectGEODE, the actual version of GEODE used, and provides the performance simulation capabilities by SDL means and additional support functions which are implemented as operators in C. EaSySim II still provides access to SES/workbench, but also to other tools and (user) software in a transparent manner.

A number of activities have been executed since 1992 when the first ESTEC project HRDMS [10] on system validation started, which especially concentrated on performance matters. Since 1992 the development approach has been continuously improved and the productivity of development steadily increased, mainly based on the powerful capabilities of SDL, but also by proper organisation of the development steps [5].

This experience now allows to give recommendations for tuning of system development, how to obtain correct verification results or how to increase system quality. Although extending the verification process to performance properties, verification becomes much simpler because notion of time and shared resources introduce an ordering scheme which reduces the number of system states. This helps to avoid state explosion and to master exhaustive simulation in such cases when it is not possible otherwise. Moreover, it was recognised that the number of system states may be taken as a measure for system quality indicating how well defined a system really is.

To conclude: when extending the verification process towards performance matters this does not only lead to more reliable results, but it also simplifies system validation and hence allows to tackle more complex systems.

While SDL is more addressing an abstract, mathematical system, the EaSySim II environment concentrates on a real, physical system and its properties. This extension of the scope is needed when dealing with a more general class of distributed systems with SDL.

2. The Impact of Performance on System Validation

This section identifies the risks which arise when the SDL capabilities for behavioural verification are applied to a larger class of distributed systems without considering all relevant system aspects such as performance. Otherwise errors in a system may remain hidden and may cause sporadic or permanent faults during later system operation.

2.1 An Extended Application Domain Requires An Extended Scope of Validation

In the past, SDL was mainly applied to telecommunication applications. Such applications form a sub-class of "distributed applications" which often can be characterised as a sequence of "one-point-to-one-point" communications. Many such communications may occur at the same time and they may compete for resources. But they do not disturb each other during execution of a protocol sequence, because there is no signal exchange between them.

Usually, no such communication request has a higher priority than any other, and the next action will not start before the previous action has been completed. This makes it reasonable to ignore time and to assume that a state transition does not take any significant time at all. Performance aspects may be important but they only impact the consumption of resources and the duration of activities, and not the system behaviour.

However when taking into account a more general class of distributed systems for which "n-point-to-m-point" connections ("anybody can communicate with anybody else at any time") are allowed, time plays a more important role: performance of the (real) distributed system may impact the validation process and the results may not match the (physical) system architecture.

The reason is: signals may not propagate with the same (average) transmission rate through a network. When they take different paths (1) the transmission rate may depend on the path, (2) the number of processing steps may be different. If transmission rate is assumed to be infinite (zero propagation time) this dependency is not recognised. Also, in case processing time is ignored the number of processing steps do not impact the final arrival time of a signal. But consumption of time makes the difference between "ideal" and physical systems. And this difference makes validation harder in case of distributed systems with arbitrary communications.

Due to zero-propagation time signals arrive in a order in a process queue which may be different from the order in the physical system. Consequently, the real sequence on the physical architecture may never occur during simulation. Hence, successful verification by simulation with SDL and SDL tools does not necessarily mean that the system will work correctly on teh architecture because the impact by performance is not known: whether it invalidates the result or not.

As it is shown in section 2.2 even in case of a synchronous master-slave protocol which is run on two uni-directional lines, time consumption of transmission and data processing cannot be neglected.

Hence, in order to obtain results which are compliant with the real, physical system we need to consider performance matters already during system validation by simulation.

Several activities are known which introduce notion of time in SDL [11,12,13,14], but they only concentrate on aspects like channel delays and response times or violation of performance constraints, but do not consider that time may impact system behaviour. They analyse time delays e.g. in the queues of application processes although the signals may not have to wait there, but e.g. in the network or the on the processors. Behaviour remains the same when time consumption in physical resources added.

As SDL tools already provide the capability of exhaustive simulation and support a priori distributed systems it is possible to extend tool capabilities such that a more general class of distributed systems is covered. The EaSySim II environment provides such enhanced capabilities on top of the ObjectGEODE tool: consequently, a user can exploit the performance of a certain system architecture and can validate such a distributed system under realistic conditions.

2.2 A Protocol Example: Succeeding with Validation of an Erroneous System

The protocol shown by Fig. 2a has been used during the project HRDMS [10] and in mean time it turned out that it is a very good example to demonstrate (a) violation of validated behaviour when introducing timing aspects, (b) the weakness of validation of system properties under artificial (simplified) operational conditions, (c) the interaction between system tuning and correctness of results of exhaustive simulation, (d) the significant reduction of system states when introducing performance aspects into exhaustive simulation.

The protocol is completely deterministic and synchronous from a logical point of view, which is the reason that people believe that performance matters can really be ignored for its validation. When taking exactly the sequence of signals as shown by Fig. 2a the protocol will *never* run free of errors on the system architecture of Fig. 2b. And this is the good point of its determinism. When starting to remove the bug (by varying the sequence of the signals and playing with timing) the protocol may loose its determinism due to performance and environmental impacts and it becomes even harder to identify the bug.

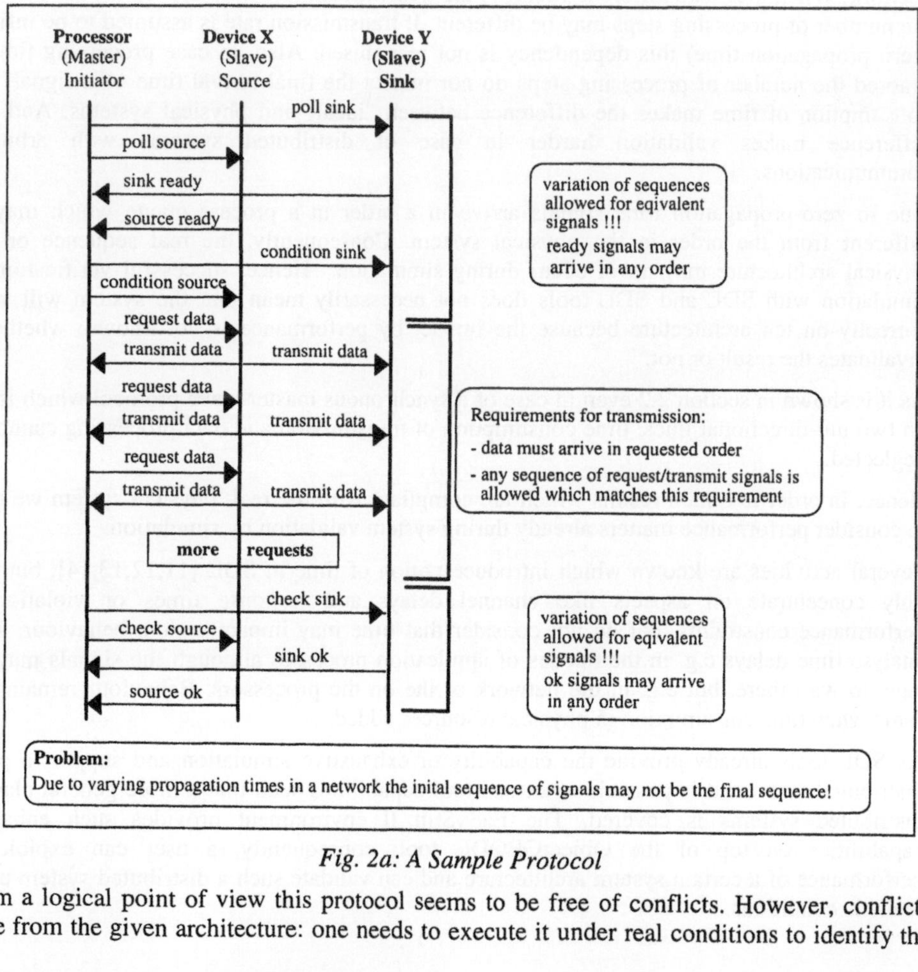

Fig. 2a: A Sample Protocol

From a logical point of view this protocol seems to be free of conflicts. However, conflicts arise from the given architecture: one needs to execute it under real conditions to identify the conflict. In consequence, one can never be sure that no error will occur in the real environment when performance aspects are ignored during system validation by simulation.

The goal of the protocol shown by Fig. 2a is to exchange data between the source and sink devices. This transfer is initiated and supervised by the processor (master) for each data request. As it is a typical "master-slave" protocol it should be free of conflicts. But this is not true.

The processor polls the source and sink devices whether they can provide data or whether they are ready to accept data, respectively. If both respond with 'ready' the processor conditions the devices and requests data, cycle for cycle. At the end of data transmission the processor checks the source and sink devices whether all data have been transmitted correctly. And this final checking sequence causes the problem (Fig. 2c)

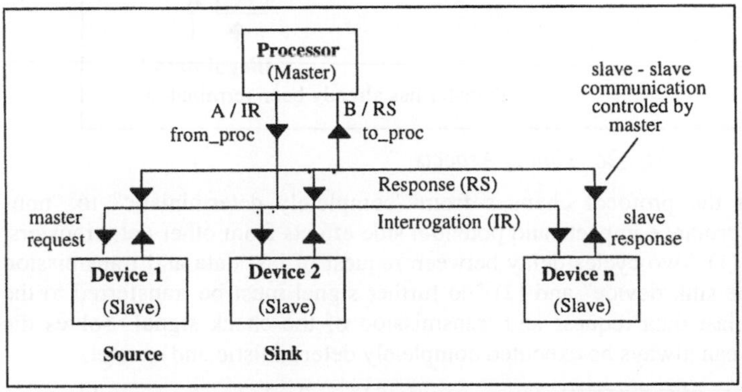

Fig. 2b: System Architecture

When ignoring transmission time all transmitted data arrive before the final checks. This is different when shared resources like bus or processor cycles are consumed on a real architecture like the one shown by Fig. 2b. Then the signal sent from the source device to the sink device is synchronised with the bus cycles. This causes the last data sent from the source to the sink to arrive later at the sink device than the check signal issued by the processor directly to the sink device. This confirms (a).

The reason is that data coming from the source are delayed by two bus cycles before they arrive at the sink. During the first bus cycle the request signal is processed by the source device and the data are written to the output registers. During the second cycle the data is transmitted to the sink device. However, the check signal is directly sent from the processor to the sink device and is therefore one cycle faster.

To solve this problem an idea could be to change the sequence of the check signals (check sink, then check source, see Fig. 2a) and to add a further cycle between the last data request and transmission of the check signal for the device, because this will delay the check sink signal by two cycles which are needed according to Fig. 2c.

However, as mentioned already above this will make life even harder. For a certain test the protocol may run correctly, but not in all cases. If several transmissions are initiated on the processor, the delay of the check signal will provide an empty bus slot which may be used by another protocol sequence running in parallel. If this sequence addresses the same sink device, the sink will again identify an error due to incompatibility of its state with the incoming data (in best case) or it will accept the wrong data (in worst case). This confirms hypotheses (b) and (c). In consequence, exhaustive simulation executed with filter conditions will deliver wrong results because such side effects may not be detected due to filtering of side effects

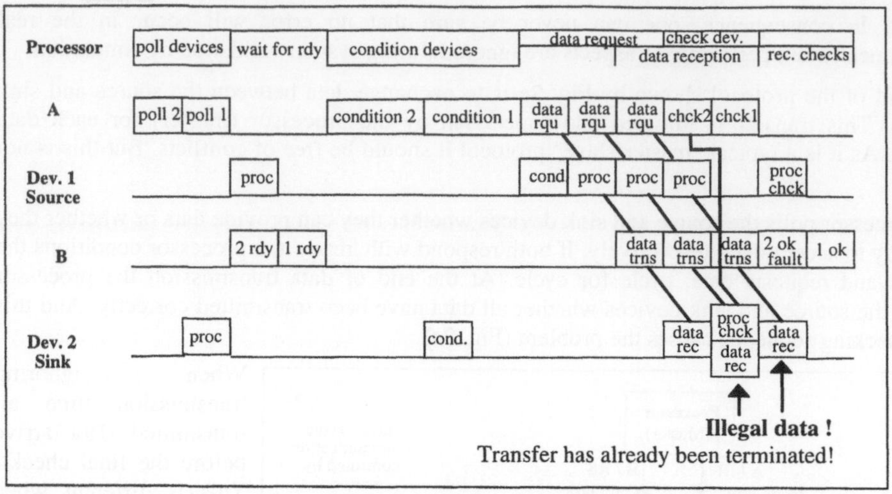

Fig. 2c: Timing Aspects

Hence, the behaviour of the protocol changes from "completely deterministic" to "non-deterministic" due to performance impacts and potential side effects from other data transfers. Only the two constraints (1) "two cycles delay between request of last data and transmission of the check signal for the sink device" and (2) "no further signal must be transferred to the sink device between the last data request and transmission of the check signal" solves the problem and the protocol can always be executed completely deterministic and correct.

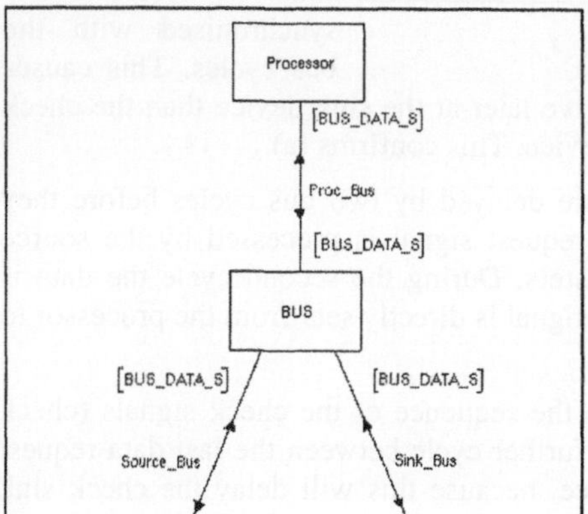

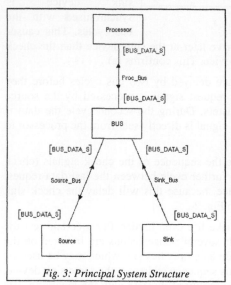

Fig. 3: Principal System Structure

The protocol of Figs. 2a-2c has been implemented in SDL for several implementations of the bus as shown by Figs. 3 - 7. The principal system structure (Fig. 3) has always been kept and mainly the bus implementation was changed. For optimisation of system performance the timing of data requests in the processor was also varied, e.g. the next request may be sent before the data of the previous request arrives.

If processing time and transmission time are ignored system performance does not matter at all. So the simplest solution is to send the next data request (or the final check) only when the requested data have been received. This ensures execution of the protocol free of errors as long as no other data transfer is running in parallel which may use the empty bus slots and may cause a state mismatch in the source or sink devices. However, when introducing time consumption this way of protocol processing becomes very inefficient because three cycles are always needed per data request yielding a bus utilisation of only 33% at most.

To achieve a higher bus utilisation, all signals following the ready signals could be issued immediately by the processor because it should be a matter of the bus interface to queue all such signals. But with SDL one cannot always proceed in this manner. If transmitting all the signals by a single burst they will be stored in a SDL queue and selected from this queue depending on which mode is used for simulation in a tool. In case "random simulation mode" is applied the sequence of the signals will be changed and the SDL simulator will detect errors in the protocol, although in practice they will not occur.

Knowing about this problem the bus clock can be used to transmit request by request synchronously from the processor not waiting for a response. Then bus utilisation remains as efficient as in case of a burst.

Such processing also reduces the number of system (SDL) states: the queue lengths are reduced to one element only at a certain time and this simplifies significantly exhaustive simulation because instead of n! mutations only 1! are considered by the tool.

Figs. 4 - 7 (Figures 5b-7 and the tables follow on the next pages) show several representations of the bus, changing from a very simple bus representation to the real bus architecture consisting of two uni-directional bus lines and a bus clock. Table 1a gives the results of verification by exhaustive simulation for the simple bus models (Figs. 4, 5a-c) which do not take into account timing aspects. Table 1b shows the results for the full bus architecture based on synchronous transfer of the data related to Figs. 6a-c and 7.

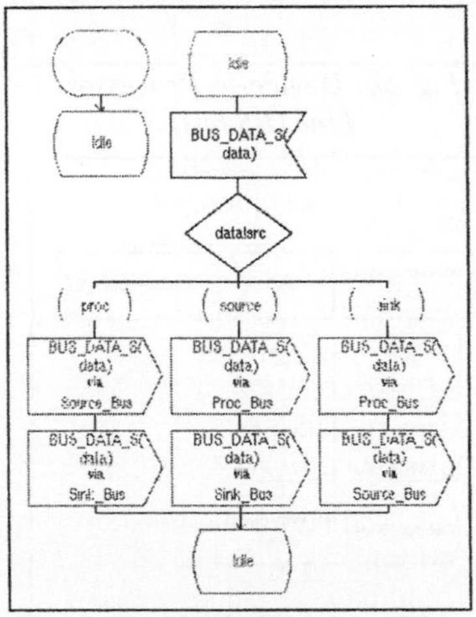

Fig. 4: Simple Bi-Directional Bus with Broadcasting

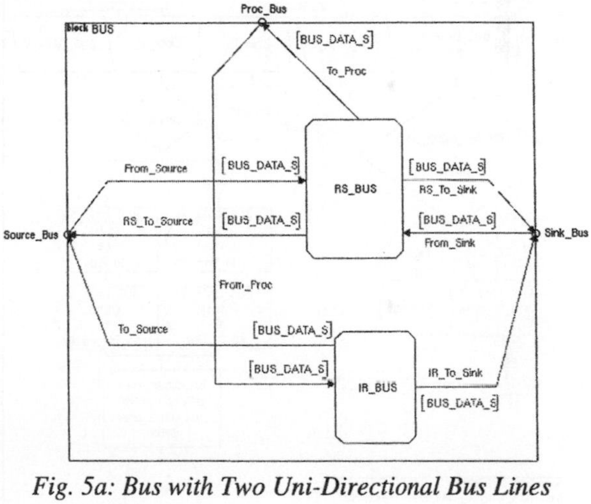

Fig. 5a: Bus with Two Uni-Directional Bus Lines

Two cases have been investigated for the full bus architecture of Fig. 6: (1) the period of the bus clock has been set to a non-zero value (the expected case) or (1) it has been set to a zero value in order to ignore transmission time.

In case of Fig. 7 an equivalent "functional" bus architecture without clock is used in order to get a comparison between non-zero bus time slots and equivalent transmission steps with zero transmission time. This means that in case of Fig. 7 a signal is immediately transferred after its reception without waiting for the bus clock.

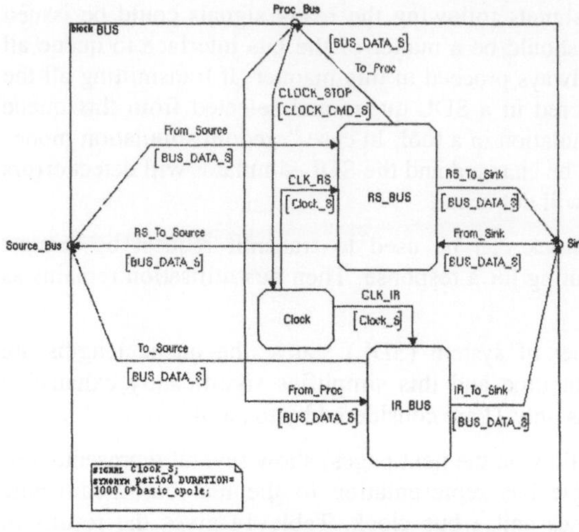

Fig. 6a: Fully Representative Bus

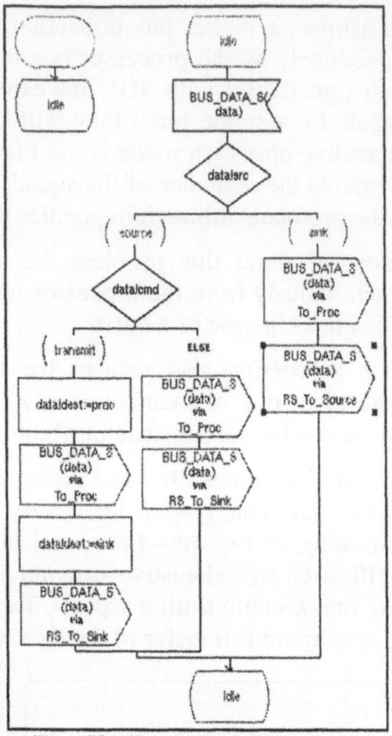

Fig. 5b: Device-to-Processor Line (RS bus)

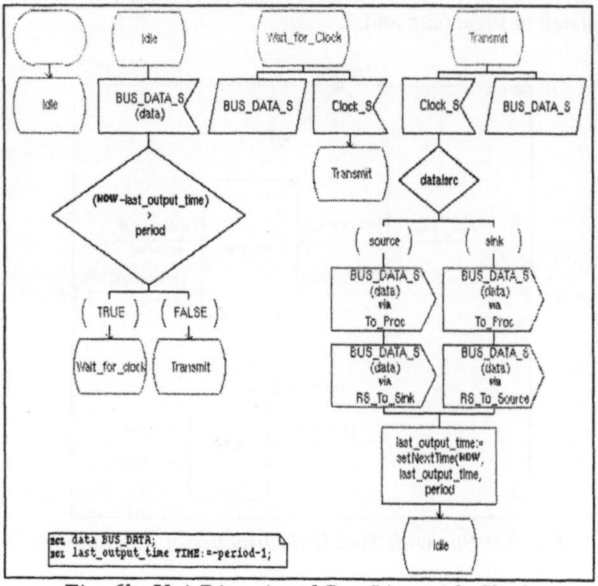

Fig. 6b: Uni-Directional Bus Line with Clock (Device-to-Processor Line)

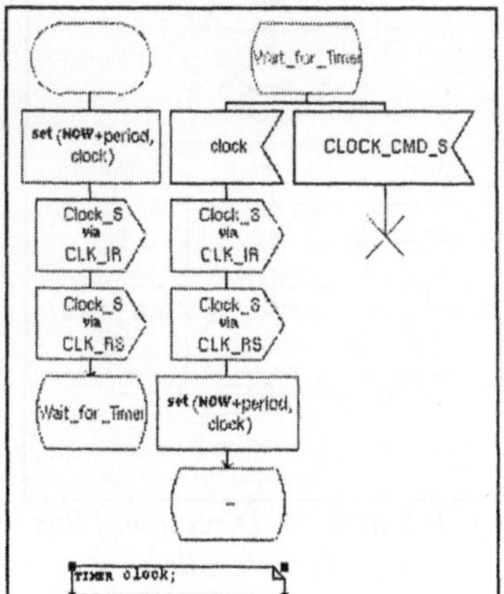

Fig. 6c: Bus Clock

Fig. 4 shows the simplest implementation of the bus: the bus just distributes the received signal to all connected devices (the sending device excepted) and acts as a bi-directional bus with one bus line. The bus shown by Figs. 5a - 5b introduce two uni-directional bus lines. So the bus of Fig. 5 already represents the real architecture but it still ignores time consumption.

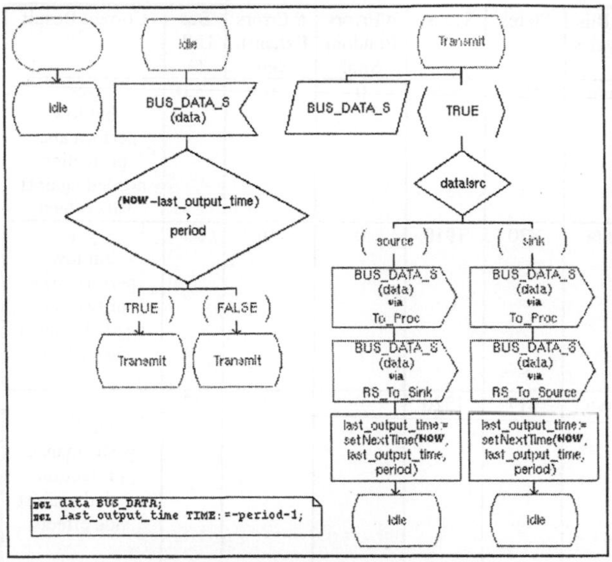

Fig. 7: Uni-Directional Bus Line (w/o clock)
(Device-to-Processor Line)

In the next step shown by Figs. 6a - 6c a bus clock is introduced driving both bus lines. This bus is a fully representative model of the real bus w.r.t. the required degree of detail. The IR bus (bus A in Fig. 2b) transfers the signals from the processor to the devices and the RS bus (bus B in Fig. 2b) takes the opposite direction. Fig. 7 shows a representation which is functionally equivalent to the one of Fig. 6b when the bus period is set to zero, but gives different simulation results.

Table 1a shows the results of simulation for three simple bus types. No error is detected, but the system has low performance. The low utilisation of the bus will be recognised later when the software is executed on the real hardware. However, then it is very expensive to change the processing algorithm for the protocol.

Although system representation for test 3 is more complex due to the two bus lines, less system states were generated. This confirms that more complex systems do not necessarily have a higher number of system states. It is a matter of possible paths through the system, and obviously the bus of Fig. 5 is more accurately defined than the one of Fig. 4. This tuning aspect is discussed in more detail in section 3. Table 1b gives the results for six different timing approaches.

In case of test 4 the same algorithm as for tests 1 - 3 was used. As the next data request is only issued when the response for the previous request arrives no error was observed, but bus utilisation is still poor. It is surprising that the number of system states is again much lower compared to tests 2 and 3 although the bus is more complex. The reduction of system states occurs because the clock synchronises the processing steps and ambiguities in system behaviour are removed. This confirms hypothesis (d) given at the beginning of this section.

A burst of data requests is issued for test 5. The SDL specific queueing mechanism caused an error during random and exhaustive simulation. Although the algorithm is correct (it includes the required delay between data requests and checks), SDL simulation will reject this algorithm because the way the SDL tool is simulating the system is the same as in real world.

Test 6 adjusted the algorithm to the needs of the SDL tool and transferred the data requests synchronously with the bus clock. The missing delay between data requests and checks was detected. For test 7 the bus period was set to zero. This increased the number of system states and exhaustive simulation did not terminate because computer resources were exhausted.

#	Functionality	Ref. to Fig.	Bus Period	# Bus Cycles	States	Trans.	# Errors Random Sim.	# Errors Exhaust. Sim.	Bus Util. %	Correct Result
1	simple bus next data request or check when previous data received 3 data requests	-	n/a	n/a	184	329	0	0	33	yes but low performance protection needed against side effects
2	simple bus with broadcasting next data request or check when previous data received 3 data requests	4	n/a	n/a	830	1910	0	0	33	yes but low performance protection needed against side effects
3	simple bus with broadcasting and two uni-directional lines next data request or check when previous data received 3 data requests	5	n/a	n/a	617	1320	0	0	33	yes but low performance protection needed against side effects

Table 1a: Results of Protocol Validation for Functional Bus Representations

Exhaustive simulation was aborted and the error in protocol processing was not yet identified.

Test 8 repeated test 7 with the equivalent bus implementation of Fig. 7 which does not use the bus clock. Again, the number of system states is significantly higher when performance aspects are ignored, bit exhaustive simulation terminates. The need for the additional delay was not detected. Test 9 runs the correct algorithm under real timing conditions and the correct result is obtained.

3. Tuning of System Development

In the previous chapter the risks and chances for system development were discussed: (1) if not all system properties (like performacne) are subject of verification and validation the system will not run correctly in the real environment although no errors have been identified during the verification and validation process, (2) if inappropriate verification and validation procedures are applied correct implementations may be rejected, (3) consideration of performance aspects simplifies the verification and validation steps because a real, physical system behaves much simpler than an abstract, mathematical system.

Although SDL provides already powerful capabilities for verification and validation of distributed systems, means are missing which allow for detailed and representative modelling of timing. In consequence, SDL has to be enhanced such that the needs of verification and validation of a real (distributed) system will be met.

According to above conclusions (1) - (3) capabilities for performance analysis and simulation and the scheduling policies like priority-based, pre-emptive scheduling need to be added. EaSySim II does it on top of ObjectGEODE.

#	Functionality	Ref. to Fig.	Bus Period	# Bus Cycles	States	Trans.	# Errors Random Sim.	# Errors Exhaust. Sim.	Bus Util. %	Correct Result
4	real bus architecture next data request or check when previous data received 3 data requests	6	non-zero	24	470	990	0	0	33	yes but low performance protection needed against side effects
5	real bus architecture burst of 3 data requests, delay before checks	6	non-zero	n/a (due to error)	715	1556	1	1	→ 100	no data requests are not processed in the right order
6	real bus architecture synchronous transfer of requests and checks, no delay between last request and checks	6	non-zero	n/a (due to error)	558	1153	1	1	→ 100	yes missing delay before checks caused an error
7	same as above	6	zero	n/a	2097150	8018550	0	0	→ 100	no missing delay not identified exh. sim. does not terminate
8	same as above but with equivalent architecture, no clock	7	n/a	n/a	18130	56760	0	0	→ 100	no missing delay not identified
9	real bus architecture burst of 3 data requests, 2 bus cycles delay between last data request and first check (check sink)	6	non-zero	17					→ 100	yes protection needed against side effects

Tab. 1b: Results of Protocol Validation for Fully Representative Bus

But tuning of system development can also be done in view of quality and feasibility. It was recognised that the number of system states provides a feedback on ambiguities left open in system definition: if undesired paths through a system's FSM's are removed then the number of system states decreases. Reduction of number of system states by more accurate implementation and by consideration of performance matters allows to master verification and validation of systems for which exhaustive simulation would not terminate otherwise.

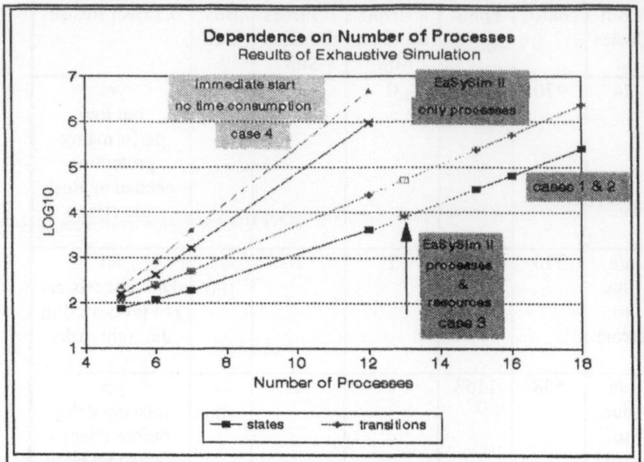

Fig. 8: Dependence of System States on Number of Processes

In fact, state explosion is a critical point of exhaustive simulation. It does not help at all to have such a powerful capability, but to fail for practical cases.

As was mentioned in section 2 filtering is not a good idea to make exhaustive simulation feasible because it may exclude critical cases, especially interaction with parallel activities. To take real advantage of exhaustive simulation one needs to reduce system states by other measures.

Fig. 8 shows the dependency of number of system states w.r.t. to number of processes for different implementations of an application. For case 4 performance aspects have not been considered. In this case systems of up to 15 processes may be validated by exhaustive simulation. It is believed that EaSySim II represents already an approach which creates a minimum number of system states (cases 1-3). But even in case of EaSySim II the number of processes are limited to about 20 - 25 processes[3]. The feasibility or unfeasibility of exhaustive simulation is also impacted by the simulation time which is about 8 hours for case 4 and 12 processes and about 1 hour for cases 1-3 and 18 processes.

3.1 Means for Tuning Verification and Validation

For tuning of verification and validation with SDL four different measures have been identified which reduce the number of system states and increase quality of a system:

1. use of a subset of SDL,
   e.g. avoid to distribute timers all over the SDL model, to use VIEW/REVEAL and EXPORT/IMPORT because such constructs may generate a lot of background traffic and a number of system states you can't control
2. enhancement of SDL tools by means which are adequate for the system under development
   EaSySim II provides optimised time managment and supports scheduling policies
3. consideration of performance aspects as described in the previous sections,
4. unambigous (and error free) definition of a system's behaviour by FSM's by evaluating the feedback from exhaustive simulation.

[3] In section 3.2 the means will be described which are provided by EaSySim II to escape from this limitation:transparent partitioning of a SDL system.

A reduction by a about four orders of magnitude was achieved for a sample application. The reduction at the beginning was obtained by means (1) and (2), while means (3) and (4) contributed to "fine tuning" at the end.

This experience is reflected by the EaSySim II Δ-approach© which is shown by Fig. 9.

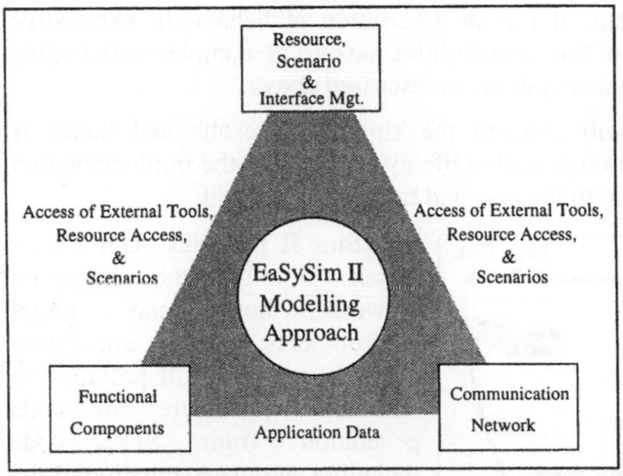

Fig. 9: The EaSySim II Δ-Approach©

EaSySim II extends ObjectGEODE. It provides support functions which help to organise a SDL system such that the number of system states can be reduced and resources can be consumed. Also, by this organisation a system can easily be distributed in a transparent manner. Moreover, this mechanism allows to communicate with other simulation tools such as SES/workbench or other software like window managers, database systems and other EaSySim II environments on the same or on remote processors.

EaSySim II divides a system into three principal parts: (1) a management part which drives the tests and system operation and provides an interface to the outside world, (2) a "functional" part which covers functional, behavioural and performance aspects of the application, and (3) a "communication" part which represents the network of the application through which the functional components are communicating with each other under consideration of performance.

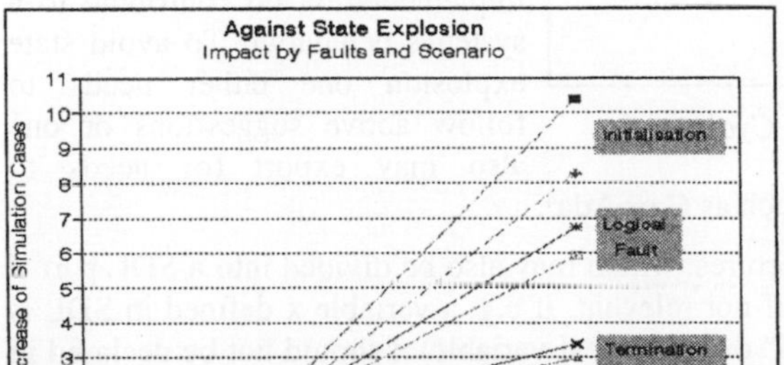

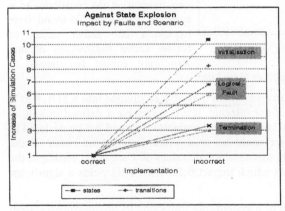

Fig. 10: Impact by Logical Faults and Performance Aspects

It is also possible to change the communication topology at run-time. This allows to perform redundancy switching for a fault-tolerant system after occurence of a fault. Hence the Fault Identification and Recovery Procedure (FDIR) can be subject of exhaustive simulation.

Fig. 10 demonstrates the impacts of (3) and (4) on number of system states during exhaustive simulation. A real, physical system is activated by switching on its components one after the other. In SDL all start transitions are executed at time "T_0". This causes a lot of additional system states as is shown by Fig. 10. The same happens when terminating a system immediately. EaSySim II provides the means to activate or de-activate a SDL system like a physical system and this reduces significantly the number of system states. The mechanisms provided by EaSySim II act like a capacitor connected across the poles of an electrical switch.

Moreover, it was observed that number of system states is also reduced when a logical fault is removed like an illegal path through the FSM's, a deadlock or an exception.

3.2 Means to Tune Efficiency of System Development

It was already pointed out that SDL provides powerful capabilities to make system development more efficient e.g. by means of formal description of behaviour, exhaustive simulation and automated code generation. Such capabilities have to be complemented when applying SDL to a broader class of distributed systems as discussed above.

Early transition to the target system will confirm the simulation results and hence is recommended. Fig. 11 shows the steps through such a life cycle and how the implementation approaches more and more the final system in the host and target environment.

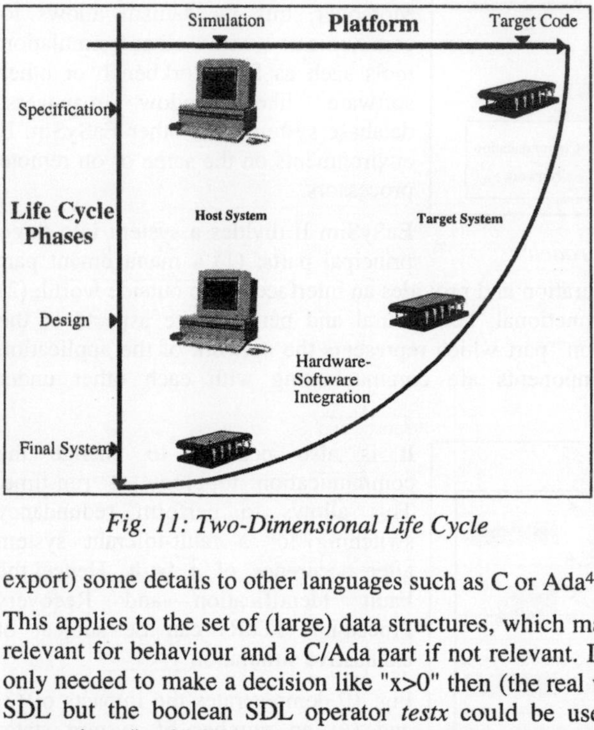

Fig. 11: Two-Dimensional Life Cycle

EaSySim II provides such means which simplify the transition between host and target environments, between simulation and generated code. It provides an automated procedure for code generation from SDL code including automated creation of the libraries speeding up the whole process to 15 mintes only. Moreover, EaSySim II tools remove performance instrumentation automatically.

Not all details of an implementation do contribute to a system's behaviour. To avoid state explosion one either needs to follow above suggestions or one also may export (or needs to export) some details to other languages such as C or Ada[4].

This applies to the set of (large) data structures, which may also be divided into a SDL part if relevant for behaviour and a C/Ada part if not relevant. If e.g. a variable x defined in SDL is only needed to make a decision like "x>0" then (the real variable) x should not be declared in SDL but the boolean SDL operator *testx* could be used which imports the result of the comparison "x>0" from C/Ada to SDL. In this case not all values of x are made visible to the exhaustive simulator but only such values which impact behaviour. This yields a significant reduction of SDL system space.

EaSySim II supports transparent partition of a system (not impacting its architecture): system processes my be included in more than one EaSySim II environment. So the scope of exhaustive simulation can be limited to some parts only, and exhaustive simulation can sequentially be applied to all system parts one after the other.

[4] The author has already successfully implemented SDL operators in Ada [15].

4. Future Issues

Currently, exhaustive simulation concentrates more on the combinatorial exploration of state space. When introducing performance, shared resources and more sophisticated scheduling policies multiple occurence of events nearly disappears and hence the need for combinatorial exploration becomes less important. What needs more detailed investigation is the timed execution of events and its consideration by exhaustive simulation, preferably in a more formal manner. When considering performance, interference between parallel system activities becomes much more important for system verification and validation.

Also, in order to master state explosion a more abstract interface should be introduced for implementation of behaviour. The object-oriented paradigm seems to be appropriate to cover this point: information hiding should be applied to such parts of an (SDL) implementation which do not impact a system's behaviour. More principal considerations are needed in this context.

5. Conclusions

Potential risks have been discussed which occur when SDL is used for development of a more general type of distributed systems and means were identified to master such risks. It was described how wrong conclusions may be derived on the correctness of an SDL implementation: a SDL system may be considered as correct after verification by SDL simulation, although it will never run correctly under real conditions. Vice versa, a correct implementation may be rejected by the SDL simulator. This is very dissatisfying and dangerous in case of safety-critical systems.

The EaSySim II environment was presented as a solution for most of the problems which are currently not solved by SDL and for optimisation of development of distributed systems.

Performance matters were identified as the main reason for such weakness of verification. Hence, verification and validation without consideration of performance is meaningless, because one does not know about its potential impact. Implementations which are considered as completely deterministic and correct may turn out as non-deterministic and incorrect in practice, even when people believe to be sure that the implementation is correct and performance cannot cause any problem.

Moreover, it was shown that consideration of performance aspects do simplify verification and validation significantly and help to master state explosion. So the extension of verification and validation from purely behavioural to performance aspects does not complicate system development, but eases it and reduces risks at early life cycle phases.

The number of system states and state transitions should be considered as a representative figure for quality of an implementation. A high figure may indicate that the system is not yet well defined.

The capabilities needed to complement SDL and SDL tools by performance evaluation issues can be provided as add-on's. However, more formal consideration of performance aspects and better support by the language to master state explosion are needed.

References:

[1] OMBSIM (On-Board Management System Behavioural Simulation, ESTEC contract no. 10430/93/NL/FM(SC), Final Report Nov. 1995, Noordwijk, The Netherlands

[2] R.Gerlich, Ch.Schaffer, Y.Tanurhan, V.Debus: EaSyVaDe / EaSySim: "Early System Validation of Design by Behavioural Simulation", ESTEC 3rd Workshop on "Simulators for European Space Programmes", November 15-17, 1994, Noordwijk, The Netherlands

[3] R.Gerlich, C. Joergensen: An Alternative Lifecycle Based on Object-Oriented Strategies, International Symposium on "On-Board Real-Time Software" , November 13-15, 1995, Noordwijk, The Netherlands

[4] R.Gerlich, Th. Stingl, Ch. Schaffer, F. Teston, G. Martinelli, Y. Tanurhan: Use of an Extended SDL Environment for Specification and Design of On-Board Operations, Systems Engineering Workshop, November 28-30, 1995, ESTEC, Noordwijk, The Netherlands

[5a] R.Gerlich: From CASE to CIVE: A Future Challenge, 'DASIA 96' - Data Systems in Aerospace, May 20-23, 1996, Rome, Italy

[5b] R.Gerlich: Experience with Simulation, Automated Code Generation and Integration, 'DASIA 97' - Data Systems in Aerospace, May 26 - 29, 1997, Sevilla, Spain

[6] R.Gerlich, N.Schäfer, A.Schäferhoff: Early Validation of DMS Design by a Reusable Environment, EUROSPACE On-Board Data Management Symposium on "Technology and Applications for Space Data Management Systems", January 25-27, 1994, Rome, Italy

[7] ObjectGEODE SDL-Tool, Verilog, 150 rue Vauquelin, F-31081 Toulouse Cedex, France

[8] SES/workbench, Scientific and Engineering Software Inc., Building A, 4301 Westbank Drive, Austin, Texas, 78746-6564, USA

[9] EaSySim II: The Enhanced Environment for System Validation, R. Gerlich BSSE, Auf dem Ruhbuehl 181, D-88090 Immenstaad, Germany

[10] HRDMS (Highly Reliable DMS and Simulation), ESTEC contract no. 9882/92/NL/JG(SC), Final Report, 1994

[11] L.Braga, R.Manione, P.Renditore: A Formal Description Language for the Modelling and Simulation of Timed Interaction Diagrams, FORTE/PSTV'96 Conference, Kaiserslautern, October 8-11, 1996

[12] M. Buetow, M.Mestern, C.Schapiro, P.S.Kritzinger: Performance Modelling with the Formal Specification Language SDL, FORTE/PSTV'96 Conference, Kaiserslautern, October 8-11, 1996

[13] S.Fischer: Implementation of multi-media systems based on real-time extension of Estelle, FORTE/PSTV'96 Conference, Kaiserslautern, October 8-11, 1996

[14] M.Diefenbruch, J.Hintelmann, B.Mueller-Clostermann: The QUEST-Approach for the Performance Evaluation of SDL-Systems, FORTE/PSTV'96 Conference, Kaiserslautern, October 8-11, 1996

[15] R.Gerlich, Y.Lejeune: How to use ObjectGEODE with Ada, January 1997, internal communication, unpublished

III

Verification and Validation I

SDL '97: TIME FOR TESTING - SDL, MSC and Trends
A. Cavalli and A. Sarma (Editors)

Telephone Feature Verification: Translating SDL to TLA$^+$

P. Gibson and D. Méry*[a]

[a]CRIN-CNRS URA 262 et Université Henri Poincaré - Nancy 1 , Bâtiment LORIA, BP239, 54506 Vandœuvre-lès-Nancy (FRANCE)
Email: {gibson,mery}@loria.fr

SDL is commonly used in the early stages of software development. It provides mechanisms for the specification of data structure, data flow, control flow, encapsulation, information hiding and abstract dependencies, through its support for concurrent objects. We propose a mechanism for translating SDL into a TLA$^+$specification, in order to provide a proof-theoretical framework. The preservation of properties through the translation is examined within the framework of a simple state-sequence semantics. We identify the strengths and weaknesses of such an approach, and introduce the translation which binds the two different semantics together. We apply the translation in the verification of two telephone features, and their interaction.

1. Introduction

This paper reports on the research that arose in response to a need for more formal means of verifying telecom feature systems. We believe that TLA$^+$holds many attractions for rigorous development and so aim to utilise it as our mathematical basis. We also believe that object oriented concepts offer real benefits at all stages of software development. Our strategy is based on combining object oriented and temporal logic models in a coherent and complementary manner. This provides us with a compositional approach to verifying systems of interacting telephone features. In this paper we examine the process of generating the first formal design models through a translation from SDL to TLA$^+$.

1.1. SDL

SDL92 [15], which we will now refer to as SDL, is an ITU (formally CCITT) standard language which provides a well accepted means of constructing reactive systems. Using SDL, it is possible to construct models which satisfy certain safety constraints. The validation techniques associated with the language provide automatic simulation environments and, in some cases, automatic code generation. These techniques are useful but not sufficiently rigorous for proving properties about systems: i.e. verifying that the defined behaviour is *correct*. SDL is particularly popular in telephone feature development [2]. The feature interaction problem is difficult, if not impossible, to solve without some form

*This work is partially supported by the contract n°06 1B CNET-FRANCE-TELECOM & CRIN-CNRS-URA262 and by the Institut Universitaire de France

of formal reasoning. SDL has been used to specify features but has not proved useful in the verification of systems of interacting features.

1.1.1. Introducing language concepts

In SDL, behaviour is defined by communicating processes. These communicate by exchanging (parameterised) signals via channels. Processes describe extended finite state machines (EFSMs) which change state only when a signal arrives. A signal may also trigger the sending of other signals and update some local variables. Processes may be grouped into blocks, the most important structural construct in SDL. A block may contain other blocks, connected by channels, or it may contain a set of processes, also connected by channels. The system is finally composed of several blocks, and is, of course, itself a block. An SDL system communicates with its environment by sending and receiving signals to/from that environment. These signals are, like internal communications, transferred by channels. Communication in SDL is asynchronous: each process has a message queue which buffers the incoming messages.

1.1.2. SDL is Object-Based

SDL provides object based conceptualisation [21], since we can view processes as concurrent objects. It provides the following facilities:

Instantiation: Processes, blocks and procedures are defined by types. Multiple instances of these types are indeed distinguishable by unique identifier.

Encapsulation: In SDL, the only way to change both state and local variables is to send a message to the appropriate process according to some well defined protocol.

Genericity: The ability to create generic behaviour expressions is very useful but not fundamentally object oriented.

Inheritance: All SDL types may be specialised by 'inheriting' all features from a supertype. This is one of the fundamental aspects of object oriented languages. However, the SDL inheritance semantics is not powerful enough to cope with the notion of class as type and the need for polymorphism. Inheritance, in SDL (and most other object oriented specification languages), is more like a code re-use mechanism [12]. Thus, we say that SDL is object-based rather than object oriented.

We choose to promote an object oriented interpretation of SDL code (wherever possible), and thus promote an object oriented style of expression which utilises our interpretation mechanisms. The underlying semantic framework is illustrated in figure 1. The object-labelled state transition semantics (O-LSTS) are taken directly from [12] and we are currently working on their implementation in TLA^+. They provide the structural consistency as we move from SDL to TLA^+, and, from our experience, they help both requirements modellers and designers to communicate.

1.1.3. Validation techniques

Message sequence charts (MSCs) provide one means of validating SDL specifications are [4]. MSCs can be used to formulate requirements of an SDL specification in terms of signal sequences. These can then be validated using an appropriate tool, like the SDL validator [7]. Such a tool is able only to validate MSCs which observe all messages between participants and thus it is limited in its application. Animators and code generators can

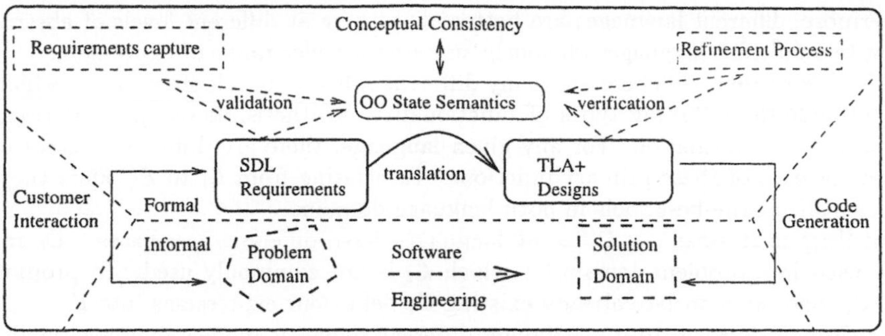

Figure 1: The Semantic Structure

also aid the validation process, which is always going to be informal[2] because of the need for the customer to be satisfied that the behaviour expressions being validated do *correctly* express their needs.

1.2. TLA+

TLA+is a specification language developed by Lamport [19] and based on his temporal logic of actions [20,18], extended by notations of set theory and syntactic structuring mechanisms. It has proved itself to be a formal, abstract and usable specification language [17]. It is founded on simple syntax and semantics which, in our opinion, can be exploited by anyone with basic mathematical ability. It provides a means of temporal reasoning which does not require a large knowledge of logic. In TLA+, a refinement relation between two specifications is simply defined as the deduction relationship in the underlying logic. The proof of a property in TLA+is simply reduced to a proof of implication: *A specification satisfies a property, if a specification implies that property.* TLA+is well supported by the theorem prover TLP [10].

1.3. Translation: A General Motivation

The translation from one language $\mathcal{L}_1$, say, into another language $\mathcal{L}_2$, say, is common in computing science. The utility of the translation is based on the preservation of the properties defined in the behavioural expression being transformed [3,22]. The difficulties of formalising such an approach must be out-weighed by the potential advantages:

Degree of Theoretical Foundation — $\mathcal{L}_1$ may not be formally defined. As such, expressions written in $\mathcal{L}_1$ are not amenable to the type of mathematical analysis (and transformation) which is becoming ever more important in safety critical systems development. By defining a mechanism for translating any given *correctly* defined $\mathcal{L}_1$ expression into an $\mathcal{L}_2$ expression, where $\mathcal{L}_2$ is a formally defined language, one effectively provides $\mathcal{L}_1$ with a rigorous semantics. Furthermore, there is potential for re-use of well-defined concepts in the framework of $\mathcal{L}_2$.

Expressiveness — Different languages have different expressional capabilities. Consequently, some problem domains are more easily modelled in one language than in another.

[2] Informality does not necessarily imply a lack of rigour.

Furthermore, different languages are better at working at different levels of abstraction. Having two different languages obviously supports a wider range of expression.

Practical Support — There are many different software development tools which generally provide the following types of functionality: synthesis, analysis, validation, verification and transformation. For any given language, there are different degrees of tool support for each of these primary functions. Translating from $\mathcal{L}_1$ to $\mathcal{L}_2$ offers the possibility of utilising the best tools in both language domains.

Expanding user-base — Different languages have different user-bases. $\mathcal{L}_1$ may be widely used in a problem domain for which $\mathcal{L}_2$ is not commonly used. To promote the use of $\mathcal{L}_2$, one can translate already existing $\mathcal{L}_1$ behaviour expressions into $\mathcal{L}_2$.

Improving understanding — Having different semantic models may also facilitate a better understanding of the problem domain being considered and of the strengths and weaknesses of each of the languages.

Re-use — An important aspect of all modelling is the ability to re-use previous work. This re-use may come in many different forms [13,16,14,11,24]. Translation between languages facilitates the transfer of all types of re-use from one domain to the other.

1.4. Translation: SDL to TLA$^+$

It is difficult to rigorously relate or transform SDL models. Furthermore, SDL, unlike TLA$^+$is not well suited to the verification of rigorously formulated properties. SDL cannot express properties such as liveness and fairness, which are becoming ever more important in telephone feature specifications. SDL tool support is strongest for model synthesis and validation. TLA$^+$tool support is strongest in the areas of refinement and verification. The translation from SDL to TLA$^+$should introduce many more developers to the advantages of formal languages, in general, and temporal logics, in particular. Through translation we understand much better the feature interactions which are due to fairness problems. Such interactions are difficult to address in the SDL framework. There is much potential for re-use of SDL code in a constructive, object-based manner. Within TLA$^+$we also promote re-use of proof components as a means of facilitating compositional verification. Translating SDL to TLA$^+$permits exploitation of the strengths of both languages in a complementary manner.

1.5. Object Oriented Methods

1.5.1. Advantages

Object oriented concepts have been shown to aid model development at all levels of abstraction and in many different problem domains [1,5,9]. They also lend themselves to a natural state-based conceptualisation [12], incorporating the notions of abstraction, composition, delegation and subclassing in a formal framework. Object oriented methods encourage different types of re-use, facilitate a better understanding of the systems being developed, aid validation and, given a formal semantics, are a step towards the type of constructive rigorous verification which is necessary for *correct* system development.

1.5.2. Objects and Classes

There are two distinct conceptualisations of the term *object* within the semantic framework which we propose. Each class has a set of *member objects*, each of which represents a potential state of an *object instance* of that class. An *object instance* is a state machine whose current state is defined by a reference to a particular *object member* of the class to which it belongs. Meyer states in [25] that 'a class is an executable entity in its own right'. We consider each class member to be an executable finite state machine (FSM), as defined in [12]. State transitions occur only in response to service requests. This model can be realised, after a degree of conceptual manipulation, in the SDL framework by the notions of block, process, channel and signal.

1.5.3. Objects and Fairness

Temporal requirements, such as liveness and fairness, must be included informally in any SDL model. These informal aspects must be formalised by hand as we translate to TLA^+: in our telephone feature case studies, the need for fairness is evident in our formal models. The O-LSTS semantics provide formal definitions for object, class, service, subclassing, polymorphism, genericity, and composition. The O-LSTS models complement our TLA^+specifications because the underlying model is that of a class as a state transition machine. The two methods share this interpretation, but at different levels of abstraction.

2. An Operational Semantics for SDL

2.1. An Overview

We are required to preserve the semantics of the given SDL models in the TLA^+specifications which result from the translation. We must ensure that the semantics which we attribute to SDL (through our translation to TLA^+) coincide with those as expressed in the SDL standard. Let us denote any given SDL specification as *sdl* and the semantics of such a specification, expressed as a set of infinite sequences of states closed by stuttering, as $S(sdl)$. Similarly, let us denote any given TLA^+specification and its semantics as *tla* and $S(tla)$ respectively. Now, given a translation function T: SDL $\rightarrow$ TLA^+, we have the mathematical structure as shown in figure 2:

> Given *sdl*, and $tla \equiv T(sdl)$ then: $S(sdl)$ and $S(tla)$ are two sets of infinite sequences of states related by the following relationship — $S(sdl) \subseteq S(tla)$. Now, we ensure that any property holding for *sdl* also holds for *tla* : if a property Φ holds for *tla*, then $S(tla) \subseteq S(\Phi)$, where $S(\Phi)$ is the semantics of the property expressed as a set of infinite sequences of states, and if $S(sdl) \subseteq S(tla)$, then $S(sdl) \subseteq S(\Phi)$. The preservation guarantees that any property derived from *tla* is also a property of *sdl*.

Now, after generating the *tla* specification we can verify our design steps as refinements. These refinements guarantee that as we add new features to our system we do not compromise the requirement properties of features already developed.

2.2. The SDL definition

The SDL syntax is represented in two different ways: textually and graphically. Informal semantic descriptions are added to these representations in the form of comments. Our method consists of studying SDL syntax defined in the ITU (CCITT) standards document for the purpose of understanding and defining an appropriate subset, which we call CROCOS [23]. A subset of SDL syntax has been examined for translation. (Work is currently being carried out to expand this subset and to incorporate the object based syntactic constructs of SDL-92. At the moment the size of the subset is constrained by

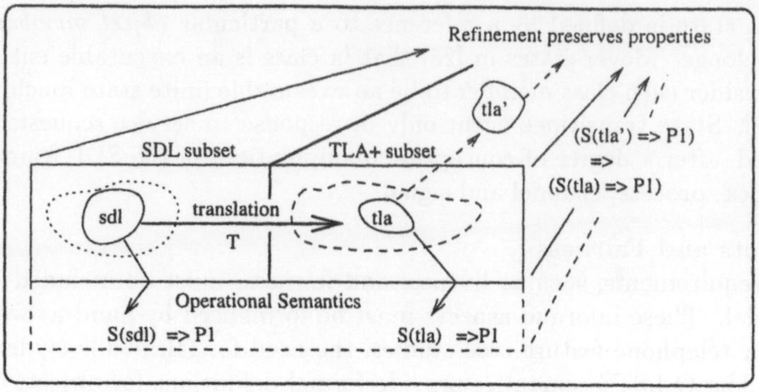

Figure 2: Mathematical Structure

the semantic framework underlying the translation process. Furthermore, we need to formalise the relation between the O-LSTS object oriented concepts and those found in the standard before the translation can be extended.)

2.3. Introducing the language constructs

An SDL text specifies a system as a set of blocks communicating through channels and using signals.

$$\texttt{System } S \triangleq \begin{cases} \texttt{Signal} & sig_1, \ldots, sig_p; \\ \texttt{Channel} & chan_1, \ldots, chan_q; \\ \texttt{Block} & B_1 \\ \ldots & \\ \texttt{Block} & B_n \end{cases}$$

A block B is either a set of blocks communicating via channels and using signals:

$$\texttt{Block } B \triangleq \begin{cases} \texttt{Signal} & B \bullet sig_1, \ldots, B \bullet sig_p; \\ \texttt{Channel} & B \bullet chan_1, \ldots, B \bullet chan_q; \\ \texttt{Block} & B \bullet B_1 \\ \ldots & \ldots \\ \texttt{Block} & B \bullet B_n \end{cases}$$

or a set of processes communicating via routes:

$$\texttt{Block } B \triangleq \begin{cases} \texttt{SignalRoute} & B \bullet r_1, \ldots, B \bullet r_p; \\ \texttt{Process} & B \bullet P_1 \\ \ldots & \ldots \\ \texttt{Block} & B \bullet P_n \end{cases}$$

An SDL process P is defined by a name, a list of parameters and a set of transitions. A transition is characterized by a starting label and final labels corresponding to the execution of different basic actions as assignment, receipt of a message, sending a message.

$$\text{Process } P \triangleq \begin{cases} \texttt{Process} & < name > (min, max) \\ \texttt{Fpar} & < formal\ parameters > \\ \ldots & \ldots \\ \texttt{state } start: & < transition_0 > \\ \texttt{state } label_1: & < transition_1 > \\ \ldots & \ldots \quad\quad \ldots \\ \texttt{state } label_n: & < transition_n > \end{cases}$$

The translation of an SDL system into a TLA text uses the hiding of variable as channel. The mapping is relatively obvious and it allows us to give a TLA-based semantics for SDL. The fact that SDL requires the definition of algebraic datatypes does not suggest any problem because we suppose that users can utilise the abstract data type of SDL as set-theoretical elements. In sections 2.4 to 2.7, we provide a semi-formal overview of the way in which the translation maintains the semantics and structure of SDL systems. (As an overview, these sections can act only as a brief justification of our approach: more details can be obtained directly from the authors.)

2.4. Naming elements of SDL text

The naming of SDL constructs leads to a simple partition of sets as variable parameters in the corresponding TLA$^+$specification.

`System`	:	set of names for system
`Block`	:	set of names for blocks
`Process`	:	set of names for processes
`Channel`	:	set of names for channels
`Signal`	:	set of names for signals
`Variable`	:	set of names for variables
`State`	:	set of names for states

module *Basic-Notations*

variable

$P, S, B, Chan, Sig$

2.5. Transforming transitions into TLA actions

A transition is written as follows:

$$T \triangleq \begin{cases} STATE & label_1 & S_1 & NEXTSTATE & label'_1 \\ & \ldots & \ldots & NEXTSTATE & \ldots \\ & label_n & S_n & NEXTSTATE & label'_n \end{cases}$$

The control state is defined as a special variable attached to every process :

- $P \bullet L$ means that L is a label variable for P of the process P.
- $P \bullet L$ is the current value of the control of P, and $P \bullet L'$ will be the next value of L.
- the process P has variables that may be modified by `TASK` and P can send or receive messages. Labels are located at the beginning of every state and before every operation. A global assertion, namely an invariant on control, is defined to handle the relationship between labels.

A control invariant for P is defined from the text of the process P : $Icontrol(P)$.
A control invariant for a block B is defined from components of B:

$$Icontrol(B) \triangleq \bigwedge_{B' \in B \bullet Block} Icontrol(B')$$

A control invariant for a system S is defined from components of S:

$$Icontrol(S) \triangleq \bigwedge_{B \in S \bullet Block} Icontrol(B)$$

The transformation of T into an action of TLA is as follows:

- T is decomposed into $T_1; T_2; \ldots; T_n$
- for any i in $\{1, \ldots, n\}$, T_i becomes $\mathcal{A}_i(T)(x, x')$
- $\mathcal{A}$ is $\mathcal{A}(T_1)(x, x') \vee \mathcal{A}(T_n)(x, x')$
- for any i in $\{1, \ldots, n\}$, $\mathcal{A}(T_i)$ is $\mathcal{A}(T_{i1})(x, x') \vee \mathcal{A}(T_{ij_n})(x, x')$

2.6. The Next relation for a system S

We require the following notation in our definition of *Next*:

- For any process P, $\mathcal{N}(P)$ is the disjunction of actions in P.
- For any block B, $\mathcal{B} \triangleq \bigwedge_{B' \in B.Block} \mathcal{N}(B')$
- For any system S, $\mathcal{N}(S) \triangleq \bigwedge_{B \in S.Block} \mathcal{N}(S)$

Finally, the global next relation for S is simply defined by a TLA$^+$module *Next*:

module *Next*

extends ...

Other modules are required for the definition of Next and are imported

$$\mathcal{GN}(S) \triangleq \mathcal{N}(S) \wedge Icontrol(S)$$

2.7. A semantics for S

The definition of a semantics for S leads us to characterize a set of behaviors for S with the help of a TLA formula; in the style of Lamport we write:

module *semantics-of-S*

extends ...

```
Other modules are required for the definition of S(S) and
are imported
```

$$\mathcal{S}(S) \triangleq Init(S) \wedge \mathcal{GN}(S) \wedge Fairness(S)$$

$Fairness(S)$ expresses a fairness condition for S. $Fairness(S)$ can be defined with the weak fairness (WF) or strong fairness (SF) predicates. $\mathrm{WF}x\mathcal{A}$ states that, if $\mathcal{A}$ is continuously enabled from a given state, then $\mathcal{A}$ will be executed, while there is a possible stuttering on x; $\mathrm{SF}x\mathcal{A}$ states that, if $\mathcal{A}$ is infinitly often enabled from a given state, then $\mathcal{A}$ will be executed.

2.8. Translation: The Formalisation

The main problem is to define the soundness of the translation with respect to a semantics of system. Intuitively, a SDL system is semantically defined as a set of traces: a trace of states allows us to observe the transformation of data with actions. A notion of action can be clearly extracted from the ITU (CCITT) documentation on SDL.

Definition 1 *Semantics of a system*
A system S over a set of variables V is modelled by a set of behaviours Behaviour(S, V,) over V: $\sigma \in Behaviour(S,V,)$ *and* $\sigma' : \sigma_0 \xrightarrow{\mathcal{A}_0} \sigma_1 \ldots \xrightarrow{\mathcal{A}_{i-1}} \sigma_{i-1} \xrightarrow{\mathcal{A}_i} \sigma_i \xrightarrow{\mathcal{A}_{i+1}} \ldots \sigma_0, \sigma_1, \sigma_{i-1}, \sigma_i$ *are states of the system S over V and are defined as mapping from V to the memory values* $\mathcal{A}_0, \ldots, \mathcal{A}_{i-1}, \mathcal{A}_i, \mathcal{A}_{i+1} \ldots$ *are actions over V : an action $\mathcal{A}$ is defined as a set of couples of states.*

A system is characterized by a set of infinite traces over a set of variables. However, SDL uses infinite communication channels that leads to a first observation that automata in SDL are generally not finite state. A second observation is that we need to use a variable for every channel. Now we turn to the translation of an SDL specification into a TLA formula and the definition of the semantics of a system S written as an SDL specification:

- Action is [TASK X := E]: $(x' = e(x) \wedge inv(x))$, where $inv(x)$ is an invariant of x.
- Action is [Start Choice Task1 Task2 Task3 ... Taskn End]: $T(Task1) \vee \ldots \vee T(Taskn)$

The question of the soundness of the translation is crucial. The result is based on equivalence by stuttering, which simply states that two traces are equivalent by stuttering, if they are equal when you forget idle actions[20].

2.8.1. Translation: work to date

The translation of SDL into a formal framework has been done in our CROCOS environment [23], and we have translated a subset of SDL using the *wp* operator for atomic actions We are currently considering translation of the full SDL language: the additional structure in the TLA$^+$logic, together with our O-LSTS semantic integration, provides a means to facilitate a more complete object-based conceptualisation of SDL. An important thing to note in the translation is the introduction of fairness assumptions which could not be expressed in the original SDL systems. These fairness assumptions reflect informal assumptions that we have made about the objects in our models. In particular, they reflect the fact that a system of concurrent objects is actually modelled using interleaving and a *nondeterministic scheduling*. The TLA^+semantics can be used to formally state our informal assumptions about the fairness of concurrent objects in the SDL models. This is important in the domain of telephone feature development. The behaviour specified by the resulting TLA^+models can be viewed as a refinment of the originating SDL models because of the way in which the nondeterminism is treated at a different level of abstraction.

2.9. Verification of SDL programs

Our technique has been developed to improve the way to prove properties about programs written in SDL. Several techniques can be applied to handle a SDL specification translated into a TLA specification. A model checking technique is applied when the TLA specification is finite-state[3] A direct consequence is that we need to translate a TLA specification into an equivalent finite automaton in order to check properties on the SDL program. Theorem proving is a more powerful approach which requires theorem prover tool. We have such a tool, namely TLP [10], for TLA. Hence, when we have translated an SDL program into an equivalent TLA specification, we prove properties of the SDL program by proving properties of the TLA^+produced in the translation. Then during design, each refinement of the TLA^+specification maintains the properties as required by the SDL model.

3. A Simple Case Study: Telephone Features

The feature interaction problem is concerned with what happens when we try to put a wide range of telephone features together in one system. An interaction is said to occur if the complete system does not fulfil the requirements of each individual component feature. Feature interaction is one of the most difficult problems in this problem domain [6,8] and must be considered in the initial stages of specification. Finite state automata have been shown to play a role in the analysis of safety properties in systems in which feature interactions can occur. However, it is now becoming clear that liveness and fairness properties can also be important in such interactions. In this simple study we show the problems that can occur when defining new features (call waiting and three-way calling are used as examples) which extend standard telephone functionality. We compare an *SDL-alone* approach with one based on a translation to TLA^+.

3.1. POTS

The Plain Old Telephone Service (POTS) requirements is represented, in figure 3, by our O-LSTS diagram of the simplest of telephones. (In the diagram we have not represented null state transitions which return some value to the external interface, through services hook and signal, but do not change the internal state of the system. Their intended semantics should be evident from the state labels.)

[3] If a TLA specification has only finite domains, then the generated automaton is finite.

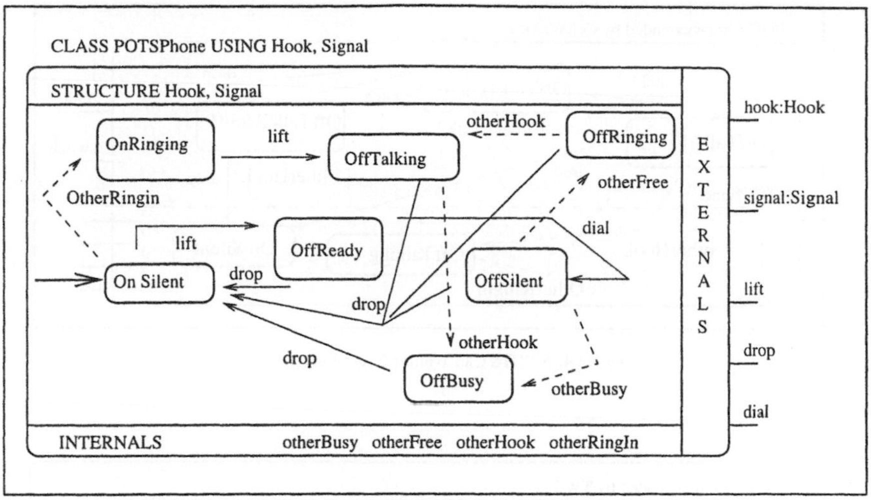

Figure 3: A POTS Phone Requirements Model

3.2. Call Waiting (CW) and POTS

CW functionality is enabled only when talking to someone else, and a third person tries to call. With CW, they will not get a busy tone (as before) but will hear a ringing tone until they are held. CW permits the talking to one person concurrently with the holding of another. It also permits the switching of the talking and held persons. Either of the two other users can hang up to leave the CW user in the standard POTS state where they are talking to one person. The CW subscriber can also hang up leaving them in the standard POTS `OnSilent` state. This is illustrated in the *partial* state transition diagram for the extended telephone (we do not show all the telephone states and transitions as they are preserved by the extension mechanism), in figure 4.

3.3. Three Way Calling (TWC) and POTS

If I subscribe to TWC then the feature is enabled only when I am talking to someone and I receive a call from a third party. I then have a new service (connect) which permits me to talk with both callers at the same time. In this new state I can also disconnect either one of the two callers. This is illustrated in the *partial* state transition diagram for the extended telephone, in figure 5.

3.4. CW and TWC: A feature interaction?

Traditionally, the argument for these two features interacting is as follows:

> What happens if both features are activated and we are talking to someone when we receive an incoming call? There is an ambiguity because the system doesn't know which feature to execute: the CW or the TWC.

We must ask whether there is really a problem here. The question is best addressed within a formal framework: below, we examine the SDL-TLA$^+$models of the behaviour. The *partial* O-LSTS diagram, in figure 6, is common to both models.

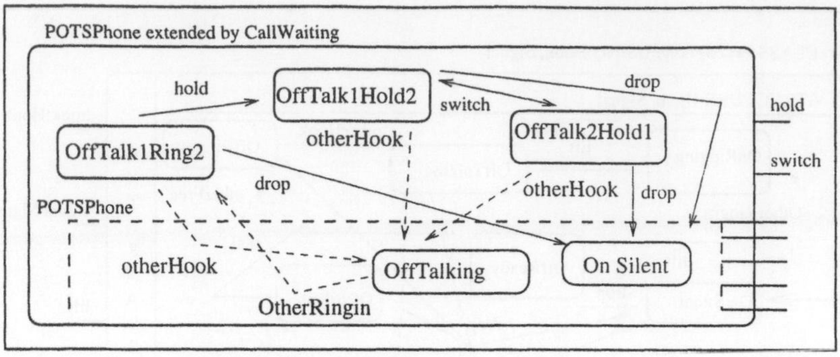

Figure 4: A POTS Call Waiting Extension

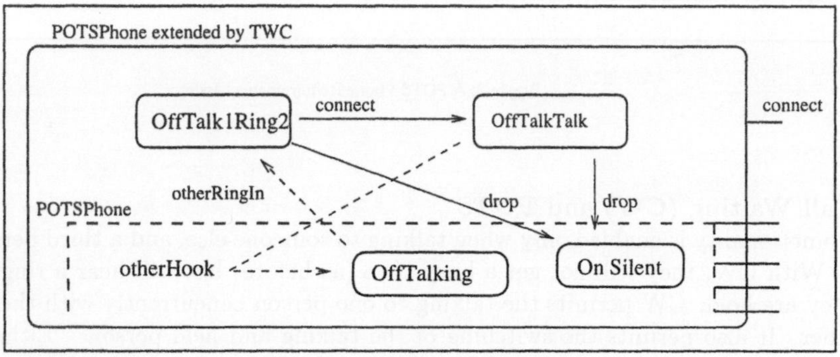

Figure 5: A POTS Three Way Calling Extension

3.5. Standard SDL Approachs

3.5.1. Informal Validation: Animation

The SDL state transition model can be animated for validation. A black-box validation is done when the animator shows only execution behaviour as a trace of actions. White-box testing also permits the user to see the internal state representation of the system during execution. Both types of validation are useful for interacting with the customer, but they are not sufficient when we consider systems with large numbers of states.

3.5.2. Rigorous Validation: Using MSCs

The SDT validator of MSCs can perform an exhaustive search on the state space of the finite state machines representing the SDL specifications. MSCs help to structure the validation process. The user no longer needs to interact directly with a large, complex machine; instead, they specify sets of requirements as MSCs and these are automatially verified against the underlying model. There are limitations to this approach:

- It is sometimes necessary to construct huge MSCs which are difficult to understand

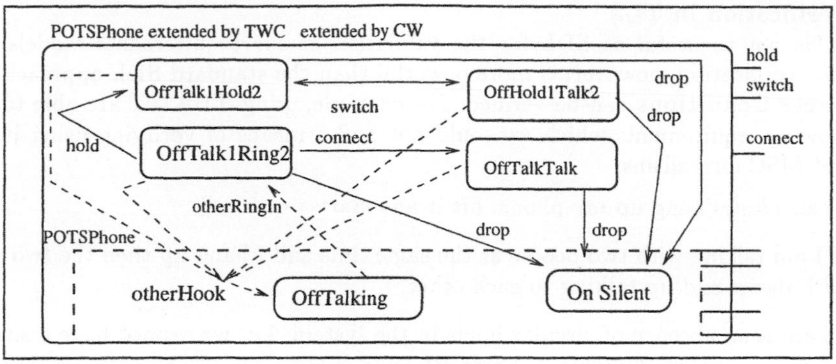

Figure 6: A Feature Composition

and ultimately may not even correctly define the requirements properties that are to be verified.

- Safety properties can be proved in this way but were found, in practice, to be too complicated to be expressed using MSCs
- Liveness properties cannot be considered
- As systems are refined or extended, the validation process must be carried out again. In other words, the approach is not compositional.

3.5.3. Verifying our Feature Composition

The process of validation does not aid us with the feature interaction problem. Consider the following situation:

The POTS telephone is validated against MSCs $p1$ and $p2$
The CW-telephone is validated against MSCs $cw1$ and $cw2$

We would like to be able to formally verify each extension of the original POTS system in such a way that the properties are preserved automatically, for example:

CW-telephone is *verified against* a POTS telephone $\Rightarrow$
CW-telephone automatically fulfils properties $p1$ and $p2$

In the standard SDL approach $p1$ and $p2$ must be separately verified against the CW-telephone specification. The state space of a simple telephone and a few features is relatively small and so is amenable to exhaustive testing. Consequently, we can verify the incremental feature extensions of the POTS phone using the standard SDL tools. However, the state space of the POTS system (where we have a set of telephones and their features) was too large for automatic verification. It was possible to validate subsets of the state space but there was no means of constructing a larger validation (or verification) of the whole system in a rigorous fashion.

3.6. Verification in TLA$^+$

TLA$^+$is not as useful as SDL for the valdiation of our requirements models Using TLA$^+$for verification, however, is more powerful than the standard SDL approach:
* **Liveness Conditions** can be verified. For example, using TLA$^+$we are able to prove the following requirements which we could not find a means of verifying using just the SDL and MSC formalisms:

- I can *always* hang up my phone, lift it and start a new call.
- If I am talking with two people at the same time and I hang up then the two people will *always* end up talking to each other.
- There is an absence of circular holds in the system: i.e. we cannot have a situation where: $P1$ holds $P2$ holds ... holds $P1$.
- When I dial a number I will *eventually* get a busy or ringing signal.

These properties are formalised in TLA$^+$as follows:

module *SPECIFICATION*

extends ...

theorems

I can *always* hang up my phone, lift it and start a new call.

$$DEFINITION1 \triangleq \Box(\text{ENABLED}\ \neg Hang\_Up\_My\_Phone \bullet Lift\_It \bullet Start\_New\_Call)$$

If I am talking with two people at the same time and I hang up then the two people will *always* end up talking to each other.

$$DEFINITION2 \triangleq \Box(\forall p1, p2. Talking(I, p1, p2) \land Hang\_On(I) \Rightarrow Talking(p1, p2))$$

There is an absence of circular holds in the system: i.e. we can never have a situation where: $P1$ holds $P2$ holds ... holds $P1$.

$$DEFINITION3 \triangleq \Box(\neg(\exists P_1, P_2, \ldots, P_n : \land\ \forall i \in \{1 \ldots n-1\} : Hold(P_i, P_{i+1})) \land Hold(P_n, P_1))$$

When I dial a number I will *eventually* get a busy or ringing signal.

$$DEFINITION4 \triangleq Dial(I, Number) \leadsto (Busy\_Toning(I.Number) \lor Ringing(I, Number))$$

* **Compositional verification** can be mechanised because verification is represented by a logical implication which can be handled directly by the TLA$^+$theorem prover TLP [10].
* **Power of expression** is better when using TLA$^+$rather than MSCs for specifying requirements properties for verification.

3.7. CW and TWC: Is there an interaction?

The two features *do* interact when the `hold` and `connect` actions are obliged (by each of their feature requirements) to occur when in the state `OffTalk1Ring2` — this is the standard model. Clearly, these two actions cannot both be performed and, in this case, an interaction is said to occur because both features cannot meet their obligations. With the TLA$^+$notion of liveness, we can guarantee that we do not stay in state `OffTalk1Ring2` whilst obliging neither of the two actions individually. Thus, we have no contradictory requirements and the two features do not interact. It is the the user who chooses which feature to execute; and if such a choice is not made liveness can be used to gaurantee that a nondeterministic action *eventually* changes the state of the system.

4. Conclusions and Future Work

This paper reports on a continuing experiment into the use of formal methods in showing the *correctness* of telephone feature requirements models (written in SDL). It is clear, even at this early stage, that there is much complexity involved. Some of this complexity is presently being 'factored out' in the development of appropriate translation tools. One of the most difficult aspects of verification is the sheer size of the task. What is clear is that the complexities of verification increase much more than linearly with respect to the size of the models to be verified (this is particularly true for our telephone feature interaction case study). At worst, the problem seems to be almost exponential in nature. What is needed is a constructive approach to verification in the same vein as the constructive approaches to validation which are evident in many of the modern object oriented analysis and requirements capture methods. However, the problem of constructive verification hinges on the definition of constructive proof operators which can be used in conjunction with the operators used in the synthesis of requirements models. This is our current area of research.

We believe that there is much to be achieved through the integration of object oriented concepts, simple operational semantics and temporal logics. This work is a small step towards achieving such an integration. SDL is useful in telephone feature development during analysis and requirements modelling. TLA$^+$is useful for formal verification of design steps and system extensions, and it also provides us with the means of reasoning about fairness aspects of telephone services. The object oriented state-transition based semantics provide us with a good basis on which to connect these two languages in a complementary fashion. We have illustrated how a subset of SDL can be translated; this subset will be expanded upon as we integrate the O-LSTS semantics with the extended finite state semantics in the SDL standard. This will also facilitate a more compositional approach to TLA$^+$verification.

REFERENCES

1. G. Booch. *Object Oriented Development.* IEE Software Engineering, February 1986.
2. L. G. Bouma and H. Velthuijsen, editors. *Feature Interactions in Telecommunications Systems.* IOS Press, 1994.
3. N. Brown and D. Méry. A proof environment for concurrent programs. In J. C. P. Woodcock, editor, *FME'93: Industrial-Strength Formal Methods*, pages 196–215. IFAD, Springer-Verlag, 1993. LNCS 670.
4. M. Broy. Towards a semantics for sdl. Technical report, PASSAU University, 1989.
5. P. Coad and E. Yourdon. *Object oriented analysis.* Prentice-Hall (Yourdon Press), 1990.
6. P. Combes, M. Michel, W. Bouma, and H. Velthuijsen. Formalisation of properties for feature interaction detection. In *ISN Conference*, 1993.
7. P. Combes, M. Michel, and B. Renard. Formalisation verification of telecommunications service interactions using SDL methods and tools. In *6th SDL Forum.* North Holland, 1993.
8. P. Combes and S. Pickin. Formalisation of a user view of network and services for feature interaction detection. In L. G. Bouma and H. Velthuijsen, editors, *Feature Interactions in Telecommunications Software System*, pages 120–135. IOS Press, 1994.
9. Brad Cox. *Object oriented programming: an evolutionary approach.* Addison-Wesley, 1986.
10. U. Engberg. *TLP Manual-(release 2. 5a)*-PRELIMINARY. Department of Computer Science, Aarhus University, May 1994.
11. R. Fairley. *Software Engineering Concepts.* McGraw Hill, New York, 1985.
12. J. Paul Gibson. *Formal Object Oriented Development of Software Systems Using LOTOS.* Technical report CSM-114, Stirling University, September 1993.
13. Joseph Gougen. Reusing and interconnecting software components. *Computer*, 20, February 1986.
14. Raymonde Guindon. Knowledge exploited by experts during software system design. *International Journal of Man-Machine Studies*, 33(3):279–304, 1990.
15. ITU. *Specification and description language (SDL) ITU-T Recommendation Z.100*, revision 1 edition, 1994.
16. R. E. Johnstone and B. Foote. Designing re-usable classes. *Journal of Object Oriented Programming JOOP*, pages 22–35, June 1988.
17. L. Lamport. Hybrid systems in TLA$^+$. In Grossman, Nerode, Ravn, and Rischel, editors, *Workshop on Theory of Hybrid Systems.* Springer-Verlag, 1992. LNCS 736.
18. L. Lamport. A temporal logic of actions. *Transactions On Programming Languages and Systems*, 21(9):768–775, September 1995.
19. L. Lamport. TLA$^+$. Technical report, Digital Equipment Corporation, 5th july 1995.
20. L. Lamport. TLA in pictures. *IEEE Trans. on SE*, 16(3):872–923, May 1995.
21. T. Lindner and C. (editors) Lewerentz. *Case Study Production Cell A Comparitive Study in Formal Software Development.* FZI-Publication, 1994.
22. D. Méry. *Une Méthode de Raffinement et de Développement pour la Programmation Parallèle.* PhD thesis, Université de Nancy 1,UFR STMIA, DFD Informatique, February 1993. Doctorat d'Etat.
23. D. Méry and A. Mokkedem. CROCOS: An integrated environment for interactive verification of SDL specifications. In G. Bochmann, editor, *Computer-Aided Verification Proceedings.* Springer Verlag, 1992.
24. B. Meyer. Genericity versus inheritance. In *Object Oriented Programming Languages Systems and Applications (OOPSLA 86) As ACM SIGPLAN 21*, November 1986.
25. B. Meyer. *Eiffel: The Language.* Prentice Hall International Ltd., 1992.

SDL '97: TIME FOR TESTING - SDL, MSC and Trends
A. Cavalli and A. Sarma (Editors)

Simulation of IP Mobility Support: An experiment in mobile protocol specification with SDL*

Mária Törö†

KFKI Research Institute for Measurement and Computing Techniques
H-1525 Budapest P.O.Box 49, Hungary
tmaria@sun60.mszki.kfki.hu

Abstract

This paper addresses the question of modeling mobile protocols with SDL using the example of the new Internet standard: IP Mobility Support. A modified channel model is presented that allows the specification of dynamically changing communication path configurations, which is the main difference between the stationary and mobile protocols, and which plays the key role in initiation of mobility handling mechanisms.

We show how this new channel concept allows us to detect some problems with the protocol, such as data loss due to the early expiration of the registration lifetime in the home agent, which occurs any time when the signal delay increases between the mobile host and its home agent.

The suggested channel modification easily fits with other SDL mechanisms. It allows the specification of features characteristic of the mobile environment without increasing the complexity of the specification, which would be required by the current SDL.

1. INTRODUCTION

Mobile users appeared several years ago in telephony, and now the technology provides the possibility of mobile computing as well. However there was still a lack of protocols supporting mobile users of computer networks. For example, on the Internet, the address and the location of a node are strictly related; this does not allow the migration of users between subnetworks. To address this problem a new document was developed for the Internet, which lies at the center of our paper. The IP Mobility Support (MIP) [1] is intended to deal with location man-

*. The work reported in this paper was carried out at the Computer Science Department of University of British Columbia, and it was supported in part by the joint grants from Motorola/ARRC and NSERC/IOR (Canada). The PROCONSUL project is supported by the National Scientific Research Foundation (Hungary) under contract number 17120.OTKA

†. *currently with*: University of British Columbia, Dept. of Computer Science
2366 Main Mall, Vancouver, B.C. V6T1Z4, Canada

agement on the Internet.

There have been many studies on the performance issues of TCP over MIP [2-7]. Several solutions were suggested to improve the performance. They range from splitting the TCP connection into two parts up to the end-to-end wireless aware TCP. Most of the suggestions rely on the experience of higher retransmission rate at TCP level over MIP, however the mechanism causing these retransmissions was only partially studied. The suggested solutions address the following problems: (1) higher data loss rate on the wireless link, which is not detected up to the IP level; (2) wide range of delivery time on the wireless link, which is detected and handled by TCP as a congestion; (3) data loss during location management. The first two problems are introduced by the wireless media and, if they are not handled appropriately, they are inherited by the protocol layers above. In [2-5] solutions are offered for these problems. Location management is addressed by MIP, therefore data loss caused during it cannot be solved by, for example, a reliable data link layer protocol. In [7] this problem was studied during the performance analysis of MIP, and not on the protocol model. We strongly believe that application of formal description techniques such as SDL can help this task, and give a solution at an earlier stage of the protocol design.

We have prepared an SDL specification of MIP, which is responsible for the location management of mobile hosts on the Internet, and we have run series of simulation of its behaviour to study both the protocol itself and the capabilities of SDL to specify mobility.

In [8] an analysis of formal approach to specify mobility is given. In our experience procedures (e.g. data transfer procedure) of mobile protocols do not differ, in general, from those in stationary protocols. The main difference is that the initiation of some procedures (e.g. location management procedures) depends on the pattern of the delivery of signals to a certain process. The system configuration changes in the sense of availability of different communication paths and not in the sense of availability of processes. The process detects the pattern of delivery of a certain signal, and decides whether this pattern can be interpreted as a motion, i.e. change in the configuration of communication paths. This means that the signal delivery pattern of channels plays a key role in the model. We have modelled different channel behaviors: beside the standard non-deterministically delaying SDL channels, the channel behaviour was declared explicitly in the specification to define 1) a channel delay and 2) a delivery constraint. The channel delay was given as a function of the global time of the SDL system. This function determined for each signal carried by the channel the delay introduced by the channel. The delivery constraint restricted the delivery of a signal when the introduced delay exceeded the calculated limit, so it modeled the effect of falling out of range.

In this paper first we describe briefly the MIP protocol and its specification in SDL. Then we give a short overview of the SDL simulator we used in our study, and we present the results of our simulations for both the protocol itself and the channel model. Finally we conclude with our experience and future plans of this work.

2. IP MOBILITY SUPPORT

The IP address is a composition of the address of the subnetwork to which a given host is connected, and a unique address on this subnetwork. This means that it determines beside the host its physical location too. The routing procedure of Internet is based on this information, cosequently this addressing mechanism is not suitable for mobile hosts, that can move between different subnetworks during the communication. To solve this problem slightly different solutions were suggested by SONY, IBM, and Columbia University, summarized in [8]. The current MIP of the Internet Engineering Task Force includes many features of these suggestions; some of them are optional. MIP introduces the concept of *mobility agents* on the network to accomplish location management for mobile hosts.

Location management of the Internet (MIP) is introduced between the TCP/UDP and IP layers as an upper sublayer of IP, in order to leave unaffected the current IP routing. At this MIP level a temporary IP address is assigned to the mobile host visiting another subnetwork, to provide the delivery of IP datagrams during its visit. The procedure of the assignment of this temporary address is called *registration*, and it results in an encapsulation of the original IP datagrams sent to the mobile host into outer IP datagrams with the new temporary address. This en/decapsulation is executed by the mobility agents and called *tunneling*. At the same time datagrams sent by the mobile host are unaffected, they are routed by standard IP routing directly to the corresponding host.

There are two types of mobility agents: *home* and *foreign agents*. The home agent is the mobility agent on the home (native) network of the mobile host, while all other mobility agents are foreign agents for the same mobile host (see Figure 1).

The home agent's responsibilities are the interception, encapsulation and forwarding (tunneling) of datagrams sent to the mobile host after the mobile host has registered with a temporary address obtained from the current foreign agent - called the *care-of address*. The mobile host applies for a care-of address by sending a registration request to the foreign agent, which registers this request and forwards it to the mobile node's home agent. The registration procedure is completed after the reception of a registration reply from the home agent first by the foreign agent and then by the mobile host. Registrations expire periodically in both mobility agents, so the mobile host has to re-register or the binding entry will be removed from the mobility agents.

Both types of mobility agents advertise their services on a regular basis, which allows the mobile host to detect its possible change of location and the possible necessity of a new registration. In the standard two motion detection algorithms are defined:

The first algorithm is based on the lifetime of the agent advertisements of the current foreign agent. As long as advertisement messages are sent three times more often than their lifetime, the mobile host may receive three messages to update its timer, failing that it assumes that the contact with the current agent is lost, so it tries to register with a new agent from which it has received a valid advertisement message.

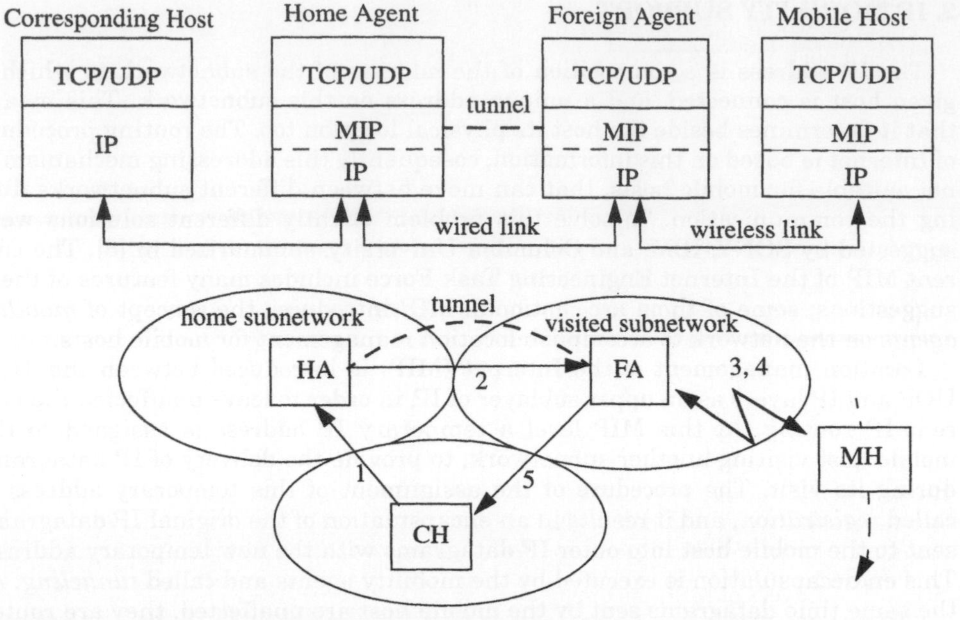

1 *Datagram to the mobile host (MH) arrives to MH's home network.*

2 *Datagram is intercepted by the home agent (HA) and is tunneled to the care-of address.*

3 *Datagram is detunneled by the foreign agent (FA) and delivered to MH.*

4, 5 *Datagram to the corresponding host (CH) routed by the visited network directly to CH.*

Figure 1. Overall concept of IP Mobility Support

According to the second algorithm the mobile host checks the subnetwork part of each received agent advertisement message. If it differs from the subnetwork address of the current agent the mobile host assumes that it has moved. After the expiration of the registration lifetime, the mobile host will make an attempt to register with the new foreign agent on the new subnetwork.

The document allows many other options: A different from the described above address allocation is possible: the so called co-located address. Its allocation is out of the scope of the MIP standard. Simultaneous bindings are also allowed - the mobile host may have simultaneous registrations with several care-of addresses. Another option provides route optimization by notification of the corresponding host of the current care-of address of the mobile host, avoiding this way tunneling of datagrams, and the triangular part of routing shown in Figure 1.

3. THE SDL MODEL

The SDL specification of the basic part of the protocol contains four types of blocks: the mobile host, the home agent, the foreign agent and the corresponding host. The mobile host is connected to other blocks by delaying channels. For IP addresses we used the process identifiers of SDL.

The simplest block is the corresponding host which is a one process block. This process provides sending of consecutive datagrams to the mobile host. All datagrams are sent to the home agent block.

The home agent is also a one-process block. It forwards the datagrams sent to the mobile host directly to the mobile host if there is no valid care-of address registered, otherwise it encapsulates them and sends to the registered care-of address. For this the home agent preforms a registration procedure at the reception of a registration request from its mobile host, and maintains this care-of address until a new registration request is received or its lifetime expires. The home agent also sends agent advertisements on the channel connecting it with the mobile host.

The foreign agent is composed of two processes: an advertiser, which sends the agent advertisements to the mobile host; and a care-of address process, which administers the registration of the mobile host, and then serves as the endpoint of the tunnel. The agent advertisement message includes the process identifier of the care-of address process, so the mobile host can address it. Both processes are connected by the same channel to the mobile host, so the introduced delay would be consistent for both of them.

The mobile host is a one-process block. It tries to register with the agent from which the first agent advertisement was received. Subsequently the host checks the agent advertisement messages, and updates the senders' timers (timers are parametrized by the senders). If an advertisement is received from a new agent, the mobile host saves the received parameters in order to use them in a later registration if necessary. At the expiration of an advertisement lifetime timer either the saved parameters received from that agent are removed, or if it is the current agent the mobile host assumes that it has moved and tries to register with another agent.

The mobile host would never register with another agent if it regularly receives agent advertisements from the current agent, so the channel delay plays an essential role in the initiation of the registration procedure. However in SDL we could use only two possibilities: either nodelay, in which case the mobile host receives all advertisements in time, and so the mobile host does not detect any motion, or else the non-deterministic delay, in which case the behaviour is rather unpredictable in respect to whether the mobile host will register with a new agent at all, and with which agent it will register.

In the reality the delay depends on two components: 1) the distance of the mobile host from the agent; and 2) the transmission conditions. The first component is rather predictable it depends on the trajectory of the motion of the mobile host, and this also determines the falling out of range condition, when no more signals can be transmitted between the agent and the mobile host, i.e. through the channel between them. The second part is a non-deterministic part. It may result in a message loss due to distortion, or in a delay if the underlaying service provides error recovery.

Accordingly we controlled the delay first by introducing channel substructures for the delaying channels, and by changing the channels themselves into non-delaying channels. The process introduced by the channel substructure provided the required delay. It set a timer for each received signal, and forwarded the signal only after the expiration of this timer. To determine the time-out period, we used a function of the global time of the SDL system. To model the effect of falling out of range the process simply dropped the received signal if the calculated delay was more than a given bound. The drawback of this channel substructure approach was that it made the specification unnecessarily complex, although many of the functions explicitly specified for the channel substructure would be obvious for a channel.

A more elegant solution is the extension of the current SDL channel definition. It was done in the following way:

<channel specification> ::=
CHANNEL <channel name> [*<channel behaviour>*]
  <channel path> [<channel path>]
  [<channel substructure definition> | <textual channel substructure reference>]
ENDCHANNEL [<channel name>] ;

<channel behaviour> ::= ([<delay>][, <nodelivery>]) | NODELAY
<delay> ::= <duration expression>
<nodelivery> ::= <duration expression>

The *delay* expression defines the function for the introduced delay. The *nodelivery* expression restricts the signal delivery: if the calculated delay exceeds the calculated nodelivery value the signal is dropped by the channel. Both expressions are optional, omitting the first one results in a non-deterministic delay, omitting the second one defines a reliable channel. Omitting the channel behaviour part or the use of NODELAY keyword are the same cases as the standard delaying or non-delaying – respectively – SDL channel. The consequence of the introduction of these expressions at the system level is that only the NOW expression can be used as a variable and the parameters should be declared as synonyms at the same level.

4. THE SDL SIMULATOR

To simulate the behaviour of the MIP specification we used the SDL simulator of the PROCONSUL workbench [10]. This simulator supports the behaviour part of SDL-92 with the exception of dynamic process creations, the predefined SDL data types and generators, and the basic three-level hierarchy extended with local procedure calls. The simulator uses a discrete global system time schedule, where in each time unit each process is allowed to make exactly one state transition provided a signal is available on its input.

Although this tool does not support all features of SDL-92, the interpreted part is enough to specify real protocols. The main advantage of using this in-house product was the availability of its source code that gave us the possibility of adding our interpretation of the channel model.

The original interpretation of channels in the tool was that each signal delivered by a channel was delayed by a random delay, but at least until the previous signal was delivered. For the random delay the user had to define its range, which was global for all of the channels of the system.

This channel interpretation was modified according to the syntax given in the previous section. That means that whenever the channel delay and/or nodelivery expressions are specified for a channel the delay is calculated in accordance or the signal is dropped if the delay exceeds the calculated nodelivery value.

The simulation output is a graphical message sequence chart that is easily understandable by the user. The simulation itself is based on the C++ code generated from the SDL specification and a simulation library providing the graphical user interface. This approach provides the consistency between the checked model and the implementation when the C++ code is used in the protocol implementation.

The SDL simulator runs on Solaris operating system and uses XView in its graphical user interface.

5. CONFIGURATION OF SIMULATED SYSTEMS

From the blocks described above we built different configurations of the MIP system.

The basic configuration contains one of each block: a mobile host, a home agent, a foreign agent and a corresponding host as it is shown in Figure 2. Beside this we built two other configurations. In the first one a second foreign agent was added to study the process of changing foreign agents. In the second configuration we duplicated all the blocks but the foreign agent, so the two mobile hosts would compete for the foreign agent, which was able to serve only one mobile host at a time.

Furthermore we studied the different channel specifications for these different configurations of the system components. We ran simulations with standard delaying channels for which we set up different ranges of the delay.

We ran simulations with our extended concept of channels. In these cases we assumed a linear motion of the mobile host at a constant speed, therefore the delay was described with the following SDL expression:

```
IF (NOW/denominator - distance)>=0
    THEN NOW/denominator - distance
        ELSE distance-NOW/denominator FI
```

The *distance* in this expression is the delay between the two endpoints of the channel at the system start. The *denominator* was used to define the speed of the motion. Both parameters were declared as synonyms. The distance parameter was different for each channel according to the assumed relative position of the endpoints.

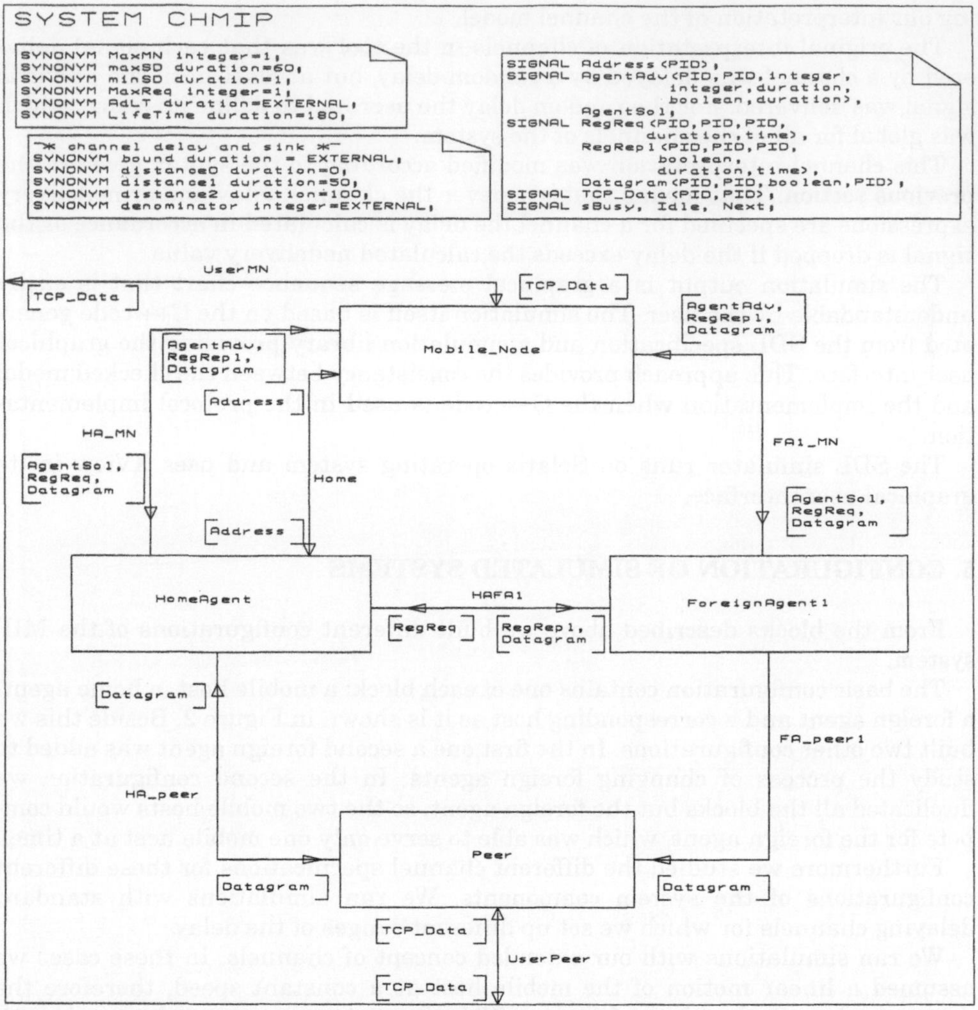

Figure 2. MIP basic system configuration

The nodelivery expression was varied, as well, for different runs. The simplest case was its omission. In other cases we varied the overlapping areas between the mobility agents.

Table 1 summarizes the cases we have studied.

As long as the main goal of our investigation was the registration procedure, and the possible data loss over the course of the registration procedure, the setting for other parameters was (in units of the global system time):

- lifetime for agent advertisements – 18,
- lifetime of registrations – 50, which means a frequent re-registration, even

when there is no shift of foreign agents.

The length of the simulation runs was at least 500 steps. To check the data loss each time when a new registration procedure was started by the mobile host the corresponding host sent 10 datagrams to it.

Table 1
Summary of simulated configurations

	Basic	Two Foreign Agents	Two Mobile Hosts
	Non-deterministic delay		
1. delay range: no bound	14, 18, 22;	14, 18, 22;	18, 22;
2. delay range: nodelivery bound:	18, 22; 20	18, 22; 20	18, 22; 20
	Linear motion		
Distances:	FA-MH: 0 HA-MH: 40	FA1-MH: 0 FA2-MH: 40 HA-MH: 80	FA-MH1: 0 FA-MH2: 23 HA1-MH1: 40 HA2-MH2: 70
3. speed: no bound	1, 1/10, 1/20	1, 1/10, 1/20	1/10, 1/20
4. speed: nodelivery bound:	1, 1/10, 1/20 20, 23, 26	1, 1/10, 1/20 20, 23, 26	1/10, 1/20 25

6. SIMULATION RESULTS

According to our two goals the simulation results can be discussed separately for the protocol and for the modified channel concept.

6.1. Experience with MIP:

Situations detected in the protocol:

(1) *Data loss happens almost at the registration even when there is no change of mobility agents due to variable delay.*

The reason of the data loss is the variation in the signal delay at different registrations. The registration entry may expire in both mobility agents, however it expires first in the home agent, then in the foreign agent, while they are updated in the opposite order. However the datagrams sent to the mobile host arrive first to the home agent. If the registration expired in the home agent the datagarms are forwarded as the mobile host is at home, so they are lost as the scenario in Figure 3 shows.

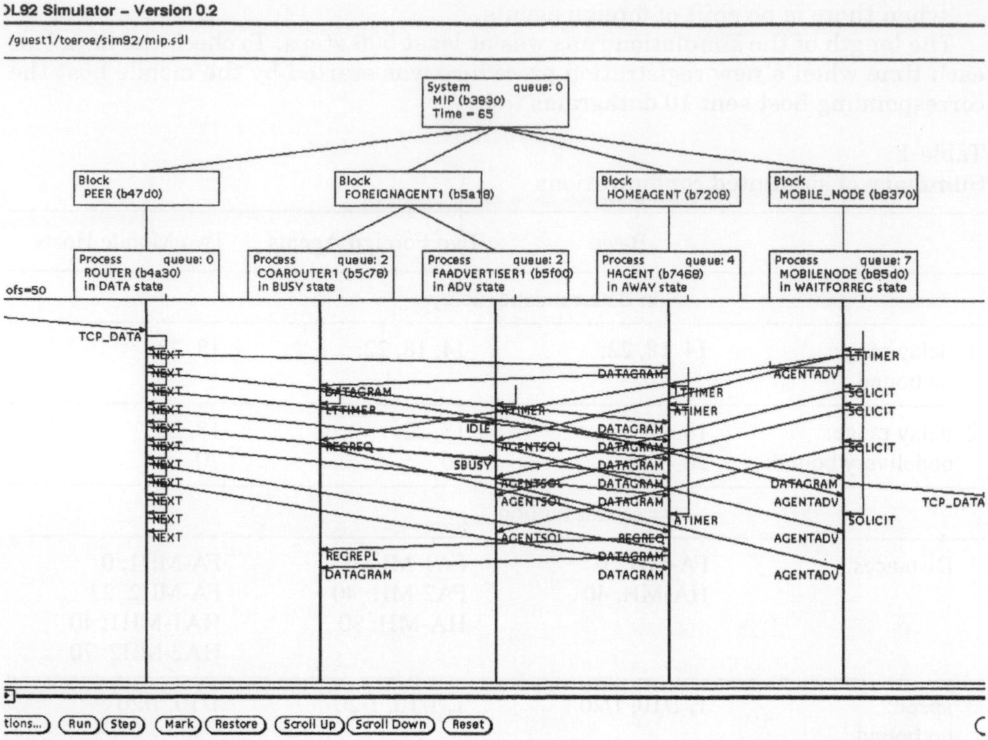

Figure 3. Scenario of data loss due to the expiration of registration (LTTIMER) in the home agent

The standard tries to take care of the entry in the home agent by setting the timer in the mobile host at the issue of the registration request and only adjusting its the accepted value at the reception of the registration reply. However in the home agent the entry expires early whenever the delay of the new registration request is greater than it was for the previous one. Each time the distance between the mobile host and the foreign agent was increasing the delay has increased, and an average 2-3 datagrams were lost in the home agent because of the lack of correct binding information. This means a retransmission at the TCP level not only, as it is usually assumed, when changing foreign agents, which is significant at high speeds, but also at relatively slow motions of the mobile host in the area of the same foreign agent, or simply because of the variation of the delay.

As a solution we suggest a longer lifetime in the home agent, for example twice as much as it was issued to the mobile host. This way the entry in the home agent either will be updated by the new registration or deregistered when the node returns home, which are the normal cases for MIP. If the update fails the home agent assumes the node away and keeps the entry still no longer then twice the registration lifetime.

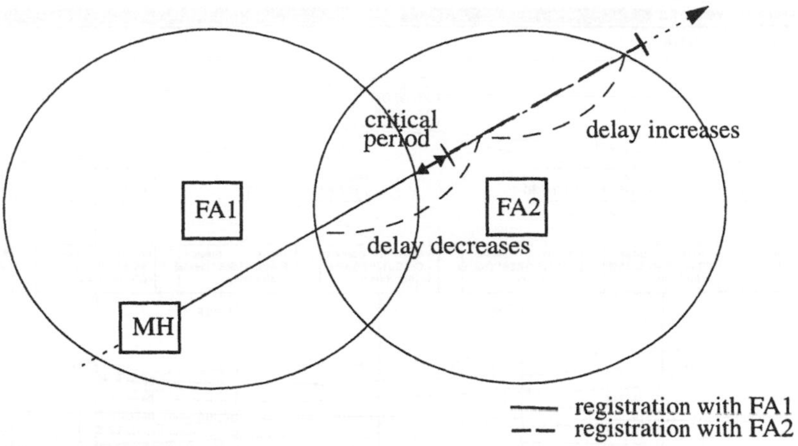

Figure 4. Changing mobility agents

(2) *The mobile host stays "loyal" to the old agent as long as it can.*

The first algorithm of motion detection of the standard – which was specified and which is based on the advertisement lifetime – forces the search for a new agent only when three agent advertisements were missed. This means that the agent tries first to register with its old agent even when it is well in in the range of a new agent and it is falling out of range of the old agent. The mobile host detects the motion only at the expiration of the advertisement lifetime, and this happens only when the mobile host is already out-of the range of that given agent. Since the mobile host is unreachable for the agent, as it is marked in Figure 4 as critical period, during this critical period all the datagrams sent to the mobile host are lost as it can be seen in Figure 5.

Even the second motion detection algorithm of the standard – based on the sub-network addresses – will not help, because in that case the mobile host also has to wait until its current registration expires after the reception of a new agent's advertisement. Since the registration lifetime is likely longer then the advertisement lifetime, again the agent advertisements play the key role.

This "loyalty" may cause also a more significant message loss due to variable delay when the mobile host crosses an area covered by an agent and overlapped by another one. As shown in Figure 4, the late registration with the new agent (FA2) causes that the mobile host has a longer period of registration with the agent on the section where the delay increases due to the increase of the distance than in the section where the delay decreases. This means that the overlapping area has influence on the performance of the protocol, as well. With a decrease of this area the mobile host is forced to make registration with the desired for that area agent. On the other hand, when there is no overlapping area the mobile host loses the connection for the time until the first advertisement will be received and the registration will be completed.

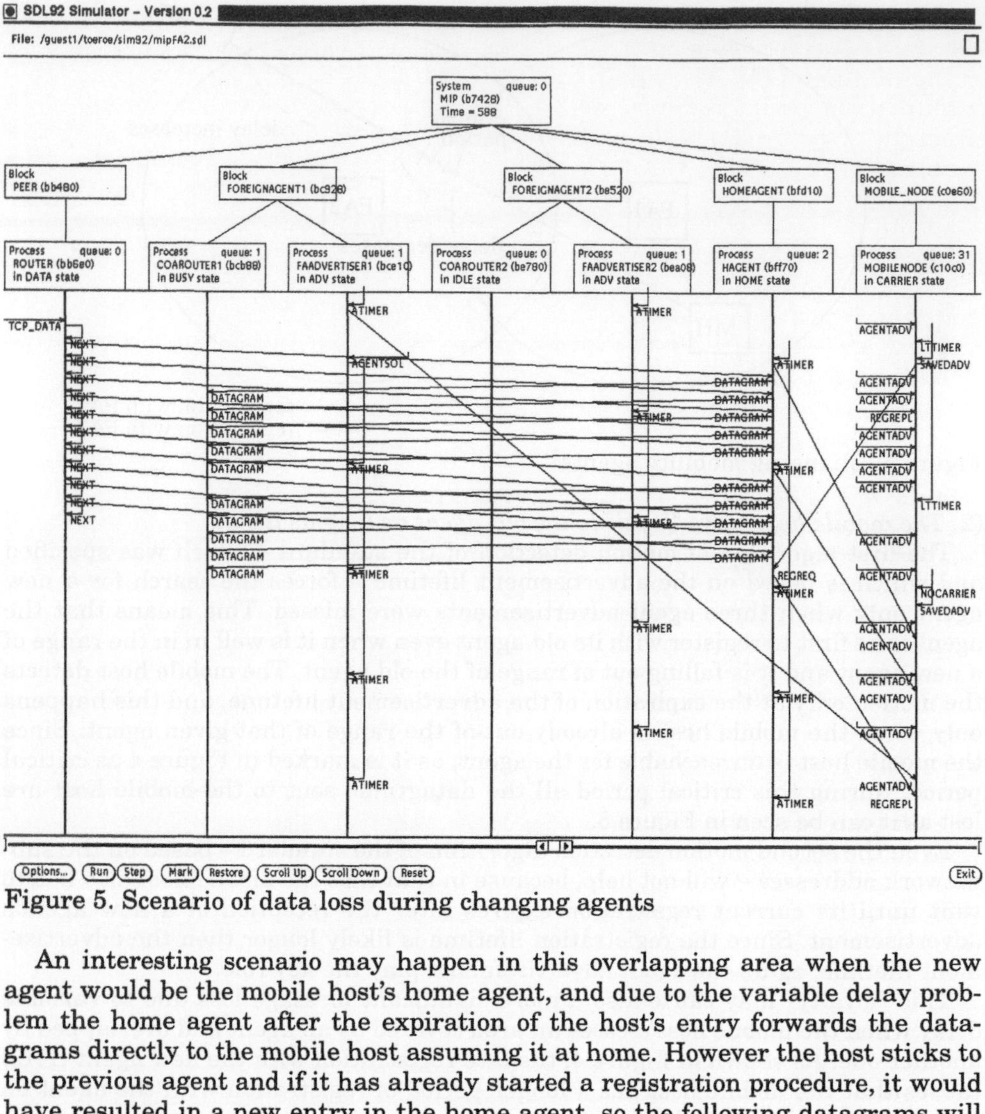

Figure 5. Scenario of data loss during changing agents

An interesting scenario may happen in this overlapping area when the new agent would be the mobile host's home agent, and due to the variable delay problem the home agent after the expiration of the host's entry forwards the datagrams directly to the mobile host assuming it at home. However the host sticks to the previous agent and if it has already started a registration procedure, it would have resulted in a new entry in the home agent, so the following datagrams will be sent to that path although it may happen that the host has already lost the contact with that agent. The new, hopefully (de)registration will be initiated by the expiration of the advertisement lifetime.

For this loyalty problem the simultaneous binding may be a solution, or a more sophisticated motion detection algorithm. The advantage of simultaneous binding is its simplicity, the disadvantage is the possible duplicated receptions of datagrams which has to be handled by the TCP level.

(3) *Occasionally the registration timer expires in the foreign agent before the re-registration request arrives.*

Beside the early expiration of registration timer in the home agent, it may expire in the foreign agent, as well, before the new re-registration request arrives from the given mobile host. More precisely, when the timer expires in the foreign agent expiration of the registration timer in the home agent always takes place. Therefore there is no data loss caused by only this third problem, however in a competitive situation, when several mobile hosts compete for the same care-of address the mobile host using the address may lose its privilege. In this case it is likely that the currently served mobile host is far from the foreign agent at this moment, which is the reason of the increase of the delay (the registration timer is set last in the foreign agent, so it has longer reserve period: the round trip time from itself to the home agent), while the "intruder" host is must be one of the closest hosts, because it must receive first an agent advertisement with non-set busy bit – the busy bit set in the agent advertisement withholds the mobile hosts from sending registration request to the agent – and answer it with a registration request within the period of the delay. Otherwise the original host will be served.

We do not consider this situation as a problem, because it was rare enough in our simulation, nevertheless it may cause problem for mobile hosts requesting service from the border area of the cell served by a foreign agent, that they are in an unfavorable position in comparison with others located closer to the same foreign agent.

In general, we can say that the protocol is very sensitive to the different timer settings. Beside the situations mentioned above, we could easily configure a system, where the mobile host's speed was too high in respect to the lifetime of agent advertisements, so the host ran out of the agents' area before finishing the registration procedure. This situation is the result of the relative values of speed and the lifetime, and not only of the high speed. Therefore the standard must be more exact regarding such timer values as advertisement lifetime and registration lifetime. However the document contains a default value only for the registration lifetime not for the agent advertisements. For this one only an assumption can be made from the statement that "the mobile node MUST NOT register more frequently than once per second on average."

6.2. Standard channel versus modified channel

As we mentioned earlier, in mobile communication the system configuration changes not in sense of process creation and termination as it is provided by SDL, but as a result of the motion different communication paths become available or unavailable for a given system component. This can be modelled by creation and termination of process instances which involves implicit creation/termination of attached signal routes, and results in a dynamically changing signal route configuration. However this involves the intermediate process, and the concept of routing signals through intermediator is alien for SDL, and requires explicit routing scheme. Using channel substructure also involves unnecessary complexity in the description.

The problems of modeling mobility by use the standard SDL channel are:

(1) *It is impossible to detect whether a signal was delivered through a channel which should be unavailable at a given moment.*

Here is an example shown in Figure 6: After the expiration of the registration lifetime in the home agent, the agent assumes the mobile host being home and forwards the received datagrams directly to the mobile host. If the mobile host is still away, that channel must be unavailable, consequently the datagrams should be lost. However in case of standard channels these datagrams are delivered properly. There is no way to determine the data loss caused by falling out of range.

(2) *Old signals contribute to the system behaviour although they are "out of date".*

It is impossible to model falling out of range with an increased delay because these signals still contribute to the system behaviour, however at a later time. This may result in a chaotic behaviour, because the mobile protocol mechanisms are *based on the assumption of falling out of range,* i.e. the mobile component is unreachable for a given part of the system, so signals between this system component and the mobile host are lost. Receiving them at a later time suggests that the component/mobile host has become reachable again, but this assumption is not true. For example, the old agent advertisements updated or set the timer, so the mobile host assumed that the sender was available. This resulted in two different scenarios: either the host had stayed with one agent, and did not register with any other agent; or if the delay was high enough, it never succeeded the registration, because the lifetime expired before the registration reply arrived.

(3) *It is difficult to design any experiment.*

As it was mentioned earlier in mobile protocols certain procedures are initiated by the pattern of the signal delivery, however when this pattern is non-deterministic it is difficult to design any experiment, which may require more investigation, or be more interesting for the user. In the case of MIP it was especially difficult to get the mobile host to register with a foreign agent once it reached the home agent. In this case the registration is not limited by the registration lifetime. The only possibility is when the host misses three consecutive agent advertisements. However on the other channels the foreign agents send advertisements with the same regularity, so the chance having high delay is the same. The FIFO feature of the delaying channel results in an increasing delay if the channel is used frequently.

Our solution for these problems is the introduction of the channel's nodelivery constraint with the delay function. Together they determine whether a channel is available, and delivers signals sent via it. This way it is easy to detect any attempt at sending a signal via a channel currently unavailable, and to decide whether it is a protocol error or not. (Sending an advertisement is not an error, while forwarding a datagram received from the corresponding host definitely means data loss.)

On the other hand, the possibility to control the channel behaviour when it plays the key role in the protocol behaviour itself is more than convenient, it is inevitable for the appropriate study of the protocol design. At the same time the suggested modification avoids the painful and totally irrelevant but complex explicit media specifications through process or substructure definition.

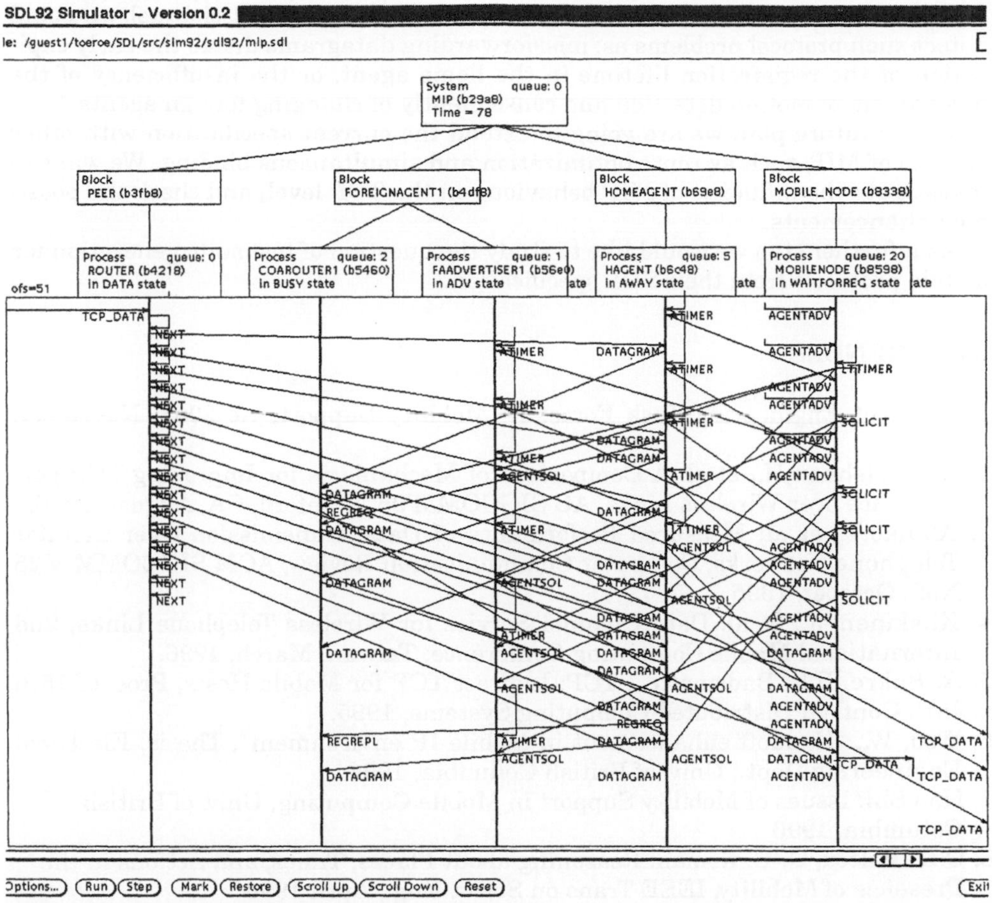

Figure 6. After the expiration of the registration lifetime (LTTIMER) in the home agent, the first datagram is delivered directly to the mobile host instead of rerouting it to the foreign agent

7. CONCLUSIONS

In this paper we have demonstrated a possible way of modeling mobile protocols with SDL. For this purpose we augmented the original channel model of SDL with a channel behaviour part, which is composed of the channel delay function and the nodelivery constraint. This extended channel allowed us to model the dynamically changing communication path configuration assumed and addressed by mobile protocols without increasing the complexity of the specification.

We demonstrated the use of this modified channel on the example of the new Internet standard: IP mobility Support, which is responsible for the location management of mobile nodes on the Internet. With the modified channel we could detect such protocol problems as: missforwarding datagrams due to the early expiration of the registration lifetime in the home agent, or the insufficiency of the mechanism of motion detection and consequently of changing foreign agents.

In our future plan we are going to extend the current specification with other options of MIP, such as route optimization and simultaneous binding. We want to investigate the influence of MIP behaviour on the TCP level, and check the possible enhancements.

As a further step we would like to study the question of test suite generation for mobile protocols from their SDL specification.

REFERENCES

1. Internet Engineering Task Force: IP Mobility Support, rfc 2002, November, 1996.
2. Balakrishnan,H., et al: A Comparison of Mechanisms for Improving TCP performance over Wireless Links, AC SIGCOMM'96, Stanford, CA, August, 1996.
3. Alanko,T., et al: Measured Performance of Data Transmission Over Cellular Telephone Networks, Computer Communication Review, ACM SIGCOMM V.25 No5, October, 1995.
4. Kiiskinen, J., et al: Data Channel Service for Wireless Telephone Links, 2nd International Mobile Computing Conference, Taiwan, March, 1996.
5. A. Bakre, B.R. Badrinath: I-TCP: Indirect TCP for Mobile Hosts, Proc. of 15th Intl. Conf. on Distributed Computing Systems, 1995.
6. Woo, W., "Handoff enhancement in Mobile IP environment", Thesis, Electrical Engineering Dept., Univ. of British Columbia, 1996.
7. Hao Shi: Issues of Mobility Support in Mobile Computing, Univ. of British Columbia, 1996
8. C.D. Wilcox, G.-C. Roman: Reasoning about Places, Times, and Actions in the Presence of Mobility, IEEE Trans on Softw. Eng., April 1996
9. Badrinath, B.R., Imielinski, T.: Location Management for Networks with Mobile Users, Mobile Computing, ed: Imielinski, T., Korth,H.F., Kluwer Academic Publishers, 1996.
10. Varga,L.Zs, et al: PROCONSUL: an SDL tool set, Computing and Control Engineering Journal, Stevenage, UK, IEE Publication, April 1994.
11. Törö, M., et al: SDL Model of IP Mobility Support, EUROMICRO'96, Prague, September, 1996
12. R. Stevens: TCP/IP Illustrated, Vol.1, The Protocols, Addison-Wesley, 1994.
13. ITU Recomendation Z.100: CCITT Specification and Description Language (SDL), 1992

SDL '97: TIME FOR TESTING - SDL, MSC and Trends
A. Cavalli and A. Sarma (Editors)

Experiences with ISDN Validation Models in SDL and Proposal for new SDL Features

Nils Fischbeck

Humboldt-University of Berlin - Dept. of Computer Science, Axel-Springer-Str. 54a, 10117 Berlin, Germany
e-mail: fischbec@informatik.hu-berlin.de

This paper shows experiences encountered during the specification of layer 3 protocols for narrowband and broadband ISDN in SDL-92. It shows a methodology how to structure a specification that it can be reused in derived specifications on structural level as well as on behavioural level. SDL provides adequate support for the composition of large specifications. There are difficulties, however, to extend signals, data and transitions in derived specifications. Details are given why and how additional features should be introduced into SDL.

1. Introduction

The more details are given in an SDL specification the more value the specification may have. Specifications with informal tasks and decisions are useful to understand a protocol. Adding data to the specification may turn a specification into an executable specification which can be used to validate a protocol through simulation.

This paper describes experiences made during the specification of an overall SDL model for narrowband ISDN (Q.71) and the specification of validation models for broadband ISDN UNI (Q.2931, Q.2971) and NNI (Q.2761-64, Q.2722.1). The paper will not go into detail of the protocols but stress the design decisions taken during specification of the protocols. The way how SDL was used may apply to other validation models in SDL as well.

The specifications had to fulfill the following requirements:

- The specification should be readable by an inexperienced SDL user.
- The specification should contain as much protocol data as possible provided the first requirement is still met.
- The specification should be reusable.
  - It should be possible to derive a specification for an extended protocol.
  - It should be possible to connect the specification with specifications of other protocols.
  - It should be possible to validate the protocol in different and not yet known connection scenarios.
  - It should be possible to reuse existing transitions.
  - It should be possible to extend the data of existing signals.

Some of these requirements could not be met since SDL does not have appropriate concepts. The following sections give details how most requirements could be fulfilled and what features are still needed in SDL.

2. Structuring a Specification

In SDL-92 a specification must be provided in one or more packages to allow reuse of the specification. A simple approach would be to specify a system type definition in a package and to allow other packages to redefine the system type. Inside the system type all blocks and processes would be defined based on virtual type definitions. A derived specification could redefine the necessary types and reuse the structure as well as the behaviour of the specification. Although this approach results in a structure which can be easily understood it has some major drawbacks:

(a) It is difficult to integrate two specifications.

(b) It is difficult to construct a connection scenario from another connection scenario.

The following sections give details why these restrictions apply and how to change the specification to overcome the difficulties.

2.1. Integrate Specifications

In SDL-92 only a system definition provides an executable specification. If two specifications are developed as system types there is no possibility to merge both into a single specification. SDL does not support multiple inheritance of system types and the interconnection of systems is outside of the scope of SDL. Before giving the details how the structure can look like it is necessary to consider the following: Two entities can only be interconnected if they share the same signal definition for signals which cross the boundary between both entities.

Therefore it is necessary to define signals that can be used in both specifications which shall be connected. This is possible through the definition of a package which contains signals and common data definition. It is also useful to provide signal list definitions in that package to harmonize the appearance of the interface.

Given that there is a common signal definition, how does the structure of the specification look like? A package which defines the main components of a protocol should define block types instead of system types on top level. These block types may be reused to define a system type which is an integration of protocols. In order to integrate the specification of protocol Q.XYZ with protocol Q.XYZext the structure could be as shown in figure 1. Note that simplified SDL is used.

In this example protocol Q.XYZ is specified in block type Q.XYZ_BT and protocol Q.XYZext is specified in block type Q.XYZext_BT. To connect both specifications an instance of each block type is created in system type Q.XYZUnified_ST. Both instances are connected with a channel.

2.2. Connection Scenarios

After the creation of at least one instance and appropriate connections the specification has a fixed structure. The term connection scenario will denote this structure throughout this paper. It is still possible to derive another connection scenario which adds blocks or processes, however it is not possible

- to insert a process or block between two communicating entities as a channel or signal route refinement,
- to change the number of initial processes of a certain kind,
- to change the upper bound of the number of processes of a certain kind.

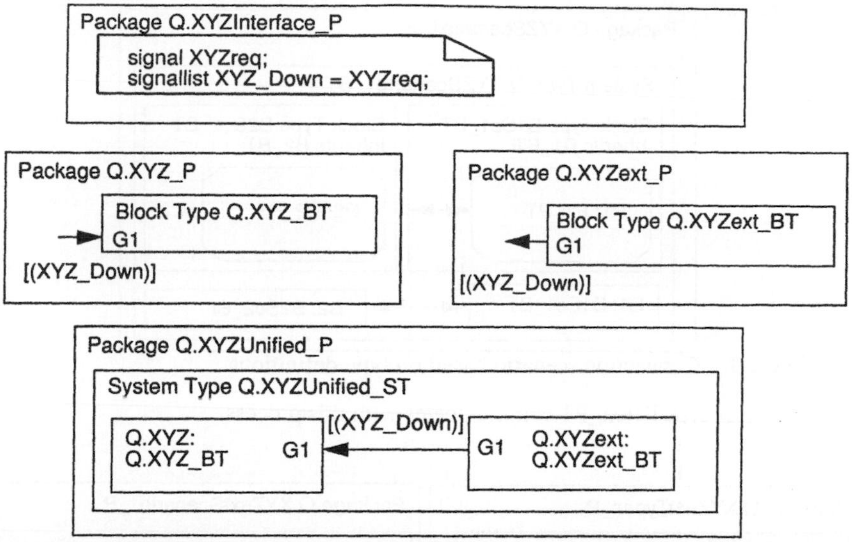

Figure 1. Two protocols are connected based on a common signal definition.

One should therefore create instances and communication paths as late as possible. The creation of a connection scenario should always be the last step when creating a system type. That means, block types are initially specified without any connection and process instance. Block types which will be used as base types contain type definitions only. All definitions like gates and signal list definitions shall be made to prepare the creation of a connection scenario but no channel or signal route shall be drawn. The following figure shows an example.

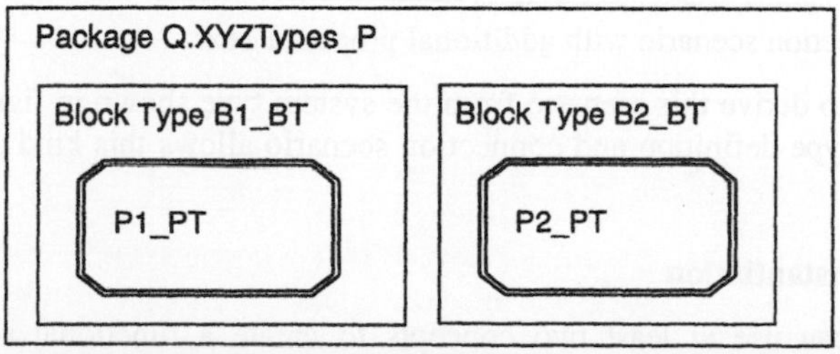

Figure 2. Definition of types in a package without instances and connections.

Package Q.XYZTypes_P defines a block type with two other block types B1_BT and B2_BT in it. Each block type contains a process type definition. Gates and other definitions are not shown. A connection scenario which uses this structure can look like in figure 3.

If the types of a specification are provided in a package, not only different connection scenarios can be constructed from the original types. It is also possible to extend the types of the specification and provide connection scenarios using these extended types. Figure 4 shows the example of an extended protocol in which process type P1_PT is changed and an

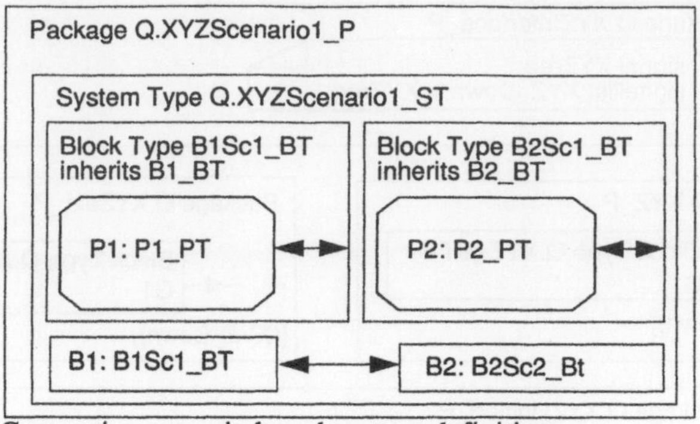

Figure 3. Connection scenario based on type definitions.

additional process type P1ext_PT communicates with this process.

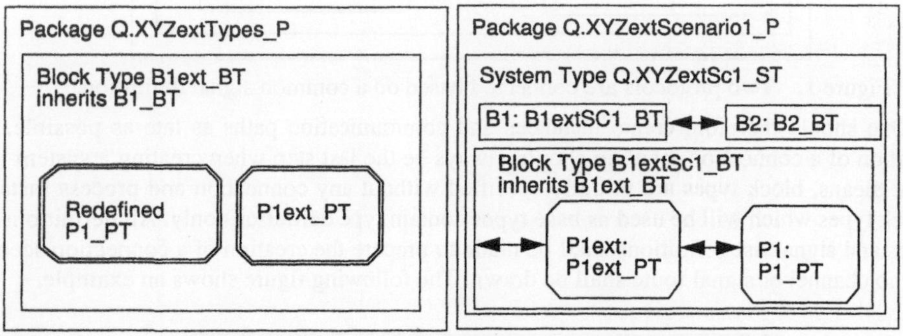

Figure 4. Connection scenario with additional process P1ext.

It is not possible to derive this scenario from the system type shown in figure 3. Only the separation between type definition and connection scenario allows this kind of extension of the protocol.

3. Dynamic Block Instantiation

In SDL-92 one can use at least two concepts to create a functional entity which is composed of several smaller entities:

- A block composed of processes (substructures are not considered here).
- A process composed of services.

Often a certain functionality has to be provided on demand, that means several smaller entities have to be created dynamically and have to be considered as a group. Although one can create dynamically a process composed of several services it is not possible to have more than one service of the same kind as part of that process. However, it is often not possible to provide a functionality without duplicating a certain part. Therefore only a block composed of processes is an appropriate concept. But blocks can not be created dynamically.

A process can create another process only if both are in the same scope unit. Therefore, to create an additional grouping of processes there must be a dedicated process inside the block which serves as creator of these processes. It is a waste of resources when a process is running all the time only to create processes in very rare cases.

SDL should allow to create an instance of a block dynamically. At the time of creation all contained processes are started with the number of initial instances as specified. The difficult part is that the creation should return an identifier of that block such that one can send messages to the block. It is necessary to identify a block instance with a PId. Which process receives that signal inside the block depends on the signal routes and the number of process instances inside the block. An uncompromising approach would allow not only an output to a PId which identifies a block but also an output to a block identifier.

These changes make a block very similar to a process composed of services but without the restriction that the entities have different input signal sets and that two entities are never running at the same time. It would be consequent to allow the definition of variables on block level as a way to communicate data between processes as it is possible to define variables on process level when the process is composed of services.

In an attempt to simplify SDL the differences between

- a system composed of blocks,
- a block composed of blocks,
- a block composed of processes and
- a process composed of services

should be reduced. Only one grouping concept should remain with the choice between its components running concurrent or exclusive.

4. Extending Signals and Data

Most protocols like the B-ISDN layer 3 protocol Q.2931 are designed to be easily extended with new messages and to carry additional information elements in already defined messages. An SDL specification should have provisions to allow such extensions. Although it is very easy to introduce new signals in a derived specification it is impossible to change the definition of data that existing signals carry. The following sections describe what features SDL should provide.

4.1. Extending Signals

In SDL signal inheritance is possible. A signal defined by

```
signal SETUP(Integer);
```

can be derived to

```
signal SETUPExt inherits SETUP adding (Boolean);
```

Through inheritance a completely new signal `SETUPExt` is created which could be created also by

```
signal SETUPExt(Integer,Boolean);
```

Inheritance between both signals does not mean that the signal `SETUPExt` can be received as a stimulus for

```
input SETUP(intvar);
```

SDL does not support signal polymorphism. Signal inheritance can be used to provide constraints for signals used as formal context parameters. Since tool support for context parameters is poor this is not used very often.

Instead of signals inheritance another concept is needed: signal redefinition. Suppose a specification of a protocol defines

```
signal SETUP(Integer);
```

The second, derived version of the specification wants to implement an enhancement of this signal which now carries an additional boolean parameter. The signal definition could look like

```
signal redefined SETUP adding (Boolean);
```

What happens to transitions in the base specification? The signal redefinition would allow to receive the redefined signal SETUP in transitions of the base specifications. A transition

```
dcl i Integer;
state x;
input SETUP(i);
output SETUP(i) to pid;
nextstate -;
```

would still allow to receive the redefined signal. However, what happens to the additional boolean parameter? Since no variable is provided this value would be discarded. The parameter is not provided in the output, therefore the parameter will be set to „invalid value". There must be another solution to allow signal redefinition, in a way that transitions in the base specification handle additional parameters automatically. This solution would introduce signals as a special kind of data.

SDL should predefine a data type `signal`. Every signal should be derived from this base type. Derivation allows to add additional parameters to the signal. Each parameter has a name. Signals provided that way can be received without giving a variable for each parameter of the signal. The input would just provide a variable for the whole signal. The same applies to output which would be an output of a value of the data type derived from the signal base type. SDL with ACT ONE or ASN.1 does not provide means to express this concept. The following code gives an example which uses intuitive syntax.

Suppose `signal` is the name of the signal base type the SETUP signal would be defined in the following way:

```
newtype SETUP inherits signal adding
call_reference Integer;
endnewtype;
```

The redefined signal can be defined with the following statements:

```
redefined newtype SETUP adding
negotiation_allowed Boolean;
endnewtype;
```

A transition which receives, manipulates and sends this signals is shown in the following code:

```
dcl setupvar SETUP;
input setupvar;
task setupvar!call_reference:=0;
```

```
output setupvar to pid;
```

If a derived specification redefines the SETUP signal the transition will handle the additional parameter correctly: the parameter negotiation_allowed will be transmitted unchanged in the outgoing SETUP signal. The redefinition of the signal changes implicit the meaning of transition of the base transitions.

This method has another advantage: the signal sender could become a parameter of the signal. Currently SDL sets magically a variable SENDER which provides the PId of the signal sender. With the new approach the signal base type should define a parameter sender which will be a parameter of any derived signal. Thus the sender of signal SETUP could be accessed by

```
setupvar!sender
```

The sender of this signal remains accessible until setupvar is assigned a new value.

A disadvantage of this method is that the input statement will contain the name of a variable instead of the name of the signal which will be received. It is more difficult to read such a specification.

Since signals are data types which can be redefined one should consequently be able to redefine other data types as well.

4.2. Redefine Data Types

When a signal has to transmit many parameters it is useful to define a separate STRUCT type and give the signal one parameter of this type. The definition of the SETUP could look as follows:

```
newtype SETUPdata STRUCT
param1 type1;
param2 type2;
paramn typen;
endnewtype;
signal SETUP(SETUPdata);
```

Based on that definition it is easy to store data received with a SETUP signal:

```
dcl setupvar,store SETUPdata;
state x;
input SETUP(setupvar);
task store:=setupvar; /* store data of signal */
```

With the new notation of a signal as a data type one would define:

```
newtype SETUP inherits signal adding
param1 type1;
param2 type2;
paramn typen;
endnewtype;
```

To store the contents of the signal one would write:

```
dcl setupvar,store SETUP;
state x;
input setupvar1;
task store:=setupvar1;
```

This method has the disadvantage that the sender of the signal is stored too, which is probably not intended. It is therefore useful to define a separate data type:

```
newtype SETUPdata STRUCT
```

```
param1 type1;
param2 type2;
paramn typen;
endnewtype;
newtype SETUP inherits signal adding
data SETUPdata;
endnewtype;
```

Only the parameter `data` would be used if the signal has to be stored:

```
dcl setupvar SETUP;
dcl store SETUPdata;
state x;
input setupvar;
task store := setupvar!data;
```

What happens when the signal should be extended in a derived specification? One would like to redefine the data type `SETUPdata` providing that the task `store:=setupvar!data` stores the additional data too. This requires the redefinition of `SETUPdata`:

```
redefined newtype SETUPdata adding
paramext typeext;
endnewtype;
```

Besides the redefinition of STRUCT types it should be possible to redefine ENUMERATED (newtype with literals only) like data types. This is necessary for instance to provide values for new decision branches when the decision is based on an ENUMERATED type. This is explained in section 5.4.2.

Redefinition of data types would be a major change in the data type concept. It should therefore be considered whether a new data type language could replace ACT ONE. ACT ONE has the following disadvantages:

- difficult or unusual syntax,
- missing built-in types like dictionaries, sets,
- no polymorphy (the explained redefinition of data types can help),
- axioms define equivalence of terms - only limited tool support possible.

SDL in connection with ASN.1 as defined in Z.105 improves the situation since it defines additional data types and has its own syntax for the definition of types. However, Z.105 uses ACT ONE for the definition of operations with these data types.

The definition of a new data type language which uses types of commonly accepted other languages like OMG IDL or TINA-C ODL could overcome the problem. This is however not elaborated here.

5. Reuse Transitions

Suppose a specification defines a process type P1_PT. This process contains a transition as shown in figure 5. A derived specification defines a process type P1Ext_PT which inherits the transition from P1_PT. The derived specification extends the transition as shown in figure 5.

The transition has been extended at two places: a new function call has been inserted after the input symbol and an output symbol has been inserted after the decision in one decision branch. In this example the whole transition has been redefined. Since the transition is not very long this is a suitable solution. But having a long transition repeating the whole transition in a derived process is not appropriate. There are at least three solutions to prepare a transition

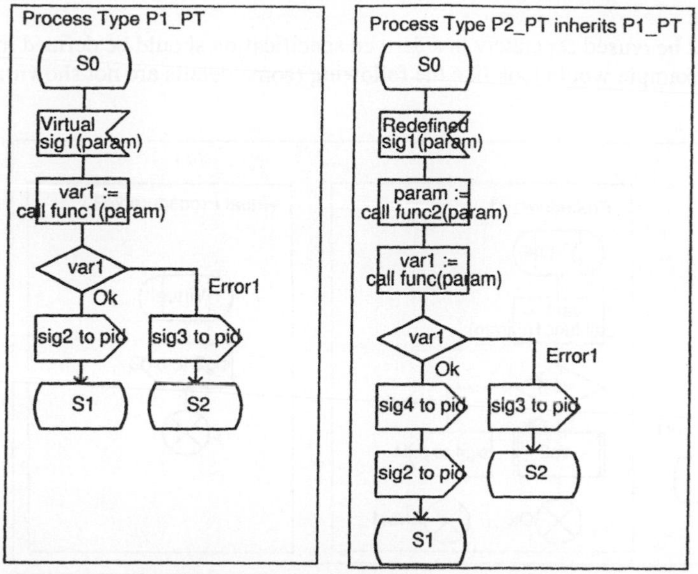

Figure 5. Extension of a transition.

such that a derived specification does not have to repeat the whole transition:

- Use of a virtual procedures.
- Use of connectors.
- Use of states with continuous signals.

These solutions are explained in the following sections.

5.1. Virtual procedures

Everything that could be reused separately in a derived specification should be defined in a virtual procedure. The example would look like the following (some details are not shown):

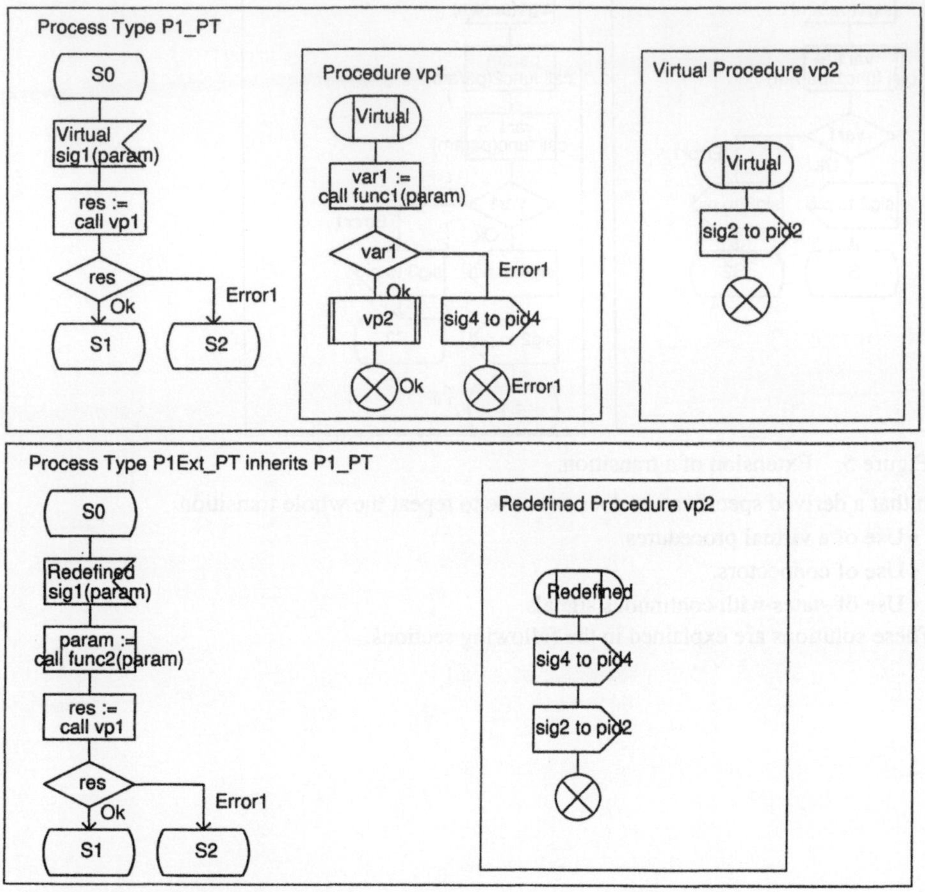

Figure 6. Reuse with redefined procedures.

This method has the following disadvantages:

- behaviour is defined at different levels,
- procedures must be defined even when they are not used for redefinition,
- the transition can be changed only at places where virtual procedures are called,
- additional types are sometimes necessary to provide the state change after a call to a procedure.

5.2. Connectors

Instead of defining procedures one could define connectors that point to reusable pieces of code. When the code is needed in derived specifications one could simply jump to that connector. An example is shown in the following figure:

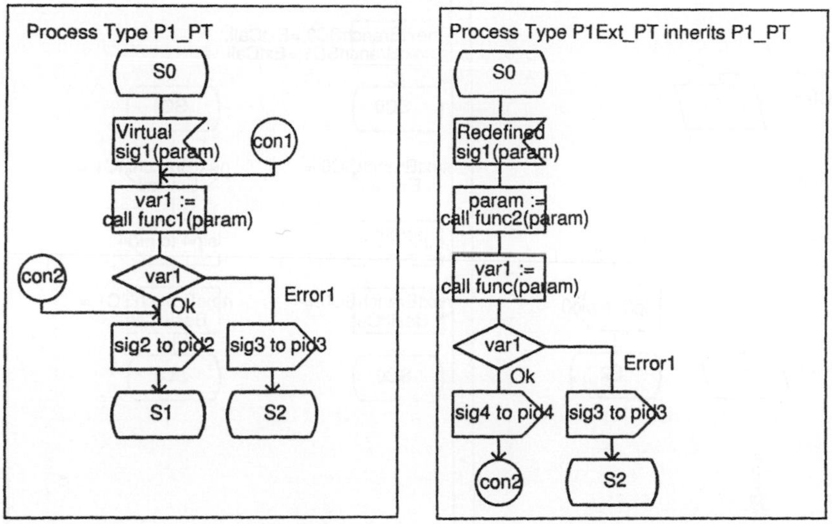

Figure 7. Reuse with connectors.

In this example connector `con1` is not used since jumping to that connector would mean that there is no way to include an output of `sig4` in the code. Therefore only the connector `con2` is used to reuse the sending of signal `sig2`. This method has the following disadvantages:

- after jumping to a connector the original transition is executed till the end,
- there must be connectors inserted at every place where reuse is foreseen even when the connector is not used in the current specification,
- using connectors it is difficult to follow the flow of an specification (connectors are like goto in C: they tend to produce spaghetti code),

However, this method has the advantage that it is easy to understand since it does not use sophisticated features of SDL.

5.3. States with Continuous Signals.

At every place in a transition where additional actions could be inserted a state is defined with a continuous signal. The additional actions are inserted using another continuous signal. The value of a variable controls the order of execution. This is shown in the next figure.

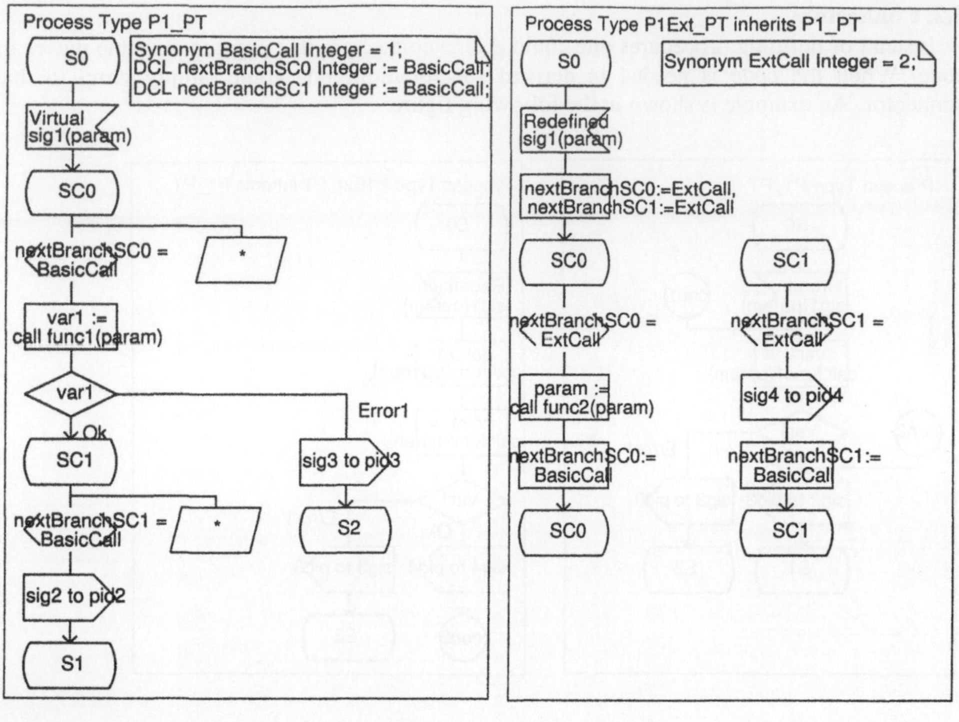

Figure 8. Reuse with additional states and continuous signals.

This method has some disadvantages too:

- It is difficult to read since it uses continuous signals and additional states.
- States must be inserted at every place where reuse is foreseen.
- A state is usually used for other purposes than for jumping to different parts of code.

Compared to the other methods this method is the most flexible since it allows You to insert code at different places in a transition at the same time. It is also possible to extend the transition in a second step of derivation. An additional continuous signal added to a state is sufficient.

5.4. Solutions

SDL-92 does not have the features necessary to solve the problem of transition reuse. The problem can be eluded, however with major drawbacks as explained in the last sections. At least two extensions of SDL are possible to provide a better solution. These extensions are:

- virtual connectors,
- extensible decisions.

Both extensions do not imply each other.

5.4.1 Virtual connectors

An in-connector (named label or free action in SDL/PR) can be virtual by writing the keyword virtual before the connector name. A derived entity can redefine that in-connector that means redefine the transition-area which follows the connector. Jumping to that connector (using an out-connector or a join in SDL/PR) will always cause the execution of the transition of the redefined connector. However, it should still be possible to jump to the original in-connector by using a qualifier. An usage of this concept applied to the problem of transition reuse could look like the following:

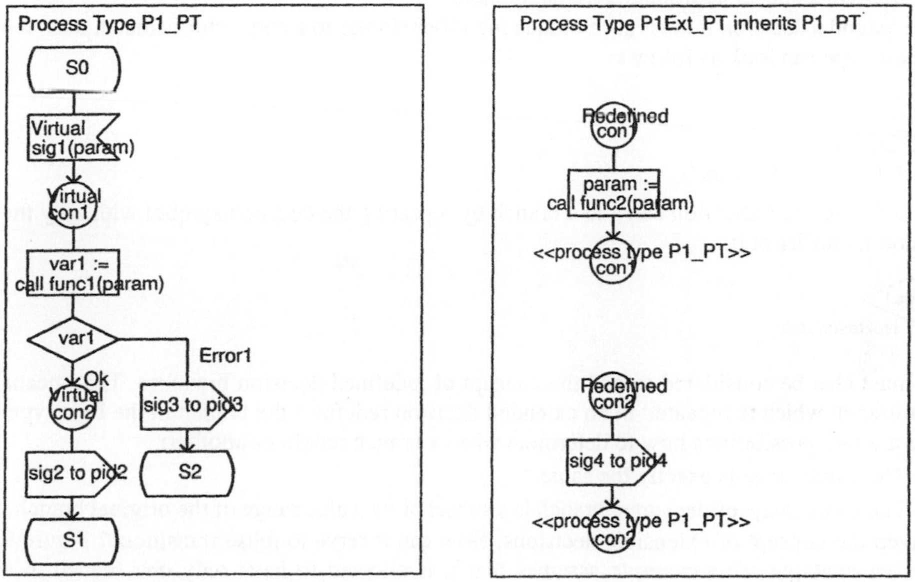

The short hand notation

stands for

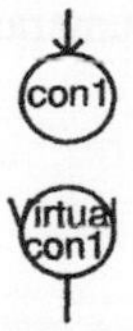

in this drawing.

This looks like an elegant solution for the problem of transition reuse. However, extending the concept of connectors tempts the user to apply jumps to other connectors where he should not use this concept (for instance to reuse code from a completely unrelated transition).

5.4.2 Extensible Decisions

In SDL-92 a decision has a fixed number of branches. Derived specifications can not add other branches. However, it should be possible to add branches at least for two purposes:

- Additional branches can serve to insert additional actions in a transition like virtual connectors can.
- Decisions are often used to take appropriate action depending from the outcome of a procedure call. In derived specifications there can be a new outcome of a procedure so there must be an additional decision branch.

To extend a decision it must get a unique identifier similar to a connector name. A decision in a base type can look as follows:

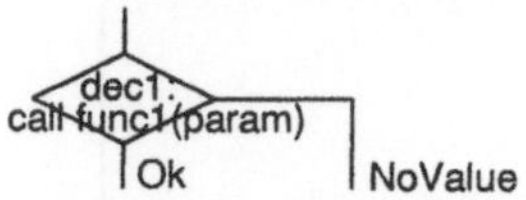

The derived specification can add a branch by repeating the decision symbol with only the decision identifier in it:

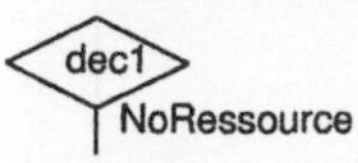

It must also be considered to add the concept of redefined decision branches. That means that a branch which is repeated in an extended decision redefines the branch in the base type. There are two possibilities how to determine when a branch redefines another:

- The value range is exactly the same.
- The value range of the added branch is a subset of the value range of the original branch.

Given the concept of extensible decisions: How can it serve to reuse transitions? Figure 9 shows an example. This example assumes that it is allowed to have only one branch in a decision which is not allowed in SDL-92.

Using extensible decision for transition reuse is very similar to the insertion of new states with continuous signals. It has the disadvantages that

- it is difficult to read,
- a decision must be inserted at every place where an extension could be foreseen.

However, this solution is very flexible and it is based on a feature which is very useful for other problems as well.

Note that the values at decision branches often are values of an enumerated type. Extensible decisions also foster the need for an extensible enumerated type.

6. Transition Local Variables

A process variable can serve two purposes:

- It serves as global data storage with a valid data value for several transitions.
- It serves as data storage for the duration of one transition only.

The main usage of the second case is the following: A signal is received with a parameter.

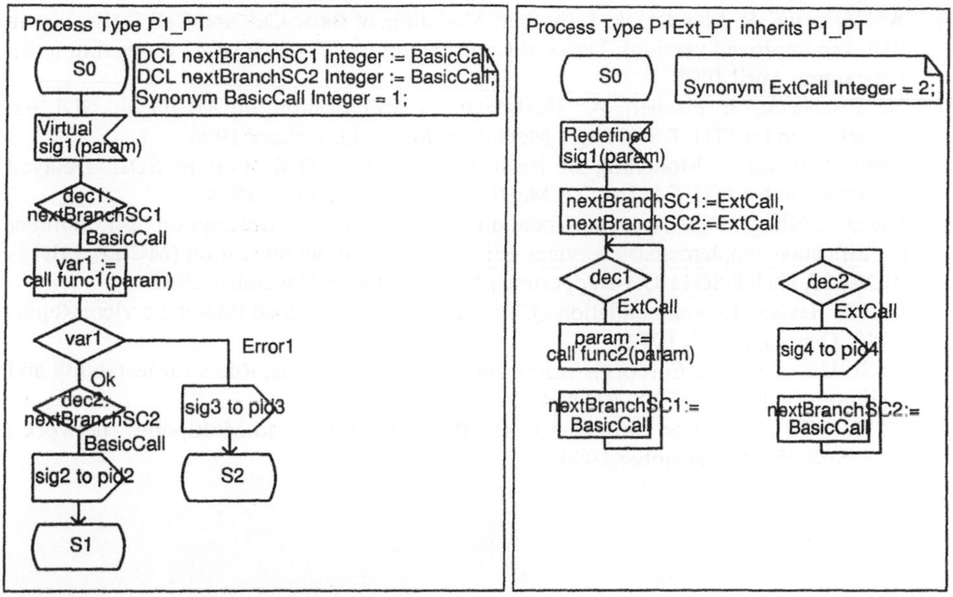

Figure 9. Reuse with extensible decisions.

The parameter is assigned to a variable. The value of the variable is processed and appropriate actions are taken in response to the signal. After the state change there is no need to store the value of the parameter any longer. However, the variable is still there. To give an example: In an ETSI specification of the B-ISDN DSS2 protocol there have been used at least twice as much transition local variables as global variables.

SDL should have the feature to define variables which are valid from the start of the transition till next state change. This could lower the need of memory a specification has as an executable and make a specification more readable since the definition of the variable will be in the context of the transition.

7. Conclusion

SDL has proved to be an appropriate language for the definition of validation models for Narrowband- and Broadband-ISDN. Although it defines means to inherit and redefine behaviour it does not have enough flexibility to extend the data model smoothly. Therefore language features like signal and data redefinition, dynamic block instantiation and extensible decisions should be introduced into SDL.

REFERENCES

[1] ITU-T: Z.100 (1993): CCITT Specification and Description Language (SDL), ITU-T Jun. 1994.

[2] J. Rumbaugh, M. Blaha, W. Premerlani, F. Eddy, and W. Lorensen: Object Oriented Modelling and Design. Prentice Hall, International Editions (1991).

[3] A. Hoffmann, R. Mundstock, J. Fischer: Modelling of Basic Call and Call Deflection in SDL (an improved version), Delayed Contribution for ITU-T SG10/Q.6 meeting in St. Petersburg, April 1995

[4] N. Fischbeck, J. Fischer, A. Hoffmann: A specification of MCID in SDL'92, Contribution for ITU-T SG11/Q.1 Meeting in Miyazaki, January 1996

[5] Lennart Månsson: Modelling of Basic Call and Call Deflection in SDL, Delayed Contribution for ITU-T SG10/Q.6 Meeting in Geneva, October 1994

[6] Dieter Müller: New Recommendation Q.81, Stage 2 Description for number identification supplementary services §7: Malicious Call Identification (MCID), Q1/11-BLN-010, ITU-T SG11/Q.1 Rapporteurs Meeting Berlin, November 1995

[7] ITU-T: Revised Recommendation Q.71: Circuit Mode Switched Bearer Service, Report R220, Geneva, March 1992

[8] ETSI: Use of SDL in European Telecommunication Standards; Rules for testability and facilitating validation; ETS 300 414; December 1995

[9] ETSI: SDL Validation Model for B-ISDN DSS2 Point-to-Multipoint (network); DTR/SPS-05128; December 1996

SDL '97: TIME FOR TESTING - SDL, MSC and Trends
A. Cavalli and A. Sarma (Editors)

Design for Testability of Communication Protocols Based on SDL Specification*

K. Karoui, R. Dssouli and N. Yevtushenko

Université de Montréal, Faculté des arts et des sciences, Département d'informatique et de recherche opérationnelle, C.P. 6128, Succursale Centre-Ville. Montréal, (Québec) H3C 3J7
{karoui, dssouli}@iro.umontreal.ca

Abstract. Conformance testing is used to verify whether an implementation under test exhibits a permissible behavior or not. Test cases derived from a reference specification are applied to an implementation under test in order to compare its behavior with the reference one. Length of test cases, facility of test generation and analysis of results of test application are important factors that affect the cost of testing. In this paper, we address the problem of augmenting a partially specified EFSM, extracted from an SDL specification, in order to have shorter tests.

Keywords. SDL, EFSM, Specification, testability, *'don't care'* transitions.

1. INTRODUCTION

Various Formal Description Techniques (FDTs), such as SDL, LOTOS or ESTELLE are used for communication protocols. Most of the FDTs possess some practical tools for automatic verification and simulation of a protocol in order to detect and correct some classes of faults before protocol's implementing. Automatic test cases generation from FDTs based specifications is still an open problem [ETS 94]. Existing test derivation methods usually start by transforming a specification to a proper model such as an FSM (Finite State Machine), EFSM (Extended Finite State Machine) or a data flow graph and others [Sari 93, Chan 93, Huan 95, Kim 95, Ural 87]. Appropriate testing methods are then used for test derivation.

Protocols are widely recognized as systems that are partially specified [Boch 94, Petr 93b]. By default, unspecified transitions in SDL specifications are usually implemented as self-loops. A process described by SDL never locks even if it reaches an unspecified transition. This paper addresses a problem of augmenting a given SDL specification in order to have shorter tests, while maintaining sets of

* This work was funded by NSERC, "Strategic Grant".

defined states and events. We use some unspecified transitions, namely those which can be interpreted as '*don't care*' transitions, to improve the testability of protocol's implementations. For this purpose, we transform an SDL specification to an EFSM, improve its testability by specifying some of its '*don't care*' transitions and transform the augmented EFSM back to SDL specification. We consider SDL specifications because of their use in various fields and their good support tools.

This paper is structured as follows. Section 2 comprises some basic definitions related to an SDL specification, an EFSM model and data flow testing methods. In Section 3, we discuss how to improve the testability of an SDL specification. In Section 4, a technique of EFSM augmenting is proposed. The approach is illustrated on a particular EFSM specification in Section 5.

2. BASIC NOTIONS AND DEFINITIONS

2.1. SDL based specifications

SDL (Specification and Description Language) is a CCITT standard specification language. It is based on an extended finite-state machine (EFSM) model. SDL specifications can be written in two different syntaxes: graphical (SDL/GR) and textual (SDL/PR); one-to-one mapping exists for the two forms. The following concepts [Beli 89, Sari 93] are important for SDL:

- System is described hierarchically by elements called systems, blocks, channels, processes, services, signal routes and signals.
- Behavior is described using the EFSM concepts.
- Data is described using the abstract data types with the addition of a notion of program variables and data structures.
- Communication is asynchronous via channels that can have infinite queues.

Most existing SDL testing methods do not deal directly with an SDL specification. A specification is transformed to an appropriate mathematical model such as an FSM [Luo 94], an EFSMs or a flow graph [Ural 87] from which tests are derived. The transformation may be difficult if an SDL specification is not written in a certain style called normalized style [Sari 93, Ural 87]. If a specification is not normalized, the transformation must be preceded by a normalization and a simplification procedures. The normalization procedure makes specification's transitions parameters clear, namely a starting state, an input clause, a decision clause, task statements and output clauses. As an example, we take an SDL specification in Figure 1a. After the normalization procedure, the *save* structure is removed and replaced by a set of transitions (Figure 1b). We derive a corresponding EFSM (Figure 1c) from the obtained SDL specification.

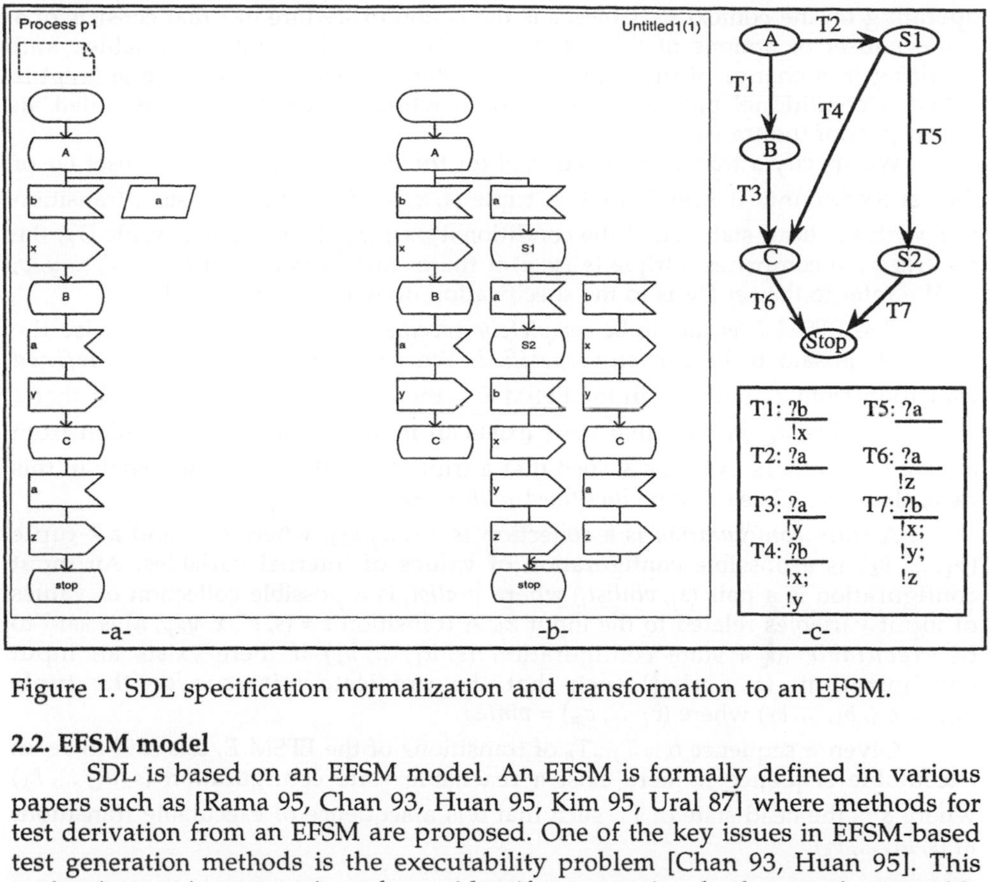

Figure 1. SDL specification normalization and transformation to an EFSM.

2.2. EFSM model

SDL is based on an EFSM model. An EFSM is formally defined in various papers such as [Rama 95, Chan 93, Huan 95, Kim 95, Ural 87] where methods for test derivation from an EFSM are proposed. One of the key issues in EFSM-based test generation methods is the executability problem [Chan 93, Huan 95]. This notion is very important in order to identify automatiquely the set of executable test sequences from the set of all derived test sequences. In this section, we give some basic definitions related to an EFSM that are necessary for presentation of our results.

An EFSM E is represented as a 5-tuple $E = (S, X, Y, T, s_o)$ [Rama 95], where S is a finite non empty set of states including a special state s_0 called the initial state, X is a finite non empty set of *input primitives*, Y is a finite non empty set of *output primitives*, T is a finite non empty set of *transitions*. Every input primitive $x \in X$ is represented as *?x(inlist)*, where x is the name of an input primitive and *inlist* is a subset of a finite set I of input variables. Every output primitive $y \in Y$ is represented as *!y(outlist)*, where $y \in Y$ is the name of an output primitive and *outlist* is a subset of a finite set V of internal variables. The union of the sets I and V is the set of context variables of the EFSM. For the sake of simplicity, we assume that the sets I and V are disjoint sets.

Each transition $t \in T$ is a 6-tuple $t = (s, s', x, y, p, a)$, where $s, s' \in S$, are called the head and the tail states of t, $x \in X$, $y \in Y$, p is the predicate of a finite set P

operating on the context variables; a is the action procedure of t that consists of a finite subset of actions of the set A operating on the context variables and resulting in a change of the values of the internal variables. The couple (x, p) is called a conditional part of the transition, while the couple (y, a) is called an action part of the transition.

We specify a transition function H for the EFSM E that maps a subset D_E of the set $S\times X\times P$ into the set $S\times Y\times A$. A triple $(s, x, p)\in D_E$ if there exists a transition $t\in T$ with the head state s, and the conditional part (x, p). For each $(s, x, p)\in D_E$, the set $H(s, x, p)$ comprises a triple (s', y, a) if there exists a transition $t = (s, s', x, y, p, a)$. We refer to the set D_E as to the specification domain of the EFSM E.

The EFSM E is said to be *completely specified* if $D_E = S\times X\times P$; otherwise the EFSM E is said to be *partially specified*. We say that there exists *undefined* transition from a state $s\in S$ in the EFSM E if there exist $x\in X$ and $p\in P$ such that a triple $(s, x, p)\in D_E$. We say that there exists an input-(I-)*undefined* transition from a state $s\in S$ if there exists $x\in X$ such that a triple $(s, x, p)\in D_E$ for each $p\in P$; in this case, the state s is said to be *undefined with respect to the input x*.

A *state configuration* is a collection $(s, b_1, ..., b_k)$, where $s\in S$ and a k-tuple $(b_1, ..., b_k)$ is a possible configuration of values of internal variables. An input configuration is a pair $(x_j, vinlist_j)$ where $vinlist_j$ is a possible collection of values of input variables related to the input x_j. A transition $t = (s, s', x, y, p, a)$ is said to be *executable* at a state configuration $(s, b_1, ..., b_k)$ if there exists an input configuration $(x, vinlist)$ such that the predicate p is true for the tuple $(c_1, ..., c_m, b_1, ..., b_k)$ where $(c_1, ..., c_m) = vinlist$.

Given a sequence $\alpha = T_1...T_n$ of transitions of the EFSM E, α is said to be an executable sequence if there exist a reachable state configuration $(s, b_1, ..., b_k)$ where s is the head state of T_1, such that α is a sequence of executable transitions at $(s, b_1, ..., b_k)$.

2.3. Data flow testing criteria

The data flow testing is used to check the correctness of flow of context variables. In practice, it is impossible to test such correctness w.r.t. all values of context variables because of huge sizes of their domains. By this reason, various criteria [Weyu 93, Ural 87, Sari 93, Huan 95, Rama 95], were proposed to test the proper features of data flow. A hierarchy of data flow coverage criteria proposed in [Weyu 93] is shown in Figure 2.

Throughout this paper, we illustrate our approaches for a test suite that covers all the DO-paths of an EFSM [Huan 95]. Informally, each DO-path is a sequence of transitions of an EFSM that allows to determine for an appropriate context variable how the actions of an appropriate transition change the variable's value or how this variable's value affects a sequence of executed transitions. The formal definition of a DO-path is given in [Huan 95].

In the paper [Huan 95], the authors propose a method for test suite derivation that covers all the executable DO-paths of a given EFSM. A test suite is a set of test cases (sequences of transitions). Each test case comprises three sequences: a preamble that allows to reach an appropriate DO-path, a test body, i.e. the DO-path itself, and a postamble that takes an EFSM back to the initial state. In fact, there can exist various preambles and postambles for a given DO-path. The shorter are these sequences, the shorter is a test suite. We propose to augment a given EFSM in such way that it becomes possible to replace some parts of preambles and postambles by a single transition.

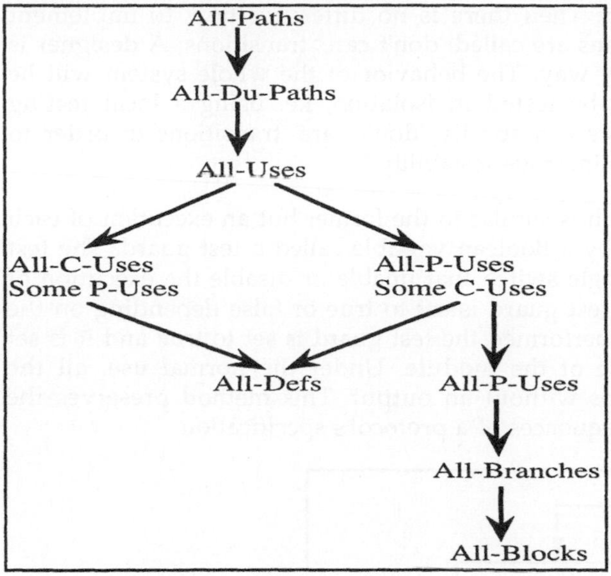

Figure 2. Data flow testing criteria.

3. IMPROVING SPECIFICATION TESTABILITY

In order to improve the protocol testability some authors [Dsso 91, Kim 95, Sale 92] propose to add some new input and output primitives into a protocol description. Those primitives are used to improve observability and/or controllability of protocol's implementations. To improve observability, the primitives are generally used to report the internal state of the protocol or a trace of the fired transitions. To improve controllability, those primitives are used to take a protocol to a particular state or to select the next transition to be executed. Kim and Chanson [Kim 95] use such primitives that improve the observability and controllability under the test mode. These methods add new primitives to the protocols.

We propose to improve testability of protocol implementations by augmenting a partially specified EFSM extracted from an SDL specification under the assumption that the cost of the testing process is inversely proportional to test suite length [Petr 93a]. We propose a technique to specify some 'don't care' transitions of a specification in order to shorten a test suite. Two approaches are proposed to maintain a protocol's behavior.

First approach. Some input sequences may never occur at an input of a module embedded within a complex system. It is the case when the module is encapsulated in a particular environment (e.g. layered architecture) and input sequences are output sequences of other modules. The latter means that some transitions may never be fired. Then there is no difference how to implement these transitions. Such transitions are called 'don't care' transitions. A designer is free to implement them in any way. The behavior of the whole system will be preserved. If the module can be tested in isolation, i.e. using a local testing architecture (Figure 3), then we can specify 'don't care' transitions in order to shorten tests, and, therefore, to improve testability.

Second approach. This approach is similar to the former but an execution of each added transition is controlled by a Boolean variable called a test guard. The test guard variable is used as a toggle switch that unable or disable the execution of the transitions (Figure 4). The test guard is set to true or false depending on the module usage. When tests are performed the test guard is set to true and it is set to false under the normal use of the module. Under the normal use, all the added transitions are self-loops without an output. This method preserves the initial set of executable input sequences of a protocol's specification.

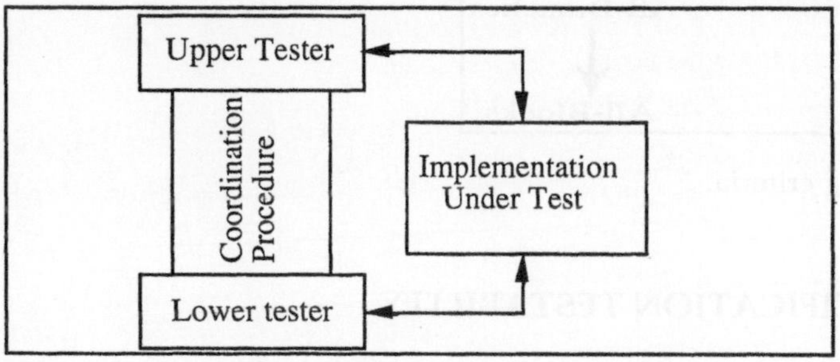

Figure 3. Local testing architecture.

Compared to the previous methods [Kim 95, Sale 92], our method does not need additional primitives and does not change the normal behavior of a protocol within its environment. In the next section, we describe a technique of augmenting an EFSM specification in order to shorten tests.

4. AUGMENTING AN EFSM SPECIFICATION

4.1. Specification of undefined transitions

Our technique is based on specifying some *I*-undefined transitions in order to shorten test cases. After specifying such transitions, we assess how much testability is improved by comparing test suite lengths of the initial and the augmented EFSMs. We use the DO-paths criterion to generate a test suite [Huan 95]. The added transitions of the module will never be fired, because of the restrictions imposed by the environment or of the value of the test guard (Section 3). We assume that the module can be tested in isolation using the local architecture (Figure 3). The upper and the lower testers can use the added transitions. We say that the module testability is improved if length of the test suite derived from the augmented specification is reduced.

A sequence α of transitions with a head state s and a tail state s' may be included in various test cases. Under some conditions, α may be replaced by a new transition t from s to s' such that α and t take the EFSM E from a state configuration $(s, b_1, ..., b_k)$, to the same state configuration. $(s', b'_1, ..., b'_k)$. For testing purposes, t may be used instead of α in order to reach $(s', b'_1, ..., b'_k)$ from $(s, b_1, ..., b_k)$. If α has at least two transitions then total length of test cases is shortened. However, if we want to use a sequence β of transitions unstead of α, the two sequences must take the EFSM from the starting state configuration to the same tail state configuration. In this case, α and β are said to be *interchangeable* sequences. In other words, the EFSM E exhibits the same behavior after sequences α and β. Given a sequence α of transitions of a partial EFSM E with a head state s, a *state configuration* $(s, b_1, ..., b_k)$ and an *I-undefined* transition t at the state s, we try to specify the transition t in such way that t and α become interchangeable sequences. For the testing process, if we use t instead of α in order to reach a state configuration, length of test cases having α as a subsequence will be shortened. The longer is α and the more is the number of test cases where α is used, the more we reduce test suite length.

In order to have an interchangeable transition t with a sequence α, the execution of t must take the EFSM to the same state configuration as a. Below we propose some sufficient conditions where it is possible.

Let $a = T_1...T_n$ be a sequence of transitions and I_j be the set of input parameters used in the input primitive of T_j (with $1 \le j \le n$). Let also I_a denote the union of I_j over $j = 1, ..., n$, i.e. $I_\alpha = \bigcup_{j=1}^{n} I_j$,

Proposition Given a sequence $a = T_1...T_n$ of transitions with the head state s , the tail state s', the action parts (y_j, a_j), $j = 1, ..., n$, let there be an I-undefined transition from the state s w.r.t. an input x. If the list of input parameters of x includes I_a and if $\bigcap_{j=1}^{n} I_j = \varnothing$ then a transition $t = (s, s', x, p, y, a)$ where p is the identity predicate that is true for any configuration of context variables, y is any output and a is a sequence actions of transitions $T_1, ..., T_n$, is interchangeable with α.

Due to the above proposition, we can specify some 'don't care' transitions to make them interchangeable with an appropriate sequence of transitions. Some equivalence transformations can be used to simplify the action parts of new transitions.

To reduce length of a test suite we can deal with preambles and postambles of test cases. In this section, we illustrate our approach for preambles. We present an algorithm that shortens length of preambles (if possible) by specifying some of undefined transitions. The algorithm replaces each possible subsequence of a preamble by a single transition interchangeable with the subsequence. The same algorithm can be used in order to shorten a predefined set of postambles.

Algorithm. Augmentation of a given EFSM *E* with predefined set of executable test cases.
Input. An EFSM *E*, a set of preambles, and a set *DT* of all t the don't care I-undefined transitions.
Output. The augmented EFSM with the set of test cases.

```
Begin
 E'<--E
 For each sub-sequence seq = T_i, T_{i+1}, ...T_{j-1}, T_j of preamble
 Do
  For k=i to j
  Do
      If DT=Ø Then exit
      Else
      If the head state of T_k is a state of at least one don't care transition of DT
      Then
        Par <-- the parameters of the don't care transition
        I <-- I_k; /* the input variables associated to the input primitive of T_k */
        I_{k+1} <-- the input variables associated to the input primitive of T_{k+1} ;
        Act <-- Act_k /*the action part of T_k */
        l <--k;
       While I«I_{l+1}=Δ and I»I_{l+1}ÕPar
        Then
            I<-- I»I_{l+1};
            Act <-- Act [sequencing] Act_{l+1};
            l<--l+1;
            I_{l+1} <-- the input variables used in the input primitive of T_{l+1} ;
        EndWhile
       If (l-k)≥2
       Then
            T^k.head_state <-- head state of T_k;
            T^k.tail_state <-- tail state of T_l;
            T^k.param <-- I
            T^k.Action <-- Act
```

```
            IF second solution
            Then
                   T^k.condition <-- Test_guard
            EndIF
            Added-Trans <-- Added-Trans »T^k
            DT <-- DT - T_k;
            k<-- 1
        EndIF
      EndIf
      EndIf
      E' <-- S(E', T^k); /* add to E' */
      seq<-- substitute(preamble, T_k...T_l, T^k); /* replace T_k...T_l by T^k in the
preamble                                                      set */
      k<--k+1
   EndFor
   next seq
  EndFor
End
```

4.2. Testability evaluation

Let *Test* be a test suite that covers all the DO-paths of a given EFSM *E* and a sequence α of length $l(\alpha)$ be appeared p times in preambles of test cases of *Test*. Then replacing the sequence α with a single transition we obtain a test suite with length being equal to:

$$l(Test) - p(l(\alpha)-1) \qquad (1)$$

The bigger are p and $l(\alpha)$, the more the testability is improved. For a nondeterministic EFSM, the advantage of use of t instead of a can be even better. It is well known that nondeterministic specifications are usually less testable than deterministic ones. One of the factors that affects cost of the testing process is facility of reaching DO-paths. When we replace a sequence α of transitions with a single transition we can specify it in such way that nondeterminism deteriorates, and therefore, a state configuration where α takes the EFSM *E* from the initial state becomes reachable with less efforts. We can compute controllability improvement by use of the formulae in [Dsso 95, Karo 96]. The detailed discussion of this advantage is remained out of the scope of this paper.

5. APPLICATION

To illustrate our algorithm, we apply it to an EFSM *E* [Huan 95] presented in Figure 4. The related SDL specification is given in Figures 6 and 7. Since we have no information about an environment of this protocol, we use our second approach (Section 3). Due to the above mentioned assumptions, not all I-undefined transitions can be specified. For example, the transition *t* with the input *U.DATA(SDU, segment, blockbound)* from the state *A* is an *I*-undefined transition *t*. Nevertheless, by default, it is defined transition since it can never be fired in any implementation.

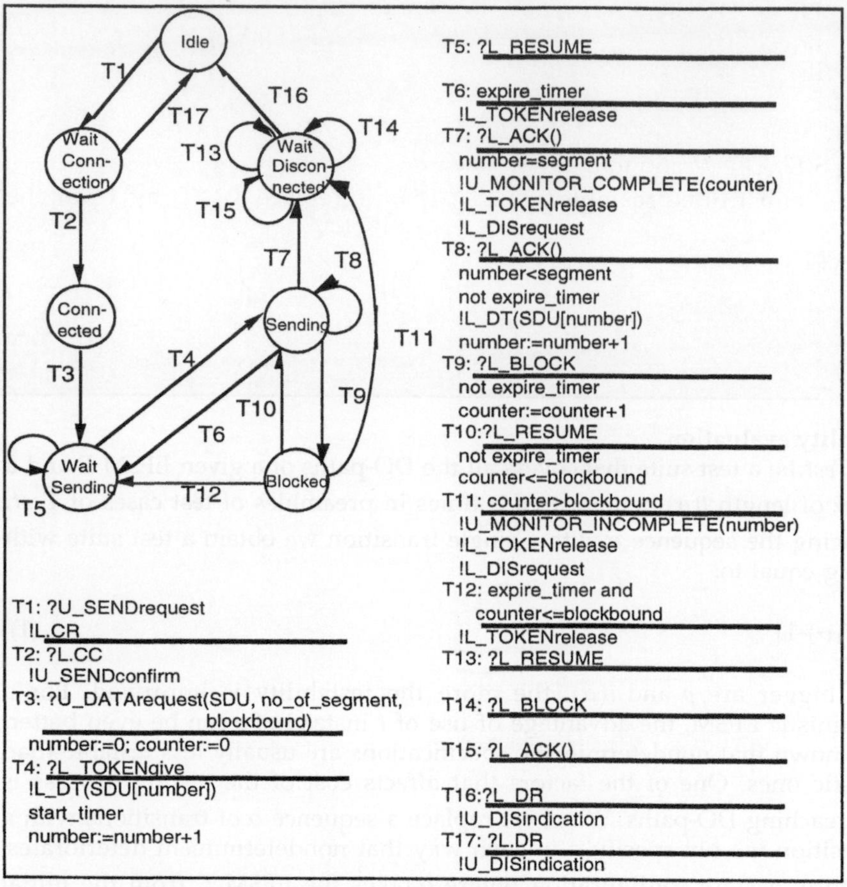

Figure 4. Example of an EFSM specification.

Consider a set of predefined executable test sequences presented in [Huan 95] (Table 1), that cover DO-paths of the EFSM. Total length of the test suite is equal to 271. We consider a transition *t* with the input *U.DATA(SDU, segment, blockbound)* from the state *idle*. By direct inspection, one can see that a preamble $T_1T_2T_3$ is interchangeable with a transition *t*, constructed from the state *Idle* to *Wait Sending*, by use of the above algorithm.

t: ?U.DATArequest(SDU, segment, blockbo
number:=0; counter:=0; !L.CR;

If we use t instead of $T_1T_2T_3$ in the testing process we improve the testability since $l(Test) - p(l(\alpha)-1) = 271 - 24(3-1) = 223$ (Formulae 1). The transition t is added to the specification with the Boolean variable as the *test_guard* that controls its execution. Figure 5 illustrates parts of the SDL and EFSM specification where we add the transition t. In the right hand side part of the figure, the bold line represents the added transition t. When *test_guard* is set to true the new transition can be used to facilitate the testing process.

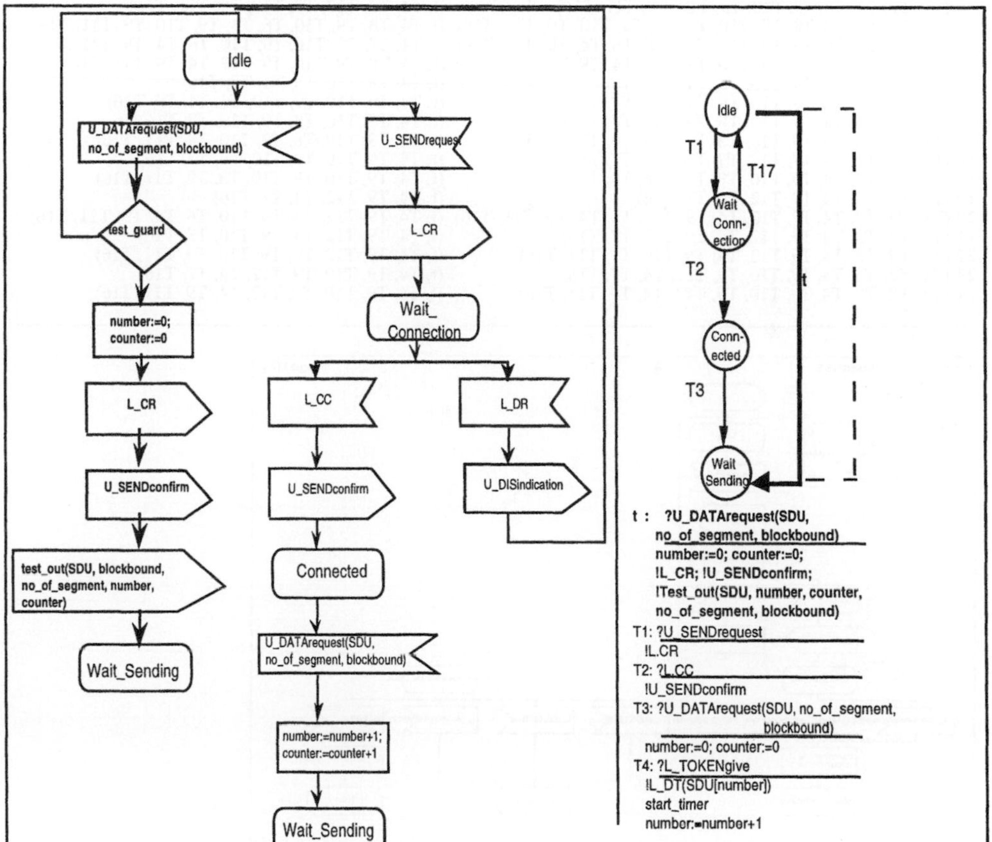

Figure 5. Specifying *I-undefined* transition.

The algorithm replaces each occurrence of $T_1T_2T_3$ in each test case by t. The set of new test cases is represented in the second column of the Table 1. Total length of the set is 223.

Table 1. The set of test sequences before and after specifying a 'don't care' transition.

No	Executable Test Sequences	Ext. Executable TestSequences
1	(T1, T2, T3, T4, T6, T4, T7, T16)	(t, T4, T6, T4, T7, T16)
2	(T1, T2, T3, T4, T6, T4, T9, T10, T7, T16)	(t, T4, T6, T4, T9, T10, T7, T16)
3	(T1, T2, T3, T4, T6, T4, T9, T10, T9, T10, T7, T16)	(t, T4, T6, T4, T9, T10, T9, T10, T7, T16)
4	(T1, T2, T3, T4, T6, T4, T9, T10, T9, T10, T9, T11, T16)	(t, T4, T6, T4, T9, T10, T9, T10, T9, T11, T16)
5	(T1, T2, T3, T4, T8, T9, T10, T7, T16)	(t, T4, T8, T9, T10, T7, T16)
6	(T1, T2, T3, T4, T8, T9, T10, T9, T10, T7, T16)	(t, T4, T8, T9, T10, T9, T10, T7, T16)
7	(T1, T2, T3, T4, T8, T9, T10, T9, T10, T9, T11, T16)	(t, T4, T8, T9, T10, T9, T10, T9, T11, T16)
8	(T1, T2, T3, T4, T8, T7, T16)	(t, T4, T8, T7, T16)
9	(T1, T2, T3, T4, T9, T10, T9, T10, T9, T11, T16)	(t, T4, T9, T10, T9, T10, T9, T11, T16)
10	(T1, T2, T3, T4, T8, T9, T10, T6, T4, T9, T10, T9, T11, T16)	(t, T4, T8, T9, T10, T6, T4, T9, T10, T9, T11, T16)
11	(T1, T2, T3, T4, T8, T9, T10, T9, T10, T6, T4, T9, T11, T16)	(t, T4, T8, T9, T10, T9, T10, T6, T4, T9, T11, T16)
12	(T1, T2, T3, T4, T8, T9, T10, T9, T12, T4, T9, T11, T16)	(t, T4, T8, T9, T10, T9, T12, T4, T9, T11, T16)
13	(T1, T2, T3, T4, T9, T10, T6, T4, T7, T16)	(t, T4, T9, T10, T6, T4, T7, T16)
14	(T1, T2, T3, T4, T9, T10, T9, T10, T6, T4, T7, T16)	(t, T4, T9, T10, T9, T10, T6, T4, T7, T16)
15	(T1, T2, T3, T4, T9, T10, T8, T9, T10, T7, T16)	(t, T4, T9, T10, T8, T9, T10, T7, T16)
16	(T1, T2, T3, T4, T9, T10, T8, T9, T10, T9, T11, T16)	(t, T4, T9, T10, T8, T9, T10, T9, T11, T16)
17	(T1, T2, T3, T4, T9, T10, T9, T10, T8, T7, T16)	(t, T4, T9, T10, T9, T10, T8, T7, T16)
18	(T1, T2, T3, T4, T9, T10, T9, T10, T8, T9, T11, T16)	(t, T4, T9, T10, T9, T10, T8, T9, T11, T16)
19	(T1, T2, T3, T4, T9, T12, T4, T7, T16)	(t, T4, T9, T12, T4, T7, T16)
20	(T1, T2, T3, T4, T9, T12, T4, T9, T10, T6, T4, T9, T11, T16)	(t, T4, T9, T12, T4, T9, T10, T6, T4, T9, T11, T16)
21	(T1, T2, T3, T4, T9, T12, T4, T9, T10, T7, T16)	(t, T4, T9, T12, T4, T9, T10, T7, T16)
22	(T1, T2, T3, T4, T9, T12, T4, T9, T10, T9, T11, T16)	(t, T4, T9, T12, T4, T9, T10, T9, T11, T16)
23	(T1, T2, T3, T4, T9, T10, T9, T12, T4, T7, T16)	(t, T4, T9, T10, T9, T12, T4, T7, T16)
24	(T1, T2, T3, T4, T9, T10, T9, T12, T4, T9, T11, T16)	(t, T4, T9, T10, T9, T12, T4, T9, T11, T16)

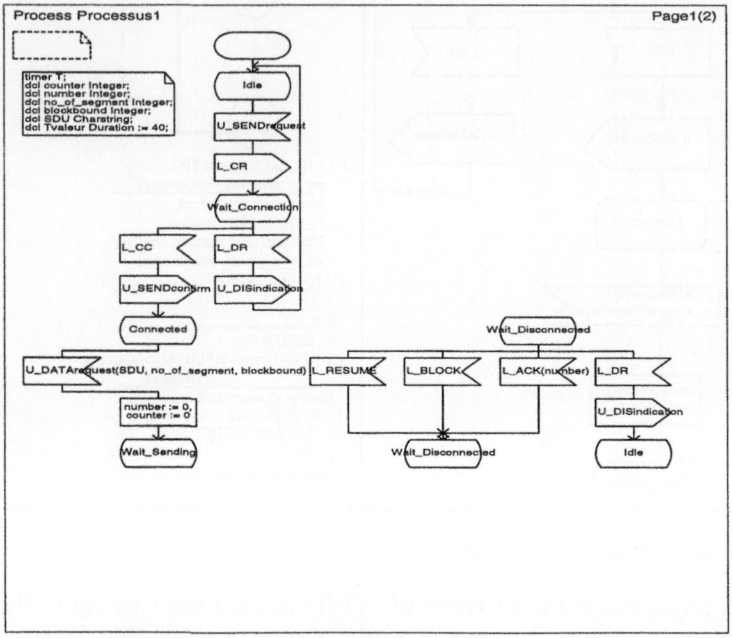

Figure 6. Extended SDL specification.

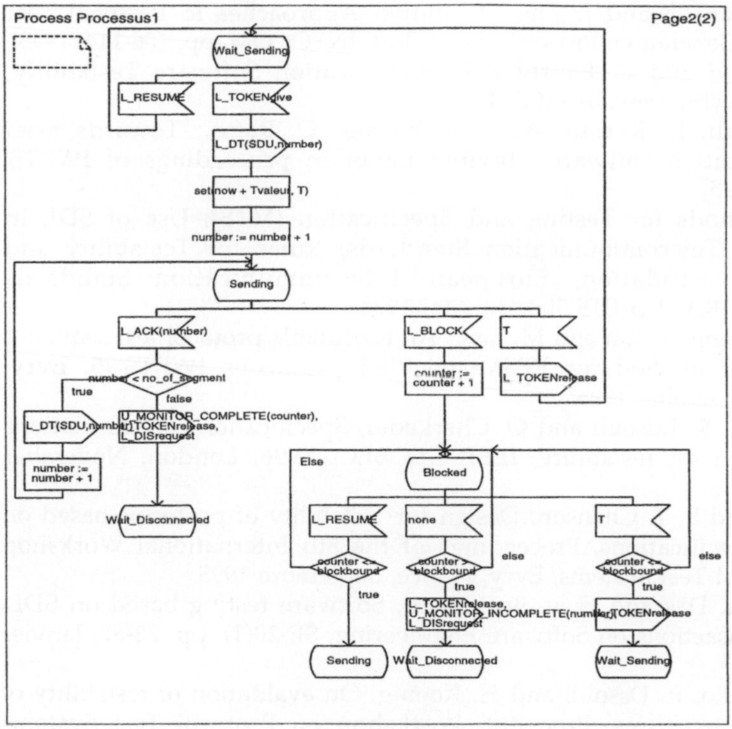

Figure 7. Extended SDL specification.

6. CONCLUSION

In this work, we have presented an approach for improving the testability of implementations issued from SDL protocol specification. The advantage of this approach is that it improves the data flow testing without changing the operational use of the protocol and without adding new primitives. In future work, we intend to extend this approach to improve the control flow testing.

REFERENCES

[Beli 89] F. Belina and D. Hogrefe, The CCITT-Specification and Description Language SDL, Computer Networks and ISDN Systems, Vol. 16, pp.311-341, 1989.

[Boch 94] G. v. Bochmann and A. Petrenko, Protocol Testing : Review of Methods and Relevance for Software Testing, publication #923, DIRO, Université de Montréal, 1994.

[Chan 93] S. T. Chanson and J. Zhu, A unified Approaches to Protocol Test Sequence Generation, Proceedings of IEEE INFOCOM, pp. 106-114, 1993.

[Dsso 91] R. Dssouli and R. Fournier, Communication Software Testability, Protocol TestSystems III - IFIP 1991.

[Dsso 95] R. Dssouli, K. Karoui, A. Petrenko and O. Rafiq, "Towards testable communication software", Invited paper in proceedings of IWPTS'95, France, 1995.

[ETS 94] ETS, Methods for Testing and Specification (MTS); Use of SDL in European Telecommunication Standards; Rules for Testability and facilating validation, European Telecommunication Standards Institute, DRAFT prETS 300 414, Mai 1994.

[Huan 95] C.-M. Huang, Y. Lin and M. Jang, An executable protocol test sequence generation method for EFSM-specified protocols, IWPTS'95, Evry, France, Septembre 1995.

[Karo 96] K. Karoui, R. Dssouli and O. Cherkaoui, Specification transformations and design for testability, IEEE GLOBECOM'96, London, November 1996.

[Kim 95] M. Kim and S. T. Chanson, Design for testability of protocols based on formal specifications, Proceedings of the 8th International Workshop on Protocol Test Systems, Evry, France, Septembre 1995.

[Luo 94] G. Luo, A. Das and G. v. Bochmann, Software testing based on SDL, IEEE Transactions on Software Engineering, SE-20(1), pp. 72-87, Janvier 94.

[Petr 93a] A. Petrenko, R. Dssouli and H. Koenig, On evaluation of testability of protocol structures, Proc. Int. Workshop on Protocol Test Systems (IFIP), Pau, France, 1993.

[Petr 93b] A. Petrenko, N. Yevtushenko, A. Lebedev and A. Das, Nondeterministic state machines in protocol conformance testing, Proceedings of the IFIP Sixth International Workshop on Protocol Test Systems, Pau, France, September 1993, pp. 363-378.

[Rama 95] T. Ramalingom, A. Das and K. Thulasiraman, A unified test case generation method for the EFSM model using context independent unique sequences, IWPTS'95, Evry, France, Septembre 1995.

[Sale 92] K. Saleh, Testability-directed service definitions and their synthesis, Proceeding of the eleventh IEEE Phoenix Conference on Computers and Communications, Arizona, USA, Mars 1992.

[Sari 93] B. Sarikaya, Principles of Protocol Engineering and Conformance Testing, Ellis Horwood Series in Computer Communications and Networking, 1993.

[Ural 87] H. Ural, Test sequence selection based on static data flow analysis, Computer Communications, Vol.10, No.5, October 1987.

[Weyu 93] E. J. Weyuker, More experience with data flow testing., IEEE Transactions on Software engineering, 19(9):912-919, September 1993.

IV

MSC I

The MSC-96 Distillery

Ø. Haugen
Ericsson AS, P.O. box 34, N-1361 Billingstad, Norway
E-mail: etooha@eto.ericsson.se

The MSC-96 Distillery is a method to produce pure and applicable MSC-96 descriptions. We take as the starting point a general method for property modeling and use MSC-96 as our formal language. The technique uses a dialectic approach to refinement where the two approaches mutually affect and support each other. The need for making descriptions more precise has aspects of formalizing, narrowing and supplementing. The need for making descriptions more detailed has aspects of decomposing, breaking down and revealing. Distilling is to summarize these two approaches to reach a clear description on two abstraction levels.

The paper also shows that MSC-96 seems to be somewhat too restrictive for practical use, and language modifications are presented.

1 INTRODUCTION

MSC-96 is a language which supersedes MSC-92 with respect to expressiveness and power. Still the standard interpretation is that an MSC document represents a set of message sequences which represent *possible* sequences in the system under consideration. In the MSC Methodology of [5] we introduced MSC documents where the interpretation was that the message sequences were *not possible*. With MSC-96 we may in some cases introduce the third interpretation that the MSC document covers *all possible* sequences which may happen in the system under consideration.

Also with MSC-96 the company strategy and the categorization of the MSCs are important for the awareness and focusing of the MSC production. This issue was properly covered also in [6].

This method has been developed through the SISU project [7] and is represented in the Integrated Methodology which is published as a development support tool on CD Rom [2].

Firstly we shall briefly introduce our general property modeling technique and then we shall apply it on our well-known *Access Control* system which was originally introduced in [1] and later applied for a number of pedagogical purposes.

2 THE DIALECTICS OF REFINEMENT

The starting point is that we have some description of behavior. We do not here take a stand on exactly how the behavior is described, but we may assume that both informal prose and more structured MSCs are used.

Our task here is then to describe the road ahead from such a description, which also represents a state of understanding in the development team.

We face two different needs which interact:

- The need for more precise description;

- The need for more detailed description.

It is important here to realize that these needs indeed are different, and that their fulfillment requires different means, and that they are interlinked. The two approaches refer to the development process and not to the descriptions themselves. Still the development will be reflected in a series of descriptions. By focusing on the development process we indicate that the developers cannot expect to make perfect descriptions at once. The traditional approach to refinement often has as an implicit assumption that perfect descriptions can be made provided the refinement steps are small enough. Thus they perceive that descriptions are always correct and need little or no maintenance. Contrary to this we believe that system development is a process of understanding where improvements are made along the way implying the discarding of older solutions.

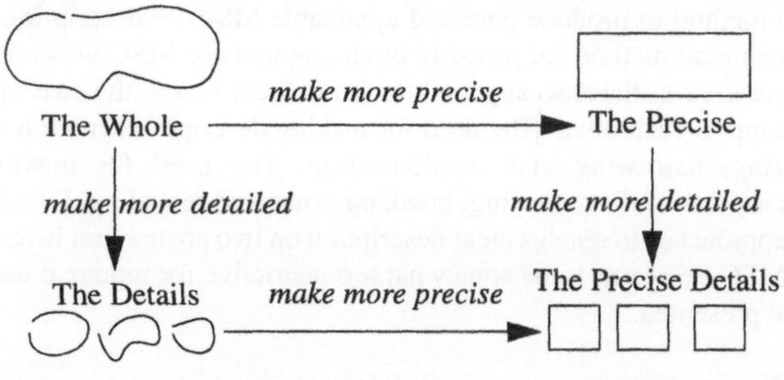

Figure 1 The Whole, The Precise and The Details

2.1 The need for more precise descriptions

In property modeling making the property descriptions more precise involves three different sub-approaches:

1. To *formalize*, meaning that we move from descriptions in prose to descriptions in a formal language. The formal language may be imperative like MSC [10; 12] or declarative like CSP [8]. The language may handle time like CTL [4] or like Focus [3].
2. To *narrow*, meaning that we add more properties such that our description is less underspecified.
3. To *supplement*, meaning that we add properties of other aspects than what we did before. This could mean adding time-dependent properties explicitly in addition to the plain MSC description.

2.2 The need for more detailed descriptions

Even though it may be the ideal to describe a situation without going into much detail, it is repeatedly shown that sometimes the understanding of the details are necessary for the understanding of the whole.

If we assume that the whole behavior is represented by an MSC, we can distinguish a set of means to make the description more detailed:

- To *decompose* the instances, meaning to see how the instances of the whole behave inside. Which instances do they consist of, and how do these instances interact to make up the already known whole?

- To *break down* the protocols, meaning that what on the upper level looks like one message or one behavioral pattern (e.g. an MSC), on the next level is a protocol of interaction.
- To *reveal*, meaning that more of the total scene is considered, more messages, more instances.

We see that several of these approaches to precision and detail can be used simultaneously, but we should be aware of which mechanisms we actually use.

During the process of making more precise and more detailed descriptions, the understanding improves and the improved understanding feeds back to the original starting point making the description of the total behavior more accurate.

2.3 Description distillery

The process of reaping the experience on the upper level from work on lower levels and from making the description more precise, we choose to call “distilling”. It amounts to making the description cleaner, more pure, and more valuable.

A central idea of our methodology is to be able to apply the same overall techniques also on the next level of detail. Then we have to make sure that the distinction between the levels is reasonably clear. We should be able to reason on one level at the time.

3 EXAMPLE: ACCESS CONTROL: CHANGE PIN

The distillery approach should be more easily grasped when we go through parts of our *Access Control* example in some detail to explain what we mean by each of the individual approaches. We shall try to apply only one individual approach at the time while in practice a development step may use more than one approach.

Our example system is an *Access Control* system where *Users* come to *Access Points* where they by presenting the proper access means (e.g. a magnetic card and a personal identification number) are allowed to enter certain *Access Zones*.

Our starting point is an informal domain statement of the domain of *Access Control* systems from which we extract:

"Users shall be able to change their secret code"

This is the service that we shall develop in this paper. It is obvious that the simple line above of the domain statement may give rise to a number of interpretations and a number of possible implementations.

4 MAKE MORE PRECISE

It is reasonable to start by trying to make the statement more precise, and we have three approaches: formalize, narrow and supplement. It is not obvious which of these approaches will give the best progress.

4.1 Formalize

Trying to formalize will often make the designers discover more about the prose statement than they first thought was in it. Assuming that there is already some description of the service in prose, we would like to formalize this in MSC-96. How do we go about doing it?

Even though MSC-96 is a formal language, MSC-96 diagrams may have comments and they may be annotated by informal, but important prose. How can the amount of important, informal information be decreased or eliminated? By eliminating such informal information more formal validation techniques can be applied.

With the prose description as starting point, make MSCs which have the active objects of the prose description as instances. In the domain property model, such active objects are *roles*.

Model communication actions by messages. Give rather coarse sketches of the message sequences possibly leaving out all messages or actions which may blur the overview picture.

Our starting point is the single line of the domain statement in Section 3. It identifies the *User* and that there should be some service providing role (say: *PINChanging*) which will make it possible for the *User* to change his secret code. We suggest the simple service as depicted in Figure 2.

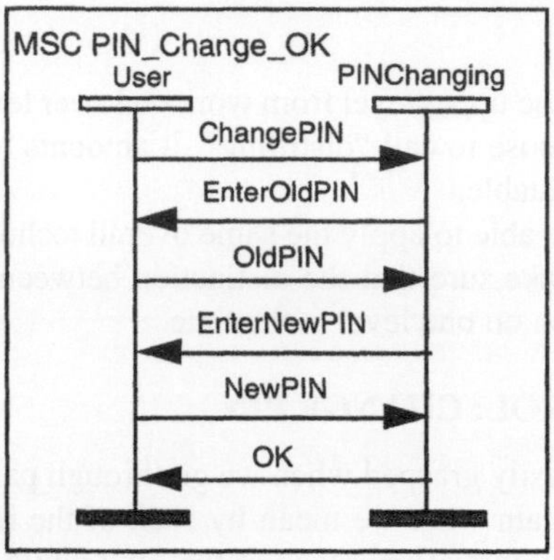

Figure 2 MSC User changing PINwith success

We should be aware, however, that our proposed formalization through an MSC is not the only possible interpretation of the domain statement. For instance the domain statement says nothing about whether the *User* is to choose his new PIN himself or the system selects it for him! In Figure 2 we have indicated that the *User* will have a chance of selecting his own new PIN, but this is actually because we have already used our next approach.

4.2 Narrow

When the prose (or formalization) gives rise to too many interpretations, we must add more properties so that the number of valid interpretations decreases.

A valid interpretation of the domain statement is that the *User* gives a command to change PIN and a new PIN is delivered from the system.

Furthermore we have not specified any requirement that the ownership of the card is to be validated before a new PIN is accepted.

By adding these new requirements to the domain statement we have narrowed the set of valid interpretations *without* formalizing.

The last requirement of Figure 3 is not merely a requirement on the situation before or after the service, but a requirement on how the service should be performed. The pre- and postcondition style is not well suited to express such requirements since the service itself is considered a black box and its results are all that matter. MSC, on the other hand, is especially tailored to express such execution sequences.

Service PIN Change

- Users shall be able to change their personal identification
- The User shall be able to choose his new PIN
- The Card shall be validated by the old PIN before a new PIN can be given. The new PIN shall subsequently also be validated.

Figure 3 PIN change narrowed

The general operation of narrowing is to restrict the possible interpretations of the description. MSC-96, however, is a language which are very explicit about which sequences it covers. While in other languages it may be difficult to overview the runs covered by a certain construct, MSC-96 is more intuitive. The MSC diagrams express explicitly the covered runs. Therefore narrowing is not applied much once an MSC description has been reached.

One possible act of narrowing in MSC may be the adding of more general ordering relations in a coregion. This does not apply in our example.

We may now validate whether the formalization in Figure 2 satisfies the informal narrowed domain statement in Figure 3 We easily see that this is not the case! The formalization does not validate the new PIN again.

4.3 Supplement

While narrowing restricted the set of valid interpretations, supplementing increases the scope of the specification. New and important aspects are considered which were not an issue earlier.

Typically, when the formalization is done in MSC, the MSC does not quite cover all the situations covered by the informal specification. There is a need to supplement with exceptional and erroneous cases and more normal cases. In MSC-96 the erroneous and exceptional cases can often be described as additions to the MSCs where the normal runs are described. Through alternative constructs like **opt**ion and **exc**eption, normal MSCs can be enriched into covering all legitimate runs.

In our example we need to specify what happens if the *Old PIN* is not properly typed in, and if the *New PIN* is not repeated properly.

In Figure 4 we have used MSC-96 with MSC references and exceptional operators. We have used substitution to show that to validate the new PIN, one can use the same sequence structure as when validating the old PIN.

Other aspects which could possibly supplement our MSC are time and capacity aspects. Are there any requirements on how fast the system should respond to the User commands and data? Such requirements could be attached here by comments in the MSC or through more textual prose.

Requirements to the response times of the User may be specified through the use of timers, but that seems more adequate as a matter of specifying the actual protocols in more detail.

For this service it would be valuable to specify some idea of how frequent the service is intended to be used. We believe that changing the PIN is a service which will occur very infrequently compared with the main service which is the access of the zones.

Supplementing and narrowing can sometimes be difficult to distinguish, but in practice it is

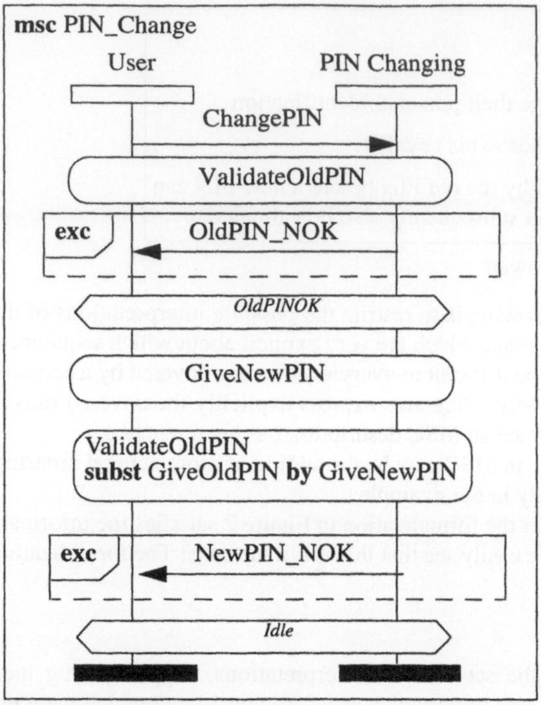

Figure 4 PINChange supplemented (MSC-96)

not critical that the designer knows whether he has applied one or the other. The goal of both approaches is to make the description more precise such that misinterpretations cannot occur.

5 MAKE MORE DETAILED

Even when we have a formal MSC-96 document, we may have reasons to go into greater detail. The instances may consist of smaller instances, the messages may actually be a whole protocol, and the MSC references must be resolved by defining the MSC diagrams which they refer to.

Furthermore when the magnifying glass is applied, entirely new aspects may be revealed which on the more coarse level were insignificant, but which on a more detailed level proves to be significant.

We have in Section 4 reached a formal description in Figure 4 which covers the informal and narrowed description of Figure 3 A reasonably smart tool would be able to simulate (execute) that description e.g. by implementing all MSC references as the empty MSC, but tracing the MSC reference occurrence. The informal descriptions do not give much clues to how the pending MSCs shall be described or implemented. This means that, regarding the top level requirements almost any implementation of these MSCs will actually be valid interpretations of the service.

5.1 Layers of MSC documents

Our overall methodology makes a distinction between the domain model and the design model. Generally speaking the design model should fulfill the domain model, but we do not demand that the design model should consist only of refinements of concepts of the domain model. Rather we say that the design model should be "inspired by" the domain model. The reason for this is partly technical and partly practical.

The technical reason is connected to the complexity which arises when the different approaches of this MSC-96 distillery is combined with role casting and requirements of formal refinements. Experiments have shown that MSC documents which combine both the domain model and the design model become less transparent than if we divide the description in two such that one MSC document represents the domain level and another the design level. It is conceivable that it is possible to formalize the relation between these MSC documents, but we believe there is a need for other constructs than what we find inside MSC-96 today. The practical reason for the division is that different persons read, construct and maintains the different levels. Larger projects organize their teams along such lines. Possibly the upper layers are used for marketing and documentation, while the lower ones are used in design. Their perfect inter-consistency is preferable, but not vitally important. Documentation MSCs may "cut a few corners" without violating the overall principles and spirit of the solution while gaining simplicity and overview.

Typically the domain model contains instances which are functional roles. These roles are seldom described in details by defining their component. Components are pieces of objects and not of functional roles. Thus the transfer from domain concepts to design concepts normally means to perform the casting of objects to roles.

In our example we have cast the role *PINChanging* to the total object *AC system*, and our "inspired" *PIN Change* service is shown in Figure 5.

5.2 Decompose

Decomposition in MSC is meant to be achieved by the **decomposed** mechanism where an instance of one MSC diagram (called the "decomposed instance") is spelt out in greater detail in another MSC diagram (called the "decomposition diagram").

Even though the principle of decomposition is a simple one and seem to be well supported in MSC-96, there are some points which should be carefully handled.

Tool support

The support for decomposition in tools may vary from little or no support to advanced consistency warnings. It is important for the engineer to know what language rules and methodological guidelines he will have to check himself without the aid of the tool. Here is a checklist for tool support:

- *No support for decomposition diagrams* at all. Unfortunately this happens.
- *Static check of messages* to/from the decomposed instance compared with the corresponding communication in the decomposition diagram.
- *Dynamic check of the communication.* This means to make sure that the sequence described on the decomposed instance in the upper level diagram is *exactly* the sequence resulting from the communication within the decomposition diagram.
- *Check of aggregate hierarchy of instances.* The tool may check that there is an underlying tree structure of decomposed instances.

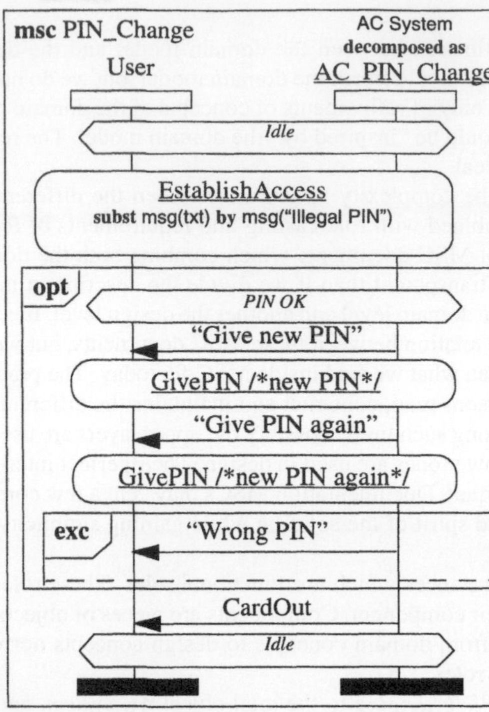

Figure 5 PIN_Change of design model

MSC environment

MSCs are used to describe interaction between instances. It may seem arbitrary which instances are considered "in the environment" and which instances are considered "inside the situation". Often we would prefer to let many instances appear inside the situation where many individual entities of the environment can be described by individual instances rather than using the frame to describe the environment.

Taking Figure 5 as an example, the standard decomposition of *AC System* (in *AC_PIN_Change*) will have no reference to the instance *User*, but for a better self-contained understanding of *AC_PIN_Change* it would help to see that the signals to and from the environment are actually sent to and received from the *User*. Our firm advice is never to repeat instances in decomposition diagrams from upper level diagrams, and rather supply the gates with adequate names or comments.

We suggest an MSC-96 extension where this is possible inspired by the "gate endpoint constraints" of SDL-92 [9; 11] where it is possible to draw instances outside the diagram frame as shown in the non-standard diagram Figure 6 This option should be attractive also for those who make their MSCs with a general drawing tool and not a dedicated MSC editor.

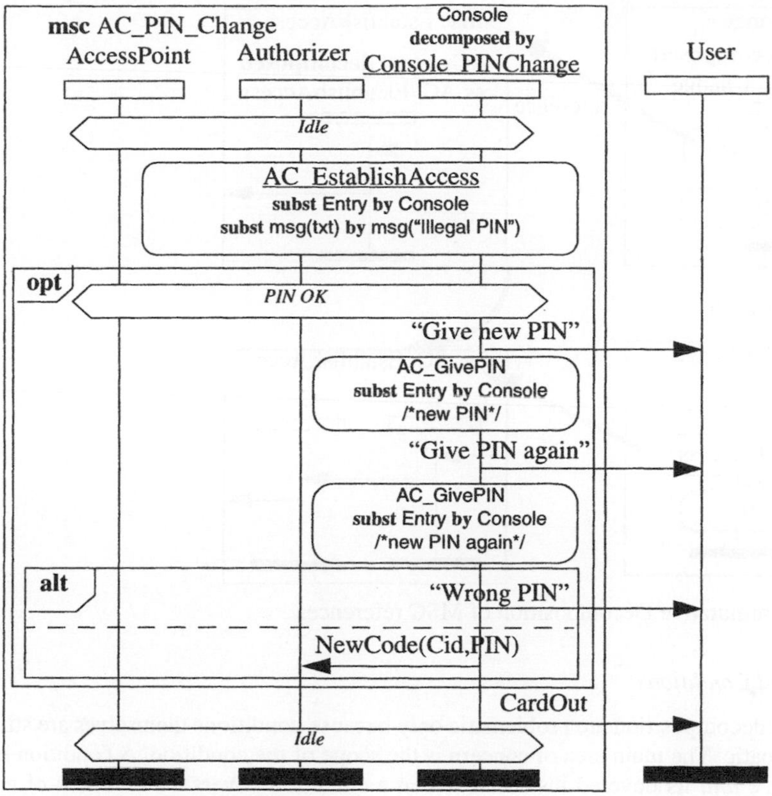

Figure 6 AC_PIN_Change

Decomposition and MSC references

Decomposition combined with MSC references is disallowed in MSC-96 because the semantic interpretation was not entirely clear. We find this restriction impractical, but realize that a faithful methodological approach is demanded in order to keep the decompositions consistent with the MSC references. In Figure 7 we present schematically the principle for consistency between decompositions and MSC references.

The following principles should hold. Whenever an instance which is covered by an MSC reference is decomposed, the decomposition should show the same structure of MSC references as the decomposed instance. The MSC references of the decomposition refer to decompositions of the instance of the referred MSC. A proper naming convention of MSCs should be provided such that the name itself describes the hierarchy of decompositions which it represents.

By following this fairly simple principle, there is no need for a more complicated consistency control procedure.

If pure MSC-96 must be used, the levels of decomposition must be contained in different MSC documents and the decomposed references must be made informally in notes.

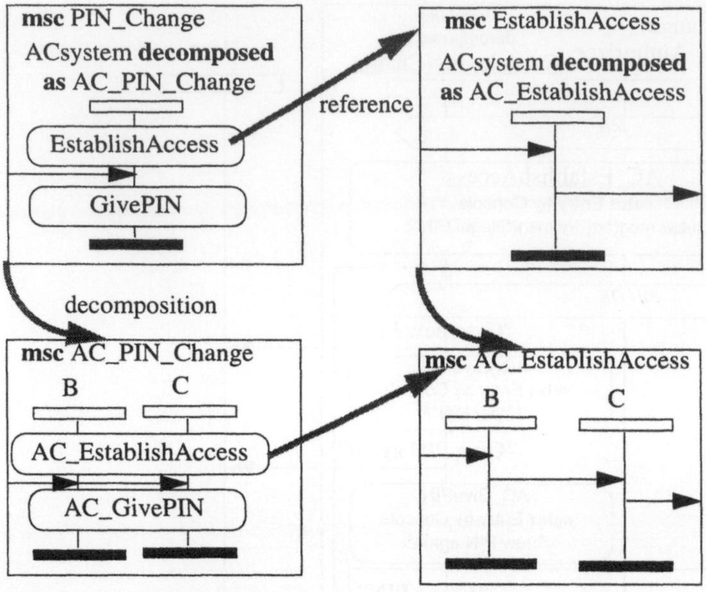

Figure 7 Commutative Decomposition of MSC references

Decomposition and Conditions

Conditions and decomposition are problematic only because conditions themselves are still somewhat problematic. The main area of concern is the scope of the condition. A condition is defined by its name *and* its covered instances. When a condition covers all instances of an MSC, is it then "global" meaning that it can be considered to cover *all* instances in the whole MSC document? The MSC language definition [12] hardly gives an adequate answer to this, but a normal interpretation is that it is a global condition if every instance in all MSCs it appears are covered. What if instance A is decomposed into an MSC with instances B and C. Does a global condition covering A also cover B and C? From what we earlier said, the reasonable interpretation is that the global condition also covers B and C (since it is supposed to cover all instances). Then a reasonable requirement is that global conditions of the decomposed instance should reappear in the decomposed MSCs. For verification and consistency purposes the global conditions are the interesting ones, while for MSC to SDL conversion purposes local conditions can also be used favorably. A local condition of a decomposed instance should reappear in the decomposition diagram as a condition shared by all the instances of the decomposition.

The instance hierarchy

There should be consistency between different decompositions of the same instance in different MSCs. The decomposition of an instance is a definition of a part of the aggregate hierarchy of instances. In Figure 6 the instance *AC System* has been decomposed into instances *AccessPoint*, *Authorizer* and *Console*.

Our first question is whether all decompositions of an instance must contain the same set of sub-instances? In principle it may be possible to find cases where different component sets could be feasible. Intermediate levels may be aggregated in different ways. In our methodology, however, we hold the view that there is *one* underlying aggregate tree-structure of instances.

The second question then is whether all decompositions must show exactly the same set of instances. Our methodological answer to this is that as long as one underlying aggregate structure can be deduced from the decompositions of the whole MSC document, there is no need for instances which are not involved in the communication to be shown in decompositions.

An example of this may be the situation where in our *Access Control* system, the *User* will always escape from the inside to the outside of the *Access Zone* by only pressing a plain button which will unlock the door. This situation can be described with the *AC System* as one instance communicating with the *User*. In this situation, however, a decomposition of *AC System* need not show *Authorizer*, because the *Authorizer* is not involved in this situation at all. Still the underlying aggregate structure will have *Authorizer* as one component of *AC System* due to other decompositions.

The designer should also be careful not to skip levels in the decomposition which would make it more difficult to deduce the underlying aggregate hierarchy.

The aggregate hierarchy of instances should match the aggregate hierarchy of the corresponding object model which is typically described in SDL.

Methodological experience and MSC semantics

We owe the reader to point out that our methodology presented here in practice seems to violate the MSC-96 semantics. In MSC-96 all MSC expressions are totally independent of each other. This may seem reasonable at first, but our experience shows otherwise. There are two different problems which are highlighted by the use presented here. One problem concerns global conditions and continuations, while the second concerns alternative expressions and decomposition.

Conditions in simple MSCs (i.e. those MSCs containing instances) have no semantics other than that of an informal comment. This is not the way it is normally perceived.

The MSC *EstablishAccess* shown in Figure 8 ends with an alternative expression which either ends in condition *Idle* or in condition *PIN_OK*. The MSC *PIN_Change* then continue with an option (which is a degenerate alternative expression) starting with the condition *PIN_OK*. The intention of course is that the option will happen if and only if the alternative of *EstablishAccess* returned in *PIN_OK*. This interpretation has no background in MSC-96 semantics where the two alternative expressions are totally independent and the option may happen also when the *EstablishAccess* has ended in *Idle*.

Concerning alternative expressions and decompositions, we may observe the option statement of *PIN_Change* (Figure 5) and the corresponding one of *AC_PIN_Change* (Figure 6). The problem is of course that the option of *PIN_Change* is not formally associated with the option in *AC_PIN_Change*. Assume for a second that the User is also decomposed and the decomposition contains a corresponding option. Assume further that we interpret the decomposition as a macro and expand the two decompositions. We would then have two independent option expressions and there is semantically no constraint that the two options either happen together or both do not happen. This is again contrary to how the construct is intuitively perceived.

Our position is that the MSC-96 semantics should be made to cope with these methodological problems.

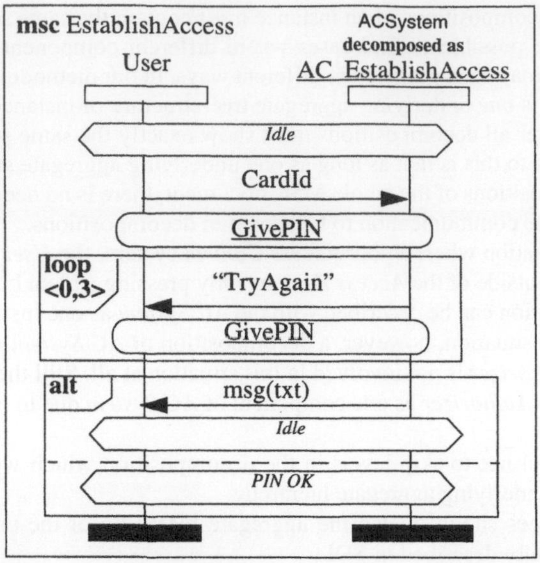

Figure 8 EstablishAccess

5.3 Break down

While decomposition defines a hierarchy of instances, breaking down means to define a hierarchy of communication concepts or protocols. There are two MSC concepts used for this: messages and MSC references.

There is no mechanism in MSC to break down a message. Still we all know that messages are on different levels often modeled by the OSI layers. While low level communication may be necessary to achieve a detailed understanding, the more upper level messages are better for coarse overviews.

Since there is no language mechanism to handle this, we must distinguish between a set of different cases.

- The MSC document as such may be divided into layers which match protocol layers such that broken down messages do not occur in the same MSC document as the aggregated message (see Section 5.1).
- A message (type) of one MSC may be broken down by an MSC. The original message is replaced everywhere by an MSC reference referring to the result of the breaking down.
- A message (type) of one MSC can be broken down by an MSC, but the original message cannot be seen directly as an MSC reference due to message overtaking.

Message as MSC reference

When the message can be understood as an MSC reference, this is exactly what we advise to do: substitute the message by an MSC reference to the broken down protocol. Unfortunately the substitution mechanism in MSC cannot be used since messages can only be substituted by messages. The change must normally be done manually for all places where this message (type) occurs. The resulting MSC document keeps the layered structure, both overview and detail are taken good care of. The only disadvantage compared with the MSC document strategy above is that the direction of the communication primitive is lost since MSC references have no direction.

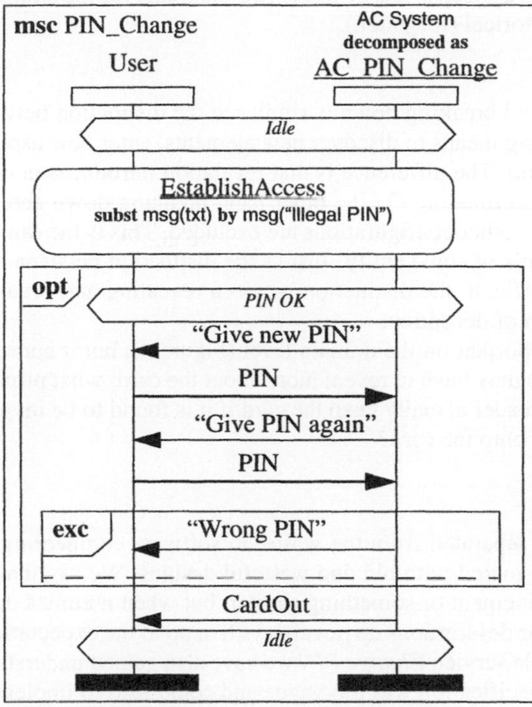

Figure 9 PIN_Change with PIN

In our example Figure 5 shows *PIN_Change* where an MSC reference *GivePIN* is introduced. On this level we could just as well have described this by the message *PIN* as shown in Figure 9. For all we know this may have been sufficient all along. We made, however, a breaking down on the fly by specifying it as a reference. This gives us the chance to go in more details about how the PIN is to be entered.

The transformation from message to MSC reference has of course also effect on decomposition.

Messages as merged protocols

Technically there is an important difference between messages and MSC references. While messages may overtake other messages, no such thing is defined for MSC references. If we have two messages which are involved in message overtaking and they are both subject to breaking down, the final result is not obvious. While a message has one sender and one receiver, a protocol may have messages going both ways. Extra instances may also be introduced in the breaking down. The actual meaning of breaking down two such messages *may* be to allow the parallel merge of the two protocols. This is normally not the case, however, that the freedom is that wide. Rather the fact is that the detailed meaning must be spelled out manually for that specific situation. In the descriptions broken down messages must be substituted not by an MSC reference, but by the content of the MSC diagram which defines the breaking down. The message overtaking of the original indicates a specific merge of the two diagrams for the situation. The original messages will become historical (forgotten).

5.4 Reveal

The distinction between revealing and breaking down is similar to the distinction between supplementing and narrowing. Revealing means to discover new elements, enter new aspects, which were what supplementing also did. The difference is that revelation introduces new instances and objects, not merely new information. On the other hand breaking down actually limits the scope as an infinite number of other configurations are excluded. This is the same as narrowing, but with respect to the details of some entity. Just as the distinction between supplementing and narrowing could be difficult, the distinction between revealing and breaking down can also be difficult or a question of definition.

In our example the card was not important on the domain level (Figure 4), but it appeared as a design decision (Figure 5). Still we may have to reveal more about the card: what prompts the entering of the card? Can the card reader actually keep the card if it is found to be invalid? Does the service write something back onto the card?

6 DISTILLERY

In distilleries the pure substance is separated from the waste. In software engineering the problem is that the purified results are mixed with old and wasteful designs. We say that we apply top-down design or stepwise refinement or something similar, but when it comes down to providing the steps and the layers, our descriptions do not always live up to the expectations.

During our progress with our example service *Change PIN* we have also gained understanding. We discovered that our original specification was too vague and could lead to implementations which were clearly undesirable.

We were able to reach a fairly complete, and fairly precise description of the whole which did not go into great detail. (Figure 4). This precise, but not so detailed description serves well as a communication medium with non-professionals and as an introduction to newcomers to the project group. Furthermore it is precise enough (formal enough) to serve as base for simulation and verification. This description is the "*distilled whole*", a description which has been purified through a process of making the initial description more precise. That process may also have benefited from the process of detailing as it may include details which on first thought appeared to be irrelevant on this level anyway.

The software engineers should not consider the precise detailed description as the only valuable result, even though it marks the next step toward realization. It is important that also the precise detailed description is verified to be an implementation of the distilled whole.

7 STRATEGIES FOR THE DESCRIPTION BY MSC-96

We have presented the principles for using MSC-96 in a stepwise fashion. In this section we summarize our findings by giving explicit guidelines and rules for the design.

7.1 Formalizing

- *Service orientation*. Make one MSC per service.
- *Role orientation*. Instances of the MSCs in the domain are roles.
- *Normal cases*. Focus first on the normal cases and make them formal.

7.2 Narrow

- *Actions and comments*. Try and minimize the use of informal text which is actually meaningful on its own. See if actions and comments can be expressed (also) by messages.
- *General ordering*. Scrutinize coregions and make sure that the allowed variability of sequencing is the desired one.

7.3 Supplement

- *Exceptions and errors*. Supplement the normal cases by cases expressing exceptional and erroneous situations. Use alternative-, exceptions- and option- mechanisms of MSC-96.

7.4 Decompose

- *Environment*. Use the frame to describe the environment for better reuse capabilities. Use good gate names or comments to describe the connection points. Informally instances outside the frame can be utilized (non-standard MSC).
- *Underlying aggregate hierarchy of instances*. Use the decompose-mechanism to define the aggregate hierarchy of instances. The hierarchy should be one tree structure. Do not skip aggregate levels in the decomposition. The instance tree structure should match a corresponding structure from the object model.
- *Decomposition consistency*. In order to keep a simple consistency between decompositions and MSC references the following principles should be kept:
  - The structure of MSC references on an instance A in MSC M shall be retained in the decomposition of A.
  - MSC references in the decomposition of A refers to decompositions of A in diagrams referred to by MSC references on A in the original MSC M.
  - Thus MSC references and decompositions make up a commutative scheme as shown in Figure 7.
- *Conditions*. Use global conditions to describe important system states. These will formalize restrictions on component MSCs when used in HMSC diagrams. Whenever a global condition covers a decomposed instance, the condition shall also appear in the decomposition.

7.5 Breaking down

- *Layers of MSC documents*. When the description of the services are made on very different abstraction levels for very different purposes (and possibly for very different people), it is possible that keeping the ultimate formal connection between the MSCs requires too much effort. The solution to this is to make more than one MSC document, but where each MSC document represents a complete understanding by itself.

- *Messages become MSC references*. Sometimes what appears as one message turns out to be a somewhat more complicated protocol. Such messages may be replaced by MSC references to a diagram showing the protocol.
- *Messages are expanded.* When the messages which turn out to be protocols cannot be substituted by MSC references due to e.g. message overtaking or other sequence merge problems, the messages should be expanded by the contents of the protocol.

7.6 Reveal

- *"Under the carpet"*. Consider details which have been pushed aside in earlier phases. As the richness in detail has increased, the significance of "forgotten" details will also increase. Reconsider the aspects which have been pushed under the carpet.

7.7 Distillery

- *Layering*. The purpose of the distillery is to make sure that the descriptions are organized in a layered manner. The upper layer should be such that it can be understood by itself in its own universe of concepts. The relation which defines the layering should be explicit and well defined. In MSC-96 MSC references and decomposition constitute such relations.
- *HMSC*. High level MSC can often be used for top level overviews. In HMSC instances are eliminated and conditions are explicitly global and restrictive.

8 REFERENCES

1. Bræk, R. and Haugen, Ø. (1993). *Engineering Real Time Systems*. Hemel Hempstead, Prentice Hall International 0-13-034448-6.
2. Bræk, R., Haugen, Ø., Melby, G., Møller-Pedersen, B., Sanders, R. and Stålhane, T. (1996). Integrated Methodology. Oslo, SISU (see: http://www.sintef.no/sisu/).
3. Broy, M. and Stølen, K. (1996). *FOCUS on System Development*. Munich, (manuscript)
4. Clark, E. M., Emerson, E. A. and Sistla, A. P. (1983). *Automatic verification of finite state concurrent systems using temporal logic specifications*. 10th ACM Symposium on Principles of Programming Languages, Austin, Texas January 24-26, 1983, Pages: 117-126, ACM
5. Haugen, Ø. (1994). MSC Methodology. SISU Report L-1313-7, Oslo. (see: http://www.sintef.no/sisu/)
6. Haugen, Ø. (1995). *Using MSC-92 Effectively.* SDL'95 with MSC in CASE. Proceedings of the Seventh SDL Forum, Oslo, Norway 26.-29. Sept. 1995, North-Holland, Elsevier
7. Haugen, Ø., Bræk, R. and Melby, G. (1993). *The SISU project*. SDL '93 Using Objects. Proceedings of the Sixth SDL Forum, Darmstadt, Germany October 12th – 16th 1993, Pages: 479-489, North Holland 0-444-81486-8.
8. Hoare, C. A. R. (1985). *Communicating Sequential Processes*. Hemel Hempstead, Prentice Hall International 0-13-153271-5.
9. ITU (1993) Z.100 ITU Specification and Description Language (SDL), ITU-T, June 1994, 237 p
10. ITU (1993) Z.120 Message Sequence Charts (MSC), ITU-T, September 1994, 36 p
11. ITU (1996) Z.100 Addendum to Recommendation Z.100: CCITT Specification and Description Language, ITU, October 1996, 31 p
12. ITU (1996) Z.120 Message Sequence Charts (MSC), ITU-T, Oct. 1996, 78 p

SDL '97: TIME FOR TESTING - SDL, MSC and Trends
A. Cavalli and A. Sarma (Editors)

Switching Software Test Environment Using MSC

Shugo Shiba, Yoshiaki Shigeta and Wataru Tanaka[a]

[a]Telecommunications, Group, Oki Electric Industry Co., Ltd.
WBG Bldg., Nakase 2-6, Mihama-ku, Chiba 261-71, JAPAN

One problem in the switching software test stage is inability to start testing before completion of the switching system hardware. It is, therefore, necessary to implement the software test environment before completion of the hardware. The central processor and speech path systems of the switching system operate independently, with control signals as the interface between them. The control signals may be regarded as messages to be transferred between the central processor and speech path systems.

In the proposed test environment, mutual conversion between control signals and MSC/PR is enabled. In the test environment control signals are event-oriented. Because the MSC/PR is instance-oriented, conversion into the MSC/PR involves low conversion efficiency and complications.

In the test environment, therefore, control signals are converted into and from event-oriented MSC/PR for efficient conversion. On the other hand, real-time conversion between event-oriented MSC/PR and MSC/GR is also enabled. Compared to instance-oriented MSC/PR, event-oriented MSC/PR allows easy conversion into MSC/GR, which also applies to real-time conversion.

Implementing an automatic regression test is desirable in the test environment. It has been realized by execution and verification using the recorded event-oriented MSC/PR.

As a result, the test environment has been established easily with improvement of testing job efficiency. It has also been confirmed that event-oriented MSC/PR is especially effective for a real-time system.

1. Introduction

Services in the communication field are being diversified and upgraded at an astonishing speed. Switching systems as cores of communication systems are inclined to be upgraded to provide more advanced services and to connect diversifying types of terminals. Against such a background, it is necessary to develop the switching software for controlling switching systems in a shorter period while it becomes much more complicated.

In the switching software design stage, introduction of multi-purpose development equipment and visual design support tools has been promoted for steady improvement of the design job efficiency. The job efficiency in the test stage, on the other hand, has not been sufficiently been improved because of the need for a special test environment that hinders introduction of multi purpose development support tools.

One big problem in the test stage is the inability to start the test before completion of the switching system hardware. To solve this problem, therefore, it is important to implement the software test environment before hardware completion. This environment is called the switching software test environment.

The message sequence chart (MSC) [1] enables general message interchange to be described in graphical representation with definite syntax, thus allowing subjective understanding of message interchange.

This paper describes the switching software test environment using MSC. Section 2 explains the switching software configuration and test procedure to clarify the range covered by this paper. Section 3 describes the test environment obtained for supporting the switching software test. Section 4 describes implementation of the switching software test environment using MSC, and Section 5 the tools in the switching software test environment. Section 6 is the conclusion.

2. Switching Software Test

The switching system components and the switching software test procedure are described below with the scope of the test discussed in this paper.

2.1. Switching System Components

Figure 1 shows the switching system configuration.

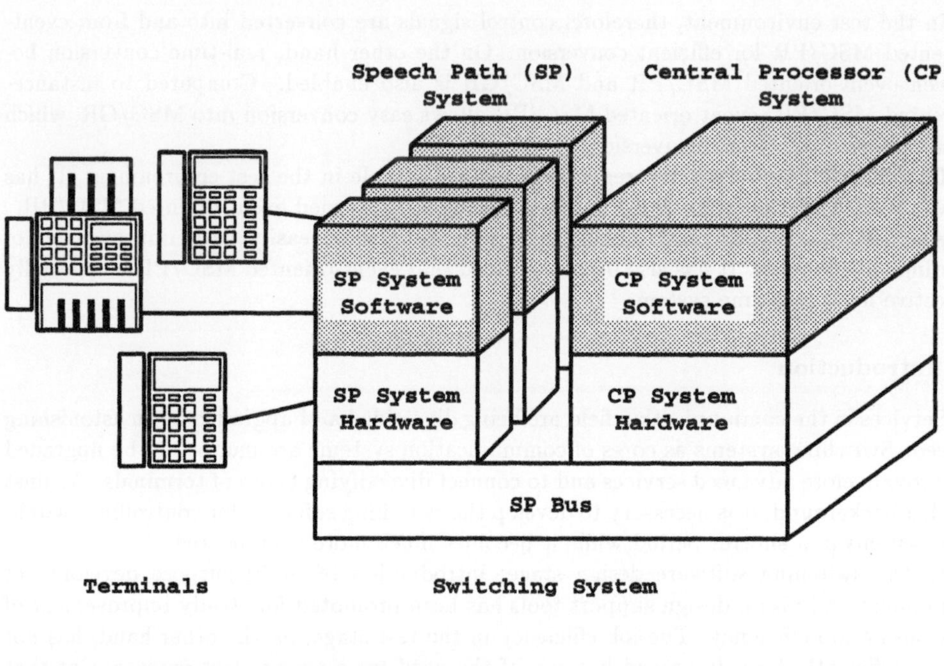

Figure 1. The Switching System Configuration

The switching system roughly consists of the Central Processor (CP) system, Speech Path (SP) system and Speech Path (SP) bus.

The CP system consists of the CP system hardware and software. The CP system hardware comprises the CPU, memory and disk for running the CP system software. The CP system software is the core portion for the switching process to provide telephone call switching and services.

The SP system consists of the SP system hardware and software. The SP system hardware connects telephone, facsimile and other terminals, and controls them by means of electrical signals. The SP system software converts electrical signals from terminals into control signals for transmission to the CP system. It also converts control signals from the CP system into electrical signals for controlling terminals.

The SP bus is used for interfacing between the CP system and SP system.

2.2. Switching System Test Procedure

The switching system is tested roughly according to the procedure shown in Figure 2.

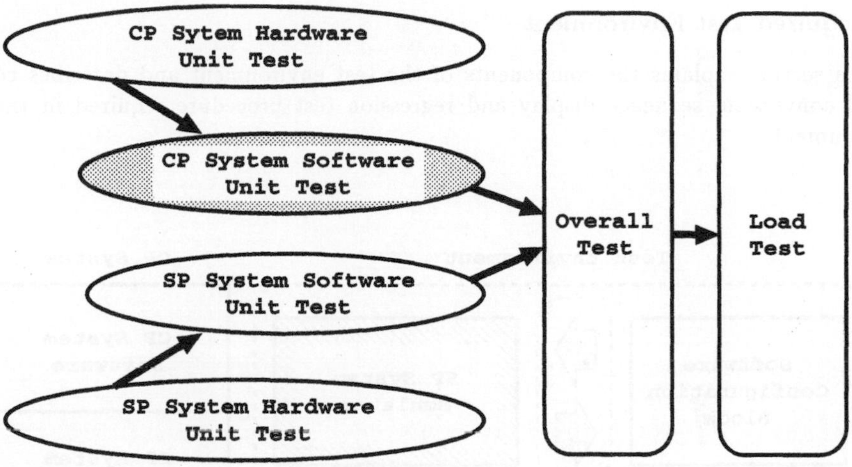

Figure 2. Switching System Test Procedure

In the CP system hardware unit test, small scale software for operation checks is used to check the normal functioning of each unit composing the CP system hardware.

The CP system software unit test individually tests each unit of the CP system software. This test checks for normal functioning of each basic functional unit such as call connection. It starts after confirmation of stabilized CP system hardware operation by the CP system hardware unit test.

In the SP system hardware unit test, small scale software for checking the functions of SP system hardware is used for checking the normal functioning of each hardware unit.

In the SP system software unit test, each control function for the SP system hardware is checked for normal functioning after confirming normal functioning, to a certain degree, of the SP system hardware by means of the SP system hardware unit test.

The overall test is conducted after the end of four unit tests by combining all portions in the same environment as in the operation stage.

The load test is conducted in the final stage to check stabilized switching system operation under heavy call traffic intensity.

2.3. Covered Range

This paper discusses the environment for the CP system software unit test out of the switching system tests shown in Section 2.2 above. The CP system software accounts for the largest portion in scale of the switching system software. In the CP system software unit test, the CP system software must be tested without the presence of the SP system. The switching software test environment is the environment required for conducting the unit test of the CP system software.

3. Required Test Environment

This section explains the components of the test environment and describes control signal conversion, sequence display and regression test procedure required in the test environment.

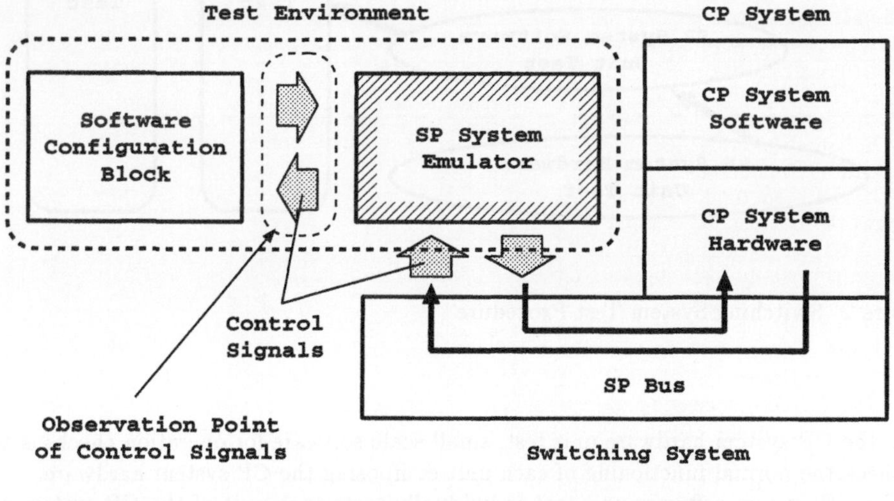

Figure 3. Configuration of Switching Software Test Environment

3.1. Components of Test Environment

The switching software test environment consists roughly of the SP system emulator and software configuration block. Figure 3 shows configuration of switching software test environment.

The SP system emulator is the hardware for emulating the SP system hardware. The SP system emulator has a single function. It writes the control signals received from the CP system hardware into the SP bus. It also monitors the control signals written by the CP system hardware and sends it to the software configuration block. Providing the SP system emulator in the form of hardware enables the CP system software to be tested in the same environment as in actual operation. Because it is unnecessary to modify the CP system software for the purpose of testing, the preparation period for the test can be eliminated.

The software configuration block is a group of multiple software packages for realizing the user interface with the testing person and testing functions.

3.2. Control Signal Conversion

In the test environment, the testing person checks the control signals sent from the CP system to the SP system by receiving them from the SP system emulator to judge the correctness of the CP system software functions. The control signal elements to be checked are the sources, destinations, time, types and parameters. The sources and destinations are checked to judge whether control signals are sent from or sent to correct terminals in communication between the CP system and multiple terminals connected to the SP system. The time must be measured in milliseconds since the executed operation varies with the time lapse. Types are control signal functions, and parameters are auxiliary information that determines the operation of control signals.

In the test environment, control signals sent from the SP system to the CP system are emulated by control signal transmission to the SP system emulator by the testing person. These control signals must be prepared beforehand.

Control signals are expressed in binary format for reducing the communication cost. It is difficult for the testing person to check and prepare control signals in binary format. It is desirable to allow easy checking and preparation by conversion to text format.

3.3. Sequence Display

Aside from checking the content of each control signal, it is necessary to check the sequence of multiple control signals in the test for judgment on the correctness of one control procedure.

It is desirable to improve the checking job efficiency by displaying the sequence visually for intuitive understanding.

3.4. Regression Test Execution

A regression test means re-execution of a test checked in the past. When any function is added to the CP system software, it is necessary to conduct regression tests for existing functions. Since the life cycle of the CP system software is too long to make addition of functions account for most of the development work, the man-hours required for regression tests are enormous

One feature of the CP system software is the modular structure exerting minimum influence on existing functions. Most regression tests, therefore, can be conducted according to exactly the same procedure. Automatic conduction of regression tests will be possible because of this characteristic.

It is necessary to realize regression tests without human intervention for automatic re-execution by storing the operation records upon each test execution.

4. Implementation of Test Environment

This section explains the MSC, followed by implementation of the mutual conversion between MSC/PR and control signals, sequence display by MSC/GR and regression test execution by MSC/PR.

4.1. MSC

MSC provides two syntaxes for describing message interchanged: MSC/GR (graphic representation allowing intuitive understanding) and MSC/PR (textual representation for mechanical processing). These represent the same meaning and allow mutual conversion. As an improved version of MSC/PR, MSC/PR using *event oriented* textual representation has been proposed recently. [2–4] Compared to the event oriented textual representation, the conventional MSC/PR representation is called the *instance oriented* textual representation.

In the instance oriented textual representation, the viewpoint is placed in a situation and the message list is described for each situation. In the message, the input or output instance is described. In the event oriented textual representation, the viewpoint is placed at the message and description is given for each message. The input and output instances are described in the message.

Event oriented textual representation is required for special uses such as checking, tracing, debugging and simulation because the message is not generated for each instance but for each event. The event oriented textual representation is characterized with easy manual editing and easy PR to GR conversion thanks to the syntax similar to graphic representation when compared to instance oriented textual representation.

When distinction of MSC/PR is required in this paper, MSC/PR using instance oriented textual representation is called instance-oriented MSC/PR and that using event oriented textual representation is called event-oriented MSC/PR.

4.2. Mutual Conversion Between MSC/PR and Control Signals

It is desirable to use a formal text format for control signals so as to obtain various values added. Since each control signal must be checked immediately in the test environment, conversion to MSC/PR must be done with each control signal as the unit. Mutual conversion between control signals and MSC/PR is discussed below on assumption of MSC/PR as the text format of control signals.

Control signals are observed at the contact between the software configuration block and SP system emulator in Figure 3. Each control signal sent from a terminal to the switching system is observed and converted upon transmission from the software configuration block to the SP system emulator. Each control signal sent from the SP bus emulator to the software configuration block is observed and converted upon transmission from the SP system emulator to the software configuration block. The instance in the converted

MSC/PR is a terminal or switching system. Since the control signal does not have time information, it is given when the software configuration block converts the control signal at the observation point. Since the time information is given at one observation point, it is the same in the input and output messages.

When considering conversion to instance-oriented MSC/PR, it is difficult to use one instance definition for the same instance. Instance definition is the message definition for one instance. For immediate conversion, the instance definition may have to end with each message. Conversion to event-oriented MSC/PR, on the other hand, can be performed with each message as the unit. Figure 4 shows an example of conversion from control signal *off_hook* from terminal *Telephone1* to switching system *Target* into MSC/PR. (a) in Figure 4 shows the case of conversion into instance-oriented MSC/PR and (b) in Figure 4 the same into event-oriented MSC/PR.

```
instance Telephone1;
  out off_hook(time$0:0:100) to Target;
endinstance;
instance Target;
  in off_hook(time$0:0:100) from Telephone1 ;
endinstance;
```

(a) Converted to instance-oriented MSC/PR

```
Telephone1: out off_hook(time$0:0:100) to Target;
Target:     in off_hook(time$0:0:100) from Telephone1;
```

(b) Converted to event-oriented MSC/PR

Figure 4. Control Signal Conversion

(a) and (b) in Figure 4 are the same in meaning. In the example of conversion into instance-oriented MSC/PR, one message should be converted to six MSC/PR lines. Since frequent instance definitions are needed, the conversion is complicated. Conversion into event-oriented MSC/PR, on the other hand, is efficient as two lines per message. Conversion is simple because there is no need to consider instance definition.

From the above, control signal conversion using event-oriented MSC/PR as the control signal text format has been realized.

4.3. Sequence Display Using MSC/GR

The control signal sequence is displayed as MSC/GR converted from event-oriented MSC/PR. Sequence display by MSC/GR should be implemented in two types: display from records and real-time display according to the requirements in check operation. The first is performed as display of event-oriented MSC/PR recorded within the time determined by the testing person. Real-time display is performed immediately after mutual conversion between control signals and event-oriented MSC/PR. For these two types of display, PR to GR conversion with each message as the unit is realized. Both requests can be satisfied as a result. Figure 5 shows event-oriented MSC/PR as the object of conversion. Figure 6 shows example of PR to GR conversion.

```
Telephone1: out off_hook,1( time$0:0:100 ) to Target;
Target:     in  off_hook,1( time$0:0:100 ) from Telephone1;
Telephone2: out off_hook,2( time$0:0:200 ) to Target;
Target:     out dial_tone_on,3( time$0:0:300) to Telephone1;
Telephone1: in  dial_tone_on,3( time$0:0:300 ) from Target;
Target:     in  off_hook,2( time$0:0:400 ) from Telephone2;
```

Figure 5. Event-oriented MSC/PR as the object of conversion

For real-time display, the message is drawn when the pair of input and output messages is resolved. In the first output message *off_hook,1*, output instance *Telephone1* is drawn as it does not exist and the message output position is marked. In the second input message *off_hook,1*, input instance *Target* is drawn as it does not exist and the message input position is marked. Since message *off_hook,1* is solved by this message, draw the message by connecting the input and output positions. This stage is (a) in Figure 6. Because output instance *Telephone2* does not exist in the third output message *off_hook,2*, draw the picture and mark the message output position. This stage is (b) in Figure 6. Since message *off_hook,3* is solved by 4th output message *dial_tone,3* and 5th input message *dial_tone,3*, draw it as a message. This stage is (c) in Figure 6. Since message *off_hook,2* is solved at 6th input message *off_hook,2*, draw it as a message. This stage is (d) in Figure 6. This message becomes over-talking. In PR to GR conversion, the instance is drawn when a new instance appears in the message and the message is drawn when a pair of input and output messages is solved.

As explained in Section 4.2, message over-talking does not exist in the test environment since one observation point is used. It, however, is not necessary to assume it as a precondition for conversion from event-oriented MSC/PR to MSC/GR. Message over-talking can easily be realized by drawing upon solution of a pair of input and output messages.

In conversion with instance-oriented MSC/PR as the input, real-time conversion is

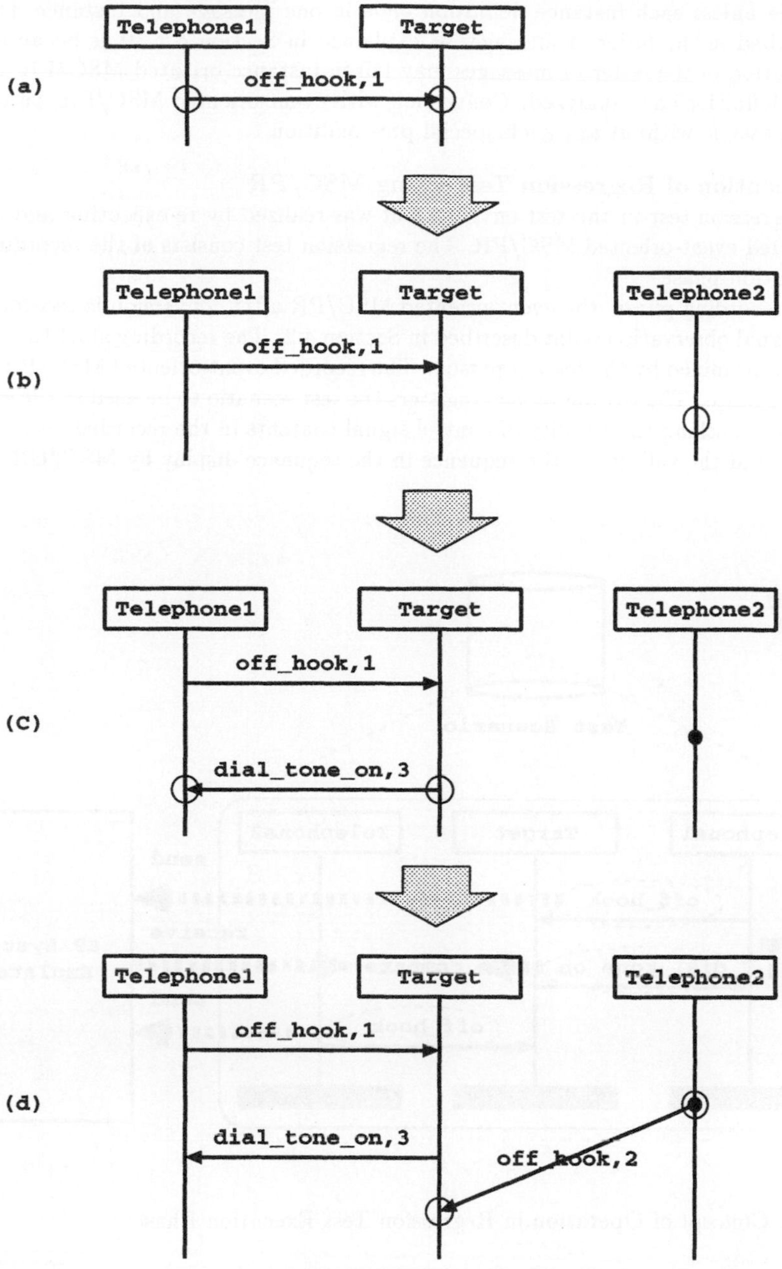

Figure 6. Example of PR to GR Conversion

impossible unless each instance definition ends in one message and instance definitions are described in the order of messages as explained in Section 4.2. It is because perfect determination of the order of messages may fail in instance-oriented MSC/PR unless all instance definitions are analyzed. Conversion with event-oriented MSC/PR, on the other hand, is possible without any such special pre-condition.

4.4. Execution of Regression Test Using MSC/PR

The regression test in the test environment was realized by re-executing and verifying the recorded event-oriented MSC/PR. The regression test consists of the recording phase and execution phase.

In the recording phase, the event-oriented MSC/PR after conversion is recorded at the control signal observation point described in Section 4.2. The recording start time and end time are determined by the testing person. The recorded event-oriented MSC/PR is called the test scenario. The testing person registers the test scenario to be used in the execution phase after checking the validity of control signal contents in the recorded event-oriented MSC/PR and the validity of the sequence in the sequence display by MSC/GR.

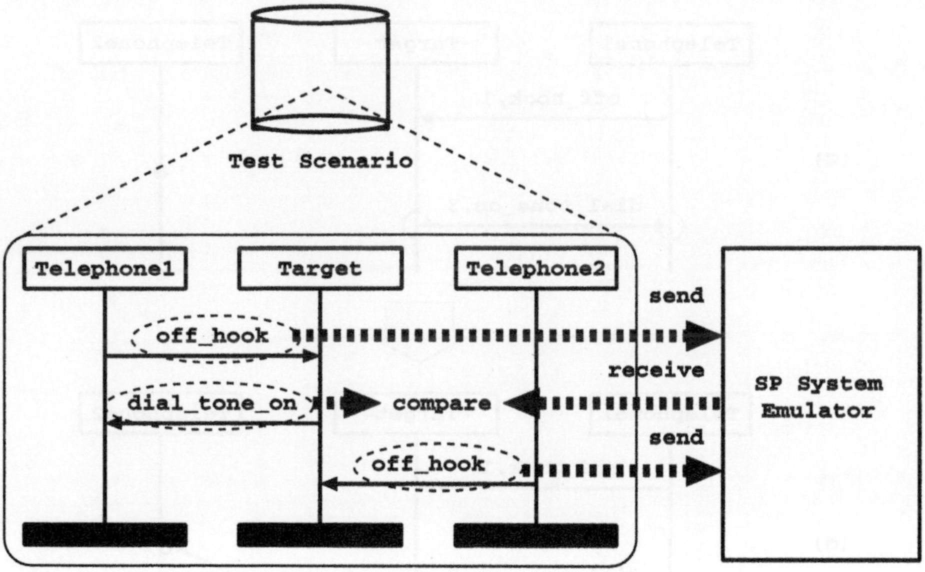

Figure 7. Concept of Operation in Regression Test Execution Phase

In the execution phase, the test is automatically tested again according to the test scenario. The validity of the test is checked by executing verification at the same time with execution. The test is executed by sending the message from the terminal to the switching system recorded in the test scenario according to the relative time between messages. Figure 7 shows the concept of operation in the regression test execution phase.

First, the message *off_hook* in the test scenario is sent using the same content as in the record. Next, the message obtained by execution is compared with message *dial_tone_on* in the test scenario. Then, message *off_hook* in the test scenario is sent using the same content as in the record.

Items compared in message comparison are the message name and parameter values. If any inconsistency is found in message comparison, it is treated as an error and the test judges abnormal result indication.

Since the sequence is formed in the order of message issuance in event-oriented MSC/PR, re-execution can be realized easily. Verification can also be achieved easily by event-oriented MSC/PR as the text format. In message comparison in verification, analysis of detailed contents is necessary because there are parameters to be excluded from the object of comparison.

5. Tools

This section explains the components of tools and using by testing job.

5.1. Components

Five tools forming the switching software test environment, or the SP system emulator, server, terminal operator, viewer and test scheduler are explained in this section. The test environment shown in Figure 3 consists of the tools shown in Figure 8.

The SP system emulator is the hardware for control signal transfer with the CP system hardware through the SP bus.

The server has the mutual conversion between event-oriented MSC/PR and control signals function in Section 4.2, and the automatic regression test execution function by the test scenario in Section 4.4 as the core tool of the test environment.

The terminal operator is the tool used as the user interface for the test. The terminal operator reads the message prepared by the testing person and sends it to the server. The control signal from the terminal to the switching system is emulated in this way. The message sent from the terminal is displayed on the screen to inform the testing person of the control signal sent from the switching system to the terminal. The terminal operator can also initiate the viewer as the MSC/GR display tool as an auxiliary tool. The viewer linked with the terminal operator is capable of real-time display of the message sequence using MSC/GR.

The viewer is the tool provided with PR to GR conversion explained in Section 4.3 for sequence display using MSC/GR. When the test scenario is input, the viewer operates individually to display one complete MSC/GR.

The test scheduler is a tool used as a user interface for carrying out the regression tests mentioned in Section 4.4. It is capable of regression test execution and check by means of the test scheduler. Since massive regression tests can be systematized for management, efficient execution of regression tests is possible.

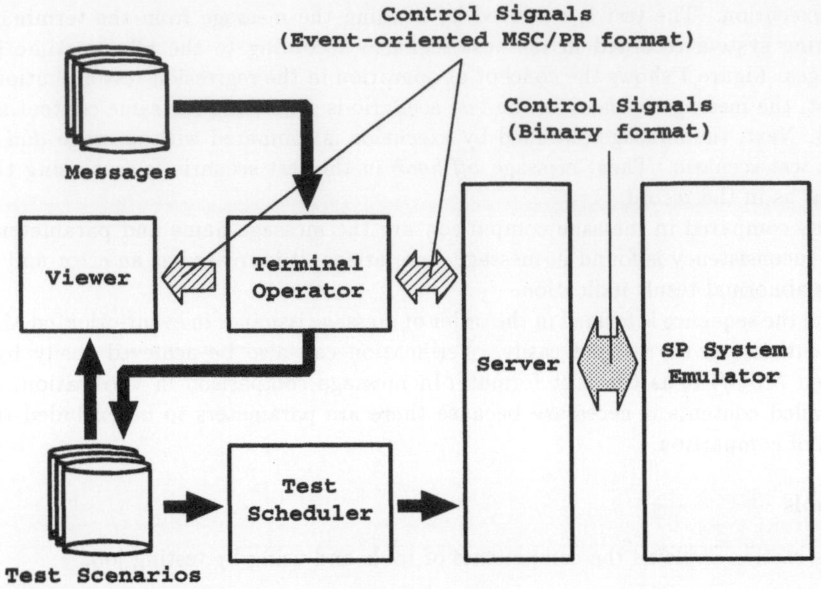

Figure 8. Test Environment Tool Configuration

5.2. Using by Testing Job

Tools forming the switching software test environment confirmed large scale PBX. This PBX has about 20,000 circuits maximum. The CP system software is developed by about 100 persons.

In an initial stage of the CP system software unit test, correctness of the CP system software functions is confirmed slightly each. The testing person transmits making control signal on the CP system software by using the terminal operator. Afterward, checks right control signals has answered from the CP system software. In the display function of the terminal operator, there is not only the function which display the control signals by event-oriented MSC/PR. The terminal operator has the function which display the watch condition of the switching system and display the real terminal action. As these various display formats, testing for beginners who is not well versed in control signals can test easily.

When control signal which had answered is not right, action of the CP system software is a problem. In this case, the testing person analyze the CP system software by using the ICE and modify the CP system software. When the testing person analyzing the CP system software, the testing person execute the CP system software on the switching system. For this reason, analyzing the CP system software is difficult and inefficient. In order to settle this problem, the testing person execute the CP system software on the machine-language instruction simulator which can execute by work station (WS) in recent days, and the testing person analyzes the CP system software in a source code level by using a symbolic debugger. In this method, a execution speed is late about 400 times from 80 doubles of the switching system. For this reason, it is applied to only an initial stage of the CP system software unit test. The execution speed of WS is higher from now on, this method can apply to a whole stage of the CP system software unit test.

When the stage of the CP system software unit test is advanced, it moves to the stage which confirms the test items which has been planned beforehand. Contents of the test items are the interface specification which aimed at functional confirmation. The confirmation process of test item is described by a sequence of the control signals. The testing person transmits control signals in accordance with a sequence of the confirmation process by using the terminal operator. By this operation, the testing person can confirms correctness of a sequence of control signals between the terminals and the CP system software. The testing person uses MSC/GR concerning a design stage of the CP system software. It is effective to use the viewer which display a sequence of control signals by MSC/GR. By a former test, a sequence has been formed of a dump of control signals by a hand. When lots of terminals appear in the confirmation process, lots of instance is needed. For this reason, the testing person was spending lots of time on the work which is converted into a sequence. By using the viewer, it can be converted mechanically and fast. Moreover, a difference with a last executed result can be also confirmed by a look by a sequence. By these, job efficiency can be improved.

However, even though a executed result dose not coincide with the confirmation process in fact, it is sometimes regarded as normal action. This is generated by control signal which is transmitted to a terminal regularly and a functional of executing priority in the CP system software inside. Regression test by the test scenarios is supporting this spot and can compare it rightly. Since the life cycle of the CP system software is too long. While a version up is repeated, the CP system software is used. The CP system software which was applied this time, it positioned at the beginning of a life cycle. For this reason, a regression test by the test scenarios is scheduled mainly to end by accumulative work of the test scenarios. At the time of a next version up of the CP system software, though it is supposed that effect of regression test appears sufficiently, the stage which can be still valued has not been reached.

6. Conclusion

This paper has introduced the switching software test environment as the environment for supporting the CP system software unit test. The following items have been implemented by applying MSC/PR to the test environment:

- Mutual conversion between event-oriented MSC/PR and control signals
- Real-time conversion from event-oriented MSC/PR into MSC/GR
- Automatic regression tests using recorded event-oriented MSC/PR

As a result, the test environment can be configured easily with improvement of the testing job efficiency. It has especially been confirmed that event-oriented MSC/PR is effective for a real-time system.

REFERENCES

1. Z.120(1993). Message Sequence Chart(MSC). ITU-T, Sep. 1994.
2. P.A.J.Tilanus. A formalisation of Message Sequence Charts, SDL'91 Evolving Methods, Sep. 1991.
3. E.Rudolph, P.Graubmann, J.Grabowaki. Tutorial on Message Sequence Charts, SDL'95 with MSC in CASE Tutorials 95.09.25, Sep. 1995.
4. A.Ek. Event-Oriented Textual Syntax TD44(Question 9/10), ITU-T Study Group 10 Meeting Geneva, Oct. 1994.

SDL '97: TIME FOR TESTING - SDL, MSC and Trends
A. Cavalli and A. Sarma (Editors)

Deriving an SDL Specification with a Given Architecture from a Set of MSCs

Gabriel Robert[a1], Ferhat Khendek[b2], Peter Grogono[a]

[a] *Department of Computer Science*

[b] *Department of Electrical and Computer Engineering*

Concordia University

1455, De Maisonnneuve Blvd. W. Montreal(Quebec), Canada H3G 1M8

Abstract

We introduce a new synthesis approach which allows the systematic derivation of SDL processes from a set of MSCs. Our approach takes explicitly into account the architecture of the target SDL specification and ensures, by construction, consistency between the SDL specification and the MSC specification. Furthermore, the SDL specification we generate is free of deadlocks. In this paper, we also discuss future extensions of our approach.

1. INTRODUCTION

The development of distributed systems goes through many phases. The initial phase, requirement analysis and specification, determines the functional and non-functional requirements in a specification with a high level of abstraction. This specification describes the required functionality of the system, but not how to realize it. In the design phase, the system development starts with an abstract specification of the design which is then refined step by step towards the implementation which is finally tested before its deployment .

Formal description techniques (FDTs) play an increasingly important role in the development life cycle of distributed systems, especially telecommunication systems. FDTs were developed to ensure unambiguous, concise, complete and consistent specification of the system under development. FDTs allow for partial or total automatization of many analysis and synthesis activities in the development life cycle. From the formal specification of the user requirements to the implementation, activities such as the validation of the design specification against formal specification of requirements and the verification of the design specification, stepwise refinement of formal specifications towards implementation, test case generation from the formal specification, etc. are at least partially automatized. Developers rely on different tools implementing these different activities for the development of distributed systems.

Among the standardized FDTs, SDL (Specification and Description Language) [7] and MSC (Message Sequencing Charts) [8] are widely used within the telecommunication

[1]Partially supported by the National Sciences and Engineering Research Council of Canada (NSERC).
[2]Partially supported by Concordia University (FRDP) and NSERC.

systems community. MSCs which capture explicitly the interactions and the message exchange between processes in the system and the environment are suitable at the requirement stage and as a basis for test case development. SDL is used at the design stage for the description of the functional behavior and the architecture of the target system. The MSC and SDL specifications of a given system are often developed independently from each other. In order to ensure consistency between requirement stage and design stage, the SDL specification has to be validated against the set of MSCs given at the requirements stage.

Instead of validating the behavior of the SDL specification against the set of MSCs, we introduce in this paper a synthesis approach which allows the systematic derivation of the SDL descriptions of the processes from a set of MSCs and a given SDL architecture of the system. Our synthesis approach ensures, by construction, consistency between the SDL specification and the MSC specification; no further validation is required. We adopt trace inclusion for the semantic consistency, also called correctness of the SDL specification. In other words, an SDL specification is consistent with a set of MSCs if and only if the the set of traces defined by the MSCs are included in the set of traces allowed by the SDL specification. Furthermore, the SDL specification that we generate is free of deadlocks.

In order to translate MSCs into SDL specification, we take into account the MSC and SDL formal semantics. During the last few years, this formal semantics of MSC and SDL as well as techniques for systematic derivation of state transition oriented specifications from a set of MSCs have been addressed [1, 16, 2, 13, 14]. In this paper, we also comment on these issues.

The remainder of the paper is structured as follows. Section 2 discusses the issues to consider in deriving SDL specifications from MSCs, such as MSC formal semantics. Section 3 introduces our approach, describes the algorithm and illustrates it with an example. Finally, in Section 4, we discuss future extensions and related work, before concluding.

2. ISSUES ON TRANSLATING MSC TO SDL

In this section, we introduce briefly the MSC and SDL languages and discuss their respective semantics, especially the MSC constructs for message exchange, the "`out` *msg* `to` *dest*" and the "`in` *msg* `from` *sender*", and the related SDL constructs, `input` and `output`. For our purpose, in the rest of the paper, we will refer to these two types of constructs, either by their construct name, or generically, as *input* and *output* events.

SDL

An SDL system is represented as a structure of blocks which may be decomposed recursively into subblocks, until the basic components, namely processes, are reached. Blocks are interconnected through channels. Processes communicate through signalroutes. Communication between processes is asynchronous. SDL allows for multiple signalroutes (channels) between processes (blocks), in each direction. However, each SDL process has a single FIFO queue for arriving messages, regardless of the source. Messages sent to a process P_i by different processes are merged into P_i single input queue, in the order of their arrivals.

The behavior of an SDL system is defined by the parallel composition of the behaviors of the process instances in the system. The process behavior is described by a diagram which is an extension of the extended finite state machine model. A process is modeled as a set of states and transitions connecting the states. Each transition consists of a series of actions, such as local actions, procedure calls, timer set and reset, signal output, etc. An SDL process, in a given state, initiates a transition by consuming an expected signal from its input queue. An input signal which is not mentioned in a state (a signal which does not initiate any transition) is implicitly consumed by the process. In this case, the signal is simply discarded and the process remains in the same state. This implicit consumption of signals may lead to a deadlock situation in successive states where the signal is needed in order to progress. In order to retain signals in the queue for later consumption, SDL provides a **save** construct. In a given state, signals mentioned in a **save** are neither removed from the queue nor consumed in that state. In other words, the **save** construct is used to change the order of signal consumption. For instance, in Figure 1, the message x is consumed, but if either y, z, or w is present, it is saved for consumption at a later step.

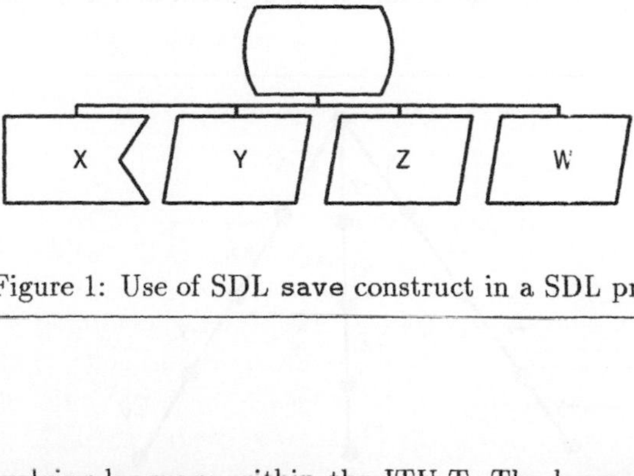

Figure 1: Use of SDL **save** construct in a SDL process

MSC

MSC is still an evolving language within the ITU-T. The language, like SDL, has two equivalent forms: a graphical form: MSC/GR, and a textual representation: MSC/PR. In this paper, we will use the graphical representations of both MSC and SDL. The recent MSC draft standard has introduced the high level MSCs, where MSCs can be composed using a set of operators [8]. In this paper, we focus on the basic MSCs (bMSC) which consist, graphically, of a set of axes (see Figure 2). Each axis represents one process and is delimited by a start and end symbol. Processes exchange messages asynchronously and in pairwise manner. In the graphical representation, message exchanges are represented by arrows where the tail corresponds to the output event and the head corresponds to the reception event. In Figure 2, for instance, we have three processes, P_1, P_2 and P_3. Process P_1 sends message x to P_2, P_3 sends message y to P_2 and P_2 consumes messages x and y. Events in a given axis are totally ordered. For instance, in Figure 2, consumption of x by process P_2 occurs earlier in time than consumption of y. The output event of a given message always precedes its input (for instance, the sending of x by P_1 precedes the reception of x by P_2). However, there is no order between the sending of message x by P_1 and message y by P_3.

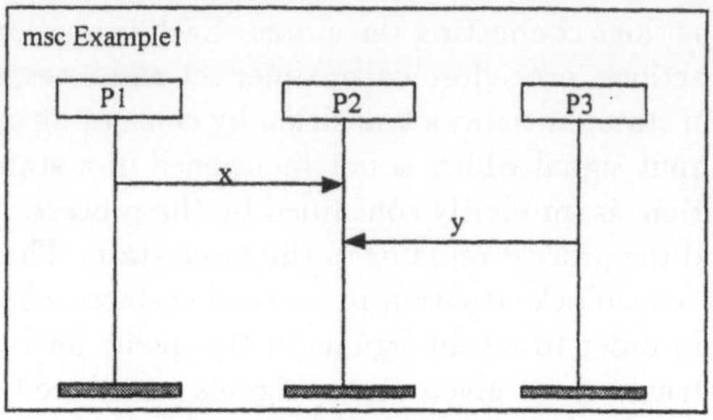

Figure 2: Example of basic MSC

The behavior of a bMSC is defined as a set of traces of output and input events [16, 13, 14]. These semantics are based on the output events and consumptions by the processes. For instance, the tree in Figure 3 represents the behavior defined by the bMSC of Figure 2. Notice that, in Figure 3, a "+" stands for an input event and a "–" stands for an output event.

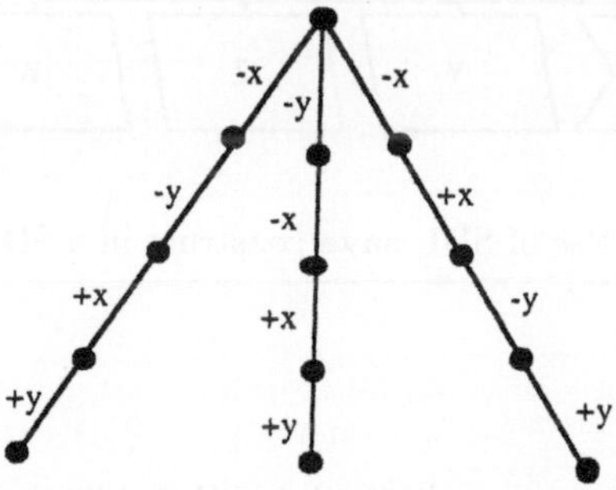

Figure 3: Behavior defined by the bMSC in Figure 2

A bMSC specifies the required order of sending and consumptions of messages, but not the actual arrival order into the input queue of each process. The actual ordering of the arrival of the messages depends on the architecture of the system and on the interleaving of the processes. While translating a bMSC into an SDL specification with a given architecture, we have to take into account the actual arrival order of signals into the input queue of each process and not discard from the input queue signals which are expected in successive states.

For instance, in Figure 2, when P_2 is ready to consume message x, the process FIFO queue may have the following contents: (we show the head of the process queue – next element to consume – at the left)

(i) The process queue is empty.
(ii) The process queue contains x.
(iii) The process queue contains y.
(iv) The process queue contains x, y.
(v) The process queue contains y, x.

In the context of translating the reception into SDL, case 1 causes no problem since the SDL process will simply wait until a message arrives. Cases 2 and 4 also cause no problem since we will consume the expected message x, which is at the head of the queue. However, cases 3 and 5, will cause a problem since SDL will simply discard the message y. This loss will prevent the process P_2 from ever reaching completion. In order to deal with this case, we can use the `save` construct in SDL to save message y if it is present and consume it at a later stage.

Consistency and Design Errors

During the development life cycle, an SDL specification has to be verified against the general properties that any distributed system specification should satisfy. Among these general properties, deadlocks (all the queues in the system are empty and there is no possible progress for any process) are of particular interest in this paper. In the area of communication protocols, analysis techniques have been developed and applied to detect design errors like deadlocks, unspecified receptions, or non-executable interactions. The best-known approach seems to be reachability analysis, usually based on the specification of protocol entities as finite state automata (see for instance [3]). Because the analysis of a sufficiently complex distributed system specification usually reveals some of the above design errors, the specification has to be revised and the analysis to be repeated until no more errors are found.

On the other hand, the absence of design errors does not ensure the semantic consistency of the specification. In order to verify its semantic consistency, a specification has to be validated against the user requirements or compared with another specification which has been validated against the user requirements. In this paper, we assume that the MSC specification has been validated against the user requirements and used as a reference for the semantic consistency of the SDL specification. Since MSCs define partial behaviors only, we say that an SDL specification is semantically consistent with respect to an MSC, if and only if the set of traces defined by the MSC are included in the set of traces of the SDL specification. This definition of semantic consistency of an SDL specification with respect to an MSC has been used first by Nahm [17]. However, the trace inclusion as a semantic relation between specifications has been in use for many years in the communication protocols domain.

3. APPROACH

For clarity of presentation, we present our approach with a single bMSC as input. We also use the term `channel` to refer to SDL `channels` and `signalroutes`. Later, in Section 4, we discuss how the approach can be generalized to more complex cases (full MSC language, multiple MSCs, etc). Basically, our approach consists of generating all the possible message interleavings that are allowed for a given bMSC, under a given SDL architecture. For instance, if there is a single channel from process P_1 to P_2, the messages sent by P_1 will arrive in the same order at P_2. On the other hand, if each message is sent through a separate channel, the order of arrival of the messages will be undetermined.

In order to build these interleavings, the algorithm must first determine the ordering of the events in time, which can be done by analyzing the constraints described by the bMSC. Once the order is established, the interleavings of messages are determined by maintaining data structures keeping the relative order of messages. Finally, after these structures has been built for all the processes and all the output events, the algorithm is able to generate SDL code to handle all the possible orders of arrival, by using the `save` construct discussed above.

In the next sections, we will describe the keypoints of our algorithm in more detail:

- Architecture of the system;
- Ordering of the events;
- Channel queue occupancy table;
- Using the SDL `save` construct to prevent deadlocks.

Architecture of the system

In our approach, the architecture of the system for which we will generate SDL specifications is given in SDL. Figures 5 and 6 give examples of two such descriptions. In order to be able to derive specifications from bMSC, the bMSC and the SDL architecture must obviously be "consistent", in terms of process types described and channels available (for example, the bMSC does not attempt to send a message between two processes that are not connected). We define this *architectural consistency* as follows:

(i) For each process instance described in the MSC there is a corresponding process type in the SDL architecture.

(ii) Each message described in the MSC is enumerated in the SDL architecture (on a `channel` statement) connecting the sending instance and the receiving one.

These two requirements ensure that the architecture given is sufficient to implement the scenario given in the bMSC. If not, the user would simply be informed of the discrepancy. Notice that we are not using SDL implicit definitions of channels and signalroutes. ¿From now on, we will assume that the bMSC and the SDL architecture are consistent.

Ordering of the MSC events

To order the events in the bMSC, we start by sequentially numbering the events (input and output) from e_1 to e_N, where N is the total number of events in all the MSC instances. We define a transitive relation *earlier* that we denote by $\ll$. We will write " $e_i \ll e_j$ " if event e_i occurs earlier in time than e_j.

According to [8], an MSC describes a time ordering of the events by two rules:

(i) In each MSC instance, the events are totally ordered: if the event e_1 is described before e_2 (in MSC/PR) or is "above" e_2 (in MSC/PR), event e_1 occurs *earlier* than e_2.

(ii) The MSC sending of a message occurs earlier than its reception.

It is possible to enumerate all the order relations that are described by the MSC. Further, since the order relation is transitive, it is possible to determine the closure of the relation. This gives us the ordering between the events: for any two events e_i, e_j, we can have only one of the three possible relations:

- $e_i \ll e_j$
- $e_j \ll e_i$
- e_i and e_j are not ordered in time with respect to each other.

Table 2 gives the transitive closure of the partial orders corresponding to the MSC diagram of Figure 4.

Channel Queues Occupancy Table

For any two processes P_i and P_j, the SDL architecture defines the channels connecting P_i and P_j and the messages they can carry. Assuming that we have m such channels in one direction (from i to j), we number them from $C_{i,j,1}$ to $C_{i,j,m}$. Likewise, if there are n channels in the reverse direction, we will number them from $C_{j,i,1}$ to $C_{j,i,n}$. However, SDL defines a single FIFO queue for all the inputs of a process. Therefore, all the $C_{j,i,x}$, for all values of j, and x (from 1 to n), will contribute in filling the process queue of process P_i. In order to maintain the relative order of the messages in the process queue, the algorithm represents the process queue of process P_i as a set of FIFO channel queues: $(Q_{j,i,x})$, corresponding to the incoming channels to P_i, for all values of j and x. Further, the contents of each of these channel queues are maintained over time. Conceptually, the algorithm maintains a table like table 1, for each process.

The table has as many columns as there are channels coming from other processes, and each column represents the FIFO queue that we associate with the channel. The rows of the table are the input events in the MSC of the process P_i (we are only interested in maintaining the table for the input events). This table will be filled by inspecting all the outputs and propagating the messages in the queues of all applicable input events. When the process will be completed, the possible contents of every queue will be known at every moment, enabling us to generate the proper SDL save statements. Tables 3 and 4 show the contents of the channels across time for our two test cases.

Event	Input Message	$Q_{1,i,1}$	$Q_{i,i,2}$	...	$Q_{j,i,n}$
...					
e_x	a	x, y, z	a, b	...	r, s, t
...					

Table 1: Channel Occupancy Table Format

Using the SDL save construct to prevent deadlocks

In order to avoid deadlocks, the algorithm uses the SDL **save** construct to keep messages in the process queue. The algorithm generates a **save** only when it is required, as shown in Figures 7 and 8. In other words, our approach generates a **save** only for signals that may be in the process queue because of the interleaving and which are needed in successive states. In the first figure, a **save** is not generated for the message y at time e_3 since it is known that y follows x in the FIFO channel. Any of the other messages (z, w) can be earlier than x in the global FIFO queue if SDL, but y cannot be. However, in the second figure, a **save** is generated since x and y are sent through separate channels.

Basic Algorithm

In this section, we describe our algorithm using pseudocode. As introduced previously, we use e_x to denote events and P_y to denote processes.

```
1. check the SDL architecture and the MSC for architectural consistency,
and build the required data structures.
2. number each event uniquely.
3. build the transitive closure of the ordering of the events

4. /* fill the receive queues */
for each instance P_i in the MSC diagram
    for each out event e_s, sending message m to instance P_j
        find the related input event e_r in instance P_j
        for each in event e_k, in instance P_j
            if not(e_k ≪ e_s) ∧ not(e_r ≪ e_k)
                add message m to the appropriate receiving queue
            end
        end
    end
end

5. /* generate the SDL code */
for each instance P_i in the MSC diagram
    for each event e_j
```

```
        if the event is an out generate a SDL output
        else if the event is an in of message m
                generate a SDL input of message m
                for each receive queue of P_i (except the queue to which m belongs)
                    generate a SDL save for all the messages in the queue.
                end
        end
    end
end
```

Notice that the association between the output event e_s and its associated input e_r is immediate in the graphical MSC representation, but not necessarily obvious in the textual representation. In MSC/GR, each message sent is associated with a specific message reception, corresponding to the arrowhead. If the same message appears at various places in the MSC, the MSC/GR representation will always indicate what is the intended reception. However, this information will be lost in MSC/PR. With this representation, we will know, for instance, that there are two transmissions of message x, and two receptions, but we cannot say which reception corresponds to which transmission. This raises semantic questions: are the two messages x, two instances of the same message, or two different messages? This difference between MSC/PR and MSC/GR is discussed in [14] and [15].
Our algorithm is guaranteed to terminate and the step that dominates the running time of algorithm is the transitive closure required to order the events, which can be done in time $O(N^3)$ with known algorithms (e.g.: Floyd/Warshall), where N is the number of events in the bMSC. Alur *et al.* [1] also describe a modified algorithm that can be used to perform this step in $O(N^2)$.

Example

In this section, we will illustrate the algorithm with two examples. We use the same bMSC in both examples, but two different architectures are used, to illustrate the workings of the algorithm.
In the first architecture description (Figure 5) there is only one channel from P_1 to P_2 and only one from P_3 to P_2.
In the second case (Figure 6), there are two channels between P_1 and P_2 and two channels between P_3 and P_2, i.e.: there is a separate channel for each message. In this situation, we can not assume any ordering between the message arrivals and SDL `save` have to be generated for every possible message interleaving.
The algorithm starts by numbering the events from e_1 to e_8 as was already shown in Figure 4. In order to determine the ordering, we start by using the fact that each MSC instance is totally ordered, giving the following order relations:

$$
\begin{array}{llll}
(P_1) & & e_1 \ll e_2 & \\
(P_2) & e_3 \ll e_4 \,; & e_4 \ll e_5 \,; & e_5 \ll e_6 \,; \\
(P_3) & & e_7 \ll e_8 &
\end{array}
$$

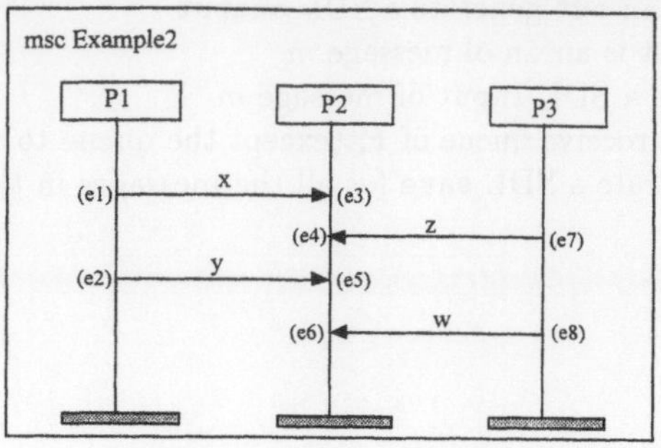

Figure 4: Example bMSC

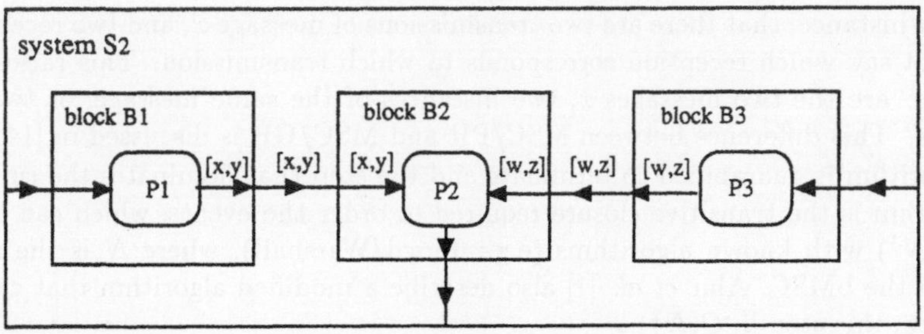

Figure 5: SDL architecture 'A'

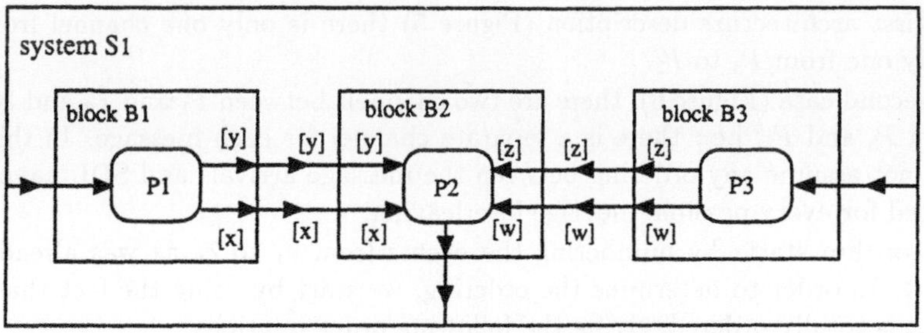

Figure 6: SDL architecture 'B'

Further, since every out precedes its in, we also have the following relations:

$$e_1 \ll e_3 \,; \quad e_7 \ll e_4 \,; \quad e_2 \ll e_5 \,; \quad e_8 \ll e_6 \,;$$

By working the transitive closure of the previous relations, we obtain the Table 2, where a **T** in matrix element (e_i, e_j) indicates that $e_i \ll e_j$.

	e_1	e_2	e_3	e_4	e_5	e_6	e_7	e_8
e_1		T	T	T	T	T		
e_2					T	T		
e_3				T	T	T		
e_4					T	T		
e_5						T		
e_6								
e_7				T	T	T		T
e_8						T		

Table 2: Transitive closure of the order relations

We now proceed to fill the channel queues occupancy table by examining each output event in turn. In the following, we apply our algorithm for the derivation of process P_2 specification only, since it is the only receiving process in this example and the application of the algorithm for the other processes is straightforward. We start by e_1, which sends message x to P_2. Since the associated input is e_3, we have $e_s \equiv e_1$ (output event) and $e_r \equiv e_3$ (input event). We then examine each of the input events of P_2 (e_3, e_4, e_5, e_6) to determine whether message x must be added to the the channel queue. It will be added if it is possible for the message to be in the process queue at the time of the input, i.e.: if the time of the input (e_3) is not earlier than the time of the output (e_s), and not later than the time of the consumption of the message (e_r). For e_1, it gives:

(i) $\text{not}(e_3 \ll e_s) \wedge \text{not}(e_r \ll e_3)$ is true: add x to the appropriate FIFO queue of event e_3.
(ii) $\text{not}(e_4 \ll e_s) \wedge \text{not}(e_r \ll e_4)$ is false: do not add x to the queue of event e_4
(iii) $\text{not}(e_5 \ll e_s) \wedge \text{not}(e_r \ll e_5)$ is false: do not add x to the queue of event e_5
(iv) $\text{not}(e_6 \ll e_s) \wedge \text{not}(e_r \ll e_6)$ is false: do not add x to the queue of event e_6

By repeating the process for each output (e_2, e_7, e_8), we obtain Table 3, which gives the contents of the channel queues for P_2 (it is the only receiving process in this example):

In case 2, where there are four channels (each message goes through its own channel), the channels occupancy table is given in Table 4.

The contents of the table are then used to generate the appropriate SDL specifications of the processes. In case 1, we generate for process P_2 the SDL code of Figure 7. Notice that, we need to generate a save for both messages z and w since it is entirely possible that both z and w arrive before x in the FIFO queue of the process P_2. For case 2, the

Event	Input Message	$Q_{1,2,1}$	$Q_{3,2,1}$
e_3	x	x, y	z, w
e_4	z	y	z, w
e_5	y	y	w
e_6	w		w

Table 3: Channels Occupancy Table for Architecture 'A'

Event	Input Message	$Q_{1,2,1}$	$Q_{1,2,2}$	$Q_{3,2,1}$	$Q_{3,2,2}$
e_3	x	x	y	z	w
e_4	z		y	z	w
e_5	y		y		w
e_6	w				w

Table 4: Channels Occupancy Table for Architecture 'B'

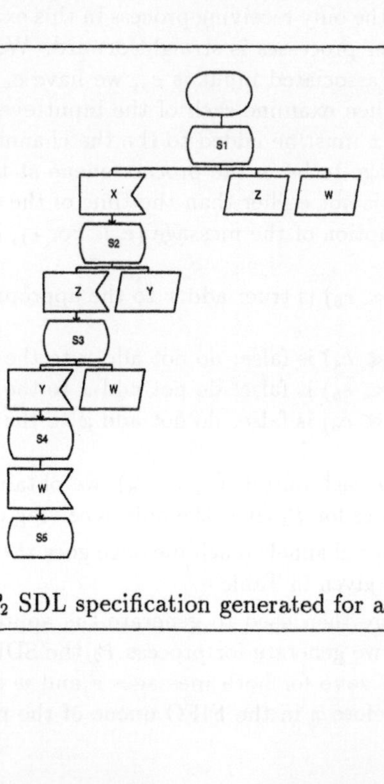

Figure 7: P_2 SDL specification generated for architecture 'A'

algorithm generates additional `saves` for messages y and w at e_1 and e_2 respectively, since we can no longer assume that y will always follow x (or w, z). The code is shown in Figure 8.

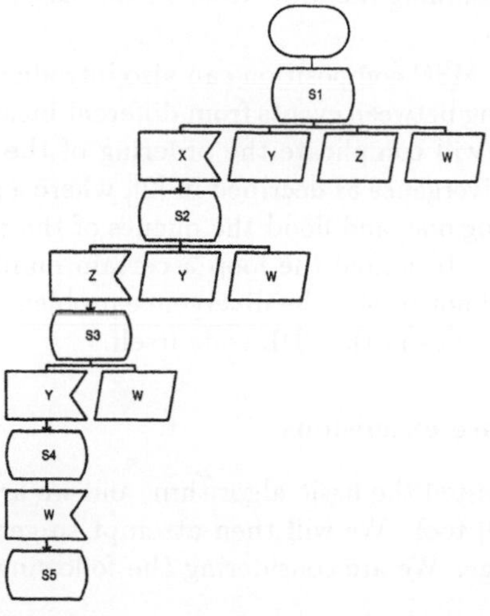

Figure 8: P_2 SDL specification generated for architecture 'B'

4. DISCUSSION

The algorithm described above, given our assumptions, will generate SDL specifications free of deadlocks by construction. Further, the generated SDL will be semantically consistent with the MSC.

The above algorithm only applies to basic MSCs. In order to extend it, some generalizations cause no difficulties. For example,

- MSC `timer` and `action` translate directly into their equivalent SDL construct as well as the MSC instance termination
- MSC process creation also translates easily. However, the action introduces one more element of ordering: the creation of a process will always occur before the initial step of the created process. This would need to be taken into account in the ordering step.
- MSC coregions and partial orderings could be handled by explicitly generating all the possible permutations of events within the coregion. However, this may lead to the distributed choice problem discussed below.

On the other hand, other generalizations introduce problems that need to be addressed. The use of MSC inline expressions like `alt` can introduce a distributed choice which may lead to the well known problem of collision when translated into SDL or any state transition based specification. The distributed choice defined by the MSC cannot be implemented in SDL in a distributed manner. The same problem can arise when translating service specifications into protocol specifications as pointed out in [12] and later by [14, 2] in the context of MSCs. However, we believe that we can determine easily the presence of a distributed choice by examining the MSC tree. In this case, the algorithm will notify the user and terminate.

The use of conditions and/or MSC composition can also introduce cycles, as can the `loop` construct of MSC. Interleaving between events from different incarnations will be possible. These possible interleavings will complicate the ordering of the MSC events. This may also lead to the problem of divergence as decribed in [2], where a sending process may run much faster than the receiving one, and flood the queues of the receiver. To handle these cycles, one approach could be to unfold the loop a certain number of times, as done by Alur *et al.* [1], but this would not resolve the divergence problem. Our preferred approach would be to implement the cycles in the SDL code itself.

Implementation and future extensions

We have implemented and tested the basic algorithm, and we are currently interfacing it with the ObjectGEODE [19] tool. We will then attempt to generalize the algorithm to handle the full MSC language. We are considering the following algorithm, but we have not yet implemented it.

(i) Process the architecture table as above.
(ii) Merge the MSCs to obtain a single MSC "tree" for each process, describing the total ordering within each process.
  - Coregions would be replaced by explicit enumeration of the possible permutations within `alt` boxes.
  - Global states (and partial global states) would be taken into consideration (as synchronizing points).
  - Cycles (MSC `loop` construct, or cycles resulting from composition with conditions) would be translated in SDL cycles, or, alternatively, unfolded a certain number of times.

(iii) Number each event uniquely.
(iv) Examine each MSC tree for the non-local choice problem.
(v) Establish the transitive closeure of the ordering between the events, based on the partial orderings of each tree, and on the additional MSC semantics.
(vi) Build the channels occupancy table.
(vii) Generate the SDL code.

We are also working on an incremental approach which consists of deriving an initial SDL specification from a single MSC and a given SDL architecture. This initial SDL specification is then enriched by new MSCs in an incremental manner following the merging approaches introduced in [10, 11].

On the other hand, the SDL process specifications we generate have to be structured using the `service` and `procedure` concepts in SDL.

Related work

Although there has been much work on the subject of protocol synthesis (for a survey see [18]), and work on translating from MSC to other languages (for instance [15, 5]), we are aware of only a few papers dealing specifically with conversion from MSCs to SDL.

Ito *et al.* [6] performs translation from MSCs to SDL by translating the MSCs into an intermediate representation as a state diagram (a finite state machine) and applying a component-based synthesis algorithm from [9] to complete the missing transitions. The authors generate a protocol free from errors, but they do not seem to conform to the semantics of the MSCs for composition, defined in [8] as the application of the `alt` operator. Their algorithm generates SDL `input` statements at any point in time where a message may appear, regardless of the allowable ordering of events defined by the MSCs. Also, the architecture of the target system is not taken into account. From our understanding, they assume a "flat architecture" where they have a single channel between each pair of communicating processes.

The work by Holzmann [4] and Alur *et al.* [1] is much closer to our work in that they take the channels architecture into account. However, they are not attempting to generate SDL specifications: instead, they develop an interactive design tool that warns the user of any possible race condition resulting from conflicts between the order assumed by the user from the MSC diagram, and the actual enforced order that be allowed under a given channel architecture. In our case, we handle these "race" conditions while generating an SDL specification that implements the MSC requirements.

Finally, many authors have worked on the semantics of the MSC diagrams and the various problems that exist in their interpretation [16, 2, 13, 14].

5. CONCLUSION

In this paper we introduced a novel approach for the synthesis of a consistent and deadlock free SDL specification from an MSC. We take into account the architecture of the target system. For different architectures, we obtain different SDL process specifications in general. We subscribe to the formal semantics of the MSC language. Our approach is based on the ordering of the messages in the MSC and on maintaining the relative order of messages. We have implemented the basic algorithm and are working on extending it to more general cases.

Our work is still in progress, we are working on an incremental approach that will handle full MSC. We are also developing a tool implementing our approach.

References

[1] Rajeev Alur, Gerard J. Holzmann, and Doron Peled. An analyzer for message sequence charts. In *Proceedings TACAS '96*, pages 35–48. Springer-Verlag, 1996.

[2] Hanene Ben-Abdallah and Stefan Leue. Syntactic analysis of message sequence chart specifications. Technical Report 96-12, University of Waterloo, November 1996.

[3] Gerard Holzmann. *Design and Validation of Computer Protocols.* Prentice-Hall, 1991.

[4] Gerard J. Holzmann. Early fault detection tools. In *Proceedings TACAS 96*, pages 1–13. Springer-Verlag, 1996.

[5] Haruhisa Ichikawa, Makasi Itoh, and Masahi Shibasaki. Protocol-oriented service specifications and their transformation into CCITT specification and description language. *The Transactions of the IECE of Japan*, E 69(4):524–534, April 1986.

[6] Atsushi Ito, Hironori Saito, Fumio Nitta, and Yoshiaki Kakuda. Transformation technique between specification in SDL and specification in message sequence charts for designing protocol specificatons. In *ICC 92*, pages 442–447. IEEE, 1992.

[7] ITU-T Z.100. Recommendation Z.100. specification and description language (SDL). Technical report, ITU-T, 1993.

[8] ITU-T Z.120. Recommendation Z.120. message sequence chart (MSC). Technical report, ITU-T, 1996.

[9] Yoshiaki Kakuda and Yasuhi Wakahara. Component-based synthesis of protocols for unlimited number of processes. In *Proceedings of COMPSAC87*, pages 721–730. Computer Society of IEEE, 1987.

[10] Ferhat Khendek and Gregor v. Bochmann. Incremental construction approach for distributed system specifications. In *Int. Symposium on Formal Description Techniques: FORTE'93*, pages 87–102. North-Holland, 1994.

[11] Ferhat Khendek and Gregor v. Bochmann. Merging behavior specifications. *Formal Methods In System Design*, 6(3):259–294, June 1995.

[12] Ferhat Khendek, Gregor v. Bochmann, and C. Kant. New results on deriving protocol specifications from service specifications. In *Communication Architectures and Protocols: ACM SIGCOMM'89*, pages 136–145. ACM, 1989.

[13] Peter B. Ladkin and Stefan Leue. An analysis of message sequence charts. Technical Report IAM 92-013, Univeristy of Berne, IIAM, June 1992.

[14] Peter B. Ladkin and Stefan Leue. Four issues concerning the semantics of message flow graphs. In D. Hogrefe and S. Leue, editors, *Proceedings of the Seventh International Conference on Formal Description Techniques.* Chapman and Hall, 1995.

[15] Stefan Leue and Peter B. Ladkin. Implementing and verifying scenario-based specifications using promela/xspin. In *The Second SPIN Workshop, Rutgers University*, 1996.

[16] S. Mauw. The formalization of message sequence charts. *Computer Networks and ISDN Systems*, (28):1643–1657, 1996.

[17] Robert Nahm. Consistency analysis of message sequence charts and SDL-Systems. In *SDL '91, Evolving Methods*, pages 261–271. Elsevier Science Publishers B. V. (North-Holland), 1991.

[18] Robert L. Probert and Kassem Saleh. Synthesis of communication protocols: survey and assessment. *IEEE Transactions on Computers*, 40(4):468–475, April 1991.

[19] Verilog. Objectgeode. Technical report, Verilog, 1995.

SDL '97: TIME FOR TESTING - SDL, MSC and Trends
A. Cavalli and A. Sarma (Editors)

MSC'96 and Beyond - a Critical Look

Stefan Loidl, Ekkart Rudolph, Ursula Hinkel[a]

[a]Institut für Informatik, Technische Universität München, D-80290 München
{loidl,rudolphe,hinkel}@informatik.tu-muenchen.de

Deficiencies and inconsistencies within the semantics and graphical syntax of the new MSC'96 concepts are outlined. Problems in the combined use of language constructs, already contained in MSC'92, and the new concepts are discussed. Main goal is the exhibition of open questions and conflicts within the new MSC'96 standard and the presentation of possible solutions. Though already positive experiences have been gained with MSC'96 in the field of protocol specification and prototype implementation, the new concepts need further completion and semantic foundation in order to be successfully applicable in all parts.

1. INTRODUCTION

During the last ITU-study period, 1993 – 1996, Message Sequence Chart has advanced to a considerably powerful and expressive language [6]. Main emphasis has been put on the development of new structural concepts: generalized ordering, new formulation of instance decomposition, inline expression, MSC references, gates and High-level MSCs. In the following, only a brief outline of the new concepts is presented since the paper essentially is addressed to a readership which already is sufficiently familiar with the MSC language. A more extensive description of MSC'96 can be found in [4].

Generalized ordering constructs serve for the definition of general time orderings between MSC events. MSC'92 is restricted to total event ordering on MSC instances (normal case) and to complete unordering of the events contained within coregions. Since MSC instances may refer to higher level entities like, e.g. SDL blocks, language constructs for the specification of more general time orderings within one instance are demanded. The same refers to the event definition on decomposed instances. As a straightforward generalization, the coregion is enhanced by ordering relations graphically represented by special symbols, called connection lines, which denote the generalized time ordering in an intuitive manner. Events between different instances within MSC'92 are ordered merely via messages. However, on an early stage of requirement specification, one often abstracts from the internal message exchange while specifying the external behaviour only. On this level of abstraction, synchronisation constructs are demanded similarly to Time Sequence Diagrams which impose a time ordering between events attached to different instances. This kind of generalized ordering in MSC'96 again is defined by means of ordering relations graphically represented by connection lines between different instances.
Since MSCs can be rather complex, there is a need for a refinement of one instance by a set

of instances defined in another MSC. By means of *instance decomposition*, a refining MSC may be attached to an instance, which describes the events of the decomposed instance on a more detailed level. The refining MSC represents a decomposition of the instance without affecting its observable behaviour, i.e. it must be possible to map the messages leaving or entering the refining MSC to the messages of the decomposed instance. Thus, instance decomposition determines the transition between different levels of abstraction.
By means of *inline expressions*, composition of event structures may be defined inside an MSC. The composition operators *alt*, *par*, *loop*, *exc* and *opt* refer to alternative and parallel composition, iteration, exception and optional region. Graphically, the inline expression is described by a rectangle with dashed horizontal lines as separators. The operator keyword is placed in the left upper corner. Each section of an inline expression in principle again describes one MSC which represents a small trace segment. Thus, inline expressions are ideally suited for the comprehensive description of small variations of system runs.
MSC references are used to refer to other MSCs of the MSC document. The MSC references are objects of the type given by the referenced MSC. Each MSC reference points to another MSC which defines the meaning of the reference, i.e. the reference construct can be seen as a placeholder for an MSC diagram. MSC references may not only refer to a single MSC, but also to MSC reference expressions constructed by means of the operators *alt*, *par*, *seq*, *loop*, *opt*, *exc* and *subst*, and MSC references. By means of the *subst* operator a textual substitution inside the referenced MSC may be defined. Graphically an MSC reference is represented by a rectangle with rounded corners containing the name of the referenced MSC or an MSC expression.
Gates are used to define connection points for messages and order relations with respect to the interior and exterior of MSC references and inline expressions. Gates on inline expressions are merely transit points on the frame of the inline expression. A message gate name can be defined explicitly by a name associated with the gate on the frame or implicitly by the direction of the message through the gate and the message name.
High-level MSCs (HMSCs) provide a means to graphically define how a set of MSCs can be combined. The composition of MSCs specified by HMSCs can be guarded by conditions in the HMSCs. The conditions can be used to indicate global system states. An HMSC is a directed graph where each node is either a start symbol, an end symbol, an MSC reference, a condition, a connection point or a parallel frame. Contrary to plain MSCs, instances and messages are not shown within an MSC. This way, HMSCs can focus completely on the composition aspects. HMSCs are hierarchical in the sense that a reference again may refer to an HMSC.

These new MSC concepts have been stimulated essentially by two main streams of modern computer science: A major input for MSC'96 was provided by the development of a formal MSC semantics within the last ITU study period, based on process algebra ([10,9]). This has led quite naturally to an enhancement of MSC with composition mechanisms which now play a central role within inline expressions, MSC references with operator expressions and HMSCs. Object-oriented techniques have been equally influential, e.g. for the reuse of MSCs by means of MSC references and substitution ([3]). In this context, also the MSC based formalization of Use Cases, which play a central role within the method Objectory ([7]), has been a major stimulus and has contributed to the development of inline expressions and HMSCs. After this period of rapid and sometimes rather hectical development of new MSC concepts, naturally a period of consolidation has to follow. Most of the new concepts need further elaboration and, in particular, a precise formal foundation. Certainly, the elaboration of a formal semantics will promote the clarification of these language parts considerably. A corresponding standard document is in preparation which is developed along the same lines as the MSC'92 semantics and therefore again is based on process algebra. An outline of parts of the new semantics can be found in [11]. We do not aim to provide a formal definition for the semantics gaps pointed out within this paper. Main goal of this paper, which is based on a diploma thesis ([8]), carried out at Technical University of Munich and Corporate Research and Development of Siemens AG, is to exhibit the deficiencies discovered in MSC'96 and to discuss possible solutions.

2. GENERAL ORDERING RELATION

General ordering is used to describe the temporal order of two events, in case where this cannot be deduced from the ordering imposed by the instances and messages. In the graphical representation, two general ordering symbols are defined - a line symbol without arrow head (general ordering symbol 1) and a line symbol with an arrow head in the middle (general ordering symbol 2). For the ordering of two events attached to different instances only the general ordering symbol 2 is allowed. This symbol can have any orientation and also be bent.

2.1. Combined general ordering and messages

Messages and general ordering relations may cause confusions in the graphical representation. Beginning and ending points of messages and general ordering relations may lead to ambiguities, in case where a message sending event is connected to a general ordering symbol 2. This situation occurs if the message and/or the general ordering symbol crosses one or more instances (see figure 1). It is not obvious whether the message1 is sent from instance1 or instance2 and this applies also for message2 with regard to instance3 and instance4.

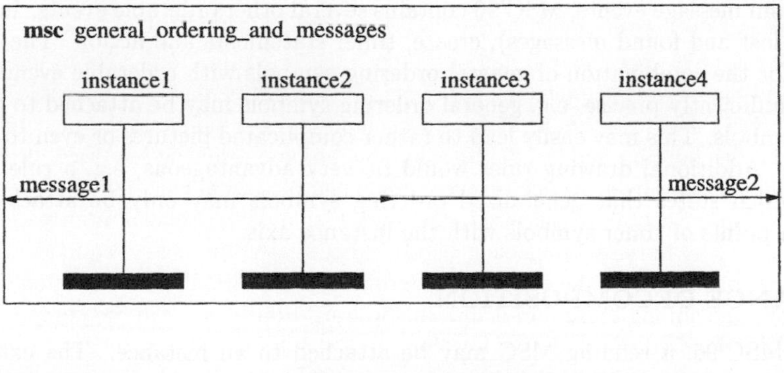

Figure 1. General ordering relation between two messages

Suggested solutions:

- In case, where the general ordering symbol is supposed to cross instances, several arrow heads may be attached to it in order to separate the ordering symbol from message line symbols (see figure 2). This solution does not demand a special arrangement of instances.
- Beginning and end of the general ordering symbol may be indicated by means of special symbols, e.g. semicircles. This solution has the same generality as the second one but needs additional symbols.

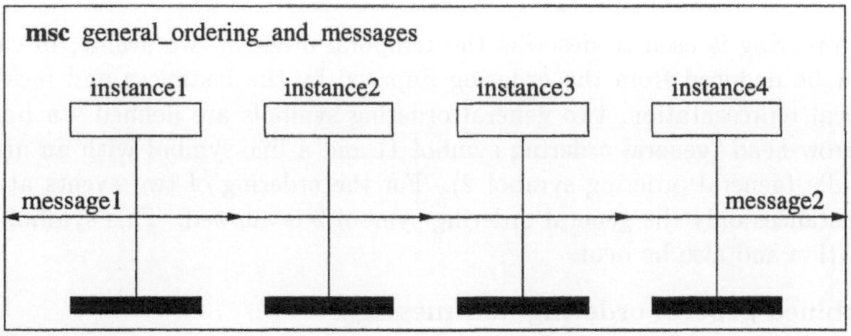

Figure 2. Representation of the general ordering relation with many arrow heads

2.2. Graphical representation of general ordering in combination with other orderable events

Apart from message events, MSC'96 contains several other orderable events: incomplete messages (lost and found messages), create, timer statements and action. The graphical grammar for the combination of general ordering symbols with orderable events appears to be not sufficiently precise, e.g. general ordering symbols may be attached to any point of timer symbols. This may easily lead to rather complicated pictures or even to misinterpretations. Additional drawing rules would be very advantageous, e.g. a rule for timer symbols which states that generalized ordering symbols may only be attached to the connection points of timer symbols with the instance axis.

3. INSTANCE DECOMPOSITION

Within MSC'96, a refining MSC may be attached to an instance. The external behaviour of the refining MSC defined by the messages entering and leaving the environment is formally related to the messages sent and consumed by the decomposed instance. No formal mapping is prescribed for other language constructs like conditions and actions.

3.1. Generalized ordering and instance decomposition

Generalized ordering relations between events on decomposed instances and events on other instances or gates are not excluded within MSC'96. Therefore, it seems to be natural to define a formal mapping between decomposed instances and refining MSCs also for general ordering relations in analogy to messages. However, the mapping is unclear in case where more than one general ordering relation are attached to one decomposed instance since no names are associated with general ordering relations. Since gates are not defined on decomposed instances also a mapping via gates is not possible (see figure 3).

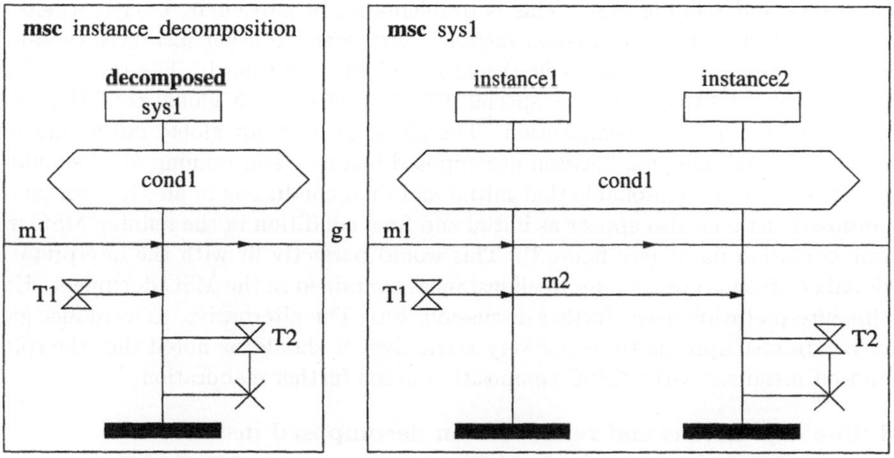

Figure 3. Instance decomposition with general ordering, timer and conditions

3.2. Timer and instance decomposition

Within MSC'96, no rules concerning the mapping of timer elements of a decomposed instance to timer elements in the refining MSC are defined. Timers, however, are essential constituents of the MSC'96 standard. One possible solution is to map each timer construct of a decomposed instance to a corresponding timer construct on one of the instances of the refining MSC. Together with the additional rule that correlated timer constructs, like timer setting and timeout of the same timer, have to be attached to the same instance within the refining MSC, a consistent mapping of timers for decomposed instances can be achieved.

3.3. Instance creation and instance stop in combination with instance decomposition

Within the MSC'96 standard, an instance may be created by a decomposed instance, however, this instance creation cannot be mapped consistently onto the refining MSC. In order to achieve such a formal mapping the standard has to be extended by including gates for instance creation events in addition to messages and general ordering relations. Otherwise, instance creation should be disallowed on decomposed instances.

Equally, it is not defined how the termination of decomposed instances by an instance stop - which is possible within MSC'96 - may be carried over to the refining MSC. Two solutions seem to be possible: Either all instances within the refining MSC have to stop or instance stop is disallowed on decomposed instances. A similar reasoning holds for the creation of decomposed instances.

3.4. Conditions on decomposed instances

Within MSC'96, there is also no formal mapping defined for conditions between decomposed instance and refining MSC. This is problematic, in particular, in case where the condition attached to the decomposed instance also refers to other instances (non-local condition) or even to all instances in the MSC (global condition). The case of global initial and final conditions deserves special attention since such global conditions play an important role for MSC composition. Therefore, at least for global initial and final conditions, a formal mapping between decomposed instance and refining MSC should be defined. It seems to be reasonable that initial and final conditions in an MSC containing a decomposed instance also appear as initial and final condition in the refining MSC with the same condition name (see figure 3). This would perfectly fit with the interpretation that global conditions always refer to all instances contained in the MSC document. However, this interpretation needs further discussion, too. The alternative, to introduce gates also for conditions, appears to be not very attractive. It should be noted that the role of decomposed instances within MSC composition needs further elaboration.

3.5. Inline expressions and references on decomposed instances

Within MSC'96, inline expressions and references must not be attached to decomposed instances. In practice, such a rule seems to be too restrictive. In particular, the use of MSC references without operator expressions in combination with decomposed instances is requested. E.g., related to SDL, it should be possible to attach references to instances of type block which may be further decomposed into refining MSCs containing instances of type process. Since decomposed instances refer to a vertical (de)composition and references or inline expressions to a horizontal (de)composition the combination seems to produce nontrivial problems. In full generality, this appears to be a challenging task for MSC2000.

4. INLINE EXPRESSIONS

Inline expressions introduced in MSC'96 contain several conflicting points: The textual and graphical grammar contain some inconsistencies and the semantics of some operators (*alt*, *opt*, *exc*, *loop*) is not sufficiently defined.

4.1. Inconsistencies of textual and graphical grammar

The textual grammar allows the use of instance creation, instance stop and the representation of instance beginning and instance end within inline expressions. Within the graphical grammar, instance stop and the beginning and end of instances are excluded inside an inline expression. A create event is not explicitly ruled out, however, this does not make sense without a new instance beginning. Apart from these inconsistencies, the use of instance creation and stop in connection with operator expressions leads to several semantic problems.

From that we conclude that for both, textual and graphical grammar, creation and stop as well as beginning and end of instances should be disallowed within inline expressions.

4.2. Inline expressions with gates

Inline expressions with message gates or general ordering gates can lead to problems. As an example (see figure 4), we take an optional region with a message 'm1' crossing an inline gate and being sent to the instance 'instance2'. Due to the optionality, it is possible that the message will not be sent from the inline expression and therefore also not be received by 'instance2' which causes a deadlock on 'instance2'. For an illustration, the semantics of the MSC 'opt_inline_expression' is modelled by a corresponding Petri net (condition event system, see [2]).

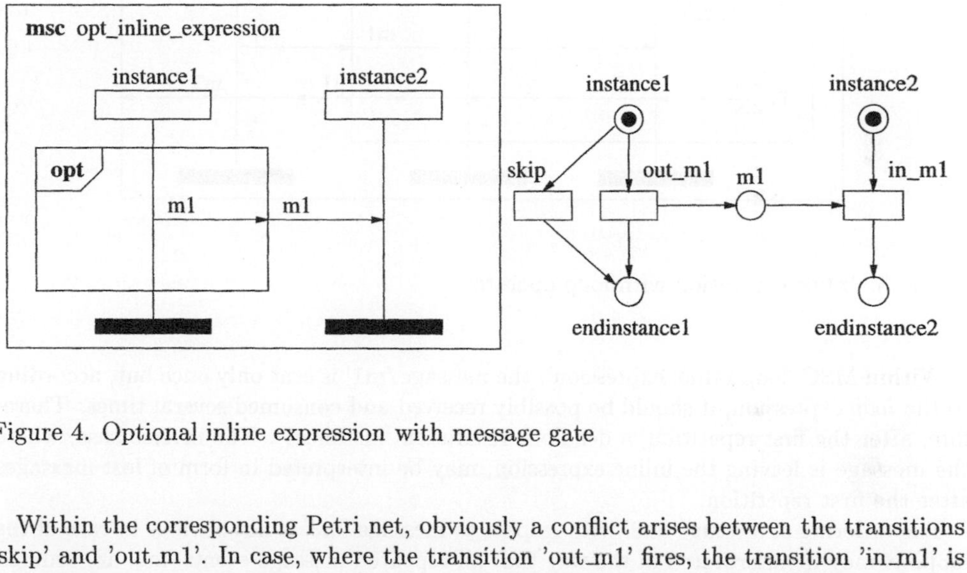

Figure 4. Optional inline expression with message gate

Within the corresponding Petri net, obviously a conflict arises between the transitions 'skip' and 'out_m1'. In case, where the transition 'out_m1' fires, the transition 'in_m1' is enabled and may fire. In case, where the transition 'skip' fires, the transition 'in_m1' is deadlocked.

Similar examples can be constructed for the *alt* operator. Gates for general ordering relations lead to corresponding problems. In case of the *alt* operator, conflicts could be avoided if all alternatives contain the same gate interface. In general, however, a considerable number of additional static semantic rules would be necessary to avoid deadlock situations. Therefore, it has been decided in MSC'96 to leave it to the user's own responsibility.

The *loop* operator may cause several problems due to the repetition of events inside the inline expression, in particular in connection with gates (see figure 5). A message entering an inline expression with a *loop* operation cannot be received several times inside if it is sent only once outside. A consistent solution may be obtained only if the messages arise from a corresponding loop expression. In case, where the gate refers to a general ordering relation, the interpretation is even more problematic: The semantics of general ordering relations in connection with the repetition of events is not defined. *Loop* expressions may lead to interpretation problems also for timer constructs. Timer in inline expressions with a *loop* operation cannot expire several times without being set again. This situation corresponds to the message gate problem, only that in the case of timer constructs the connection between individual timer events is not defined via gates but via name identification.

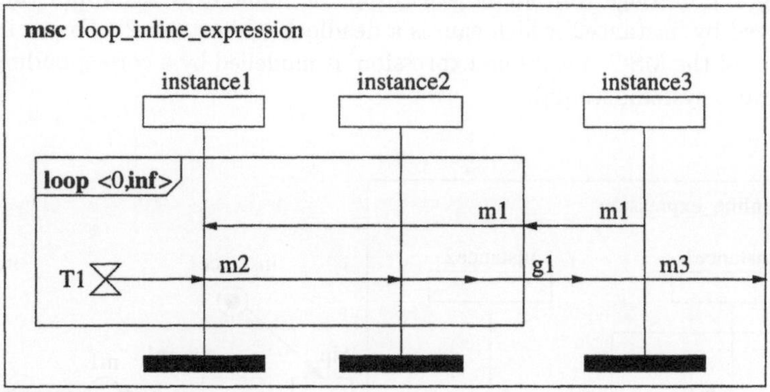

Figure 5. Inline expression with loop operator

Within MSC 'loop_inline_expression', the message 'm1' is sent only once but, according to the *loop* expression, it should be possibly received and consumed several times. Therefore, after the first repetition, a deadlock results on 'instance1'. The inverse case, where the message is leaving the inline expression, may be interpreted in form of lost messages after the first repetition.

The ordering of message 'm2' with respect to message 'm3' is not obvious in case of the loop. It may be interpreted in the way that all repeated message events 'm2' are ordered with respect to the single message event 'm3'.

MSC 'loop_inline_expression' also contains the expiration of timer 'T1' which according to the *loop* expression may possibly be repeated several times. Again, this leads to a deadlock on 'instance1' after the first repetition.

4.3. Inline expressions containing the exc operator

The *exc* operator may be employed within inline expressions and MSC references containing operator expressions. The semantics is defined in MSC'96 in form of a shorthand notation: The *exc* operator can be viewed as an alternative inline expression where the second operand is the entire rest of the MSC. The meaning of the operator is that either the events inside the *exc* inline expression are executed and then the MSC is finished or the events following the *exc* inline expression are executed. For nested inline expressions this rule may lead to inconsistencies. For an *exc* inline expression in one of the sections of a parallel inline expression, the semantics is not precise. It is not clear whether the events in the other sections of the parallel expression shall be executed or not.

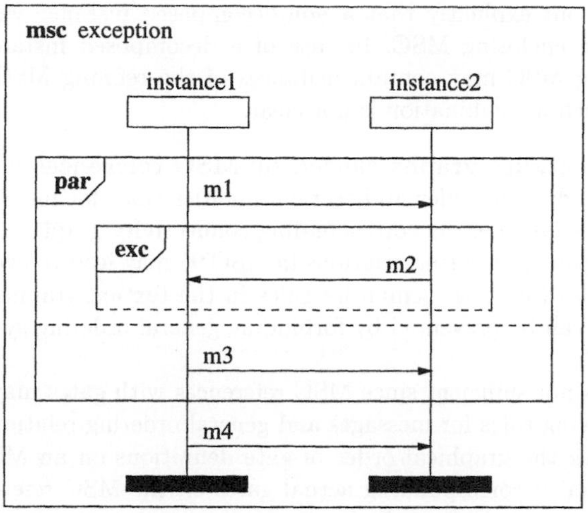

Figure 6. MSC with nested *exc* inline expression

Within MSC 'exception' in figure 6, the message 'm3' is exchanged in parallel with the exception region containing the message 'm2'. It is not clear how to interpret the entire rest of the MSC with respect to the exception region. One possibility to solve this ambiguity concerning nested expressions would be to relate the *exc* region to the section in which it is contained. After the execution of the exception inline expression the rest of the section in which it is contained is skipped. A probably more realistic solution would be to forbid exception regions within nested inline expressions. The same problems occur in MSC references with operator expressions (see section 5).

5. MSC REFERENCES

MSC references are comparable in their functionality with inline expressions. Inline expressions can be represented equivalently by references with operator expressions. The gate interface of an inline expression corresponds to the gate interface of an MSC reference together with the gate interface of the referenced MSCs. The other way round, apart from some minor discrepancies, MSC references may be substituted by inline expressions with the additional rule that simple expressions containing only one MSC reference or sequentially composed MSC references are replaced by their expanded form. Because of this equivalence, we discuss only problems specific for MSC references in this section. All conflicts listed for inline expressions apply to MSC references as well.

5.1. Decomposed instances in MSC references

Decomposed instances must not be attached to MSC references according to MSC'96. Contrary to that, decomposed instances may appear within referenced MSCs. This is consistent since the decomposed instance may only appear in the referenced MSC but it has to be ruled out explicitly that a non-decomposed instance with the same name is contained in the enclosing MSC. In case of a decomposed instance in a referenced MSC, the enclosing MSC may contain instances of the refining MSC. Within MSC'96, the semantics of such a combination is not clear.

5.2. Cyclic connectivity graphs caused by MSC references with gates

According to the drawing rules and static semantics rules for messages, deadlocks are excluded within MSC'92, i.e. the corresponding connectivity graph cannot contain loops. Contrary to that, general ordering relations in MSC'96 may lead to cyclic graphs since no special drawing rules (or static semantics rules in the textual grammar) are prescribed. Possible deadlocks can be prevented by forbidding general ordering symbols with upward slope.

This, however, is not sufficient since MSC references with gates may lead to deadlocks even if special drawing rules for messages and general ordering relations are obeyed. The problem arises since the graphical order of gate definitions on an MSC frame need not agree with the order of corresponding actual gates on the MSC reference. This may be illustrated by the example in figure 7:

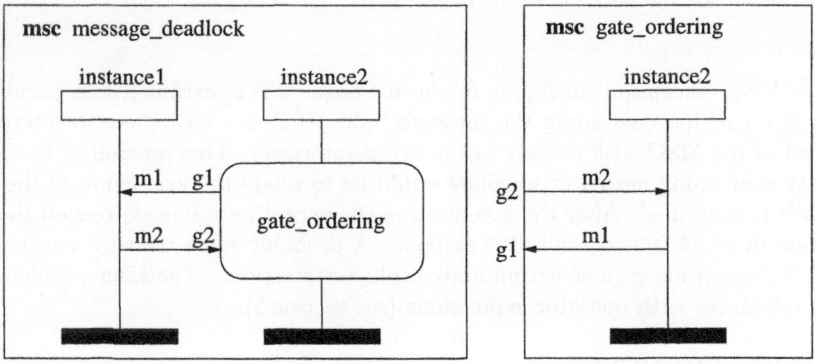

Figure 7. Deadlock caused by message gates

Obviously, the MSC 'message_deadlock' with the MSC reference 'gate_ordering' leads to a deadlock since the order of gate definitions, 'g1' and 'g2', in 'MSC gate_ordering' has been interchanged for actual gates in MSC 'message_deadlock'. This problem may be solved by an additional drawing rule: The graphical order of actual gates has to agree with the order of gate definitions. In the textual grammar, additional static semantics rules are necessary which exclude loops of the connectivity graph including message events for the referenced MSC. Similar problems occur if the gates refer to generalized ordering relations.

5.3. Gate interface of MSC reference expressions

Within MSC'96, the relation between the gate interface of the MSC reference and the interface of the MSCs referenced in the expression may be quite intricate. Not all gate definitions of the referenced MSCs must have a correspondence in the gate interface of the MSC reference. Gate definitions of the referenced MSCs which have no corresponding gate interface are propagated to the environment. The other way round, the interface of the MSC reference must match the interface of the MSCs referenced in the expression, i.e. any gates attached to the reference must have a corresponding gate definition in the referenced MSCs. However, the interface of the MSC reference in general does not match the interface of only one of the referenced MSCs. It is not always obvious how the gate interface of an operator expression is built of the gate interfaces of the individual referenced MSCs. The referenced MSCs of an alternative expression may have different gate interfaces so that the gate interface of the expression has to be adjusted accordingly. For parallel and sequential operator expressions, it even seems that the gate interfaces have to be different for the individual referenced MSCs in order to be meaningful. In any case, a clear semantics definition is demanded urgently.

5.4. Substitution in MSC references

MSC'96 essentially contains four semantic rules for the substitution in MSC references:

- All substitutions in a substitution list are thought to be applied in parallel. Thus the order in which the substitutions take place is not relevant.
- The substitution of an MSC name must share the same gate interface as what it replaces.
- If an MSC definition to which substitution is applied contains MSC references, then the substitution should be applied also to the MSC definitions corresponding to these MSC references.
- An MSC containing references and substitutions is illegal if the application of the substitutions results in an illegal MSC.

In some cases, additional static semantics rules are necessary: The parallel substitution of the same element is not excluded. The following MSC expression is syntactically correct: 'MSC1 *subst* msg m1 *by* m2, msg m1 *by* m3'. The result, however, is unclear. It is not defined which operation has to be executed first.

As the substitution is defined recursively within MSC'96, all substitutions in an MSC definition are carried over to the MSCs, referenced within this MSC. In case that the referenced MSCs contain further substitution lists, this may lead to undefined overlapping, i.e. it is not clear which substitution has to be carried out first. Apart from such semantic problems, the substitution concept seems to be too narrow in practice: Only instance names but not instance types may be replaced. For messages, only the message names may be substituted but in practice also the substitution of message parameters is requested. Beyond that, also the substitution for other language constructs, like timer and conditions, may be useful.

6. HIGH LEVEL MSCS

Whereas in MSC'92 the composition was based completely on the merging of final and initial conditions, within MSC'96, the composition of MSCs is defined by means of HMSCs. The conditions in MSC'96 play a restrictive role defined by a set of static semantics rules. Compared with MSC'92, the composition mechanisms of MSC'96 are much more flexible, e.g. MSCs may be composed with or without initial or final conditions. This flexibility, however, leads to some semantic problems which need further clarification.

6.1. HMSCs without end symbol

According to the MSC'96 standard, an HMSC need not contain an end-symbol, i.e. it may be completely cyclic. In case, where an MSC reference refers to a cyclic HMSC, this leads to a dead branch because the events following the MSC reference will not be executed any more. Therefore, an MSC reference pointing to a cyclic HMSC should be disallowed.

6.2. Conflicts in the semantics of MSC composition

For HMSCs, similar problems as for operator expressions may occur in connection with instance creation, instance stop and timers contained in the referenced MSCs. The following situations which are allowed for HMSCs according to MSC'96 lead to inconsistencies:

- Instances which are terminated within one referenced MSC may be contained in the subsequent referenced MSC or in a parallely executed MSC.
- In HMSCs containing free loops, instances in referenced MSCs may be created several times.
- In HMSCs containing free loops, instances in referenced MSCs may be terminated several times.
- Instances with the same name may be contained in one referenced MSC as decomposed, in another one as non-decomposed.
- Instances with the same name may vary in different MSC references by the instance type.
- The same timer may expire in subsequent referenced MSCs without being set between them again.

These inconsistencies should be disallowed by additional static semantics rules.

6.3. Composition rules for HMSCs

At a first glance the role of conditions on the level of HMSCs is not immediately visible. Since the HMSC conditions are not mandatory, they only play a restrictive role. Their use becomes more obvious in examples taken from practice: HMSCs without conditions become difficult to handle since conditions, representing global system states, provide natural check points.

Nevertheless, conditions on the HMSC level could play a more significant role if they are employed for a dynamical choice in form of guards. In fact, such a mechanism is demanded urgently. Within MSC'96, alternatives defined within a referenced MSC cannot be continued differently outside of the reference. In practice, this makes the specification, in particular of exception handling, quite clumsy. E.g. in figure 8, within the HMSC 'setup_attach', the choice made in the referenced MSC 'connect_request' between failure (first alternative) and successful connection (second alternative) cannot be carried over to the subsequent branching in the HMSC. That means, according to the present standard, both branches inside of MSC 'connect_request' can be continued by both branches outside (with the HMSC conditions 'failure' and 'connection'). It would be advantageous to change the semantics and to employ HMSC conditions as guards.

Some immediate deficiencies of the present standard may be removed by a reformulation of the static semantics rules. In case of the composition of simple MSCs without (unique) global initial (final) conditions, the set of initial (final) conditions is defined to be the set of all possible condition names. By means of this default value no empty sets of initial or final conditions can be produced. Such a rule is not carried over consistently to referenced HMSCs and referenced MSC expressions. E.g. the sets of initial (final) conditions of *alt* and *par* MSC expressions are defined as the intersection of the sets of initial (final) conditions of the referenced MSCs. This way, the sets can be empty. Similarly to simple MSCs, the default value in this case should be the set of all possible condition names. Beyond that, for the *exc* operator expression any definition is lacking in the standard.

7. CONCLUSION AND OUTLOOK

Contrary to MSC'92 ([5]), the new standard MSC'96 offers the promising possibility of a fairly comprehensive system specification in an intuitive and transparent manner. In this respect, MSC'96 has been applied already successfully to an ISDN service specification ([12]) and to the formalization of Use Cases ([1]). Practical experience has been gained by the implementation of one of the new MSC'96 concepts (MSC reference) as a prototype component within the Siemens SICAT tool. This has been part of the diploma thesis on which this paper is based ([8]).

Nevertheless, as was pointed out in the preceding chapters, MSC'96 still contains a number of obvious deficiencies, inconsistencies and semantic gaps. Most evidently, MSC inline expressions and MSC reference expressions combined with gate concepts need further elaboration and precise mathematical foundation. This, of course, also demands an intense feedback from tool makers, users and the academic community since standardization is a highly interactive process. Certainly, the completion of the formal semantics for MSC'96 based on process algebra will contribute considerably to a further consolidation

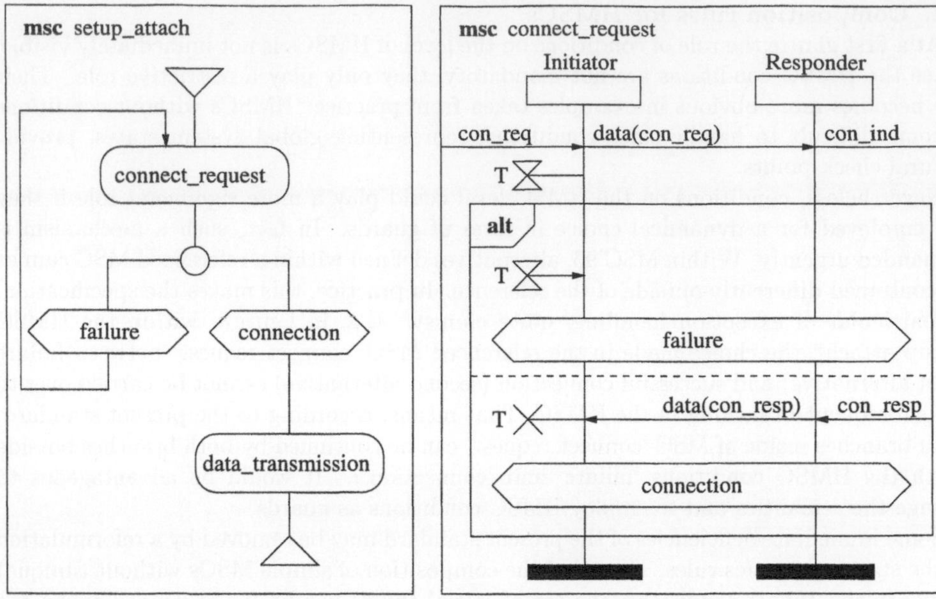

Figure 8. HMSC and MSC reference for connection setup

of the language.

Whilst most of the new MSC'96 concepts need further elaboration, a number of important concepts have been left out in the Z.120 since they were found either to be not sufficiently mature or they have not been sufficiently supported yet by the standardization community. The list contains disruption and interruption operator, parallel composition with synchronisation mechanism, strong sequencing operator, concepts for synchronous communication, formal data concepts, inclusion of non-functional properties. The list may be easily extended. All these open items are included in the working program for the next ITU-study period which is supposed to result in an addendum to MSC'96 in 1998 and in a new recommendation in 2000 (MSC2000).

ACKNOWLEDGEMENTS

We thank Dieter Kolb for interesting discussions about MSC'96. We are grateful to Sjouke Mauw and Michel Reniers for having a critical look at our paper.

REFERENCES

1. M. Andersson and J. Bergstrand. Formalizing Use Cases with Message Sequence Charts. Master's thesis, Lund Institute of Technology, 1995.

2. P. Graubmann, E. Rudolph, and J. Grabowski. Towards a Petri Net Based Semantics Definition for Message Sequence Charts. In O. Færgemand and A. Sarma, editors, *SDL'93 - Using Objects*. North-Holland, 1993.
3. Ø. Haugen. MSC'96 – The advanced MSC. SISU Report L–2002–4, September 1996.
4. Ø. Haugen. The MSC-96 Distillery. In A. Cavalli and A. Sarma, editors, *SDL'97*. North-Holland, 1997.
5. ITU-T. *Z.120 – Message Sequence Chart (MSC)*. ITU-T, Geneva, 1994.
6. ITU-T. *Z.120 – Message Sequence Chart (MSC)*. ITU-T, Geneva, 1996.
7. I. Jacobson. *Object-Oriented Software Engineering – A Use Case Driven Approach*. Addison-Wesley, 1992.
8. S. Loidl. Interpretation und Werkzeugunterstützung von Message Sequence Charts (MSC'96). Master's thesis, Technische Universität München, 1996. in German.
9. S. Mauw. The formalization of Message Sequence Charts. *Computer Networks and ISDN Systems - SDL and MSC*, 28(12), June 1996.
10. S. Mauw and M.A. Reniers. An algebraic semantics of Basic Message Sequence Charts. *The Computer Journal*, (37), 1994.
11. S. Mauw and M.A. Reniers. High-level Message Sequence Charts. In A. Cavalli and A. Sarma, editors, *SDL'97*. North-Holland, 1997.
12. E. Rudolph, P. Graubmann, and J. Grabowski. Tutorial on Message Sequence Charts (MSC'96), Forte/PSTV'96, Kaiserslautern, October 1996.

V

SDL and MSC in International Organizations

SDL and MSC in International Organizations: ITU-T

Rick Reed[1]

Telecommunications Software Engineering Limited, 13 Weston House, 18-22 Church Street, Lutterworth, Leicestershire, LE17 4AW. Email: rickreed@tseng.co.uk

This paper gives an overview of the development and use of SDL in ITU-T up to 1997 and the plans for SDL to take it into the 21st Century. It covers a short history of SDL, the use of SDL within ITU-T and its members, the status of the standards in 1997, the role of the SDL Forum Society and the plans for SDL-2000. Conformance to the Z.100 standard within ITU-T is examined. The use of MSC is considered in relation to the use of SDL. The current plans in 1997 will lead to a new Recommendation in the year 2000. There are other plans for increased support of SDL (in ETSI, by tool vendors, and possibly other organisations such as OMG) that are outside the scope of this paper.

Keywords: SDL-88, SDL-92, current SDL, SDL-2000, MSC, MSC-92, MSC-96, MSC-2000, ITU-T, Z.100, Z.105, ASN.1, Z.120, Conformance, Standards, Recommendations, Data, Simplification.

1. HISTORY OF SDL

In 1968 CCITT (replaced by ITU-T in 1993) proposed that its study group 11, which dealt with signalling and switching, should include in its studies the impact of the "stored program control" (SPC) systems on telecommunications standards. These software controlled systems were just coming into use, and at that time only a few visionaries imagined that eventually software would become the major technology to replace much of the electro-mechanical and hard-wired electronic elements of systems. In fact the SPC systems were often "programmed" by threading wires through large (several cms.) ferrite rings: each wire represented one machine instruction, and was threaded (or not threaded) through rings for each bit so that either a 0 or 1 would be read. In 1972, at the end of the 4 year study period, the result was a recognition that studies were needed on languages for human machine interaction (called "man-machine language" (MML) at that time), specification and description, and programming.

The study continued on the specification and description language (SDL) and the first standard (23 pages containing some symbols for "state transition diagrams", definition of concepts and a few examples) was published in the CCITT Orange book in 1976. It was assumed that the rules for use and semantics were intuitively understood, as many organisations were using different forms of state transition diagrams. This proved not to be the case, but software was not a top priority for ITU-T. In any case a group normally had to wait for the publication of the next CCITT coloured book before updating a standard (this changed in 1993), so it was the 1980 CCITT Yellow book that had the first real description of SDL in 72 pages. This was still very informal but it was realized that to find errors at the specification stage and to provide good tool support, the meaning of SDL drawings needed to be defined more formally. The real metamorphosis from a graphical drawing technique with loose semantics to a formal description technique took place in the next four years, so that the 1984 CCITT Red Book recognized an interpretation model that treated the drawings as the basis of mathematical graphs. Additional language features were added which recognized that

[1] Rapporteur ITU-T Study Group 10 Question 6 (Maintenance and support of SDL) study period 1996-2000.

drawings represented processes (of which there could be several concurrent instances that might be created or stopped dynamically) and that branchings in the graphs and information passed by signals between processes relied on existence of data! The basic language of states and transitions triggered by signals between processes did not change, but the 1984 version enriched the language with many features. Data was added to the language, in a way which later had mixed consequences. One unique feature added was to have a program-like textual form as well as a graphical form. The Red book also contained user guidelines.

In 1984 the increasing importance of software was reflected in the creation of study group 10 (Languages for telecommunication applications)[1] which between 1984 and 1988 tackled the task of improving the formal basis for SDL, which was given an added incentive by the work on support tools. The semantics were defined in an abstract way independent of whether the concrete language was the textual Phrase Representation (PR) form, or the Graphical Representation (GR) form. The structure of the current standard [1] was established. Work was accelerated to complete the formalisation in two years by early 1987 so that users within CCITT could use the improved standard for their own standards to be completed in 1988. The SDL-88 standard [2] in the CCITT Blue book was about 200 pages (not including the formal definition in VDM and tutorial material such as the user guidelines). Also during this period the data definitions part was aligned with the evolving ISO standard LOTOS [3] using the same algebraic model. This required few changes to the syntax of the language, but gave data a sound mathematical basis.

At the start of the next period, 1988 to 1992, there was a major requirement to keep the language stable, but it was also recognized that there were major user benefits if the language could allow for re-usable objects. The main evolution in this period was therefore the addition of object oriented features as an extension. Remote procedure calls and non-determinism and were added to meet user needs. The SDL-92 standard [1] was about 10% larger than the SDL-88 standard [2] (comparison by counting pages is not precise; for example, the SDL-92 version has a slightly smaller type-face). Significant work was also done in the period on methodology which is a difficult area to handle within the framework of standardisation since many aspects are organisation dependent. This was issued as methodology guidelines to replace the user guidelines of the Blue book.

The World Telecommunication Standards Conference (WTSC) in Helsinki 1993 that formally approved SDL-92, enabled and encouraged study groups to issue standards when ready rather than wait for the end of a four year period. Thus work on using SDL in combination with ASN.1 to introduce sorts of data was approved in March 1995 [4], which as far as possible was an extension of SDL-92. Otherwise in the 1992 to 1996 period stability was the major objective and allowed tools to catch up with the standard. A common graphical interface between tools was standardized in Z.106 [5], and a new methodology framework document was produced as Supplement 1 to Z.100 [6]. Some extensions to SDL-92 were agreed to meet user needs, generally relaxing rules of SDL-92 to make it easier to use and some corrections were made to the language definition where it was unclear, ambiguous or inconsistent. These were collected into the 35 pages of Addendum 1 to Z.100 [7] which together with SDL-92 defines "current SDL"[2]. Though the texts (Z.106, Addendum 1, Methodology) were approved for publication in 1996, printed copies were not available by May 1997.

2. HISTORY OF MSC

The Message Sequence Chart (MSC) language was first standardized in Z.120 in 1992 as MSC-92 [8], although they had been suggested since 1984 as auxiliary diagrams to be used

---

[1] Before 1993 roman numerals were used, so SDL actually moved from study group XI to study group X.

[2] From SDL-88 to SDL-92 adding types was signficant and Z.100 was re-isssued., whereas Addendum 1 is a much smaller update so "current SDL" = SDL-92 + Addendum 1 is more appropriate than "SDL-96".

with SDL. Standardization of MSC was suggested in the 4th SDL Forum October 1989 [9] and agreed in June 1990 by ITU-T study group 10. The first standard was rapidly produced and so was approved by WTSC in March 1993 at the same time as SDL-92.

The main objectives in standardizing MSC were to formalize the informal auxiliary diagrams so that they could always be understood in the same way, and (perhaps more important) the existence of a standard encourages tool producers to support the language. MSC tools now exist that are linked to SDL tools. It can also be noted that very often MSC-like diagrams were being used within other study groups (for example "time sequence diagrams") and study group 10 took the initiative to propose a single well defined language rather than rely on less formal descriptions.

Once MSC-92 had been standardized, it was obvious that it could be significantly improved in some areas: better overview and more structuring capabilities were the major needs. These issues were tackled between 1992 and 1996, and included in MSC-96 [10].

3. USE WITHIN ITU-T

SDL originated in study group 11, and one of the main concerns was to be able to describe signalling protocols for standards. SDL-like diagrams can be found in signalling protocols in the CCITT Yellow book, and SDL has continued to be used until the present day. In earlier uses the diagrams very rarely (if ever) conformed even to the syntax of SDL, though it was argued by the protocol designers that the SDL was only illustrative of the natural language text in the standards which was definitive. Also the diagrams were often quite simple, so it was reasonable to claim that the meaning was intuitive. Transitions often ended in text saying "to be defined". It was quite common for a signal which carried information to be mentioned only by name in an input symbol, even though the subsequent tasks and decisions relied on the information. Since early versions of SDL did not support data and relied on human interpretation of tasks and decisions, the loose adherence to Z.100 is understandable. Paper [11] presented at SDL '87 gives some examples.

The introduction of SDL-88 to ITU-T work was not an overwhelming success as reflected in paper [12]. The main problem from the point of view using rapporteurs "using" SDL, was that there were a lot more rules in SDL-88, and although these had been introduced in SDL-84, rapporteurs were still using SDL-80. They were used to sketching process diagrams informally. Nevertheless two standards [13, 14] were introduced in this period by study group 11 that outlined a three stage methodology for ISDN services work that specifically require the use of SDL as in Z.100.

More recent versions of the standards covered in [11] such as the Q.931 (03/93) therefore adhere to more SDL rules, but still show a high degree of informality. In particular, it is still the case that in most standards that claim to use SDL, the structure is not shown in valid SDL and signals are not properly defined in SDL. Often such standards, for example Q.921(3/93) specifically show a limited number of SDL symbols (state, input, output, save, task, decision, procedure call, option, procedure start, procedure return) as relevant. Often the data and signals are not defined. Within tasks there is no distinction between informal text

(Get last transmitted I frame)

and more formal text

(V(S) = V(S) + 1).

The general impression is that (at least up to 1992) most protocol designers were *still* using something more like the 1980 version of SDL, and were not taking advantage of the possibility to check and validate the descriptions in standards. Fortunately the situation gradually seems to be changing and some more recent standards (such as Q.2971 [15]) conform more closely to Z.100, and SDL has been used in the Open Distributed Processing standards to define a reference model for the Trader. A good example of what can be done is provided by the INAP CS-2 protocol that is formally defined in SDL and this description is considered to be definitive. However, this work originates from ETSI.

Tools are available through ITU for rapporteurs to produce good models, and those cases where proper SDL models have been produced have shown that it enables errors to be found and ambiguities to be resolved in standards before they are published. An ITU-T Recommendation (Z.110 [16]) has been available since 1988, giving criteria for the use of formal description techniques that suggested a gradual move from informal use of SDL to the formal use. Z.110 (10/96) is a minor update to reflect changes since 1988.

4. USE BY ITU-T MEMBERS

Almost all the major participants in the telecommunications industry are members of ITU-T either as Recognized Operating Agencies (such as France Telecom), or Scientific and Industrial Organizations (such as Alcatel). These members often take the SDL-like descriptions in standards and use these as the basis for specifications and implementations of systems. It is at this stage that the deficiencies and errors in the SDL in ITU-T recommendations are often found. The result is that in different systems these flaws in the standards may be fixed in different ways, so that as well as increasing costs, different implementations may not be inter-operable.

The major difference in the industry compared with ITU-T until recently has been the use of tools. These have enabled the industry to check the specifications and to generate implementations. However, not every ITU-T member uses SDL in the same way: in many cases the focus is on implementation [17], but in some cases SDL is used for very abstract specifications using abstract data types or for investigating feature interaction. SDL is used for specification, design and implementation.

Of course, once SDL is used with tools then it must conform to the language, or in reality to the tool version of SDL. The informal versions of SDL in ITU-T standards is then only partially helpful, because of incorrectness, incompleteness and sometimes inconsistency. The issue of the technical quality of standards was, however, raised by Canada at the 1996 WTSC, citing ASN.1, SDL, MSC and TTCN as languages that should be exploited properly and this there an ITU correspondence group [18] treating this issue. The ideal situation would be to start from machine readable versions of the standards, and it seems that as the initiative from Canada is followed then this may be achieved in the future.

SDL is also used in industries such as aerospace, medical and automobile applications, but it can be very difficult to obtain information about SDL from ITU-T. To quote an Ovum report

> *The latest and current version of the standard, SDL(1996) was formally approved in October 1996. However it is still to be published and ITU-T does not make it easy to obtain pre-publication text. We understand that this is not the first time - delays of one to two years have occurred with previous versions.*
>
> *The ITU's approach to publication is absurd. In many ways SDL is a model of international and intercompany co-operation. It is very difficult to collaboratively develop a rigorous specification language, and its even more difficult to keep it up to date. The last thing that is needed is for the ITU-T to announce it as a standard, but delay its publication.*

5. CURRENT SDL, Z.105 AND MSC-96

The current standards in force[1] related to SDL and MSC are:

- SDL: Z.100 (3/93) with Addendum 1 (10/96) and Supplement 1 (10/96); [1, 6, 7]
- SDL with ASN.1: Z.105 (3/95); [4]
- MSC: Z.120 (10/96); [10]
- Use of FDT's: Z.110 (10/96).[16]

[1] The standards dated (10/96) were still in the publication process within ITU-T in May 1997.

5.1 Current SDL

Current SDL is essentially a superset of SDL-92 which in turn was superset of SDL-88, so that valid SDL-88 is still valid in current SDL, except in a few obscure cases that are unlikely to arise in practice. Current SDL can therefore be considered as SDL-92 with some corrections and a few extensions. The extensions simplify SDL by harmonizing concepts and improve the expressive power of SDL. There have been no changes to the underlying models.

Harmonising signals, remote procedures and remote variables

Remote procedure definitions, remote variable definitions all define communication primitives, but in SDL-92 remote procedures and remote variables cannot be used:

- to show the communication on interfaces (signal routes, channels and gates);
- for communication with the environment of the system

The use of remote procedures and remote variables have been harmonized with signals, such that whenever a signal can be mentioned, a remote procedure or remote variable can also be mentioned, a remote variable in an input or save symbol is not allowed because it does not make sense. Remote procedures and remote variables can be included in signal lists, so that, like signals, can be used when defining channels, signal routes, gates, signalsets, inputs and save. If a remote procedure or remote variable is mentioned on a gate, channel or signal route of a diagram then the diagram need not include an **imported** specification. To use remote procedures and variables for communication with the environment, they must be mentioned on the channels connected to the environment.

A related improvement is to allow a signal list identifier (in brackets) in an input. The reason that this was prohibited in SDL-92 and SDL-88 could not be remembered, and many users are surprized when they encounter this peculiarity.

There is now a possibility of a clash of names between signals, remote procedures and remote variables. If there is a visible signal with that name then it is denoted, and a procedure (or variable) with the same name must be preceded by **procedure** (or **remote** respectively). These keywords are, of course, optional at other times, so can be used to annotate the procedure and variable names, and this allows the SDL-92 syntax to be used in inputs. The SDL-92 style may be preferable in some cases, for example when a remote procedure is used in a number of blocks, the diagram would be cluttered by the mentioning of the remote procedure on all the relevant channels.

The communication with the environment by remote procedure calls in current SDL is useful when:

- building large systems, to allow a part of the system to be modelled as a system on its own in order to apply testing, reuse and encapsulation principles in a modular way, so that in addition to using signals, the part may also communicate with its environment through remote procedures and variables;
- using SDL for a distributed client-server system, where there are a number of servers (which may be SDL systems) offering interfaces to clients, and because the number and type of clients is not fixed, the clients must be located in the environment of each server SDL system.

External procedures and operators

Current SDL allows for the use of procedures and operators defined outside the SDL-description. The format of an external procedure definition is a <procedure-heading> with the keyword **external** inserted at the very end. For example a C library function in an SDL description could be:

procedure strcmp **fpar** op1,op2 Characterstring; **returns** Integer; **external**;

Simplifying and harmonizing channels and signal routes

The changes are:

- channels are optional in block substructure and system diagrams, just as signal routes are optional in block diagrams;

- to allow structure diagrams to be less complex and thereby more readable, the names and signal lists of channels and signal routes may be omitted.

The names of channels and signal routes are only used in **output via** (and in the **connect** statement of SDL/PR), and the signal lists can be derived from their endpoints.

The consequence is that in current SDL the use of channel, signal route and signal list names in diagrams can be restricted to just those places where they are needed (that is if they are referred to in some part of the description), or if they serve a useful explanatory function. Nevertheless signallists are useful to check the interfaces between different parts of a system, especially for descriptions which are built by several people, so for readability of diagrams it is strongly suggested to introduce and use signallist names even though they are not essential in current SDL.

Channels or signal routes connected to same entity in both endpoints

In SDL-92 it was not possible to draw a signal route from one process instance set back to the same one, or to draw a channel from a block set and back to itself. Therefore it was not possible to denote the interface between one member of the set and another. This restriction has been removed. So that the construct is not ambiguous, it must be a one-way communication path, but two or more distinct one way paths are allowed so two way communication is possible.

Block, process or service considered a system

Often, the SDL view of an SDL system, that it is a self-contained entity which communicates with it environment, is too restricted. Consider for example a computer. It can be regarded as a well-defined system on its own, but it can also be a component of a larger system, for example a computer network. It must therefore be possible to compose a system from other self-contained systems. Such component systems are often rather simple. When a simple system is defined, it is cumbersome and it decreases readability if a complete SDL-92 system has to be formed, consisting of at least system, a block and a process, even if these are drawn directly nested on a single diagram. Furthermore, tool support for these nested diagrams is difficult to provide. Finally when a loosely coupled system is being defined (for example, a client-server based system - often consisting of one server process and a number of client processes) it is easier to define each item as a separate system.

Current SDL therefore allows a service, process, or block to be considered as a system with the surrounding constructs (that is for a service the process, block and system) implied.

Extended use of packages

In SDL-92, packages can only be attached to packages and the system diagram. The disadvantage of this is that all definitions in a package will be visible in the whole system scope. There is a need to include definitions from a package at a lower level, for example, when some sorts of data are only needed in a single process in the system, but in SDL-92 the sort of data would be visible everywhere thus making mistakes more likely. In current SDL it is possible to restrict the visibility of names defined in a package by allowing package references to be attached to other scope units than just packages and the system level. For example, a package reference attached to a process diagram, has the effect that the names in the package are visible only inside the process diagram.

State expression

This is an additional imperative operator (like SELF, OFFSPRING and NOW) which when called returns the name of the current state as a charstring expression.

Dashed lines in comment symbol

The difference between a text extension (connected to another symbol by a solid line) and a comment (connected to another symbol by a dashed line) is not always obvious in SDL-92. An alternative comment symbol consisting of dashed lines is introduced in current SDL. Users may be surprized that this is a new symbol, because it was already implemented by tools, and this is an example of language maintenance in line with user wishes.

Nullary operators

These are operators without arguments defined just as any other operator, but with no argument sorts of data in its operator-signature. Its behaviour is defined as for operators, and it is normally used exactly as a literal. However, the implicit ordering rules of SDL for literals do not apply to nullary operators, therefore it is useful when defining sort of data with the **ordering** property.

5.2 Methodology

This is not part of the Z.100 standard: the 1992 guidelines are in an appendix which is therefore *informative* (as compared to an *Annex* which is normative, so that Annex F of Z.100 - the formal definition - is a normative part of the SDL standard). The methodology associated with Z.100 can only suggest approaches, but SDL can be used validly in many other ways. The work done in the 1992-96 period on methodology is published in Supplement 1 to Z.100 – "SDL+ methodology: use of MSC and SDL (with ASN.1)". Supplements contain additional information considered to be useful.

The SDL+ methodology does replace the 1992 guidelines, but provides a more detailed framework that can be elaborated for a particular use to develop a formal specification in SDL. It covers to some extent MSC and use of ASN.1, and can be applied from the level of requirements capture. It suggests the use of the OMT object model notation for forming the initial classes. An overview [19] was presented at the SDL '95 Forum.

5.3 Z.105

This only became a standard in 1995, and is now being supported by tools. It allows data used within SDL processes and in signals to be defined using a subset of the ASN.1 notation. This then also implies that ASN.1 encoding can be used, at least for signals to and from the SDL system. This is an advantage over SDL, because SDL does not define encoding of data. ASN.1 is also an advantage because it has been widely used to define protocol data units conveyed by messages between systems: in standards and sometimes in real systems.

The use of SDL with ASN.1 is of benefit to ASN.1 users, because ASN.1 allows data values to be defined, but does not define any operators between those values. For example, ASN.1 defines the Integer values 1 and 2, but does not define "+" or any way of writing expressions and therefore cannot be used to describe behaviour. SDL can be used to describe structure and behaviour, and in particular can define operators for data. Z.105 brings these two worlds together, and an overview was presented [20]at the SDL '95 Forum.

Z.105 also brings some useful features to SDL that were lacking: optional fields in structures and CHOICE (that is, union) sorts. There are also some very useful additional predefined sorts of data for Bit, Bit_String, Octet, Octet_String and Bag (or **set of**). Z.105 also allows a definition of a sort of data to be written in places where Z.100 insists on a sort name, even if is only used once. For example:

dcl a Array(Integer(0:255), Boolean);

is allowed with Z.105.

5.4 MSC-96

An excellent overview [21] of MSC-96 was presented at FORTE '96.

The key advances since MSC-92 are:

- MSC references for substructuring;
- high level MSC (HMSC) that graphically define how MSCs are combined;
- inline expressions for alternative, parallel, and looping constructs;
- general partial ordering.

In general MSC-92 is a subset of MSC-96, but in a few cases diagrams may to be updated, for example because the syntax rules for intance heads was changed. The references for substructuring is a most useful feature, already implemented in at least one tool.

6. TOWARDS MSC-2000 AND SDL-2000

SDL and MSC are living languages, which means they are used frequently with new applications in new areas. If they were natural languages then new uses, features and vocabulary would come into use, and some language constructs would become unused, unfamiliar or even unknown. Similarly for MSC and SDL users have new needs, and have innovative ideas for changing the languages. But SDL and MSC are formal languages, that need to be well defined and machine processable, so that all users and tools can understand and manipulate them. Changes to the languages need to be carefully managed. Formally this is the task of ITU-T study group 10, with the study of SDL under Q.6/10 and the study of MSC under Q.9/10[1].

The languages are quite complex. This means that there is plenty of scope for clarifying the language definitions so that they are not misinterpreted, and also it is quite likely that there are still some ambiguities, inconsistencies or just defects in the languages (that is "bugs") that may need correcting. The studies therefore specifically include defect correction. Maintenance also includes the possibility to change the language, and for SDL the maintenance rules and change request procedure are defined in Addendum 1 of Z.100.

For both MSC and SDL there are plans to produced revised Recommendations in the year 2000 as further detailed below. In the meantime master lists of changes will be issued, which include clarifications and corrections (effective immediately), extensions and modifications (in theory only effective in 2000), a list of open items still being studied and a list of closed items.

6.1 MSC-2000

There is an intent to seek harmonization with other notations similar to MSC. In this respect study groups 7 and 11 have similar notations, and there is also an initiative on a Unified Modeling Language (UML) by the Object Management Group (OMG) that contains a similar notation. The 1997 study group 10 meeting of MSC experts planned to promote MSC within OMG as *the* language for event sequence modelling.

Within the current study period it is planned to focus on four special topics: control logic, decomposition, advanced communication primitives and real time constructs. The "control logic" is epxected to contain such items as a data concept, guards on expression alternatives, break out of loops and continuation conditions. It is recognized that decomposition in MSC-96 has some interpretation problems that need attention. Some corrections to the MSC-96 standard will be needed Already at the first meeting a number of issues had been identified, and more are likely to be found as tools implement the full language, or from the work on formalizing the semantics of MSC-96. The work for MSC therefore includes both innovation and maintenance.

6.2 SDL Simplification and Maintenance

There are differing opinions as to precisely what "simplification" means: it could just be deletion of some language concepts, or it could extend to modelling blocks, processes and services all as variants of some building block object. The working definition is "removal of unnecessary restrictions and differences in language concepts and perhaps unnecessary, unused features".

A long list of open items being considered for inclusion in SDL-2000 has been agreed ranging from trivial items such allowing the keyword **call** to be optional, to major changes such as the introduction of block identities similar to Pids. An important topic that has been specifically recognized for study, is a way of modelling performance using SDL.

Whatever changes are made it is agreed that in future there ought to be implementation in at least one tool to prove feasibility, before a feature is finally accepted into the language.

---

1 Rapporteur ITU-T Study Group 10 Question 9 (Maintenance Message Seqeunce Charts (MSC) syntax and semantics) study period 1996-2000: Øystein Haugen - email: etooha@eto.ericsson.se

6.3 Exceptions and Timer Handling in SDL

SDL is mainly used for implementing systems. More focus is therefore being given to constructs for using SDL for design and implementation. The study question includes a proposal for exception handling, but this needs more consideration. A short requirements list for exceptions is:

- handle run time errors (which implies there are language defined errors);
- compatibility with IDL/ODL;
- avoid any conflicts between exceptions in SDL and in other languages (such as IDL/ODL, Java);
- user defined exceptions and causing exceptions.

It is also recognized that there could be some improvement in the handling of timers.

6.4 Incorporation of Z.105 and the Data model

Consideration was given to incorporating Z.105 completely into Z.100, but the view was taken that Z.105 should remain a separate document describing how the ASN.1 syntax can be used with SDL. However, it was also agreed that some parts of Z.105 should be incorporated into Z.100, so that Z.105 (2000) is a simple extension of Z.100 (2000). This is not the case between SDL-92 and Z.105: for example, SDL-92 allows "[" and "]" in names whereas Z.105 does not.

Use of ASN.1 is strongly related to the data model of SDL, and it has been agreed to consider changing the underlying data model of SDL. The rationale is:

- it has not been possible to properly incorporate *error!* in the existing ACT One model;
- the existing approach for defining new sorts of data is difficult to master and it is difficult to make efficient implementations from ACT ONE;
- the existing model produces some undesirable language rules (such as not permitting a **struct** field as an **in/out** parameter.

A call for proposals to revise that data model has been sent out.

6.5 More methodology

It is anticipated that more work will be done on the SDL+ methodology, in particular elaborating the description to cover implementation and adding more examples. The exact results will depend on what contributions are made and how they are consolidated. The plan is to issue a revised document in 2001, so that it can be sure to be consistent with SDL-2000.

7. SDL FORUM SOCIETY

This organisation was originally set up to organize the SDL Forums, and to pass any profit from one forum to the next. Although it had informally existed from 1989, it was formally set up only in 1995. It aims and objectives are to promote SDL and to disseminate information about SDL. As well as the Forum, there is support of the www.sdl-forum.org site which is the primary site for SDL information, and the paper SDL Newsletter.

The modern method of developing standards is for much of the work to be done with a common specification group. Clearly for SDL the SDL Forum Society is a suitable group for this role. The Society already has formal recognition by ITU-T SG10, and it is proposed that many of the working experts meetings can be considered joint SG10 experts and SDL Forum Society meetings. This should allow more open access to the standards work, and hence better meet the real user needs,

8. CONCLUSION

The ITU-T is taking the lead in standards for the Global Information Infrastructure (GII). Within this area SG10 has a role to play in providing languages and architectures, and has drafted project plans for several projects, including one for object oriented environments for which Q.6/10 is nominated as the lead body. The objective is to provide sound technologies for the GII reference descriptions, that allow these descriptions to contain objects that can specialized and re-used. This is fully in line with the MSC and SDL work, and the results will be more use of the languages in ITU-T.

The project description includes study of special object features required by GII, enhancement of the SDL+ framework methodology, provisions of an example of the use of the methodology on a GII element, outline of tool requirements with a feasibility demonstration, and guidelines on use for good quality descriptions. This work, like the work in section 6 of this paper, requires participation and effort. If everyone is an observer, nothing will move. By using a combination of the SDL Forum Society and ITU-T facilities it should be possible to meet everyone's requirements in a flexible way.

The future looks solid for SDL and MSC, and so the author looks forward to seeing many new participants on the work of supporting the standard to the benefit of all.

9. REFERENCES

1. Z.100 (03/93) CCITT Specification and Description Language (SDL), ITU-T, 1994.
2. Z.100 - Functional Specification and Description Language (SDL), CCITT Blue book, Volume X, fasc. X.1, ITU-T Geneva, 1989.
3. Information Processing Systems - Open Systems Interconnection - LOTOS - a Formal Description Technique based on the Temporal Ordering of Obsevational Behaviour, ISO/IEC 8807, ISO Geneva.
4. Z.105 (03/95) SDL Combined with ASN.1 (SDL/ASN.1), ITU-T,1995.
5. Z.106 (10/96) Common Interchange Format for SDL, ITU-T, to be published (May 1997).
6. Supplement 1 (04/96) to Rec. Z.100 (03/93) SDL+ Methodology: Use of MSC and SDL (with ASN.1), ITU-T, to be published (May 1997).
7. Z.100 Addendum 1 (10/96) Corrections to Recommendation Z.100 (03/93), ITU-T, to be published (May 1997).
8. Z.120 (03/93), Message Sequence Chart (MSC), ITU-T, 1994.
9. J. Grabowski and E. Rudolph, Putting Extended Sequence Charts to Practice, in SDL '89 The Language at Work, Elsevier North-Holland, 1989.
10. Z.120 (10/96), Message Sequence Chart (MSC), ITU-T, to be published (May 1997).
11. M. Regan, J. Colton and R. Reed, Experience Using CCITT SDL, in SDL '87 State of the Art and Future Trends, Elsevier North-Holland, 1987.
12. O. Færgemand, Introducing SDL-88 to CCITT WP XI/5, in SDL '89 The Language at Work, Elsevier North-Holland, 1989.
13. I.130 (11/88) Method for the characterization of telecommunication services supported by an ISDN and network capabilities of an ISDN, CCITT Blue Book Fasc. III.7, ITU, 1989.
14. Q.65 (11/88) Stage 2 of the method for the characterization of services supported by an ISDN, CCITT Blue Book Fasc. VI.1, ITU, 1989
15. Q.2971 (10/95) Broadband Integrated Services Digital Network (B-ISDN) – Digital Subscriber SignallingSystem No. 2 (DSS 2) – User-Network Interface Layer 3 Specification For Point-To-MultipointCall/Connection Control, ITU, 1996.
16. Z.110 – Criteria for the Use of Formal Description Techniques, CCITT Blue book, Volume X, fasc. X.1, ITU-T Geneva, 1989. Revision (10/96) to be published.
17. L, Mitchel and S-C. Lu, Specifications and validations of Inmarsat Aeronautical system protocols, in SDL '93 Using Objects, Elsevier North-Holland, 1993.
18. The ever-dynamic TSAG continues to show the way, ITU News, 4/97.

19. R. Reed, Methodology for Real Time Systems, in Computer Networks and ISDN Systems Volume 28 Number 12 June 1996, Elsevier North-Holland.
20. L. Verhaard, An introduction to Z.105, in Computer Networks and ISDN Systems Volume 28 Number 12 June 1996, Elsevier North-Holland.
21. E. Rudolph, J. Grabowski and P. Graubmann, Tutorial on Message Sequence Charts (MSC '96), FORTE/PSTV '96, Oct. 96.

VI
Testing

SDL '97: TIME FOR TESTING - SDL, MSC and Trends
A. Cavalli and A. Sarma (Editors)

Towards the Industrial Use of Validation Techniques and Automatic Test Generation Methods for SDL Specifications

Anders Ek[a], Jens Grabowski[b], Dieter Hogrefe[b], Richard Jerome[c], Beat Koch[b], and Michael Schmitt[b]

[a]Telelogic AB, P.O. Box 4128, S-20312 Malmo, Sweden, eMail: anders.ek@telelogic.se

[b]Institute for Telematics, University of Lübeck, Ratzeburger Allee 160, D-23538 Lübeck, Germany, eMail: {jens,hogrefe,bkoch,schmitt}@itm.mu-luebeck.de

[c]Ericsson Limited, Public Systems Division, Ericsson Way, Charles Avenue, Burgess Hill, West Sussex RH15 9UB, England, eMail: etlrdje@etlxdmx.ericsson.se

Due to increasing demands from companies and standardisation bodies, Telelogic AB and the University of Lübeck started a research and development project in October 1996 which aims at improving the validation and, especially, the automatic test generation facilities of the SDT/ITEX tool set. The project is driven by practical experiences and practical needs, but also takes care of research results. In this paper, we present two short experience reports and describe the project.

1. INTRODUCTION

The ITU-T Specification and Description Language (SDL) [16] is worldwide the most successful standardized formal description technique. SDL has been used successfully in industrial projects and for standardization purposes. Lots of SDL success stories can be found in the proceedings of the past SDL Forum conferences [1,6–8].

The SDT/ITEX tools from Telelogic AB are one of the most successful commercial SDL tool sets. They provide a complete environment for the development of SDL specifications, SDL based implementations and TTCN based test suites. For this, they include graphical editors, analysers, simulation tools, various browsers, application code generators adapted to different real time kernels and further support tools.[1] Besides SDL, SDT/ITEX support the specification languages MSC [17] and TTCN [14].

One tool of SDT/ITEX is the Validator [4]. The Validator is aimed at providing engineers with the possibility to increase the quality of their work and to automate time-consuming tasks. More specifically, the tool is designed to help engineers in three situations:

1. *During an incremental design*, by providing an automated fault detection mechanism that finds inconsistencies and problems in an early stage of development.

[1]An overall view of SDT/ITEX can be found in Section *'XII Demonstrations'* of [1].

2. *When verifying the system against requirements*, by providing an option for automatic MSC verification.
3. *When developing test cases*, by providing options for automatic test generation.

The items 1 and 2 are referred to by the term *validation*, whereas item 3 is referred to by *automatic test generation.* Validation and automatic test generation are closely related, because basically the same techniques can be used for both.

The Validator is based on the *state space exploration* technique (e.g., [12]), which is a well known technique for the automatic analysis of distributed systems. Using this technique a system property is validated by building up and examining the system's state space. Examples for properties which can be verified are freedom of deadlocks or the fulfilment of an MSC.

In general, for automatic test generation we are also interested in finding a property. Furthermore, we need to find a trace which can be used for testing the property in a system implementation. In this context a property is referred to by *test purpose.* Automatic test generation becomes a little bit more complex, because we also have to follow testing methodologies [13] and to transform the resulting test sequences into the TTCN format.

Validation and automatic test generation both have to deal with complexity. Due to the *state space explosion* problem it is often impossible to perform an exhaustive validation or to generate test cases automatically even for small systems.

Currently, we observe an increasing demand for advanced validation techniques and automatic test generation methods from SDT/ITEX customers. Research and case studies have shown that automatic test generation becomes feasible [2,9,10].

Therefore Telelogic AB and the University of Lübeck have set up a research and development project called AUTOLINK. AUTOLINK improves the validation and especially the test generation facilities of SDT/ITEX. The project is driven by practical experiences, but it also considers research results.

The paper continues as follows. In Section 2 the Validator is sketched. SDL validation experiences from Ericsson are presented in Section 3. The need for automatic test generation methods will be explained by an ETSI experience report in Section 4. The AUTOLINK project, its current status and the future plans are described in Section 5. Finally, the conclusion and outlook are given.

2. THE SDT VALIDATOR

The Validator is based on the state space exploration technique (e.g., [12]). In the SDL context this means that the state space of an SDL system is built up, stored in a directed graph and examined. The directed graph is referred to by *reachability graph* and represents the behaviour of the SDL system. The nodes of the reachability graph represent global SDL system states. The edges describe SDL events that can take the SDL system from one global system state to the next global system state. A global SDL system state, i.e., a node in the reachability graph, is characterized by:

- the active process instances,
- the variable values of all active processes,
- the SDL control flow state of all active process instances,
- the active procedures (with local variables),

- the signals (with parameters) that are present in the queues of the system,
- the active timers,
- etc.

The edges in a reachability graph define the atomic events of the SDL system. These can be SDL statements like tasks, inputs, outputs etc., but also complete SDL transitions depending on how the state space exploration is configured.

During validation the reachability graph is analysed. Properties of the reachability graph describe properties of the system behaviour. For example, a system is free of deadlocks if all nodes in the reachability graph have at least one outgoing edge.

2.1. MSC verification

The Validator provides two options to check an SDL specification against system requirements. The requirements have to be expressed in form of observer processes (see Section 2.2) or MSC diagrams. State space exploration techniques are used for both options. For an MSC requirement, the Validator explores the state space, i.e., it simulates the SDL specification, and searches for a path in the reachability graph which includes the MSC. If such a path exists the SDL system has the MSC property, i.e., the MSC is verified.

2.2. Observer processes

An observer process allows to check more complex requirements on systems than can be expressed by MSCs. The notion is to use a special kind of SDL processes, called *observer processes*, to describe the requirements that are to be checked. Then the observer processes are included in the SDL system. Typical application areas for observer processes are test case generation, feature interaction analysis, or the analysis of safety-critical systems.

To be useful, observer processes must be able to inspect the SDL system without interfering with it, and also to generate reports that convey the success or failure of whatever they are checking. To accomplish this, three features are included in the Validator:

1. *The observer process mechanism.* By defining processes to be observer processes, the Validator starts to execute in a two-step fashion. First, the rest of the SDL system executes one transition, and then all observer processes execute one transition and check the new system state.

2. *The assertion mechanism.* The assertion mechanism enables the observer processes to generate reports during state space exploration. These reports will show up in the list of generated reports in a special report viewer.

3. *The Access abstract data type.* The purpose of the Access abstract data type is to give the observer processes a possibility to examine the internal states of other processes in the system. Using the Access ADT it is possible to check variable values, contents of queues, etc., without any need to modify the observed processes.

There are two main characteristics of observer processes:

1. Continuous signals are used which check the internal state of other processes using the Access operator.

2. Assertions are used to report the result of the test.

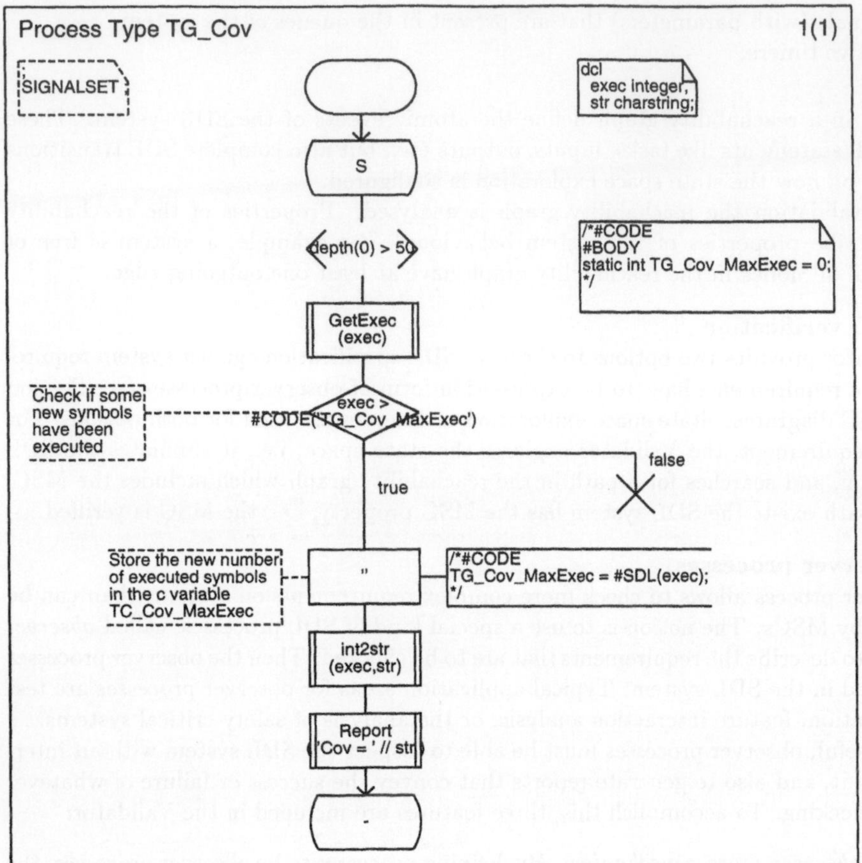

Figure 1. A simple observer process

A simple observer process type is shown in Figure 1. *TG_Cov* realizes a symbol coverage based strategy for the generation of reports. Each time a trace with length 50 is found that covers an additional SDL symbol, a new report is generated. SDT provides a mechanism for accessing variables and functions of the Validator's C Code in an SDL statement. This allows to retrieve information about the current status of the state space exploration. The observer process and its application for test generation will be described in detail in Section 5.2.

2.3. Using the Link tool for semi-automatic test generation

SDT/ITEX offers the option to link SDL specifications and TTCN descriptions by means of the Link tool. For this a *.link* file is generated from the SDL specification. This file is an executable program which in combination with ITEX supports the semi-automatic

(a) Existing system (b) Required system

Figure 2. Existing and required system

construction of TTCN test suites. The Link tool allows to generate the following parts of a test suite:

- ASP (Abstract Service Primitive) definitions are generated automatically. All SDL signals appearing on channels to the environment are translated to ASN.1 ASPs.
- PCOs (Points of Control and Observation) are generated automatically. All channels to the environment are considered to be PCOs.
- If the SDL signals are structured, then these structures are translated to ASN.1 type definitions.
- The test case behaviour can be constructed semi-automatically. The user chooses a *send* event appropriate for the test purpose, and the Link tool adds the following correct *receive* events to the test case description. Then the user has to select the next *send* event.
- A single default behaviour description for the test suite is generated.
- There is a limited generation of constraint definitions.

3. ERICSSON EXPERIENCES

Ericsson is a global telecommunications company that supplies a vast range of hard- and software solutions to network operators all around the world. For one of the current projects in the UK, Ericsson has used SDT/ITEX to design new application software for Ericsson AXE10 telephone exchanges. These exchanges are already in use and form an integral part of the UK switching network.

Customer requirements for such projects are normally provided in form of lengthy textual descriptions. These can prove imprecise when, for example, describing signalling systems or protocols. For the project in the UK there was an agreement to express the requirements in form of an SDL specification. Furthermore SDL was used for the system design.

3.1. The SDL requirements model

The project required to introduce a new signalling system into the existing network. As shown in Figure 2a, the *existing system* consists of the two in- and outputs A and B, with associated functionality X and Y, respectively. The *required system* (Figure 2b) consists of the three in- and outputs A, B and C, with associated functionality X, Y and Z, respectively.

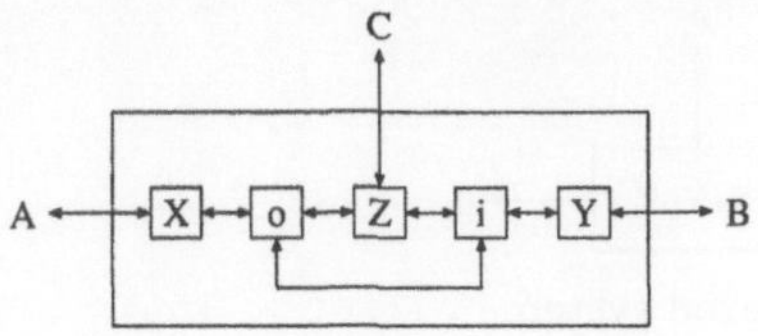

Figure 3. Design model

The system in Figure 2b can be seen as a black box model for the functional requirements to be fulfilled by the existing and the new functionality. The system has been described in SDL and served as functional requirements model (FRM) for validation purposes.

3.2. The SDL design model

The interfaces between the signalling in- and outputs A, B and C, and the functionality of X, Y and Z are clearly understood. The new components of the required system, i.e., the signalling system C with functionality Z already existed. Thus, single SDL specifications for A/X, B/Y and C/Z were developed.

For the required system design (Figure 3), the new functionality C/Z was incorporated in and interfaced with the existing system functionality by means of the additional software blocks o and i.[2] SDL models for o and i were produced and the (functional) SDL design model (FDM) completed. The FDM can be seen as a protocol conversion exercise, with o and i as conversion blocks.

3.3. Validation

The problem of software development is to detect faults as early as possible. For the Ericsson project, a small inter-work fault at FDM level might take an hour to fix, but it could take hundreds of hours if it is not found until the software starts to work on an AXE10 telephone exchange. Thus, the sooner the FDM can be validated against the FRM, the better.

The SDT Validator was used for the validation of FRM and FDM. Early thoughts were that this could just be used to ensure that the FDM did not have any inherent errors like deadlocks or infinite loops; that it described some kind of reliable and stable system. But as a result of the design process two SDL specifications FRM and FDM were developed which had identical external interfaces A, B and C. Therefore the Validator could be used to check if the FDM met the requirements provided by the FRM.

The validation was done in a two step procedure. In a first step all relevant execution traces of the FRM were generated. In a second step each trace was transformed into an MSC and loaded into the FDM. By using the MSC verification feature of SDT/ITEX the traces of the FRM were shown to exist in the FDM.

[2]It should be noted that this design includes abstraction and simplification. Depending on the call type, the system may have two instances of i and none of o. Furthermore, the system may be instantiated more than once. During operation a telephone exchange may maintain up to 64000 instances of the system.

Step 1: Recording FRM traces

Step 1 was performed by adding an observer process (Section 2.2) to the FRM. The observer process was used to control the exploration of the FRM state space. It recorded the path from the *idle* state to predefined global system states and determined the state-space coverage at these states. If the actual path increased the coverage, it was saved. If not, exploration continued. Further improvement of the result of step 1 was achieved by doing some fine tuning, e.g., considering only significant signal parameter values, i.e., the one causing branches in SDL processes.

After several days of execution, ~200 usable paths had been generated. The paths had a length of ~100 transitions and provided about 70% coverage of the system. Further 20% of coverage were achieved by manually navigating to the roots of unexplored branches in the state space and by implementing a rule which prevented to return to the *idle* state during the exploration.

Step 2: MSC verification

In step 2, the paths generated in step 1 were transformed into MSCs. Then each MSC was loaded into the FDM validator and, if possible, verified. An *unverified* MSC corresponded to an error in *either* of the models. Errors in the FDM model are easily rectified, but faults in the FRM cause a repetition of step 1, because MSCs generated from an erroneous specification may reflect the errors. In the AXE10 project the MSCs had to be regenerated only twice.

3.4. Results and discussion

It took three weeks for two people to (re)generate the MSCs and work through the faults. About 80 discrepancies between the FRM and FDM were detected and corrected. The majority of these were inter-working errors, usually the hardest of all errors to find. All errors were removed and the SDL specifications of FRM and FDM were corrected until all 260 MSCs were verified. It has been estimated that the 260 verified MSCs covered more than 60% of the FDM and approximately 90% of the FRM.

Quantifying the benefit of the Validator in this project is hard. Certainly without the validation process, errors would have slipped through to subsequent design phases. Inter-work errors are notoriously hard to find, and they cause large problems in software projects. It may be enough to say that the software has progressed from the SDT/ITEX environment through testing on AXE10 emulators and onto real AXE10 exchanges with no major difficulty. Normally projects of this magnitude prove rather more troublesome.

Subsequent demonstrations to the customer made a good impression. Test cases running on the SDT Simulator and on Ericsson's AXE10 emulators showed the required signalling interaction, which matched precisely in both environments. Without doubt, the SDT Validator will be used again. Additional options for automatic test case generation would be most useful, although most of the generated MSCs do not translate well into real-life test cases.

4. ETSI EXPERIENCES

Within Project Team 65 ETSI started an effort to experiment with test case generation methods [3]. Three different protocols were selected for experimentation: INRES [11],

INAP CS2 [5] and B-ISDN [15]. The protocols were specified with SDL. For each protocol one or two test purposes were specified as an example. Then the tools SDT Link from Telelogic and TTCgeN from Verilog were taken to generate test cases. For detailed results, see [3].

Some general observations can be derived from these experiments.

The automatic generation of the static declarations (PCOs, ASP types, ...) is very useful. The test case developer is freed from a time consuming task, all provided that the SDL specification already exists and is correct.

The dynamic test case generation is semi-automatic and performed in a step-by-step manner. In the case of SDT Link, a test purpose is performed by sending an appropriate signal to the SDL specification together with the constraint. The tool then generates all possible responses together with their constraints automatically. This is repeated until the test case is defined. The approach of TTCgeN is slightly different on first sight. It takes a complete MSC as input and then generates the TTCN in one go. The MSC has to be developed in a step-by-step manner with simulation. Therefore in effect the tools follow approximately the same strategy.

Most of the time is spent with defining the constraints. The first constraint has to be entered manually. Then SDT Link generates the outputs together with their constraints. In TTCgeN this is done on the MSC basis. Usually these automatically generated constraints can then be used, maybe in a slightly modified form, to serve as constraints for further inputs. Due to the tool support the user can speed up the constraint development considerably by reusing automatically generated constraints.

The use of the tools normally tempts into making rather large test cases compared to the single state transition test cases which are typically developed by hand. The resulting test suite then consists of a smaller number of large test cases compared to the traditional large number of small test cases. The reason for this is the fact that the SDL model allows to very easily perform a complete scenario in a simulative way. This has certain advantages and disadvantages over the state-by-state approach, which for some test case developers tends to be rather boring. The advantage is that the complete scenarios can be used as acceptance tests for a tested product. The test is performed from a user's perspective. The disadvantage is that the coverage may not be as complete as if every single state transition was tested.

The tool-supported test generation seems to be of particular benefit for those protocols which define a lot of states and transitions instead of data. These state oriented protocols can very naturally be defined in SDL (and they usually are nowadays). Therefore the effort to produce an SDL specification suitable for test case generation is acceptable. This was the case for INRES and INAP CS2. For data oriented protocols an SDL specification may not be so natural. Most of the protocol is defined in terms of parameter variations instead of dynamic behaviour. The effort of producing an SDL specification suitable for test case generation is considerable. This was the case for B-ISDN.

To sum up, the experience made by ETSI within PT65 was promising enough to continue one of the experiments in a follow-up project. A project team has been set up to generate a test suite for INAP CS2 from the SDL specification using software tools. The results from this first tool-supported test case generation with the aim of creating a complete test suite within ETSI will be available in early 1998.

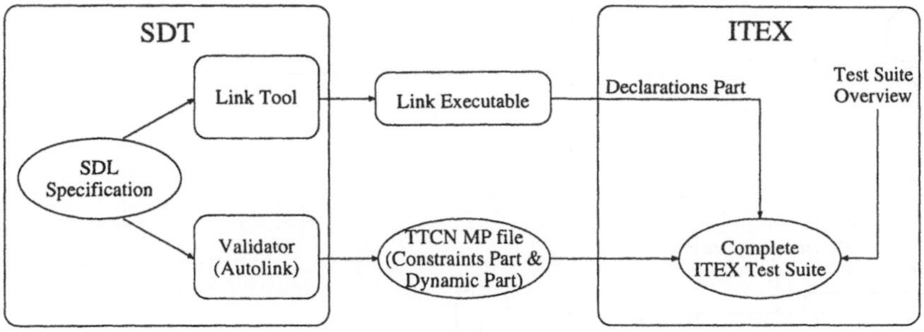

Figure 4. System overview

5. THE AUTOLINK PROJECT

The main objective of the AUTOLINK project is the development and implementation of an SDT component which supports the automatic and semi-automatic generation of TTCN test suites based on SDL specifications.

While SDT allows the user to construct an SDL specification and test it with the Validator, ITEX on the other hand supports the user in the development of TTCN tests suites. So far only the Link tool has served as a bridge between SDT and ITEX (Section 2.3).

With the AUTOLINK component the connection between SDT and ITEX becomes even tighter (Figure 4). Now, the user can specify the test cases within the SDT Validator and let the system generate a TTCN test suite with constraints and dynamic behaviour tables. This test suite can then be completed in ITEX with the declarations provided by the Link tool.

5.1. The first step: path based test generation

The generation of a TTCN test suite with the first AUTOLINK version proceeds in several steps. These are outlined in Figure 5. Most of them can be executed repeatedly as indicated by the loops. In the following we describe each step in more detail.

Define paths

The basis for the generation of a TTCN test case is a *path*. A path is meant to be a sequence of events that have to be performed in order to go from a start state to an end state. The Validator provides several mechanisms for selecting such a path in the state space of an SDL specification. They are sketched in Section 5.2. For AUTOLINK, the externally visible events of a path describe the test sequence to which a *pass* verdict is assigned.

All defined paths are transformed into and stored as *system level MSCs*. By doing this, we omit all internal events of the specification. A system level MSC shows the external interaction that is supposed to take place between an implementation and the test system when executing the test case.

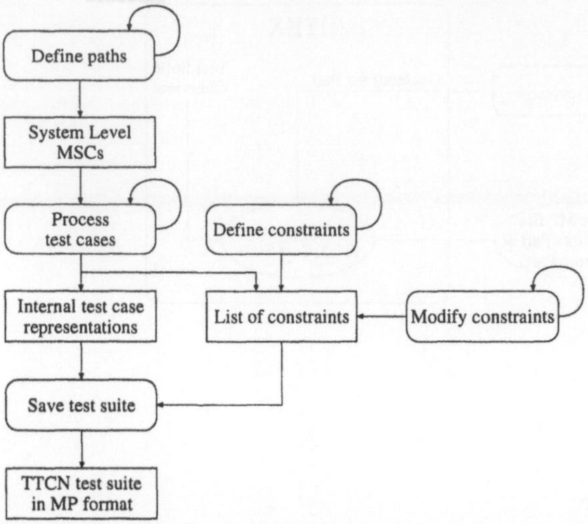

Figure 5. Test Suite Generation

Process test cases

During the processing of a test case, a sequence of send and receive events leading to a TTCN *pass* verdict is created. In addition, all alternative receive events are looked up and added to the test case with a TTCN *inconclusive* verdict.

The processing of test cases consists of three distinctive parts. After some preparatory work, a state space exploration algorithm is used to build up the internal data structure which represents a test case. Finally, post-processing of the internal test case data structure is needed.

A modified version of the Validator's bit-state exploration algorithm is used to build up the internal data structure which represents the current test case. The data structure basically is a tree. Each node of that tree represents an event on a path to a TTCN *pass* verdict. It contains information about the current event, a list of the event nodes with *pass* verdict on the next level, and a list of events with TTCN *inconclusive* verdict on the next level. Here is a short description of the exploration algorithm. Figure 6 shows the data structures involved in the exploration. The state space is represented as a graph. Let us assume that we are in state 4 on level n and $p2$ is the current node in the Autolink event tree. Now state 5 on level $n+1$ is computed. This produces a list of events.

Event $e1$ of the list is checked against the system level MSC. The test shows that $e1$ is not relevant to the MSC, so $e2$ has to be checked next.

$e2$ is an observable event and it satisfies the MSC. Therefore it is appended as *pass* event $p3$ to the current node in the Autolink event tree. $p3$ also becomes the new current node in the Autolink event tree.

$e3$ is not an observable event, therefore it can be ignored. It is also the last event in the list. This means that the transition is completed and state 5 in the state space graph

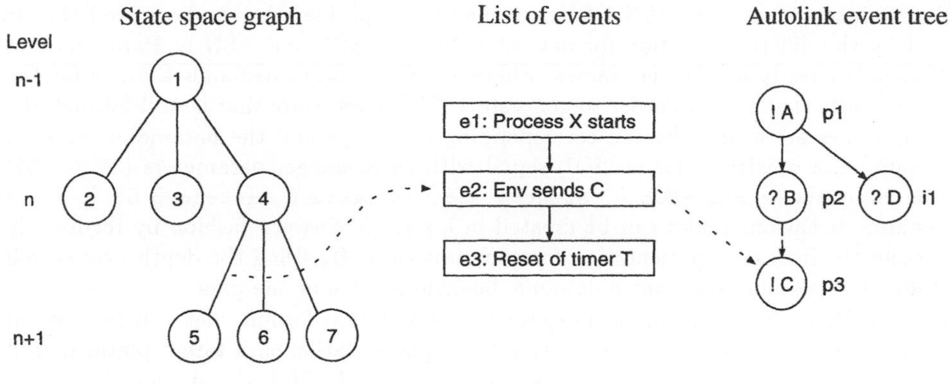

Figure 6. Test case processing algorithm

has been reached. To continue the exploration, the first state following state 5 on level $n+2$ has to be computed.

An *inconclusive* node is appended to the Autolink event tree if an event e in the list of events is observable but does not satisfy the MSC. To continue the exploration, the next state on the same level has to be computed. If we had such an event in the transition from state 1 to state 2 in Figure 6, e.g., then the transition from state 1 to state 3 would be computed next.

For every level n the current node $p(n)$ in the Autolink event tree is saved. If there is no next state on level n, then the next state on level $n-1$ is computed and the saved $p(n-1)$ becomes the current node in the Autolink event tree. The exploration ends if no more states are found below the start state.

Post-processing removes unwanted events from the Autolink event tree. First, it is assumed that the environment always sends signals to the system as soon as possible, whereas receive events occur with an undefined delay. Therefore, alternative receive events to a send from the environment are removed from the Autolink event tree. Second, incomplete pass paths may have been generated during the state space exploration. The first event in a branch which does not end with a *pass* verdict is reassigned as an event with *inconclusive* verdict, and the rest of the branch is discarded.

Define and modify constraints
Constraints are automatically created during test case processing. Additionally, the user can define and remove signal constraints at any time. It is also possible to assign more reasonable names to constraints generated by AUTOLINK and to merge two constraint definitions. This is useful if the constraints have the same meaning or if a signal parameter with different values in the two constraints is irrelevant.

Save test suite
The TTCN test suite generated by AUTOLINK is written in MP format. It mainly consists of two sections – the constraints part and the dynamic behaviour part.

Constraints are saved in ASN.1 format. Thereby a problem has to be solved that is caused by the different notation for data structures in SDL and ASN.1. Parameters of SDL signals have types, but no names, whereas ASN.1 always demands a name for the fields of a data structure. In order to generate a TTCN test suite that is well-formed, the missing names are formed by the corresponding data type and the parameter number. For example, a constraint for an SDL signal with three integer parameters (55, 0, -55) will be mapped onto `SEQUENCE { integer1 -55, integer2 0, integer3 55 }`.

Dynamic behaviour tables can be created in a straight-forward fashion by recursively traversing the internal representation for each test case. By using the depth first search strategy, it is possible to output a dynamic behaviour table in one pass.

The TTCN format is a general purpose test description format that can be used in many testing situations; both when testing an implementation on a target platform and when testing SDL systems in a simulated environment. In SDT the support for target testing is given by the ITEX TTCN environment and SDL level testing is provided by a co-simulation possibility between the SDL and TTCN simulators available in the SDT/ITEX tool set.

5.2. State space navigation

The SDT Validator offers several different ways to specify paths (and thus test cases), including both selective and brute force strategies. Some examples are:

- Manual navigation/simulation in the state space
- Using MSCs as input
- Using observer processes for a brute force strategy

All three methods to define a path can also be combined.

Manual navigation

The SDT Validator provides a special window called the *Navigator* (Figure 7) that allows users to manually explore the state space and thereby to define paths in an efficient way.

MSC verification

MSCs provide another way to define paths. In this case the idea is to create an MSC, either manually or by using, for example, the SDT Simulator, and then make the Validator search for a path that satisfies the MSC. This path is then used as the test purpose.

Observer processes

Observer processes are sophisticated constructs that allow a completely automatic definition of a large set of tests for an SDL system.

The general idea when using observer processes for test generation is to encode a high-level test purpose in an observer process. Each time a path is found by the Validator which satisfies the condition defined in the observer process, a report is generated. At the end of the state space exploration, the reports can be converted into MSC test cases.

To simplify things for users a special SDL package called the *TestGen* package has been developed. This package includes a number of utilities including two observer process types that can directly be used in test generation applications:

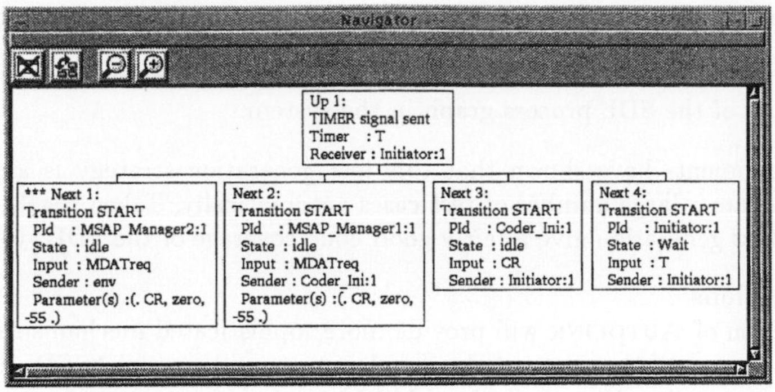

Figure 7. The SDT Navigator

- A process type for random test generation.
- A process type for test generation based on process graph coverage.

Both process types are delivered in source code and can be modified by users to suit the needs of special applications.

The random test generator process simply encodes the following rule:

> Whenever a path is found that contains more than a given number of transitions, a test is generated.

This observer process is intended to be used together with the *random walk algorithm* in the Validator. If it is included in an SDL system and a random walk through the state space is executed with a certain number of repetitions, one test case will be generated for each path that contains the given number of transitions.

The observer process is mainly included in the package in order to let users modify it with application specific test purpose conditions. If it is used as is, it will generate many equivalent test cases.

The second observer process is a very useful modification of the first one. It encodes the following test purpose condition:

> Whenever a path is found which contains more than a given number of transitions, and this particular path includes SDL process graph symbols that have *not* been covered by previously generated tests, then a test is to be generated.

This observer process is also intended to be used in combination with the random walk algorithm in the Validator. If it is included in an SDL system and a repeated random walk through the state space is executed with a certain number of repetitions, the following happens:

- The first random walk will generate a test case when the indicated depth is reached.
- All subsequent random walks will generate new test cases for all paths that cover new parts of the SDL process graph in the system.

Practical experiments have shown that this test generation strategy is a very efficient means to generate a large number of test cases automatically. Taken together, these two methods for test generation give a fairly good code coverage of the SDL system.

5.3. Future plans

The next version of AUTOLINK will provide more sophisticated mechanisms for the definition of test cases. At the moment the user has to provide complete SDL paths leading to a TTCN *pass* verdict. Via system level MSCs, these paths are transformed into TTCN notation. Additionally, all responses leading to an *inconclusive* verdict are computed. In the next version of AUTOLINK it will also be allowed to specify a test case by providing only a part of a trace leading to a *pass* verdict. Such parts are often referred to by the term *test purpose*. AUTOLINK will search for adequate completions, and pre- and postambles for a given test purpose. A test purpose may be given in form of an MSC, an observer process, or a piece of an SDL diagram which has to be executed during the test.

From research we know that the main problem of finding completions, pre- and postambles is the explosion of the state space during its exploration. Therefore our work will focus on developing strategies and mechanisms for dealing with this problem. Especially, we will start to implement tools for a *static* and a *dynamic pre-investigation* of SDL specifications and for performing *measurements of the test generation capabilities*.

Static pre-investigation of an SDL specification. A static pre-investigation may be based on a data flow analysis. It will provide information about all message parameters that influence the behaviour of the SDL specification. This information helps to manually define concrete parameter values, which have to be provided by the test equipment during the test run.

Dynamic pre-investigation of an SDL specification. A dynamic pre-investigation may be based on a symbolic execution of the SDL specification. It allows to calculate the 'optimal input data' automatically and to propose stable testing states.

Measurement of the test generation capabilities. While the number of states which can be examined by test case generators in a certain amount of time is almost constant, the complexity of the search within the state space of an SDL specification depends on the options and search heuristic chosen by the user. The complexity and thus the capabilities of a test case generator for a particular SDL specification can be measured by a number of simulation runs. An automatic comparison of the results will provide information for a reasonable choice of options and heuristics.

With test suite validation we recognized another important problem. Due to the different nature of TTCN and SDL it is nearly impossible to generate complete TTCN test descriptions from SDL specifications only. Therefore a generated test suite has to be refined manually. This on the other hand may introduce new errors or ambiguities into the test suite. Our work will also focus on providing tools for performing test suite validation against an SDL specification.

6. SUMMARY AND OUTLOOK

We have shown the current possibilities for tool assisted test case generation using the SDT Validator and ITEX. Practical use of these methods has indicated that an improvement of the test case generation facilities is needed and possible. Therefore, the AUTOLINK project has been set up. The first, basic version of the AUTOLINK tool has been described in this paper. In the future, AUTOLINK will be enhanced to include a pre-investigation of the SDL specifications, the measurement of the test case generation capabilities and additional test case generation mechanisms.

REFERENCES

1. R. Bræk, A. Sarma (editors). *SDL'95 with MSC in CASE.* North-Holland, 1995.
2. L. Doldi, V. Encontre, J.-C. Fernandez, T. Jéron, S. Le Briquir, N. Texier, M. Phalippou. *Assesment of Automatic Generation of Conformance Test Suites in an Industrial Context.* In 'Testing of Communicating Systems' (B. Baumgarten, H.-J. Burkhardt, A. Giessler, editors). Chapman & Hall, 1996.
3. ETSI MTS 10/96 TD42. *Report on Automatic Generation of TTCN from SDL.* ETSI, 1996.
4. A. Ek. *Verifying Message Sequence Charts with the SDT validator.* In [8].
5. ETSI STC SPS 3. *Intelligent Network (IN); IN Capability Set 2 (CS2); Scoping of Intelligent Network Application Protocol (INAP).* DTR/SPS-03043, ETSI, 1996.
6. O. Færgemand, M. M. Marques (editors). *SDL'89: The Language at work.* North-Holland, 1989.
7. O. Færgemand, R. Reed (editors). *SDL'91: Evolving Methods.* North-Holland, 1991.
8. O. Færgemand, A. Sarma (editors). *SDL'93 - Using Objects.* North-Holland, 1993.
9. J. Grabowski, D. Hogrefe, R. Nahm. *Test Case Generation with Test Purpose Specification by MSCs.* In [8].
10. J. Grabowski, R. Scheurer, D. Hogrefe. *Applying SAMSTAG to the B-ISDN Protocol SSCOP.* Technical Report A-97-01, Medizinische Universität zu Lübeck, Schriftenreihe der Institute für Mathematik/Informatik, Lübeck, January 1997.
11. D. Hogrefe. *OSI Formal Specification Case Study: The Inres Protocol and Service* (revised). Technical Report IAM-91-012, University of Bern, Institute for Computer Science, May 1991, Update May 1992.
12. G. J. Holzmann. *Design and Validation of Computer Protocols.* Prentice-Hall International, Inc., 1991.
13. ISO/IEC. *Information Technology - OSI - Conformance Testing Methodology and Framework.* International ISO/IEC multipart standard No. 9646, 1994.
14. ISO/IEC. *Information Technology - OSI - Conformance Testing Methodology and Framework - Part 3: The Tree and Tabular Combined Notation (TTCN).* ISO/IEC IS 9646-3, 1996.
15. ITU-T Rec. Q.2931. *Broadband Integrated Services Digital Network (B-ISDN) - Digital Subscriber Signalling System No. two (DSS2) protocol.* Geneva, 1995.
16. ITU-T Rec. Z.100 (1996). *Specification and Description Language (SDL).* Geneva, 1996.
17. ITU-T Rec. Z.120 (1996). *Message Sequence Chart (MSC).* Geneva, 1996.

SDL '97: TIME FOR TESTING - SDL, MSC and Trends
A. Cavalli and A. Sarma (Editors)

Automating the process of test derivation from SDL specifications

G. v. Bochmann, A. Petrenko*, O. Bellal, and S. Maguiraga

Université de Montréal, CP. 6128, Succ. Centre-Ville, Montréal, H3C 3J7, Canada, bochmann@iro.umontreal.ca

* CRIM, Centre de Recherche Informatique de Montréal, 1801 Avenue McGill College, Suite 800, Montréal, H3A 2N4, Canada, petrenko@crim.ca

In this paper, we present a set of automated tools for the development of conformance tests following a methodology based on a partial unfolding of a given SDL specification, describing the behavior of the system under test. The methodology relies on FSM-based test derivation methods which focus on the fault coverage aspect of testing. The tool kit offers to the test designer a number of options for achieving different levels of fault coverage. In particular, it provides support for partial specifications, grouped transitions and timers. The tests, which are generated in SDL or in TTCN must be completed by hand concerning certain aspects related to signal parameters, however, most of these adjustments are relatively straightforward and certain parts of the original SDL specification can be reused without change. We also report on our experience of using the tool kit for the development of a test suite for the ATM PNNI signalling protocol.

1. INTRODUCTION

The specification of a system component or a protocol entity is the basis for any implementation or testing effort [1]. In order to (at least partially) automate these efforts, it is necessary that the specification exists in a form which is machine processable. Formal description techniques, such as SDL, have been developed with essentially two objectives:

(1) encouraging the development of precise specifications which do not allow for any ambiguities, and

(2) allowing the partial automation of the system development activities, such as the verification and evaluation of the system design (e.g. protocol specification); the implementation process, as existing (SDL) tools allow to produce implementation code [2]; and the test development process, in particular semi-automated development of test purposes, abstract test suites (written in TTCN, SDL or some ad hoc notation, possibly including sequences of API calls) and their validation and finally automatic translation into executable tests (Note: the automation of test suite development is most advanced for the FSM-related aspects of the specifications).

While the use of formal specifications has many advantages, there are also some important shortcomings:

(a) It takes time to build a formal specification.

(b) The performance of the automatically generated implementation is less than optimal.

(c) The aspect of PDU encoding is often difficult to express in the formal language. Coding routines written by hand may be used.

(d) Concerning test development, the following observations can be made:

- Most tools only automate part of the test development process.
- The test development process may be more difficult to be controlled by the test designer because certain decisions are taken by the tool (for instance the choice of a particular preamble, among several possibilities, for a given test case).
- Most testing tools address the control flow (FSM) aspects only, and neglect the aspects related to interaction parameters.

In this paper we concentrate on the problem of automatically deriving tests from a given specification in SDL. We present a tool kit which partially automates the derivation of a test suite from a specification and shortly describe its use for the development of a test suite for the ATM PNNI signalling protocol. Our approach to the design of testing tools, further discussed in Section 2, is based on the automatic extraction of a partially unfolded FSM model from the given SDL specification and the use of existing test derivation tools for partially specified FSM specifications. Using a pragmatic approach for the partial unfolding, the FSM model allows us to exploit the fault coverage guarantees provided by FSM-based test development methods (in an approximated manner) for the tests obtained from the SDL specification. We believe that our attention to <u>fault</u> coverage aspects, as compared to <u>code</u> (or transition) coverage considered by many other testing methods, leads to better test suites. Section 3 describes the proposed test development process and the tools we have developed for this purpose. Sections 4 and 5 discuss certain tool extensions which concern the efficient testing of groups of coherent transitions (such as erroneous or unexpected inputs) and the testing of the behavior of timers. Our experience with the application of the methodology to the ATM PNNI signalling protocol is described in Section 6, which is followed by the conclusions.

2. OUR APPROACH TO THE DESIGN OF TEST TOOLS FOR SDL

The underlying model of an SDL specification is an Extended Finite State Machine (EFSM). Its most general form has not only internal (context) variables, but also input parameters such that a transition can only be executed if its enabling condition (usually in the form of a predicate depending on input parameters and state variables) is satisfied. It is a well-known difficult problem to derive a parameterized input sequence which either transfers an EFSM to a desired state or which distinguishes a pair of states. Compared with the classical FSM model, the EFSM model may give a very compressed behavioral description of the system, but at the same time, it is much less tractable for verification and test derivation purposes. If certain limiting assumptions are made about the form of the predicates and actions, the analysis of the behavior of the specification and systematic test selection remains decidable [3], but in general, in particular when the actions may include loops, the question of deciding which input parameters should be used in order to force the execution of a particular transition becomes undecidable, like the question of deciding the executability of a given branch of a program in software testing.

Several researchers have proposed to use dataflow analysis for the systematic selection of test cases for EFSM, and therefore for SDL specifications. Dataflow analysis involves the input and output parameters and the additional state variables. By selecting appropriate test cases involving appropriate transitions, it is possible to satisfy the testing criteria that have

been developed for software testing, such as "all definition-use pairs", etc. [4]. The aspect of fault detection is, however, not directly addressed within these approaches. An alternative approach is to view an EFSM as a compressed notation of an FSM. The intention behind this approach is to retain the applicability of the FSM-based methods to generate tests. In this approach, at least three solutions exist to obtain a more tractable state-oriented specification:
(1) to derive a pure FSM by ignoring all the extensions (parameters, predicates, and actions) to basic FSM model;
(2) to unfold the EFSM into an FSM by expanding the values of the input parameters;
(3) to extract an FSM by the partial unfolding of variables of enumerated types, while using enabling conditions as a part of the corresponding FSM inputs.

The main drawback of the first option is that all the tests derived from the obtained FSM should be verified for executability. The second option, a straightforward unfolding of an EFSM, easily leads to an explosion of the number of states and inputs. In our work, we have decided to follow a compromise solution. The partial unfolding approach is based on the observation that most real protocols have not so many complicated predicates, a majority of transitions are not guarded by any predicate at all, while internal variables of enumerative types can easily be eliminated by unfolding (see also the normalization, as suggested in [5]). This observation has been reported by a number of researchers. It supports an optimistic view that "the worst usually does not come to the worst". More precisely, we approximate the behavior of the SDL specification by an FSM (called an *approximating machine*), where an input of the FSM corresponds to a pair of an input signal and an enabling condition (if any), while states of the FSM mostly correspond to the control states of the SDL specification, except for unfolded states which are control states augmented with values of enumerative variables. In Section 3.2, we present the tool FEX (FSM extractor) which construct such an approximating machine from a given SDL specification. We believe that this approach has a number of attractive features:

- the state/transition explosion is alleviated compared with "complete" unfolding;
- the construction of an approximating machine can easily be automated;
- FSM-based methods can be applied to generate tests with high fault coverage;
- a good number of sequences derived from such an approximating machine usually remains executable with respect to the original SDL specification;
- the number of non-executable sequences and, thus, of human interruptions needed to adjust them is controlled;
- existing commercial SDL tools can be used to check the executability of sequences modified by hand;
- once a major part of a test suite with a certain fault coverage (in terms of the FSM-based fault models) needs no adjustments, the final test suite is expected to have a high fault detection power, as well.

Of course, the approach becomes less attractive for an EFSM with rather complicated enabling conditions, when most test sequences should be adjusted by hand. However, it never becomes inferior to the approach completely neglecting the predicates and parameters.

3. OUR TOOL KIT FOR TEST DERIVATION

3.1. The process of test derivation

A number of different tools have been developed at the University of Montreal for partially automating the test development process. Most tools use an underlying FSM model, that is, the behavior of the system to be tested is expressed in terms of a number of states and inputs, and the outputs and state transitions produced by the arrival of a given input in a given state. These tools are therefore useful for systems that can be characterized by FSM-oriented specifications, such as communication protocols.

In the following we focus on a chain of tools for the development of test cases from SDL specifications, as shown in Figure 1.

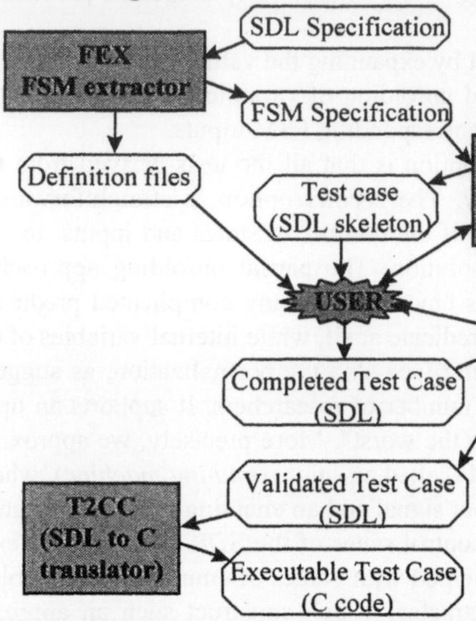

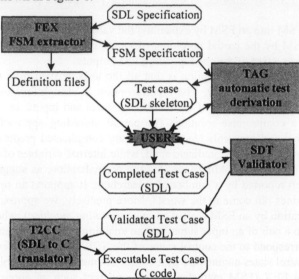

Figure 1: Test suite development from SDL specifications

The diagram of Figure 1 shows in the middle column the description of objects leading from the formal specification in SDL of the component to be tested to the executable test cases written in C code. On the left and on the right are shown the tools that can be used during the test development process. The first tool, called FEX (FSM Extractor) extracts from the SDL specification a partial view of the behavior represented in the form of an FSM. At the same time, files containing SDL declarations of interactions (called "signals") and channels are created which can be later used for obtaining complete test cases written in SDL. The FEX tool generates an FSM transition for each branch of each SDL transition in the specification; thus each branch corresponding to a particular input and particular conditions of the input parameters gives rise to a separate transition (for each state of the specification). We note that the resulting FSM model is quite similar to the "test matrix" which is commonly used for the (manual) development of protocol conformance test suites. The TAG (Automatic Test Generation) tool [6] is a generic tool for test suite development based on FSM specifications. It accepts as input a partially specified, deterministic FSM and generates test cases according to the options provided by the test designer. The options include the following:

(a) Automatic generation of a complete test suite with guaranteed coverage of output and transfer faults (assuming that the number of states of the implementation under test (IUT) is not larger than the number of states of the specification);

(b) Generation of tests for a specific transition (corresponding to a given "test purpose") selected by the test designer;

(c) The use of state identification sequences for checking transfer faults is optional;

(d) Separate generation of test preambles, postambles and state identification sequences;
(e) Generation of tests related to timers (setting, resetting and time-out transitions, further discussed in Section 5)
(f) Generation of tests for grouped transitions (corresponding to a single SDL transition having several starting states, or several input signals, further discussed in Section 4).

It is important to note that the TAG tool supports several output formats for the generated test cases:

(1) I/O sequences: This format is easy to read and relatively condensed.
(2) SDL skeletons: The generated SDL skeletons represent test cases, preambles, postambles and state identification sequences. They are complete SDL procedures, except that the details concerning the signal parameters are not included. (Note: If the SDL signals of the specification have no parameters, the generated SDL skeletons are complete SDL procedures).
(3) TTCN-MP skeletons: The generated skeletons represent test cases, preambles, postambles and state identification sequences. They are complete TTCN dynamic behavior trees, except that the details concerning the signal parameters are not included.

The generated test suite (in SDL or in TTCN) must in general be completed by hand (see below) in order to add the information concerning the signal (interaction) parameters, that is the checking of the conditions to be satisfied by the input parameters and the determination of the parameter values of the output signals.

The next development step shown in Figure 1 is the validation of the obtained test cases against the original SDL specification, using an existing SDL development environment. After this validation step, the test cases may be compiled into executable C code, thus resulting in executable test cases. An SDL-to-C translator developed at the University of Montreal has been enhanced with a facility for automatically generating PDU coding and decoding routines. It has also been extended to partially automate the variation of parameter values used by the test cases. This tool, described in Section 3.5, allows the test designer to control the automatic variation of interaction parameters for obtaining a repeated execution of a given test case with varying interaction parameters. In the case that the generated test cases should be obtained in the TTCN language, the TTCN output option of the TAG tool could be used. The resulting test cases should be completed by hand in a way similar to what is described above. In this case, it would be profitable to generate the definition files in TTCN-MP, however, this would require the automatic translation of the declarations from SDL to TTCN.

3.2. Generating an FSM model from an SDL specification: the FEX tool

The FEX tool applies a normalization algorithm on a given SDL[1] specification in order to extract an FSM model from it. One or more transitions in the generated FSM correspond to a given input at a given state in the SDL specification. This is due to the fact that the tool uses partial unfolding to preserve constraints on the values of message parameters. In addition, FEX generates additional files to be included in the SDL skeletons of test cases generated by TAG. They contain data type declarations, signal declarations, channel and signal route definitions and related information.

The FSM format used by TAG and generated by FEX is simple and intuitive. It consists of four sections specifying the FSM states, inputs, outputs and transition lists. Input signals are usually parameterized as shown in Example 3.1, for input `I2`. In this case FEX generates

[1] We use a subset of SDL which allows the description of one-process specifications.

several transitions for the parameterized input using partial unfolding of parameters. Each transition corresponds to a different value of the parameter as specified in the subsequent decision statement. In Example 3.1, two transitions are generated for input `I2` at state `S0`; corresponding to values 0 and 1 of parameter **n**. TAG treats `I2(n=0)` and `I2(n=1)` as two different inputs.

Example 3.1

SDL specification:

```
state S0;
   input I1;
   output O1;
   nextstate S1;

   input I2(n);
   decision n;
      (0): output O2;
           nextstate S2;
      (1): output O3;
           nextstate S3;
   enddecision;
```

FSM transitions generated:

```
S0 ?I1 !O1 >S1;
S0 ?I2(n=0) !O2 >S2;
S0 ?I2(n=1) !O3 >S3;
```

As mentioned in the introduction, TAG produces SDL skeletons of derived test cases which are completed manually by the test designer. The information present in the reference SDL specification related to input/output parameters can be very useful to the user in this sense. FEX carries this information and reproduces it in the FSM specification, which is then reproduced by TAG as comments in appropriate places in the generated SDL skeletons of test cases. This helps the test designer avoid referring to the SDL specification each time he wants to complete a test case. Example 3.2 shows how assignment statements and timer operations are gathered and reproduced for a corresponding transition. Assignment **`task p := 7;`** and timer setting **`set(now+100,T);`** are associated to the second transition.

Example 3.2

SDL specification:

```
state S0;
   input I1;
   output O1;
   nextstate S1;

   input I2(n);
   decision n;
      (0): task p := 7;
           set(now+100,T);
           output O2(p);
           nextstate S2;
      (1): output O3;
           nextstate S3;
   enddecision;
```

FSM transitions generated:

```
S0 ?I1 !O1 >S1;
S0 ?I2(n=0) !O2 >S2 {(p := 7), set(now+100,T)};
S0 ?I2(n=1) !O3 >S3;
```

The main process of the SDL specification may make calls to procedures. These have their own FSM part. It may also make several calls to the same procedure, however, recursive calls are not supported. FEX produces one global FSM for the entire specification. FSM parts of called procedures should be linked to the main process FSM. When FEX encounters a procedure call, it produces a transition to the start state of this procedure. It then generates all of its transitions. The states generated for a given procedure must be different for each call of the procedure. To avoid state name collision, FEX prefixes a procedure state name with two things: the name of the procedure (to avoid collision with state names of other procedures), and a call number (to distinguish state names of different calls of the same procedure). For instance, `p_2_S1` denotes state `S1` of the second call of procedure `p`.

The tool only accepts a single-process SDL specifications and does not support recursive procedures. Besides, some control aspects related to state variables cannot be captured and preserved in the process of FSM extraction. For instance, the iteration of some transitions expressed by a counter variable cannot be reflected in the generated FSM. Typically, another transition is triggered whenever the counter reaches a specified value, i.e. after a number of iterations on other transitions. The FSM transition which corresponds to this latter case contains the iteration information only in the form of a condition associated with the input which cannot be interpreted in the proper way by the TAG tool. Therefore the generated test case(s) for this transition do not contain the sequence of input/output corresponding to the iteration part. In such cases, the test designer should be able to add the necessary interactions to obtain executable test cases. An example is given in [7].

3.3. Test derivation: the TAG tool

TAG implements the so-called transition identification approach for test derivation from an FSM. In particular, to achieve a particular test purpose which is a certain transition to be tested, the following steps have to be performed:

- bring the FSM from its initial state to the starting state of the transition under test using the shortest input sequence possible (called a preamble of the test case);
- execute the transition and check the observed output;
- check a tail state of the transition by observing its reaction to a pre-selected set of state identification sequences, which can verify the correctness of the tail state (a test body to achieve the test purpose);
- apply an input sequence to return to the initial state of the FSM (a postamble of the test case).

The user may specify a so-called homing sequence which is expected to take the FSM from any state back to the initial state. The set of all preambles is called a state cover; the set of sequences used to execute all specified transitions is called a transition cover. State identification sequences are input sequences which distinguish states by their output reactions. Some FSMs may have indistinguishable states for which there exists no sequence which tells them apart. If this is the case for the given FSM then the tool still produces test cases, however, certain transfer faults in implementations might not be detected. A reduced or minimal machine has no indistinguishable states, and the tool produces a test suite for such a machine with the guaranteed coverage of all output and transfer faults within the specified number of states. The tool, further described in [6], implements the so-called HSI method [8], [9] which is similar to the widely known W-method [10] in which a characterization set is used for state identification. However, the HSI-method uses a tuple of subsets of a W set for the identification of each state and can be applied to partially specified FSMs. The tool supports the following two modes of test derivation:

- complete test derivation, when a test suite has to test all transitions specified in the given FSM (according to the HSI method);
- selective test derivation, when a test case has to test a single transition given as a test purpose.

Before starting the tool, the user must have a text file containing the FSM specification with suffix ".fsm". This file can be produced by transforming an SDL specification through the tool FEX, or directly by using a text editor. The FSM specification is required to be deterministic and initially connected, but it may be partially or completely specified.

An FSM description consists of six parts: (1) the state definitions, (2) the input definitions, (3) the output definitions, (4) the transition definitions, (5) the variable declaration and (6) the homing sequence definition; parts (5) and (6) are optional.

The user may use keyword "homing" to give a sequence of input names as a homing sequence of the FSM specification, that is, it leads the FSM from any state to the initial state. The names in the homing sequence may be undefined input names. The principle is that TAG adds a postamble in a test case, if there is a postamble for a tail state, the postamble is used; otherwise, if the homing sequence is given, the homing sequence is used. If there is no postamble and no homing sequence is given, no postamble is included in the test case.

The FSM specification is analyzed, the tool displays the related information, such as whether or not it is initially connected, it has indistinguishable states, equivalent states, and states with no postamble. If there are non-deterministic transitions in a certain state in a given specification, one among these non-deterministic transitions is kept in the compiled FSM and the others are ignored. Test derivation for an FSM with indistinguishable states is also possible, though some faults in these states might not be detected. In these two cases the tool will prompt a warning message. The tool derives preambles and postambles (if required) for all the states of a given machine. A transition cover is also generated when a complete generation of tests is chosen.

To obtain a minimal characterization set for a given FSM, as well as minimal harmonized state identification sets, may be an NP-hard problem. The tool TAG uses, therefore, an heuristic solution attempting to obtain minimal HSI sets. As the experiments show this method constructs state identifiers in a nearly polynomial time [6]. The user may select just one sequence from a state identifier to confirm the tail state of a transition.

We note that the TAG tool supports three different formats in which the tests can be generated. An easily readable mnemonic format in the form of I/O sequences, SDL skeletons and TTCN behavior tables. A complete example of the test case generated for a given transition of the INRES protocol is given in [7].

3.4. Completing the generated test skeletons

SDL skeletons of the generated test cases must be completed by the test designer with respect to the aspects:

- to supply values for all output signal parameters, where needed;
- to supply variables to store all input signal parameters, where needed;
- to add decision statements after input statements in order to check parameter values, where needed;
- to supply the necessary declarations of variables and associated type definitions.

The type definitions can be imported from the original SDL protocol specification, however, the other three aspects must be written by the test designer for each specific test case. As an example, we consider second FSM transition of Example 3.3 above. Part of the SDL skeleton generated by TAG is shown below. We note that the test case specifies the behavior of the tester, therefore the inputs of the FSM specification become the outputs for the tester and vice versa.

```
  ...
  /* USER: make n = 0 */
  output I2(/* USER: fill parameters */);
  nextstate wait_O2_in_S0;

state wait_O2_in_S0;
  /* (p := 7), set(now+100,T) */
  input O2;
  /* USER: Check parameters */
  ...
```

Completed by the test designer, this part of the test case may look as follows. Note in particular the assignment statement `(p := 7)` is replaced by a decision statement which checks the assigned value of the parameter `P` of input `O2`.

```
  ...
  task n := 0;
  output I2(n);
  nextstate wait_for_O2_in_S0;

state wait_for_O2_in_S0;
  input O2(P);
  decision P;
    (7): RETURN;
    (else): MACRO fail('param. of O2 expected to be 7');
          return;
  enddecision;
  ...
```

Except for the handling of interaction parameters, the test case skeletons generated by TAG are complete SDL specifications, including all necessary BLOCK, CHANNEL and PROCESS definitions. A test suite is represented as an SDL process which contains the test preambles, state identification sequences and postambles as procedures. Each test case is also represented as a procedure calling, in order, the preamble, the transition under test, optionally the state identification sequence and the postamble.

3.5. Parameter variation

One of the difficulties encountered during test design is the generation of different tests for the different values of input parameters to be tested. The Test Parameter Variation tool can be used to generate such tests with different representative valid and/or invalid values. It first generates additional representative values for each test parameter according to its declared type, and then generates tuples of test values possibly varying simultaneously the values of several test parameters. The scheme of variation can be specified by the test designer in the test script. The test designer is given the possibility to specify some or all of the representative valid and/or invalid values for a given test parameter; the Test Parameter Variation tool completes the lists of valid and invalid values, if left open by the test designer. Tuples of parameter values to be used in tests are output in files which are used by the generated code during test execution.

Since it is impossible to test an implementation under test with all possible values of test parameters, a representative set of values has to be chosen. Both normal and abnormal situations should be applied to the IUT. Therefore test parameter values should include both representative valid and invalid values. In this respect, two kinds of problems are to be addressed. The first one is related to the generation of sets of representative values from determined data types; the second involves the organization of these sets of values in value tuples, which can be applied in a single execution of a test case.

Most methods for value generation use the idea of dividing the set of values of a given data type into equivalence classes, where each equivalence class regroups values of the given type that are considered to lead to the same testing effect. One representative value is then chosen from each equivalence class. Equivalence classes are determined for invalid values as well. Some methods use the limit values in types to determine valid and invalid values. In contrast, other methods rely on the test designer's intuition. We choose here a combination of these methods where valid and invalid values are automatically generated and/or determined by the test designer (see also [11], [12]). Values tuples are then automatically calculated, and the test designer may suppress some of these value tuples or add others that he believes appropriate for testing based on his expertise.

After the generation of the possible values (representative "normal" values and "invalid" values) for each parameter to be selected by a test case, it is important to determine which combination of values should be applied in a test run. If all parameter values are varied independently of one another, a combinatorial explosion of test runs could easily occur. Therefore the test designer should indicate which combination of parameter values should actually be used in the test runs. The problem here is to generate a set of combinations that cover all of the valid and invalid representative values. This is not straightforward because dependencies may exist between some of the parameters, for instance between a string (one parameter) and its length (another parameter). Moreover, a test designer may want to have some parameters varied in parallel and others in a dependent way. Three methods of value variation can be specified: variation in combination, in parallel, and free variation.

4. COHERENT TRANSITIONS RESULTING FROM SDL SPECIFICATIONS

In spite of the fact that state/transition explosion does not usually occur when an approximating machine is derived from an SDL specification, the number of transitions specified in the obtained machine can yet be very high. As a result, the total length of tests derived by means of TAG tool could be quite big, as well. This often happens when a single transition of the given specification yields in the resulting machine multiple "similar" transitions having the same output. The basic idea is to test only one (or a few) transition among a set of similar ones. In the following, we first take a closer look at the source of multiple transitions and then we describe how these transitions could be handled, involving some pragmatic decisions, in order to further reduce the number of generated tests.

First, it is well known that a single statement in SDL may be used to describe multiple transitions. For example, the fragment

state * (s1, s2, s3);

input i1, i2;

output o;
nextstate s4;

corresponds to many transitions from all states, except **s1, s2, s3**, under input i1 or i2. Each of these transition has the same output **o** leads to the same next state **s4**. We call such a group of transitions *convergent* transitions. If the next state is specified as "-" (meaning to remain in the same state), then the statement describes the set of transitions which we call a group of *looping* transitions. In addition, the symbol "*" may be used to describe a set of inputs.

Second, according to the SDL semantics, all unspecified inputs in a given state must be ignored (the so-called completeness assumption). Speaking formally, any approximating machine should therefore be completely specified by enumerating all transitions implied the completeness assumption. An exception could apparently be made for inputs representing primitives from an upper layer, as they are usually left undefined in standardizing documents. Extracting a finite state machine from any specification, the "ignored" inputs imply a number of looping transitions labeled with the dummy "null" output. The test designer may decide to test whether the (completeness assumption) [4] is correctly implemented by applying a limited number of inputs (PDU's) in certain states, leaving the majority of the implied transitions untested.

Finally, multiple transitions also result from unfolding the parameter values of input signals and/or the values of control state variables. Such groups of transitions are considered by the parameter variation tool described in Section 3.5, but are not considered in the following.

In general, we call a group of convergent or looping transitions a group of *coherent* transitions. These groups can be distinguished according to the sets of starting states and/or the sets of inputs; all transitions of a group have the same output. The information about coherent transitions may either be deduced automatically from a given SDL specification or given by the test designer in the form of a list of coherent groups (in addition to the list of individual transitions).

In our extended TAG tool, the following notation is used to specify coherent transitions. "**E !I ?O** > -" represents a group of cycling transitions for the set of states **E**, labeled with all inputs of the set **I** and the output **O**. A similar notation "**E !I ?O > S**" is used for convergent transitions. The sets **E**, **I** can be specified explicitly by enumeration; the expression "***\P**" is used for the complement of **P**.

The decision to test a single representative among convergent transitions is based on the following "fault-coupling" hypothesis. In particular, if a single transition has a fault then all coherent transitions in the group are faulty; all of them have a wrong output or/and wrong tail state. Testing just one among the group would be sufficient. Theoretically speaking, fault detection power of the resulting test suite may not always correspond to what is often called "complete fault coverage" [13]. However, deriving tests only for selected transitions gives a good tradeoff between the length of tests and the fault coverage. Again, it is up to the user of the tool to make a proper selection of transitions to be tested. Note that in the case of cycling transitions, not one, but at least two transitions should be selected. The reason is that, an implementation error may convert them into convergent transitions leading to the same state which, by chance, may have been chosen for testing the cycling transition of the specification.

The extended TAG [14] performs such "selective" test generation. However, it does not take coherence into account for the generation of state identifiers; therefore the same state identifiers (if requested by the test designer) are used for complete or selective test derivation.

5. HANDLING TIMERS AND RELATED COUNTERS

Error-recovery functions of communication protocols often rely on timers which invoke limited retransmission of PDU's. At the expiration of a timer, a specific output is sent and the timer is restarted if the maximum number of retransmissions is not yet attained. If the maximum number is reached, usually a different transition with a different output is taken, for example, to release the current connection. Certain received input messages may stop a running timer.

The classical model of an FSM has no notion of time, yet it is quite common to use, in state-oriented specifications, a dummy input *T* to represent a silent time period which leads to the expiration of time *T*. To model the behavior triggered by timers and related counters, one typically augments FSM transitions between (control) states by internal actions "start *T*", "stop *T*" and adds transitions guarded by timer expirations (time-outs), as shown in Figure 2.

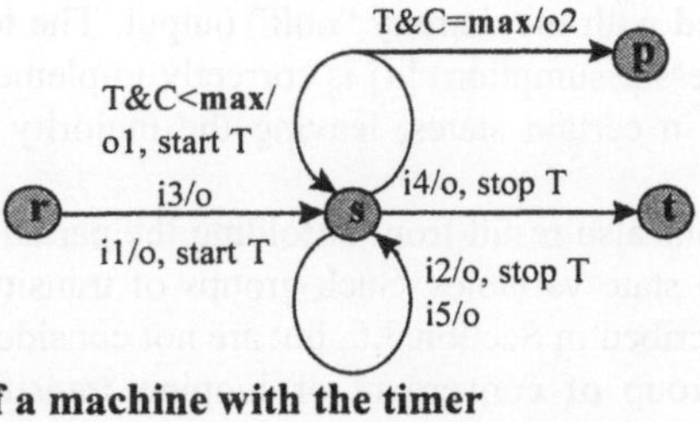

Figure 2: The fragment of a machine with the timer

Here, *C* represents a counter used by the protocol entity to ensure that the number of timer expirations never exceeds a given limit *max*. As this fragment of a specification indicates, an FSM with timers and related counters is a special case of the model of an extended FSM (EFSM). The difference from a general case is that the problem of test sequence executability is alleviated in this case, since the semantics of timers directly enables the derivation of executable tests, as discussed in the following.

A specification of the timer-regulated behavior should be consistent, in the sense that the presence of a timer should influence the observable behavior of the protocol and should be detectable by an external observer. In particular, as the above fragment shows, if timer *T* can be active in state *s*, there should be at least one incoming transition labeled with "start *T*" as well as at least one outgoing transition labeled with "stop *T*". Once *max* is reached, a time-out should cause an output different from the one produced by the previous time-outs, i.e. $o1 \neq o2$, and in general a transition to a different next state. All transitions setting up a timer for the first time are not cycling, i.e. states *r* and *s* (Figure 2) are not equivalent. In addition, to be consistent, a specification should, in case that several timers can be active at the same state, have no transition simultaneously starting several timers. Under the above assumptions, our extended TAG tool [14] provides the automatic derivation of test cases for checking the timing behavior, as explained below.

The test derivation strategy is based on the following assumptions about implementation errors related to timers and accompanying counters. First, we suppose that an implementation under test has successfully passed all tests derived from the "pure" FSM specification. Thus, testing the timer-related behavior, we may well assume that all the states of the specification are present, and all transitions not related to timers are correctly implemented. Implemented time-outs may violate the specification, but the maximal waiting time interval to cause expiration of any active timer should be known. Once the waiting time elapses, and no observable output was produced, one assumes that all timers (if any) were not active.

Potential implementation errors related to timers may either change the expected behavior or cause an unexpected behavior. Faults of the former group may occur in transitions labeled with **start *T*** (expected **start**); transitions labeled with ***T* and [C=max]** (expected **max**); and transitions labeled with **stop *T*** (expected **stop**). Faults of the latter group may create unexpected actions with timers, such as transitions labeled with **start *T*** (unexpected **start**) and transitions labeled with **stop *T*** (expected **stop**). In the following, we discuss the structure of test cases which are needed to check the above transitions, using the example in Figure 2.

***Expected* start**: To check whether or not the input *i*1 sets the timer *T*, we use the test sequences defined by the following expression: $\alpha[r]$. *i*1. *T*. *W*[*s*], where $\alpha[r]$ is a preamble to bring the machine from the initial state to the state *r*; *T* indicates that the tester should have time-out *T*, *W*[*s*] is a set of identification sequences for the state *s* (optional, in case we wish to confirm the tail state of the transition caused by the first expiration of the timer). Once the IUT passes all these tests, the following tests could be applied.

***Expected* max**: To check whether or not the implemented counter reaches the specified limit **max**, we use the test sequences defined by the following expression: $\alpha[r]$. *i*1. *T*(1). *T*(2). ... *T*(**max**). *W*[*p*], where **max** consecutive signals *T* indicate that the tester should have its time-out *T* expired **max** times observing repeated output *o*1 followed by *o*2. An earlier reception of *o*2 indicates that either the related counter was not properly initialized or the implemented value is less than **max**. In the case when a timer should expire only once (no counter is used), an additional time-out may be included into the test to verify if any unforeseen counter is implemented for this timer.

***Expected* stop**: To check whether or not the input *i*4 arrived after *i*1 stops the timer *T*, we use the test sequences defined by the following expression: $\alpha[r]$. *i*1. *i*4. *T*. *W*[*t*], where the use of the state identifier *W*[*s*] is optional. Any output produced by the IUT during the time-out period indicates that the input *i2* did not stop the timer *T*.

***Unexpected* start**: To check whether the input *i*3, for example, sets the timer *T* on, we use the test sequences defined by the following expression: $\alpha[r]$. *i*3. *T*. *W*[*s*]. Any output produced by the IUT during the time-out period indicates that the input *i*3 unexpectedly set the timer *T*. Tests of this type applied to all states at which the specification has no active timers would reveal an unforeseen timer. Assuming that, in the implementation under test, all timers are placed at the correct states, one may skip many tests related to unexpected **start**.

***Unexpected* stop:** To check whether or not the input *i5* stops the timer *T*, we use the test sequences defined by the following expression: $\alpha[r]$. *i*1. *i*5. *T*. *W*[*s*]. The IUT is expected to produce the output *o*1 after the time-out *T*, the failure to do so signals an error.

6. EXPERIMENTAL RESULTS

We applied the above test development methodology described in Section 3 to the ATM PNNI signalling protocol (ATM Forum version 1.0, excluding the routing functions). The first step in our work was the formalization of the PNNI protocol specification. Since a test architecture involving two PCO's was selected, as shown in Figure 3, we decided to write a combined specification for the behavior of the two PNNI entities shown in the figure, one playing the succeeding role and the other playing the preceding role.

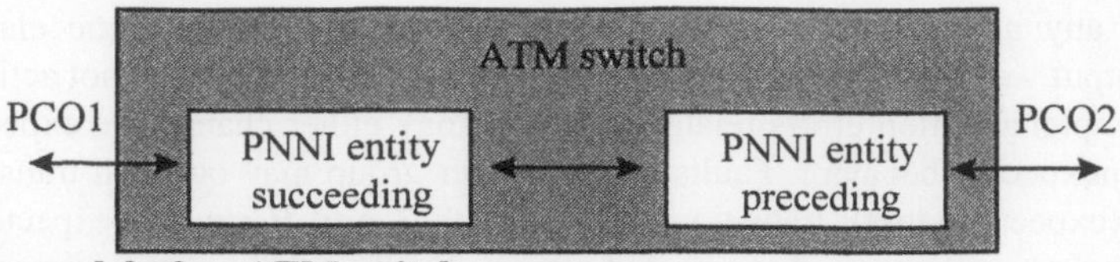

Figure 3: The model of an ATM switch

The development of the SDL specification was done in two phases. During the first phase, we studied the (informal) PNNI signalling protocol specification and developed a state table. Each state of the combined system shown in Figure 3 consists of a pair of states, one for the succeeding and one for the preceding PNNI entity. The resulting state table has 8 states (i.e. pairs of states) and a varying number of inputs including various conditions on the input parameters. For connection establishment (normal mode of operation), there are 6 table entries, and 36 for disconnection. Each table entry correspond to a given state, or a group of states, and an input with conditions. In addition, there are 8 entries concerning timers, 12 concerning status inquiry, and 71 entries for error handling situations.

During the second phase, we developed a specification in SDL. The information contained in the state table was easily translated into SDL. However, to obtain a complete specification of the protocol behavior, the type declarations related to the PDU parameters had to be written and the conditions associated with the different transitions had to be formalized. Since the interaction parameters of the PNNI protocol are very complex, this activity was time consuming. The resulting SDL specification has 8 states, and represents 13681 lines of SDL in the machine processable format. (This SDL code was generated by the SDT tool from the graphic SDL representation of the specification using the option of suppressing comments; with the automatic comment generation option of SDT, one obtains 31481 lines of code. The verification of the non-mandatory data elements was not included). The main activities for test derivation were the following:

(1) **Generating an FSM model using FEX:** The execution time of the tool for the processing the whole specification was 25 minutes. (As noted above, the tool was improved over time; we had to do this execution many times). The resulting FSM specification includes 628 inputs (corresponding largely to the different data conditions associated with the different branches in the SDL specification) and a total of 1508 transitions (ignoring groupings).

(2) **Generating test skeletons in SDL and TTCN using TAG:** The test cases were generated individually for selected test purposes. The processing time by TAG is negligible.

(3) **Completing test cases by hand:** The completion of the first test cases took more time, since (a) we had to learn how to do it, and (b) a number of routines had to be written (see discussion below). We have completed 10 test cases. We estimate that the time to complete the first 10 test cases is of the order of 4 days, the time for completing the next 100 test cases would be 10 days, and the time for completing 600 additional test cases would be 30 to 45 days.

(4) **Validating the test cases against the SDL specification:** We have used the SDT tool for validating the completed test cases. The time required for validating 10 test cases is about half a day. (Note: This could be further shortened if certain routine tool commands could be invoked automatically).

This experiment with PNNI let us to develop a method for completing test skeletons by hand along the following lines:

(1) The declarations from the protocol specification in SDL can be directly used for the test cases.
(2) The procedures of the protocol specification which check various conditions of the input parameters can be directly used in the corresponding test cases. They correspond to TTCN constraints that are used with input clauses.
(3) A number of procedures have to be written which select appropriate output parameters for the test cases, at least one procedure for each type of PDU. They correspond to TTCN constraints that are used with output clauses.
(4) The remaining additions to the skeletons are quite straightforward and some of them could be automatically generated by an improved TAG tool.

7. CONCLUSIONS

The automatic derivation of a test suite from a given SDL specification of the system under test is a challenging problem, especially if a certain guarantee of fault coverage is desired. We have presented a set of automated tools which can be used for the development of conformance tests following a methodology based on a partial unfolding of the SDL specification. This approach assures not only that all branches of the SDL specification are covered, but also that transfer faults are detected. A complementary tool for parameter variation has also been developed. We note that the tests generated from the SDL specification using our development process are quite similar to conventional conformance tests which are generated by hand. This test development is partly automated and leaves much freedom to the test designer to chose various options of fault coverage. The tests, which are generated in SDL or in TTCN must be completed by hand concerning certain aspects related to signal parameters, however, most of these adjustments are relatively straightforward and certain parts of the original SDL specification (e.g. data type, signal and channel definitions, conditions of DECISION statements) can be reused without change.

We have applied this methodology and our tools to the development of a test suite for the ATM PNNI signalling protocol and found that it is quite efficient compared with the conventional approach of developing the complete test suite by hand. A similar application to the ATM UNI signalling protocol is described in [15]. The main effort within our development process is the writing of the SDL specification. However, it is to be noted that this specification is not only a step towards the generation of the conformance tests, but can also be used to automatically generate code for a reference implementation of the protocol. We are presently working on extending our methodology and tools to the testing of systems consisting of several processes. This includes the case where the implementation under test (IUT) has a specification consisting of several SDL processes, but also the case of embedded testing where the IUT is not directly accessible, but only indirectly through other processes [16].

The tests generated from the SDL specification using the development process described above are quite similar to conventional conformance tests which are generated by hand. The main effort within this development process is the writing of the SDL specification. However, it is to be noted that this specification is not only a step towards the generation of the conformance tests, but can also be used to automatically generate code for a reference implementation of the protocol.

Acknowledgments. This work was partly supported by the NSERC strategic grant STRGP200 "Methods for the systematic testing of distributed software systems". The PNNI experience was supported by the Hewlett-Packard - NSERC - CITI Industrial Research Chair on Communication Protocols at the University of Montreal. The original version of the TAG tool was developed by Q.M. Tan and the extensions concerning coherent transitions and timers were implemented by W. Mainvis. The authors would like to thank their colleagues for many fruitful discussions, in particular, Q.M. Tan, W. Mainvis, D. Ouimet and R. Dssouli.

REFERENCES

1. G. v. Bochmann, *Protocol specification for OSI*, Computer Networks and ISDN Systems, 18, 1990.
2. G. v. Bochmann, G. Gerber and J.-M. Serre, *Semiautomatic implementation of communication protocols,* IEEE Trans., SE-13, No. 9, 1987, pp. 989-1000.
3. T. Higashino and G. v. Bochmann, *Automatic analysis and test derivation for a restricted class of LOTOS expressions with data parameters,* IEEE Trans., SE-20, 1, 1994.
4. G. v. Bochmann and A. Petrenko, *Protocol testing: Review of methods and relevance for software testing,* in Proc. of the ACM Intl. Sym. on Software Testing and Analysis (ISSTA'94), USA, 1994.
5. B. Sarikaya, G. v. Bochmann, *Obtaining normal form specifications for protocols,* in Proc. COMNET'85, IFIP, North Holland, 1985, pp. 601-613.
6. Q. M. Tan, A. Petrenko, and G. v. Bochmann, *A test generation tool for specifications in the form of state machines,* in Proceedings of the International Communications Conference, 1996, pp.225-229.
7. O. Bellal, *Example test cases for the INRES protocol generated by the FEX and TAG tools,* University of Montreal, Technical Report 1997, Web URL <ftp://ftp.iro.umontreal.ca/pub/teleinfo/TRs/Bell97.ps.gz>
8. A. Petrenko, *Checking experiments with protocol machines,* in Proceedings of the IFIP 4th International Workshop on Protocol Test Systems, the Netherlands, 1991, pp. 83-94.
9. G. Luo, A. Petrenko, and G. v. Bochmann, *Selecting test sequences for partially-specified nondeterministic finite state machines,* in Proc. of the IFIP IWPTS, Japan, 1994, pp. 95-110.
10. T. S. Chow, *Test Design Modeled by Finite-State Machines,* IEEE Trans. SE-4, 3, 1978.
11. G. J. Myers, *The Art of Software Testing*, John Wiley & Sons, 1979, 177p.
12. P. Gamache, *Générateur intelligent de tests adapté au domaine des protocoles de communication*, M.Sc. Thesis, Dépt. IRO, Université de Montréal, 1991.
13. A. Petrenko, G. v. Bochmann, and M. Yao, *On fault coverage of tests for finite state specifications,* Computer Networks and ISDN Systems, 29, 1996, pp. 81-106.
14. W. Mainvis, *Intégration de nouvelles fonctionnalités dans un outil de dérivation de tests pour les protocoles.* DEA Thesis, Université de Montréal (in collaboration with CRIN, Nancy, France), 1996.
15. D. Hristov et al., *Developing tests for the ATM signalling protocol using automated tools,* University of Montreal, submitted for publication.
16. A. Petrenko, N. Yevtushenko, G. v. Bochmann, and R. Dssouli, *Testing in context: framework and test derivation,* Computer Communications, 19, 1996.

SDL '97: TIME FOR TESTING - SDL, MSC and Trends
A. Cavalli and A. Sarma (Editors)

Test generation for the SSCOP-ATM networks protocol

Ana Cavalli[a], Boo-Ho Lee[b] and Toma Macavei[a]

[a]Institut National des Télécommunications
Les Epinettes
9, rue Charles Fourier
91011 Evry Cedex
France
[b]Electronics and Telecommunications Research Institute
Yusong P.O.Box 106 Taejon 305-600, Korea

E-mail: Ana.Cavalli@int-evry.fr
Toma.Macavei@int-evry.fr
bhlee@pec.etri.re.kr

Abstract: This paper presents the application of a test generation method to the testing of the SSCOP protocol for ATM networks. Test sequences have been generated automatically in an optimized and non optimized way from the SDL specification of the protocol. To illustrate the advantages of the presented method we have translated a test sequence generated using the method into the MSC formalism to show that tests obtained in an automatic way have the same form that tests obtained manually, as is the case for one of the tests scripts proposed by the standard.

Keywords: test generation, conformance testing, finite state machines, SDL, MSC, TTCN, SSCOP protocol (ATM networks).

1. Introduction

The increasing complexity of telecommunication systems based on ATM networks requires the development of testing techniques to be applied to their services and protocols. Testing is an important phase in the development of these systems. It is well known that the introduction of a new product in the network or the introduction of a new service, assumes that these systems have been tested in order to be sure they accomplish their functionalities.

In general, tests are performed manually by experts starting from informal specifications but this procedure is very costly. Telecommunication industries have become conscious of the importance of the testing phase in the development of distributed software applications. This explains the intensive research developed in the last years in order to automatise the test generation procedure. This research activity has produced a great number of test generation methods that have been integrated into existing tools and have been applied successfully in several industrial projects. In particular, at INT we have developed a method for the automatic generation of tests from the SDL specification of a system [1]. This method has been implemented in the TESTGEN tool and has been already applied to real protocols [2].

We present here the application of this method to the test generation from the SDL specification of the SSCOP (Service Specific Connection Oriented Protocol) [3] protocol for ATM networks. One of the aims of this paper is also to show the possibilities and difficulties to efficiently perform the testing of a real system at a reasonable cost. In fact, the testing of the SSCOP protocol presented some difficult tasks, as for instance, the treatment of a big number of parameters into the PDU transmitted by the protocol.

The paper is organized as follows. Section 2 presents a short description of the SSCOP protocol. In section 3, the SDL specification of the protocol is presented as well as the modifications done in the original specification in order to improve its testability. In section 4, we give a short presentation of the test generation method and in section 5, we present and comment the results obtained. Finally, section 6 gives the conclusions of the work.

2. The SSCOP protocol

The ATM (Asynchronous Transfer Mode) technique has been chosen by ITU-TS to support the communication in the broadband ISDN network. ATM provides a well adapted answer to the requirements of broadband ISDN systems such as the integration of different types of traffic (video, audio, data), an important rate requirement, highly variable with time, and the possibility of dynamic allocation of resources.

2.1. ATM signalling

The SSCOP (Service Specific Connection Oriented Protocol) is a signalling protocol (layer 2) for ATM networks. The SSCOP (Service Specific Connection Oriented Protocol) is located in the Service Specific Convergence Sublayer (SSCS) of the ATM Adaptation Layer. The SSCOP protocol has been defined to provide the fonctionnalities required by the SAAL (Signalling ATM Adaptation Layer) level. The AAL (ATM Adaptation Layer) resides above and makes use of the service provided by the ATM layer. Its function is to adapt layer information, such as video, voice, user data and signalling so that it may be transported by the cell-based service provided by the ATM layer. At the SAAL level, the SSCS (Service Specific Convergence Sub-Layer) is functionally divided into the SSCOP and a SSCF (Service Specific Coordination Function), which maps the services provided by the SSCOP to the needs of the user of the SAAL. This structure allows a common connection oriented protocol with error recovery (the SSCOP) that provides a generic reliable data transfer service for different AAL interfaces defined by the SSCF. Two such SSCFs, one for signalling at the User Network Interface (UNI) and one for signalling at the Network to Network Interface (NNI), have been defined in recommendations Q.2130 and Q.2140, respectively. It is also possible to define additional SSCFs over the common SSCOP to provide different AAL (ATM Adaptation Layer) services. Figure 1 illustrates this architecture.

2.2. Functions of SSCOP

The SSCOP protocol performs the following functions:

- Connection Control: performs the establishment, release, and resynchronization of an SSCOP connection. It also allows the transmission of variable length user-to-user information without a guarantee of delivery;
- Transfer of User-Data: is used for the conveyance of user data between users of the SSCOP. SSCOP supports both assured and unassured data transfer;
- Sequence Integrity: preserves the order of SSCOP SDUs that were submitted for transfer by SSCOP;
- Protocol Error Detection and Recovery: detects and recovers from errors in the operation of

the protocol;
- Error Correction by Selective Retransmission: Through a sequencing mechanism, the receiving SSCOP entity can detect missing SSCOP SDUs. This function corrects sequence errors through retransmission;
- Local Data Retrieval: allows the local SSCOP user to retrieve in-sequence SDUs which have not yet been released by the SSCOP entity;
- Keep Alive: verifies that the two peer SSCOP entities participating in a connection remain in a link connection established state even in the case of a prolonged absence of data transfer;
- Flow Control: allows an SSCOP receiver to control the rate at which the peer SSCOP transmitter entity may send information;
- Error Reporting to Layer Management: indicates, to layer management, errors which have occurred;
- Status Reporting: allows the transmitter and receiver peer entities to exchange ATM Signalling.

3. SDL modelling of SSCOP

The specification of the protocol has been written in the SDL language [4] following the natural language and SDL description of the SSCOP standard (Q.2110). This specification has been completed and transformed in order to be tested. We describe in the following sections the main aspects of the SDL modelling and transformations of SSCOP and present the test architecture used for testing.

The following figure shows the state machine description of SSCOP proposed in the standard[3].

3.1. The know-how of experts

The role of designers during the test phase is the role of an expert, able to weigh up the importance of each branch of the specification, corresponding, for instance, to parts of some service. He assists the tester, if necessary, to simplify intelligently the specification: if the branch that manages data retrieval is too complex and causes a problem during the exhaustive simulation, he can help replace, at some phase of the test generation, this branch with 2 provided clauses : data retrieved or data lost.

There exist also in the specification, transitional states, which are very difficult to reach and test and that don't have a relevant signification for the SSCOP protocol. The experience of the experts allows to focus the tester capabilities on the kernel part of the SSCOP specification, in order to cover primarily this part and later the remaining ones.

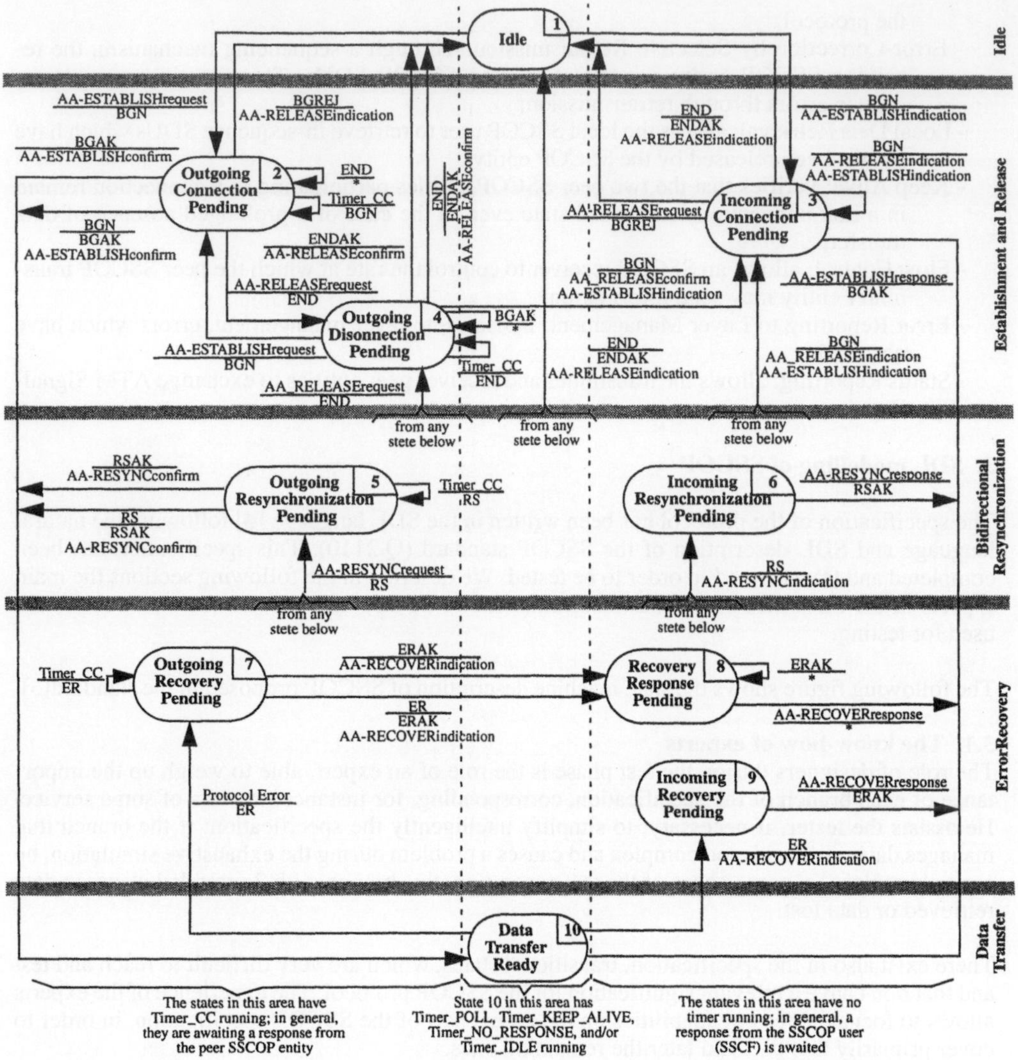

Figure 1. State machine representing the SSCOP protocol

3.2. SSCOP features & testing make-up

The SSCOP SDL specification is an example of significant size: 2400 lines of SDL-PR, it contains 10 states and supports 11 services using 25 types of signals. In the CPCS_UNITDATA, one of the

SSCOP signals, 15 PDU messages are used as parameters. An overview of the specification shows that each state receives input signals from the SSCF (AA), from the CPCS or internal signals. In all states there are messages to the Management Layer (MAA). The treatment of such signals in the specification is different depending on their complexity. In the case of signals exchanged with the SSCF or the Management Layer, the transitions are generally very simple. In the case of signals exchanged with the CPCS, the exchanges are more complex, for instance the depth of the branches is of about 17 decisions linked together.

3.3. Treatment of decisions

For some decisions, we can control the "useful" variables (useful variables act in decisions) from the environment and we can restrict the graph generation by fixing values of parameters of incoming messages (mechanism allowed in the Geode tool by using feeds). Some useful variables are VT_S (related to N_S parameter), VT_PS (N_PS), VR_R (N_MR) or VT_SQ (N_SQ) and VR_MR (window size). Unuseful variables (variables which, directly or indirectly, don't participate in decisions) are ignored. But for some decisions it is not possible to control variables, and we must transform previous formal decisions in informal ones. In this case, during the generation of the reachability graph, each branch of such decision will create two or more different transitions. Each branch of the transformed specification will correspond to a unique test case, even if it corresponds to a selection of data. This choice allows to obtain a full state coverage and a good coverage of transitions .

3.4. Treatment of procedures and macros

During simulation, huge transitions play important roles in the accessibility graph size because of the number of combinations of scenarios. The SSCOP protocol contains 11 macros and many procedures that are described in natural language. We have transformed these procedures into SDL procedures. Most of them are relatively simple, but some are really big, like DataRetrieval, SDexist, or RemoveMU. We have decided to replace some of them by their SDL code and others, depending on the implementation, have been replaced by tasks. Some procedures manage the contents of buffers where the lost information could be retrieved if functioning under the assured-mode. For the purpose of testing, the contents of those buffers are hidden, we have thus decided to remove these procedures (or macros).

We have kept some procedures as found in the original specification, like DataRetrieval or DeliverAll, and also some macros like InitializeXXX, ReleaseBuffers, PrepareRetrieval or DeliverData.

3.5. PDUs representation

In order to manage a large number of parameters, we decided to describe PDUs like structures, with fields following closely the SSCOP standard. The use of this kind of description is very easy, and allow sending signals with only one parameter (at most 3 in CPCS signals). This choice turns out to be effective for the SDL language but embedded structures are not easily managed by the simulator tool. For instance, cpcs_unitdatasignal(idle_bgak , 1 , 1 , 1), includes *idle_bgak* that is a container that includes about 60 parameters. This can be seen in the generated test sequences.

3.6. Treatment of timers

There are five kinds of timers, and they are replaced by the following signals from the environment:

```
SIGNAL bt_Timer_KEEP_ALIVE;
```

SIGNAL bt_Timer_IDLE;
SIGNAL bt_Timer_POLL;
SIGNAL bt_Timer_NO_RESPONS;
SIGNAL bt_Timer_CC;

All set and reset messages are eliminated. Timers are considered as external signals, so that timing is still considered but the specification for testing is simplified.

3.7. Treatment of internal signals

The actual SSCOP standard (Q.2110) requires to use some internal signals, as for example SD_PDUQueuedUp, which are hidden for all possible PCOs. They are used to indicate that a new data is ready to be sent. Some proposals, inside of the SDL normalisation groups, require forbidding this kind of internal messages. Such a message is subjected to a SAVE clause. This clause is used in order to put the save event in the queue until the system transits to another state where the event can be treated. In our case, we have decided to rewrite the specification without the SAVE clause and to replace this internal signal with an external one. In this case, the priority information at the time the state change is lost, as well as the internal nature of the signal, but this modification allows to test the behavior of the protocol to these signals.

There are three kinds of internal signals: QueuedUp signals, MD_PDUQueuedUp, UD_PDUQueuedUp, and SD_PDUQueuedUp. When MAA_UNITDATArequest and AA_UNITDATArequest signals are received from the environment via channel 'fromLM', they are queued, and consumed when the lower layer is not busy. For simulation, we have modified these two signals, MAA_UNITDATArequest and AA_UNITDATArequest, to be consumed directly when these signals are received from the environment. When MAA_UNITDATArequest and AA_UNITDATArequest signals are received from the environment via the 'fromLM' channel, they are queued, and consumed when the lower layer is not busy.

When AA_DATArequest signal is received from the environment via channel 'fromUser', SD_PDU is queued and the SSCOP generates an internal signal, SD_PDUQueuedUP. This AA_DATArequest can be received from the state 7(OutgoingRecoveryPending) or the state 10(DataTransferReady). We have removed all the OUTPUTs of SD_PDUQueuedUp signals from the specification. Instead, we have done the following modification: the SD_PDUQueuedUp signal is fed from the environment via the 'fromUser' channel as follows: SIGNAL SD_PDUQueuedUp. We also delete all SAVEs and inputs associated to this internal signal.

3.8. Test architecture

The testing architecture is represented in Figure 2. The IUT (Implementation Under Test) is composed by the SSCOP protocol. The upper tester is composed by the combination of the services and functions provided by the SSCF and the lower tester simulates the behavior of the CPCS. There is no service access points defined between SSCF and SSCOP. In the standard the term *signal* is used instead of *primitive* in order to describe the exchanges between SSCF and SSCOP. The IUT exchanges AA-signals with the SSCF and PDUs (SSCOP Protocol Data Units) with the lower tester.

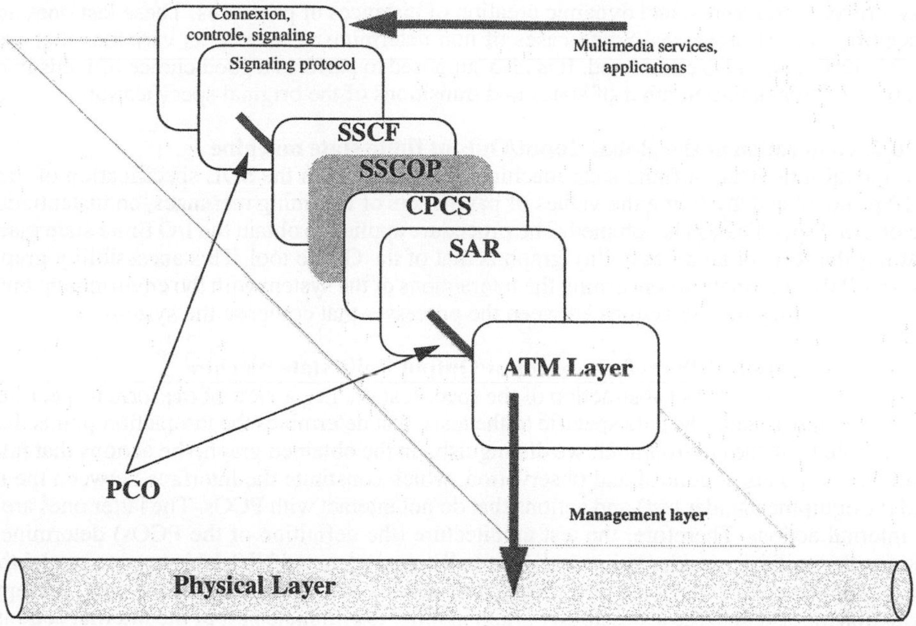

Figure 2. Test architecture

4. The method for test generation

The method for test generation adapts methods based on input/output finite state machines [5] to the SDL language. These methods allow to detect output faults, by means of a traversal of all the transitions of the finite state machine; and transfer faults, by defining signatures for all the states of the finite state machine. In our method, we call these signatures characterizing sets and they are based on the concept of UIO (Unique Input/Output) sequences and PUIO (Partial Unique Input/Output) sequences. [1]. This method has been implemented in the TESTGEN tool.

The finite state machine required by test generation is obtained by a transformation of the accessibility graph computed by a commercial tool, Geode, developed by Verilog [6] (the transformation is used to format the data so it can be used by the test generation tool).

The main steps of the method are the following:

Step 1. Specification treatment
The principal modifications of the original specification have been already described in detail in the precedent section, but we want to mention here that this step is necessary in order to obtain a simpler and more testable specification. In the case of SDL specifications, we eliminate some constructors that impeach the generation of a finite state machine, as for instance, save construc-

tors, procedures, macros, and dynamic creation of instances of processes. These last ones are replaced by normal processes. Some cases of non determinism, as well as variables that are not used in testing, are also eliminated. It is also supposed to perform a good choice of feeds in order to cover the maximum number of states and transitions of the original specification.

Step 2. Generation of the global Input/Output finite state machine
The global Input/Output finite state machine is obtained from the SDL specification of the SSCOP protocol and, by fixing the values of parameters of incoming messages, an instantiation of the original specification is obtained. The procedure applied to obtain the I/O finite state machine that has the form of an accessibility graph is that of the Geode tool. This accessibility graph includes all the information concerning the interactions of the system with the environment but also those concerning the interactions between the processes that compose the system.

Step 3. Generation of the reference Input/Output finite state machine
In order to obtain a correct abstraction of the specification, i.e., a view of the formal specification that takes into account the data specific to the tests, that determines the interaction points that are observable from the environment, we distinguish, in the obtained graph, the actions that interact with PCOs (points of control and observation, which constitute the interface between the tester and the equipment under test) and actions that do not interact with PCOs. The latter ones are seen as internal actions. Therefore, the test architecture (the definition of the PCOs) determines the actions that will be considered internal. The null signal (denoted NULL) is used to model the input of spontaneous transitions, or the output of actions that do not produce events. We apply a reduction algorithm to the accessibility graph in order to eliminate part of the internal actions and null signals, obtaining a new graph with fewer states. The experience of the application of this algorithm has shown that the resulting graph has fewer nodes but, on the other hand, the number of transitions increases. The reason for this is that when one state is eliminated the number of resulting transitions correspond to the number of incoming transitions multiplied by the number of outgoing transitions on that state. However, if the number of states eliminated is important, the number of transitions also diminishes.

Finally, a minimization to eliminate redundancies is applied. In the case of the SSCOP protocol, this minimization produces an automaton with 731 states and 23233 transitions, from an automaton of 15139 states and 64886 transitions.

We have also integrated in our tool a new composition algorithm that is based on a progressive elimination of internal actions [7].

Step 4. Generation of test sequences
The tests are composed of a preamble, the testing of the transition to be tested and the signature of the arriving state of the transition. The test sequences can be obtained in a non optimized or an optimized way. In the first case, the test sequence is composed by the concatenation of subsequences of test. Each one of these subsequences corresponds to the testing of one transition of the reduced accessibility graph.

Optimized testing can be performed in two different ways : one using UIO sequences and PUIO combined with the rural Chinese postman tour algorithm and the other using overlapping and multiple UIO sequences [8], [9].

Figure 3 illustrates the main steps performed for test generation.

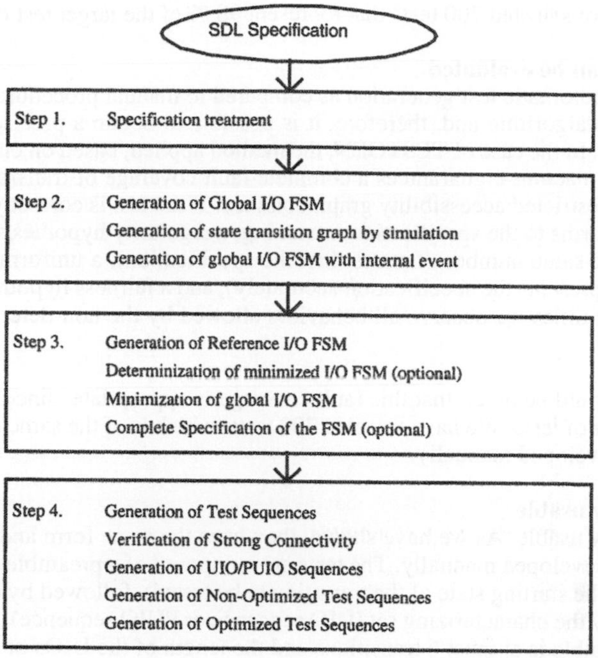

Figure 3

5. Results obtained

In this section we provide a short presentation of the main results obtained.

1. The method can be applied to real protocols

One of the goals of our work is to apply the methods we develop to real protocols. We have already applied our method to real protocols [2] and the SSCOP protocol is a new example of significant size: 2562 lines of SDL/PR, 10 main states, supporting 11 services using 25 types of signals.

The phases of traitment of the specification, simulation to eliminate errors in the original specification and simplification and validation phases takes around 4 months/months, which is a raisonnable time.

We generated a restricted accessibility graph by fixing the values of parameters of incoming messages (mechanism allowed by the Geode tool). We thus obtained a graph of manageable size which represents one instantiation of the original specification that represents the global behavior of the system. For the SSCOP example, by simulation we have obtained a graph of 15139 states and 64886 transitions. This graph has been reduced to one with 731 states and 23233 transitions. The simulation takes 12min 12 sec and the transition coverage rate was of 85.47 % and the state coverage rate was of 86.67 %. Taking into account the size of the graph and the big number of transitions, we have selected 700 tests that represent 98 % of the target test objectives.

2. The coverage can be evaluated

The advantage of automatic test generation as compared to manual procedures is that test selection is made by an algorithm and, therefore, it is possible to obtain a precise evaluation of the coverage achieved. In the case of TESTGEN, the method applied, based on classical methods for testing finite state machines, guarantees a complete fault coverage of transfer and output faults in relation to the restricted accessibility graph obtained. If the test is correctly executed, the implementation conforms to the specification; assuming, a regularity hypothesis (the implementation has less or the same number of states than the specification), a uniformity hypothesis (the restricted graph represents the specification accurately), and a fairness hypothesis (by executing the system several times we observe all behaviors allowed by the non-determinism of the system).

Furthermore, it should be noted that this fault coverage is appropriate, since it corresponds to a reasonable number of tests. We have selected 700 tests, which is of the same order of magnitude of the test suite developed manually.

3. Tests are really usable

The tests are really usable. As we have shown, they have the same form and are of comparable size to test suites developed manually. The tests are composed of a preamble (shortest path from the initial state to the starting state of the transition to be tested), followed by the transition being tested, followed by the characterizing set (UIO sequence or PUIO sequence). For the SSCOP the length of the preamble is at most 6 transitions and the length of the UIOs or PUIOs varies from 1 to 6 transitions. The structure and the length of the tests produced by our tool therefore correspond to the usual standards.

4. Tests can be produced in the TTCN or MSC notation

The tests obtained can be produced in both notations TTCN [10] or MSC [11]. The translation to MSC can be useful to illustrate that the test purposes to be tested can be produced automatically. Figure 4 gives the MSC of a test produced by our method. This part coincides with the test scenario proposed in the standard. Our experience shows that tests obtained in an automatic way have the same form as tests obtained manually, like in the case for the test scripts proposed by the standard [3]. Figure 5 presents the same test produced in the TTCN notation.

6. Conclusions

We have shown in this paper how automatic test generation methods can be applied to real specifications. The application of TESTGEN to test generation from the SDL specification of the SSCOP is encouraging: it is actually possible to generate useful tests for this protocol. We shall also remark that the method produces the tests in a totally automatic fashion; this is an advantage with respect to existing commercial tools that permit only the assisted generation of tests. The test sequences are generated in an optimized and a non optimized fashion and the user can choose the way best adapted for their application.

As was mentioned in Section 5, we have obtained a graph of manageable size which represents one instantiation of the original specification representing the global behavior of the system. For the SSCOP example, by simulation we have obtained a graph of 15139 states and 64886 transitions.

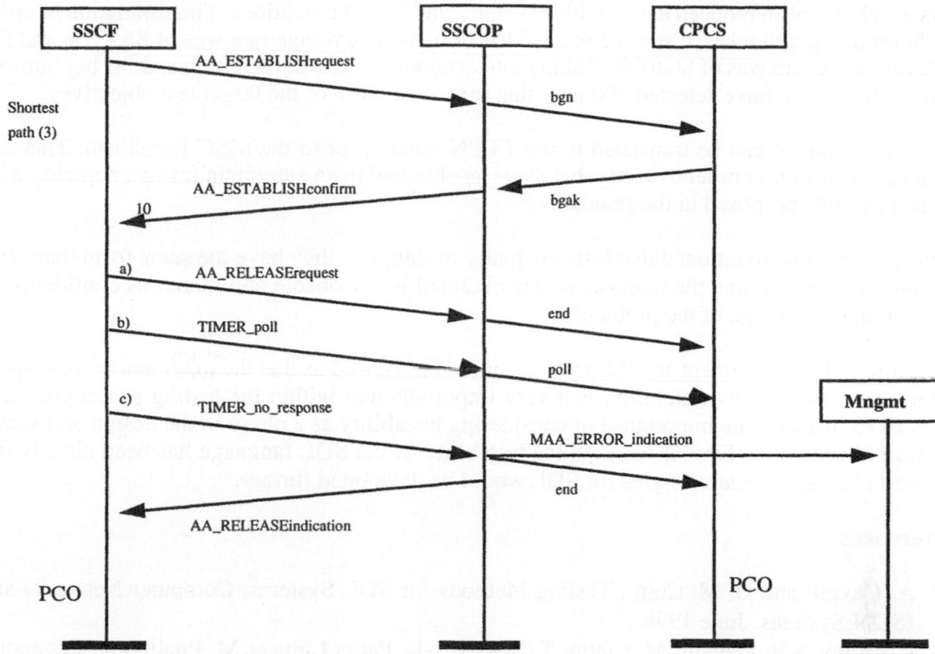

Figure 4. MSC obtained from the test sequence generated automatically by TESTGEN

Test Case Dynamic Behaviour				
Test Case Name:	SSCOP			
Group:	SSCOP/OCP_DTR_ODP			
Purpose:	connexion phase, step ODP			
Default:				
Comments:				
Label	Behaviour Description	Constraints Ref	Verdict	Comments
1	!AA_ESTABLISHrequest			
2	?BGN	bgn_contraint_table		2, OCP
3	!BGAK	bgak_contraint_table		
4	?AA_ESTABLISHconfirm			10, DTR
5	!AA_RELEASErequest			
6	?END	end_contraint_table	PASS	4, ODP
7	?MAA_ERRORindication	maa_err_table	INCONC	
8	?BGN	bgn_contraint_table	INCONC	
9	?RS	rs_contraint_table	INCONC	
10	?BGN	bgn_contraint_table	INCONC	
11	?END	end_contraint_table	INCONC	
12	?MAA_ERRORindication	maa_err_table	INCONC	

Figure 5. Example of a test produced by TESTGEN

This graph has been reduced to one with 731 states and 23233 transitions. The simulation in order to obtain this graph takes 12min 12 sec and the transition coverage rate was of 85.47 % and the state coverage rate was of 86.67 %. Taking into account the size of the graph and the big number of transitions, we have selected 700 tests that represent 98 % of the target test objectives.

The tests obtained can be translated to the TTCN notation or to the MSC formalism. This last form can be useful in order to verify that the tests obtained in an automatic fashion coincide with the tests scripts proposed in the standards.

Finally, it must be mentioned that tests are really usable, i.e., they have the same form than tests obtained manually, and the faults coverage obtained is reasonable and increases confidence in the complete coverage of the protocol.

In addition, this experiment and the previous ones [2], showed us that the treatment of SDL specification to improve its testability, is a very important step within the testing procedure. This leads us to insist on the importance of considering testability as a phase in the design and specification of protocols. Even if work on the testability of the SDL language has been already developed [12], specification styles for SDL would be developed further.

References

[1] A. Cavalli and B. M. Chin , Testing Methods for SDL Systems, Computer Networks and ISDN Systems, June 1996.

[2] R.Anido, A.R. Cavalli, M. Clatin, T. Macavei, L. Paula Lima et M. Phalippou, Engendrer des tests pour un vrai protocole grâce à des techniques éprouvées de vérification, CFIP'96, Octobre 1996.

[3] CCITT Final Draft Recommendation Q2110 , SSCOP protocol, March 1994.

[4] CCITT, Specification and Description Language, CCITT Z.100, International Consultative Committee on Telegraphy and Telephony, Geneva, 1992.

[5] Z. Kohavi, Switching and Finite Automata Theory, Tata McGraw-Hill Publishing Company Limited, New Delhi, 1978.

[6] Verilog, Geode Editor - Reference Manual, France, 1993.

[7] L. Paula Lima and A. Cavalli, Service Validation, Proceedings of Eunice Summer School, Lausanne, September 1996.

[8] A. Aho, A. Dahbura, D.Lee and M. Uyar, An Optimization technique for protocol Conformance Test Generation Based on UIO Sequences and Rural Chinese Postman Tours, Proceedings of the 8th International Symposium on Protocol Specification, Testing and Verification, Atlantic City, June1988.

[9] M.S.Chen, Y. Choi and A.Kershenbaum, Approaches utilizing segment overlap to minimize test sequences, Proc. 10th International IFIP Symposium on Protocol Specification, testing and Verification, Canada, June 1990.

[10] ITU-T Rec. Z.120 (1996), Message Sequence Chart (MSC), Geneva, 1996.

[11] ISO/IEC. Information Technology - OSI - Conformance Testing Methodology and Framework. International ISO/IEC multipart standard No 9646, 1994.

[12] Ellsberger J. and Kristoffersen F., Testability in the context of SDL, Protocol Specification, Testing, and Verification XII, Lake Buena Vista, Florida, June 1992.

VII

MSC II

SDL '97: TIME FOR TESTING - SDL, MSC and Trends
A. Cavalli and A. Sarma (Editors)

High-level Message Sequence Charts

S. Mauw and M.A. Reniers

Eindhoven University of Technology, P.O. Box 513, NL-5600 MB Eindhoven,
The Netherlands. E-mail: {sjouke,michelr}@win.tue.nl

We study High-level Message Sequence Charts – a concept incorporated into *MSC*96 for composing *MSC*s explicitly. A formal semantics is given which extends the accepted process algebra semantics of *MSC*92. We assess the language by studying a simple example, which leads us to consider the extension of *HMSC* with gates.

1. INTRODUCTION

The standardization of Message Sequence Charts (*MSC*s) [8] in 1992 by the CCITT has increased the interest in and use of *MSC*s considerably. Due to the variety of applications, many extensions have been proposed since 1992 for increasing the use of *MSC* in specific application domains or in general. Several of these proposed new language constructs were selected when extending the *MSC* language to *MSC*96 [7].

The composition of *MSC*s has been a main issue for the upgrade of the recommendation. In *MSC*92 composition of *MSC*s was hardly covered, while in *MSC*96 there are several new language features for constructing *MSC*s from simpler *MSC*s. In this paper we will focus on one of these composition techniques, namely High-level Message Sequence Charts (*HMSC*s).

An *HMSC* is a graphical overview of the relation between the *MSC*s contained. It helps in keeping track of the control-flow. In an *HMSC* alternative, sequential and parallel composition as well as recursion are captured in an attractive graphical layout: references to *MSC*s are related by means of arrows connecting them. One can look at *HMSC* as the synthesis of the roadmap approach [16,18] and the operator approach [6].

One of the current aims is to also extend the semantical definitions for *MSC*92 [11,9] to the *MSC*96 language. Because *MSC*96 has become quite a large language, we propose to study the new constructs first in isolation and get a full understanding of these features before combining them into one semantics definition.

In this paper, we will give a definition of the semantics of the sub-language *HMSC* of *MSC*96, based upon the recommended process algebra semantics of *MSC*92. Further, we discuss the use of *HMSC* by studying the well-known Alternating Bit Protocol (*ABP*) from different views. This case study motivates to extend *MSC*96 with gates on *HMSC* nodes.

This paper is structured as follows. First, we give an introduction to High-level Message Sequence Charts (*HMSC*s). As a basis we take Basic Message Sequence Charts (*BMSC*s). Then, in Section 3, we present a denotational and indirectly an operational semantics for *HMSC*. In Section 4, we focus on a layered description of the well-known *ABP*. In Section 5 we argue in favour of an extension of *HMSC*s based on gates. We conclude with some remarks and topics for further research.

Acknowledgements
We would like to thank Anders Ek, Loe Feijs, Jens Grabowski, Øystein Haugen, and Ekkart Rudolph for their participation in the discussions on our ideas.

2. HIGH-LEVEL MESSAGE SEQUENCE CHARTS

2.1. Basic Message Sequence Charts

A Basic Message Sequence Chart (*BMSC*) contains a description of the asynchronous communication between instances. Additionally local actions can be specified on instances. An instance is an abstract entity of which one can observe (part of) the interaction with other instances or with the environment. The *BMSC P* in Figure 1 defines the communication behaviour between instances i, j, k, l and the environment. An instance is denoted by a vertical axis. The time along each axis is running from top to bottom.

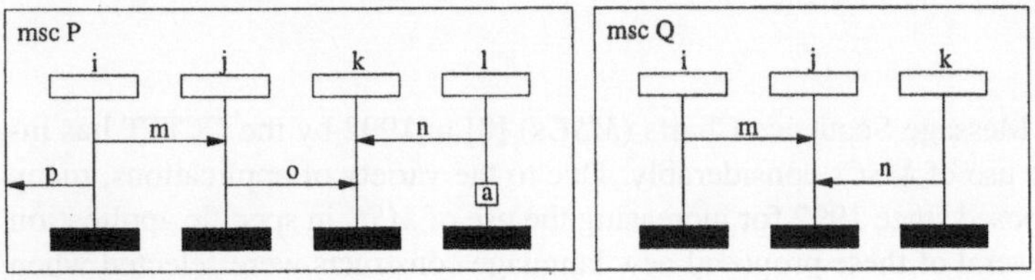

Figure 1. Example Basic Message Sequence Charts.

A communication between two instances is represented by an arrow which starts at the sending instance and ends at the receiving instance. In *BMSC P* from Figure 1 we consider the messages m, n, o, p. Message p is sent to the environment. The behaviour of the environment is not specified. For instance l a local action a is defined.

Although the activities along one single instance axis are completely ordered, we will not assume a notion of global time. The only dependencies between the timing of the instances come from the restriction that a message must have been sent before it is received. For *BMSC P* this implies for example that message o is received by k only after it has been sent, and consequently, after the reception of m by j. For the sending and receiving of m and n no order is specified. Since we have asynchronous communication it is even possible to first send m, then send and receive n, and finally receive m.

2.2. High-level Message Sequence Charts: *HMSC*

The most simple *HMSC* is a *BMSC*, as in Figure 1. The purpose of the compound *HMSC*s is to describe the relations between the *MSC*s contained in a graphically attractive way. A compound *HMSC* consists of a collection of components, enclosed by a frame. The components are thought of as complex *MSC*s that operate in parallel. Every component consists of a number of nodes and a number of arrows that imply an order on the nodes. We make a distinction between three kinds of nodes. Every component has exactly one start node, indicated by an upside-down triangle (▽). Further, it may contain a number of end nodes, indicated by a triangle (△), and several *HMSC* references. An *HMSC* reference consists of a frame with rounded corners enclosing the name of the referenced *HMSC*. We require that within a component every node (including the end nodes) is reachable from the start node. In Figure 2 an *HMSC* is shown. For simplicity we do not draw the abundant frame from *MSC*96 to denote parallelism.

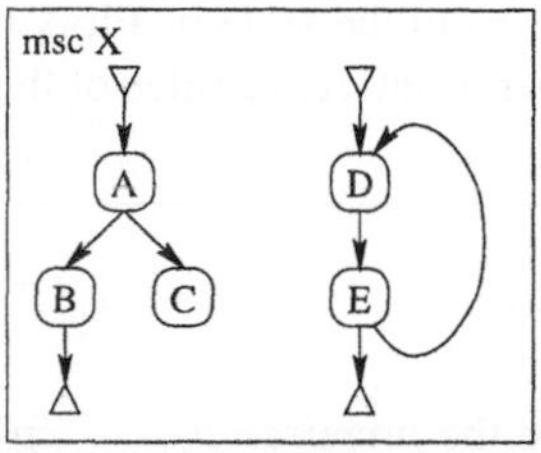

Figure 2. Example *HMSC*.

An arrow between two *HMSC* references implies that they are composed vertically. Splitting of an arrow denotes that the successors are alternatives. A cycle connecting a number of *HMSC* references expresses a repetition. In this way infinitary behaviour can be described.

Diagrams with many nodes and arrows can easily become unreadable for the human eye. By introducing *connectors* we can improve a lot on this problem. A connector is indicated by a circle (∘). Every combination of an incoming and an outgoing edge of a connector represents an arrow between the source of the incoming arrow and the destination of the outgoing arrow. A transformation of *HMSC*s with connectors to *HMSC*s without connectors can, in the presence of a formal definition of *HMSC* diagrams, easily be given. An example of an *HMSC* with connectors is given in Figure 7 (see Section 4).

3. SEMANTICS

This section is devoted to the semantics of *HMSC*. With respect to *MSC*92 formal semantics were defined based on Petri nets [5], Büchi automata [10], process algebra [11] and, more recently, partial order methods [1]. Since the process algebra approach was selected for standardization [9], we will use this approach as a starting point. First, we recapitulate the semantics of *BMSC*. Next, we define the operators needed for relating the *MSC*s contained in an *HMSC*. Finally, we define the semantics of *HMSC* based on an abstract syntax.

3.1. Basic Message Sequence Charts

In [11] a semantics for *BMSC* is presented. We will give a short explanation of this semantics. To each *BMSC* a closed process expression is associated. With every event specified in a *BMSC* an atomic action is associated as follows: The sending of a message *m* by instance *i* to instance j (or the environment) is represented by $out(i, j, m)$ (or $out(i, env, m)$), the reception of a message m by instance j from instance i (or the environment) is denoted $in(i, j, m)$ (or $in(env, j, m)$), and a local action a on instance i is denoted $action(i, a)$. Together with the constants ε and δ which denote successful termination and inaction (or deadlock) respectively, the atomic actions mentioned above constitute the constants of the term algebra used for the semantics. Furthermore, the term algebra consists of binary operators $+$ and $\cdot$ for non-deterministic choice and strong sequential composition, respectively. The process expression that can be associated to a *BMSC* defines the order in which events may be executed by means of an operational semantics.

Next, we present a structured operational semantics for closed terms in the style of Plotkin [14] (see Table 1). Such an operational semantics consists of a number of inference rules of the following form:

$$\frac{p_1, \cdots, p_n}{c}.$$

This inference rule means that for every instantiation of variables in the *premises* $p_1, \cdots, p_n$ and the *conclusion* c we can conclude c from $p_1, \cdots, p_n$. If no premises are present, i.e., $n = 0$, then c is a tautology (often called an axiom). Premises and conclusions are constructed from the predicates $\downarrow$ and $\xrightarrow{a}$. The intuition of the unary predicate $\downarrow$ is as follows: $p\downarrow$ indicates that p has an option to terminate successfully. The intuitive idea of the predicate $\xrightarrow{a}$ (for every $a \in A$) is as follows: $p \xrightarrow{a} q$ denotes that process p can execute action a and after the execution thereof the resulting process is q.

With this operational semantics, we define the behaviour of a *BMSC*. By defining the usual notion of strong bisimilarity [13], we can also reason about the equality of *BMSC*s.

Table 1
Structured operational semantics for the constants and operators ($a \in A$).

$$\frac{}{\varepsilon\downarrow} \qquad \frac{x\downarrow}{x + y\downarrow} \qquad \frac{y\downarrow}{x + y\downarrow} \qquad \frac{x\downarrow, y\downarrow}{x \cdot y\downarrow}$$

$$\frac{}{a \xrightarrow{a} \varepsilon} \qquad \frac{x \xrightarrow{a} x'}{x + y \xrightarrow{a} x'} \qquad \frac{y \xrightarrow{a} y'}{x + y \xrightarrow{a} y'} \qquad \frac{x \xrightarrow{a} x'}{x \cdot y \xrightarrow{a} x' \cdot y} \qquad \frac{x\downarrow, y \xrightarrow{a} y'}{x \cdot y \xrightarrow{a} y'}$$

Based on this structured operational semantics, to every closed process expression (and thus to every *BMSC*) a labeled transition system can be associated as follows: the initial node of the labeled transition system is given by the term under consideration. A state s has an outgoing edge labeled with a to a state s' iff $s \xrightarrow{a} s'$ is derivable from the inference rules and tautologies. Also, s is labeled by a termination arrow iff $s\downarrow$ is derivable.

Example 3.1 Consider the *BMSC* Q from Figure 1. For our convenience we denote this *BMSC* with its name Q. The semantics of this *BMSC* is given by

$$\begin{aligned} S_{BMSC}(Q) = \; & out(i,j,m) \cdot (out(k,j,n) \cdot in(i,j,m) \cdot in(k,j,n) \\ & \qquad\qquad\quad + in(i,j,m) \cdot out(k,j,n) \cdot in(k,j,n) \\ & \qquad\qquad\quad) \\ + \; & out(k,j,n) \cdot out(i,j,m) \cdot in(i,j,m) \cdot in(k,j,n). \end{aligned}$$

The labeled transition system that is associated to this *BMSC* is given in Figure 3.

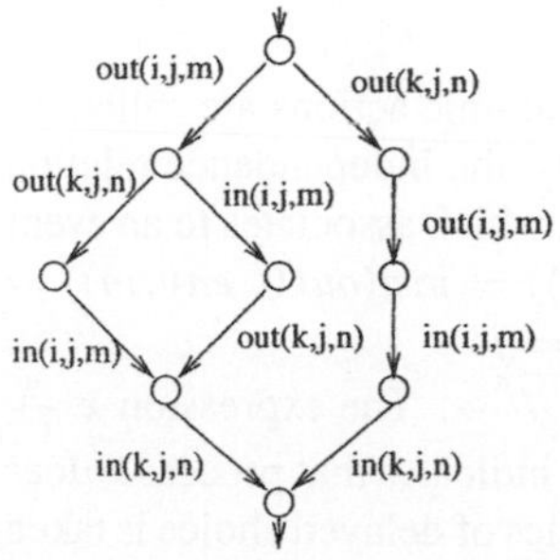

Figure 3. Labeled transition system.

3.2. The composition operators

The relations between the composing *MSC*s of an *HMSC* are graphically defined by arrows and semantically by using three operators.

The delayed choice operator ($\mp$) was introduced by Baeten and Mauw [2]. It acts as a deterministic choice in the context of strong bisimulation. The delayed choice between processes x and y, is the process obtained by joining the common initial parts of x and y and continuing with a non-deterministic choice ($+$) between the remaining parts.

The weak sequencing operator ($\circ$) is based on the interworking sequencing operator [12]. A generalization of this operator was studied in [15]. The weak sequencing of the processes x and y denotes their parallel execution with the restriction that an action from y can only be executed if that is permitted by x. In Figure 4 we give a typical example of vertical composition by means of the weak sequencing operator.

The free merge operator ($\|$) denotes the interleaved execution of its arguments without synchronization. It is well-known in concurrency theory.

A structured operational semantics for the operators $\mp$, $\circ$, and $\|$ is provided in Table 2. Auxiliary predicates $\overset{a}{\cdots\rightarrow}$ (for $a \in A$) are introduced. The predicate $x \overset{a}{\cdots\rightarrow} x'$ means that x allows y to execute event a in a context $x \circ y$. Thus, this predicate is used to restrict the collection of possible events that can be executed by y. The process x' that results from permitting a to be executed in the permission relation $x \overset{a}{\cdots\rightarrow} x'$ is obtained by omitting from x all alternatives that do not allow the execution of a by y. The basis for this so-called *permission relation* is provided

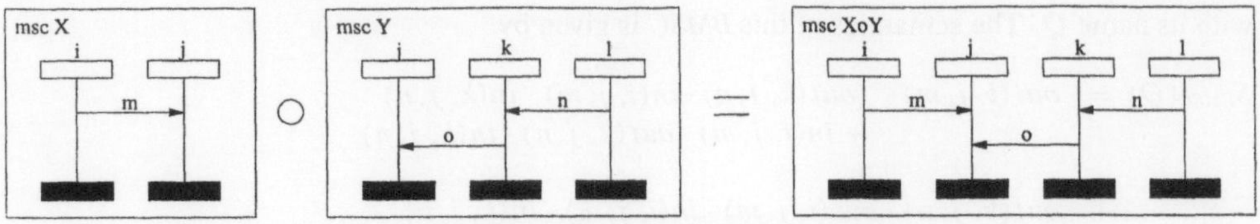

Figure 4. Vertical composition.

by the relation $I \subseteq A \times A$, called the *independence relation*. Two atomic actions are called independent, aIb, if they are defined on different instances. Formally, the independence relation I is defined as follows: aIb iff $inst(a) \neq inst(b)$. The function *inst*, which associates to an event the instance on which it is specified, is defined by $inst(out(i,j,m)) = inst(out(i,env,m)) = inst(action(i,a)) = i$ and $inst(in(i,j,m)) = inst(in(env,j,m)) = j$.

The inference rules also contain *negative premises* $x \not\xrightarrow{a}$ and $x \cdot\!/\!\cdot\!\xrightarrow{a}$. The expression $x \not\xrightarrow{a}$ means that process x cannot execute an action a. Similarly, $x \cdot\!/\!\cdot\!\xrightarrow{a}$ indicates that process x does not permit the execution of atomic action a. The operational semantics of delayed choice is taken from [2], the operational semantics of the weak sequencing is based on [15], and the structured operational semantics of the free merge is taken from [3].

Table 2
Structured operational semantics for $\mp$, $\circ$, and $\|$ $(a, b \in A)$.

$$\frac{aIb}{b \overset{a}{\cdots\rightarrow} b} \qquad \frac{}{\varepsilon \overset{a}{\cdots\rightarrow} \varepsilon} \qquad \frac{}{\delta \overset{a}{\cdots\rightarrow} \delta} \qquad \frac{x \overset{a}{\cdots\rightarrow} x',\ y \overset{a}{\cdots\rightarrow} y'}{x \cdot y \overset{a}{\cdots\rightarrow} x' \cdot y'}$$

$$\frac{x \overset{a}{\cdots\rightarrow} x',\ y \cdot\!/\!\cdot\!\xrightarrow{a}}{x + y \overset{a}{\cdots\rightarrow} x'} \qquad \frac{x \cdot\!/\!\cdot\!\xrightarrow{a},\ y \overset{a}{\cdots\rightarrow} y'}{x + y \overset{a}{\cdots\rightarrow} y'} \qquad \frac{x \overset{a}{\cdots\rightarrow} x',\ y \overset{a}{\cdots\rightarrow} y'}{x + y \overset{a}{\cdots\rightarrow} x' + y'}$$

$$\frac{x\downarrow}{x \mp y\downarrow} \qquad \frac{y\downarrow}{x \mp y\downarrow} \qquad \frac{x \xrightarrow{a} x',\ y \xrightarrow{a} y'}{x \mp y \xrightarrow{a} x' \mp y'} \qquad \frac{x \xrightarrow{a} x',\ y \not\xrightarrow{a}}{x \mp y \xrightarrow{a} x'} \qquad \frac{x \not\xrightarrow{a},\ y \xrightarrow{a} y'}{x \mp y \xrightarrow{a} y'}$$

$$\frac{x \overset{a}{\cdots\rightarrow} x',\ y \cdot\!/\!\cdot\!\xrightarrow{a}}{x \mp y \overset{a}{\cdots\rightarrow} x'} \qquad \frac{x \cdot\!/\!\cdot\!\xrightarrow{a},\ y \overset{a}{\cdots\rightarrow} y'}{x \mp y \overset{a}{\cdots\rightarrow} y'} \qquad \frac{x \overset{a}{\cdots\rightarrow} x',\ y \overset{a}{\cdots\rightarrow} y'}{x \mp y \overset{a}{\cdots\rightarrow} x' \mp y'}$$

$$\frac{x\downarrow,\ y\downarrow}{x \circ y\downarrow} \qquad \frac{x \overset{a}{\cdots\rightarrow} x',\ y \overset{a}{\cdots\rightarrow} y'}{x \circ y \overset{a}{\cdots\rightarrow} x' \circ y'} \qquad \frac{x \xrightarrow{a} x'}{x \circ y \xrightarrow{a} x' \circ y} \qquad \frac{x \overset{a}{\cdots\rightarrow} x',\ y \xrightarrow{a} y'}{x \circ y \xrightarrow{a} x' \circ y'}$$

$$\frac{x\downarrow,\ y\downarrow}{x \parallel y\downarrow} \qquad \frac{x \overset{a}{\cdots\rightarrow} x',\ y \overset{a}{\cdots\rightarrow} y'}{x \parallel y \overset{a}{\cdots\rightarrow} x' \parallel y'} \qquad \frac{x \xrightarrow{a} x'}{x \parallel y \xrightarrow{a} x' \parallel y} \qquad \frac{y \xrightarrow{a} y'}{x \parallel y \xrightarrow{a} x \parallel y'}$$

Since the operators $\|$ and $\mp$ are symmetric and associative and ε is a unit for $\|$ and δ for $\mp$ ([3,2]), we can generalize these as follows for a finite set I:

$$\mathop{\mp}_{i\in I} P_i = \begin{cases} \delta & \text{if } I = \varnothing \\ P_j \mp \left(\mathop{\mp}_{i\in I\setminus\{j\}} P_i \right) & \text{if } j \in I \end{cases}$$

and

$$\mathop{\|}_{i\in I} P_i = \begin{cases} \varepsilon & \text{if } I = \varnothing \\ P_j \,\|\, \left(\mathop{\|}_{i\in I\setminus\{j\}} P_i \right) & \text{if } j \in I \end{cases}$$

The language *HMSC* can be used to describe infinitary behaviour. Therefore, we will extend our semantic domain with recursive specifications. Let Σ be an arbitrary signature, and let V be a set of recursion variables. A recursive specification $E(V)$ is a set of equations

$$\{X = s_X(V) \mid X \in V\}$$

where each $s_X(V)$ is a term over the signature Σ and the set of variables V. The set of terms constructed like this is denoted by $Rec(\Sigma)$.

Next, we will present an operational semantics for recursion (see Table 3) which generates exactly one solution for every recursive specification. Let E be a recursive specification in which X occurs as a recursion variable. Then $\langle X \mid E\rangle$ denotes the solution for X with respect to the recursive specification E. The process $\langle X \mid E\rangle$ can terminate or execute an action if its defining equation (in the context of E) can do so. For t a term possibly containing recursion variables, the process $\langle t \mid E\rangle$ denotes the process t with all occurrences of recursion variables r replaced by their solution $\langle r \mid E\rangle$. The function *eqs* is defined by $eqs(\langle r \mid E\rangle) = E$.

Table 3
Structured operational semantics for recursion ($X = s_X \in E$, $a \in A$).

$$\frac{\langle s_X \mid E\rangle{\downarrow}}{\langle X \mid E\rangle{\downarrow}} \qquad \frac{\langle s_X \mid E\rangle \xrightarrow{a} y}{\langle X \mid E\rangle \xrightarrow{a} y}$$

More difficult is the definition of the permission relation for recursive specifications. The reason for this is that the recursive specification itself must be adapted.

Suppose that the recursive specification E is given by $\left\{ X^i = t^i \circ \left(\mathop{\mp}_{j\in J} X^j \right) \middle|\, j \in I,\, J \subseteq I \right\}$, where t^i is a closed term and I and J are index sets. All recursive specifications that are required for describing the semantics of High-level Message Sequence Charts are of this form.

The set of equations that result from transforming E due to the permission of action a is denoted by E_a and consists of a fresh recursion variable X^i_a for each variable X^i from E. For the equation $X^i = t^i \circ \left(\mathop{\mp}_{j\in J} X^j \right) \in E$ we introduce the equation:

- $X_a^i = t_a^i \circ \left(\mp_{j \in J} X_a^j \right)$ if $t^i \overset{a}{\cdots\rightarrow} t_a^i$ and $i \in J$, or

- $X_a^i = t_a^i \circ \left(\mp_{j \in J} X_a^j \right)$ if $t^i \overset{a}{\cdots\rightarrow} t_a^i$, $i \notin J$ and there is at least one equation for the variables X_a^j that is not of the form $X_a^j = \delta$, or

- $X_a^i = \delta$, otherwise.

Then $\langle X \mid E \rangle \overset{a}{\cdots\rightarrow} \langle X_a \mid E_a \rangle$ provided that the equation for X_a is not of the form $X_a = \delta$. We give a simple example to illustrate this. Suppose that we have the recursive specification $E = \{X = a \circ (Y \mp Z),\ Y = b \circ X,\ Z = c \circ X\}$, where a, b, and c are pairwise independent actions. Suppose that we are interested in the process $\langle X \mid E \rangle \circ b'$ where b' and b are dependent. The action b' can only be executed if the process $\langle X \mid E \rangle$ permits the execution of b'. Then we must construct the recursive specification $E_{b'}$: $E_{b'} = \{X_{b'} = a \circ (Y_{b'} \mp Z_{b'}),\ Y_{b'} = \delta,\ Z_{b'} = c \circ X_{b'}\}$. Hence $\langle X \mid E \rangle \overset{b'}{\cdots\rightarrow} \langle X_{b'} \mid E_{b'} \rangle$. Thus the process $\langle X \mid E \rangle \circ b'$ is capable of performing the action b' and thereby evolves into the process $\langle X_{b'} \mid E_{b'} \rangle$. This example shows that by permitting action b' the choice for executing the b actions is resolved.

The following theorems express the soundness of the definitions so far. They are proven using standard techniques.

Theorem 3.2.1 *The term deduction system that consists of the deduction rules introduced so far uniquely defines a transition relation.*

Theorem 3.2.2 *Strong bisimulation is a congruence with respect to the operators* $\mp$, $\circ$, *and* $\|$.

3.3. Abstract syntax of *HMSC*

A *hierarchical graph* is a mathematical structure that represents the information contents of an *HMSC*. The set *HGid* represents the set of all *HMSC* names. Obviously, this includes the names of *BMSC*s. Since we did not provide a formal graphical syntax for *HMSC* we cannot provide a formal mapping from *HMSC* to hierarchical graphs. However, the intuition is clear. A node in an *HMSC* contains a reference to another *HMSC* via its name.

Definition 3.3.1 (Hierarchical graphs) A hierarchical graph is either a *BMSC* or a tuple $\langle id, Nodes, Starts, Ends, Edges, l \rangle$, where

- $id \in HGid$ is the name of the hierarchical graph;

- *Nodes*, *Starts*, and *Ends* are pairwise disjoint sets of *HMSC* reference nodes, start nodes and end nodes respectively with $Starts \neq \emptyset$;

- $Edges \subseteq (Nodes \cup Starts) \times (Nodes \cup Ends)$ is a set of edges. An edge (n, n') is denoted by $n \to n'$;

- $l : Nodes \to HGid$ is a labeling function which associates to a node a reference to an *HMSC* by means of an *HMSC* name;

such that every node and end node is reachable from exactly one start node, and an *HMSC* is not referenced from one of its own nodes (recursively). The set of all hierarchical graphs is denoted by *HG*.

An *HMSC*-document contains a number of *HMSC*s. It is required that all *HMSC*s in an *HMSC*-document have different names. Then, an *HMSC*-document can, in the abstract syntax, be represented by a (partial) mapping $H : HGid \rightarrow HG$. For technical reasons we require that the nodes (including start and end nodes) of any two hierarchical graphs are disjoint.

3.4. Denotational semantics for *HMSC*

We will associate a recursive specification to every hierarchical graph by means of a mapping S. Since the nodes of a hierarchical graph may contain references to other hierarchical graphs, the semantic mapping S is labeled with the mapping $H : HGid \rightarrow HG$ which represents an *HMSC*-document.

A recursive specification for a hierarchical graph (say with name id) is obtained by introducing a recursion variable $\overline{id}$ and a recursion variable $\overline{n}$ for every node n in the hierarchical graph (this includes start and end nodes). The relation between these nodes is formalized by defining one recursive equation for every recursion variable introduced as follows.

- The overall behaviour of the hierarchical graph is obtained by the parallel execution of the behaviours associated to the start nodes: $\overline{id} = \mathop{\|}_{s \in Starts} \overline{s}$.
- For every start node s of the hierarchical graph a recursive equation $\overline{s} = \overline{n_1} \mp \cdots \mp \overline{n_m}$ is introduced, where $n_1, \cdots n_m$ are the successor nodes of start node s.
- For every *HMSC* reference node n which refers to an *HMSC* with name i (i.e., $l(n) = i$) a recursive equation $\overline{n} = \overline{i} \circ (\overline{n_1} \mp \cdots \mp \overline{n_m})$ is introduced, where $n_1, \cdots, n_m$ are the successor nodes of node n.
- For every end node e the equation $\overline{e} = \varepsilon$ is introduced.

Furthermore, we also have to add equations describing the behaviour of the referenced *HMSC*s. The formal definition is given below.

Definition 3.4.1 Let $H : HGid \rightarrow HG$ be a function that represents a set of hierarchical graphs. The function $S_H : HG \rightarrow Rec(\Sigma)$ is defined as follows. If X is a *BMSC* with name id, then $S_H(X) = \langle \overline{id} \,|\, \{\overline{id} = S_{BMSC}(X)\} \rangle$ and if $X = \langle id, Nodes, Starts, Ends, Edges, l \rangle$ then $S_H(X) = \langle \overline{id} \,|\, E \rangle$ where

$$E = \left\{ \begin{array}{l|l} \overline{id} = \mathop{\|}_{s \in Starts} \overline{s}, \quad \overline{s} = \mathop{\mp}_{s \to n \in Edges} \overline{n}, & s \in Starts, \\ \overline{n} = \overline{l(n)} \circ \left(\mathop{\mp}_{n \to n' \in Edges} \overline{n'} \right), & n \in Nodes, \\ \overline{e} = \varepsilon & e \in Ends \end{array} \right\} \cup \bigcup_{n \in Nodes} eqs(S_H(H(l(n)))).$$

From now on, if no confusion can arise, we will denote a recursion variable by n instead of $\overline{n}$.

Example 3.4.2 Consider the *HMSC* shown in Figure 2. In Figure 5 the same *HMSC* is shown with the names of the nodes in the abstract syntax as annotation. Suppose that the semantics of the *HMSC*s A, B, C, D, E are given by $\langle r_A \mid E_A \rangle, \cdots, \langle r_E \mid E_E \rangle$ respectively. Then the semantics of *HMSC* X is given by $\langle X \mid E \rangle$ where E consists of the equations of $E_A, \cdots, E_E$, and additionally the equations shown in Figure 5.

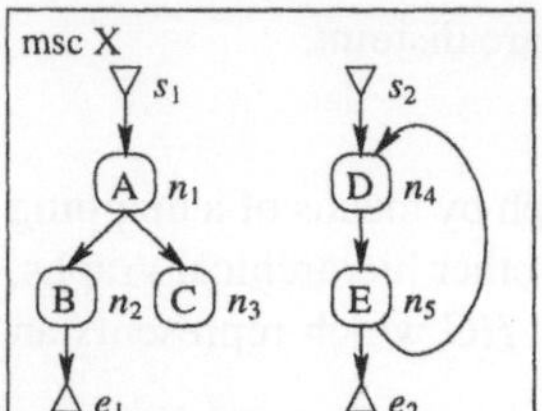

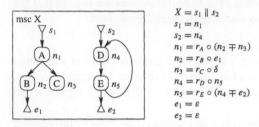

$$
\begin{aligned}
X &= s_1 \parallel s_2 \\
s_1 &= n_1 \\
s_2 &= n_4 \\
n_1 &= r_A \circ (n_2 \mp n_3) \\
n_2 &= r_B \circ e_1 \\
n_3 &= r_C \circ \delta \\
n_4 &= r_D \circ n_5 \\
n_5 &= r_E \circ (n_4 \mp e_2) \\
e_1 &= \varepsilon \\
e_2 &= \varepsilon
\end{aligned}
$$

Figure 5. *HMSC* annotated with the recursion variables and the equations for those variables.

4. EXAMPLE: THE ALTERNATING BIT PROTOCOL

In this section, we will give a description of the behaviour of the Alternating Bit Protocol (*ABP*) in *HMSC*. The *ABP* is developed for the transmission of data from one entity (the sender *S*) to another entity (the receiver *R*) by means of an unreliable communication medium; channel *K* from *S* to *R* for messages and channel *L* from *R* to *S* for acknowledgements (see Figure 6).

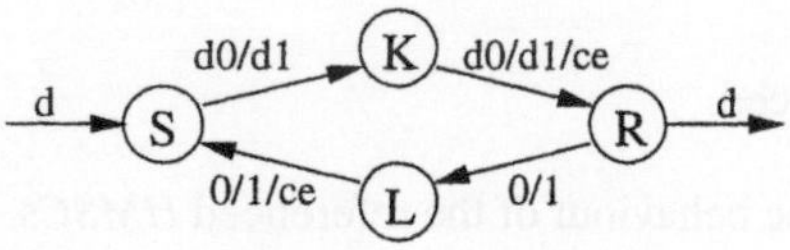

Figure 6. The architecture of the *ABP*.

It is assumed that media errors can be detected, e.g., by means of a checksum error (*ce*). Other faults, such as message loss will not occur. In Figure 6 we have added which messages may be transferred between the entities. In communication with the environment, only plain data items *d* play a role. From *S* to *R* frames are transmitted which consist of a data item and a bit value (e.g. *d*0). Furthermore channel *K* may send checksum errors (*ce*) to the receiver. Channel *L* is used to transmit acknowledgment bits 0 and 1 and it may produce a checksum error.

The specification will be presented in a top-down fashion. From the overall description in Figure 7 (msc *ABP*), we learn that it operates in two alternating phases: a *0-phase* and a *1-phase*.

The two phases are similar, except that the bits 0 and 1 are swapped. In Figure 7 we will give the 0-phase only. It shows that there is one main scenario, namely successful transmission. This trace starts with an input of a datum from the environment (*S-in*), followed by successful transmission of this datum in phase 0 (*tr-ok-0*). Next, the datum is sent to the environment (*R-out*) and the transmission of the acknowledgement in phase 0 succeeds (*ack-ok-0*).

There are two places where a deviation of the main scenario may occur (viz. the two loops in the msc *0-phase*). The first problem that is anticipated at, is an erroneous transmission (the upper loop in msc *0-phase*). If this happens, a phase 1 acknowledgement is issued and, regardless whether this acknowledgement arrives correctly, the transmission is repeated. In the same way an error in the acknowledgement channel is solved (the lower loop).

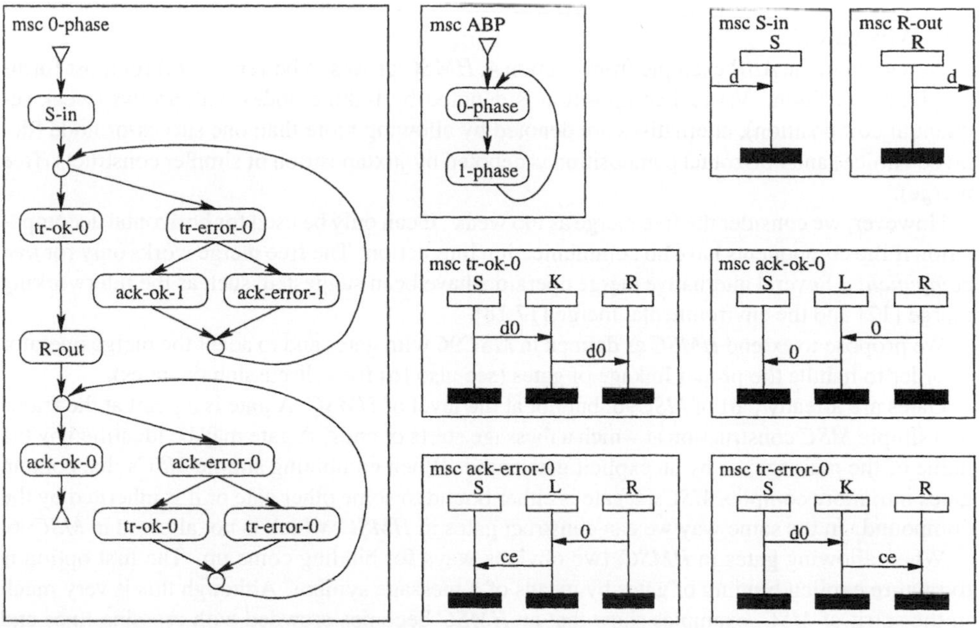

Figure 7. Specification of the *ABP*.

Finally, we give the lowest level definitions of the *MSC*s that occur in the phase descriptions (see Figure 7). For instance, msc *tr-ok-0* contains the description of correct transmission of a datum *d* in phase 0 from *S* to *R*. Notice that the datum is attributed with the phase bit. The *MSC*s *tr-ok-1*, *tr-error-1*, *ack-ok-1* and *ack-error-1* are not displayed. They can be easily derived from their 0-phase counterparts.

We can draw several conclusions from this example. First, the decomposition elaborated here is just one of many possible descriptions of the same protocol (see e.g. [4]). It has the virtue that it helps in understanding the overall operation of the protocol. If one is interested in understanding the behaviour of the entities in separation, a horizontal decomposition technique can be used. This way, we obtain the parallel composition of the four instances involved. Since there is communication between these components, we need a notion of *gates* for defining the interface between the components (see [6]). We elaborate on this issue in Section 5.

Next, observe that we have defined several *MSC*s that differ only in the phase bit. A shorter specification can be easily obtained by introducing parameterized specifications. This is closely related with extending the *MSC* language with data types. In the current description, it is not stated that the sender can receive any datum *d* from the environment. It rather says that the same input message *d* is repeated every time an input occurs. This can only be viewed as an abstraction.

5. GATES IN *HMSC*

5.1. Why gates?

As shown in the *ABP* example from Section 4, *HMSC* proves to be very useful for most forms of (de)composition. Vertical composition is denoted by linking nodes with arrows (weak sequential composition), alternatives are denoted by allowing more than one successor node (delayed choice) and horizontal composition is denoted by juxtaposition of simpler constructs (free merge).

However, we consider the free merge as too weak. It can only be used for horizontal decomposition if the components have no communication interaction. The free merge works only for *free components*. Several alternative merge operators have been suggested, such as the Interworking merge [12] and the environmental merge [17,18].

We propose to extend *HMSC* as defined in *MSC*96 with gates and to adapt the merge operator in order to handle the proper linkage of gates (see also [6] for a discussion on gates).

Gates are already part of *MSC*96, but not at the level of *HMSC*. A gate is a point at the frame of a simple *MSC* construction at which a message starts or ends. A gate may be identified by the name of the message, or by an explicit gate name. When combining simple *MSC*s that contain gates into more complex *MSC*s, a gate is either bound to some other gate or it is inherited by the compound. In the same way we can construct gates in *HMSC*, which is not allowed in *MSC*96.

When allowing gates in *HMSC*, two obvious ways for binding come up. The first option is to require explicit binding of gates by means of a message symbol. Although this is very much in the spirit of *MSC*, examples show that an *HMSC* becomes crowded with crossing lines and looses its purpose for overview specification.

The second possibility is to bind gates by name identification. That is, an input and an output gate are connected if they have the same gate name. This makes it harder to find out which gates are connected, but yields a much more quiet picture. In order to have this binding by gate name identification, a possibility must exist for renaming gates. Unfortunately, in *MSC*96 substitution of gates is not allowed. Since we cannot find any semantical or logical reasons to exclude gates from substitutions, we propose to extend *MSC*96 in this respect.

5.2. The Alternating Bit Protocol revisited

The purpose of this section is to give an *MSC* specification of the *ABP* from an instance oriented point of view. In the previous *ABP* specification the emphasis was on the overall behaviour of the complete system. This is a nice way to get an overview of the protocol itself, but it does not describe as clearly the behaviour of each component in isolation.

Here, we have a more implementation directed view, closer to the *SDL* way of specification. The components of the system are represented by separate *HMSC*s that operate in parallel. They communicate via gates. The behaviours of the components are clearly separated. This style of specification is very suitable as an intermediate stage between the *classical* use of *MSC* and *SDL*.

Before giving an explanation of the *ABP* in Figure 8, we will first point out some additional differences between our diagrams and *MSC*96. First, we allow complete Basic Message Sequence Charts to occur in *HMSC* nodes, rather than references to *BMSC*s. Experience showed that this makes the drawings much easier to understand. Second, we omitted the *instance start* and *instance end* symbol for making the drawing less crowded. The third difference is that we omit the abundant frame surrounding a parallel construct.

The *ABP* specification in Figure 8 can be understood as follows. It consists of four concurrently operating entities. The sender S and the receiver R and two channels. Channel K connects the sender to the receiver and channel L connects the receiver to the sender (see Figure 6 and see the names of the gates in Figure 8). Looking at the behaviour of the channels first, we see that channel K repeatedly receives some data frame via gate g and sends either the same frame to gate h, or some specific value called *ce* (for checksum error). Channel L exposes the same behaviour, be it that input is received from gate i and sent to gate j. This channel is only capable of transmitting bits.

Notice that we have sketched the behaviour of the channel using four scenarios. Two basic scenarios in which transmission succeeds and two faulty scenarios leading to a checksum error. The alternative composition of these scenarios does not imply that the choice between correct operation and faulty operation is resolved before the reception of the input. Due to the use of the delayed choice operator, the choice is rather made after reception of the frame.

The behaviour of the sender S is a repetition of the following. The sender starts in the so-called zero-phase. First some data d to transmit is received from the environment. This data is extended with the bit 0 and yields the frame $d0$ which is sent along gate g. Then the sender awaits an incoming message from gate j. In case this is a negative acknowledgement (1) or a checksum error (*ce*) generated by channel L, the transmission of frame $d0$ is repeated. In case of a positive acknowledgement (0), the zero-phase is concluded and the process starts the one-phase, which is the converse of the zero-phase.

The behaviour of the receiver R can be explained likewise. The receiver also starts in the zero-phase and awaits the correct transmission of a zero-frame via gate h. The first time this frame is received the data contained is copied to the environment. Then the receiver enters the one-phase.

6. CONCLUDING REMARKS

The expressive power of the *MSC* language has increased considerably since the recent introduction of new constructs. We have studied the sub-language of *HMSC*s in isolation, in order to assess this feature's use and semantics.

It is perfectly feasible to define a semantics of *HMSC* in the line of the already existing process algebra semantics of *MSC*92. It is based upon the known process algebra operators for weak sequencing, delayed choice and free merge. These operators are already incorporated into *MSC*96 on the level of *MSC* expressions. In order to capture the infinite behaviour of a system description in *HMSC*, we have used recursive equations. This yields a sound operational semantics.

By explaining the use of *HMSC* by means of the well-known toy example of the *ABP*, we

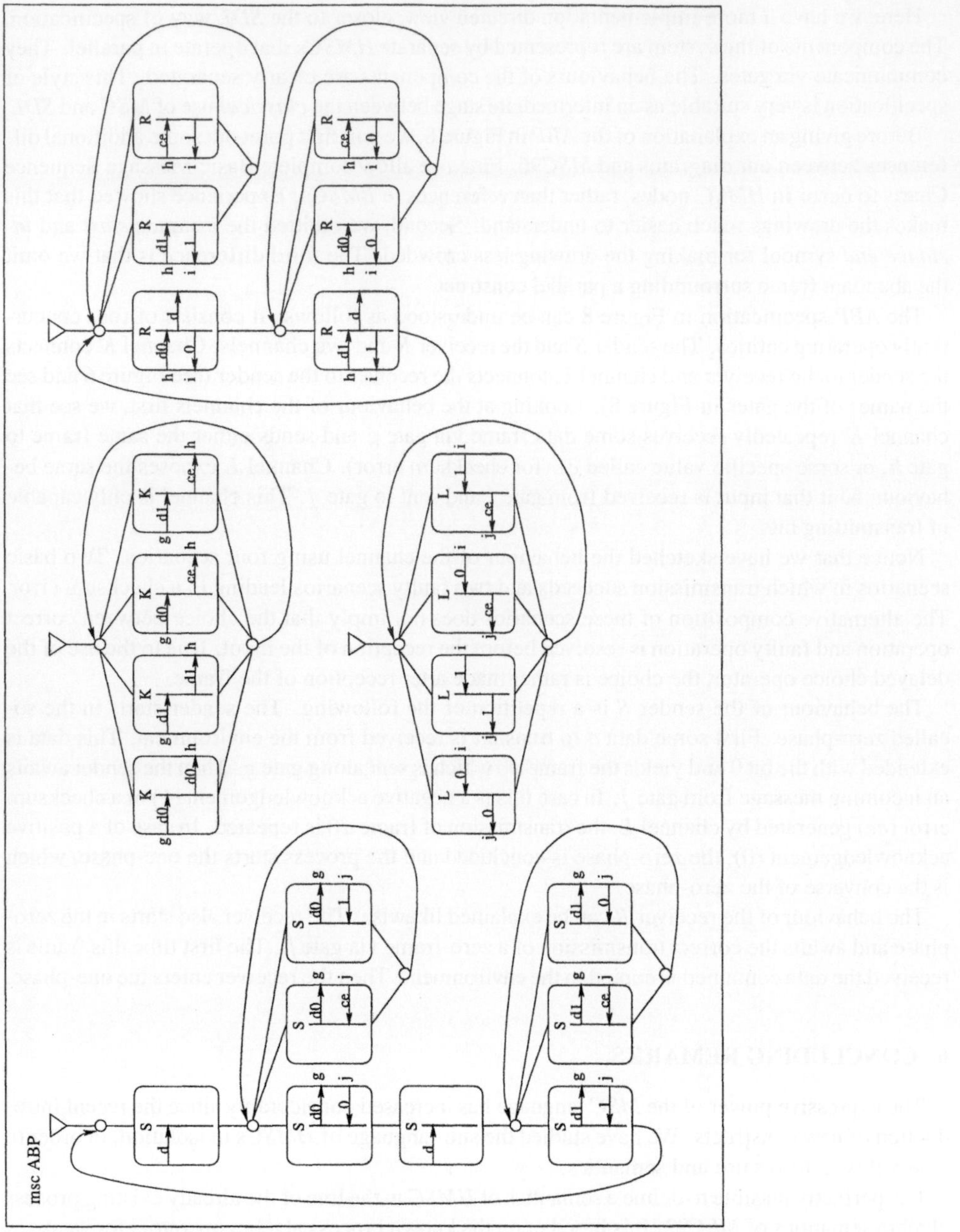

Figure 8. The *ABP*: process oriented specification.

have argued that *HMSC* is very suited for overview descriptions. *HMSC* is mainly used here for vertical decomposition and displaying alternative scenarios. However, a more process oriented view, in which the system is decomposed into communicating subsystems, is hard to achieve with *HMSC*. Therefore, we propose to add gates to the language. By using gates, we were able to give a specification of the components of the *ABP* in a more *SDL*-like style.

We have presented two views of the *ABP*: an overall description expressing the control-flow and an instance oriented description. In principle an instance oriented description can be obtained from the overall description as follows. For every instance we first make a copy of the *HMSC* and then delete all other instances from the *MSC*s. If in this process we break a complete communication into an output and an input event, we need to introduce a gate which is later used to connect the two parts of the communication. In general this will result in an instance oriented description which may not be optimal with respect to readability. We can transform this initial instance oriented description into a more tractable form. The result of this transformation on the *ABP* example is shown in Figure 8. Of course we need to show that these transformation are semantically correct. For this purpose a formal definition as as presented is necessary.

We think that the possibility to switch between different views within the same language fits very well with the variety of uses of the *MSC* language. A thorough study on the (formal) relation between these different views is apparently an important step towards the (semi-) automatic derivation of *SDL* code from *MSC* scenarios. It may be expected that the extension of *HMSC* with gates does not introduce semantical difficulties.

Our simple case study also revealed two more shortcomings of *MSC*96. First, since data is not incorporated in the language, we were not able to give a full specification of the *ABP*. We abstracted from the actual set of data to be transmitted by giving them the same name d. Second, our specification would benefit from being able to reuse *MSC*s that only differ in the value of the alternating bit. A parameterization mechanism will show helpful.

Finally, we mention two minor issues. The *HMSC* specification of the *ABP* benefits from the possibility to consider complete *MSC*s as a node in an *HMSC* specification, rather than a reference. Additionally, there are reasons for removing the restriction that a gate can not be substituted.

REFERENCES

1. R. Alur, G. J. Holzmann, and D. Peled. An analyzer for Message Sequence Charts. In T. Margaria and B. Steffen, editors, *Tools and Algorithms for the Construction and Analysis of Systems (TACAS'96)*, volume 1055 of *Lecture Notes in Computer Science*, pages 35–48, Passau, Germany, 1996. Springer-Verlag.
2. J. C. M. Baeten and S. Mauw. Delayed choice: an operator for joining Message Sequence Charts. In D. Hogrefe and S. Leue, editors, *Formal Description Techniques VII*, IFIP Transactions C, Proceedings Seventh International Conference on Formal Description Techniques, pages 340–354. Chapman & Hall, 1995.
3. J. C. M. Baeten and W. P. Weijland. *Process Algebra*, volume 18 of *Cambridge Tracts in Theoretical Computer Science*. Cambridge University Press, 1990.
4. L. M. G. Feijs. Synchronous sequence charts in action. Technical Report CSR 95-25, Eindhoven University of Technology, Department of Computing Science, 1995.
5. J. Grabowski, P. Graubmann, and E. Rudolph. Towards a Petri net based semantics defini-

tion for Message Sequence Charts. In O. Færgemand and A. Sarma, editors, *SDL'93 - Using Objects*, Proceedings of the Sixth SDL Forum, pages 179–190, Darmstadt, 1993. Amsterdam, North-Holland.
6. Ø. Haugen. MSC structural concepts. Technical Report TD 9006, ITU-T Experts Meeting SG 10, Turin, 1994.
7. ITU-TS. *ITU-TS Recommendation Z.120: Message Sequence Chart (MSC)*. ITU-TS, Geneva. Publication scheduled 1997.
8. ITU-TS. *ITU-TS Recommendation Z.120: Message Sequence Chart (MSC)*. ITU-TS, Geneva, September 1993.
9. ITU-TS. *ITU-TS Recommendation Z.120 Annex B: Algebraic semantics of Message Sequence Charts*. ITU-TS, Geneva, April 1995.
10. P.B. Ladkin and S. Leue. Interpreting message flow graphs. *Formal Aspects of Computing*, 7(5):473–509, 1995.
11. S. Mauw and M. A. Reniers. An algebraic semantics of Basic Message Sequence Charts. *The Computer Journal*, 37(4):269–277, 1994.
12. S. Mauw, M. van Wijk, and T. Winter. A formal semantics of synchronous Interworkings. In O. Færgemand and A. Sarma, editors, *SDL'93 - Using Objects*, Proceedings of the Sixth SDL Forum, pages 167–178, Darmstadt, 1993. Amsterdam, North-Holland.
13. D. M. R. Park. Concurrency and automata on infinite sequences. In P. Deussen, editor, *Proceedings 5th GI Conference*, volume 104 of *Lecture Notes in Computer Science*, pages 167–183. Springer-Verlag, 1980.
14. G. D. Plotkin. A structural approach to operational semantics. Technical Report DIAMI FN-19, Computer Science Department, Aarhus University, 1981.
15. A. Rensink and H. Wehrheim. Weak sequential composition in process algebras. In B. Jonsson and J. Parrow, editors, *CONCUR'94: Concurrency Theory*, volume 836 of *Lecture Notes in Computer Science*, pages 226–241, Uppsala, 1994. Springer-Verlag.
16. E. Rudolph. MSC roadmaps. Towards a synthesized solution. Technical Report TD 9017, Experts Meeting ITU-TS SG 10, 1995.
17. E. Rudolph, P. Graubmann, and J. Grabowski. Message Sequence Chart: composition techniques versus OO-techniques - 'tema con variazioni'. In R. Bræk and A. Sarma, editors, *Proceedings Seventh SDL Forum*, Oslo, 1995. Amsterdam, North-Holland.
18. E. Rudolph, P. Graubmann, and J. Grabowski. Tutorial on Message Sequence Charts. *Computer Networks and ISDN Systems*, 28(12):1629–1641, 1996. Special issue on SDL and MSC, guest editor Ø. Haugen.

SDL '97: TIME FOR TESTING - SDL, MSC and Trends
A. Cavalli and A. Sarma (Editors)

An Annotational Extension of Message Sequence Charts to Support Performance Engineering *

Nils Faltin[a], Lennard Lambert[a], Andreas Mitschele-Thiel[a], Frank Slomka[a]

[a]Friedrich-Alexander-Universität Erlangen-Nürnberg
Lehrstuhl für Informatik VII
Martensstraße 3, 91058 Erlangen, Germany
Email: {nsfaltin,ldlamber,mitsch,fkslomka}@informatik.uni-erlangen.de

With the development of complex systems based on SDL, performance issues often play a major role. However, this is neither reflected by the SDL methodology nor by the specification techniques suggested by the methodology, namely SDL and MSC. To remedy this problem, we propose Performance Message Sequence Charts (PMSC). PMSC represents an extension of MSC-96 to include performance aspects into the language. The extensions allow for the formal specification of various performance aspects, e.g. performance requirements, resource requirements and the specification of the available resources. In order to support the use of tools based on MSC-96, the language extensions are embedded in comments of the original MSC-96 language.

PMSC allows for the co-specification of functional and performance aspects. This joint specification of functional and performance aspects eases the task of software engineers. It saves effort otherwise needed to maintain two different models. In addition, the co-specification based on MSC, rather than on SDL, supports the early evaluation of the performance of the system.

1. Introduction

Performance issues play a major role in the software engineering process. Nevertheless, the integration of performance aspects in the software engineering process has not been well studied. Rather, software engineering and performance evaluation are being considered as two rather independent areas. Each world has its own specialists and uses its own models, methods and tools. Thus, different models are used to deal with different aspects of the system under development. The major drawback of the use of disjunct models is the extra effort needed to keep the models consistent. This extra effort necessary to derive a separate performance model in addition to the functional model is often avoided by putting off performance issues as long as possible in the engineering process.

Considering performance as "afterthoughts" is especially dangerous in the major application area of SDL. In the telecommunication sector, product families are offered which evolve over many years and which have to be maintained and updated for a period of 20 years or more. With such systems, the "afterthought approach to performance" often results in a gradual destruction of the system architecture. In order to quickly meet performance requirements of the system at

*The research described is supported in part by the *Deutsche Forschungsgemeinschaft* under grant He 1408/2-1 and grant SFB 182, B3 and C1.

a stage where the system is already fully implemented and integrated, solutions are selected that are not in accordance with the system architecture (kernel bypasses, etc.). If this approach is taken for several iterations of a product line, complexity is gradually added to the system. This typically results in enormous cost and delays for system integration and testing. In the worst case, the system runs completely out of control due to its enormous complexity.

In order to acknowledge the importance of performance issues, we propose its early and systematic integration into the development process. We propose the co-specification of functional aspects and aspects related to performance, i.e. the use of a consistent model that jointly describes functional as well as performance aspects. Our approach is based on Message Sequence Charts (MSC), a standardized technique heavily used in the telecommunication sector to specify use cases. So far, MSC only supports the functional reasoning about the system.

The scope in which MSCs are typically employed ranges from the requirements specification down to the testing of the implemented system. This wide range for the usage of MSCs makes it a prime candidate for the specification of performance aspects. Thus, the performance information added to MSCs can be used in various phases of the development process. The extended MSC notation described in this paper can be employed to support performance evaluation in all phases in which traditional MSCs are used, i.e. from the early design phases down to detailed design and testing. For example, performance requirements identified during the requirements analysis and specified with the extended MSCs can be validated by model based performance evaluations during the design of the system and later on by means of measurements of the implemented system.

In the paper, we describe an extension of MSC-96 [12] (see [17] for an introduction) to integrate performance aspects. This allows to employ MSCs for performance evaluation. The co-specification has several advantages. The use of a single model ensures the consistency between the functional and the performance model. This saves effort and valuable time. In addition, the use of a description technique that is employed during several phases of the development process allows to easily reuse information once it is specified. This motivates engineers to formally specify performance aspects and to employ performance evaluation. Other advantages of MSCs for performance evaluation result from its orientation towards use cases. This allows to concentrate on specific, important uses of the system. In addition, MSCs are highly deterministic even if they are used in early design stages. This eases the evaluation of the performance of the system. Especially the evaluation of the performance data for different use cases, e.g. response time figures, can be easily supported by our approach. In addition, the extension of MSC allows for the functional validation of the system in the presence of time. This is especially important to evaluate mechanisms to handle overload.

The language extensions for MSC-96 described in this paper are based on earlier work on MSC-92 reported in [7] and [15]. An approach to extend MSC-92 by language constructs rather than by annotations has been described in [19]. [4] report on a language that has some similarities with MSC-96. The language is specifically designed to support performance simulation and supports structural and hierarchical modeling.

Most approaches to support performance evaluation of SDL systems are based on extensions of the SDL language itself to specify various performance aspects. Extensions to SDL to specify performance requirements are described in [14] and [6]. In [13], the separate specification of performance requirements with a temporal logic is proposed. Most approaches known from the literature specify the resource requirements for the execution of the SDL system with extensions added to SDL itself (e.g. the approaches described in [1,2,5,6,14,19]). A hybrid approach to specify resource requirements in SDL and/or MSC has been presented in [7]. Available resources of the system are typically specified by special constructs added to the SDL language, e.g. in [6], or separately specified in a simulation environment that also serves for the performance evaluation (e.g. [18]). Most approaches for performance evaluation of SDL systems are based on simulation, e.g. the approaches described in [6,5,14,18,3]. Performance evaluation of SDL systems based on numerical analysis is described in [1].

The paper is organized as follows: section 2 discusses the integration of performance aspects into the development process of systems based on SDL and MSCs. Our extensions to MSC-96 to support performance engineering are described in section 3. Section 4 concludes the paper and outlines the application areas of our extended MSC notation.

2. Performance Engineering

2.1. Traditional Development Process in the Context of SDL and MSC

The use of SDL and MSC in the development process has been described in [10]. An update of the methodology is currently being devised [11] (see [16] for an overview). The documents focus on functional aspects of the system under development. Performance or other quantitative aspects are not considered. In addition, implementational issues are not dealt with in detail. Instead, the methodology is focusing on the requirements analysis and the design phases (draft design and formalization). The methodology suggests the use of an object-oriented method to classify the information derived during the requirements analysis. MSCs are employed to specify the functional requirements of the system. Thus, the typical and important use cases of the system to be developed are specified by respective MSCs. Once the use cases have been identified, SDL is used during draft design to specify the raw structure of the system. During the detailed design, the behavioral aspects of the system are subsequently added to the specification. This is also called formalization. For the formalization, the SDL specification and the MSC specification are concurrently refined. Thus, if details are added to the SDL specification, e.g. blocks are refined by processes, also the respective MSCs are refined to model the processes rather than the blocks. When the refinement is completed and the SDL/MSC specification has been checked for correctness, the implementation is derived from the SDL specification in a further step.

The major advantage of the use of SDL and MSC for system specification is their support for functional validation. During draft design, SDL structures can be derived from the given MSCs. In addition, the check of consistency between the MSCs and the structural SDL specification is supported by tools. Once behavioral details have been added to the SDL specification during detail design, the SDL specification can be checked for functional correctness, e.g. for deadlocks, livelocks, reachability and unexpected arrivals. MSCs can be used to simulate the functional behavior of the SDL specification. Functional validation is supported by several commercial tools, e.g. SDT [20] and GEODE [21].

2.2. Integration of Performance Aspects

An important prerequisite for the integration of performance issues in the software engineering process is the identification and formal specification of all aspects relevant to performance.

2.2.1. Performance Aspects

The performance aspects relevant for the design and implementation of the application are as follows:

Performance requirements denote the requirements related to performance which are imposed on the implementation. Examples of performance requirements comprise the response time of the system for different arrivals or the system throughput, i.e. the number of arrivals that can be handled within a given time period. Note that the requirements may change over time and that there may be different classes of performance requirements imposed on the application. Performance requirements can be hard or soft requirements. Hard requirements need to be enforced strictly to ensure the functional correctness of the system whereas the violation of soft requirements may be tolerable under certain conditions.

Implementation alternatives describe the possible freedom of choice for the implementation (and the design). Implementation alternatives describe a set of implementation techniques that are applicable to the different parts of the SDL specification and specify how the SDL units can be mapped on the available resources. Examples of implementation alternatives are the possible assignments of the SDL units on the underlying runtime system and the possible implementation models.[2] The description of implementation alternatives allow for the mapping tools to choose the most relevant implementation alternatives regarding all requirements and the preconditions imposed by the machine. The specification of implementation alternatives for the application opens a large possible solution space from which synthesis tools can choose the most appropriate solution. Note that the implementation alternatives are often given implicitly. For example, the alternatives to map SDL units on processors are not explicitly specified. Instead, only restrictions of the possible mappings are given. Note also that the selection of the implementation alternatives is a prerequisite for the evaluation of an implementation.

Resource requirements specify the cost caused by the assignment or execution of the parts of the SDL specification on the available resources. The resource requirements of the implementation or parts hereof may depend on the selected implementation alternative. In this case, the resource requirements have to be derived for each implementation alternative either explicitly or implicitly. In the latter case, the cost are given in a parameterized manner from which the resource requirements can be derived. The resource requirements are given either absolutely (e.g. the delay time of a data transmission) or relatively (e.g. the volume of the transmitted information). The granularity of the parts for which the resource requirements are specified may differ. It may vary from the course-grain specification of the requirements of an SDL block down to the fine-granular specification of the execution cost per transition or even per single SDL statement.

The *available (limited) resources* denote the units which are available for the application, i.e. the assignment of the load as well as its execution. The most important resources are the processors and the communication channels of the system. Further important resources concern the available memory. Besides the capacity of resources, their service strategies are of importance.

The *implementation decisions* are an important prerequisite for performance evaluation. The implementation decisions determine which of the specified implementation alternatives are chosen for the realization of the system. This also influences the resource requirements of the parts of the system. The most important implementation alternatives are the choice of the implementation models for the different SDL units and the mapping of the code derived from the SDL specification on the system. The mapping determines how the units of the SDL specification with their resource requirements are distributed on the available limited resources of the system.

The specification of performance aspects is typically done in a behavior-oriented fashion or use-case oriented. In the case of the behavior-oriented specification of performance aspects based on SDL, performance aspects are associated with the units of the SDL specification (blocks, processes, channels, transitions, etc.). In case of the use-case-oriented specification, performance aspects are associated with the description of execution sequences of the system. For this, mostly MSCs extended by special constructs are employed.

---

[2] See [9] for a description of different implementation models for SDL specifications.

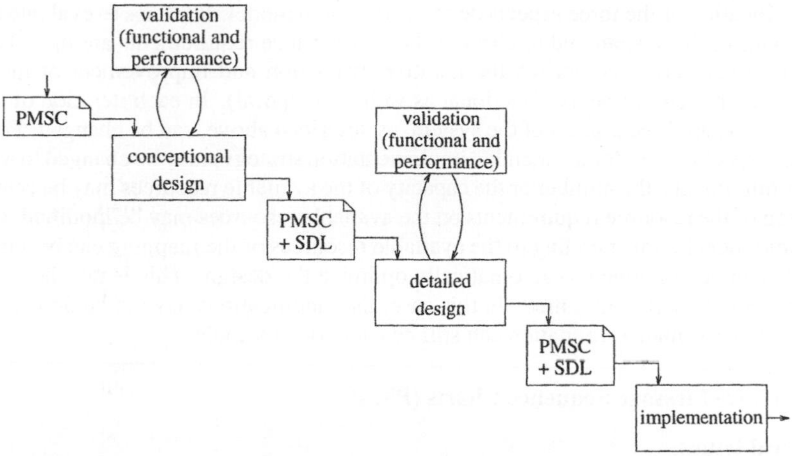

Figure 1. Outline of the performance engineering methodology

2.2.2. Methodology for Performance Engineering

Our methodology represents an extension of the methodology described in [11] to deal with performance issues in addition to functional aspects. The outline of our methodology for performance engineering is depicted in figure 1. In the figure, feedback areas are omitted for simplicity. Similar to the methodology described in [11], our approach is not limited to a specific development process model, e.g. the waterfall or spiral model. Our approach to performance engineering is based on the annotational extension of the MSC language to describe performance aspects.

With our approach performance engineering is supported as follows: During the functional specification of the use cases with MSCs, the performance requirements of the system are also formally specified with the same MSCs. The most important examples of such performance requirements are response time and throughput requirements.

With the traditional methodology, only functional aspects are validated during the design. We add the validation of performance aspects to the methodology. Thus, functional and performance validations are performed during the design of the system. Different from functional validation, there is no principle difference between the performance evaluation of the system during draft design and detailed design. This is because the performance validation is based on MSCs rather than on the SDL specification. The focus on MSC allows to support performance validation of the draft design already. The performance validation counterchecks the performance figures of the specified system with the performance requirements. In order to derive the performance figures, the following issues are of particular importance: First the resource requirements of the operations of the system as specified (executed) by the MSCs have to be identified. Second, the available resources to handle the resource requirements have to be identified. Third, the mapping of the parts of the application with its respective resource requirements on the available resources has to be defined. This comprises the decision on open design or implementation alternatives, the specific distribution of the load on the resources and the strategies to handle contention of the resources, e.g. the dynamic scheduling strategy.

The specification of the three aspects defines the system model. It allows to evaluate the temporal behavior of the system and to check if the performance requirements are met. Typically, performance engineering comprises the iterative evaluation and improvement of the system model to meet the requirements (functional as well as temporal). In each iteration of the optimization process all three aspects of the system, as described above, can be changed. For example, the SDL specification (or its intended implementation strategy) may be changed to reduce its resource requirements, the number or the capacity of the available resources may be changed, or the mapping of the resource requirements on the available resources may be modified. Changes to the system model corresponding to the available resources or the mapping can be automized. Thus, tools can be employed to automatically optimize the design. This is not the case if the SDL specification itself is modified. In this case, the modifications have to be done manually. However, the performance validation can still be supported by tools.

3. Performance Message Sequence Charts (PMSC)

3.1. General Issues

In order to describe the performance aspects of a system, a description language is needed. Using this language as input, the performance of the system can be evaluated using analytical techniques, measurement or simulation. We have defined the description language *Performance Message Sequence Chart (PMSC)*. PMSC extends MSC-96 [12] with performance aspects. The extensions are embedded in comments of the original language. At present we concentrate on a subset of MSC-96. As far as we know, this subset has the same expressive power as the original language.

3.1.1. Embedding Annotations

One goal of the PMSC language is, that MSCs adjunct with performance information can still be processed by tools expecting input in the MSC-96 format. To accomplish this, all performance aspects are embedded in textual parts of the specification that have no formal meaning in MSC-96, but mostly serve for communication among human users. We will call the syntactical elements of MSC, that allow this embedding, *host constructs*. For PMSC, the following host constructs are used:

- *<comment>*
- *<text definition>*
- *<action>*
- *<note>*

A *<comment>* is always attached to an object of the MSC specification, e.g. an action, an input event or an instance. Comments are used in PMSC to specify attributes of the object they are attached to. A *<text definition>* is used for global annotations. *Global annotations* are annotations whose meaning do not depend on the place they are written, but contain all information within themselves. Global annotations may also be given as separate input files to an evaluation tool. An *<action>* describes an internal computation within an instance. Annotations concerning the action can be placed directly inside the action. The *<note>* is the only construct, that normally is invisible in the graphical representation of MSC. It is only visible, when it is used inside a textual part of an MSC diagram, e.g. a reference expression. A note is used in PMSC to annotate reference expressions.

Performance annotations have to be given at the beginning of a host construct and may be followed by a regular user comment. The annotation part begins with a dollar sign and can contain several annotations, separated by comma and enclosed in curly brackets. It has the following structure:

```
${annotation1, annotation2, ...} user comment
```

If for some reason a dollar sign can not be used, a user defined keyword can be defined to mark the beginning of the annotation part. This keyword has to be given as a parameter to the PMSC parser.

3.2. Functional Specification of System Behavior

3.2.1. MSC-96 in PMSC

The *functional specification* describes which *operations* (instance events) the system performs. It describes precedence relationships and potential parallelism between operations and between MSCs. We use a subset of MSC-96 for functional specification. To specify performance aspects, we introduce performance annotations which are attached to MSC objects.

The subset of MSC-96 used consists of plain MSCs, instance decomposition and reference expressions. *Plain MSCs* consist of instances and instance events, but do not contain or reference other MSCs. The only exception is that an instance may be refined by a sub-MSC. This refinement is called *instance decomposition.* In this case, the instance is a composite object and the sub-MSC defines how messages are processed within the object by computations and message exchange between the subobjects.

A *reference expression* is a construct from MSC-96 that specifies the relation in between several plain MSCs. It models the system behavior on a higher level than the plain MSCs. Reference expressions logically form a tree with operators at the inner nodes and plain MSCs at the leaves (see figure 3 for an example). The following operators are used in PMSC.

Sequence: `A seq B` specifies that subexpression A is executed before subexpression B. We use strict ordering semantics here, which means that the execution of A must be completed before B starts. Original MSC-96 uses a weak sequencing, where this ordering relation only must hold within each instance.

To express that a subexpression A runs several times, the *loop* construct is used. The semantics is that of repeatedly using `seq`. MSC gives an upper and lower limit for the number of iterations.

The *parallel composition* of two expressions means that the expressions can run truly in parallel as long as no other constraints apply, e.g. limited resources.

If the system may proceed in two different ways, the *alternative* is used. A special case of an alternative is the *optional* construct. Here expression A is executed or nothing is done.

3.2.2. Transition Semantics for MSC

MSC is mostly used to describe the message flow between SDL processes. An SDL process can only execute one transition at a time. A transition in SDL typically starts with an input and is followed by actions and outputs in any order. If MSCs are used to describe an SDL system, the use of this *transition semantics* when making a performance evaluation is an obvious choice. Figure 2 gives an example of an instance axis containing two transitions. Our definition of a transition semantics for MSC is as follows:

1. A transition is a sequence of events of a local MSC instance.
2. A transition starts with an input and ends before the next input. To cover all cases, an extra rule is defined: The first instance event begins a transition (even if it is not an input), the last event ends a transition.
3. All local instances (in several MSCs) with the same name form a *global instance*. Each global instance has its own input queue for incoming messages. If a PMSC system is sim-

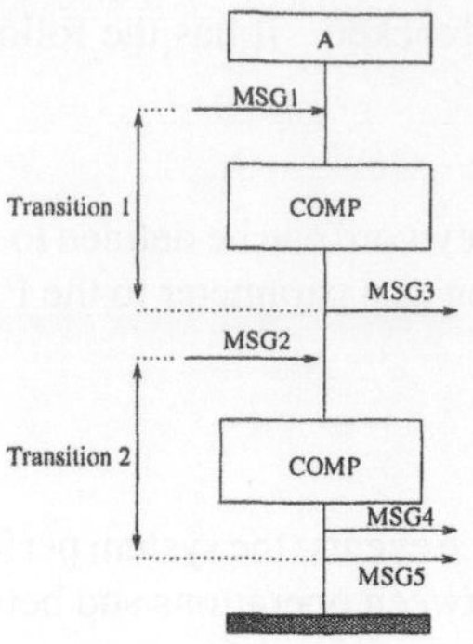

Figure 2. Transition definition

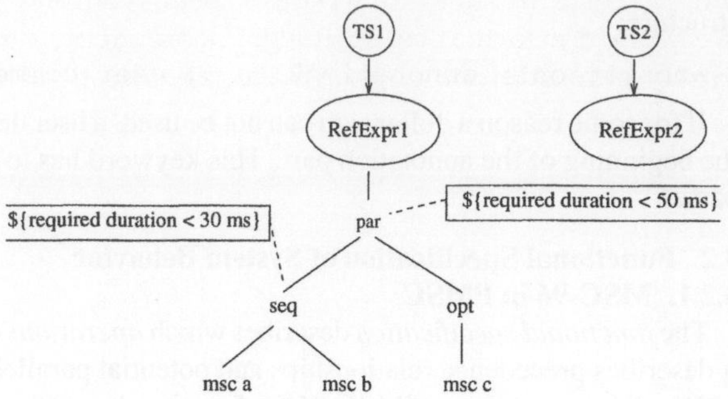

Figure 3. Traffic sources and duration times

ulated, messages can arrive in a different order than expected e. g. because of message overtaking. To allow processing in the correct order, a message will remain in the queue until the instance reaches the corresponding input.

4. A global instance executes a transition exclusively. Thus, while the transition is executed, no other events are processed by the same instance.

3.3. Performance Requirements

3.3.1. System Stimulation

The performance model of PMSC consists of a number of reference expressions, each with an own traffic source. A *traffic source* generates *service requests* to be handled by the PMSC system. A reference expression describes how an PMSC system processes a *service* by employing instance processing and exchange of messages between the instances.

Figure 3 shows a system with two services, described by RefExpr1 and RefExpr2. Requests are generated by the traffic sources TS1 and TS2. The structure of RefExpr1 is detailed graphically.

The interarrival times of the service requests are deterministic. The user specifies a repeat count and a list of interarrival times. The traffic source will wait as long as the first time indicates and then produce a service request. It will then wait the next specified time interval and produce another service request until it has worked through the list. The whole procedure will be repeated the specified number of times. If no repeat count is given, it defaults to one. The name of a reference expression is defined by inserting a <*note*> inside the reference expression. It contains the keyword **name** and the name of the expression.

In the following example the traffic source will generate a service request for reference expression Ref1 at the times 2 ms, 5 ms, 7 ms, 10 ms, 12 ms and 15 ms. The name of the expression is defined inside the expression:

```
...  /* ${name Ref1} */ ...
```

The traffic source is specified somewhere as a global annotation:

```
source for TS1 loop 3 interarrival det {2 ms, 3 ms}
```

Each reference expression is implicitly started, when its service request arrives. There can be several executions of the same expression active at once, e.g. started shortly after each other by

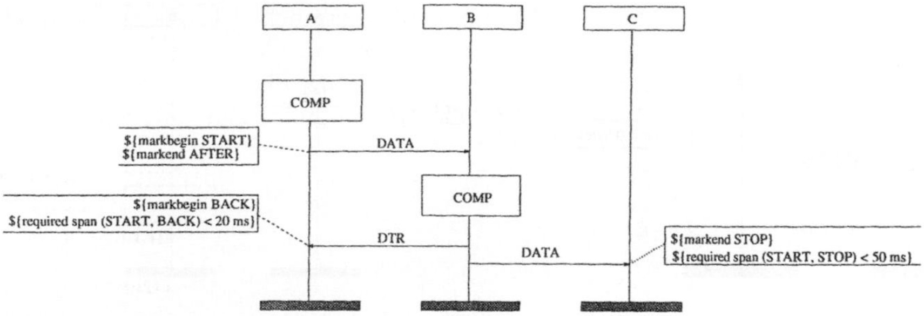

Figure 4. The markbegin, markend and span annotation

subsequent service requests.

The traffic sources produce service requests independently of each other. Here too, the processing of requests from different traffic sources proceed in parallel. All these executions have to share the same MSC instances and the same resources. An MSC instance will only execute an input event, when the corresponding message has arrived. Because the sender of messages from the environment is not modeled directly, such messages are considered available when needed. The load imposed by the traffic sources constitutes an implicit performance requirement (throughput) because the system has to be able to handle this load.

3.3.2. Elapsed Time

The *elapsed time* is the time that elapses between two defined events. The elapsed time is the sum of the computation time, transmission time and waiting time. All instance events, e.g. action, input and output, consume time in our model. It is possible to mark the beginning or the end of the instance event and thereby define a *timestamp event* and give it a name. Timestamp events are typically used by a simulation or measurement tool to record the time an event occurs. The beginning of an instance event is marked with the keyword **markbegin**, the end is marked with **markend**.

With the function **span**(s,e) the elapsed time between the timestamp events s and e is specified. Timing requirements formulated with span() are typically written in a text symbol of a MSC or in a comment. Figure 4 shows several performance requirements for elapsed time between timestamp events. For example, the time between the sending of message DATA (timestamp event START) and the reception of DTR (BACK) has to be less than 20 ms.

It is also possible to specify the elapsed time of the execution of a reference expression and of subparts of the expression (figure 3). Each subexpression corresponds to the operator, that binds it together. After the operator, a <note> comment is added. Within this <note>, the keyword **duration** is written. Duration and span are well suited to specify a response time requirement. Figure 3 states two requirements. The duration of the whole reference expression has to be below 50 ms and the duration of the subexpression (a seq b) has to be less than 30 ms.

3.4. Resource Requirements

Resource requirements specify the amount of resources needed for an operation. The resource requirements are specified with abstract parameters by annotating the MSC. The absolute resource usage can be derived from the abstract parameters and the attributes of the resource the operation runs on. The available resources and their attributes are described in the machine

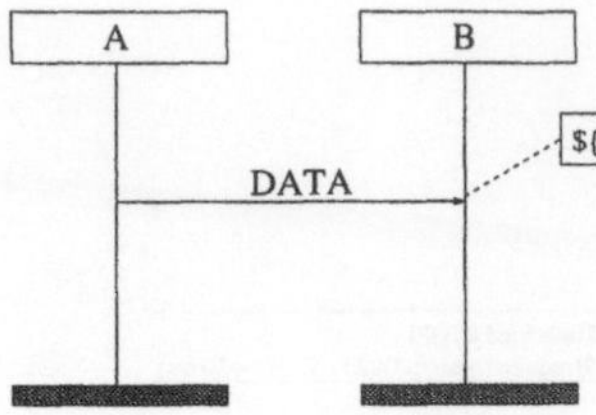

Figure 5. PMSC annotation of message size

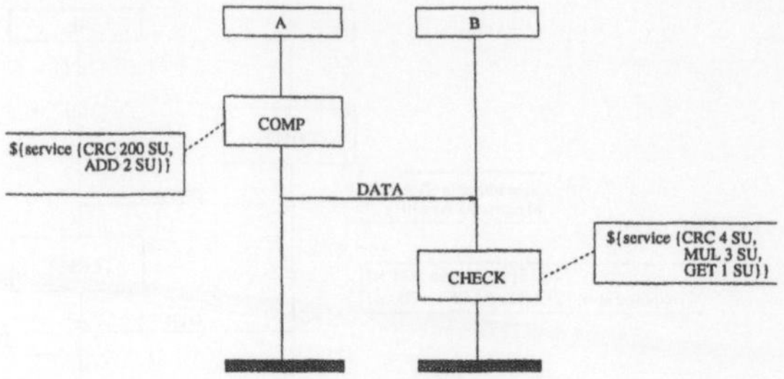

Figure 6. PMSC annotation for service usage of MSC actions

model. In PMSC the ressources needed for message transmission and computation can be specified.

3.4.1. Message Size

For messages, only the message size in bytes is given. It can be annotated either at the corresponding input event or output event (figure 5). The message arrow cannot be annotated directly. This is because the arrow is only present in the graphical representation and does not have a counterpart in the phrase representation of MSC. A message size of 100 byte is defined by:

```
size 100 byte
```

The sending and receiving of a message consumes processor time. If a message is transmitted over a communication link, it will use that link (resource) for some time. Both times depend on the message size, the processor characteristics and the link characteristics. Additionally, waiting time may be needed until the resources are available.

3.4.2. Service Usage

In order to model that an operation needs computation time, the concept of services is used. An *operation* is an MSC action, that runs on a processor and uses services. Each operation states which services it uses. It also specifies for each service the amount it requires from the service. The service usage is annotated inside the action event or in a comment attached to it.

An example is given in figure 6, where the action COMP computes a checksum (CRC) of a payload field of size 200 units and also makes two additions.

The unit of a service usage is stated as **su** (service unit). It must be specified in the machine model which services are available and how long the execution of a service unit will take.

Our model for resource usage is powerful enough to express different instruction mixes as well as the direct specification of the execution time.

1. *Instruction mix.* The processor usage is specified by stating how many basic processing instructions, e.g. addition, comparison and load/store are needed to perform the operation. For example, the instructions may correspond to statements in SDL, C or assembly language. In the simplest case, computing requirements are modeled by stating how many "standard" instructions an operation needs. Then there is only one instruction type and thus only one service needed.
2. *Runtime per processor.* In this model, the runtime of each operation for each type of processor available is specified. For each processor type, a service is introduced. The service

unit corresponds to a time unit, e.g. microseconds. When there is only one type of processor in the system, only one service is needed. This approach can be especially interesting, when there is a sequential (non-parallel) prototype implementation available, which can be measured. These data can then be used to simulate a parallel implementation more accurately than with abstract service usage.

3.5. Machine Model

The *machine model* describes the available system resources. It consists of processors, clusters and links. The machine model is well suited to model a parallel computer consisting of several processor clusters. Within a cluster, processes communicate via shared memory and in between clusters by message passing via communication links. In the following, we describe the resources, their attributes and how computation time of operations and communication time of messages are derived. The machine model may be given inside the MSC specification in a <*text definition*> or as a separate document.

3.5.1. Processors and Clusters

Processors are computing devices that offer services to operations. Each processor belongs to a *processor cluster*. The processors of a cluster dynamically share the load assigned to that cluster and can communicate without using a link. All processors in a processor cluster are equal, i. e. offer the same services at the same speed. A cluster can offer several services. The service set offered may differ from cluster to cluster. For each service and each cluster, the computation time per service unit (**su**) is given.

The total computation time of an operation is obtained by adding up the service times of the operation. Each service time is calculated by multiplying the number of service units with the computation time per service unit. The number of service units is given in the resource requirements.

A message transmission consists of an output event and an input event. As stated in section 3.4.1, both input and output events consume computation time on the processor they run on. The computation time (per event) depends on the message size and the two attributes latency and capacity of the cluster the processor belongs to. It is calculated according to the formula:

```
computation time = latency + message size * capacity
```

The idea behind this is that the latency models the time needed for message transmission that is independent of the message size. If each byte of the message has to be processed in some way, e. g. copied in main memory, the time needed for each byte is expressed by the capacity. If the actual implementation does not have such a processing, the value can simply be set to zero (0 ns/byte). Using time per byte instead of byte per time also makes this model fit better with the service model used for determining computation cost. An example is a cluster C1 with two processors that offers the service of calculating a checksum at a speed of 20 nanoseconds per word and an addition at a speed of 10 nanoseconds per operand. For communication within the cluster it has a latency of 7 microseconds and a capacity of 10 nanoseconds per byte.

```
cluster C1 processors 2 service {checksum 20 ns/su,add 10 ns/su}
latency 7 us capacity 10 ns/byte
```

3.5.2. Mapping and Scheduling

A global MSC instance is statically mapped to a cluster. Each instance has its own input queue of messages waiting to be processed (Fig. 7). Once an instance has received an input message, it

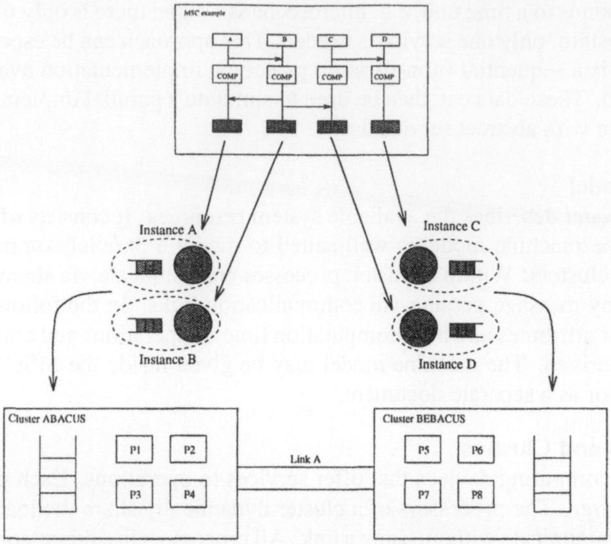

Figure 7. Mapping of instances to clusters

needs a processor and queues up in a ready queue shared by all processors of the cluster. So far we assume that the instances have static priorities specified with integer numbers. The smaller the number, the higher the priority. Once an instance reaches an input event, it can be descheduled. In PMSC, the mapping is described for each cluster as in the following example where the cluster ABACUS is assigned instance A with priority 1 and instance B with priority 2:

```
mapping ABACUS contains {A 1, B 2}
```

3.5.3. Links

A *link* is a bidirectional, reliable communication line connecting two clusters. It consists of two channels, one for each direction. Both have the same attributes. For each pair of clusters, a link must be specified. A message that travels from one cluster to another will use the link connecting the clusters. Messages will always be transmitted unfragmented. Only one message can use a channel at a time. Additional messages will wait in a FIFO queue. Message sending is asynchronous, i.e. processors are free to proceed when the message is in this FIFO queue. The transmission time over a link depends on the message size and the two attributes latency and capacity of the respective link:

```
transmission time = latency + message size * capacity
```

An example for a link L1 connecting the clusters C1 and C2 with latency 2 milliseconds and capacity 100 nanoseconds per byte is:

```
link L1 connects C1 C2 latency 2 ms capacity 100 ns/byte
```

Figure 7 gives an overview of the mapping principles. Local instances from different MSCs with the same name form global instances, each with its own input queue. Instances A and B

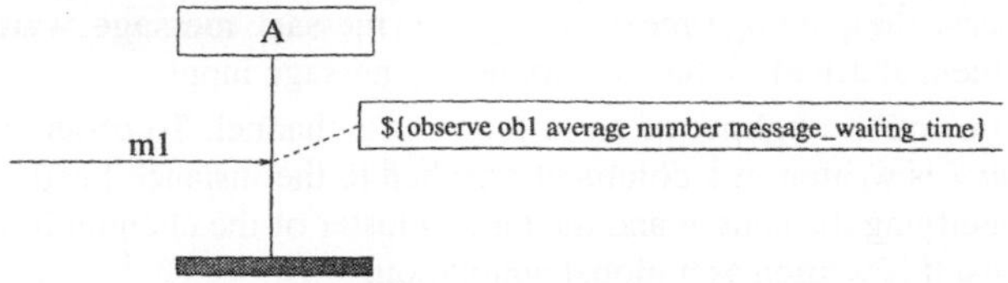

Figure 8. Observing message waiting time

are mapped to cluster ABACUS, instances C and D to cluster BEBACUS. Cluster ABACUS consists of four processors P1, P2, P3 and P4 that share a ready queue. Cluster ABACUS and BEBACUS are connected by the link A.

3.6. Observations

For performance evaluation it is possible to define *observations* in PMSC. They provide the user with an insight into the system. Performance evaluation tools will observe the system behavior at these points and report an aggregated performance measure. Besides the observations declared by the user, the performance requirements stated in section 3.3 must also be observed and controlled by the evaluation tool.

In the example of fig. 8 the user wants to know how long message m1 arriving at instance A has to wait in the instance input queue. Because the msc of fig. 8 is executed several times, there are also several arrivals of message m1 and thus several *samples* of message waiting time. The user is only interested in the *average* of the samples and the *number* of samples. Other *result values* that can be requested are the *standard deviation* and the *list of samples*. As the user may specify several observations, each one gets a unique *observation name* (here ob1), so the derived values can be identified in the output of the evaluation tool. The output format of the evaluation tool is not specified in PMSC, but an output line might look like this:

```
observation ob1 average:  1.2 ms number:  16
```

To state that the *observation object* he wants to monitor is the message input, the user attaches a comment with the observation statement to it. If it is not possible to specify the object by attaching a comment, an *at clause* is used. This is the case when monitoring a communication channel, as in the following example.

observe `chan` **at channel** `c1 c2` **value utilization**

Here the *utilization* of the channel carrying messages from cluster c1 to cluster c2 is monitored. Even if several messages run over the channel, there is only one utilization *value*, so average, deviation, number and samples make no sense here.

The observation point states what attribute of an object shall be monitored. The following types of observation points can be defined in PMSC:

1. The queue length of an instance. The length can be given in number of messages (**queue_length_messages**) or memory size of all messages including their parameters (**queue_length_bytes**). The <*observation*> is written in a comment attached to the instance head.
2. The queuing time of messages at the receiving instances. To observe the queuing time of all messages **messages_waiting_time** is written in a comment attached to the instance

head. To observe the queuing time of one specific message **message_waiting_time** is written in a comment attached to the corresponding message input.

3. The utilization and throughput of an instance or a channel. To observe an instance, the *<observation>* is written in a comment attached to the instance head. A channel is observed by specifying the source and the target cluster of the channel in an at clause. The observation itself is written as a global annotation.
4. The elapsed time between two defined timestamp events and the duration of a complete reference expression (see section 3.3). The observation for a reference expression is written in a note behind the operator of the subexpression to be observed. Observations of elapsed time with the span() function are written as global annotation.

4. Conclusions

In the paper Performance Message Sequence Charts (PMSC), an extension of MSC-96 to include performance aspects into the MSC language, have been described. The language extension allows for the co-specification of functional and performance aspects. This joint specification of functional and performance aspects eases the task of software engineers. It saves effort otherwise needed to maintain two different models. PMSC supports the formal specification of a variety of aspects related to performance. This includes performance requirements (e.g. response time requirements and throughput requirements), resource requirements (e.g. the computational cost of MSC operations), the specification of the available resources as well as the specification of the mapping of the MSC instances on the available resources.

The proposed language extensions are embedded in comments of the original MSC-96 language. Thus, standard tools based on MSC-96 can still be employed. The major advantage of PMSC is its support for early performance evaluation. Since MSCs are employed from the requirements specification down to detailed design and testing, it is a prime candidate for the integrated specification of performance aspects. The wide spectrum of use of MSCs allows to employ a single specification technique to specify and evaluate performance issues in various phases of the development cycle.

Different from extensions to model performance aspects with SDL, PMSC supports the early performance evaluation of systems. This is because of the orientation of MSCs towards use cases, which allow for the early specification of specific, selected executions of the system. Thus, a highly deterministic and also accurate model is available at an early design stage, which is a valuable base for performance evaluation. PMSC especially supports the evaluation of the response time of the system under various loads in an early design stage. This rather deterministic evaluation of specific uses of the system at an early design stage is not possible with performance evaluations based on SDL. This is due to the orientation of SDL towards structural and behavioral aspects, rather than on use cases. Thus, performance evaluation based on extensions of SDL are typically based on probabilistic branching which prohibits the accurate evaluation of the response-time behavior of the system for different classes of services.

We are currently working on a set of tools based on PMSC. A PMSC parser has been implemented.The parser is based on the Kimwitu tool [8] and supports the fast extension of the PMSC language to quickly include new annotations (performance constructs) as they are needed.

In addition, we are working on a PMSC simulator that supports performance evaluation and validation. The PMSC simulator will support deterministic as well stochastic simulation. In case of a deterministic simulation, or the simulation with bounded times, the simulator will allow us to validate the performance requirements as specified in the PMSC description.

The PMSC language is also an integral part of the DO-IT toolbox. The DO-IT toolbox provides an integrated set of tools to support the early and systematic integration of performance aspects in the development process of SDL systems. The DO-IT toolbox is a joint project of the Universities of Erlangen and Cottbus and aims at the derivation of efficient code from SDL specifications. With the DO-IT toolbox, the implementation is derived in four steps: First, the cost for the execution of the different components of the SDL specification are analyzed. Second, a semantical analysis of the SDL specification determines where certain code optimization strategies can be applied and provides hints to the user where a modification of the SDL specification may result in the derivation of more efficient code. The derived information are described with the PMSC language. In the third step, an appropriate implementation design is derived for the available target machine. This is done based on the information derived in the first and second step and an abstract specification of the available machine. In order to evaluate different implementation designs, simple evaluation techniques as well as complex simulations based on the PMSC simulator currently developed may be employed. Next, the actual code is derived for the SDL specification. The code generator is in charge of implementing the design decisions made in the previous step. Last, the implementation is measured and the performance figures of the implementation are counterchecked with the performance requirements specified with the PMSCs. The techniques employed by the DO-IT toolbox to derive efficient code are described in [9]. The application of the DO-IT toolbox to implement a multimedia conference system has been described in [15].

Besides the implementation of pure software systems based on SDL, we are also working on a rapid prototyping system that supports the codesign of hardware/software systems based on SDL, PMSC and VHDL.

REFERENCES

1. F. Bause, P. Buchholz. Qualitative and Quantitative Analysis of Timed SDL Specifications. Kommunikation in Verteilten Systemen, Reihe Informatik aktuell, Springer, 1993.

2. F. Bause, H. Kabutz, P. Kemper, P. Kritzinger. SDL and Petri Net Performance Analysis of Communicating Systems. Proc. 15. Int. Symp. on Protocol Specification, Testing and Verification (PSTV'95), P. Dembinski, M. Sredniawa (Ed.), June 1995.

3. S. Böhmer, R. Klafka. A new Approach to Performance Evaluation of Formally Specified Protocols. Formal Description Techniques for Distributed Systems and Communication Protocols (FORTE), VIII, 1994.

4. L. Braga, R. Manione, P. Renditore. A Formal Description Language for the Modelling and Simulation of Timed Interaction Diagrams. Joint Int. Conf. on Formal Description Techniques for Distributed Systems and Communication Protocols (IX) and Protocol Specification, Testing and Verification (XVI) (FORTE/PSTV'96), Gotzhein, Bredereke (Eds.), p. 245-260, Chapman & Hall, 1996.

5. M. Bütow, M. Mestern, C. Schapiro, P.S. Kritzinger. Performance Modelling with the Formal Specification Language SDL. Joint Int. Conf. on Formal Description Techniques for Distributed Systems and Communication Protocols (IX) and Protocol Specification, Testing and Verification (XVI) (FORTE/PSTV'96), Gotzhein, Bredereke (Eds.), Chapman & Hall, 1996.

6. M. Diefenbruch, E. Heck, J. Hintelmann, B. Müller-Clostermann. Performance Evaluation of SDL Systems Adjunct by Queuing Models. SDL '95 with MSC in CASE (Proc. Seventh SDL Forum), R. Braek, A. Sarma (Ed.), Elsevier, 1995.

7. W. Dulz. A Framework for the Performance Evaluation of SDL/MSC-specified Systems. Proc. ESM'96, Budapest, June 1996.

8. P. van Eijk, A. Belifante. The Term Processor Kimwitu, http://wwwtios.cs.utwente.nl/doc/tp.man/tp.man.html, March 1993.
9. R. Henke, H. König, A. Mitschele-Thiel. Derivation of Efficient Implementations from SDL Specifications Employing Data Referencing, Application Level Framing and Activity Threads. Submitted to SDL-Forum '97.
10. ITU-T. Z.100, Appendix I. ITU, SDL Methodology Guidelines. ITU, 1993.
11. ITU-T. SDL+ Methodology: Manual for the use of MSC and SDL (with ASN.1). Draft document, ITU, March 1996.
12. ITU-T. Z.120, Message Sequence Chart. ITU, 1996.
13. S. Leue. Specifying Real-Time Requirements for SDL Specifications – A Temporal Logic-Based Approach. Proc. 15. Int. Symp. on Protocol Specification, Testing and Verification (PSTV'95), P. Dembinski, M. Sredniawa (Ed.), June 1995.
14. J. Martins, J. Hubaux. A New Methodology for Performance Evaluation Based on the Formal Technique SDL. Proc. Design and Analysis of Real-Time Systems (DARTS '95), Bruessels, Nov. 1995.
15. A. Mitschele-Thiel, P. Langendörfer, R. Henke. Design and Optimization of High-Performance Protocols with the DO-IT Toolbox. Joint Int. Conf. on Formal Description Techniques for Distributed Systems and Communication Protocols (IX) and Protocol Specification, Testing and Verification (XVI) (FORTE/PSTV'96), Gotzhein, Bredereke (Eds.), p. 45-60, Chapman & Hall, 1996.
16. R. Reed. Methodology for real time systems. Computer Networks and ISDN Systems, 28, 1685-1701, 1996.
17. E. Rudolph, P. Graubmann, J Grabowski. Tutorial on Message Sequence Charts. Computer Networks and ISDN Systems, 28, 1629-1641, 1996.
18. C. Schaffer, R. Raschhofer, A. Simma. EaSy-Sim: A Tool Environment for the Design of Complex, Real-Time Systems. Proc. Int. Conf. on Computer Aided Systems Technologies, Innsbruck, Springer-Verlag, May 1995.
19. C. Schaffer. MSC/RT: A Real-Time Extension to Message Sequence Charts (MSCs). Interner Bericht TR140-96, Institut für Systemwissenschaften, Johannes Kepler Universität Linz, 1996.
20. Telelogic Malmö AB: SDT 3.1 User's Guide, SDT 3.1 Reference Manual. 1996.
21. Verilog. ObjectGEODE – Technical Documentation, 1996.

SDL '97: TIME FOR TESTING - SDL, MSC and Trends
A. Cavalli and A. Sarma (Editors)

MSCs at Siemens A/S - towards the usage of MSC-96

Astrid Nyeng and Svanhild Gundersen

Siemens A/S,
P.O.Box 10 Veitvet
0518 Oslo, Norway
e-mail: asny@fs.osl.scn.re and sgu@fs.osl.scn.de

During a period of four years, Siemens Defence has extensively used MSCs for different purposes. MSCs are regarded useful for clarifying requirements, for verifying design decisions, as a base for the SDL design and as test cases in the integration test. The paper focus on problems in current MSC practice and how constructs from MSC-96 can be used in order to improve the uses.

1. INTRODUCTION

Formal use of SDL and MSC was introduced in Siemens Defence in 1992/93. Experiences from this introduction was reported in [1]. One specific problem encountered was that the large number of MSCs produced in the analysis phase of the project caused problems when it came to keeping the MSCs updated during the project. However, despite this problem, MSCs were seen as a very useful tool in the projects.

Siemens Defence has during eight years participated in the Norwegian SISU project. The SISU project is a Norwegian technology transfer program aiming to improve the productivity and the quality of Norwegian companies that develop systems within the real-time domain. The project is presented in [2]. In 1995 we decided to cooperate with one of the research partners in SISU (a socalled SISU consultant) in order to improve the use of MSCs. His job was to point out deficiencies in our usage of MSC and to suggest corrective actions. This paper reports which problems that were discovered and what we have done to improve our MSC practice.

Before going into details about MSC problems and improvements, we describe our software development model with emphasis on SDL and MSC.

2. SOFTWARE DEVELOPMENT MODEL

Figure 1 shows the Siemens Defence development model.

In the Invocation phase the project is staffed, planned and organized. The process model is tailored to the project taking the project's characteristics into account.

In the Analysis phase the system to be developed is analysed as a black box. In this phase MSCs are used to clarify the textual requirements stated in the Customer Requirements Specification (CRS). These MSCs are called System Interaction Diagrams (SID) and describe interactions between the system and its environment.

In the System Design phase we decompose the system into blocks, processes and services according to the static part of SDL. In this phase MSCs are used to describe the interaction between the blocks in the system, Block Interaction Diagrams (BIDs), and between processes in a block or between services in a process, Module Interaction Diagrams (MIDs). The block level MSCs and process level MSCs are verified in review meetings against the system level MSCs and block level MSCs respectively.

In the Detailed Design phase the complete SDL system is produced. The SDL description is then checked against the MSCs. The Implementation phase consists of coding abstract data types implemented in C before automatically generating code for the system.

The Integration phase is performed using the SDT simulator [5] running one simulator script corresponding to each block level and process level MSC. The simulator logs are manually compared with the MSCs.

In the System Test phase the system is tested on the target machine. The system level MSCs may be used as a base for writing the test cases, however, since we have had problems of having either too many or too few MSCs produced in the Analysis phase, this has not always been an appropriate test suite.

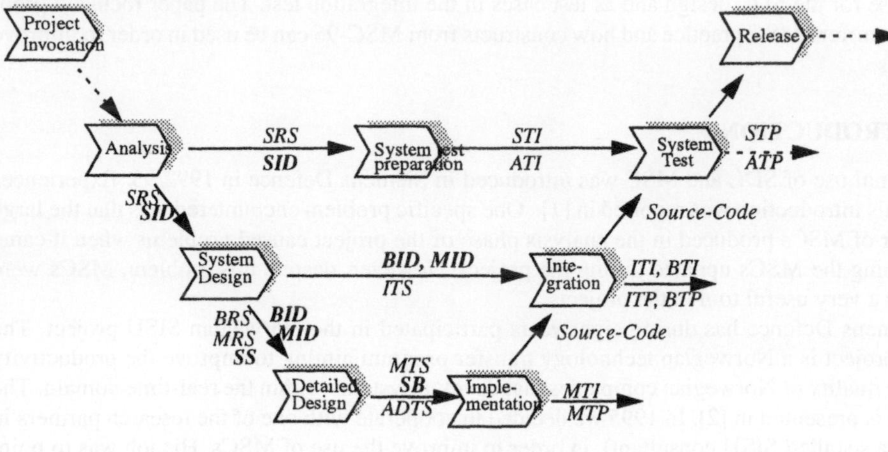

Figure 1: Process Model

SS	-	Static Structure (SDL)
SB	-	System Behaviour (complete SDL description)
ADTS	-	Abstract Data Type Specification
SRS	-	System Requirement Specification
SID	-	System Interaction Diagram. MSCs at system level.
BRS	-	Block Requirement Specification
BID	-	Block Interaction Diagram. MSCs at block level.
ITI	-	Integration Test Instructions: SDT scripts deduced from the BIDs
ITP	-	Integration Test Protocol: Generated test log by the SDT simulator
MRS	-	Module Requirement Specification
MID	-	Module Interaction Diagram: MSCs at the process level.
ITS	-	Integration Test Specification
BTI	-	Block Test Instructions: SDT scripts deduced from the MIDs.
BTP	-	Block Test Protocol: Generated test log by the SDT simulator.
MTS	-	Module Test Specifications
MTI	-	Module Test Instructions
MTP	-	Module Test Protocol: Generated test log by the SDT simulator.

Box 1: Abbreviations

To summarize, MSCs are used for the following purposes in our process model:

- to analyse and clarify requirements in the Analysis phase,
- to verify the decomposition into blocks and processes in the System Design phase,
- as a base for a complete SDL description in the Detailed Design phase, and
- as test cases in the Integration phase.

3. PROBLEMS IN PAST MSC PRACTICE

During the summer 1995 a new project was initiated at Siemens Defence. This project consisted of three sub projects. After the second sub project we invited a participant in the SISU project [2] (SISU consultant) to analyse the SIDs produced in the Analysis phase of these two subprojects. This person has been actively involved in the standardization of MSC-96 and had the needed knowledge to give advice on how to prepare for the use of MSC-96.

The system to be developed was a communication system consisting of a link layer, a network layer and a transport layer (according to the ISO Reference Model) and an application using the services of the transport layer to send application messages.

The following problems were spotted:

- lack of MSC strategy leading to a random selection of MSCs,
- consistency problems, e.g. different naming conventions, different use of conditions
- difficulties of getting the overview of the connection between the MSCs in the MSC document

- difficulties of updating frequently repeated signal sequences

Each of these problems are treated in detail in the following subsections.

3.1. Lack of MSC strategy

The Generic Engineering Handbook of Siemens Defence states precisely when, i.e. in which phases and activites, to use MSCs in the development process. This generic handbook is tailored to the specific projects. However, the book gives less advice to the analysts and designers regarding how many MSCs to produce and selection criteria for the MSCs.

In the very first project to use formal MSC in Siemens Defence more than four hundred MSCs were produced in the Analysis phase. The strategy then was to cover all functional requirements to the system including normal cases and error cases. It soon turned out that this amount of MSCs were impossible to keep updated and they were "thrown away" in a later phase of the project. In the next project, the participants were afraid of getting into the same problems. They therefore made significantly fewer MSCs. These were more or less randomly selected by the analysts. No written statement about the purpose and usage of these MSCs existed.

The SISU consultant adviced us in coming projects to write down an MSC strategy covering the following questions:

- What tools will be used to produce and maintain the MSCs?
- How do the MSC documents cover the universe of MSCs?
- Which MSC documents are to be produced?
- How is information not expressible in MSC attached?

Details about these questions can be found in [3].

3.2. Consistency problems

In order to analyse the functionality of the communication system we decided to produce a set of SIDs focusing on the higher layer (HLCOM) and a separate set of SIDs focusing on the network layer (NET). Figure 2 shows one example of a SID, logoff_N1, decsribing how two communicating systems (WTCOM and TESTCC) interact when one party initiates a logoff procedure. The details on how this procedure is performed at the network layer are suppressed. Figure 3 shows how the request to clear the virtual call (vcClearRq) is handled on the network layer.

These two MSCs illustrate some typical problems:

- The instances are named differently at the two communication levels. WTCOM at the higher layer SID (logoff_N1) corresponds to WT(HLCOM) at the network level SID (n_vcClear_N1) and TESTCC corresponds to TESTCC(HLCOM).
- The sequence of the instances are different in the two SIDs.
- The naming conventions are not obvious to an outsider of the project.
- The connection between the logoff procedure at the higher layer and the network layer is not obvious.

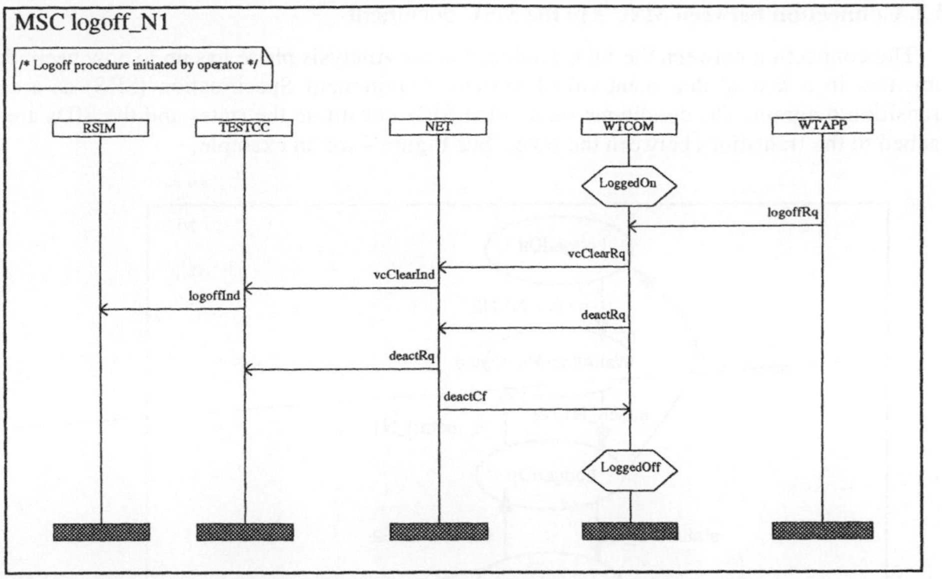

Figure 2: Logoff procedure (higher layer)

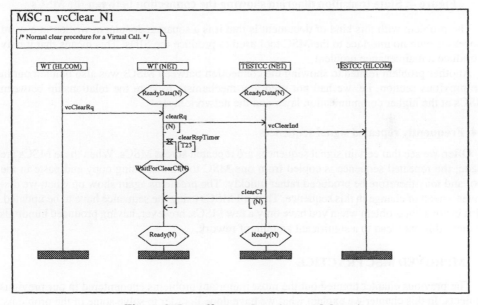

Figure 3: Logoff procedure (network layer)

3.3. Connection between MSC's in the MSC document

The connection between the SIDs produced in the Analysis phase has up to now been documented in a textual document called System Requirement Specification (SRS) as a state transition diagram. The conditions used in the SIDs constitute the states and the SIDs are attached to the transitions between the states. See Figure 4 for an example.

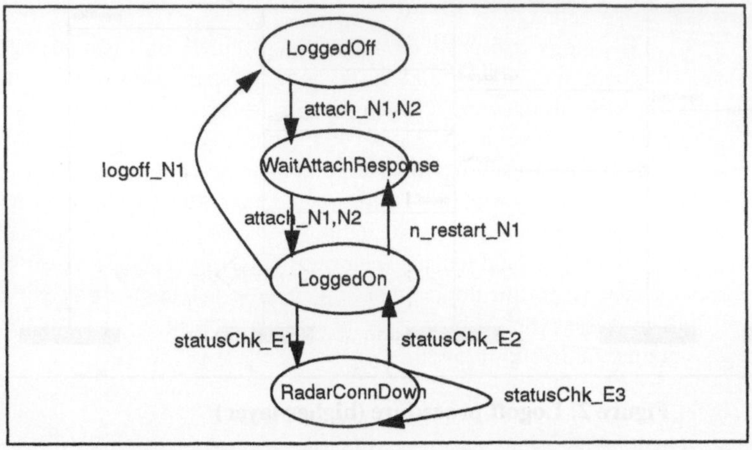

Figure 4: State transition diagram showing the connection between the MSCs

The problem with this kind of document is that it is a separate document written in a word processor with no interface to the MSC tool used to produce the SIDs. This means that it may introduce a maintenance problem.

Another problem related to showing the connection between MSCs was also pointed out in the previous section, i.e. we had not used any mechanism to state the relationship between MSCs at the higher communication layer and the network layer.

3.4. Frequently repeated signal sequences

Often we see that certain signal sequences are repeated across MSCs. When these MSCs are made, the repeated sequence is copied from one MSC to another using copy and paste in the tool and may therefore be produced rather quickly. The problems again show up when we discover a need of change in this sequence. Then all MSCs using the sequence have to be updated. This is not a big problem when you have only a few MSCs, however, having produced hundreds of them this may lead to a significant amount of rework.

4. IMPROVED MSC PRACTICE

The previous chapter pointed out the most important problems encountered in our previous projects. In this chapter we explain what we have done in order to solve some of the problems.

4.1. MSC strategy

During the period when the SISU consultant looked into our MSC practice, the third sub project started. We then decided to write down a MSC strategy for this project. The MSC strategy answered the questions stated in Section 3.1. The most important result was not the MSC strategy document itself, but the process of discussing the contents of it in the project group. For this spescific project it was decided to focus on the changed requirements since this was a project redesigning and enhancing an existing product.

We now have stated in the Generic Engineering Handbook that all projects shall write down their MSC strategy in their tailored version of the handbook.

4.2. Consistency problems

The following actions were taken to improve the clarity of the MSC document:

- All MSCs in a MSC document shall have the same left to right order of the instances.
- All instances shall be named consistently througout the document. In a retrospective perspective, this is quite obvious, but often different persons produce MSCs in the same MSC document and some common rules have to be established
- The naming conventions are documented in the Generic Engineering Handbook, see Figure 5.

```
<nameOfMsc> ::= <typeOfMsc>_[<scope>]_<function>_<case><number>
<typeOfMsc> ::= sid | bid | mid
<scope> ::= <nameOfSystem> | <nameOfBlock>.
<case> ::= N | E
<number> ::= 1|2|3|...
```

Figure 5: MSC naming conventions

4.3. Connection between MSCs in the MSC document

The SISU consultant suggested a solution to achieve an explicit relationship between the MSCs at different levels of the communication protocol. The solution is shown in Figure 6 and Figure 7. In Figure 6, the sequences in the higher layer MSC involving the network layer are referred to as separate MSCs. Figure 7 shows one of these referenced MSCs, wClear. wClear contains the sequence showing how the higher layer asks the network layer to clear the virtual call. The way the network layer handles this request is found in the decomposed MSC, n_vcClear_N1. This MSC is the same MSC as introduced in Figure 3. There is now an explicit relationship between the MSC logoff_N1 and the MSC n_vcClear_N1.

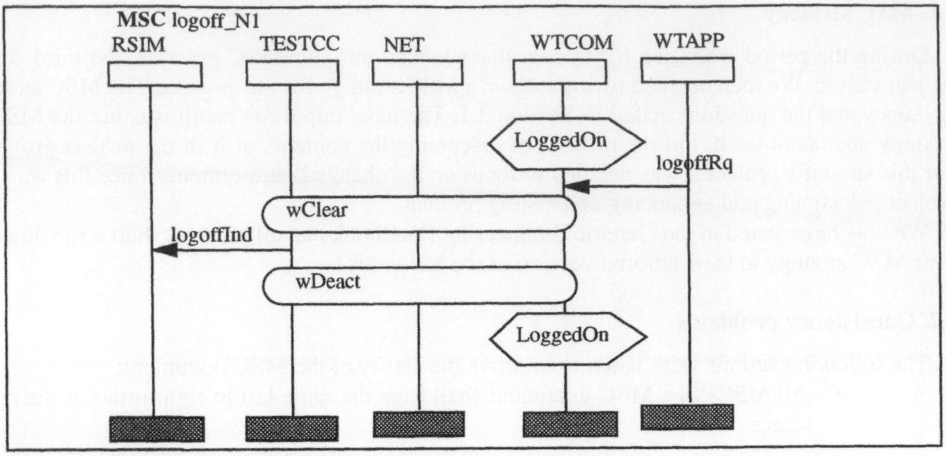

Figure 6: Use of MSC references to hide details on lower layers

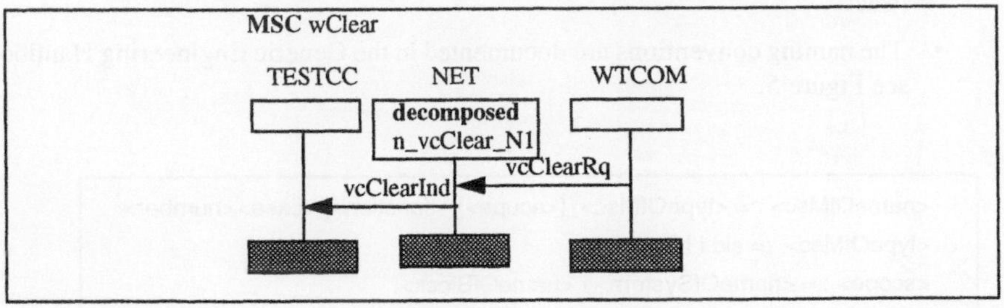

Figure 7: The referenced MSC

MSC reference has now become a construct in MSC-96. However, this construct was not supported by our MSC editor. Figure 8 shows how we used the global condition symbol to "simulate" a MSC reference. This is at present the way we do it in our projects.

Another new part of MSC-96 is the Hig Level MSCs, HMSC. HMSC looks like a promising solution in order to get rid of the state transition diagram in the SRS document. Figure 9 shows one example corresponding to the state transition diagram in Figure 4.

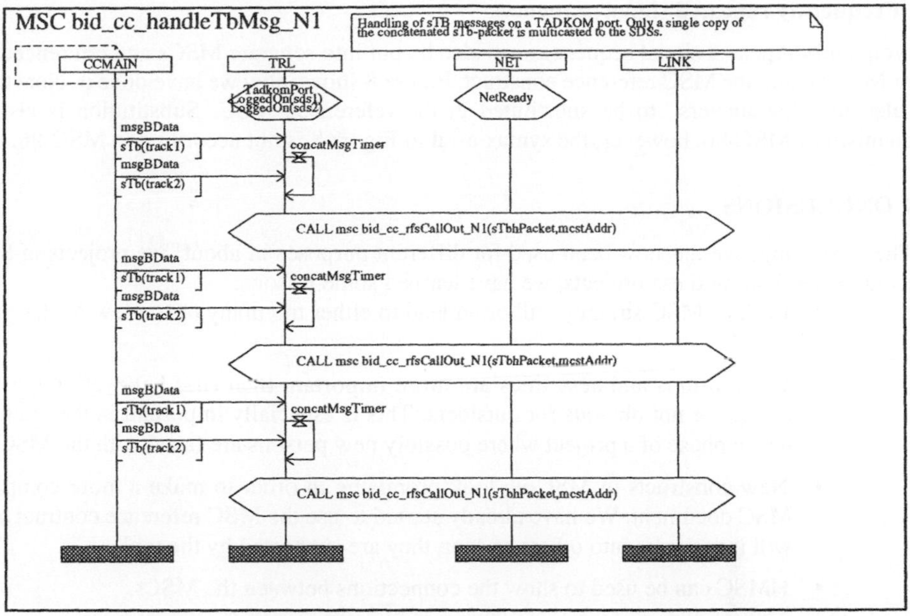

Figure 8: "Simulated" MSC reference using global condition

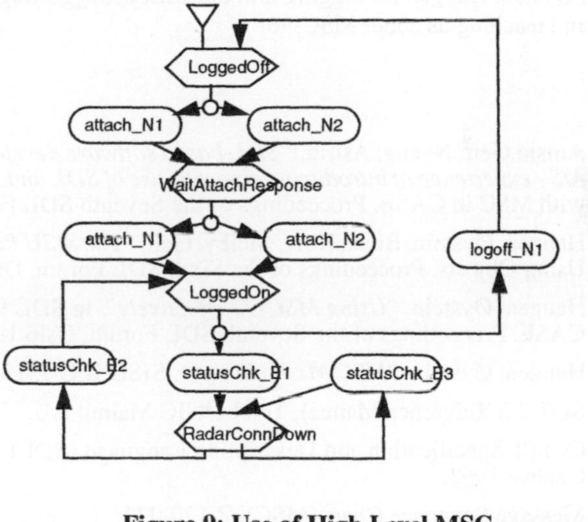

Figure 9: Use of High Level MSC

4.4. Frequently repeated signal sequences

Frequently repeated signal sequences can also be put into separate MSCs and referenced in other MSCs using the MSC reference construct. Figure 8 shows how we have done it. Note that we also use "parameters" to be substituted in the referenced MSC. Substitution is also a mechanism of MSC-96, however, the syntax used in Figure 8 is not according to MSC-96.

5. CONCLUSIONS

The MSC language has now been used for different purposes in about five projects in Siemens Defence. During these projects, we have learned some lessons:

- Lack of MSC strategy will often lead to either too many or too few MSCs produced.
- Conventions and aestethics are more important than first believed. Obvious things are not obvious for outsiders. This is especially important in the maintenance phase of a project where possibly new persons are faced with the MSCs.
- New constructs in MSC-96 look promising in order to make a more compact MSC document. We have already started to use the MSC reference contruct and will investigate into others as soon they are supported by the tool.
- HMSC can be used to show the connections between the MSCs.

Acknowledgements

Special thanks to Øystein Haugen for digging into our MSCs, suggesting better ways to use the MSC language and teaching us about MSC-96.

References

[1] Amsjø,Geir, Nyeng, Astrid. *"SDL-based software development in Siemens A/S - experience of introducing rigorous use of SDL and MSC."* In SDL'95 with MSC in CASE. Proceedings of the Seventh SDL Forum, Oslo 1995.

[2] Haugen, Øystein, Bræk, Rolv, Melby, Geir. *"The SISU Project"*. In SDL'93 Using Objects. Proceedings of the Sixth SDL Forum, Darmstadt 1993.

[3] Haugen, Øystein. *"Using MSC-92 effectively"*. In SDL'95 with MSC in CASE. Proceedings of the Seventh SDL Forum, Oslo 1995.

[4] Haugen, Øystein. *"MSC Methodology"*. SISU II L-1313-7. January 96.

[5] SDT 2.3 Reference Manual, TeleLOGIC Malmø AB.

[6] CCITT Specification and Description Language (SDL), Z.100, ITU, Geneva 1993.

[7] Message Sequence Chart (MSC), Z.120, ITU, Geneva 1996.

VIII

SDL and other languages I

SDL '97: TIME FOR TESTING - SDL, MSC and Trends
A. Cavalli and A. Sarma (Editors)

Automated Iteration between OMT* and SDL

Kurt Verschaeve

Laboratory for System and Software Engineering, Vrije Universiteit Brussel, Pleinlaan 2, 1050 Brussel, Belgium. kaversch@info.vub.ac.be

During the development of large systems in SDL, an Object Oriented Analysis Technique like OMT can be used as a front-end to SDL. This combination is promising, but only on one condition. The iteration process between OOA and SDL must be automated and must preserve manual changes in the SDL specification. In this paper, we present automated support for iteration between OMT and SDL based on hierarchical links and incremental code generation. Each OMT entity is linked with its corresponding SDL entities. Changes made to an OMT entity are forwarded locally to the corresponding SDL entities in such a way that as much as possible of the manual changes in SDL are preserved. This is carried out in hierarchical fashion which makes it possible to integrate the dynamic model of OMT in the iteration process.

Keywords: OMT, SDL, iteration, software engineering

1. INTRODUCTION

Today's major SDL tool builders (Verilog, Telelogic) are currently combining SDL [BHS91] with Object Oriented Analysis (OOA) techniques like OMT [RPB91]. OMT provides many abstraction mechanisms that give the developer a better overview of the system than is possible in SDL. The object model of OMT allows classes from different subsystems to be brought together in one module. The dynamic model provides nested state diagrams and entry/exit actions, allowing a more concise view on state diagrams.

The weak link between OMT and SDL, however, is the iteration process. That is, it should be possible to develop concurrently in OMT and SDL whereby both models are automatically kept consistent. At each synchronization point, changes made on a higher level of abstraction should be merged with the changes on the more concrete level.

The necessity of an automated iteration between OMT and SDL is apparent. Without automatic support for iteration, maintenance will probably be done on the SDL level only because no one likes to make the same change twice. By not updating the OMT model, it might be unclear what impact a change has on other parts of the system. Moreover, the OMT model gets outdated and it becomes difficult to maintain the system.

In this paper we present a automated support for iteration between OMT and SDL. First the object model and dynamic model are combined to generate an equivalent SDL system specification. The generated SDL code may then be changed without firm constraints. From then on, only the *changes* in the OMT model are translated instead of the complete model. These changes are automatically detected, translated to SDL and applied locally on the specification with maximal preservation of detailed design changes in SDL. Hierarchical links between OMT and SDL syntactic elements provide the context in the SDL system where to apply changes.

1.1 OMT*

We apply the INSYDE methodology [HWW96] to state our ideas. According to this methodology analysis is done in OMT [RBP91], system design in OMT* [WWV95] and detailed design in SDL [BHS91] for software subsystems and VHDL for hardware subsystems (Figure 1).

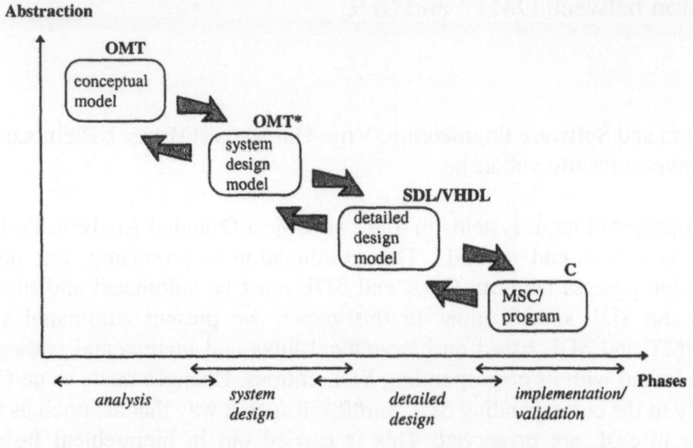

Figure 1. Iterations in the INSYDE methodology

During the analysis phase of the INSYDE methodology, OMT is used to capture the requirements of the system resulting in a conceptual model.

During system design, subsystems are identified, communication is formalized and the behavior for each active class is specified. To describe these aspects a new language, OMT* [WWV95] was developed, aimed to meet the requirements of system design. OMT* is a formal variant of OMT defined during the INSYDE project [INS95] and is better suited for system design for two reasons. First, ambiguous constructs are removed from OMT* and the semantics of OMT* constructs are clearly described. Second, the definition of OMT* includes translation rules to SDL'88, SDL'92 and VHDL. These translation rules comprise the object model as well as the dynamic model (state diagrams) of OMT*. In Section 2 we explain some important aspects of OMT*.

Before starting detailed design, the OMT* model is first translated automatically into SDL. During detailed design, the generated SDL specification is then further improved. Except for some specific cases, it is not possible to generate perfect SDL specifications immediately because OMT lacks a number of features like timers, addressing, object creation and switches.

Figure 1 shows three different iterations: between analysis (OMT) and system design (OMT*), between system design and detailed design (SDL) and between detailed design and implementation (C).

In this paper we will only focus on the iteration process between system design in OMT* and detailed design in SDL. More specifically, we limit our scope to SDL'88. We did not use SDL'92 for pragmatic reasons, but plan to cover SDL'92 in the future.

1.2 Overview of the Iteration Process

Figure 2 shows the successive steps in an iteration. ① First the complete system design model in OMT* (M-OMT*) is translated into an SDL specification (M-SDL). ②The developer then uses M-SDL as a base for detailed design. We call the detailed design changes Δ_1. ③ Then the developer returns to system design and makes changes to M-OMT*. We call these changes Δ‘. ④ Finally, in order to synchronize M’-OMT and M_1-SDL, the changes Δ_1 and Δ‘ must be merged. This is achieved by translating Δ‘ to Δ'_{SDL} and applying it to M_1-SDL.

In a second iteration (not in Figure 2), step ① is skipped. The developer continues with detailed design in M_1’-SDL (Δ_2) and system design in M’-OMT* (Δ”). At the end of the second iteration Δ” and Δ_2 must be merged, resulting in M_2”-SDL.

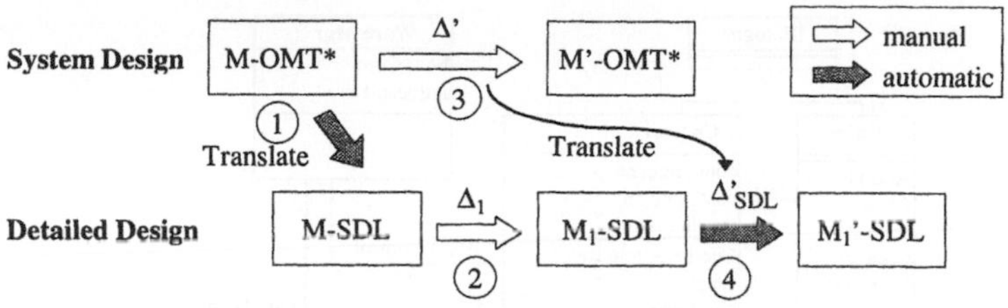

Figure 2. iteration scheme

The most important aspect of step ④ is that as much as possible of the manual changes in SDL are retained. Therefore the changes in Δ'_{SDL} are applied locally in the SDL specification, instead of overwriting existing code. In order to find the location where certain changes must be applied, the OMT* model is linked to the SDL specification during the translation. Changing an entity in M-OMT only affects the locations in M_1-SDL that are linked to that entity. The parts of the SDL specification for which the corresponding OMT* in not modified are unaffected and thus preserve every detailed change.

There exists also another approach to merge Δ_1 and Δ‘. M’-OMT* could be translated completely into SDL, resulting in M’-SDL. Applying Δ_1 to M’-SDL would also result in M’$_1$-SDL. Today’s iteration schemes ([Ratio], [Aonix]) are usually based on this approach. This works well for iterating between OMT and C++ because there Δ_1 is easy to detect (the implementation of functions). But finding all detailed changes in SDL is virtually impossible. This is because in SDL changes are made on different levels and to make the changes the same syntactic constructs are used as in the generated code. This approach has also the disadvantage that Δ_1 continues to grow with each iteration.

1.3 Structure of the Paper

The structure of the rest of the paper will be as follows. In section 2 we present the Toffee Vendor example that will be used throughout the paper. Then the four steps of Figure 2 are elaborated. ① In section 3 we present how OMT* models are translated into SDL specifications. ② In section 4 we will explain what kind of changes are allowed in SDL. ③ Section 5 shows a few system design changes in the example. ④ Section 6 explains the essence of the paper. It shows how we detect changes in OMT*, how we translate them to SDL and apply them on an SDL model. Finally, sections 7, 8 and 9 respectively give an overview of related work and of future work, and a conclusion.

2. TOFFEE VENDOR EXAMPLE

Throughout this paper we will use the toffee vendor (presented in [BHS91]) as an example to explain our ideas. Due to space limitation we will skip certain behavior of the toffee vendor as presented in [SDL]. In this section we present the initial system design model in OMT* of the toffee vendor. At the same time we explain some important semantic differences between OMT and OMT*. For a complete formal definition of OMT* see [WWV95], for a comprehensive outline of OMT* see [VWJ95].

Object Model. Like in OMT, classes represent the basic components of a system in OMT*. Unlike in OMT, aggregations are specifically used to create hierarchical subsystems. Also, associations specifically identify communication between two classes, instead of a general relationship.

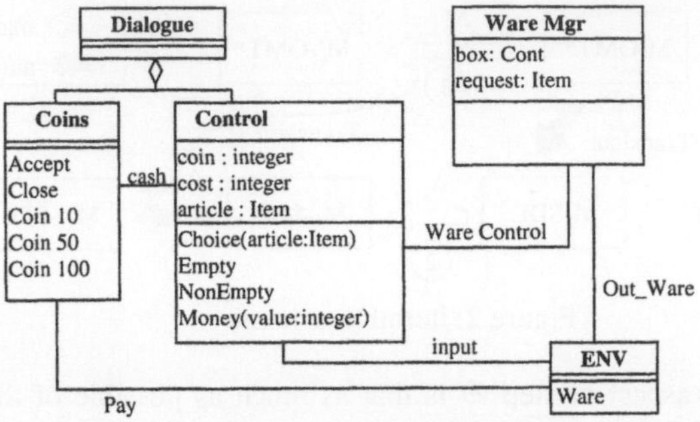

Figure 3. Initial Object Model of the Toffee Vendor

Figure 3 shows the object model of the initial system design of the toffee vendor. The *Dialogue* subsystem contains two components *Coins* and *Control*. The *Control* class is central to the operation of the toffee vendor, it manages the overall behavior and it communicates with *Coins* and *Ware Mgr*. The *Coins* class accepts coins and translates these into values that are sent to *Control*. The *Ware Manager* checks the existence of a specific article and delivers it after it is paid. The class named ENV is special class that represent the environment of the system.

Attributes are used to store values. An attribute declared in a certain class, may be used only in the state diagram of that class. For example the *article* attribute of the *Control* class is used in the state diagram to store user's requested.

Operations in OMT* are primarily used as input event declarations. Each class should declare all the events it receives, and their parameters, as an operation. For example the *Control* class can receive 4 events. The *Choice* event has one parameter to indicate the *article* the user has chosen. The *article* is of type *Item*, which is new type. The events *Empty* and *NonEmpty* are sent by the *Ware Mgr* to indicate whether the requested *Item* is available or not. The *Money* event, finally, is sent by *Coins* whenever a coin is accepted. The parameter *value* of the *Money* event indicates the value of the coin.

Dynamic Model. The dynamic model of OMT* is very similar to that of OMT. States, transition, entry and exit actions, output events, initial and terminal states and nested state diagrams, are all used in the same manner. OMT*, however, explicitly differentiates three kinds of actions: assignment, output event, function call and informal text. Each of them can automatically be recognized and accordingly translated to SDL.

Figure 4, 5 and 6 respectively show the state diagrams of the three classes *Control*, *Ware Mgr and Coins.* The overall behavior of the state diagrams should be easy to understand, so we limit our explanation to some OMT* specific aspects. The *payment* state in Figure 4 has two entry actions. The first entry action is an assignment, recognized by the ':=', and initializes the cost for the article. The second entry action *Accept* is an output event to *Coins*, because *Coins* declares it as an input event.

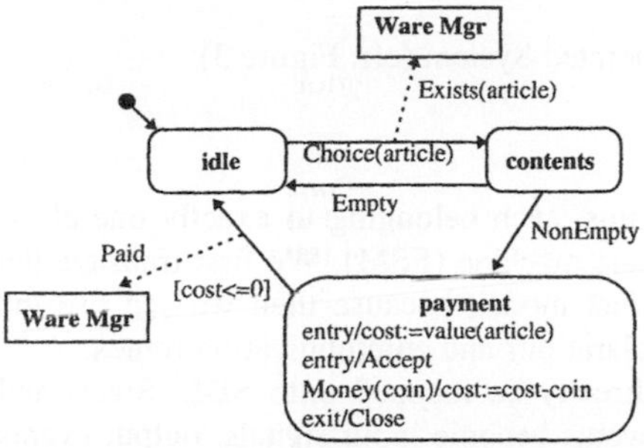

Figure 4. State Diagram of the *Control* Class

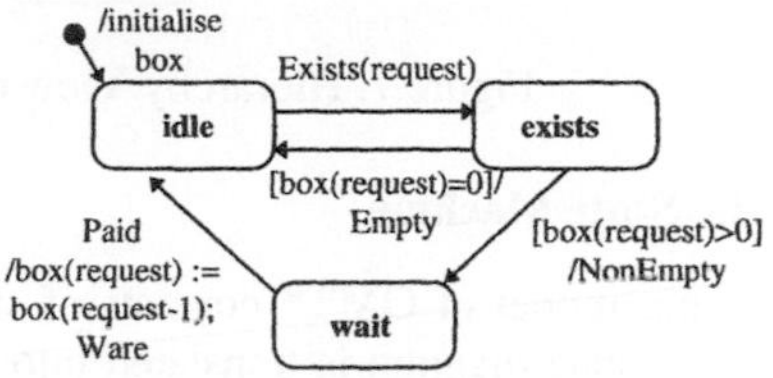

Figure 6. State Diagram of the *Ware Manager*

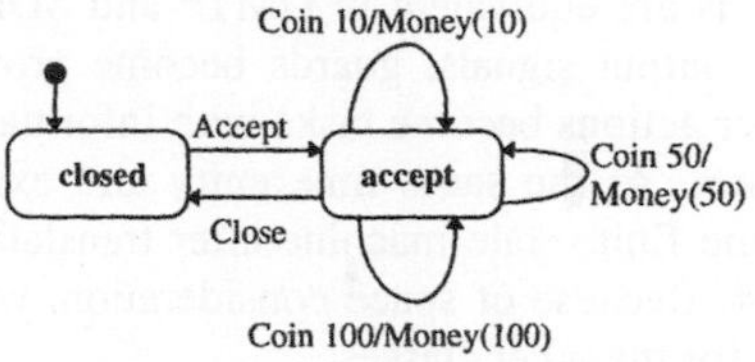

Figure 5. State Diagram of *Coins*

3. TRANSLATING OMT* TO SDL

The first step in iterating between OMT* and SDL is the generation of an SDL specification as a base for detailed design (step ① in Figure 2). The translation of OMT* to SDL is part of the formal definition of OMT* [WWV95]. The translation itself is defined as translation rules that specify the SDL code that is generated for a given OMT* construct. These translation rules are designed to generated readable SDL specifications that are a good base for detailed design. For a comprehensive explanation about the translation, see [VJW96].

Here we present an outline of the translation rules and apply them to the Toffee Vendor example of Section 2. We divide the translation rules in three parts. First we generate the structural objects of the SDL description. Then a finite state machine is generated for each process. Finally the processes are interconnected and declarations are generated for each structural level.

3.1 Hierarchical Structure

The classes and aggregations of an OMT object model are translated into a static SDL structure specification. Classes become blocks and aggregation is used to identify nested blocks. If a class owns a state diagram, a process is created in the corresponding block. Figure 7 shows the resulting hierarchical structure after translating the object model of the toffee vendor (Figure 3). Note that the spaces in the identifiers are automatically converted to underscores.

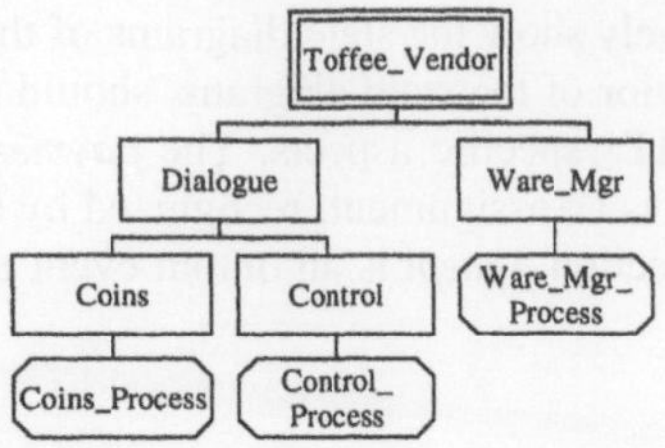

Figure 7. Hierarchy View of the Generated System (cfr. Figure 3)

3.2 Finite State Machine

The dynamic model of OMT* consists of state diagrams, each belonging to exactly one class. Each OMT* state diagram is translated into a finite state machine (FSM). We first translate the dynamic model of OMT* prior to the rest of the object model, because then we can use the information on input and output signals to generate declarations and communication routes.

Most constructs in an OMT* state diagram can directly be mapped onto SDL. States and transitions are equivalent in OMT* and SDL. Input events become input signals, output events become output signals, guards become provided constructs, assignments become assignments and other actions become tasks with informal text. Nested state diagrams are flattened before the translation. At the same time entry and exit actions are moved onto the transitions. Figure 8 shows the finite state machine after translating the state diagram of the *Control* class shown in Figure 4. Because of space consideration, we only work out the behaviour of the *Control* class and not for the other classes.

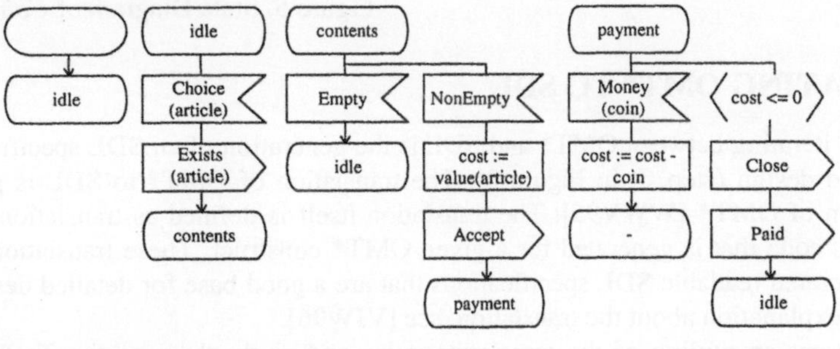

Figure 8. Generated FSM for *Control_Process* (cfr. Figure 4)

3.3 Declarations and Communication

Signal declarations are an important aspect of an SDL system. Each signal used within a process, either as input or as output signal, should have a declaration within the scope of that process. The best place the declare a signal is thus the deepest block that is visible to all processes that use the signal. The same holds for type declarations.

Another important issue is to connect processes that communicate. For every association between two classes, a communication path is generated between the corresponding processes. Channels are generated to reroute the communication path via the first common visible block. The direction of the channels and the associated signal lists are obtained from the intersection of output events of the source process and input events of the destination process.

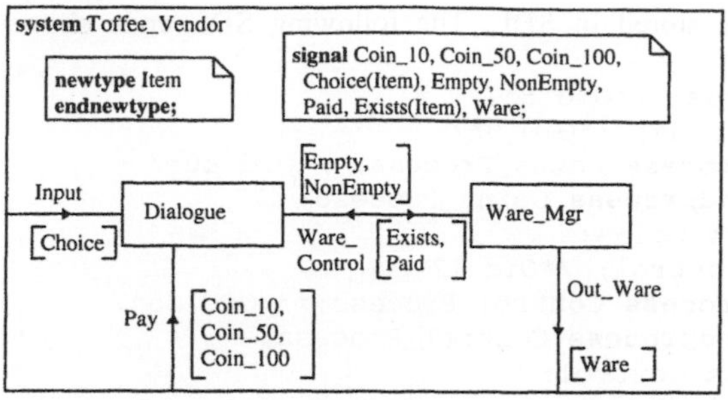

Figure 9. SDL System Specification after Translation

Figure 9 shows the declarations and the block interactions of the system after having translated the complete OMT* model of the toffee vendor example. An empty newtype declaration is created for *Item*, which is a new type. All signals needed on system level are declared. The signals *Accept*, *Close* and *Money* are not defined here, because they are only used within the *Dialogue* subsystem. The channel *Sync* is the result of rerouting the association Sync between the classes *Control* and *Ware_Mgr*.

3.4 Linking OMT* and SDL models

As explained in section 1.2, we need a link between the OMT* model and the the SDL specification. During the translation we maintain hierarchical links between both. Each entity in the OMT* model is linked with its corresponding SDL entities. For example, a class is linked with the generated block. An association is linked with all generated signal routes and channels. An activity is linked with the process, and so forth. Figure 10 shows the hierarchical structure of OMT* and SDL and the links between the corresponding constructs.

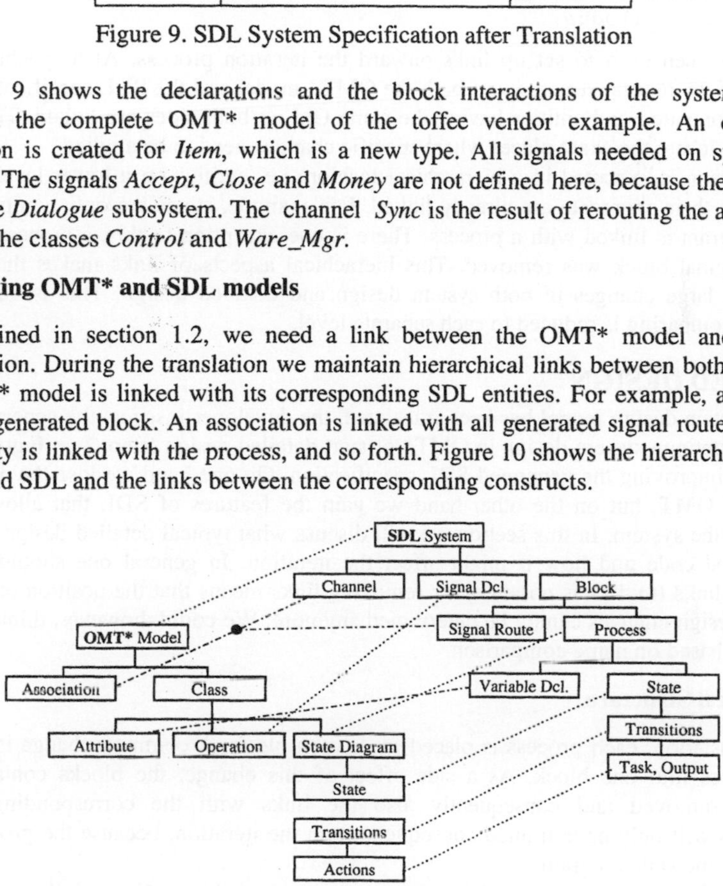

Figure 10. Hierachical Links between OMT* and SDL

The generated SDL is stored in a separate file, using standard SDL. We need a way to restore the links afterwards. This is implemented by storing unique identifiers in SDL. In our OMT tool [Verilog] each OMT construct has a unique object identification number (Oid) that is preserved as long as the construct is not deleted. This number is stored in SDL with the same technique as graphical information is stored in SDL. The following SDL code shows the Oid's in the generated code:

```
block Dialogue; /*Oid 5*/
    block Coins; /*Oid 8*/
        process Coins_Process; /*Oid 40*/
        endprocess Coins_Process;
    endblock Coins;
    block Control; /*Oid 12*/
        process Control_Process; /*Oid 25*/
        endprocess Control_Process;
    endblock Control;
endblock Dialogue;
```

These Oid's are then used to set up links onward the iteration process. At a synchronization point, we construct internal structures of both the OMT* model and the SDL specification. Both structures are compared and entities having the same Oid on both sides are linked. These links are then used to locate the exact places where specific changes need to be applied.

The comparison is executed in a hierarchical fashion, i.e. entities on a lower level are only compared when their aggregate are already linked. For example, states are only compared if an OMT state diagram is linked with a process. There is one exception to this, a process is linked even if the original block was removed. This hierachical aspects of links makes the iteration more robust to large changes in both system design and detailed design. This is because the complexity of comparing is reduced to each separate level.

4. DETAILED DESIGN

After the system design model has been translated, the developer inspects the generated SDL. He can either continue system design in OMT* or start detailed design (step ② in Figure 2), i.e., modifying and improving the generated SDL specification. On one hand we lose the abstraction mechanisms of OMT, but on the other hand we gain the features of SDL that allows one to exactly specify the system. In this section we will discuss what typical detailed design embraces on the generated code and how it might affect the iteration. In general one should strive to remove as less links (Oid's) as possible, for removing links means that the position of where to apply system design changes cannot be determined anymore. We could, however, think of a way to restore links based on name comparison.

4.1 Hierarchical Structure

During the translation, each process is placed in its own block. A common change is to group several processes into one block. As a side effect of this change, the blocks containing the processes are removed and consequently also the links with the corresponding classes. Fortunately this will only have limited consequences on the iteration, because the processes are still linked with the state diagrams.

For example, in the toffee vendor *Coins_Process* must be visible to *Control_Process* in order to let the latter create an instance of the former. Figure 11 shows the hierarchical structure after removing the blocks Coins and Control and grouping their processes in the *Dialogue* block. Compare this figure with Figure 7.

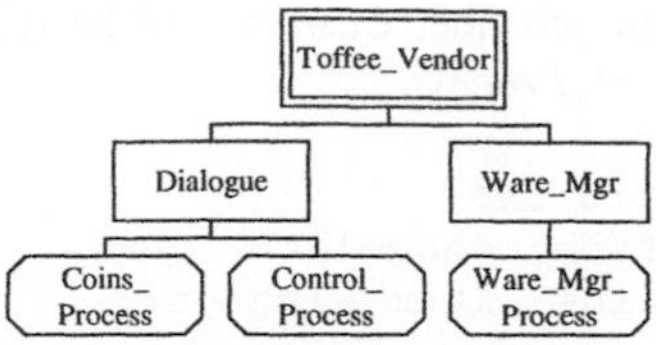

Figure 11. Hierarchy after Detailed Design (cfr. Figure 7)

4.2 Dynamic Behavior

Adding detail to the process specification is probably the most important aspect of detailed design. Here, issues like timers, addressing and switches are tackled.

On the initial transition processes can be created and their addresses queried and stored. Output events can then be modified to send signals to specific processes. Tasks can be added or improved. Transitions can be grouped together using the decision constructs, which is not avaible in OMT(*). Also error handling can easily be modeled in SDL using the asterisk state construct.

For some changes, the only purpose is to make the FSM more compact, like using state lists and signal lists. This should be avoided as it removes many links important to the iteration.

Figure 12 shows the FSM of the Control process after detailed design. The gray areas indicate the changes compared to Figure 8. On the initial state transition a process *Coins* is created, the output events have changed and the two transitions of the payment state have merged.

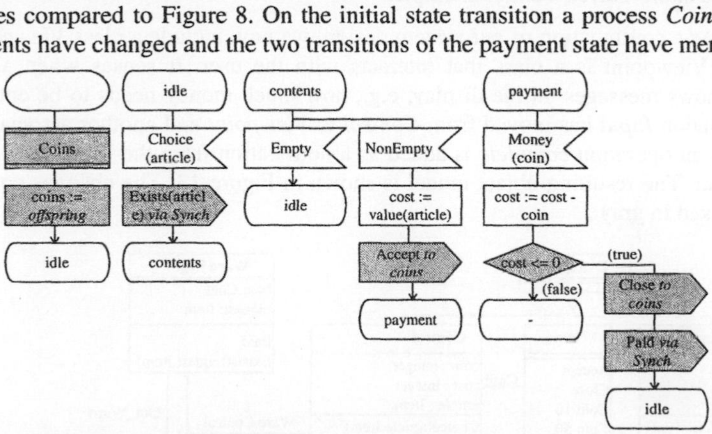

Figure 12. *Control_Process* after Detailed Design (cfr. Figure 8)

4.3 Communication and Declarations

Together with changing the block structure or the process specification also the communication paths and declarations must be adapted to the new situation.

- Wherever blocks or processes are moved, new channels or signal routes must be made or existing ones must be reconnected. Use existing ones whenever possible.
- New signals, variables, types or timers used in the process specification must be declared manually.
- Generated (empty) type declarations should be filled in.

In our example we only had to make a few changes.

- In the *Dialogue* block, the channel *Cash* should be replaced by a signal route between *Coins_Process* and *Control_Process.*
- The type *Item* becomes:

```
newtype Item; /*Oid 31*/
      literals toffee, chocolate, gum;
      operators value: Item->Integer;
endnewitem;
```

5. SYSTEM DESIGN

The system design model has been translated to SDL and improved during detailed design. Now we want to switch back to system design without loosing the detailed design (③ in Figure 2). This could be for a number of reasons.

- SDL has been used for validation and after simulation the developer continues with system design.
- New requirements make it necessary to extend the system design model.
- The developer simply continues the development within an iterative development life-cycle.

Unlike with detailed design, we cannot identify typical system design changes. Anything can be added, moved, deleted or renamed. Therefore we limit our discussion here with a number of changes we made in the Toffee Vendor example.

Object Model. As a continuation of our system design, we now include a class *Viewpoint* to the Toffee Vendor. Viewpoint is a class that interacts with the user. It senses when a button is pressed and it shows messages on the display, e.g., how much money needs to be entered. One end of the association *Input* has moved from *Control* to *Viewpoint* and another association *Displ* is added. Finally an operation *complete* is added as a notification from the Ware Mgr that it has delivered the item. The resulting object model is shown in Figure 13. The changes compared to Figure 3 are marked in gray.

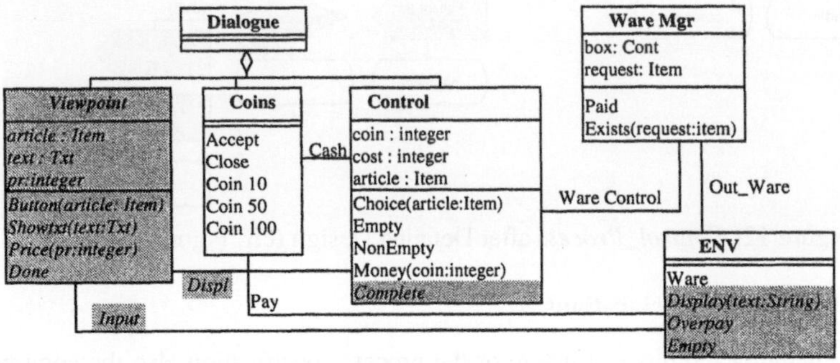

Figure 13. New System Design Model (cfr. Figure 3)

Dynamic Model. For the dynamic model we only discuss the changes in the state diagram of the *Control* class. Most changes are related to the communication with *Viewpoint.* The events *Showtxt*, *Price* and *Done* are all sent to *Viewpoint.* An extra state *releasing* is needed to wait for the event *Complete* from the Ware Mgr. Figure 14 shows the resulting state diagram.

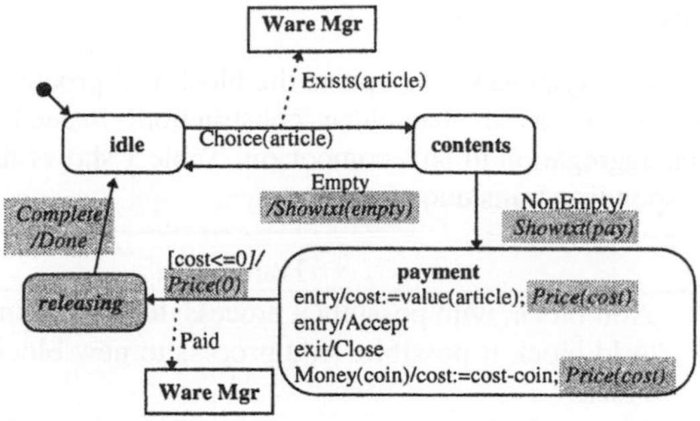

Figure 14. New State Diagram of Control (cfr. Figure 5)

6. ITERATION

After having changed the system design model, the detailed design model needs to be synchronized (④ in Figure 2). As explained in section 1.2, we will accomplish this by translating the changes in the system design model and apply them to the detailed design model.

The problem is threefold. How do we detect the system design changes (deltas), how do we translate them and how do we apply them to a specification that may be different than we expected.

6.1 Determine delta's

The first important aspect is to determine the deltas between two OMT models or two OMT* models, i.e., determine the changes made to the model during development. We have two major approaches to determine changes in a model. Although we have chosen the first approach, the rest of the iteration is independent of this choice as they both produces a set of changes.

Structural comparison. One way to determine the changes made to an OMT* model is to compare the models before and after editing. Whenever (re)entering a certain phase, the current model is stored before editing. After having changed the model, it is saved as a second version and then a standalone program compares those models.

Thanks to the structural nature of OMT, it is possible to compare two models at different levels. First it is checked whether classes or associations are added or deleted. Then the attributes and operations for each matching class are compared. There is a similar strategy for the dynamic model. The matching of entities is based on their Oid, in this way renamings can also be detected.

Track changes in Structural Editor. Another approach to determine changes is to track every edit commando during editing, together with its context. It is preferable to have a structural editor in order to store useful context information during tracking. Most graphical editors, however, are already structural editors.

6.2 Translate and Apply Deltas

The essence of the iteration is of course the actual synchronization of the system design model and the detailed design model. The changes detected during system design must be translated and applied the SDL specification. We divide this translation in the same way as in Section 3 and 4.

6.2.1 Hierarchical Structure

First we consider only classes and aggregation to update the block and process structure in SDL. We do not deal with aggregation as a standalone construction, instead we consider the combination of a class and an aggregation to be a component. Table 1 shows the possible system design changes and the corresponding translation.

System Design Change	Translation
Add Class	Add block, with possibly a process, to the system
Add Component	Add block if possible. Add process to new block or aggregate block.
Move Component	Move block or contents to new position. Create block if necessary. "Move" associations of component and sub-components.
Rename Class	Rename block and/or process
Delete Class	Promote components and remove block

Table 1: Translation Rules for Changes in Static Structure

In our example a component *Viewpoint* was added to *Dialogue*. So we simply add a process *Viewpoint_Process* to the *Dialogue* block. The result is shown in Figure 15.

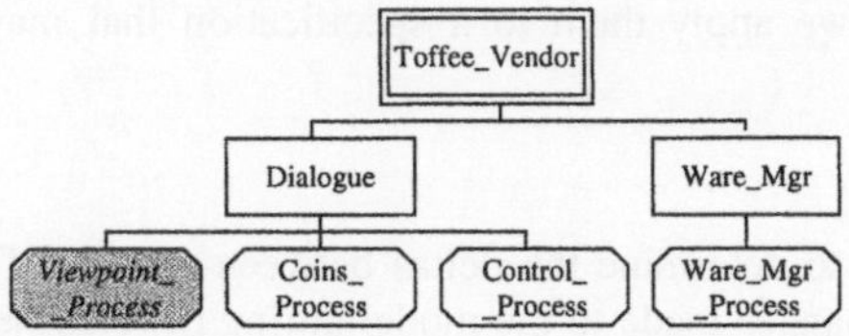

Figure 15. Static Structure after Iteration (cfr. Figure 11 &13)

6.2.2 Dynamic Behavior

Because OMT* and SDL state diagrams map very well onto each other, translating changes in the dynamic model is simple. Things are further eased by the fact that state diagrams are always flattened before comparison. So we do not have to consider nested state during iteration. The flattening algorithm [VJW95] also removes entry and exit action within the states and replaces them with actions on the transition. Table 2 shows the translation of several changes in state diagrams.

System Design Change	Translation
Add/Delete state	Add/Delete state
Rename state	Rename state
Add/Delete Transition	Add/Delete Transition
Rename transition	Rename transition
Add/Delete Action	Add/Delete Action

Table 2: Translating Changes in the Dynamic Model

During system design of the Toffee Vendor example, a number of actions and a state were added. These changes are translated accordingly, but applying them causes a conflicts. During detailed design the internal and external transitions starting from *payment* were merged

(Figure 8) and the link of the external transition was removed. So the system design changes could not be forwarded to the transition. Instead, the transitions are translated again from the new system design model. Find more about conflicts and conflict resultion in section 6.3. The result is shown in Figure 16, the gray areas are system design, the hatched areas are detailed design.

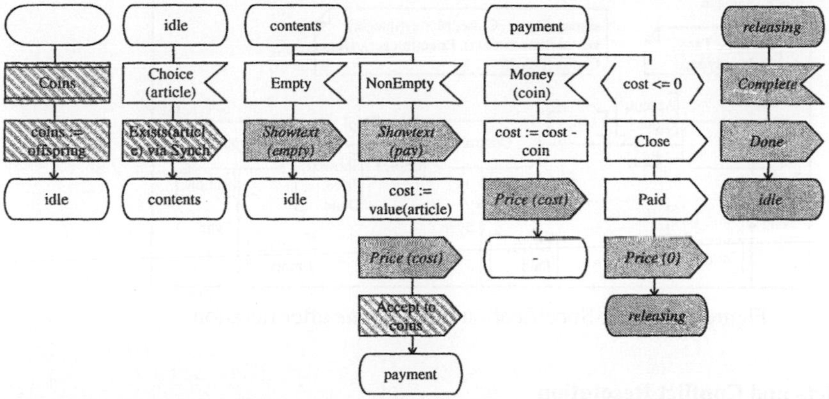

Figure 16. FSM of Control_Process after Iteration (cfr. Figure 12, Figure 14)

6.2.3 Interconnection and Declarations

Interconnection is a difficult issue during iteration. Moving one end of an association may involve the removal of many channels and/or changing of all the signal declarations along the path. For this purpose we defined "intelligent" operators that simply connect or disconnect two processes. Table 3 shows the translation of adding, deleting or moving associations.

System Design Change	Translation
Add Association	Connect the processes with signal routes and channels
Delete Association	Disconnect processes
Move Associations	Combine delete association and add association

Table 3: Translating Changes concerning Interconnection

Synchronizing declarations is similar to generating declarations the first time. The major difference is that only new declarations must be handled. Table 4 shows the translation for new declarations. The syntactical position of existing declarations is only reconsidered if the block structure has changed or if the signal or type is used on a different place.

System Design Change	Translation
Add new type	Add empty newtype declaration
Add input event dcl	Add signal declaration on the correct level
Add attribute	Add variable declaration to the process

Table 4: Translating Changes concerning Interconnection

The delete and rename operations for all three kind of declarations are straightforward, so we did not include these in the table.

In the Toffee Vendor example, not much has changed on system level. Only the *Input* channel going from the environment to Dialogue carries different signals. Instead of the *system*, we therefore show the block specification of *Dialogue* after iteration, see Figure 17.

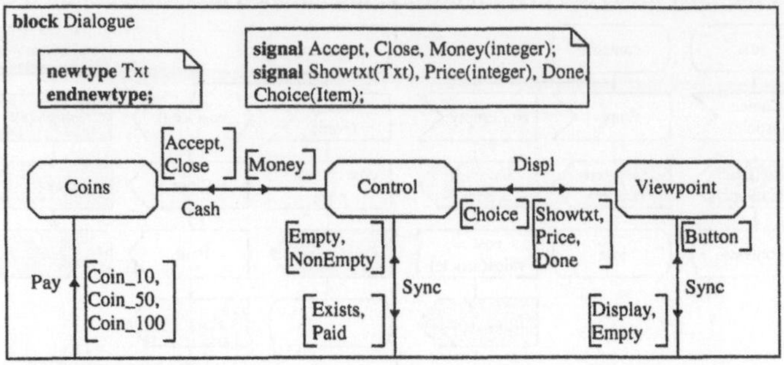

Figure 17. Block Specification of *Dialogue* after Iteration

6.3 Conflicts and Conflict Resolution

If the SDL specification is modified at the place where a change needed to be applied, a conflict may arise. Therefore we need a conflict resolution mechanism that applies changes in another fashion if necessary. This may result is duplicated code or other problems in the SDL code. A report of all conflicts, together with their context, is generated during the iteration. In this way the developer can check the problematic areas in the system by hand. We now discuss two common types of conflicts.

The most common conflict is that the link of the entity that need to be changed is not available anymore. The default conflict resolution is this case is to regenerate the part of the specification that is missing. For example if a transition is added to a state that not exist anymore, the state is created. There is one exception: if a block is not available, the process takes over the role of the block.

Another conflict arises when the developer adds the same entity in both OMT* and SDL. For example he adds a block in SDL and adds a class with the same name in OMT*. A conflict arises because it is not allowed to have two blocks with the same name on the same scope level. One way to resolve this conflict is to append a suffix to the name of the block. This problem does not apply to states or transitions, because they can have the same name.

These conflicts illustrate that translating and applying changes actually interact. As we gain more experience, we will be able to make this process more intelligent.

7. RELATED WORK

We combine many existing techniques about generating code, linking models and iteration. Our work is unique in the combination and extension of these techniques.

Most tools for object oriented analysis and design have the possibility to generate code. ObjectPartner [Verilog], The Rational Rose family [Ratio] and Paradigm+ [Plati] all include the generation of Java, C++ and many more. The programming group at CERN [AKPR93] describes a configurable code generator for OO methodologies. These approaches, however, only translate the object model and not the dynamic model.

Some tools allow incremental code generation. For example, Software trough Pictures [Aonix] will not overwrite user-written code, permitting to do design and implementation iteratively. This is realized with structural comments that indicates user modifiable code. However, these comments cannot be nested and consequently do not allow the iteration on different hierarchical levels as needed for SDL.

The SOMT [And95] method combines OMT with SDL by allowing the user to copy and paste OMT entities into an SDL specification. A so called implementation link (ImpLink) links the pasted entities with its source. This link is then used for tracing, but there is no support for iteration.

8. FUTURE WORK

A first priority work is to target SDL'92. We are convinced that our approach also works perfectly for SDL'92. The translation rules of OMT* to SDL'92 are defined in [WWV95]. The translation of changes could be deducted from these translation rules.

It would be interesting to see whether the extended features of the Unified Method Language [BR95] could improve the generation of SDL and hence also the iteration. For example the composite diagrams and the object message diagram of UML look promising.

We would also like to extend the iteration life-cycle with analysis. Changes in the conceptual model in OMT should be forwarded to the system design model. Basically, the same strategy can be applied as in this paper, except that changes do not have to be translated. Combining both iteration processes would then allow the spiral model of systems development [Boe88].

Finally, it might be interesting to combine this work with reverse engineering. A large number of existing SDL systems need maintenance. In order to start iteration, an OMT* model could be created from the SDL specification. The OMT* model could then be used as an abstract description of the system and a convenient way to maintain the system.

9. CONCLUSION

In this paper we presented automated support for iteration between OMT* and SDL.

The first iteration starts with a complete translation of the OMT* model to SDL. The translation of OMT* to SDL is the result of extensive research with industrial and academic partners. It combines the object model with the dynamic model to build an equivalent SDL specification. Because of its similarity with the OMT* model, the generated SDL is also a proper base to start detailed design.

After the first translation, the developer iteratively carries out detailed design in SDL and system design in OMT*. At the end of each iteration, the detailed design model is automatically made consistent with the system design model. This is done by forwarding changes from the latter to the former. This is different from existing techniques which usually translate the complete model and reapply the detailed design changes. Our approach is better suited for targeting SDL because it is much easier to detect changes in OMT than in SDL.

The main problem, however, is how to forward changes. There are three aspects to this: detect changes in OMT*, translate these OMT* fragments to SDL and apply the changes to the SDL specification. The changes in an OMT* model are detected by hierarchically comparing the previous version of the model with the current version. These changes can range from adding a number of classes to changing the name of an event. Translating these changes is directly based on the translation rules for a complete model. Adding entities is equivalent to a partial translation and deleting entities does the inverse. What is more important, is that the changes are applied in SDL in such a way that as much as possible of the manual changes in SDL are preserved. This is accomplished by applying the changes locally and on the correct structural level instead of re-translating a part of the system. In order to find the exact location of where to forward a modification, each OMT* entity holds a link to its corresponding the SDL entities. Because the links are structured in a hierarchical tree, a divide and conquer strategy can be applied to rebuild the links and to make the modifications. This makes our strategy robust enough to handle large changes as well as sensitive enough to handle minor changes.

10. REFERENCES

[AKPR93] A. Aimar, A. Khodabandeh, P. Palazzi, and B. Rousseau. *A configurable code generator for OO methodologies*. Technical report, Programming Techniques Group, 1993.

[And95] E. Anders. *The SOMT Method*. Preliminary product information, Telelogic, September 19, 1995

[Aonix] Aonix Worldwide Headquarters. *Software through Pictures*. 595 Market Street, San Francisco, CA 94105. (http://www.ide.com/)

[BHS91] F. Belina, D. Hogrefe, and A. Sarma. *SDL, with Applications from Protocol Specification*. Prentice Hall, 1991.

[Boe88] B. Boehm. *A spiral model of software development and enhancement*. Tutorial of Software Engineering and Project Management, 1988.

[BR95] G. Booch, J. Rumbaugh. *Unified Method for Object-Oriented Development*. Rational Software Corporation, 1995.

[HWW96] E. Holz, M. Wasowski, D. Witaszek, S. Lau, J. Fischer, P. Roques, K. Verschaeve, E. Mariatos, and J.-P. Delpiroux. *The INSYDE Methodology*. Deliverable INSYDE/WP1/HUB/400/v2, ESPRIT Ref: P8641, January 1996.

[Plati] Platinum Technology, Inc. *Paradigm Plus*. (www.platinum.com/clearlake)

[Ratio] Rational Software Corporation. *Rational Rose Family*. (www.rational.com)

[RBP91] J. Rumbaugh, M. Blaha, W. Premerlani, F. Eddy, and W. Lorensen. *Object-Oriented Modeling and Design*. Prentice Hall, 1991.

[SCV95] D. Sinclair, L. Cuypers, K. Verschaeve. A formal approach to HW/SW Co-design: The INSYDE Project.

[Verilog] VERILOG. *ObjectPartner*. (www.verilogusa.com)

[VJW95] K. Verschaeve, V. Jonckers, B. Wydaeghe, L. Cuypers, and J. Heirbaut. *OMT*, bridging the gap between analysis and design*. FORTE'95 proceedings, p.23-39. IFIP, Montreal, Canada, 1995.

[VJW96] K. Verschaeve, V. Jonckers, B. Wydaeghe, L. Cuypers. *Translating OMT* to SDL, Coupling Object-Oriented Analysis with Formal Description Techniques*. Method Engineering 96 proceedings, p.126-141. IFIP, Atlanta, USA, 1996.

[WWV95] M. Wasowski, D. Witaszek, K. Verschaeve, B. Wydaeghe, E. Holz, and V. Jonckers. *The Complete OMT**. Deliverable INSYDE/WP1/HUB/300/v3, ESPRIT Ref: P8641, December 1995.

Introducing SDL in the development of CORBA-compliant applications

Justo Carracedo[a], Carlos Ramos[a], Rubén de Diego[a], Carlos González[a], Juan José Gil[b], Emilio Rodríguez[b], Morgan Bjorkander[c].

[a]Telematic Architectures and Engineering Department,Technical University of Madrid, Spain
{ carracedo, cramos, rdiego, cgonzalez } @diatel.upm.es

[b]Telefónica I+D,Madrid, Spain
{ jgil, err } @tid.es

[c]Telelogic AB, Malmö, Sweden
mbjorkander@telelogic.se

This paper summarises the experience of introducing SDL for the development of distributed applications, based on object-oriented execution platforms. Firstly, the life cycle model used in the OTELSO* project is described. In this project, an architectural decomposition has been defined, in such a way that each of the components is developed separately using different technologies.

The use of SDL[1] in the design of some of these components offers some advantages in testing and prototyping tasks. The use of this methodology in the development of a specific prototype system in the context of Intelligent Network services has permitted the evaluation of different alternatives for the integration of SDL-developed components onto distributed execution platforms. This work has also contributed to identify the requirements that the SDL development tools must cover in order to facilitate such integration.

1. INTRODUCTION

One of the objectives of the OTELSO project, as it is described in [10], has been to combine the use of different technologies for the development of distributed applications, thus gaining the advantages derived from the specific use of each of them. In the development explained in this paper, the referred technologies are: Object-Oriented Analysis and Design (OOA/OOD), Formal Description

---

* OTELSO is an EUREKA Project partly sponsored by the Spanish Research Agency CDTI and the Spanish Plan for electronics and computer science (PEIN).

Techniques* (SDL) and object-based distributed architectures, specifically the Common Object Request Broker Architecture (CORBA), from the Object Management Group (OMG). Each of these technologies by themselves provides proved and well-known advantages.

Our interest was centred on combining and making use of each of them during different phases of the life cycle, with the aim of improving the software development. This has made it possible to know and address the issues related to the integration of these technologies, specifically SDL and CORBA.

Although the main objective of the work presented here is the introduction of SDL into the distributed application design phase, a summary of the complete development methodology used in the project is described in the next section.

In Section 3, the issues related to the integration of SDL-CORBA are addressed. Firstly, the steps used for the development of client/server applications executable on a CORBA platform are presented in a general way. Finally, the specific solution adopted for such integration is described, bearing in mind the special features of the environment and the available development tools.

Section 4 displays the case study used to evaluate the methodology, pointing out the software architecture, as well as the distribution of the implemented system, and thus showing the different components developed using heterogeneous environments.

Bearing in mind the experience obtained with the development of the case study, Section 5 underlines a set of requirements that must be satisfied by the SDL-based development tools, in order to allow the automatic generation of client/server applications to be integrated on a CORBA-compliant platform.

Finally, section 6 presents the obtained conclusions and future work lines to evaluate other integration possibilities between SDL and CORBA.

2. METHODOLOGY

The OTELSO project defines a life cycle model that incorporates an architectural decomposition for the development of distributed applications on heterogeneous environments. Such decomposition permits parallel development of the different components in which an application is structured. The detailed design of each subsystem may be carried out using different technologies, although the interest is mostly centred in the use of formal description techniques.

Finally, using a CORBA implementation as an interoperation platform, the integration of the different subsystems on a distributed and heterogeneous environment is undertaken.

---

* In the framework of the OTELSO project, similar experiences using LOTOS have been carried out [10].

The life-cycle can be viewed as a waterfall model inside the development part of a generic cycle of a spiral model [8]. It includes the following phases:

- **Conceptualisation.** It deals with the capture of end-user and software requirements. For the capture of user requirements the use-cases of the Jacobson's Use Case method [6] are employed and serve as the main input for the OOA. The project plan must be defined according to the risk assessments and the development needs.
- **Object-Oriented Analysis (OOA).** It is based on the OMT [5] object model, with modifications to specify, using MSCs [3], the inter-object dynamic behaviour, and the functional behaviour, using the operational model from the Fusion method [4] and SDL. The objective of such modifications is to introduce more formal aspects within this phase, thus allowing the validation of the analysis model.
- **Architectural Design (AD).** In this phase, the functionality of the system is distributed among a set of subsystems, based on the concept of *contract*. The different subsystems' interfaces are specified in CORBA IDL, in such a way that its interoperation is guaranteed. In addition, formal notations ADL [7] and MSCs are used to describe the assertions on the IDL operations and to show the interaction between the different components of the application.
- **Detailed Design (DD).** The resulting subsystems are developed using specific object-oriented techniques as OMT, or using FDT-based methods as SDL, according to the specific characteristics of each component and to the required functionality for evolutionary prototyping [12] purposes.
- **Implementation.** It includes the codification, hand coded or automatically generated by FDT Tools, and the integration of the final system as a distributed application on a CORBA-compliant platform.

Validation activities (prototyping and testing) will be carried out in each of the conceptualisation, OO analysis, architectural design, detailed design and implementation phases.

3. INTEGRATION SDL-CORBA

This section describes how the integration between an application developed by using SDL and a CORBA-compliant platform can be tackled in a general way. Such integration may be carried out following two different approaches [11]:

- **The CORBA-oriented approach.** It uses as a starting point the IDL specification of the application or component to be developed. From such a specification the SDL system which implements the services defined in the interface is generated, as well as the code needed for the interoperation with the ORB.

- **The SDL-oriented approach.** Starting from the SDL system specification, the IDL specification of the interfaces is obtained. The number of resultant IDL interfaces will depend on the desired system distribution. Each of the created subsystems must have its own interaction functions with the environment, and is by itself a CORBA application that interacts with the rest of the subsystems in order to implement the SDL target system.

In our case, the CORBA-oriented approach has been used, since this approach is more pragmatic and matches better the methodology defined in the project. This is due to the fact that, using the IDL specification, the development of some components can be continued with SDL, while the rest of the subsystems or components can be developed using other technologies.

In the following paragraphs the process used in order to obtain an SDL application able to be integrated on a CORBA platform is described, following the CORBA-oriented approach. An SDL application will basically be a server application in the sense that it offers services to other components, but in order to accomplish this task it could require the access, as a client, to other servers.

3.1. Mapping IDL-SDL

As it has been mentioned above, the result of the architectural design phase is a set of components that interact among themselves to satisfy requirements of the distributed system. Such interaction is specified through *contracts*, and IDL is used as the language for the definition of the services offered by each of the components. Once determined the components which development will be continued by using formal techniques, it is necessary to create the SDL system from the IDL specifications of the interfaces. This can be carried out in an automatic way if the appropriate mapping rules between both languages are established.

As it is indicated in [2], the mapping between IDL and another language must define the translation to that language of:

- All IDL basic data types
- All IDL constructed data types
- References to constants defined in IDL
- References to objects defined in IDL
- Invocations of operations, including passing parameters and receiving results.
- Exceptions, including what happens when an operation raises an exception and how the exception parameters are accessed.
- Access to attributes
- Signatures of the operations defined by the ORB, such as dynamic invocation interface, the object adapters, etc.

In the following paragraphs, a possible mapping between IDL and SDL, for main part of the above-mentioned concepts, is presented. The mapping of another IDL concepts (such as *any*, *octet*, *exceptions*, *raises* and *context expressions,)* is at the moment being studied by the authors. Other works [9] have also made contributions on this subject.

- **Modules.** An IDL module is mapped directly as an SDL block type.

- **Interfaces.** An *IDL interface* includes the definition of the operations offered by an object, as well as the attributes and types used in the interface. An IDL interface is represented in SDL by *a process type*. If the IDL interface is part of an IDL module, the SDL process type will be part of the corresponding SDL block type.
- **Operations.** An *IDL operation* describes a specific service offered by an object. An IDL operation may be *synchronous*, i.e. the client is blocked until the execution of the service is completed, or *asynchronous*, in such a way that the client continues its execution. Obviously, an asynchronous operation cannot send back any information to the client. A synchronous operation must be mapped as an *external remote procedure calls* and an asynchronous operation is mapped as an *SDL signal.*
- **Parameters.** An *IDL operation parameter* may be one of the following three types: *in*, *inout*, and *out*. Since in SDL only the two first parameters exist, an IDL out parameter is mapped as an *SDL in/out parameter*.
- **Attributes.** An IDL interface can have *attributes*. An IDL attribute is mapped as the declaration of a variable in the corresponding process type and two remote procedures to get and set its value. If it is a *readonly* attribute, only a remote procedure is generated in order to obtain the value of the attribute.
- **Constants.** A *constant* in IDL is mapped as an *SDL synonym*.
- **Types.** A *typedef* in IDL is mapped to a *syntype* in SDL.
- **Basic types.** The mappings between *IDL basic types* and SDL are shown in Table 1.

Table 1. Mapping between IDL basic types and SDL.

IDL	SDL	Syntype of
long	CORBA_long	Integer
short	CORBA_short	Integer
unsigned long	CORBA_unsigned_long	Integer
unsigned short	CORBA_unsigned_short	Integer
double	CORBA_double	Real
float	CORBA_float	Real
char	CORBA_char	Real
boolean	CORBA_boolean	Real

- **Constructed types.** The mappings of the IDL *constructed types* to SDL are as follows:
    - **Enums**.- An *IDL enum* is mapped as an *sdl newtype* with the corresponding *literals*.
    - **Structs**.- An *IDL struct* is mapped to an *SDL struct type*.
    - **Unions**.- The *IDL type union* is not directly supported in SDL and is mapped as an SDL *struct type*.
- **Template types.** There are two different template types: *sequence* and *string*. n IDL sequence is mapped to a *string* in SDL, while an IDL string is mapped to a *charstring*.
- **Complex declarators**
    - **Arrays**.- An *IDL array* is mapped to both a specific *range type* to define the index and an *SDL array*.

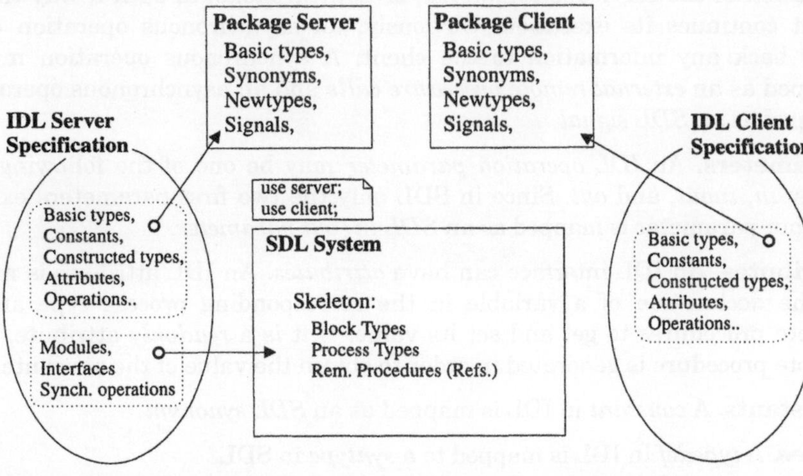

Figure 1. SDL system skeleton created from the client/server IDL interface.

3.2. Creating an SDL application

As it has already been mentioned, the development of an application in SDL using the CORBA-oriented approach has as a starting point the IDL specification of such application. Therefore, as a first step, it must be converted to an equivalent SDL system by using the mapping described in section 3.1.

From this mapping, an SDL system is obtained which contains the following parts:

- **A server interface package** containing the definitions for basic types, synonyms, newtypes, signals and remote procedures, and associated parameter types corresponding to the definitions of basic types, constants, constructed types, attributes and operations of the IDL interface.
- **An SDL system** that contains the definitions for block types, process types and remote procedure references which correspond to modules, interfaces and synchronous operations.

If the SDL system is a client/server application, it is also necessary to generate **a client interface package** from the IDL specifications of the components to which it is requesting services. This interface contains the definitions described for the server interface package and both of them must be included in the SDL system through the SDL use clause.

The SDL system (Figure 1) created from the client/server IDL interfaces is only a skeleton, since information regarding the interaction between blocks and process instances cannot be deduced from the IDL specification, nor, of course, information regarding the required behaviour. Therefore, the next step is to complete the static structure of the SDL specification and to describe the behaviour of the process types and procedures.

The complete SDL system, including the access to other servers, must be analysed and simulated to verify if it satisfies the required functionality. Finally, an executable that can be integrated on a CORBA platform must be created. Such an executable is obtained by compiling and linking the code obtained from the different parts implied in the integration.

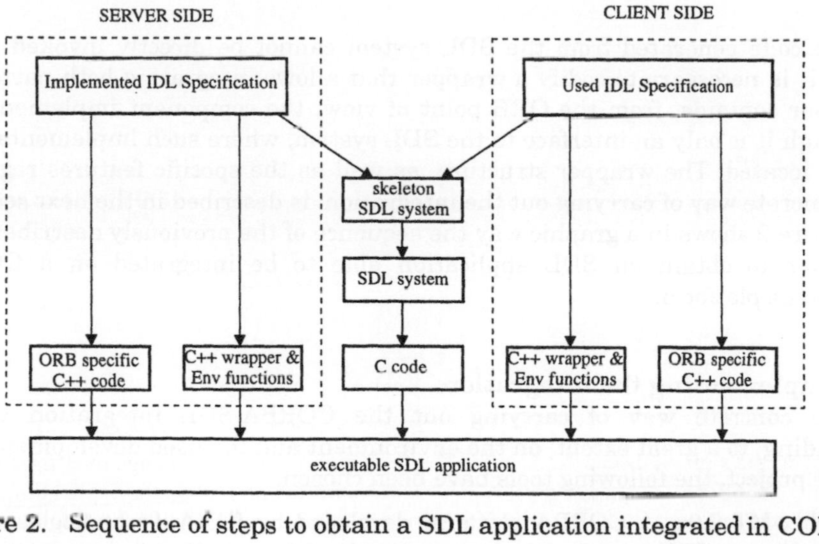

Figure 2. Sequence of steps to obtain a SDL application integrated in CORBA.

On one hand, by using the automatic code generation provided by the SDL development tools, the code that implements the services offered by the component is obtained.

On the other hand, it is necessary to generate the needed code so that the specific ORB can manage the interaction between the clients and the application, as well as between this application and the servers to which it has access (server side and client side, respectively). This code is generated in an automatic way by an ORB specific IDL compiler, usually provided by the implementations of the CORBA platform.

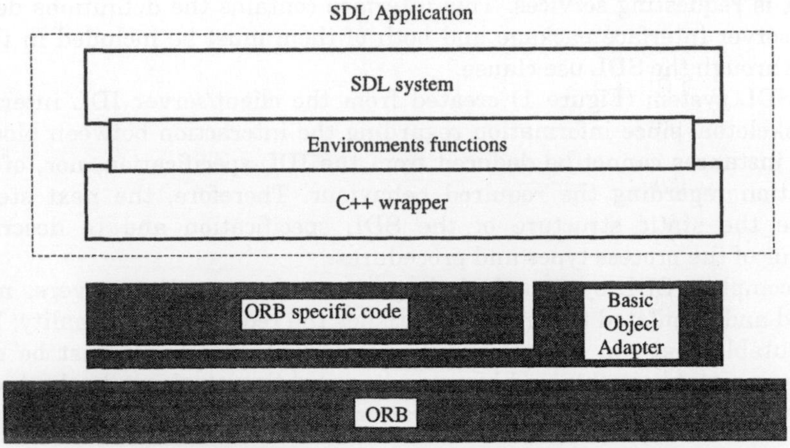

Figure 3. SDL client/server application parts.

The code generated from the SDL system cannot be directly invoked by the ORB; it is necessary to codify a wrapper that allows integrating both parts. This wrapper contains, from the ORB point of view, the component implementation, although it is only an interface to the SDL system, where such implementation is really located. The wrapper structure, as well as the specific features regarding the concrete way of carrying out the integration, is described in the next section.

Figure 2 shows in a graphic way the sequence of the previously described steps in order to obtain an SDL application able to be integrated on a CORBA-compliant platform.

3.3. Implementing the integration.

The concrete way of carrying out the CORBA-SDL integration will be depending, to a great extent, on the environment and the used development tools. In our project, the following tools have been chosen:

- Orbix-MT 2.0x. A CORBA platform developed by IONA Technologies, Ldt. It contains an IDL compiler that generates the C++ code that is necessary for the interaction between the ORB and the applications using the IDL specification.

- SDT3.02. An SDL Development Tool developed by Telelogic. It is an integrated environment for the development of SDL applications, including automatic code generation. It also includes different kernels with simulation and application generation purposes.

All in all, the SDL client/server application developed using SDT is composed of the following parts (figure 3):

- The SDL System. It contains the implementation of the component. It will be constituted by a set of process instances, some of which interact with the environment to offer certain services (server side), and to request services to other servers (client side).
- A C++ wrapper. It contains the implementation of the component from the ORB point of view. It constitutes the environment of the system from the SDL point of view. It also includes the needed code to request services to other components.
- The environment functions. They provide the required functionality for the interaction between the SDL system and the C++ wrapper.
- The ORB specific code. In conjunction with the ORB, it manages the interoperation between clients and servers.

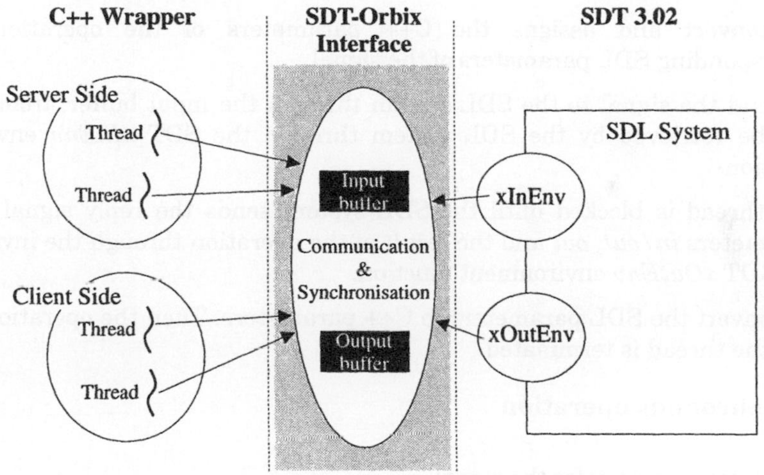

Figure 4. The SDL Orbix Interface.

The SDT 3.02 version has some restrictions that condition the functionality of the C++ wrapper and the way of implementing the integration. On one hand, due to the fact that this tool matches with SDL92, it does not accept external remote procedure call to and from the SDL system environment. This fact compels to mapping each synchronous operation as a pair of signals: one signal with the *in* and *inout* parameters, and another reply signal with the *inout* and *out* parameters, and the result of the operation.

Besides, the Kernel used to generate the SDL application provides a single Unix process which contains the SDL system, the environments functions and the C++ wrapper. This sets some problems when dealing with the synchronous operations requested by the clients: when the invocation to such operations is received, the C++ wrapper must send a signal to the SDL system and cannot go back until receiving the corresponding answer; but, since there is no a parallel processing, the SDL system cannot progress and, therefore, cannot execute the transition that implements the operation.

In order to solve this problem, a threaded approach has been used. For each synchronous or asynchronous operation requested to and from the SDL application, a new thread is created that is executed in parallel to the SDL system, which is the main thread. The used approach is shown in figure 4.

When a client requests an operation over the SDL application, the ORB invokes the corresponding method on an object in the C++ wrapper, creating a new thread. The actions to be carried out in the C++ wrapper depend on the requested operation type.

Synchronous operation

- To allocate memory for the signal.
- To convert and assigns the C++ parameters of the operation to the corresponding SDL parameters of the signal.
- To send the signal to the SDL system through the input buffer, from where it will be retrieved by the SDL system through the SDT *xInEnv* environment function.
- The thread is blocked until the SDL system sends the reply signal with the parameters *in/out*, *out* and the *result* of the operation through the invocation of the SDT *xOutEnv* environment function.
- To convert the SDL parameters to C++ parameters. Then the operation returns and the thread is terminated.

Asynchronous operation

- To allocate memory for the signal.
- To convert and assigns the C++ parameters of the operation to the corresponding SDL parameters of the signal.
- To send the signal to the SDL system through the input buffer, from where it will be picked up by the SDL system through the SDT *xInEnv* environment function.
- The thread is terminated.

In many cases, it will be necessary that the SDL system which implements a certain application acts as a client, requesting services to other components in a distributed environment. The SDL system invokes an operation by sending a signal to the environment. For each sent signal a new thread is created and the sequence of actions to be carried out inside the thread is very similar to the one previously described. In both cases of synchronous and asynchronous operations, the thread invokes the method that implements the operation. If the operation is asynchronous no other action is necessary and the thread is terminated. If it deals with a synchronous operation, the reply signal, with the adequate parameters obtained from the answer received from the ORB, is sent to the SDL system, and the thread is terminated.

If different clients request the same synchronous operation over the same object of the SDL application, there will be several threads, one for each invoked operation, being executed in parallel. In order for each thread to receive its corresponding reply signal and so that this is not affected by the racing conditions, it is necessary to send the identification of the thread that deals with each operation as an additional parameter of the signal that is sent to the SDL system.

Finally, the functions provided by SDT 3.02 for the appropriate handling of signal instances *-xGetSignal, xReleaseSignal, SDLOutput,* etc- are not multithread safe. This makes it necessary to implement strong synchronisation measures between the C++ wrapper and the environment functions, in order to avoid different threads to execute the same functions simultaneously.

4. THE CASE STUDY

To evaluate the methodology proposed in the project and, specially, to analyse the use of SDL for the development of CORBA-compliant applications, the Network Performance Manager Centre, integrated in the context of the Intelligent Network services, has been developed

In the following paragraphs, the architecture of the prototype system developed to achieve the objectives of the project is presented in a summarised way.

4.1. Software architecture of the system.

In figure 5 it is shown the context diagram of the prototype, from which the software architecture can be easily obtained, that is, the division or decomposition in subsystems and the interactions among them.

The specifications of the public parts of each subsystem have been carried out using IDL, which makes possible the fact that different subsystems implementations, offering and using the same interfaces, can exchange themselves. This characteristic permits to carry out an incremental prototyping, where certain subsystems have been completely developed, in this case the Network Performance Manager Component, while other subsystems are only partly simulated or implemented, according to the interactions described in the interfaces.

This type of development allows a rapid incremental prototyping on heterogeneous distributed systems, using design methods appropriate to simulate a reduced functionality of those system components that are been developed in parallel.

The different subsystems in which the system is structured is shown in figure 5. To make possible the interoperation, an IDL interface for the interaction between the Network Performance Manager Component and each of the other subsystems has been defined.

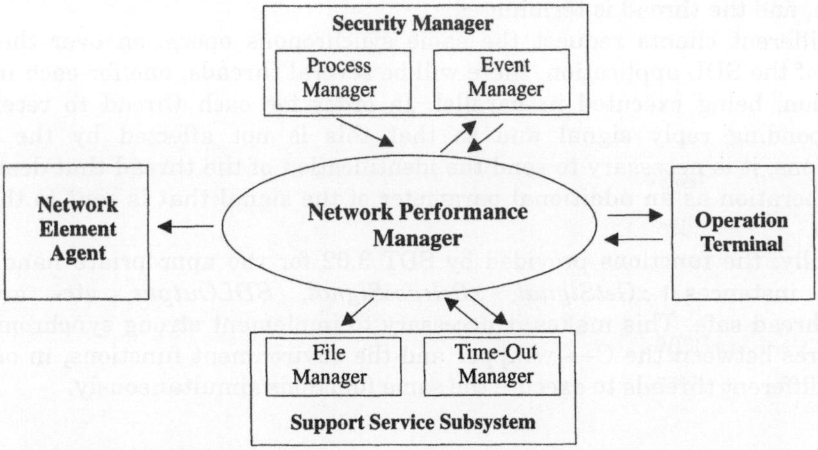

Figure 5. Context diagram of the prototype.

- **Network Performance Manager Component**.- This component manages the measures over different Elements and Services of the Intelligent Network and the generation of statistic data from such measures. The detailed design and the implementation of this component have been carried out using formal description techniques (SDL).
- **Operation Terminal Subsystem.-** It permits to program the operations to be carried out on the different network elements and services, activating and deactivating the measure taking, consulting their state and requesting the generation of reports from the obtained results. The detailed design and the implementation of the subsystem have been carried out using design object-oriented techniques and languages for the development of user graphic interfaces, specifically Visual C++.
- **Security Manager Subsystem**.- This subsystem is divided into:
  - **Process Manager.-** It undertakes tasks such as start, stop, state consulting and restart of the system.

- **Event Manager.-** This component registers and notifies the events and alarms produced in the Network Elements, in such a way that the rest of the components can process in a proper way the alarms produced during the taking of measures.

This subsystem functionality has been simulated also using Visual C++.

- **Network Element Agent Subsystem.**- The Network Performance Manager Component does not have a global vision of the network elements and services. The operations that it requests are sent to the Network Element Agent responsible of the communication with these elements. A reduced functionality of this component, specifically oriented to simulate its interaction with the Network Performance Manager, has been implemented using Visual C++.
- **Support Service Subsystem.**- It offers temporisation services to control the taking of measures, as well as services for the handling of files. Part of this component has been developed using SDL, specifically the temporisation services. The other part, the file management services, has been developed through design object-oriented techniques and C++.

All the described subsystems have been developed in parallel in heterogeneous environments and finally all of them have been integrated on a CORBA platform –in our case, Orbix 2.0x.

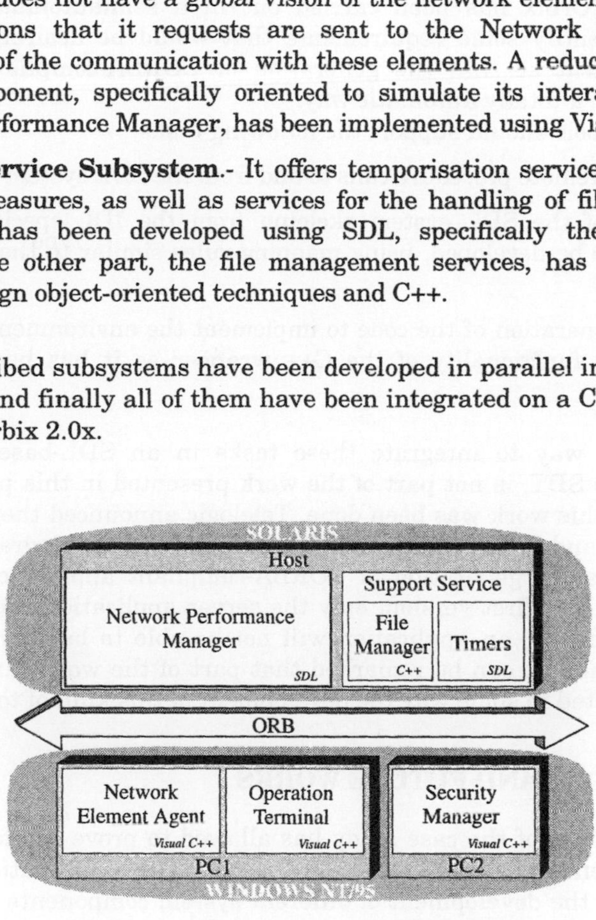

Figure 6. Distribution of the prototype.

4.2. Distribution of the system.

The different developed components or subsystems have been distributed physically as it is shown in figure 6. This configuration proves the aspects of distribution and heterogeneity of the development.

Specifically, the Network Performance Manager Component and the Support Service Subsystem have been finally integrated in a host with Orbix 2.0x installed on a Solaris 2.5. The Operation Terminal Subsystem has been developed and installed in a PC on Orbix 2.0x for Windows NT, as well as the Security Manager and the Network Element Agent.

5. SDL TOOL REQUIREMENTS

Although the development through SDL and the final integration of these components on Orbix has been carried out in a semiautomatic way, it has permitted to identify some requirements that would be desirable in an SDL-based environment so that the generation of CORBA-compliant applications could be made in a totally automatic way.

Specifically, tools should support the following tasks:

- Definition of remote procedure calls to and from the SDL system environment.
- Generation of the SDL system skeleton from the IDL specifications of the component to be developed, using mapping rules similar to those presented in section 3.1.
- Automatic generation of the code to implement the environment functions and the complete functionality of the C++ wrapper as it has been described in section 3.3.

The concrete way to integrate these tasks in an SDL-based development environment, as SDT, is not part of the work presented in this paper. However, at the moment this work was been done, Telelogic announced they were working on these topics, and in the version SDT3.1 it is planned to integrate a set of tools which facilitates the generation of CORBA-compliant applications in a totally automatic way. In a first version, only the server applications development will be supported, that is, an application will not be able to be client/server at the same time. Finally, it can be remarked that part of the work carried out in the project has affected in some way the development of this kind of tools.

6. CONCLUSIONS AND FUTURE WORKS

The development of the case study has allowed to prove the feasibility of the methodology defined in the OTELSO project. The combination of different technologies for the development of different system components permits to gain some benefits regarding the time needed to develop a system. This advantage is especially evident in tasks related to evolutionary prototyping.

The use of SDL in the development of distributed system components, according to the CORBA-oriented approach, permits to easily integrate such components on a CORBA platform. This should facilitate the development of tools, which generate, in a totally automatic way, objects that offer services in an

OMA architecture. Moreover, it will allow to apply simulation and validation mechanisms to such objects.

As future work guide lines, we aim at the experimentation of the viability of the SDL-oriented approach in the development of distributed systems. We also aim at the settlement of the requirements that the SDL tools should fulfil for the generation (probably in a semiautomatic and user-guided way) of components able to be integrated on CORBA platforms.

Other points of interest are centred in the analysis of some other alternatives in the integration of CORBA and SDL, for example by means of the definition of SDL specific Object Adapter in the CORBA architecture.

REFERENCES

1. ITU-T. SDL Specification and Description Language. Z.100. 1993.
2. OMG-X/OPEN. "Common Object Request Broker: Architecture and Specification". Working Paper OMG TC Document 91.12.1, Object Management Group, Framingham, MA (USA), September 1992.
3. ITU-T. Message Sequence Charts. Z.120. 1996.
4. C. Coleman, P. Arnold, S. Bodoff, C. Dollin, H. Gilchrist, F. Hayes and P. Jeremaes. Object Oriented Software Development. The Fusion Method. Prentice-Hall International Editions, 1994.
5. J. Rumbaugh, M. Blaha, W Premerlani, F. Eddy and W. Lorensen. Object-Oriented Modelling and Design. Prentice-Hall International Editions, 1991.
6. I. Jacobson. Object-Oriented Software Engineering - A Use Case Driven Approach. Addison-Wesley, 1992.
7. S. Sankar and R. Hayes. "ADL- an interface definition language for specifying and testing software". ACM SIGPLAN notices, Jan 1994.
8. B. Boehm. "A spiral model of software development and enhancement". IEEE Computer, May 1988.
9. M. Born, M. Winkler, J. Fischer. "Formal language mapping from CORBA IDL to SDL-92 in Combination with ASN.1". Contribution to ITU Q6 Expert Meeting, Lutterworth, June 1995.
10. S. Pickin, C. Sánchez, JC Yelmo, JJ Gil, E. Rodríguez. "Introducing formal notations in the development of object-based distributed applications". Proc. FMOODS'96. Chapman and Hall editors. Paris, March 1996.
11. A. Olsen and B.M. Jorgensen. "Using SDL for targeting services to CORBA". In A. Clarke, M. Campolargo and N. Karatzas, editors, Bringing Telecommunication Services to the people 3rd International Conference on Intelligence in Broadband Services and Networks. LNCS 998, Springer-Verlag 1995.
12. A.M. Davis. Operational prototyping: a new development approach. IEEE Software, September 1992.

SDL '97: TIME FOR TESTING - SDL, MSC and Trends
A. Cavalli and A. Sarma (Editors)

A practical experience on validating GDMO-based Information Models with SDL'88 and '92

Samir Tata, Laurent Andrey, Olivier Festor [a]

[a] INRIA Lorraine - CRIN/CNRS
Technopôle de Nancy-Brabois - Campus scientifique
615, rue de Jardin Botanique - B.P. 101
54600 Villers Lès Nancy Cedex, France
Tel: (+33) 83.59.20.11, Fax: (+33) 83.27.83.19
E-mail: {tata,andrey,festor}@loria.fr

This article presents the results obtained in several activities within which we have used SDL for the validation and interactive simulation of OSI-based Management Information Models. In this paper we present a result from a field trial in the area of Information Model validation using SDL'88. We also present a consequent work : an experience in developing a tool called MODERES for the automated generation of SDL'92 specifications from a GDMO/GRM-based specification for the purpose of Management Agent simulation.

Keywords: GDMO, GRM, Information Model, MODERES, OSI, SDL'88, SDL'92, TMN, Validation

1. Introduction

Within the last few years, the area of Telecommunication Network Management (TMN) evolved very fast. With the todays advent of service management, many new information models emerge and cover more and more features of interest towards integrated network, system and service management. All these information models share common characteristics. They are described using the standardized GDMO (Guidelines for the Definition of Managed Objects) notation [15] and most people which design those models express an increasing demand on combining their Interface Definition Notation with formal methods.

For this purpose, several proposals have been made so far but few of them have been applied to large size information models. In this paper we present the work achieved in our group to provide case studies and tool support to promote the use of Formal Description Techniques in the area of service and network management. Here we present the results of a case study in which we have specified in SDL a complete information model. Based on the lessons learned from this trial, we present a tool we developed to automate the translation from GDMO to SDL'92 specifications.

The remainder of the paper is organized as follows. Section 2 presents the results obtained from a field trial which was concerned with the validation of a Management Information Model using SDL'88. Section 3 presents the SDL'92 generator of the MODERES environment. It details the algorithm implemented in the MODERES platform and outlines all extensions provided to the generation algorithms presented so far. Section 4 concludes the paper and outlines orientations for future work.

2. A practical experience in MIB validation

The main question that arises when discovering the GDMO notation is *why is this notation used in Network Management instead of SDL'92 ?*[3]. The answer to that question is fairly simple. GDMO is an interface description language suitable for modelling system or network managed resources in the OSI framework. This framework is the one of X7** ITU recommendations serie and ISO related standards [16,14] where equipments, communication softwares, operating systems are modelled by objects. These objects are grouped into Management Information Base (MIB) where some naming and containment rules are ensured. A manager access to a MIB through an agent.

Moreover GDMO was designed and standardized before the development of SDL'92. In the next pages we present the proposals which have been made so far to combine FDT's and GDMO. We also present the results we obtained from a field trial in using SDL for the validation of a complete information model.

2.1. Related work

Several proposals other than SDL'92 have been made for the formal specification of information models behaviors but few have been applied to complete models taken from the standards.

One approach which was applied successfully to large systems, is the TIMS (*TMN-based Information Model Simulator*)[23] language and toolkit developed at the EURECOM Institute. TIMS provides a behavior language based on rules encapsulated into pre- and post-conditions. These rules are always defined in the context of relationships between managed objects. The notation is supported by a simulator and the environment has been successfully applied to a real case study on configuration management for access networks.

Another approach taken so far focusses on extending GDMO with behavioral notations. The most advanced work in this approach is GDMO+ [13,17] which proposes several extensions to GDMO for pre- and post-condition based formal behavior definition.

We have made several studies on combining FDTs and OSI-based information models. Some of these studies have been made using our own specification technique [6,11,7] whereas others are based on most popular FDTs [21,1]. Several other studies have been made by other research groups. One can mention the work done with VDM [24,19] and LOTOS [18].

2.2. The SIM-CM model

To perform a first validation trial on a "real world" information model, we have selected the SIM-CM [22] model from the Network Management Forum. This model provides all Managed Object classes required for the configuration management of switch interconnection. The model is located at the network level of the TMN hierarchical architecture.

Figure 1 provides an overview of the different abstraction levels of the model. These levels are:

(a) the managed elements and their interconnections,

(b) the interconnection model in terms of circuits and termination points,

(c) the managed objects specification representing the identified components and their organization within a Management Information Base (MIB).

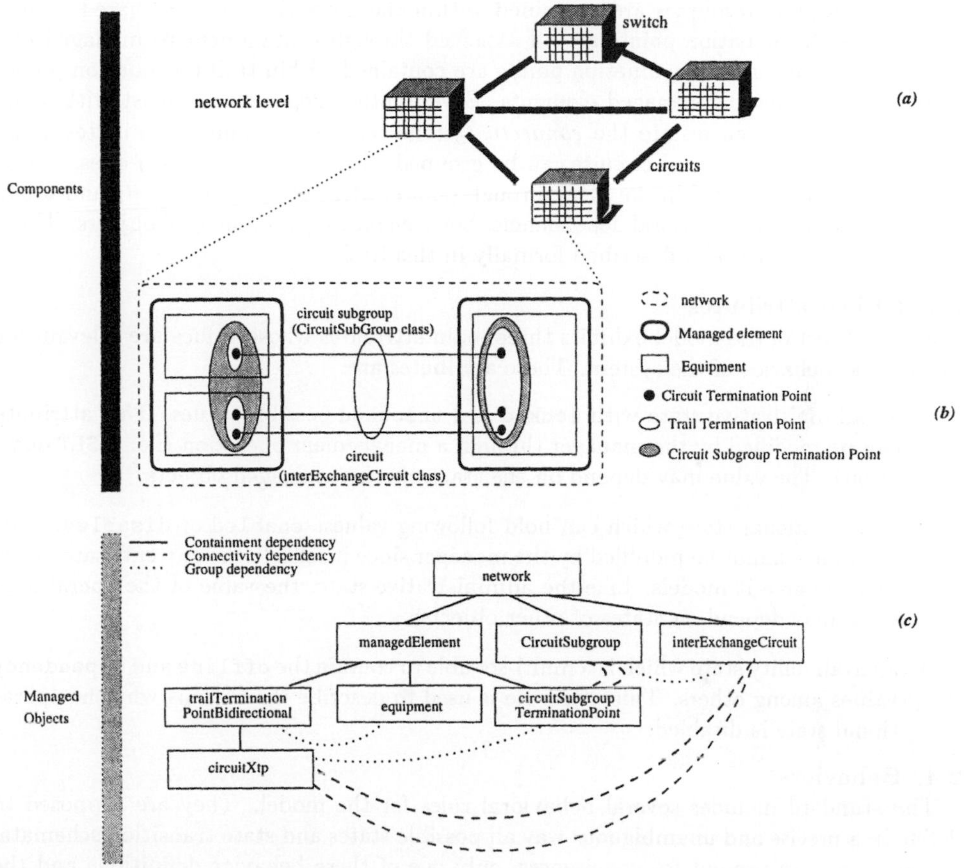

Figure 1. The SIM-CM model.

A first level of abstraction is provided in the second part of the figure (*b*). At this level, the network is divided into managed elements, themselves composed of equipments. Interconnection links between equipments are modelled through circuits and circuit subgroups.

Circuits as well as circuit subgroups are terminated by termination points (`cTp`, `CsTp`) attached to trail termination points (`trailTerminationPointBidirectional` (`TTP`)).

The termination points are hosted on equipments and managed elements.

All these elements are specified in the management interface as Managed Object classes within a Management Information Base (*(c)* part of the figure). The sole explicit dependency that exists in the MIB between those elements is the containment relationship expressed through NAME-BINDINGS. Those bindings are used to support the naming scheme and the hierarchical architecture of the MIB.

All connectivity resources are contained within the network and thus shared among equipments. Termination points are all attached through containment to managed elements. Only the circuit termination points are contained within trail termination points themselves attached to managed elements. Several other dependencies exist within the MIB. These dependencies are the *connectivity* (one termination point terminates a circuit) and the *group* (several circuits can be grouped within a circuit group) ones. These dependencies are realized in the MIB through pointer attributes. *Connectivity* and *group* relationships denote behavioral dependencies between participant managed objects. These behaviors are studied and described formally in this trial.

2.3. Object attributes

Every object of the model exhibits three main attributes whose values are relevant for the general behavior of the system. These attributes are:

1. an administrative state with `locked` and `unlocked` possible values. This attribute can be modified by the manager through a management operation (i.e. a `SET` operation). The value may depend on the state of other managed objects;

2. an operational state which can hold following values: `enabled` or `disabled`. This attribute cannot be modified by the manager since it reflects the current state of the real resource it models. Like the administrative state, the value of the operational state may depend on states of other objects;

3. an availability state which is a multi-set able to contain the `offline` and `dependency` values among others. This attribute is used to describe the reasons why the operational state is disabled.

2.4. Behaviors

The standard includes several behavioral rules for the model. They are supposed to define in a precise and unambiguous way all possible states and state transition schemata. In this paper we present for conciseness, only one of these behavior definitions and the associated formal specification. The definition chosen for this case study is "*the effect of issuing an administrative state locking operation on a circuit object*". For this operation the standard defines the following rules:

R1 a transition from `unlocked` to `locked` of a connectivity object implies the transition to `locked` of the administrative state and the transition to `disabled` of the operational state of all associated termination points;

R2 the transition of a termination point's administrative state to `locked` must be propagated in form of a transition to `disabled` of the operational state to the connectivity object and to the opposite termination point;

R3 depending on the transitions of either administrative or operational state within an object, the **offline** and/or **dependency** values must be added to the availability status if and only if the above transitions are due to a behavior propagation.

In the next section we will present the formal specification of this sub-model.

2.5. The formal specification and validation

Starting from the above presented Information Model, we have built an SDL'88 specification including all behavioral aspects of the model. Figure 2 below contains the architecture of a subset of the specification. In this example, the equipment and managed element objects are not represented still for conciseness purpose.

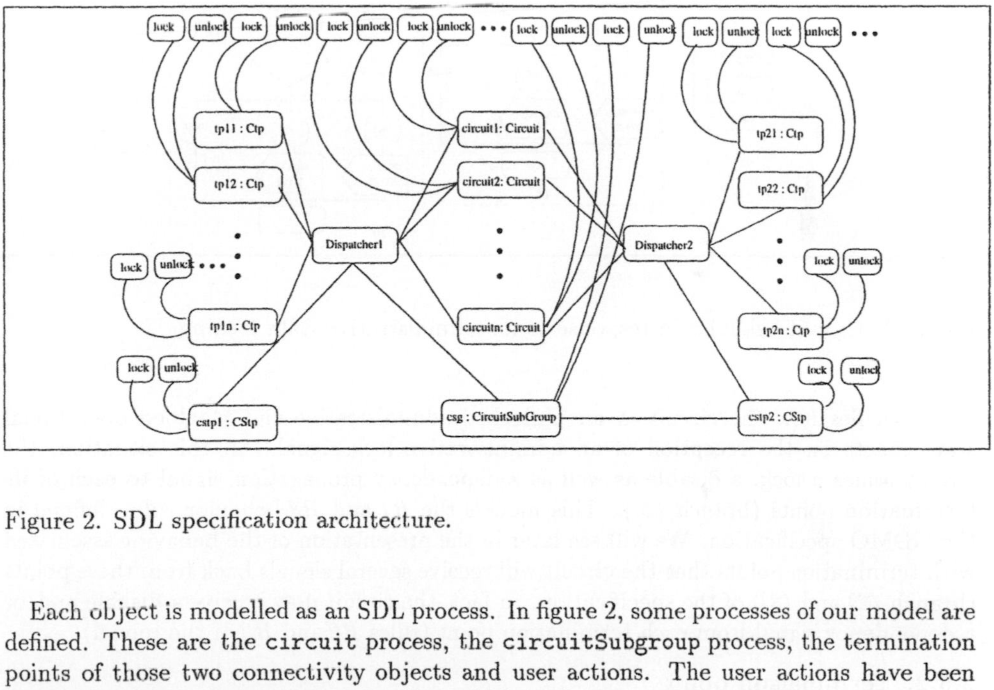

Figure 2. SDL specification architecture.

Each object is modelled as an SDL process. In figure 2, some processes of our model are defined. These are the `circuit` process, the `circuitSubgroup` process, the termination points of those two connectivity objects and user actions. The user actions have been designed as two separate processes. One which performs a `lock` operation on a Managed Object and another which performs the `unlock` operation. Those user processes always regenerate themselves so that the associated operations are always available. As the system may evolve in terms of new managed object instances creation, the communication between the managed objects is realized by `dispatcher` objects responsible for redirecting signals to associated managed objects. For conciseness let's only consider the `circuit` and termination points in the behavior description part below.

2.5.1. Circuit

Figure 3 illustrates a small part of the behavior specification associated to a circuit. We consider here a restriction of the previous architecture built of:

- one circuit (*circuit*),
- two termination points (*c1* and *c2*),
- two dispatchers (*d1* and *d2*) to link the circuit to its termination points.

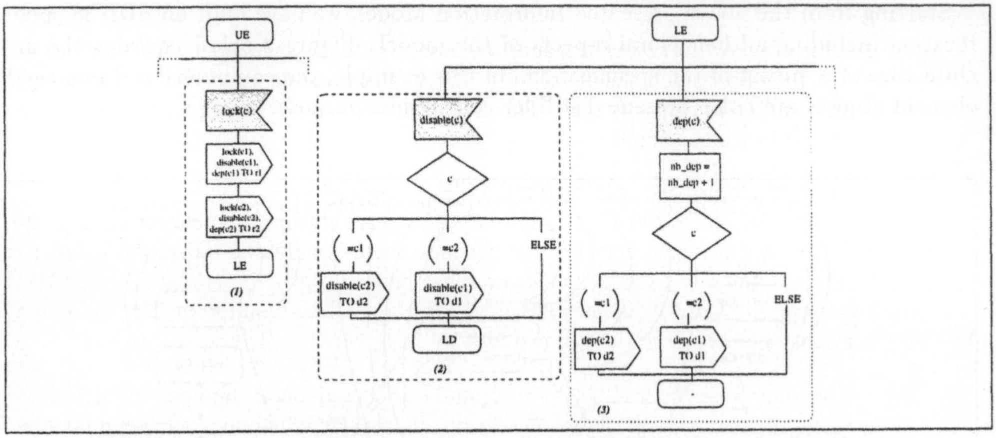

Figure 3. Circuit behavior in response to an administrative state locking.

It specifies how the circuit in an **U**nlocked administrative and **E**nabled operational state reacts on the reception of an administrative lock signal. In this situation, the circuit issues a lock, a disable as well as a dependency propagation signal to each of its termination points (branch *(1)*). This models the *R1* and *R3* behavior rules defined in the GDMO specification. We will see later in the presentation of the behavior associated with termination points that the circuit will receive several signals back from these points (branch *(2)* and *(3)*) of the specification. In fact, the circuit may receive a disable and/or a dependency signal from each termination point (rules *R2* and *R3* of the model).

2.5.2. Terminaison point

Within a circuit termination point, the behavior related to dependencies with the associated circuit is depicted in figure 4. Within the circuit, we saw that several signals may be sent to the termination points (administrative state locking, operational state change and dependency addition). These three signals are treated within the three branches of the figure 4. In this example, we consider only the situation where the termination point is initially in the **U**nlocked administrative and **E**nabled operational state.

Other behavior branches within the specification consider all other states in which the termination point may be and which behavior it exhibits in those situations. In this initial case (operational state **E**nabled, administrative state **U**nlocked) the termination point will, on the reception of a lock signal from the circuit or the operator (branch *(1)*),

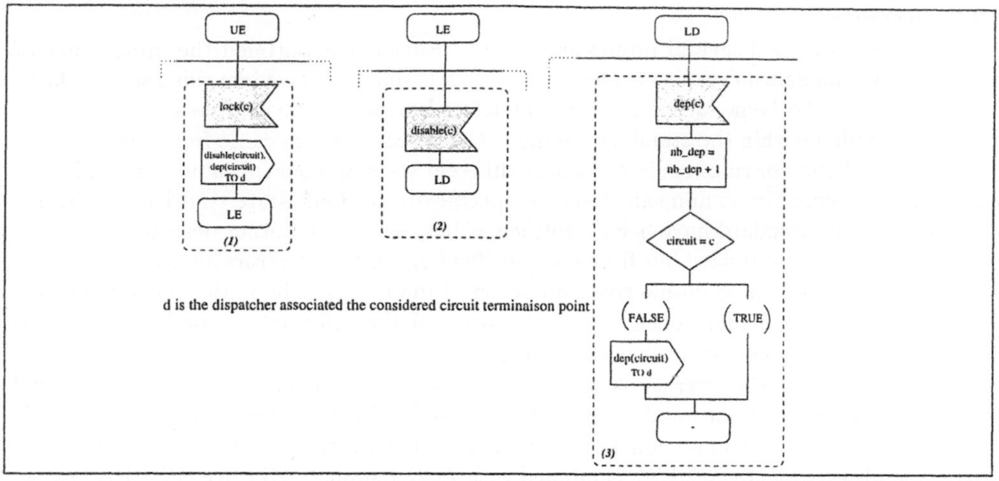

Figure 4. Termination point behavior towards administrative locking of a circuit.

propagate a disable and a a dependency propagation signals to the circuit (*R2* and *R3* rules). On the receipt of a **disable** signal from the circuit, the termination point switches to the **L***ocked***D***isabled* state (branch *(2)*). If an additional dependency is received, the dependency counter is incremented but no signal is propagated back (branch *(3)*).

2.6. Used tools

To build and simulate the model, we have used the *Object*GEODE environment from VERILOG. Within the environment, we have made an extensive use of the SDL editor as well as the simulator. To validate our model the following simulation facilities were avalaible:

1. interactive simulation;
2. random simulation with coverage (state/transitions) over the managed object processes;
3. exhaustive simulation.

For formally described MIBs, we have used the simulator to trace the evolution and follow dynamic creation of new process instances. The **interactive** simulation was used to follow and verify some **specific** parts within our model. Towards other trials we made on simulating this model with other FDT's it appears that the support of **automated** (random) simulation within the SDL environment is really helpful. It must be note that the use of **exhaustive simulation** was not really applicable on our specification as the user process was a the **self-generating** one.

The combination of all these facilities was useful to detect errors in the model, behavior branches in which the system did never enter, and some other troubles in our specification.

2.7. Results

This trial provided several interesting results. First it has outlined the importance of building formal specifications of information models since we have identified several lacks (no errors) in the behavior rules of the model and errors in the sample state transition tables provided within the standard. Some of the detected errors came from the standard in which all behavior rules could be read in different ways and our initial understanding of the model directed us to non safe behavior specifications. Some state transition diagrams provided in the standard have been identified as bugged. Several other detected errors did not come from the standard but from our specification. All these errors have been detected during either random or interactive simulation of the model. The major outputs of that phase were: a good knowledge within the team of the information model; respecified behavior rules and new state transition diagrams.

The second lesson we learned is that it is quite easy and manageable to build a formal model for an information model and the availability of mature tools helps a lot in this task. Moreover, the translation to a formal specification becomes more and more easy with the object-oriented SDL'92 combined with ASN.1 support [4] since ASN.1 is heavily used in GDMO for attribute and parameter types.

One of the current limits in the combination of SDL'92 and GDMO is the difference in the underlying object models. In fact SDL'92 is not based on a strict inheritance paradigm and does not offer support for multiple inheritance. Despite these differences, one can shift most of the time a GDMO specification so that these differences do not cause any trouble in the model. A second limit to the combined use of SDL'92 and GDMO is, due to the high availability of GDMO specifications and their impressive size (some models have more than 100 Managed Object classes), the absence of translation tools from GDMO to SDL'92. We are currently working on such a tool and a first prototype is already available and distributed over the Internet (`http: //www.loria.fr /exterieur/equipe/resedas/mode.html`). The underlying translation algorithm as well as the tool are described in the next section.

3. An extended translation algorithm for SDL'92 generation

3.1. Related work

Several proposals for combining GDMO and SDL'92 have been made so far. Mazaher and Moller-Pedersen [20] have proposed a set of translation schemata starting from a GDMO specification to an SDL'92 formal specification. Bartocci, Larini and Romellini [2] also proposed a translation focussing mainly on the attribute and parameter type translation into ACT One. They also made an in-depth study more recently (see SDL FORUM'95 proceedings), but we unfortunately do not have this reference yet. Additional studies comparing and extending those approaches have been made in [25].

We have used those proposals in our translation algorithm with a few changes. In this section we will only focus on the changes. The reader is invited to refer to the previous publications for the initial algorithms.

3.2. Our approach

As already stated above, we have kept most of the features of existing algorithms. Thus we will present here only the changes made to those algorithms. These changes concern the following GDMO constructs: parameter, attribute, actions and notifications.

3.2.1. Parameter

A parameter is a data type defined in GDMO with the **WITH SYNTAX** or **ATTRIBUTE** clause. This type is used for the parameterization of an attribute, an action or a notification. This is done within the **CONTEXT** clause. The proposed translation for a parameter clause to SDL'92 is as follows:

GDMO PARAMETER	SDL'92
parameter-label **PARAMETER** **CONTEXT** *context-type* ; **WITH SYNTAX** *type_syntax* | **ATTRIBUTE** *attribute_label*;	**newtype** *parameter_label* **inherits** *type_syntax* | *attribute_label* **struct** *type_context* : CONTEXT; **endnewtype**

where *attribute_label* corresponds to a generated ACT/One type associated to the referenced attribute. CONTEXT is defined as follows:

Type SDL'92 (ACT/One)
syntype *CONTEXT* = **charstring** **constants** (*'ACTION-INFO'*, *'ACTION-REPLY'*, *'EVENT-INFO'*, *'EVENT-REPLY'*,*'SPECIFIC-ERROR'*) **endsyntype**

3.2.2. Attribute

An attribute is translated according to the following principles:

- the **DERIVED FROM** clause identifies the attribute from which the current attribute inherits the properties. This construct is translated into the **inherits** *attribute_label* SDL clause;
- **WITH ATTRIBUTE SYNTAX** identifies the ASN.1 type associated to the attribute if it is not derived from another attribute. In our algorithm, the translation is identical as the one in case of a derived clause, i.e. **inherits** *attribute_label*;

The translation schema is as follows:

ATTRIBUT GDMO	TYPE SDL
attribute-label **ATTRIBUTE** **DERIVED FROM** *attribute-label2* | **WITH ATTRIBUTE SYNTAX** *asn1-type* ; **PARAMETERS** *p1, p2,.., pk*;	**newtype***attribute_label* < newtype *p1* ; newtype *p2* ; ... newtype *pk* ; > **inherits** [*attribute_label2* | *asn1_type*] [a]; **endnewtype** *attribute_label* ; [a]This is not a pure SDL syntax but rather a kind of translation template coping with the options in the GDMO syntax.

3.2.3. Action

A GMDO action is translated into an SDL'92 exported procedure which can be invoked from outside the process modelling the managed object which encapsulates the action. The associated translation schema is as follows:

GDMO ACTION	SDL PROCEDURE
action-label ACTION **PARAMETERS** $p_1, p_2, \ldots, p_k$; **WITH INFORMATION** **SYNTAX** *wis*; **WITH REPLY SYNTAX** *wrs*;	**procedure** *action_label* **fpar in** *par_wis* $wis(p_{i_1}, p_{i_2}, \ldots, p_{i_m})$; **returns** *par_wrs* $wrs(p_{i_1}, p_{i_2}, \ldots, p_{i_n})$; ... **endprocedure**;

$$i_m + i + n \geq k$$

The **WITH INFORMATION SYNTAX** and **WITH REPLY SYNTAX** GDMO clauses define respectively the input value and the reply structure of the action. The *wis* and *wrs* declaration may lead to parametric ASN1 types. The $p_1, \ldots, p_k$ parrameters are the effective types to use into those parametric ASN1 types. The **CONTEXT** field of any p_i paramater allows us to assign it to the procedure formal parameter type or the procedure result type:

- a **ACTION-INFO** is assigned to the procedure formal parameter type ;
- an **ACTION-REPLY** is assigned to the procedure result type ;
- a **SPECIFIC-ERROR** may be assigned to both cases.

3.2.4. Notifications

The notification translation schema is very close to the one defined for an action. The main difference is that the notification procedure is not exported and can only be invoked from the object in which it is defined.

3.3. MIB Architecture generation and inter-object communication

In a more generic approach we have also considered the whole architecture of a Management Information Base together with its agent.

Since an object does not just have the interface supporting behavioral dependencies among objects seen in the trial of the previous section, the generated SDL skeleton for an object may require additional interfaces.

To catch those dependencies from a GDMO specification, we use the General Relationship Model (GRM [5]). Each time an object is referenced in a relationship at the information model specification level, an interface is defined in SDL'92 for this object in the context of the relationship.

We can say that we need a kind of "agent toolkit" in SDL.

3.4. The MODERES toolkit

MODERES [10] is a generic environment for manipulating both GRM and GDMO specifications. The toolkit provides a GRM/GDMO parser over which an object-oriented Application Programming Interface allows access to all parts of a Management Information Model specification. In its first release, MODERES was provided with four main back-ends:

- a TEXgenerator allowing the generation of well formatted GDMO/GRM documents according to editorial constraints [9];
- a HTML generator allowing Information Models to be read over intranets with navigation facilities [8];
- a relational database back-end for the generation of a specification repository;
- an interface to management applications for relationship management through GRM specifications (the RelMan application).

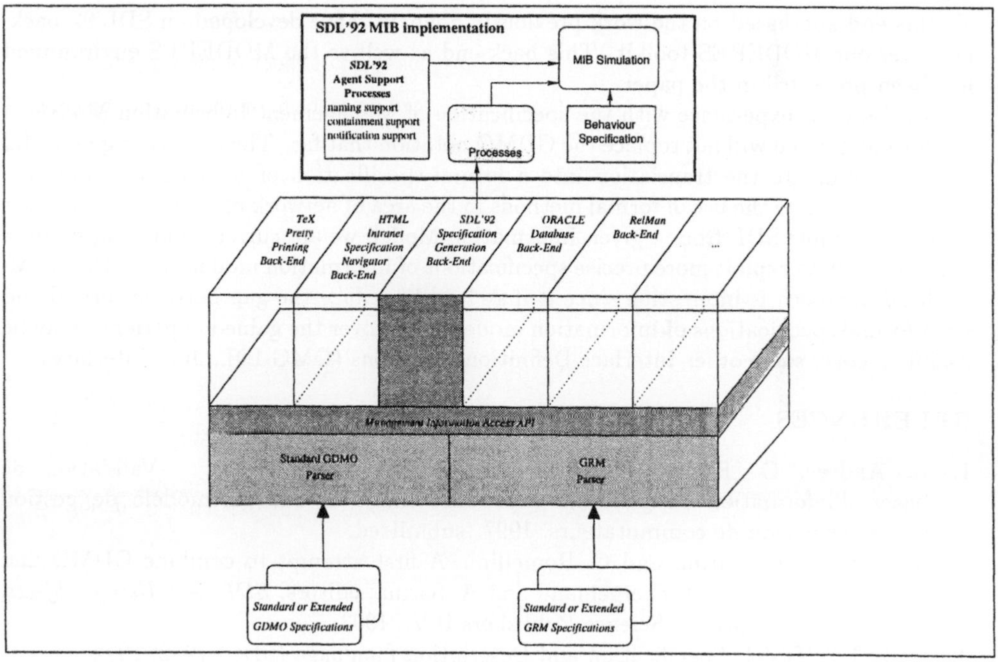

Figure 5. Architecture of the MODERES toolkit.

In order to ease the development of formally defined Information Models and to encourage people from the Network Management world to write formal specifications of their model, we have built on top of the MODERES environment an SDL'92 generator which performs the GDMO/GRM to SDL'92 translation as presented in the previous section.

The SDL back-end within the MODERES toolkit is illustrated in figure 5. The back-end is supposed to generated a generic agent model responsible for performing all CMIS requests and scoping and filtering aspects. It also generates the SDL'92 skeletons for the data types as well as one process skeleton for each GDMO managed object class. In the first release of the back-end, only the data-type and process generator is provided. Tests have been successfully performed on several standard GDMO libraries which have been translated into SDL'92. We are currenlty working on the generic SDL agent part.

4. Conlusion and future work

In this paper we have presented our practical experience in describing formally TMN-oriented Information Models using both SDL'88 and SDL'92. We have motivated the importance of deploying a validation activity on such models and shown the feasibility of this activity on a relevant example.

During this trial we have also identified the need to provide translation facilities from GDMO to SDL'92 in order to speed-up the process of Information Model formalization. To this end and based on the work previously done, we have developed an SDL'92 back-end over our MODERES toolkit. This back-end as well as the MODERES environment has been presented in the paper.

Based on our experience with the specification of Management Information Models, a full formal method will not replace the GDMO notation that far. Thus, providing powerful tools to automate the translation into a formal specification of information models is crucial to promote the use of formal methods in the area of network management. In order to generate more SDL from a given Information Model, we are currenlty looking more in depth on how to exploit more precise specifications of information models using the GRM. Such an approach is interesting since it may lead to reduce the gap between formal and semi-formal specifications of information models. Moreover the gained experience may be useful to cover some other Interface Definition Notations (OMG-IDL, Java interface).

REFERENCES

1. L. Andrey, O. Festor, E. Nataf, A. Schaff, and S. Tata. Validation de bases d'information de gestion: expérience multi-fdt sur un modèle de gestion d'interconnexion de commutateurs. 1997. submitted.
2. A. Bartocci, G. Larini, and C. Romellini. A first attempt to combine GDMO and SDL techniques. In O. Faergemand and A. Sarma, editors, *SDL '93: Using Objects*, pages 333–345. Elsiever Science Publishers B.V., 1993.
3. CCITT-Z-100-92. Specification and Description Language (SDL) 1992, 1992.
4. CCITT-Z-105. SDL Combined with ASN.1 (SDL/ASN.1), 1995. SG.10 Q.6 Proposed New Recommendation.
5. CCITT.X.725. Information Technology - Open Systems Interconnection - Structure of Management Information - Part 7: General Relationship Model, 1995.
6. O. Festor. *Formalisation du comportement des objets gérés dans le cadre du modèle OSI.* PhD thesis, 1994.

7. O. Festor. OSI Managed Objects Development with LOBSTERS. 1994. Fifth International Workshop on Distributed Systems: Operations and Management, 12-16 Septembre 1994, Toulouse, France.
8. O. Festor. Mode-pp html: A gdmo/grm to html translator -release 1.0- reference manual. Technical Report 0199, INRIA Lorraine, 1996.
9. O. FESTOR. Mode-pp tex: A grm/gdmo pretty printing library based on mode-fe for the generation of tex documents. -release 1.0- reference manual. Technical Report RT-0192, INRIA, May 1996.
10. O. Festor, E. Nataf, and L. Andrey. MODE-FE: A GRM/GDMO Parser and its API -Release 1.0-
Reference Manual. Technical Report 0190, INRIA Lorraine, 1996.
11. O. Festor and G. Zoerntlein. Formal Description of Managed Object Behavior - A Rule Based Approach. pages 45–58, 1993. in [12].
12. ISINM'93. *Integrated Network Management, III (C-12).* Elsiever Science Publishers B.V. (North-Holland), 1993. Proc. IFIP IEEE 3rd Int. Symp. on Integrated Network Management, San Francisco, CA, 18-23 April, 1993.
13. ISO. GDMO+: Working Document on Extension of GDMO for the Specification of Managed Object Behaviour, 1996. ISO/IEC SC 21 N 1115.
14. ISO-10040. System Management Overview, 1992.
15. ISO-10165.4. Structure of Management Information - Part 4: Guidelines for the Definition of Managed Objects, 1992.
16. ISO-7498.4. Basic Reference Model - Part 4: Management framework, 1989.
17. J. Keller. An Extension of GDMO for Formalizing Managed Object Behaviour. 1995. FORTE'95.
18. A.J. Kouyzer and A.K. van den Boogaart. The LOTOS framework for OSI Systems Management. In I. Krishnan and W. Zimmer, editors, *Integrated Network Management, II*, pages 147–156. Elsiever Science Publishers B.V. (North-Holland), 1992.
19. L.S. Marshall and Simon L. Using VDM to Specifiy Managed Object Relationships. 1992. FORTE'92, Lannion, Fr., 13-16 Oct, 1992.
20. S. Mazaher and B. Moller-Pedersen. On the use of SDL-92 for the Specification of Behaviour in OSI Network Management Objects. In O. Faergemand and A. Sarma, editors, *SDL '93: Using Objects*, pages 317–331. Elsiever Science Publishers B.V., 1993.
21. E. Nataf, O. Festor, A. Schaff, and Andrey L. Validation du modèle de gestion d'interconnexion de commutateurs à l'aide de systèmes de transitions étiquetées. In A. Bennani, R. Dssouli, A. Benkiran, and O. Rafiq, editors, *CFIP'96*, pages 83–97. Eyrolles, Octobre 1996. Rabat, Maroc.
22. NMF. Switch Interconnection Management: Configuration Management Ensemble, 1994.
23. D. Sidou, S. Mazziotta, and R. Eberhardt. TIMS: a TMN-based Information Model Simulator, Principles and Application to a Simple Case Study. 1995. in Sixth Int. Workshop on Distributed Systems: Operations and Management, IFIP/IEEE, Ottawa - Canada.
24. L. Simon and S. Marshall. Using VDM to Specifiy OSI Managed Objects. 1992. Bell-Northern Research Ltd., P.O. Box 3511 Station C, Ottawa, Ontario, Canada.

25. L. Verhaard. Using SDL for the Specification of Behaviour of Managed Objects, 1995. Liaison Statement to SG.10 Q.6.

IX

Code generation

SDL '97: TIME FOR TESTING - SDL, MSC and Trends
A. Cavalli and A. Sarma (Editors)

Combining SDL and C

Pär-Olof Håkansson, Jan Karlsson, Louis Verhaard

Telelogic AB, PO Box 4128, S-203 12 Malmö, Sweden
email {Par-Olof.Hakansson, Jan.Karlsson, Louis.Verhaard}@telelogic.se
http://www.telelogic.se

Keywords: SDL, C

This paper describes how C can be used in combination with SDL by adding C-specific data types to SDL and adding a few new features to the SDL language, thus allowing an automatic translation from C headers to SDL packages. The described C support has been implemented in SDT.

1. INTRODUCTION

SDT has traditionally taken the approach that the SDL system describes the whole system that is to be developed. However, in most applications, SDL is only used for a small part of the total system, that has to be integrated with other components, like lower layer protocols, data bases, or other software and hardware. For the new SDT 3.1 release it was decided to make a shift towards this more realistic viewpoint. One of the implemented improvements towards this goal is improved support for integration with applications written in ANSI C, as many of our customers have a large existing software base written in C that must work together with SDL applications.

As a side effect of this improved C support, another problem was tackled as well. In practise, SDL is mostly used as a programming language. But because SDL was not directly intended to be an implementation language, it lacks some concepts (like pointers) which are necessary to get high performance, mostly because it is hard to avoid unnecessary data copying.

The rest of this paper describes the improved support for C in more detail. Chapter 2 describes a mapping from C to SDL and backward. For this purpose, SDL was extended with some new constructs and data types. Chapter 3 gives an example of an SDL system that uses some types and functions defined in C. It also shows the tool support from a user's point of view.

2. TRANSLATING C TO SDL

In the programming language C, the major tool for integration is the concept of C headers (.h files). Such headers usually contain definitions of data types, functions, and variables that are common to several C modules in the total system. SDL has no concept for direct definition of interfaces. However, the package concept of SDL comes rather close, because definitions in a package can be used in several SDL systems. Thus, the package serves as some sort of interface.

To achieve a tighter connection between an application implemented mainly in C and a new module in the application, implemented as an SDL system, we have therefore chosen to translate C headers to interface packages in SDL. When C code has to be generated for such a package, actually no C definitions are generated, but the information in the original C header is used, by performing `#include "ex.h"`. In this way it is ensured that the SDL system and the C application interpret data in the same way, and at the same time make the data from C available to the SDL system.

To make this model work, there is a major restriction on the mapping between C and SDL. The mapping rules have to be two-way, i.e. starting from any C type, translating it to SDL and then back to C again must give the original C type. On the other hand, it is not necessary that an SDL type that is translated to C and then back again, gives the same SDL type.

The remaining part of this section will give an overview of the mapping rules C->SDL->C that are used, and the extensions of SDL that have been required to implement these mapping rules. The complete mapping rules are described in [2].

2.1 Basic C Types

We have introduced a special package called `ctypes`, which contains SDL definitions for many of the standard types in C, like `long int`, `unsigned short int`, etc. This package has in some sense a similar status as the package `predefined`, as it implements a number of "predefined" C-specific types and generators in SDL. However, this package must be explicitly "used". The package `ctypes` is listed in appendix 1. Given the types in this package, we have the following mapping rules for the basic C types:

```
int                   Integer              (predefined)
long int              LongInt              (ctypes)
short int             ShortInt             (ctypes)
unsigned int          UnsignedInt          (ctypes)
unsigned long int     UnsignedLongInt      (ctypes)
unsigned short int    UnsignedShortInt     (ctypes)
char                  Character            (predefined)
unsigned char         Octet                (predefined, Z105)
float                 Float                (ctypes)
double                Real                 (predefined)
void *                VoidStar             (ctypes)
void **               VoidStarStar         (ctypes)
char *                CharStar             (ctypes)
```

Together with the new data types, new operators are also introduced to utilize the predefined operators in C. For example the predefined type `Octet` (a Z.105-specific predefined type), that corresponds to `unsigned char`, has been extended with a number of operators to make it more useful:

```
ShiftL  : Octet, Integer -> Octet; /* shift bitwise left */
ShiftR  : Octet, Integer  -> Octet; /* shift bitwise right */
"+"     : Octet, Octet     -> Octet;
"-"     : Octet, Octet     -> Octet;
```

```
"*"      : Octet, Octet    -> Octet;
"/"      : Octet, Octet    -> Octet;
"mod"    : Octet, Octet    -> Octet;
"rem"    : Octet, Octet    -> Octet;
I2O      : Integer         -> Octet; /* integer to octet */
O2I     : Octet          -> Integer; /* octet to integer */
BitStr   : Charstring      -> Octet;
   /* e.g. BitStr('1010') == I2O(10) */
HexStr   : Charstring      -> Octet;
    /* e.g. HexStr('1A') == I2O(26) */
```

In the CharStar type there are conversion operators between CharStar and the predefined data type Charstring, as well as conversion operators between CharStar and VoidStar.

```
CStar2CString : CharStar   -> CharString;
CString2CStar : CharString -> CharStar;
CStar2VStar   : CharStar   -> VoidStar;
VStar2CStar   : VoidStar   -> CharStar;
```

2.2 Arrays in C

Arrays in C and in SDL have some differences, which makes it unsuitable to translate an SDL array to a C array. First we have the problem with the index type, as SDL allows any type as index type, while C only takes integer indexes starting from 0 to a given upper limit. Second, we also have the problem with parameter passing of array values. In an operator in SDL, array values are copied when used in parameters or in results. In C, arrays are always passed by reference. To map an SDL array to a C array would introduce hard restrictions on the usage of arrays in SDL. In SDT, an SDL array is therefore translated to a C struct containing the C array. In this way the semantics of operator parameter passing can be preserved in SDL.

To achieve a true C array in SDL, we have introduced a new generator, CArray, in the package ctypes. An application of this generator will become an array in C (with all its limitations). The generator parameters to a CArray are the length and the component type, just as in C.

For example in the below figure, type myarray is an array of 10 integers, with indexes 0-9. The example also shows that CArray elements are indexed in the same way as normal SDL arrays. However, no Make! operator is available, so it is not allowed to write

```
v := (. 4 .)
```

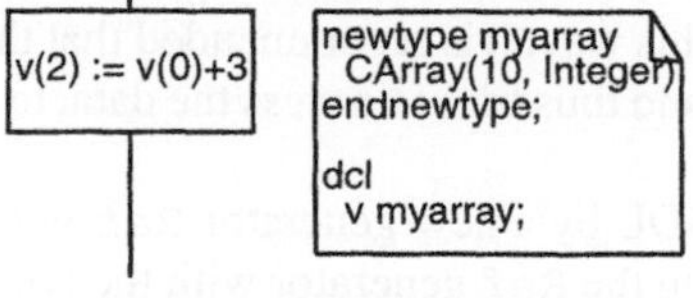
v(2) := v(0)+3
newtype myarray
CArray(10, Integer)
endnewtype;
dcl
v myarray;

Figure 1: Use of CArray

2.3 Structs in C

The struct concepts in SDL and C are almost identical and can in most cases be directly translated to each other. The only difference is that in C it is possible to optimize the space required for the struct components by using bit fields. A bit field is a specification of the number of bits for the component. In C this is only allowed for int and unsigned int components. To be able to handle C structs with bit fields, we have introduced the same facility in SDL. It is now possible to write in SDL:

```
newtype mybitfield struct
   a Integer       : 4;
   b UnsignedInt : 2;
   c UnsignedInt : 1;
                   : 0;
   d Integer       : 4;
   e Integer;
endnewtype;
```

The interpretation of the bit fields is according to the semantics of C.

2.3 Unions in C

SDL has no concept that matches C's union. It is not even possible to express the properties of a C union in SDL, because C's union has the unfortunate property that it does not follow from a union value, which of the union fields is selected. Therefore we map unions to SDL structs that is accompanied by a special code generator directive that tells the C code generator to generate a C union instead of a C struct. Pointers are not allowed in unions, as memory leaks would occur when used in SDL.

The properties of C's union cannot be expressed with SDL. Also, possible tool support for validation of unions is limited, so it is not recommended to use them in combination with SDL. Z.105 offers a better alternative, viz. choice types.

2.4 Pointers in C

A very important feature in C is the usage of pointers. Pointers are also extremely dangerous to use in real-time applications, as data inconsistency may occur when several processes try to access the same data area via pointers. Despite this, we decided to introduce pointers in SDL, because the benefits of pointers, if correctly used, are substantial.

There are two areas where pointers are useful and where the risk of using them is limited. First, pointers can be used to build data structures that are local to a process instance, for example lists and trees. Second, pointers can be used to send references to large data areas between different process instances, instead of copying the data area, assuming that the processes share the same address space.This saves data copying, and can significantly improve performance. If pointers are used in this way, it is recommended that there is only one process instance at a time "owns" the pointer and thus tries to access the data, to avoid the above mentioned data inconsistency problems.

Pointers are included in SDL by a new generator `Ref` in the package `ctypes.` A pointer type is created by instantiating the `Ref` generator with the type that is pointed to as parameter. Note that the properties of this pointer generator cannot be expressed in standard SDL. For example if we change the contents of a pointer to some variable, then the variable itself is also changed, which is a property that cannot be expressed with axioms.

The below defined data type `mybitfieldRef` is an example of a pointer to `mybitfield` (see previous example)

```
newtype mybitfieldRef
  Ref(mybitfield)
endnewtype;
```

There are a number operators that can be used to work with pointers in SDL:

- There is an operator to go from the pointer to the object that the pointer refers to. This is very similar to extract and modify for array and struct types. We introduced a new syntax for dereferencing pointers. If `P` is a pointer, `P*>` is the object referred to by the pointer. This is an extension of Z.100's syntax, to mark clearly that this operator can not be defined in standard SDL.
  ```
  dcl P mybitfieldRef;
  task P*>!a := 2; /* corresponds in C to P->a = 2; */
  ```
- The opposite operator is the address-operator, which given a variable returns its address. For example if `V` is a variable, `&V` gives its address. Also here the Z.100 syntax is extended to mark clearly that this is an operator with properties that cannot be expressed in standard SDL.
- Memory can be dynamically allocated with parameterless operator `Alloc`. For example if `P` is a pointer to `mybitfield`, `p := Alloc` would create a memory area for one `mybitfield`, and `P` would point to it. Dynamically allocated memory has to be freed by calling procedure `Free`, that is also defined in `ctypes`.
- There are conversion operators to and from VoidStar. They are mainly used when calling C functions that have `void *` parameters, or that return `void *`.

2.5 C Function Prototypes

A C header usually contains a number of function prototypes that provide an interface to functions implemented in C. With the new SDL-96 concept of external procedures, such C function prototypes can be directly mapped to external procedures.

For example the C function prototype

```
int myfunction (char *s);
```

is in SDL represented by

```
procedure myfunction;
  fpar s CharStar;
  returns Integer;
external;
```

The C function can be called from SDL by means of a procedure call:

```
dcl i Integer;

task i := call myfunction (Null);
```

Functions with a variable number of arguments cannot be mapped to SDL, as SDL procedures always have a fixed number of arguments. In the next chapter it will be shown how this restriction to some extent can be circumvented.

2.6 External variables

SDL has no concept for global variables. Therefore external variables are mapped to two external procedures in SDL, one to get the value and one to set the value. The use of such variables is dangerous, since there are no synchronization mechanisms to prevent several processes updating the same variable at the same time, which may lead to data inconsistency.

2.7 Constants

Constants in C can be mapped to a 'normal' synonym or to an external synonym. As an example we consider:

```
#define MAX 1000
```

This C macro definition can be mapped to a normal synonym or alternatively to an external synonym:

```
synonym MAX Integer = 1000;
synonym MAX Integer = external;
```

The same mappings are valid for C constants defined with `const`. For example the below C constant is from an SDL point of view the same as the above macro:

```
const int MAX = 1000;
```

As will be explained in the next chapter, macros cannot be automatically translated to SDL in the current implementation of SDT, so the latter way of defining constants is preferred.

3. USING C HEADERS IN SDT

The translation rules described above have been implemented in a utility named H2SDL which is included in SDT 3.1. The H2SDL utility is integrated with the other Telelogic tools to simplify the use of C headers in SDL systems. It can also be used as a stand-alone tool to create SDL packages from header files.

3.1 Organizing C Headers

Including a C header in SDL is straightforward and consists of a few operations in the SDT Organizer and writing a template file to describe how to compile and link the C code generated by SDT with external C sources.

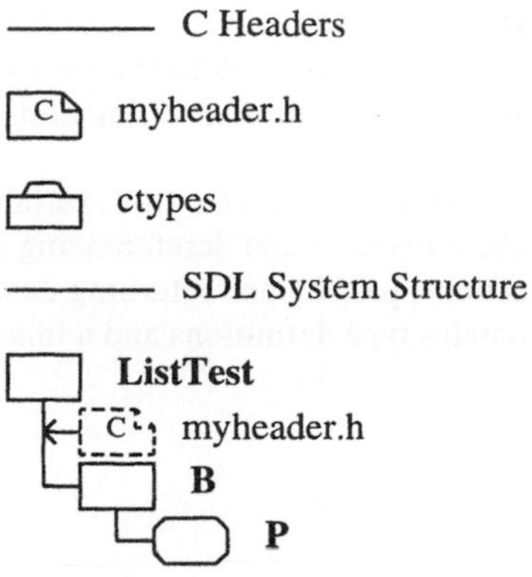

Figure 2: Organizer view of an SDL system that uses a C header

The illustration above shows the view of a small system in the SDT Organizer tool. The user includes the header file, in this case myheader.h, and makes a dependency link between the SDL substructure and the header file.

The SDL system can make use of the definitions in the C header by means of a `use` clause at the system diagram. The user must also include the `ctypes` package to get access to the C-specific data types needed to connect C and SDL. The `use` clauses are shown in figure 3 below.

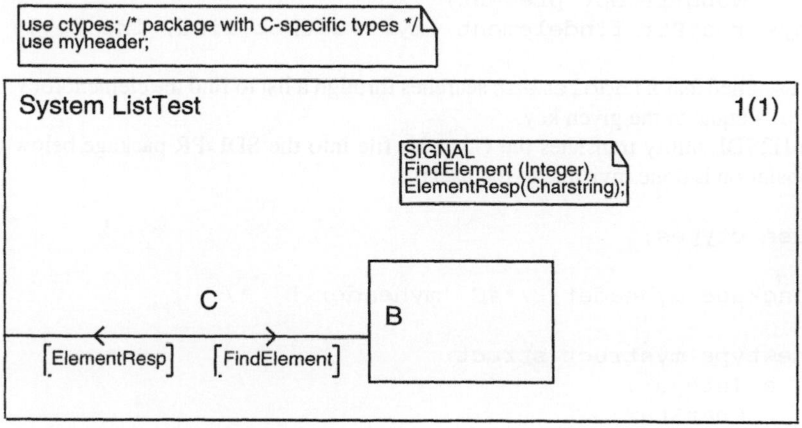

Figure 3: SDL system that uses a C header

Once these preparations are made, SDT handles everything automatically; when the user analyses the system, SDT will start the H2SDL utility and from the user's point of view the header file is just another SDL package.

3.2 Using C Definitions in SDL

The simple system seen above, is described in detail below to illustrate a few of the features implemented in SDT to facilitate the use of external C functions and definitions.

The example illustrates:

- Using external C type definitions to declare SDL variables.
- Pointers; using the address operator and dereferencing pointers to get the contents.
- Calling external C functions; passing and returning data via pointers.

The following header file contains type definitions and a function which will be used in the SDL system:

```
/* myheader.h */
/* structure */
typedef struct {
  int a;
  char *b;
  } mystruct;

typedef mystruct myarray[3];

typedef mystruct *mystructPtr;

  /* finds first element in list that has given int
     (NULL if not present) */
  mystructPtr findelement (mystructPtr list, int key);
```

It is assumed that `findelement` searches through a list to find the element for which component a is equal to the given key.

The H2SDL utility translates the C header file into the SDL/PR package below (although this translation is done invisible to the user)):

```
use ctypes;

package myheader; /*#C 'myheader.h' */

newtype mystruct struct
  a Integer;
  b CharStar;
endnewtype mystruct;

newtype myarray
  CArray(3,mystruct);
endnewtype myarray;

newtype mystructPtr
  ref(mystruct);
endnewtype mystructPtr;
```

```
procedure findelement;
  fpar
    list mystructPtr,
    key Integer;
  returns mystructPtr;
external;

endpackage myheader;
```

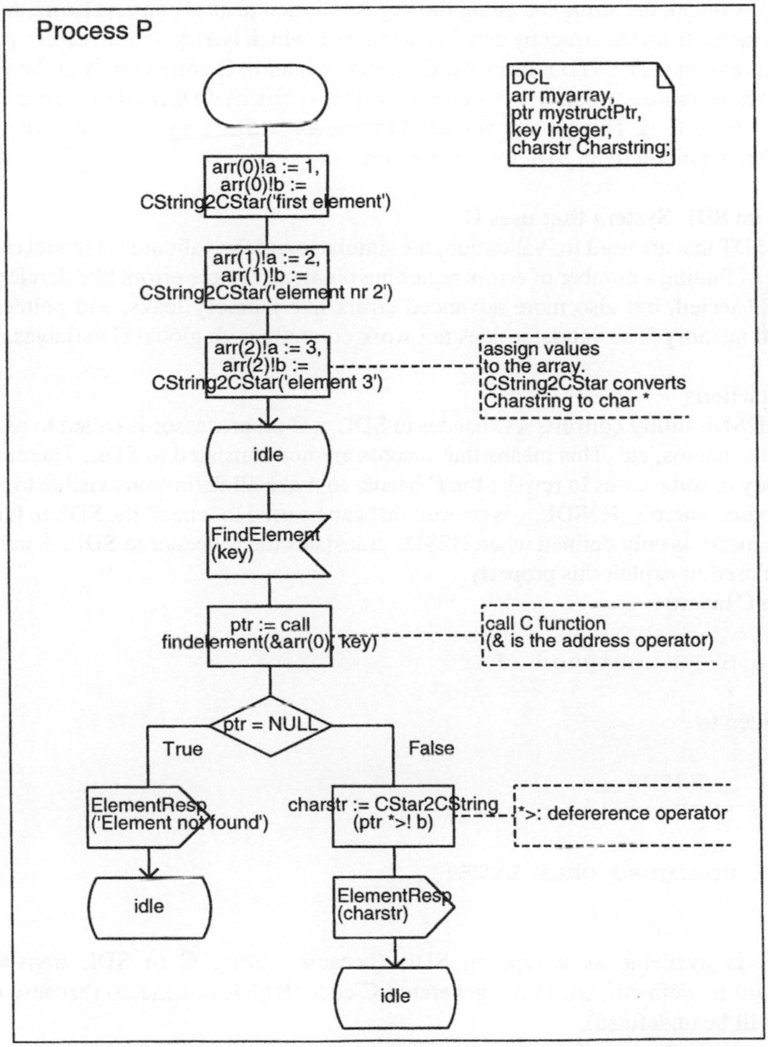

Figure 4: A process that uses types and functions defined in C

Figure 4 shows a process in the system that uses the C definitions. The three task boxes that follow directly after the start symbol initialize the array variable `myarray`. The function `CString2CStar` converts the SDL charstrings to C `char` pointers which is the type of the `myarray` struct member `b`.

After the start transition the process awaits a `FindElement` signal. When a `FindElement` signal arrives the C function `findelement` is called with a pointer to the start of the array of structs to be searched, and the integer key to search for. `findelement` is translated to SDL as a value returning procedure, and if an element with a matching key is found, a pointer to the element is returned and assigned to the variable `ptr`.

If an element is found, the string matching the key is returned in an `ElementResp` signal. The string is extracted from the struct by dereferencing `ptr` which is a `myStructPtr` pointer. The SDL expression `ptr*>!b` returns the CharStar pointer b. It corresponds to the C expression `ptr->b`, or more correct: `ptr*>` corresponds to `(*ptr)` in C, and thus `ptr*>!b` corresponds to `(*ptr).b`. This pointer is passed to `CStar2CString` which in turn transforms a `CharStar` pointer to an SDL `Charstring`.

3.3 Validating an SDL System that uses C

The tools in SDT that are used for validation, the simulator and the validator (a model checker), are capable of finding a number of errors regarding pointers. Simple errors like dereferencing NULL are detected, but also more advanced errors like memory leaks, and pointers to already released memory. The validator does not work correctly with global C variables.

3.4 Some Restrictions

Before the H2SDL utility converts a C header to SDL, a C preprocessor is called to resolve conditional code, macros, etc. This means that macros are not translated to SDL. Therefore it may be necessary in some cases to rewrite the C header to make all definitions visible to SDL.

For this purpose, macro __H2SDL__ is present that can be used to 'cheat' the SDL to C code generator. This macro is only defined when H2SDL translates the C header to SDL. A number of tricks can be used to exploit this property.

For example C macro

```
#define BYTE unsigned char
```

can be rewritten to

```
#ifndef __H2SDL__
#define BYTE unsigned char
#else
typedef unsigned char BYTE;
#endif
```

Now BYTE is available as a type in SDL (because during C to SDL translation, `__H2SDL__` will be defined), but in the generated C code, BYTE is a macro (because then, `__H2SDL__` will be undefined).

Another example is the fprintf function that of the standard C library, which has a variable number of arguments. Its prototype is:

```
int fprintf( FILE *, const char *, ...);
```

H2SDL will map this function to an external procedure with two parameters (with parameters pointer to FILE and pointer to Character respectively). We can add functions to make specific parameter combinations available in SDL. Below, two extra functions are provided for printing one respectively two integer parameters.

```
int fprintf( FILE *, const char *, ...);

#ifndef __H2SDL__
#define fprintf1 fprintf
#define fprintf2 fprintf
#else
int fprintf1(FILE *, const char *, int);
int fprintf2(FILE *, const char *, int, int);
#endif
```

4. CONCLUSIONS AND FUTURE WORK

By extending SDL with some new language constructs and a package with C-specific data types and generators, a C header containing data types and functions can be translated to a corresponding SDL package. These translation rules have been implemented in a C to SDL compiler that is integrated with the rest of SDT. Thus SDL systems can use C headers as if they were SDL packages. The user only has to know the translation rules from C to SDL, and the package with C-specific data types and generators.

The same principle can be applied for integrating SDL with many other languages. For example the ASN.1 support in SDT has been implemented in the same way: ASN.1 modules can be added to the Organizer structure, and when they are used by an SDL system they are translated to corresponding SDL packages, according to translation rules derived from Z.105 ([3]). C++ is one of the candidates that is next on our list.

REFERENCES

1. American National Standard X3.159, ANSI C, ANSI, 1989.
2. Telelogic Tau 3.1 Reference Manual, Telelogic, 1996.
3. Z.105 (1995), Specification and description language (SDL) combined with abstract syntax notation one (ASN.1), ITU-T May 1995.

APPENDIX: PACKAGE CTYPES

```
package ctypes;

/*---------------------- ShortInt ----------------------*/
/* Corresponds to C types : short int, short           */
/*------------------------------------------------------*/
syntype ShortInt = Integer
endsyntype ShortInt;
```

```
/*---------------------- LongInt -------------------------*/
/* Corresponds to C types : long int, long                */
/*--------------------------------------------------------*/
syntype LongInt = Integer
endsyntype LongInt;

/*----------------- UnsignedShortInt ---------------------*/
/* Corresponds to C types : unsigned short int,           */
/*                          unsigned short                */
/*--------------------------------------------------------*/
syntype UnsignedShortInt = Integer
endsyntype UnsignedShortInt;

/*-------------------- UnsignedInt -----------------------*/
/* Corresponds to C types : unsigned int, unsigned        */
/*--------------------------------------------------------*/
syntype UnsignedInt = Integer
endsyntype UnsignedInt;

/*----------------- UnsignedLongInt ----------------------*/
/* Corresponds to C types : unsigned long int,            */
/*                          unsigned long                 */
/*--------------------------------------------------------*/
syntype UnsignedLongInt = Integer
endsyntype UnsignedLongInt;

/*---------------------- Float ---------------------------*/
/* Corresponds to C type : float                          */
/*--------------------------------------------------------*/
syntype Float = Real
endsyntype Float;

/*--------------------- CharStar -------------------------*/
/* Corresponds to C type : char *                         */
/*--------------------------------------------------------*/
newtype CharStar
  operators
    /* conversion operators SDL Charstring <-> char * */
    CStar2CString : CharStar -> CharString;
    CString2CStar : CharString -> CharStar;
    /* conversion operators CharStar <-> VoidStar */
    CStar2VStar : CharStar -> VoidStar;
    VStar2CStar : VoidStar -> CharStar;
endnewtype CharStar;
```

```
/*--------------------- VoidStar -----------------------*/
/* Corresponds to C type : void *                       */
/*------------------------------------------------------*/
newtype VoidStar
endnewtype VoidStar;

/*------------------- VoidStarStar ---------------------*/
/* Corresponds to C type : void **                      */
/*------------------------------------------------------*/
newtype VoidStarStar
endnewtype VoidStarStar;

/*--------------------- CArray -------------------------*/
/* Corresponds to C arrays                              */
/*------------------------------------------------------*/
generator CArray(constant Length, type Itemsort)
  operators
    /* usual array operators, only Make! is not allowed */
    Modify! : CArray, Integer, Itemsort -> CArray;
    Extract! : CArray, Integer -> Itemsort;
endgenerator CArray;

/*--------------------- Ref ----------------------------*/
/* Corresponds to C pointers                            */
/*        The properties of this generator cannot       */
/*        be expressed with axioms!                     */
/*------------------------------------------------------*/
generator Ref( type Itemsort)
  /* Alloc is used for dynamic memory allocation. It
     should actually be a parameterless operator, but this
     SDL-96 construct is not yet supported in SDT 3.1 */
  literals Null, Alloc;
  operators
    /* dereferencing operators (postfix) */
    "*>" : Ref, ItemSort -> Ref;
    "*>" : Ref -> ItemSort;
    /* address-of operator (prefix) */
    "&" : ItemSort -> Ref;
    /* pointer arithmetic operators (C compatible) */
    "+" : Ref, Integer -> Ref;
    "-" : Ref, Integer -> Ref;
    /* every pointer type gets conversion operators to
       and from VoidStar, and to VoidStarStar */
    Ref2VStar : Ref -> VoidStar;
    VStar2Ref : VoidStar -> Ref;
    Ref2VStarStar : Ref -> VoidStarStar;
```

```
  default Null;
endgenerator Ref;

procedure Free;
/* used to free memory allocated by "Alloc" */
fpar
  p VoidStarStar; external;
endpackage ctypes;
```

Derivation of Efficient Implementations from SDL Specifications Employing Data Referencing, Integrated Packet Framing and Activity Threads*

Ralf Henke[a], Hartmut König[b], Andreas Mitschele-Thiel[a]

[a]Friedrich-Alexander Universität Erlangen-Nürnberg, Lehrstuhl für Informatik VII, Martensstraße 3, 91058 Erlangen, Germany, email: mitsch@informatik.uni-erlangen.de

[b]Brandenburgische Technische Universität Cottbus, Institut für Informatik, Postfach 101344, 03013 Cottbus, Germany, email: koenig@informatik.tu-cottbus.de

Implementations automatically derived from SDL descriptions often do not fulfill the performance requirements of performance-sensitive applications. In the paper, we describe how three different techniques mainly known from the manual implementation of protocol architectures can be applied to automatically derive efficient implementations from SDL specifications. The three techniques are data referencing, integrated packet framing and activity threads. Data referencing is employed to optimize communication between process instances. Integrated packet framing allows to minimize copying overhead within process instances. The activity thread model supports the minimization of overhead for process management. In the paper, we analyze the prerequisites to apply the different optimization techniques and show how the techniques can be employed for the automatic derivation of efficient implementations from SDL specifications. Finally, we present measurements comparing the performance achievable with the different optimization techniques. The measurements are made for different implementations of the Xpress Transfer Protocol derived from an SDL specification. Our results show that a considerable speedup can be achieved with each of the optimization techniques.

1 Motivation

The performance of communication systems is decisively determined by the protocols used. Experience with practical protocol implementations shows that protocol performance depends as much, and usually more, on the implementation than on the design [4], [19]. Communication protocols are usually implemented by hand. The implementations are typically based on informal (verbal) standards provided by ISO, ITU-T or other organizations. The techniques employed for hand-coded implementations have been continuously improved. Examples range from the simple elimination of copy operations between protocol layers by data referencing to more sophisticated optimizations as application level framing [2], [5], common path optimization [11] and integrated layer processing [1], [3], [5]. In addition, the exploitation of various kinds of parallelism to derive efficient protocol implementations has been investigated. The re-

* The research described is supported in part by the *Deutsche Forschungsgemeinschaft* under grant He 1408/2-1 and grant Ko 1273/7-1.

sults indicate that with most protocol architectures the granularity of the parallel units is too small to be exploited efficiently on multiprocessor systems.

Implementations automatically derived from formal descriptions are less reported, although approaches for the computer-aided derivation of implementations have been investigated for more than ten years. So far, the use of automatically derived implementations is limited due to their lack of efficiency. Thus, they are mainly used for prototyping or for applications, where optimal performance is not crucial.

The main obstacle for the successful application of computer-aided implementation techniques (and probably of formal description techniques in general) is the insufficient efficiency of the generated code. There are several reasons for this [9]:

(1) The implementation model prescribed by the transformation tool is elaborated during tool design. It does not take into account the context in which the implementation is used.
(2) Formal description techniques are based on formal semantics. The semantics highly influence the design of the implementation model. Optimizations can only be introduced by ensuring correctness and conformance criteria.
(3) So far, automated protocol implementations are mainly focused on one-layer implementations (due to their orientation on prototyping).

Current transformation tools mostly follow a straight-forward implementation of the semantics of the formal description technique. The process model typically employed is the server model [15]. All code generators for SDL known to us solely support the server model (e.g. [7], [14], [16], [17], [18]). Some proposals to increase the efficiency of automatically generated implementations exist. In [9], the use of a variable implementation model for Estelle is proposed. It allows to configure the (hand-coded) runtime system depending on the implementation context. An approach to derive application specific protocol architectures from Esterel specifications has been described in [6]. In the reported research, the concepts of integrated layer processing and application level framing are applied.

So far, the approaches have not yet achieved the derivation of implementations that exhibit a performance close to the performance of hand-coded implementations [8], [9]. As far as SDL is concerned, the inclusion of implementation strategies known from the hand-coded implementation of high-speed protocols as application level framing or the activity thread model are not considered at all. An approach for the optimization of implementations derived from (a subset of) SDL that has been studied to some extend is the integrated-layer-processing approach. However, the work reported in [11] is focusing on the analysis of SDL specifications for data and control dependences and the integration of data manipulation operations on a common execution path rather than the automatic derivation of code. For the automatic derivation of code that supports the integrated processing of data manipulation operations of various layers, also the protocol executions that differ from the common path have to be handled. Our research indicates that this can not be done automatically.

Our research is focusing on three techniques to improve the efficiency of automatically derived code, namely

(1) the replacement of data copying between process instances by data referencing,
(2) the elimination of data copying operations within the process instances employing a technique similar to application level framing [5], and
(3) the application of the activity thread model instead of the server model [4], [15].

All three techniques are well known from the manual implementation of protocol architectures.

The paper is structured as follows: in section 2, we review the state of the art of the automatic code generation from SDL. Two techniques to minimize data copy operations are described in section 3, namely data referencing and integrated packet framing. In section 4, we describe the activity thread model and show where and how it can be applied for the automatic derivation of code. In order to evaluate the performance improvements achievable with the three optimization techniques, performance results for the Xpress Transfer Protocol (XTP) [13] are given in section 5. Conclusions are drawn in section 6.

2 State of the Art

Formal description techniques possess formal semantics that guarantee the exact interpretation of the specification. Automatically deriving implementations from formal descriptions requires transformation rules which preserve the semantics of the specification, i.e. the conformance of the implementation with the specification. This adds overhead to the implementation which is not present with implementations manually derived from informal descriptions.

Deriving implementations from SDL specifications, several alternatives exist. Two issues are of particular importance for the efficiency of the derived implementations.

(1) The first issue relates to the manner used to map the process instances of the SDL specification on the active entities provided by the system, i.e. on the threads or processes provided by the operating system or the runtime environment.

(2) The second issue deals with the question how communication between process instances is implemented.

Due to the semantic similarities between SDL and the server model (asynchronous computation and communication), current code generators known from industry and academia all resort to the server model. In this section, we describe the server model and the typical approach to handle communication between process instances.

2.1 Implementation of Process Instances - The Server Model

With the server model, each process instance of the SDL specification represents a server that processes signals or other events (e.g. timeouts, continuous signals or spontaneous transitions). Thus, process instances can be considered as active entities of the runtime environment or the operating system. Typical implementations map each process instance on a thread (or a process). The thread may be handled by the thread library provided by the operating system or a specific library that implements the SDL runtime environment. In either case, the library contains a scheduler that typically schedules the process instances in a round-robin fashion. Thus, each process instance gets a fair chance to test its trigger conditions and in case a trigger condition holds, executes the respective transition. This strategy also allows the system to handle continuous signals, i.e. to execute a transition not triggered by an input signal. Depending on whether transitions are preemptable by the underlying system or not, operations to ensure mutual exclusion have to be employed.

2.2 Communication between Process Instances - Data Copying

Typical protocol architectures follow the structure depicted in Fig. 1. The figure outlines the processing of an outbound packet.

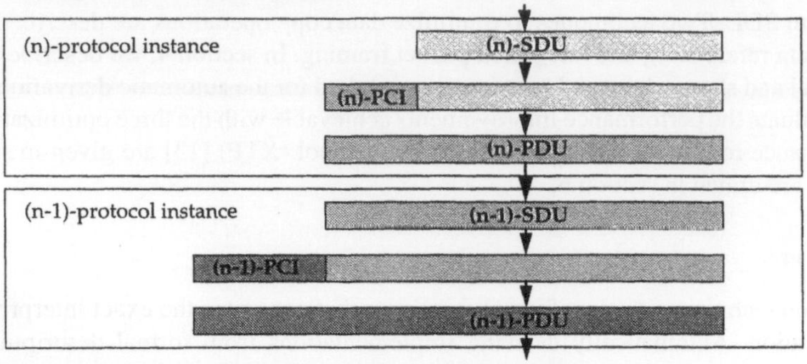

Fig. 1: Outline of protocol processing (outbound traffic)

The Service Data Unit (SDU) received by the (n)-protocol (i.e. the (n)-SDU) is processed by the (n)-protocol instance. Protocol processing for outbound traffic comprises two parts, handling the data provided in the SDU and the generation of the Protocol Control Information (PCI). The PCI is typically added as a prefix to the packet*. With many protocols, the SDU provided by the upper layer is simply copied into the Protocol Data Unit (PDU). Thus, the (n)-PDU typically results from adding the (n)-PCI to the (n)-SDU. For inbound traffic, the reverse is the case, i.e. the (n)-SDU passed to the upper layer is typically derived by stripping of the (n)-PCI from the (n)-PDU provided by the lower layer.

Conceptually, SDL assumes asynchronous buffered communication between process instances. Employing SDL for the specification of protocol architectures, the typical structure of an implementation derived from an SDL process is depicted in Fig. 2. The figure shows the processing of an outbound packet by a protocol instance. The processing of a packet by a single SDL process instance (i.e. a protocol instance or a part hereof) typically involves the following five data copy operations:

(1) *Input SDU*: First, the SDU is copied from the input queue of the process instance into its internal address space. The copy operation makes the SDU accessible for the receiving process instance.

(2) *Prepare PDU*: With communication protocols, often only a header (PCI) is added to the SDU before it is passed to the lower protocol instance (i.e. another SDL process). As a prerequisite for this, the SDU is copied in a different address area to provide space to add the header information (PCI).

(3) *Add PCI to PDU*: In order to complete the PDU, the SDU is typically prefixed with the PCI. This involves copying the PCI into the PDU.

(4) *Output PDU*: Next, the completed PDU (i.e. the SDU for the lower protocol instance) is copied into the output buffer of the process instance. The reasons for this copy operation are twofold: First, the copy operation saves the current state of the PDU which otherwise could be manipulated by actions following the output statement. Second, the buffering of

* Some protocols additionally add some PCI data as suffix to the SDU. Since there is no principle difference in dealing with prefixes and suffixes, we only describe the addition of a prefix.

the output ensures that the result of the transition is not provided to the other SDL processes before the transition is completed. This ensures that the atomicity of the transition is guaranteed, which might otherwise be violated, e.g. if a transition contains more than one output statement.

(5) *Transmit PDU*: Once the transition is completed, the PDU (i.e. the new SDU for the lower protocol entity) is transmitted to the input queue of the process instance that implements the lower protocol instance.

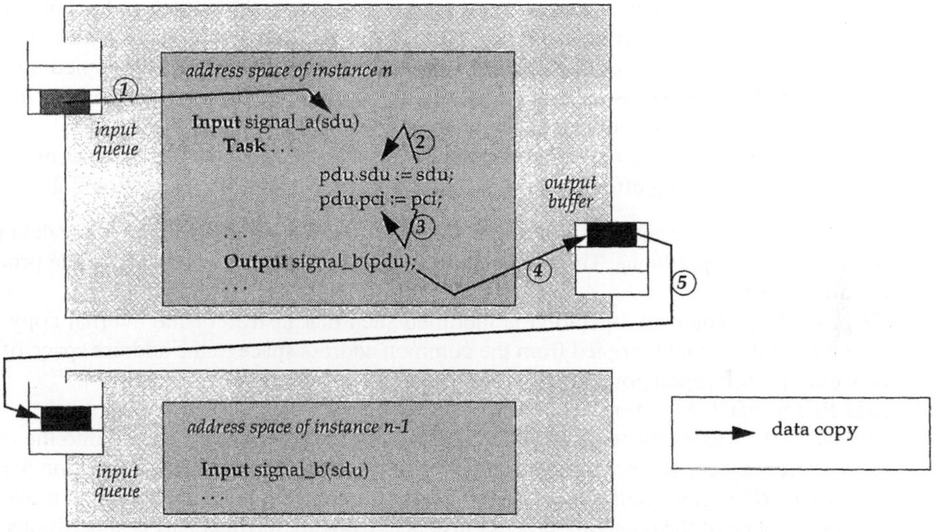

Fig. 2: Copy operations involved with the processing of a process instance

Typical commercial code generators employ additional copies to transmit signals between process instances. For example if a signal contains several parameters, the parameters are first copied in a contiguous data area before they are copied into the output buffer. A similar approach is taken for the input of signals with several parameters.

3 Elimination of Data Copies

Specifying protocol architectures with SDL, typically rather large messages are transmitted between the process instances. On the other hand, the actual amount of computation performed by the process instances that implement the protocol functionality is rather small. Thus, the elimination of copy operations provides a large potential to increase the efficiency of the derived implementation.

We suppose the application of two strategies to eliminate copy operations, namely data referencing and Integrated Packet Framing (IPF). While data referencing aims at the elimination of data copying between process instances, IPF is targeting at the elimination of data copying within the process instances.

3.1 Data Referencing

Data referencing deals with the elimination of copy operations employed to transmit signals between process instances. In order to support this, we divide the information transmitted between the process instances in two parts, namely a data and a control part. The data part contains the actual parameters of the signal. The control part contains the signal identification and a reference to the data part. The data part of a signal is of variable size. Conversely, the control part is of fixed size.

With data referencing, the control part of the signal is transmitted as before, employing queues. Conversely, the data part of the signal is stored in a common data area that is shared by the process instances. Thus, the data part is no longer copied into the queues and is not copied into the address space of the process instance. Instead, the data part is referenced by the process instance with the reference given in the control part. As a result, the data part is copied into the address space of the process instance only if an explicit copy operation is performed that copies the data into a variable of the address space of the process instance.

The application of the data referencing technique is depicted in Fig. 3. The application of the technique has the following effect on the five copy operations identified in section 2.2:

(1) *Input SDU*: Since the signal is kept in the common address space, the copy of the data part of the signal is superfluous. The control part is copied into the address space of the process instance as before.
(2) *Prepare PDU*: The copy operation is modified such that instead of the internal copy, the data part of the signal is copied from the common address space to the address space of the process instance (operation 2').
(3) *Add PCI to PDU*: As before.
(4) *Output PDU*: Analogous to operation 2, the data part of the signal is copied into the common address space. The control part is put in the output buffer as before (operation 4').
(5) *Transmit PDU*: As a result of operation 4', only the control part of the signal is moved to the input queue of the receiving process instance. Copying the data part is superfluous.

Applying the data referencing technique, two out of five operations to copy the data part could be removed. In addition, the technique allows for a simplification of the queuing mechanisms due to the queuing of structures of fixed sized, compared to the large variable-sized structures needed to hold the whole signal. A similar approach is applied by the SDT Cmicro codegenerator [17].

The described technique does not violate the semantics of SDL. This is because our implementation of output statements still ensures that a copy of the current state of the respective signal is made. In addition, the signal can be referenced by the receiving process instance only after the sending process instance has completed the transition. This is because the reference to the signal is copied into the input queue of the receiving process instance after the transition has been completed.

The only prerequisite for the application of the data referencing technique is the availability of a shared address space accessible by the communicating process instances. For example, if the sending process instance communicates with a network adapter card or another processor that does not share the same memory, the copy operation 5 can not be eliminated.

A comparison of two implementations of XTP according to the server model, one with and one without data referencing shows a performance gain of a factor of 6.1 for the implementation that employs data referencing (see section 5 for details).

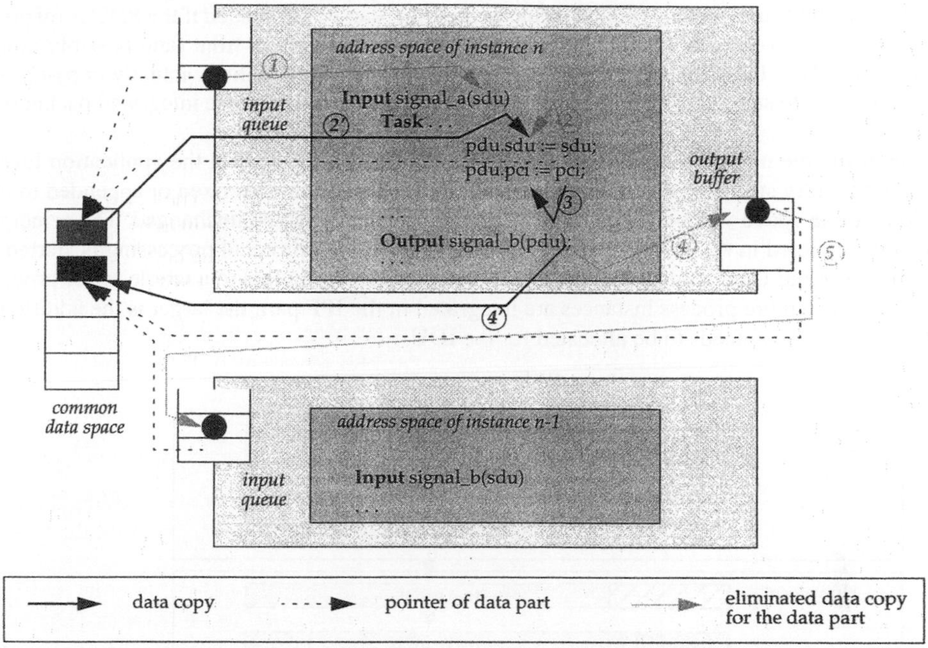

Fig. 3: Copy operations with the application of data referencing

3.2 Integrated Packet Framing (IPF)

Different from the data referencing technique described above, IPF aims at the elimination of copy operations within the process instances. The motivation for the strategy is the fact that with many protocol instances only a small part of the packet is changed, while most of the data contained in the packet are passed-through unchanged.

In general, four cases can be identified:

(1) The input signal is passed to the output without changes. Examples are multiplexers and to some extend routers.
(2) Some additional data are added to the front or/and the tail of the packet. This is typically the case with outbound traffic.
(3) Some data are removed from the front or/and the tail of the packet. This is typically the case with inbound traffic.
(4) The output signal derived is completely different from the respective input signal. This is the case with protocol instances employing encoding/decoding, encryption, segmentation, fragmentation or stuffing.

The last case is the only case where the data are completely changed by the process instance. All other cases pass at least a part of its input data directly to the output. These cases carry a potential for optimizations by eliminating copy operations. In the first and the third case, the copy operation can be eliminated completely.

In the second case, the copying of the incoming SDU can be eliminated if the SDU is mapped in the address space such that enough memory space is available in front (and possibly at the tail) of the SDU. In this case, the PCI can be added to the SDU without actually copying the SDU. In order to support this for a set of protocol instances, we introduce integrated packet framing (IPF).

The principle of IPF is to allocate at a higher protocol layer (typical the application layer) enough memory space for an SDU such that all PCIs subsequently prefixed or appended to the packet can be added without actually copying the part that is passed unchanged. The principle of IPF is depicted in Fig. 4. The memory space allocated when protocol processing is started is called Integrated Data Unit (IDU). Note that IPF is typically applied to a whole set of process instances. The more process instances are integrated in the IPF part, the larger is the additional memory space that needs to be allocated for the IDU.

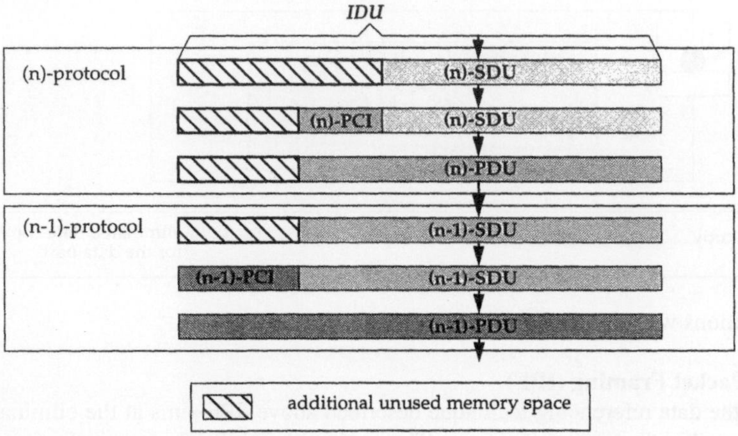

Fig. 4: Reservation of memory (IDU) for the application of IPF

The application of IPF to a process instance is shown in Fig. 5. The application of IPF (in conjunction with data referencing) has the following effect on the copy operations: Copying the SDU into a new address area is no longer needed. Thus, the copy operation 2' (see Fig. 3) can be eliminated. The copy operation 3 is modified such that the PCI is copied directly into the IDU, i.e. the common data space (operation 3'). In case no PCI is added to the SDU, the copy operation 3' is not present. This is often the case for inbound traffic and with multiplexers and routers. Provided that there is no write access to the IDU after it is output and the transition contains a single output for the IDU only, the copy operation 4' can be eliminated as well. This is often the case for protocol processing. In case a write access exists after the output, a change of the SDL specification can replace the write access to the IDU by equivalent operations without changing the semantics of the specification. In case the IDU is output more than once in a transition, the elimination of the copy operation 4' can be applied to one of the outputs only. For the other outputs, the IDU needs to be copied to avoid conflicts.

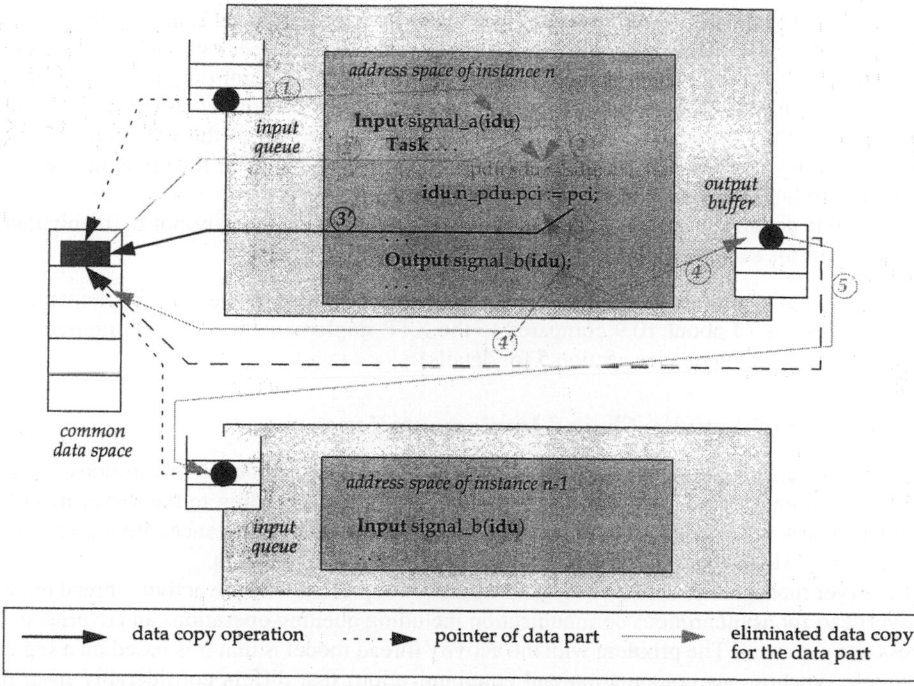

Fig. 5: Copy operations with the application of IPF and data referencing

In general, the automatic transformation of an arbitrary SDL specification to an equivalent SDL specification that applies IPF is rather complex. In addition, the effective application of IPF involves knowledge not present in the SDL specification itself, for example the probabilities for the execution of different execution branches of the SDL specification. A related issue is the selection of the appropriate size of the IDU to hold the PCIs subsequently added. This may vary depending on the state of the process instances as well as the exact contents of the packet.

In case the SDL specification has been prepared to support IPF, the derivation of code that implements IPF is straight-forward. The prerequisites for the SDL specification to support the automatic derivation of code that implements IPF are as follows:

(1) The respective IDUs have to be defined such that enough free memory space is available to allow the process instances manipulating the IDU to add the respective PCIs. In case no data are added, no extra memory needs to be allocated.
(2) The manipulation of a copy of the input signal (i.e. the parameters) has to be replaced by the direct manipulation of the input signal. Thus, the input signals can be manipulated directly in the shared address space.
(3) The parameter name of the input signal has to be identical to the parameter name of the output signal on which IPF is applied. This allows the codegenerator to identify the cases where IPF can be applied.
(4) In case several outputs of a transition specify the same parameter name on which IPF is applied, IPF may only be applied to one of the outputs. For the other outputs, the parame-

ter has to be copied to avoid the case that several process instances concurrently manipulate the same data. However, since in SDL it is not possible to specify to which output IPF is applied, we do not recommend to apply IPF in case of several outputs with identical parameters names. This is because an arbitrary selection of one of the outputs to apply IPF may violate the semantics. This is due to the fact that the size of the IDU is determined based on the path the IDU takes through the SDL system. Thus, an IDU may not be large enough to hold the data added to it on a different path.

(5) The input parameter which is passed with the output statement may not be manipulated later on in the same transition.

The joint application of IPF and the data referencing technique to the XTP implementation exhibits a speedup of about 10.9 compared to the XTP implementation solely employing the data referencing technique (see section 5 for details).

4 Derivation of Activity Thread Implementations

Due to the semantic similarities between SDL and the server model (asynchronous computation and communication), the automatic derivation of code according to the server model is straight-forward. In contrary, with the activity thread model, process instances are implemented by procedures. Thus, communication is implemented by procedure calls.

The server model exhibits extra overhead which is not present with the activity thread model, e.g. overhead for asynchronous communication including queuing operations and overhead for process management. The problem with the activity thread model is that it is based on a semantic model (synchronous computation and communication) that differs considerably from the SDL model. Thus, special care has to be taken to correctly map the semantics of SDL on activity threads.

In order to apply the activity thread model rather than the server model to derive code, the following differences between the two models have to be taken into account:

- The active elements in the server model are the protocol entities. In general, each entity is implemented by a thread (or process) of the operation system or the SDL runtime environment. The execution sequence of the events is determined by the scheduling strategy of the operating system or the runtime environment. Communication is asynchronous via buffers.
- The activity thread model is event-driven. It supports an optimal execution sequence of the events. With the activity thread model, one event is handled at a time. Processing of subsequent events is not started before the first event has been completely processed. The complete processing of an external input event by the system is denoted as activity thread. Communication is synchronous, i.e. no buffers are employed. Thus, the model is well suited for the layer-integrating implementation of protocols.

4.1 Principle and Problems with Activity Threads

The transformation strategy chosen in our approach is outlined in Fig. 6. The SDL specification (or a part hereof) is mapped on the main procedure *AT* which controls the execution of the activity thread. Each SDL process is implemented by a procedure. For the moment, let's assume that each output statement of an SDL process is replaced by the call of the respective procedure which implements the SDL process that receives the signal.

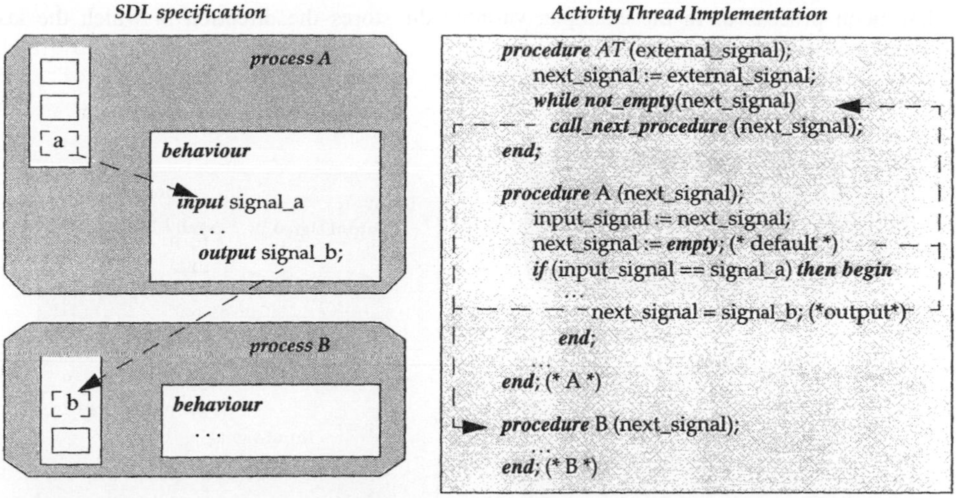

Fig. 6: Basic strategy for the derivation of activity threads from SDL specifications

Thus, the next executable transition is defined by the signal itself, the state and the input statement of the process receiving the signal. The sequence of the output and input statements (output'input ... output'input ...) results in a sequence of procedure calls, i.e. an activity thread. The activity thread is completed when the event has been completely processed by the respective SDL processes. Each procedure call corresponds to a transition executed on a signal. In case the transition has a simple structure, i.e. input'action(s)'output, the simple transformation strategy described above can be applied. Thus, each output can be directly translated to a procedure call. However, SDL also allows to specify the following variants:

- transitions not triggered by an input signal,
- transitions performing an action after an output,
- transitions with multiple outputs, and
- transitions without output.

A transition without an output simply results in the termination of the activity thread. For the other cases, special care has to be taken to ensure conformance with the semantics of SDL. In particular, the simple transformation of an output statement to a procedure call is no longer possible. In the following, we discuss the semantic problems with these transition types and provide solutions to preserve the semantics.

- **Transitions performing an action after an output**

  The simple replacement of an output statement by the call of the respective procedure (implementing the SDL process receiving the signal) may violate the atomicity of the transition. An example for the possible violation of the atomicity of a transition is given in Fig. 7. The figure shows two communicating process instances, L2 and L3. For example let's assume that L3 implements a routing function. A signal e1, received by process instance L2 is routed to process instance L3. From L3 it is transmitted to the medium via L2. Within L2, the variable dir is employed to store information about the last event that has been processed. In the example, variable dir stores the direction in which the last signal has been transmitted.

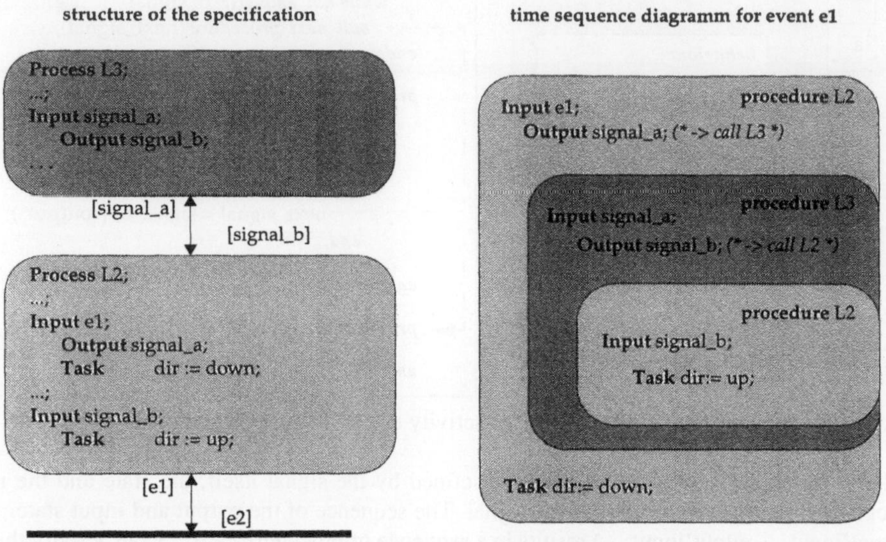

Fig. 7: Example for the possible violation of the atomicity of a transition

Our approach is to defer the procedure call until the transition has been completed. Depending on the instructions following the output statement, a copy of the output signal may be needed in order to preserve the semantics. As outlined in Fig. 6, this is implemented by the generic procedure *call_next_procedure* which calls the respective procedure after the transition has been completed. From the viewpoint of the communicating process instances this represents a transformation of synchronous communication to asynchronous communication. This is because the procedure implementing the receiving process instance is no longer called by the sending process itself. Instead, the procedure is called by the main procedure *AT*.

- **Transitions not triggered by an input signal**
  In SDL exist transitions which are not triggered by input signals. These are called *continuous signals*. These transitions are triggered only if the following conditions hold: First, there is no signal available that activates a transition. Second, its boolean condition evaluates to true. Since there is no signal to be mapped on a procedure call, transitions with no input signal cannot be implemented by an activity thread. Thus, transitions with no input signal have to be removed during the refinement of the specification or an alternative implementation strategy has to be applied.

- **Transitions with multiple outputs**
  A transition may contain several output statements. In this case, a sequential call of the procedures, which implement the SDL processes to which the signals are sent, is not always possible. Fig. 8 shows an example where this may violate the semantics of SDL. In

the figure, the sequential execution of the two outputs of process P2 results in an overtaking of signal_c by signal_e. In other words, signal_e, which results from signal_d, reaches process P4 before signal_c. In case the processes P2, P3 and P4 communicate via non-delayed channels or signal routes, this clearly violates the semantics of SDL.

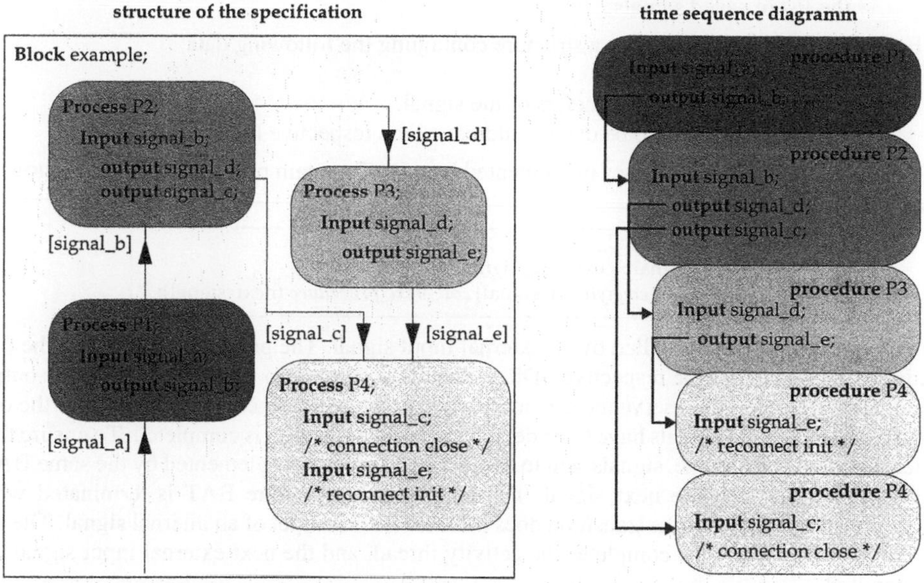

Fig. 8: Example for the overtaking of signals

The sequential call of the procedures may violate the semantics of SDL. This is due to the possibility of overtaking of signals. An approach to handle this is to split the activity thread in several activity threads. Thus, an additional activity thread is created for each additional output. To handle these additional activity threads, we have devised two process models, namely the *basic activity thread* model (BAT model) and the *extended activity thread* model (EAT). In the paper, we focus on the BAT model. The EAT model, which additionally supports parallel processing of events, is described in [10].

4.2 The BAT Model

With the BAT model, the SDL specification (or a part hereof) is mapped on a procedure. The procedure is triggered by a signal at one of the external interfaces of the BAT. The interfaces of the BAT implementation are synchronous, i.e. the external signals are always processed sequentially. No interleaving of the processing of two external signals (i.e. external to the BAT) is possible. Subsequent external signals are blocked until the previous signals have been processed.

A BAT is derived from a set of SDL processes by mapping their specification on the following structures:

- Each SDL process is transformed into a reentrant procedure that contains the executable code. With each procedure call, a single SDL transition is executed.

- With each instantiation of an SDL process, an Instance Control Block (ICB) is created. The ICB contains the following information:
  - all internal information (e.g. state information, internal variables),
  - the addresses of SDL processes (*offspring*, *parent*, *self*, *sender*),
  - the address of the reentrant procedure,
  - the list of saved signals.
- Each signal is implemented by a structure containing the following data:
  - the signal type,
  - the reference to the parameters of the signal,
  - the next procedure to be called (address of the respective ICB).

For each set of SDL processes implemented by a BAT, a main procedure with the following structure is generated:

```
procedure BAT (external_signal)
        next_signal := external_signal;
        while not_empty(next_signal) call_next_procedure (next_signal);
```

The procedure BAT is called by an external input signal. The procedure BAT calls the procedures implementing the respective SDL processes according to the structure of their output statements. In order to preserve the semantics of SDL in the presence of an action after the output statement, output signals have to be delayed until the transition is completed. To ensure this, internal output signals (i.e. signals sent to another SDL process implemented by the same BAT) are stored in the variable next_signal. The loop of the procedure BAT is terminated when next_signal is empty, i.e. the transition does not execute an output of an internal signal. The termination of the loop also completes the activity thread, and the next external input signal can be handled.

As described above, special care has to be taken for the case that the BAT contains an SDL process with multiple outputs within a transition. With our approach, multiple outputs are handled by the creation of additional activity threads. One additional activity thread is created for each additional output statement within a transition. These additional activity threads are managed by the AT_list. The management of the activity threads in the AT_list guarantees an execution order that is in accordance with the semantics of SDL. However, note that with the BAT approach, the term „activity thread" does not refer to a thread of the operating system. Instead the activity threads are managed by the main procedure BAT itself. The term „activity thread" denotes the execution path a signal takes through the SDL specification. The AT_list is used to schedule the activity threads currently present in the BAT. Note that after the arrival of an external signal, the AT_list contains exactly one activity thread. Several activities only emerge when a transition with multiple outputs is executed. In this case, the activity threads in the AT_list are scheduled according to the Round Robin principle. Only one procedure, i.e. one transition, is executed per iteration of the loop. Thus, the activity threads (or with other words, the internal signals) of the BAT are executed in a quasi-parallel manner. When an activity thread terminates, it is removed from the AT_list. The main procedure returns after the last activity thread of the BAT has terminated.

In the case that the BAT implements SDL processes with several output statements within a transition, the following procedure is generated for the BAT:

```
procedure BAT (external_signal)
        put external_signal in AT_list
        while (list_not_empty(AT_list)) do
                for_all_elements AT in AT_list do begin
                        next_signal := signal_of(AT);
                        next_signal := call_next_procedure (next_signal);
                        if empty(next_signal) then remove AT from AT_list;
                end
```

Special care has to be taken to handle save constructs. In case a save construct is encountered, i.e. there is a signal that has to be saved for the next state, the activity thread has to be deactivated. Since the BAT model does not support concurrency, the activity thread has to be removed from the AT_list and put in the save list of the ICB. The respective signal is again added to the AT_list after the next transition of the instance has been executed.

5 Measurements of the Xpress Transfer Protocol - A Case Study

In order to evaluate the performance improvements achievable with the introduced strategies, we have applied our optimization techniques to the Xpress Transfer Protocol (XTP), rel. 3.6 [13]. For our experiments, we have semi-automatically derived code according to the activity thread model (BAT) and the server model and have applied the two optimization techniques described, namely data referencing and IPF. All the measurements were taken for a single connection of the XTP. The implementation platform has been a SUN SPARC 20 with two processors running the *Solaris* operating system (rel. 2.5).

For the measurements, a test environment has been implemented that comprises the service user which generates the data stream and measures its duration, and a virtual medium (i.e. an SDL process) to implement the communication between the protocol entities. The size of the packets transmitted in the experiments was 64 bytes, the number of packets transmitted for each experiment were 100, 300 and 500, respectively. The XTP service we used was the connection-oriented unconfirmed data transfer. The measurements do not take into account the initialization phase.

The first series of experiments compare different server model implementations. **Fig. 9** shows the time to process 100 packets with the different server model implementations.

The plain server model implementation without any of the optimization techniques applied exhibits a runtime of 2065 msec. to process 100 packets. With the application of data referencing, the runtime dropped to 337 msec. This corresponds to a speedup of 6.1. Additionally applying IPF to the implementation, a further reduction of the runtime to 31 msec. could be achieved. This corresponds to an additional speedup of 10.9 compared to the implementation solely applying data referencing. The overall speedup achievable with the two optimization techniques compared to the plain server model implementation is 66.6.

The second series of experiments compares the server model with the activity thread model. For all the measurements, the data referencing technique as well as integrated packet framing has been applied. The results of the measurements are given in **Fig. 10**. The measurements show that the activity thread implementation achieves a considerable speedup compared to the server model implementation. The time to process 100 packets with the optimized activity thread implementation is 4.7 msec. Compared to the optimized server model implementation, the optimized activity thread implementation exhibits a speedup of 6.4.

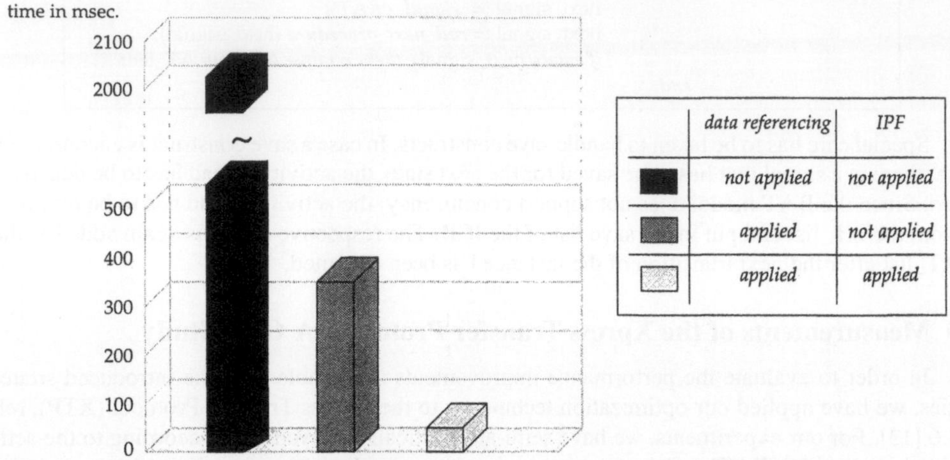

Fig. 9: Applying data referencing and IPF to the server model implementation of XTP

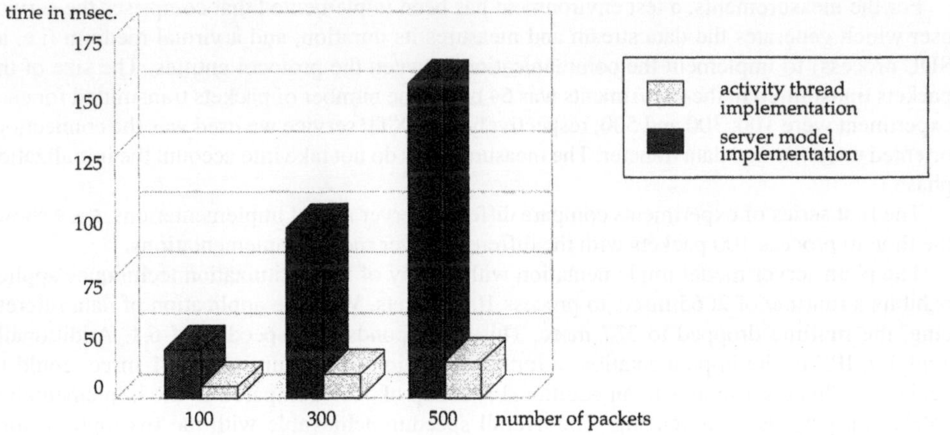

Fig. 10: Quantitative comparison of the server model and the activity thread model (applying data referencing and IPF)

The overall speedup that has been achieved with the joint application of the activity thread model, data referencing and integrated packet framing is 431. The measurements also show that with an increasing number of packets imposed on the system, the runtime of the server model is increasing in a nonlinear fashion. For example, the speedup of the activity thread implementation compared to the server model implementation is 7.1 for 500 packets, compared to a speedup of 6.4 for 100 packets. This is probably due to the increase of the overhead incurred with the server model to handle the queues which is not present with the activity thread model.

6 Conclusions

In the paper, three techniques to improve the efficiency of code derived from SDL specifications have been described. The data referencing technique supports the minimization of communication cost between process instances that share a common address space. Integrated packet framing allows to minimize copying overhead within process instances. The activity thread model supports the minimization of overhead for process management. Besides integrated packet framing, the techniques are well known from the manual implementation of protocol architectures. We have shown how and under which circumstances these optimization techniques can be applied. While the data referencing technique can be applied to arbitrary SDL specifications, some prerequisites have to be fulfilled to apply integrated packet framing and activity threads. However, the changes necessary for the SDL specification to automatically apply the two optimization techniques are rather small. In any case, no additional information is needed that is beyond the scope of SDL.

In order to evaluate the usefulness of the three optimization techniques for the automatic code generation from SDL specifications, we have semi-automatically applied the techniques to the Xpress Transfer Protocol (XTP). The measurements show that an enormous speedup can be achieved with each of the techniques. The data referencing technique and the activity thread model represent approaches that can be applied to a wide range of applications. Conversely, integrated packet framing provides a gain only for applications where a large part of the data are passed through the SDL processes without actually modifying them.

Currently, we are working on a codegenerator for SDL that supports the described techniques. The codegenerator is part of the DO-IT toolbox [12], an approach to support the efficient implementation of SDL specifications on sequential as well as parallel systems. The DO-IT toolbox aims at the systematic integration of performance aspects in all phases of the development process. The toolbox supports the specification of performance requirements as well as the analysis of SDL specifications for performance bottlenecks and constructs that prevent the automatic derivation of efficient code.

References

1. Abbott M., Peterson L.: Increasing network throughput by integrating protocol layers. IEEE/ACM Transaction On Networking, 1(5), 1993, pp. 600-610.
2. Ahlgren B., Gunningberg P., Moldeklev K.: Increasing Communication Performance with a Minimal-Copy Data Path Supporting ILP and ALF. Journal of *High Speed Networks*, 5(2), 1996, pp. 203-214.
3. Braun T., Diot C.: Protocol implementation using integrated layer processing. *ACM SIGCOMM*, 1995.
4. Clark D.D. et al: An Analysis of TCP-Processing Overhead. *IEEE Communications Magazine*, 1989.
5. Clark D.D., Tennenhouse D.L.: Architectural considerations for a new generation of protocols. *ACM SIGCOMM*, 1990, pp. 200-208.

6. Diot C., de Simone R., Huitema C.: Communication protocols development using Esterel. In HIPPARCH '94, First International Workshop on *High Performance Protocol Architectures*, INRIA, Sophia Antipolis, France, 1994.
7. Fischer J.: An Environment for SDL'92. *Systems Analysis Modeling, Simulation*, Sydow A. (ed.), Gordon & Breach Science Publ., New York 1993, pp. 107-124.
8. Gotzhein R. et al: Improving the Efficiency of Automated Protocol Implementation Using Estelle. Computer Communications 19 (1996) 1226-1235.
9. Held T.; Koenig H.: Increasing the Efficiency of Computer-aided Protocol Implementations. *Protocol Specification, Testing and Verification XIV*, Vuong S., Chanson S. (eds.), Chapman & Hall, 1995, pp. 387-394.
10. Henke R., Mitschele-Thiel A., König H., Langendörfer P.: Automated Derivation of Efficient Implementations from SDL Specifications. Technical Report 006/96, FIN / IRB, Otto-von-Guericke-Universität Magdeburg, 1996.
11. Leue S., Oechslin P.: On Parallelizing and Optimizing the Implementation of Communication Protocols. IEEE/ACM Transactions on Networking, 4(1), 1996.
12. Mitschele-Thiel A., Langendörfer P., Henke R.: Design and Optimization of High-Performance Protocols with the DO-IT Toolbox. In Bredereke J., Gotzhein R. (eds.): Protocol Specification, Testing and Verification XVI / Formal Description Techniques IX, Chapman & Hall, 1996, pp. 45-60.
13. Protocol Engines Inc.: Xpress Transfer Protocol Definition. Revision 3.6, 1992.
14. Steigner C., Joostema R., Groove C.: PAR-SDL: Software design and implementation for transputer systems. Transputer Applications and Systems '93, R. Grebe et al. (Ed.), vol. 2, IOS Press.
15. Svobodova L.: Implementing OSI Systems. IEEE Journal on *Selected Areas in Communications*, 7(7),1987, pp. 1115-1130.
16. Telelogic Malmö AB. SDT 3.0 User's Guide, SDT 3.0 Reference Manual, Telelogic, 1995.
17. Telelogic Malmö AB. SDT Cmicro Package - Technical Description, Telelogic, 1996.
18. Verilog: GEODE - Technical Presentation, Verilog, 1994.
19. Watson R.W., Mamrak S.A.: Gaining Efficiency in Transport Services by Appropriate Design and Implementation Choices. *ACM Transactions on Computer Systems*. 5(2), 1987, pp. 97-120.

SDL '97: TIME FOR TESTING - SDL, MSC and Trends
A. Cavalli and A. Sarma (Editors)

Industrial Strength Code Generation from SDL

N. Mansurov [a] A. Chernov, A. Ragozin

[a]Institute for System Programming Russian Academy of Sciences
25 B. Kommunisticheskaya
109004 Moscow Russia
e-mail: nick@ispras.ru

Tool support for *refinement* of SDL models into industrial-strength software is discussed. We present a very industry–oriented approach to automatic code generation controlled by annotations. Our *coarse-grained annotations* control the gross structure of the generated code. Our *fine-grained annotations* are used to integrate automatically generated and hand written code. The refinement process consists in adding hand written annotations to the SDL model and re-running automatic code generation. We propose *target language extensions* (TLE) to SDL for representation of refined SDL models. Advantages and limitations of this approach are discussed.

1. Introduction

SDL-based software development attracts growing attention of telecommunication industry [10]. Other industries where embedded control software is being developed also become interested in SDL [11]. Usually SDL is combined with other languages and/or notations e.g. [5,6]. Currently SDL is used in several industrial strength methodologies [1,9]. The following features of SDL are important for industrial software development:

- SDL allows to describe architecture aspects of software systems (unlike most mathematical–based formal methods and implementation languages);
- SDL has intuitive graphical representation;
- SDL allows to model implementations at very detailed level;
- SDL models are executable;
- SDL finite state machines provide powerful framework for real–time, reactive applications:

To summarize, SDL provides the right level of abstraction and presentation for both the functionality and the architecture of applications. This makes SDL adequate for detailed design modeling. Same features make SDL adequate for automatic derivation of applications from models. Indeed several SDL code generators exist [7]. However surprisingly few industrial projects are known, where automatically generated code is used in final products [4].

In this article we investigate approaches to formal design modeling and automatic code generation which might be more acceptable for industry. The result of this investigation is "annotation–based" approach to automatic code generation which supports refinement of SDL models.

We tried to keep our approach and this presentation independent of a particular target language for code generation. Any issues of readability, performance and the actual structure of the generated code will be addressed elsewhere.

The paper is organized as follows. In section 2 we analyze industrial requirements for formal design modeling and automatic code generation and present the main ideas of our approach. Refinement process of SDL models is discussed in section 3. In section 4 we outline several design issues for support of refinement. Section 5 presents the syntax and semantics of our extensions to SDL. A small example of SDL/TLE notation is provided in section 6. Section 7 describes our approach to coarse grained annotations to code generation from SDL. In section 8 we discuss existing tool support for the suggested approach. Finally, in section 9 we discuss advantages and limitations of our approach.

2. Automatic code generation in an industrial process

Most of the existing approaches to code generation from SDL could be characterized as "*traditional compilation*". Indeed, most SDL code generators use the "syntactic and semantic material" available in the target language to represent semantics of SDL constructs. The generated code has the same status as the code produced by a traditional compiler: it is supposed to be executed as a part of the final product but is never expected to be inspected or modified. Usually, any syntactic similarity between the original SDL model and the generated code is lost. Development team has to "trust" the code generator that the resulting code is correct with respect to the original SDL model. Usually, generated code has a limited number of interfaces with the environment. Thus, SDL is viewed as a programming language for some sophisticated SDL–machine. The "object code" for SDL machine is represented in a procedural language (e.g. C, or C++).

Industry in general seems to be reluctant to follow this approach. One of the reasons may be a considerable semantic gap between the SDL machine and the "target language machine" with numerous issues arising from trying to integrate code for these "machines". Obviously, *some* hand written code will always be required regardless of the progress in automatic code generation. This hand written code needs to be implemented at the level of some lower–level machine (e.g. C–machine, or even at the level of the "physical" target machine, i.e. in assembly language).

Another reason is that automatically generated code is often inefficient and typically consumes considerably more memory compared to hand-written code [4].

This builds a "barrier of trust" on introducing automatically generated code in industrial environments. Much more reports are available where SDL is used for design followed by manual implementation of code from SDL models. Note that this is a strict waterfall development process. There is high enough risk that the SDL model developed for design becomes obsoleted as soon as implementation activities starts. The cost of maintaining both the implementation and the code may be considered too high.

Our suggested approach is an attempt to lower this "barrier of trust". The status of the automatically generated code needs to be changed in several aspects.

Our proposed approach to code generation from SDL could be called "*code generator as a team member*". The new requirements for SDL code generator are as follows:

- generated code should be able to pass code inspections in the same way as any hand written code;
- generated code should be as close as possible to the original SDL model.
- seamless integration of hand written and automatically generated code should be achieved;
- generated code should conform as much as possible to the coding standards of the company;

This paper emphasizes the issues of integrating hand written and automatically generated code in such a way that SDL models are never abandoned after the design is finished, but are refined into a production–quality implementation while keeping the benefits of SDL.

SDL code generator should produce the **framework** of the application with the emphasis on *architecture aspects* (distribution and packaging of code, blocks, processes) and *functionality aspects* (input and output of signals, remote procedure calls, states and transitions).

Developers should be able to further **refine** this framework into the product by manually adding implementation details using the target language. Two modes of integration of the framework with hand written code need to be supported: 1) when the generated code is designed as a part of a hand written system ("SDL code in a non–SDL environment") and 2) when hand written code is added to the framework generated from SDL.

Adequate support is required for refinement of SDL models into final products. In our approach the code generator is controlled by **annotations**. Coarse grained annotations control various structural aspects of the system as well as run—time behaviour. Fine grained annotations attach implementation details to SDL model.

We propose certain language extensions to SDL for seamless integration of hand written and automatically generated code. We call our fine grained annotations "target language extensions" (TLE) and the resulting extended version of SDL - SDL/TLE.

In the next section we discuss the refinement process in more details. In section 4 we analyze several design issues for support of refinement. SDL/TLE constructs are discussed in section 5.

3. Refinement process

Several scenarios for the refinement process are possible depending on the level of tool support. One scenario would be to develop an SDL model using informal text for operations on data. This model could be kept as a compact and high–level reference document to the architecture of the system and its essential control flow. The code generator should be able to generate the framework of the implementation. At the next phase, the implementation language could be used to annotate the SDL model with the missing functionality.

Another scenario for the refinement of SDL models is to provide data operations using algebraic specifications [3], simulate the model and use SDL/TLE afterwards (when performance issues are considered). This scenario provides more guarantees for correctness since both the control framework and data handling are validated at SDL level. However we find this scenario very costly with respect to the learning curve which is required for providing an algebraic specification.

Yet another scenario is to use SDL/TLE during design modeling. Data definitions and operations can be specified directly in the target language without the need to learn data model of SDL [3]. To support this scenario, SDL tools need to simulate SDL/TLE. Since in most commercial SDL toolkits simulation is done by executing the suitable instrumented generated code produced by the code generator this requirement is easy to meet (see section 8).

We believe that the use of language extensions for implementation language refinements will allow to move from the strict waterfall development process (when SDL model is abandoned as soon as implementation activities starts) to spiral development process (when implementation details are added to the existing SDL model using language extensions).

In the next section we analyze several design issues for support of language extensions for refinement.

4. Design issues for support of refinement

In this section we consider the general design requirements for language support for process of refinement of SDL models into final products. Key idea of the suggested approach is to use language extensions to SDL so that hand written code can be seamlessly integrated with source SDL models.

1. The main design decision is to determine places of SDL specification where target language constructs could be used during refinement. In suggested approach refinable code includes all data–related constructs, including definition of datatypes, variables, operations on data, expressions, etc.

2. Target language constructs should be allowed in formal and actual parameters of signals, processes and procedures, etc. There is no way of transparent integration of target language expressions and target language formal parameters into SDL i.e. in such a way that syntactic correctness of the specification is preserved. We think that the use of special comments is not an adequate mean of introducing implementation language expressions into SDL. The syntax of SDL has to be extended and this extended language has to be supported by SDL tools. Suggested extensions allows much more tight integration with the implementation language than proposed in the forthcoming SDL–96 standard.

3. Target language part should not be analyzed or modified by SDL tools. This will allows to have a single front-end which can be reused for code generators for different target languages.

4. Integrating target language data into SDL does not require any new SDL/GR symbols. Some TLE constructs are provided in SDL/GR text symbols (target language

type definitions, operator definitions and variable definitions). Target language expressions occur inside other SDL/GR symbols.

5. Extended SDL should be independent of the target language. It should not contain any assumptions about lexical, syntax or semantic features of a particular target language.

6. Annotations for code generator should be separated from SDL specification whenever possible. SDL specification should provide compact and high–level document of the system.

The most challenging part of the dcsign is to integrate target language expressions. Let's consider the three groups of constructs:

Container constructs are independent of the SDL framework and can be refined into implementation language without restrictions (e.g. in `TASK`). Several additional TLE constructs are provided for various target language definitions (see section 5);

Built–in constructs are tightly integrated with SDL framework and can not be refined into target language. This group includes any expressions of the certain predefined sorts (`PID`, `DURATION` and `TIME`);

Transit constructs introduce some dependency to SDL framework (e.g. in `INPUT`, `OUTPUT`, `CALL`, `CREATE`, `VIEW`, `DECISION`). Transit expressions are passed between SDL objects or between different parts of code.

5. SDL Target Language Extensions (TLE)

Target Language Extensions to SDL are used to integrate hand written code directly into SDL models so that the SDL model is not abandoned at the implementation phase of development. The following TLE constructs are proposed:

- target language type definitions;
- target language operator definitions;
- target language variable definitions;
- target language expressions;

We would like to keep our approach target language independent. However there are certain assumptions for the structure of the generated code that should be done. We assume that the generated code consists of *modules*. Each module consists of two parts: *interface* part and *implementation* part. This distinction corresponds well to definition and implementation modules in MODULA-2 language or to a class definition and implementation in C++ language. When C language is considcrod as an implementation (or *target*) language, this corresponds to one header file and one `.c` file.

The following sections describe syntax and semantics of proposed extensions to SDL.

5.1. Uniform representation of target language code

The following construct is used for uniform representation of any target code annotations to SDL models:

Syntax:

```
<target code> ::=   '{' <text> '}'
```

Semantics:

The `<text>` can be an arbitrary text with the only assumption that "{" and "}" are properly nested. No escape characters inside the `<text>` are interpreted. Strings in target code are not distinguished, so "{" and "}" must be nested properly even in strings. Comments are also not interpreted. Symbols "{" and "}" are used as lexical delimiters of target code annotations and must not be used in SDL names.

5.2. Container constructs

SDL constructs in this section can be viewed as simple "containers" for target code. The main difference concerns the place in the generated code where the target code is emitted. There are no syntactic dependencies between the SDL framework and the target language constructs which can be used in container constructs. Semantic restrictions are described below.

Container constructs are considered as special forms of standard SDL constructs with the same keywords.

5.2.1. Target language type definition

Target language type definition is an extension of a `NEWTYPE` construct in SDL. Target language type definition is a container for implementation language data types.

Syntax:

```
<target newtype> ::= 'NEWTYPE' <target code>
```

Semantics:

Target language constructs in curly brackets after the keyword `NEWTYPE` are emitted to interface part of the module. Interface part is visible in the generated code for the current scope unit.

Any "type-related" definitions (e.g. class definitions, typedef, #define, #include, etc.) can be placed into this scope. It is guaranteed that the target code in all `NEWTYPE` scopes in one `sdl` scope unit is emitted in the same order as they occur in the SDL/PR source of this scope unit; Nothing can be said about the order in which target code from `NEWTYPE` scopes of different modules is emitted. In general, there is no guarantee that no other target code will be inserted between the contents of two successive target language `NEWTYPE` constructs (which means that target language type definitions should not be broken between several `NEWTYPE` scopes).

Target language `NEWTYPE` constructs which are contained in SDL Packages are transferred to the level of the `SYSTEM`. There is no particular order in which this is done.

5.2.2. Target language operator definition

Target language operator definition is an extension of OPERATOR construct of SDL.Target language operator definition is a container for any procedure definitions in implementation language.

Syntax:

```
<target operator> ::= 'OPERATOR' <target code>
```

Semantics:

Target language constructs in curly brackets after the keyword OPERATOR are emitted to the implementation module corresponding to the current scope unit. Target language code contained in OPERATOR construct is emitted at the global level **before** any other generated code for the current module. OPERATOR construct is expected to contain procedure definitions. Target language OPERATOR construct is not attached to any particular target language NEWTYPE construct (neither syntactically nor semantically). It is guaranteed that the constructs from all OPERATOR constructs are emitted in the same order in which they occur in the SDL/PR text of the scope unit. It is not guaranteed that other target language constructs are not emitted between the contents of two successive target OPERATOR constructs (which means that target language procedures should not be split between two OPERATOR constructs). No particular order of generation of OPERATOR constructs from different SDL scope units is guaranteed.

5.2.3. Target language variable definition

Target language variable definition is an extension of DCL construct of SDL. Target language variable definition is a container for variable definitions in implementation language.

Syntax:

```
<target dcl> ::= 'DCL' <target code>
```

Semantics:

Target language constructs in curly brackets after the keyword DCL are emitted to the area of variable definitions for the same scope unit where this construct occurs. This construct is expected to contain target language variable definitions.

The target code from all DCL constructs is guaranteed to be emitted in the same order as they occur in the SDL/PR source. Definitions from DCL construct are guaranteed to be visible throughout the whole module in which they occur. Some other variable definitions may be generated by the code generator. There are also several predefined variables (e.g. SELF, SENDER, PARENT, OFFSPRING) and predefined sorts (PId, Duration, Time) which can be used in hand written code.

5.2.4. Target language TASK

Target language TASK is an extension of TASK construct of SDL. Target language TASK is a container for complete executable statements of the implementation language.

Syntax:

```
<target task> ::= 'TASK' <target code>
```

Semantics:

Target language constructs after the keyword TASK are emitted into the body of the function which corresponds to the current SDL transition. The code for this function is generated to the implementation module for the current SDL scope unit. Target code from the TASK construct is guaranteed to be emitted into such a place relative to the generated code for other actions (SDL-generated or target language) that the order of execution is preserved.

5.3. Transit constructs

Transit constructs are used to integrate implementation language expressions into SDL models. Transit constructs operate on finer level of details compared to target language TASK construct, which only inserts complete statements. The main difficulty is that expressions are syntactically constrained by some non–trivial context is generated by the SDL code generator for the "host" construct.

To handle transit constructs, three semantically different forms of `<target code>` are introduces (all forms share the same syntax of `<target code>`):

- target language formal parameters
- target language expressions
- target language type

5.3.1. Target language formal parameters

Target language formal parameters extend SDL formal parameters in processes, procedures and remote procedures.

Syntax:

```
<target formal> ::= <target code>
```

Semantics:

Formal parameters (in processes, procedures and remote procedures) can be defined using target language. Each `<target formal>` is emitted unchecked into the corresponding context of the generated code. Both the type and the name of the formal parameter must be provided within the same annotation according to the particular syntax of the target language.

It is assumed that the information about the target language formal parameter includes its type. This assumption is important, since it does not allow us to e.g. to generate C code in the so called "traditional" (Kernighan-Ritchie) style where the information about the type of formal parameter is provided elsewhere.

5.3.2. Target language expressions

Target language expressions extend SDL expressions.

Syntax:

```
<target expr> ::= <target code>
```

Semantics:

Any target language code can be used instead of an SDL expression. This code is emitted unchecked into the corresponding context in the generated code (e.g. actual parameters in output, create request or procedure call).

The front-end views all target language types as a single type. The only form of semantic control is that the target language actual and formal parameters are used in corresponding positions. This approach allows to mix SDL and target language parameters in a single call.

5.3.3. Target language type

Target language type extend SDL formal parameters of procedures and timers.

Syntax:

```
<target type> ::= <target code>
```

Semantics:

This construct allows to use target language to define parameters of SDL signals and timers. Only the target language type of the parameter is contained in this scope. This construct is very similar to the `<target formal>` described above. In contrast, the name of the formal parameter is not provided here since the code generator should be able to generate its own names for parameters of the signal (to access them in `INPUT`, etc.).

Omitted parameters in outputs could not be supported because this requires certain assumptions about types of arguments (i.e. existence of an *undefined* value, etc.). It is only to check that the corresponding parameter has target language sort and in this case complain when the actual parameter is omitted (all target language sorts are viewed by the compiler front-end as one sort). Note also that `<target formals>` can be "non-transparent" for the front-end.

5.3.4. Target language decision

Target language decision extends `DECISION` construct of SDL.

Syntax:

```
<decision> ::= 'DECISION' <question> <end>
               <decision body> 'ENDDECISION'

<question> ::=    <expression> | <informal text>
               | 'ANY'         | <target formal> <target expr>

<answer> ::=
        <range condition> | <informal text> | <target expr>
```

Semantics:

SDL decisions are adapted to be used with target language extensions. **<target expr>** can only be used in rage when the question was provided as a target language expression. SDL **<range conditions>** must not be used with the target language question.

There exists a very strong dependency between target code and the generated framework in case of **<question>** expression in DECISION construct. **<question>** expression is matched to **<answer>** expressions using some ordering operators. This is a strong dependency because the SDL framework is responsible for switching to one of the transitions, but the value is provided by the expression.

Unfortunately, SDL decision needs a kind of counter–intuitive extension in order to support target language properly. Target language **<answer>** is a **complete** expression (as compared to SDL **range condition** which is a special syntactical unit). Our decision is to introduce a special variable (*question placeholder*) which stores the result of computation of the decision question. The question placeholder should then be used in **<target ranges>**. Question placeholder variable is introduced in **<target formal>** field of the question. This target language formal parameter must include both variable name and its type.

In the code generated for DECISION it is guaranteed that the value of the target question is computed once and then assigned to the question placeholder. It is guaranteed that the question placeholder is visible only in the code generated for the current DECISION. **<target range>** constructs are used to generate a cascade of if-then-else constructs in the target language, which compute the number of the transition to be executed.

5.4. Imperative operators

As it was mentioned in section 4 no transformation of target language expressions is performed. The consequence of this decision is that imperative operators can not be extracted from such expressions. The following three operators are provided as functions of the SDL framework.

The following operators are supported:

- Timer active expression;
- Now expression;
- PId expression;

Other operators (e.g. import(), view(), export(), any(), value returning procedure call) are not supported for target language extensions (but are of course fully supported for SDL expressions).

6. Example of sdl/tle notation

In this section we present a small example of the proposed SDL/TLE notation. Figure 1 demonstrates the use of target language variable declarations, target language TASK and target language decision constructs. Note the use of question placeholder in target language decision.

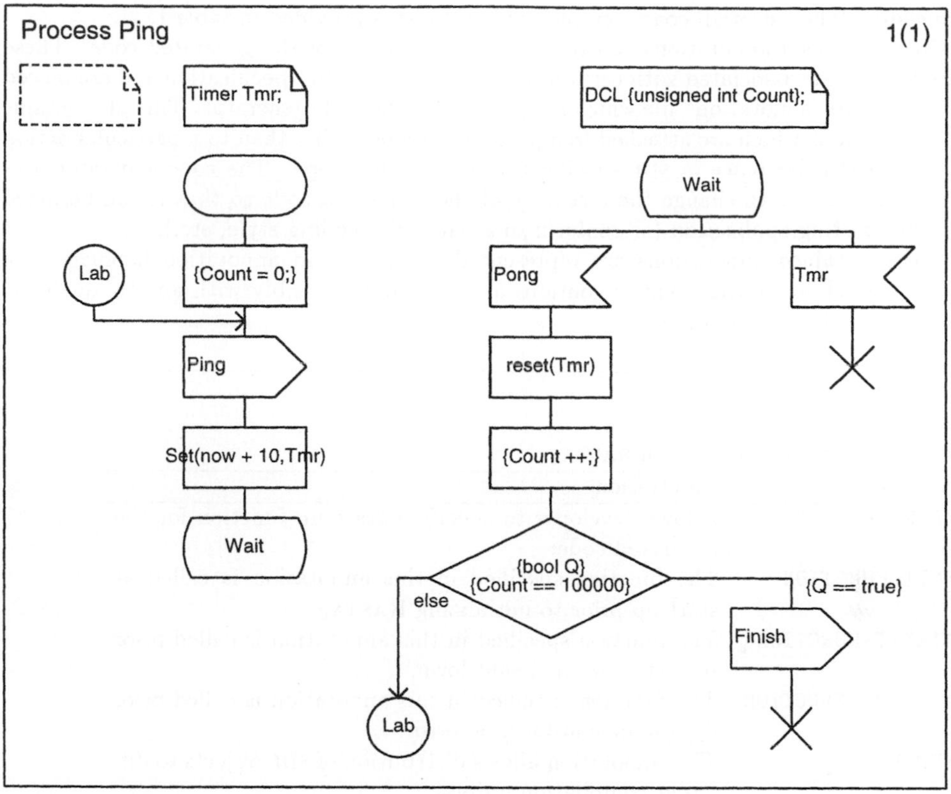

Figure 1. Example of SDL/TLE notation.

Figure 1 represents one of the processes from a well-known Ping–Pong model. On start transition process `Ping` sends the first `Ping` signal to its partner and enters state `Wait`. When reply from the partner (signal `Pong`) is available, process `Ping` increments message counter (implementation language variable `Count`) and checks whether the upper limit of messages is achieved. When the upper limit is achieved, `Ping` sends the farewell signal `Finish` to its partner and stops. Otherwise, `Ping` jumps to the label `Lab` and repeats the loop. As a precaution against infinite wait, timer `Tmr` is introduced. Before transition to state Wait the timer is set to expire after ten time units. When the timer signal is available in state `Wait`, the partner is considered unable to continue the game. In this case `Ping` stops.

7. Coarse grained annotations

In this section we describe coarse grained annotations for code generation supported by our RASTA translator [2]. Figure 2 outlines typical use of annotations in RASTA translator. The list of all coarse grained annotations is provided in table 1.

Coarse grained annotations control the gross structure of the generated code. These annotations are associated with certain scope units of the SDL specification and are placed in a separate "annotation" file which is available for the code generator. This file contains all annotations which are attached to a particular scope rather than to a particular action or to a particular place in SDL specification within the scope. The code generator uses these annotations to change the structure of the generated code so that it can be fitted into an existing application (or conform to a particular coding style, etc.).

Coarse grained annotations are represented as phrases in annotation language (see below). Each annotation phrase contains an SDL name (possibly with an SDL qualifier) plus some other information.

Table 1
Coarse grained annotations in RASTA

Keyword	Description
`MAIN-FUNCTION`	Allows developer to specify a start up function for the generated code;
`INIT-FUNCTION`	The function specified in this annotation is called at start-up prior to initializing RASTA;
`ATEXIT-FUNCTION`	The function specified in this annotation is called prior to system normal shutdown;
`ATERROR-FUNCTION`	The function specified in this annotation is called prior to system shutdown on error;
`SEPARATE`	This annotation allows distrbution of SDL objects to different compilation units;
`LIBRARIES`	This annotation allows developer to provide a list of libraries which are used for final linking of the SDL system;
`TASK`	This annotation allows developer to specify a set of blocks that should constitute a single task of a distributed SDL system. RASTA translator supports separation of a SDL system into a number of tasks. Each task executes in a separate address space as a separate process of the operating system. Tasks communicate between each other using a dedicated process called PostMaster;
`TASKLIB`	This annotation allows developer to provide a list of libraries which are used for linking of a particular task;
`SIGNAL`	This annotation allows developer to treat particular signal as a call of the procedure with the same signature. The name of the procedure is provided in the annotation;

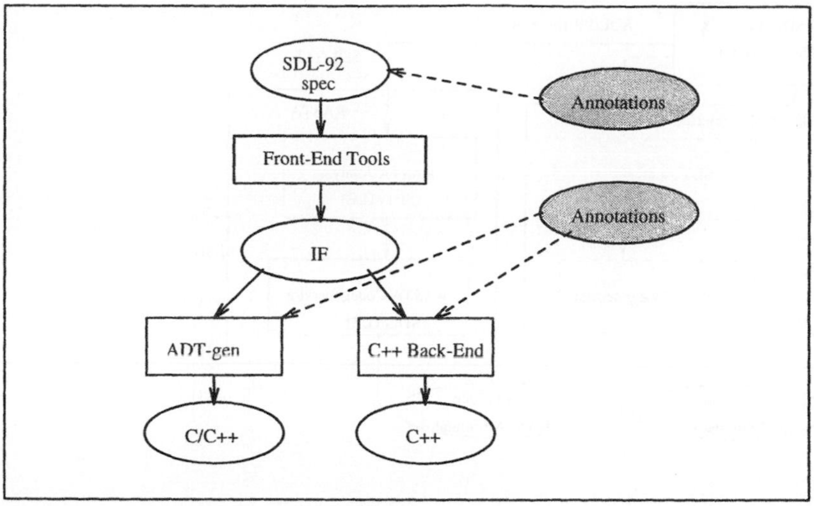

Figure 2. Annotations in RASTA toolkit.

8. Tool support

Our RASTA toolkit [2,3] provides support for all scenarios of refinement using SDL/TLE described in section 3.

Figure 2 outlines the architecture of the annotations–directed code generation in our SDL toolkit RASTA [2]. At figure 2 C++ Back-End is an annotations–driven code generator. ADT-gen is a code generator for algebraic specifications of data [3].

Figure 3 demonstrates our experience in using SDL/TLE with commercial tools. We used the SDL Graphical Editor of SDT [8] to produce SDL/TLE programs. With the syntax checking option turned off, the Editor is capable for generating SDL/PR with target code. SDL/PR output is re-routed to RASTA toolkit (analyzer and code generator) which translates SDL/TLE into C++ code instrumented for simulation. SDT Public Interface [8] is used to control simulation of SDL/TLE models using SDT Simulator GUI.

9. Conclusions

We presented our approach to industrial–strength code generation from SDL. In this approach, the code generator is viewed as a "member" of the development team rather than as a traditional compiler. We believe that instead of generating some kind of "object code" the SDL code generator should generate the framework of the embedded control application (processes, input and output of signals, remote procedure calls, states and transitions) and allow developers to refine this framework into the product by using the actual target programming language. Such code generator might be usable in an industrial environment.

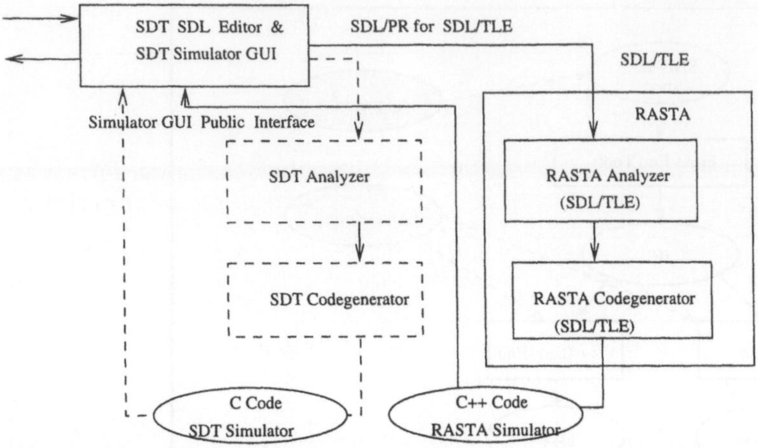

Figure 3. SDL/TLE support using SDT SDL Editor and RASTA toolkit.

The generated code should be readable enough to be able to pass code reviews (unlike "object code" produced by a traditional compiler). The main requirement for our code generator is to provide great flexibility of the interfaces to the generated code so that other developers can refine SDL specifications into products.

We view this refinement process as adding annotations to the SDL specification. We distinguish coarse-grained annotations which control the gross structure of the generated code and fine-grained annotations which are used to refine SDL model into implementation. "Target language extensions" (TLE) to SDL are proposed which can be used to represent refined SDL models.

SDL/TLE language provides more support for seamless integration of hand written and automatically generated code than is available SDL–92/96 standard. For example, SDL/TLE language allows to declare global variables outside processes and to mix SDL expressions and implementation language data in an SDL model.

Approach suggested in this paper has certain limitations. Introducing implementation language constructs into SDL models can make them less robust and will significantly complicate any in–depth semantical analysis of such models, including formal verification. Another limitation of our approach is that detection of errors in target language annotations is delayed until the compiler of the target language is run. This is a consequence of our decision to keep SDL/TLE front–end independent of the target language (see section 4).

Last limitation is easy to overcome simply by parsing error messages from the compiler of the target language and mapping them back to SDL model (e.g. in diagram editor). Robustness issue is not a limitation of our approach *per se*, since designers are using implementation languages anyway. Complicated semantical analysis of SDL/TLE models represents the major trade–off of our approach.

Our approach is very much oriented towards the needs of designers. The main goal of SDL/TLE is to promote transition from manually developing code towards using automatic code generation. In this sense, SDL/TLE can be viewed as a powerful extension to the target language with the following benefits:

- SDL can be used for architecture description (features not available in implementation languages);
- SDL can be used for explicitly describing finite state machines;
- additional static control and verification can be provided by SDL tools;
- SDL/TLE code has more intuitive visual representation which makes it much more suitable for code inspections and documentation;
- automatic code generation controlled by annotations leads to a more uniform coding style;
- attractively low learning curve for introducing SDL into industrial environment (since designers need not learn how to use SDL data);

Language extensions for implementation language refinements allow to move from the strict waterfall development process (when SDL model is abandoned as soon as implementation activities starts) to spiral development process (when implementation details are added to the existing SDL model using language extensions). We believe that our approach allows wider acceptance of automatic code generation in industry.

REFERENCES

1. Z.100 (1993), CCITT Specification and Description Language (SDL), ITU-T, June 1994.
2. N. Mansurov, A. Kalinov, A. Ragozin, A.Chernov (1995), Design Issues of RASTA SDL-92 Translator, in SDL'95 with MSC in CASE (ed. R. Bræk, A. Sarma), Proc. of the 7-th SDL Forum, Oslo, Norway, 26-29 September, 1995, Elsevier Science Publishers B. V. (North–Holland), pp. 165–174.
3. N. Mansurov, A. Ragozin, A. Chernov, I. Mansurov, Tool Support for Algebraic Specifications of Data in SDL–92, in Formal Description Techniques IX: Theory, application and tools, (ed. R. Gotzhein, J. Bredereke), Proc. of the FORTE/PSTV'96 symposium, Germany, Kaiserslautern, 8-11 October 1996, Chapman & Hall, pp. 61–76
4. A. Mitschele–Thiel, P. Langendörfer, R. Henke, Design and Optimization of High–Performance Protocols with the DO-IT Toolbox, in Formal Description Techniques IX: Theory, application and tools, (ed. R. Gotzhein, J. Bredereke), Proc. of the FORTE/PSTV'96 symposium, Germany, Kaiserslautern, 8-11 October 1996, Chapman & Hall, pp. 45–60
5. D. Witaszek, E. Holz, M. Wasowski, S. Lau, J. Fischer, A Development Method for SDL-92 Specifications Based on OMT, in SDL'95 with MSC in CASE (ed. R. Bræk, A. Sarma), Proc. of the 7-th SDL Forum, Oslo, Norway, 26-29 September, 1995, Elsevier Science Publishers B. V. (North–Holland), pp. 339–348.

6. E. Inocêncio, M. Ricardo, H. Sato, T. Kashima, Combined Application of SDL–92, OMT, MSC and TTCN, in Formal Description Techniques IX: Theory, application and tools, (ed. R. Gotzhein, J. Bredereke), Proc. of the FORTE/PSTV'96 symposium, Germany, Kaiserslautern, 8-11 October 1996, Chapman & Hall, pp. 451–466
7. Demonstrations, in SDL'95 with MSC in CASE (ed. R. Bræk, A. Sarma), Proc. of the 7-th SDL Forum, Oslo, Norway, 26-29 September, 1995, Elsevier Science Publishers B. V. (North–Holland), pp. 373–388.
8. TeleLOGIC SDT 3.02, TeleLOGIC, Malmö AB, P.O. Box 4128, S-203 12 Malmö Sweden.
9. R. Bræk, Ø. Haugen, Engineering Real Time Systems in SDL, Hemel Hempstead, Prentice Hall International 0-13-034448-6.
10. G. Amsjø, A. Nyeng, SDL-based software development in Siemens A/S — experience of introducing rigorous use of SDL and MSC, in SDL'95 with MSC in CASE (ed. R. Bræk, A. Sarma), Proc. of the 7-th SDL Forum, Oslo, Norway, 26-29 September, 1995, Elsevier Science Publishers B. V. (North–Holland), pp. 339–348.
11. F. Goudenove, L. Doldi, Use of SDL to specify Airbus Future Navigation Systems, in SDL'95 with MSC in CASE (ed. R. Bræk, A. Sarma), Proc. of the 7-th SDL Forum, Oslo, Norway, 26-29 September, 1995, Elsevier Science Publishers B. V. (North–Holland), pp. 359–372.

X

SDL and other languages II

SDL '97: TIME FOR TESTING - SDL, MSC and Trends
A. Cavalli and A. Sarma (Editors)

IS OPEN-EDI A POTENTIAL AREA FOR USE OF MSC AND SDL?

Odile Troulet-Lambert

Eutelis SA, director consultant, Chairperson of ISO/IEC JTC1 SC30 on Open-edi. *

1. INTRODUCTION

Companies use EDI for the interchange of data between partners to conduct business transactions. Today, EDI requires the partners to have a prior agreement on the technical specifications serving as the basis for the interchange. In other words, EDI partners have to precisely define with their partners how the data is to be exchanged, as well as the exact semantic of the data and the context in which this data is exchanged. This restricts the use of EDI to long term business partnerships.

Enabling companies to perform EDI without the need of such prior agreement on technical specifications requires new standards that are currently being developed in ISO/IEC JTC1 SC30. These new standards need to be based on formal descriptive techniques.

The purpose of this paper is to inform the MSC-SDL community about this work and to identify some requirements on the Formal Descriptive Techniques that open-edi requires. This information should help the community to decide whether they have an interest in this work and whether they want to make the EDI community aware of the potential interest of the MSC and SDL environment for Open-edi.

The first section of this paper contains a summary of the International Standard that ISO and IEC recently approved, that is ISO IEC IS14662, entitled The Open-edi reference model. The second section contains a description of the type of specifications in Open-edi which require the use of formal descriptive techniques. The third section identifies a set of requirements on these formal descriptive techniques. Finally the paper identifies some potential benefits for the MSC-SDL community in case these languages are chosen for open-edi standards.

---

*EUTELIS SA, 26 rue Bénard, 75 014 Paris, FRANCE

E-MAIL : s=lambert-o O eutelis A= atlas C=fr; lambert-o@eutelis.atlas.fr;

2. ISO IEC IS 14 662, THE OPEN-EDI REFERENCE MODEL

This international standard specifies the framework for the integration of existing standards and the development of future standards for the inter-working of organisations via Open-edi. The concepts of open-edi scenario and open-edi transaction are the basis of this standard. An *open-edi scenario* is the formal specification of a class of business transactions having the same business goal. An *open-edi transaction* is a business transaction that is in compliance with an Open-edi scenario.

As an example of a business transaction, we will consider a "sales transaction", the goal of which is the transfer of ownership of some goods, against payment, between two parties, the supplier and the buyer. At a given time there is an infinity of occurrences of such business transactions that occur. This set of business transactions that have the same business goal forms a class. The formal specification of this class of business transactions is the open-edi scenario. This formal specification will in particular identify the event which initiates the business transaction, that is the dispatch of an order by the buyer. Also it will identify possible terminations for the business transaction. There are at least two possible terminations for this transaction : 1) the effective transfer of ownership of the goods, after the buyer has paid the supplier; 2) the refusal of the transaction by the supplier.

Any occurrence of this business transaction, for example between company A and company B is an open-edi transaction if it occurs in compliance with the formal specification, that is the open-edi scenario.

The Open-edi reference mode, ISO IEC IS 14 662, addresses two perspectives of business transactions. The first one is called the Business Operational View (BOV). It is limited to those aspects regarding the making of business decisions and commitments among organisations, which are needed for the description of a business transaction. The second perspective is called the Functional Service view (FSV). It is a perspective of business transactions limited to those information technology interoperability aspects of Information Technology Systems needed to support the execution open-edi transactions.

A set of standards is associated to each of these perspectives. The first one is called the BOV related standards. These standards provide the tools and rules to permit and ensure :

- the specification of an Open-edi scenario,
- the reusability of components of an Open-edi scenario,
- the harmonisation of components of an Open-edi scenario among different user communities.

The BOV related standards provide a specification of how to model the business and associated requirements as an Open-edi scenario, and includes the modelling standards containing the Open-edi description technique to be used. An *open-edi description technique* is a specification method such as a formal description technique, another methodology having the characteristics of a formal description technique or a combination of such techniques as needed to formally specify the components of an Open-edi scenario in a computer processible form.

The second set of standards is called the FSV related standards. It addresses the information technology (IT) interoperability aspects required from the IT systems used by organisations to engage in Open-edi transactions.

The BOV related standards are used for the production of Open-edi scenarios by user communities and the registration of open-edi scenarios by registration authorities. The FSV related standards are used by IT designers to produce IT systems compliant with these standards. These systems can be configured with Open-edi scenarios to enable the execution of Open-edi transactions. The following figure illustrates the use of these two sets of standards.

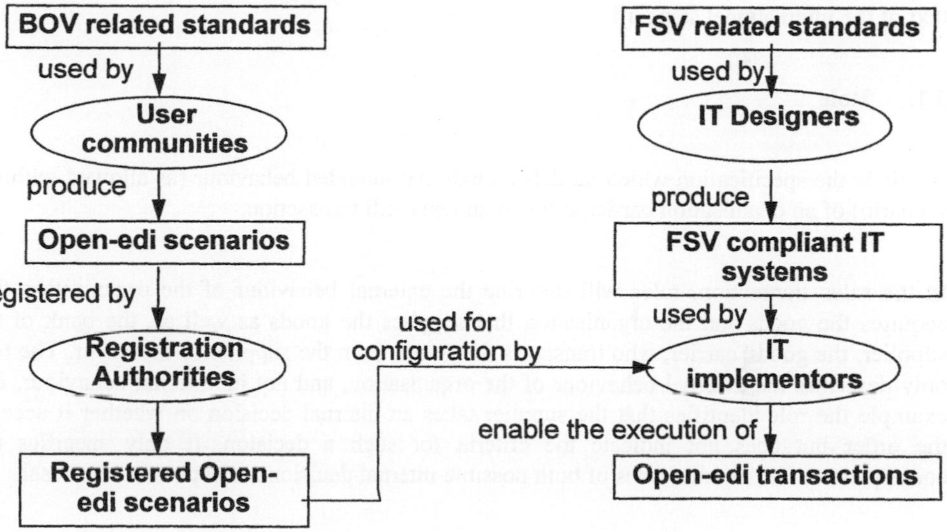

Figure 1. The use of BOV and FSV related standards

Both set of standards, will make use of formal descriptive techniques. However the BOV related standards are presently the first priority. The rest of this paper will therefore mainly concentrate on the use of FDT's within the BOV related standards.

Having briefly presented the content of the open-edi reference model, we will now describe the components of the open-edi scenarios. The specification of these components requires the use of formal descriptive techniques which will be included in the BOV related standards.

3. THE OPEN-EDI SCENARIO COMPONENTS

The open-edi reference model identifies three components of the open-edi scenario :

- roles,
- information bundles,
- scenario attributes.

Specifications of these components are made at an abstract level and are independent of matters such as data representation, coding or encoding. The open-edi reference model identifies different characteristics of each component which are to specified in the open-edi scenario. For each component, the present section describes only the characteristics that are pertinent for the purpose of this paper. For further information, the reader should refer to the text of the international standard.

3.1. Role

A role is the specification which models an external intended behaviour (as allowed within a scenario) of an organisation participating in an Open-edi transaction.

In the sales transaction, roles will describe the external behaviour of the organisation that acquires the goods and the organisation that supplies the goods as well as, the bank of the supplier, the goods' carrier, who transports the goods from the supplier to the buyer. The role only describes the external behaviour of the organisation, and not its internal behaviour. For example the role identifies that the supplier takes an internal decision on whether it accepts the order but does not indicate the criteria for such a decision. It only specifies the consequences for the other roles of both possible internal decisions, acceptation or refusal.

A role includes the specification of the allowable sequences of information bundles exchanges and the conditions in which a role is allowed to send an information bundle, such as : receipt of an information bundle, internal decision, timer expiration, exceptional condition or error.

A role also includes registration and management information related to the reusability of the role, such as : purpose of the role, business goal of the role, business rules controlling the role, regulations governing the role. Registration and information management will help different user communities to identify open-edi scenarios which fit their business needs and promote the reusability of open-edi scenarios by different communities.

3.2. Information bundles

An *information bundle* is the formal description of the semantics of the information exchanged by organisations participating in an Open-edi transaction. Information bundles are constructed using semantic components. A *semantic component* is a unit of information unambiguously defined in the context of the business goal of the business transaction. A semantic component may be atomic or composed of other semantic components.

An example of an information bundle is the formal description of an order, an invoice, a remittance advice. It could be for example a conceptual data model of the order, including the definition of each entity and attribute and the relationships between them with their cardinality. The account of the seller is an example of a semantic component, as well as the site to which the goods are to be delivered and the site to which the buyer is to be billed.

The specification of an information bundle is independent of data representation, coding and encoding. It describes the semantic (meaning) of semantic components and their relationship. In other words, these formal descriptions describe the semantics of the information that are exchanged between the organisations and are independent of the representation which is used to transfer the data values between the systems and to store the data on the local system.

3.3. Scenario attributes

Scenario attributes are the formal specification of information relevant to the whole of an open-edi scenario, i.e. information that is neither specific to a role nor to an information bundle. The scenario attributes include for example the relationships among roles, the relationships among different Information bundles.

Considering this short description of scenario components, it is possible to identify the requirements on the formal descriptive techniques which are needed in the BOV related standards.

4. REQUIREMENTS ON THE FORMAL DESCRIPTIVE TECHNIQUES

4.1. Introduction

The experts within working group 1 (WG1) of SC30 are presently working on the identification of requirements on formal descriptive techniques which need to be included in the open-edi descriptive technique, in the BOV related standards. This work is not completed at the time this paper is being written. The goal of SC30 WG1 is to produce a document identifying these requirements. This document can then serve as a call for proposals in order to receive information on existing standards which can fulfil these requirements. Once these formal descriptive techniques have been chosen by SC30, writing the BOV related standards can start.

This section of the paper includes requirements which were discussed within SC30 WG1 (see document [1]), as well as requirements stemming from the author, not yet discussed or agreed within WG1 at the time this paper is being written. It should therefore be seen as representing solely the opinion of the author.

4.2. General requirements on FDT's for open-edi

Open-edi scenarios will be written by different user communities and shall be compliant with the BOV related standards. For this reason, it is obvious that FDT's included in the BOV related standards need to be standardised.

In order to produce open-edi scenarios, the user communities will need to use modelling tools which help them in producing specifications based on these FDT's. In order to speed up the use of open-edi, it is of the highest importance that such tools already exist on the market at the time the FDT's are chosen for the BOV related standards.

Moreover, it is highly desirable that several tools exist on the market and that the standards of the FDT's provide for a neutral format of exchange between the tools in order that specifications produced on one tool of the market can be reused and modified on another modelling tool of the market.

Open-edi scenarios will be specified by user communities which are composed of business people, which are experts in their business area but not IT experts. It is therefore necessary that the FDT's include a human readable form which is easy to understand, such as a graphical form.

Also as mentioned in the summary of the open-edi reference model, part of the open-edi scenario is to be implemented in the IT system that supports the execution of the open-edi transactions. This requires that the FDT's include a computer processible form.

In addition, since the FDT's will be included in the BOV related standards, compliance to the standard will need to be assessed. Therefore test environment for these FDTs will be necessary.

Finally, organisations will have a need for both generic and specific scenarios. Therefore the FDT's and the tools on the market shall allow for both hierarchical decomposition of the models and a modular approach of the specification of open-edi scenarios.

4.3. Requirements on the FDT for roles

Compared to the specification of a complete telecommunication system such as those presently described in MSC and SDL, a role is a very simple specification. The following characteristics are necessary for the FDT used for role specification :

- It should be capable of representing efficiently both choice and concurrency.

- It should offer the possibility of describing choices in terms of conditions on data values of instances of a given semantic component in an information bundle. For example it should be possible to specify that if the value of the order is higher than a certain level, a specific insurance should be subscribed and therefore the insurer role needs to be sent a copy of the order.

- It should be able to represent internal choices, although it is questionable whether the actual rules governing these choices should be modelled, since they are usually specific to a given organisation and may be confidential for this organisation. Therefore, only the possible outcomes of these internal choices need to be represented.

- Events that trigger internal decisions need to be represented. Such events include timer expiration as well as the receipt of information bundles.

- The state of each of the partners participating in the open-edi scenario needs to be represented to enable analysis of the dynamic properties of a scenario.

- The ordering of exchanges of information flow may have strict temporal specifications. Therefore one should be able to express both absolute and relative temporal constraints.

As part of an open-edi scenario, a role will be registered in a repository. It will be necessary to verify the compliance of a role, the specification, with the BOV related standard. Therefore, the FDT shall be such that the modelling tools have the capability of checking the compliance of the specification with the standardised FDT. The capability of checking automatically the validity of a role would also be useful, e.g. to check that no deadlock exists in the role.

In addition, the role will be implemented in the IT system of some of the EDI partners. It will thus also be necessary to check the compliance of such implementations with the role.

4.4. Requirements on the FDT for Information bundles

The FDT for information bundles needs to provide the capability of describing both atomic and compound semantic components.

It should also be able to represent mandatory semantic components as well as optional semantic components and information on their cardinality.

It needs the capability to express constraints between semantic components, such as : if semantic component A is present, then semantic component B is mandatory. Another example would be : if the value of the instance of semantic component A is XX, then semantic component B is mandatory.

As part of an open-edi scenario, a semantic component will be registered in a repository. It will therefore be necessary to verify the compliance of the information bundle with the BOV related standards. The FDT should be such that the modelling tools can provide the capability of checking automatically the compliance of the information bundle with the standardised FDT.

Information bundles are models of data which is to be exchanged between the IT systems of the partners involved in the Open-edi transaction. The instances of Information bundles will be composed of data values which are encoded in a transfer syntax. The open-edi reference model indicates that the FSV related standards will include a generic mechanism used to translate the data values of Semantic components into a generic transfer syntax from the information bundle specification and vice versa. In addition, it will be necessary to check the compliance of instances of information bundles with the specification, including the constraints.

4.5. Scenario attributes

At present, the complete set of scenario attributes which are needed has not been fully identified. However, since open-edi scenarios will have to be evaluated by user communities and compared with other open-edi scenarios, it seems appropriate to include, in the open-edi scenario attributes, a global view of all possible sequences of information bundles which can be exchanged between the different partners playing the different roles.

5. POTENTIAL BENEFIT FOR THE MSC AND SDL COMMUNITY

This presentation of some requirements on the FDTs needed for the BOV related standards is aimed at helping the MSC and SDL community in making a first evaluation of the suitability of MSC and SDL for Open-edi. As a complement to this presentation, we will now identify some potential benefits for the MSC and SDL community, should these languages be chosen as part of the Open-edi BOV related standards.

Companies are today faced with a double challenge : first they are competing with more and more companies because of world-wide market globalisation. Their organisation and processes are therefore constantly evolving to adapt their manufacturing and services to the customer requirements. Secondly, there is a constant evolution towards the "immaterial economy." That is, manufacturing relies more and more on complex information systems for the design and production process. Services, whether in the private or public field, also require information systems of increasing complexity.

In this environment, the productivity of a company depends on its capacity for retrieving and processing the information necessary to its business. Such information is held in different information systems, including those of their business partners, and must be integrated in the design, manufacturing, distribution, and commercial process. This economic environment makes EDI unavoidable from an economic viewpoint.

The use of modelling techniques in the EDI environment has already started. The EDIFACT community is already using modelling techniques (IDEF0) as a first step in message design. Some users are including models in the prior agreement on technical specifications that they establish with their partners. The BOV related standards will provide the common language which is needed so that all user communities can share their specifications and harmonise them.

EDI relates to all sectors of activity. In the same way, the area of application of open-edi standards crosses all sectors. Therefore, the use of MSC and SDL in these standards could have a major impact on the dissemination of MSC and SDL across all sectors.

In addition, in the course of EDI implementation, the users have to establish a correspondence between the models of the EDI transaction between partners, and the model of their internal application which is concerned by the electronic transaction (stock management application, invoicing application, order application, ...). Therefore, the use of MSC and SDL in the BOV related standards could have a side effect on the use of MSC and SDL modelling tools for the internal applications of EDI users.

6. CONCLUSION

In this paper, we briefly presented the new ISO IEC International standard IS 14662, entitled "The open-edi reference model." Through this presentation, we identified the areas of Open-edi which require formal descriptive techniques. In the last sections, we identified some requirements on the formal descriptive techniques for open-edi and the potential benefits that the MSC and SDL community could get, should MSC and SDL be included into the Open-edi standards.

The objective of this paper is to help the MSC and SDL community to decide if MSC and SDL is adequate for Open-edi standards. Should they see an interest in promoting MSC and SDL to that effect, the next step could be to work in co-operation with ISO/IEC JTC1 SC30. This co-operative work could make use of the existing liaison with ITU SG10 or any other appropriate mechanism.

7. REFERENCES

[1] ISO IEC IS 14 662 (to be published) "The Open-edi reference model"

[2] ISO IEC JTC1 SC30 WG1 Working document on Topic 15 Identification of requirements on Formal Description Techniques for open-edi scenarios.

SDL '97: TIME FOR TESTING - SDL, MSC and Trends
A. Cavalli and A. Sarma (Editors)

The Unification of OMT, SDL and IDL for Service Creation

C. Loftus[a], E. Sherratt[a], E. Inocêncio[b] and P. Viana[bc]

[a]Department of Computer Science,University of Wales Aberystwyth, Ceredigion SY23 3DB, Wales, UK

[b]Instituto de Engenharia de Sistemas e Computadores (INESC), Praça da República, 93 - R/C, 4000 Porto, Portugal

[c]Instituto Superior de Engenharia do Porto (ISEP), Rua de S.Tomé, 4200 Porto, Portugal

Like many other subjects, SDL is embroiled in the fusion of the Telecom and Information systems worlds. This represents a shift from the predominant use of SDL in relatively closed Telecom areas to the more and more widely used open distributed processing environments. ACTS project AC227, SCREEN, is working to improve the creation of distributed telematic services. This paper presents some of the issues and challenges that these new environments present to SDL language, and the rationale for combing SDL with OMT and the targeting to CORBA compliant environments.

1. INTRODUCTION

OMT, SDL and CORBA represent some of the best known technologies to emerge from software engineering and telecommunications. Used in combination, they promise to provide an excellent basis for creating advanced telematics services. Combinations of OMT and SDL have previously been proposed, and tools to support these are available; for example, SOMT [1] combines OMT analysis with SDL design, and allows component interfaces to be specified using CORBA IDL.

This paper presents a unification of OMT, SDL and CORBA IDL which departs from previous approaches in that OMT is used as the primary basis for both analysis and structural design, with SDL supplying the detailed signal passing and timing information essential to accurate specification of service behaviour. The approach taken here goes well beyond previous combinations of these technologies by providing more detailed information about targeting than has hitherto been available.

The following section discusses the rationale behind the SCREEN approach to combining OMT, SDL and CORBA IDL. It discusses the advantages of using OMT as a primary basis for both analysis and object design, and the need for

SDL to provide precise definitions of communicating service components. In particular, it provides a detailed presentation of OMT as a basis for specifying architectural design, public and implementation interfaces, and targeting information.

Section 3 then addresses a specific problem caused by the fact that exceptions are supported by CORBA IDL, but not by SDL. A mechanism to solve this problem by translating from OMT to IDL is described. This complements the translations from OMT concepts to SDL concepts discussed in Section 2.

Section 4 summarises the previous sections, together with the main conclusions of the paper – viz., that using OMT as a primary source of analysis and design information results in highly flexible, traceable service designs, that SDL provides the power for describing communicating entities lacking from OMT, and that OMT combined with IDL and SDL facilitates practical service targeting to CORBA-based distributed processing environments.

2. THE UNIFICATION OF OMT, SDL AND IDL

2.1 Aim and Rationale

Object Modelling Technique (OMT) [2] is a highly successful object oriented analysis and design method. It is particularly applicable to analysis and design of services targeted at distributed processing environments of the kind typified by CORBA implementations.

SDL is a well established method for designing telecommunications systems [3-5]. It provides all the concepts needed to define the static and dynamic characteristics of the communicating entities that together constitute a telecommunications service, and is well supported, enabling a variety of analytical and dynamic checks of the proposed service.

IDL [6] is the CORBA interface definition language. It defines components as objects, specifying the services offered by each component as a component interface. Where a CORBA distributed processing environment forms the target environment for service implementation, it is clearly advantageous to produce IDL interface definitions for components reasonably early in system design

The idea of combining the strengths of OMT, SDL and IDL is not new in itself. Their notations and modelling approaches are complementary; between them they cover system analysis, architectural design, behaviour, interfaces and targeting. Using them together to provide alternative modifiable views on the same underlying architecture (structure and interfaces) is highly desirable, given the varying activities and experience of system engineers.

There are two ways to combine OMT with SDL. The first results in a hybrid in which OMT is used for analysis and architectural design and SDL only used for defining behaviour[1]. However, this requires significant changes to practice, as well as considerable re-engineering of existing toolsets, and is therefore unlikely to gain commercially acceptance. It also removes the ability of engineers to view architectural design using different notations.

The second approach, favoured by SCREEN, extends OMT with some additional labelling to enable engineers to express, to varying degrees, structural design, interface and targeting information. It does however, demand that adequate tool support is provided for the maintenance of consistency between duplicate views — the greater the overlap and modifiability of models the greater the support required. Indeed, existing toolsets (such as ObjectGEODE 1.1 [7] and SDT 3.1 [8]) provide translation paths between OMT, SDL and IDL. However, none of these give the service creator the option of using OMT as thc principal means of expressing analysis, structural design, interfacing and targeting information. This contrasts with SOMT [1], an approach that uses OMT for analysis only and SDL for all design.

The SCREEN approach also provides detailed guidance for targeting CORBA-based distributed processing environments (DPEs), which goes into much greater detail than is provided by any existing modelling approach. This is discussed in Section 2.3; SCREEN is also adapting existing toolsets to support the mappings described there.

There are advantages to using OMT as the primary basis for design as well as for systems analysis. OMT facilitates incremental refinement of class diagrams, enabling a seamless transition from analysis to design. Some OMT editors support the concept of views, so that classes can be viewed as analysis classes, design classes, or both. Other editors support dependency links between analysis and design classes. Thus OMT and its supporting environments encourage the construction of a continuum of analysis and design products.

Moreover, transition from design OMT to SDL is also very straightforward, and can, in principle, be automated. This contrasts with the more semantically demanding transition from analysis OMT to SDL, which characterises other approaches[9,10].

While OMT dynamic and functional models can be used in the analysis phase, SCREEN does not intend to develop the generation of SDL-92 behaviour skeletons from these models. Although there is considerable research on the subject, it is envisaged that the coherence between the OMT and SDL behaviour cannot be maintained through all phases of the development process. Instead SCREEN keeps the Object Model in all phases and design iterations, combined with MSC for analysis, SDL for behavioural design and IDL for DPE targeting.

OMT provides simple, powerful, flexible object-oriented structuring concepts which provide a good alternative to SDL for expressing structural design. These provide a good overview of a distributed multimedia system, whose behaviour

[1]It could be argued that UML is moving in this direction, where Activity diagrams are used to define behaviour. The UML documentation[12] does however state that other state machine languages such as SDL could be used instead.

can then be defined using SDL, whose extended finite state machines (EFSMs), signal passing and timers provide a well-tried basis for service specification.

The SCREEN approach pays detailed attention to service targeting. Section 2.3 shows how OMT constructs can be used to indicate how a service should be configured within a CORBA distributed processing environment (DPE). It illustrates specification of public and private class interfaces, and goes on to specify the mapping of active and passive classes to CORBA client and server tasks and physical nodes. This goes well beyond previous combinations of OMT, SDL and CORBA IDL, and also provides a basis for specifying mappings to other DPEs.

The SCREEN approach has been developed with a view to taking advantage of future developments. In particular, the proposals for Unified Modelling Language (UML) [11,12] suggest that it will eventually prove even better than OMT for unifying object-oriented analysis, architectural design, behavioural design (SDL) and targeting (IDL). For example, UML directly includes the notion of dependency relationships both between classes and objects within a single model and as traceability links between entities in different models (perhaps developed during different development phases). UML also provides more comprehensive support than OMT for targeting. At present, though, UML is in a state of flux, and is not well supported by software tools. For these reasons, SCREEN has adopted OMT, with a view to making the transition to UML when that notation has stabilised and has acquired suitable tool support.

In summary, OMT provides a good overarching modelling notation which both complements and unifies SDL and IDL, and also provides a clear evolutionary path towards its own replacement by UML, should that become appropriate in the future.

2.3 OMT as a unifying notation

SCREEN has started investigating the automatic generation of SDL and IDL from design OMT (and UML), as well as generation and targeting of C++ and Java code from SDL EFSMs, OMT and ADTs. This is described and further developed in the following sections[2]. We present one way of using OMT for this purpose along with a possible set of inter-model translation rules. This demonstrates feasibility of the approach, and does not preclude other strategies.

2.3.1 Defining architectural design information in OMT

OMT can be used to represent architectural design information which, if required, can then be translated automatically to SDL. We examine the main SDL structural constructs and propose how they can be represented in OMT. This mirroring of SDL structure in OMT will only be successful if it is not stilted but rather represents a natural use of the notation. Furthermore, since other

[2]Some of these uses of OMT are described in [13], others are extensions developed for the purpose of this paper.

mappings are possible, any automated support should allow users to define their own translation rules, or to manually guide the translation.

Figure 1 presents a simplified OMT model of a distributed digital library, one of the SCREEN project trials. In this model there are two main entity sets: the distributed servers and the clients. Each client connects to the nearest server which will then disseminate the request to other servers in order to obtain a global network. The model identifies two associations described by IDL interfaces, client to server (ClientIDL) and server to server (ServerIDL) — these will be the attachment points of the library implementation to the CORBA network.

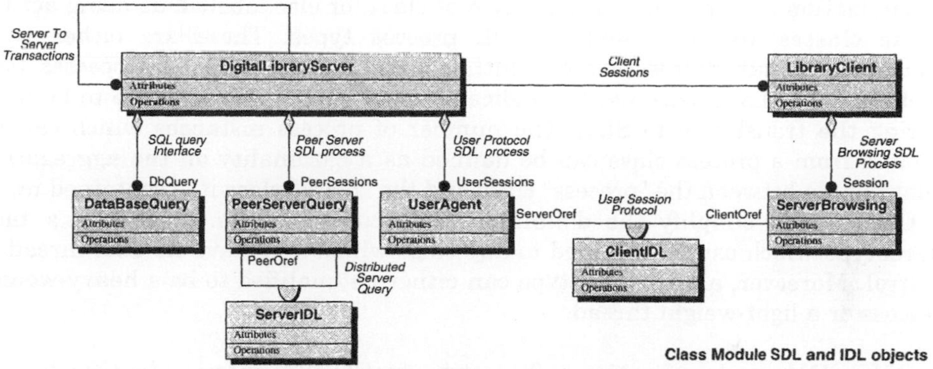

Figure 1. OMT model of Digital Library.

We have not strictly followed OMT notation in one major respect. We have used labels (not shown on the diagram) to add SDL design information used during translation. Such labels are not part of OMT but instead taken from UML's notion of stereotypes and properties which enable the definition of meta-information. These labels are also used when defining interfaces (Section 2.3.2) and targeting information (Section 2.3.3). Figure 2 shows the SDL implementation of the digital library server object.

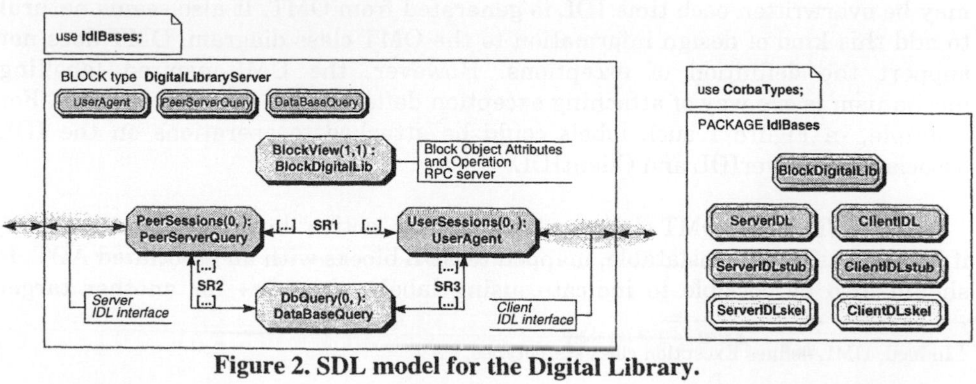

Figure 2. SDL model for the Digital Library.

SDL System/Block. In Figure 1 it can be seen that the DigitalLibraryServer object contains, besides it own attributes and operations, a number of aggregated object sets labelled as "SDL process". Hence this object is to be mapped to a SDL block that contains three SDL process sets that implement the actual object behaviour. The shaded signal routes in Figure 2 are the conceptual IDL interface paths, optionally they can be used for SDL simulation. A fourth process type (BlockView) acts as local attribute and operation server. By means of server RPCs the enclosed SDL processes gain access to parent object data.

SDL Process. Those classes representing concurrency could either be a specialisation of a specific concurrency root class, or else labelled as being active. These classes are translated to SDL process types. These are either local processes or stub processes representing external environment processes (see Section 2.3.2). Labels are used to indicate which OMT constructs are to be used during the translation to SDL. The number of process instances which can be created from a process class can be defined as a cardinality on the aggregation relationship between the "process" class and the "block" class it is contained in.

UML would simplify the definition of concurrent tasks. It defines a task stereotype which can be assigned to any class which is to have its own thread of control. Moreover, a task stereotype can either be qualified to be a heavy-weight process or a light-weight thread.

OMT, IDL and exceptions. Targeting to CORBA entails identification of relationships between OMT objects (SDL processes) described by IDL interfaces. These processes will directly communicate with the ORB by means of stubs and skeletons automatically generated from the OMT objects/IDL interfaces. In SDL this functionality is implemented by base process types (grouped in the SDL package on the right hand side of Figure 2). Section 3 will detail this targeting approach.

Since exceptions will be required in a generated service they must be defined either within OMT and then translated to IDL, or else manually inserted in the IDL. The latter causes problems since manual additions to IDL specifications may be overwritten each time IDL is generated from OMT. It also seems natural to add this kind of design information to the OMT class diagram. OMT does not support the definition of exceptions. However, the UML-inspired labelling mechanism is one way of attaching exception definitions to class operations[3]. For example, in Figure 1 such labels could be attached to operations on the IDL associations ServerIDL and ClientIDL.

SDL ADT. Those OMT classes which are not "active" but have operations are, if labelled as SDL translatable, mapped to SDL blocks with an associated ADT. It should also be possible to indicate, using labels, that C++ (or another target

[3] Indeed, UML defines Exception class stereotypes.

language) code stubs are to be generated. The form of these stubs will depend on whether the OMT class is defined as an Interface or Implementation class (Section 2.3.2) and on default or user-defined code generation templates.

2.3.2 Defining public and implementation interfaces in OMT

SCREEN [13] has defined two basic kinds of OMT class:

1. Interface classes (not to be confused with UML Interface stereotypes), which define the external interfaces of a telematic service, i.e. its interface to the external environment.
2. Implementation classes, which define local, private interfaces to be used internally within a service.

UML-style labelling is used to indicate the category to which a class belongs. This is a good case for the use of user-defined UML stereotypes since the alternative in OMT would be either to require that each class inherit from an interface or implementation superclass, or else to group the two kinds of class within different class modules. We prefer to use modules to group classes, whether interface or implementation, that contribute to specific functions of the service.

Interface classes. Interface classes will be translated to SDL and IDL. SDL translation depends on whether the class is also labelled as "active" (see Section 2.3.1) generating either an SDL process, SDL block or SDL block with associated server process. The IDL translation will generate an interface — for any class providing publicly accessible operations and attributes making it a server — using rules discussed in Section 3. "Active" classes will also result in the generation (from SDL EFSM) of CORBA client and server operating system processes or threads. Figure 3 shows the translation paths from OMT to SDL, IDL and C++ for the *DigitalLibraryServer* object.

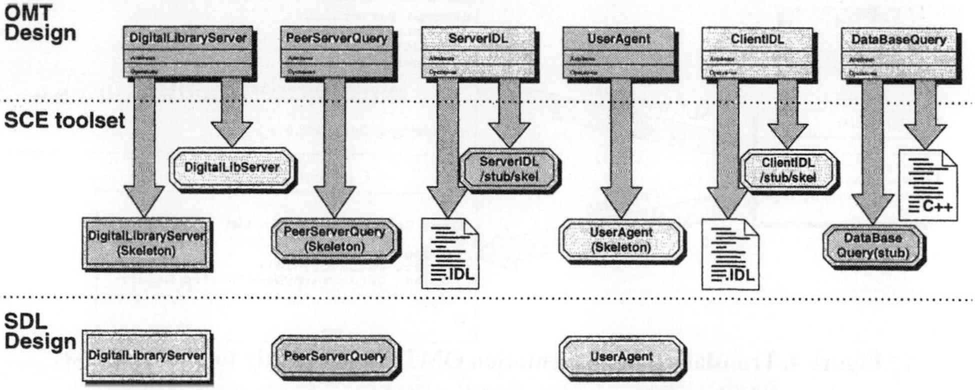

Figure 3. Translating Interface OMT classes to IDL and SDL.

A qualifying label could be used to indicate that a class is implemented externally (not shown in the diagrams). If this is the case, an SDL process stub is generated for "active" classes, and "passive" classes with operations are translated to blocks with ADTs. Both are expected to be implemented externally (not using SDL EFSMs or operator diagrams). IDL interfaces are not generated for external classes since they are defined externally. It must also be possible to configure the application generated from SDL to enable these stub proxies to interface to these external CORBA servers. One way of automating this would be to provide the code generation tool with the IDL interfaces of these external objects. This would also allow editors to check the consistency of this IDL with corresponding OMT class definitions.

It may also be appropriate to define the scope of a published IDL interface, to assist targeting. For example, a CORBA server may be registered with an ORB Implementation Repository, or it may also be registered with an OMG Object Management Architecture Name Service or Trader Service [6]. Clearly, each progressively widens the scope of the interface.

Implementation classes. These are classes of the service which contribute towards the functions of a service but are not meant to be published to external entities. Implementation classes can be translated to SDL, or directly to a target language (such as C++) or a combination of both. It is important that where both C++ and SDL are jointly generated for a class that the translations are compatible. For example, a "passive" Implementation class which is also labelled to allow C++ and SDL generation should result in the generation of a C++ class stub and SDL block with an ADT which are consistent so that the ADT provides an internal interface onto its C++ implementation (Figure 4). "Active" classes will be translated to SDL process types, instances of which will form concurrent threads of control within CORBA client and/or server applications generated from SDL.

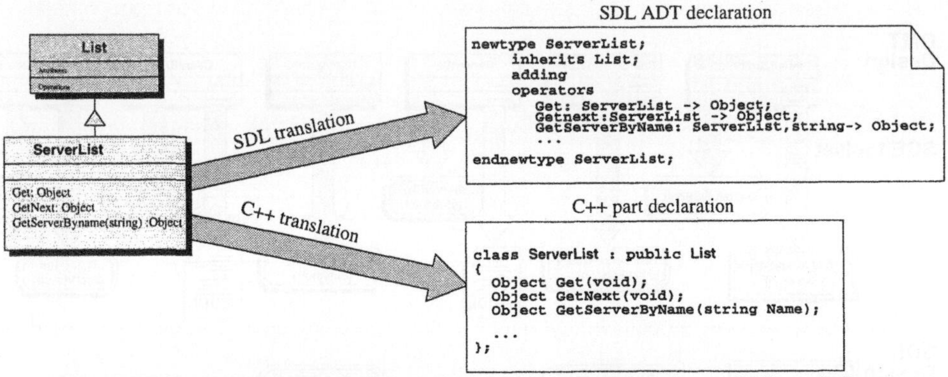

Figure 4. Translating Implementation OMT classes jointly to SDL and C++.

A service engineer may prefer active Implementation classes to be translated to server programs with separate process address spaces — within distinct CORBA server OS processes — rather than as concurrent threads. However, this will require the generation of IDL which is normally associated with Interface classes. We believe that some overlap here is appropriate, with perhaps the proviso that the scope of IDL publication should be constrained to ORB Implementation Repository registration.

As with Interface classes, it is also useful to allow the labelling of classes as external where the target language code is provided from an external source and not generated from OMT or SDL. Examples, would include external libraries (such as math or OS interface libraries) and application GUIs developed independently of OMT/SDL toolsets. The former "passive" objects could be accessed via SDL ADTs (and most tools already support this). It is likely that GUIs would require their own thread of control (e.g. for the X event loop) and so an IDL interface would need to be provided and used to enable CORBA-based communication between the SDL process stub representing the GUI and its external implementation.

UML. UML defines another concept which might be adopted by SCREEN for representing Interface and Implementation classes. This is the concept of Interface Stereotypes (analogous to Java Interfaces), where a class labelled using this stereotype can be used to define "public" operations of a server class. The server class is then linked (implements) to this Interface class using special "supplier" relationships. Client classes are linked to the Interface class via "client" relationships. Other operations on the server, but not included in the Interface class, can then be considered private.

2.3.3 Defining targeting information in OMT

Sections 2.3.1 and 2.3.2 have demonstrated already how OMT can be used to provide targeting information: targeting to SDL, the definition of active and passive classes and, hence, concurrency, and the generation of public and private interfaces. At least two other kinds of targeting information could be specified using OMT:

1. Definition of non-functional requirements such as persistency, performance, reliability etc. Again an elaborate labelling mechanism could be used to associate this kind of information with OMT constructs. UML provides significant flexibility for this kind of user-defined information; for example, it is even possible to create new class partitions. It is beyond the scope of this paper to explore this further.
2. Definition of deployment information. OMT could be used to associate OMT design classes and objects with a particular software and hardware configuration. The use of labelling to allocate OMT classes to CORBA client/server processes and threads was briefly discussed in Section 2.3.1. The

location of those clients and servers could also specified using OMT. One mechanism would be to define an architectural class/instance diagram of the target hardware. This could then be associated with service architectural classes and/or instances via suitably labelled OMT associations.

UML provides a far more comprehensive solution through its predefined Distribution stereotypes and Deployment view diagrams. Not only does UML support the definition of concurrency (processes and threads), but also the static and dynamic allocation of such classes and their instances to physical nodes. It also enables the clustering of classes/objects defining the unit of migration of generated OS processes. For CORBA DPEs support for the definition of dynamic migration would be particularly useful where mobile code system languages such as Java and Tcl are used (e.g. modelling the downloading of CORBA-based Java applets onto Web browsers).

3. TARGETING ISSUES

SDL tool vendors[7,8] are currently offering off the shelf solutions to deploy SDL applications on a CORBA compliant DPE. Language mappings are proposed in which IDL modules and interfaces are respectively mapped to SDL-92 block and process types. Quite naturally these mappings explore the apparent similarly between SDL and IDL communication mechanisms:

- IDL operations. These are mapped to SDL remote procedure calls, where both ends are synchronous blocking transactions that accept, modify or return values to the caller.
- IDL oneway operations. These are mapped to SDL signals. Here the similarly assumed is that both concepts involve a unidirectional, unconfirmed transaction.
- IDL attributes. IDL interface attributes are encapsulated with two operations: *_set_xxx(value)* modifies the value of attribute *xxx* and *_get_xxx()* returns the value of the attribute.

3.1 Mapping of oneway asynchronous operations

Asynchronous *oneway* operations map quite naturally to SDL signal exchange sequences (Figure 5). Both client and server share a signal definition equivalent to the IDL operation, i.e., a signal that has the same name and arguments list. Since the information flow is unidirectional the invocation involves just two steps:

1. The client SDL machine outputs the signal *op*, which involves the calling of a homonymous IDL stub member. The client ORB will immediately return without blocking the caller process.

2. The remote ORB receives the request and calls the appropriate skeleton member. This skeleton member will place the incoming SDL signal in the server process queue. At some later time the signal will reach the head of the queue and trigger a transition in the server process.

This mapping is almost perfect for the current semantics of CORBA *oneway* operation, the only limitation is the inability to detect system exceptions that may be raised by the local ORB. Furthermore, the OMG is considering the problem of blocking in *oneway* operations (Section 3.3). For these reasons, the alternative mapping presented in Section 3.2 is being considered for *oneway* operations.

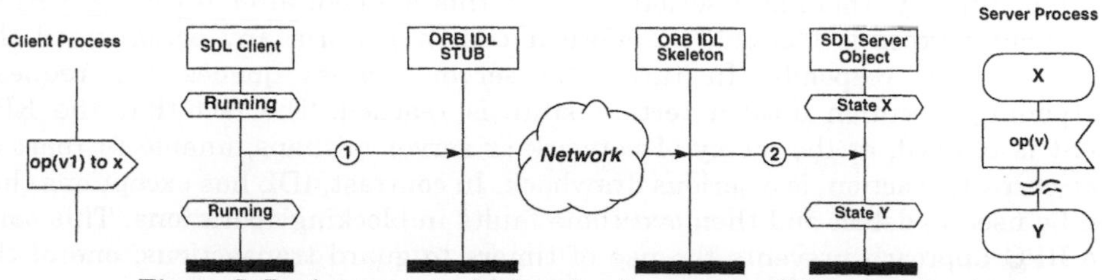

Figure 5: Basic conceptual Mapping for oneway IDL operation.

3.2 Mapping of synchronous IDL operations to SDL RPC

The informal MSC in Figure 6 depicts the mapping of an IDL operation to an SDL remote procedure call. The SDL server process, exports a procedure with a signature equivalent to the IDL operation — same name, return type and parameter type sequence with *(in)out* types as required. The IDL operation invocation involves four steps:

1. The client SDL machine calls the remote Procedure *op*, this step involves the calling of a homonymous IDL stub member. At this point, the ORB blocks the calling process.
2. The target ORB (which might be remote) receives the request and calls the appropriate skeleton member. Through an ORB dependent mechanism the skeleton will transfer the call to the server SDL process (in many C++ implementations this translation just involves a virtual function call). At this point, the SDL implementation handles the request by executing procedure *op*.
3. As soon as the execution of the remote procedure terminates, the server process returns control to the server ORB. At this point, the return value and any in/out arguments will be updated.
4. Eventually, the response reaches the originating ORB which passes updated arguments and return values to the client process. Now the client can resume the execution of the next statement in the current SDL transition.

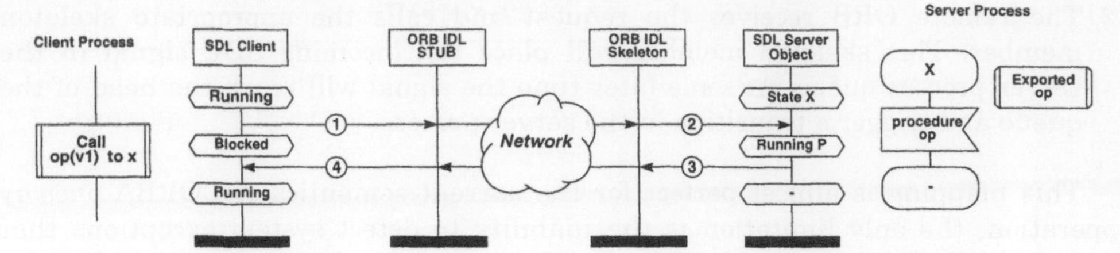

Figure 6: IDL operation mapped to SDL Remote Procedure Call

Unfortunately, there is a serious flaw in this method: after invoking a RPC, the client process is blocked, therefore it cannot perform any action until the server process responds. In turn, the server process queues the request, postponing execution until a certain state is reached. The fact that the RPC client is blocked, at the mercy of network or server mishaps, unable to react or take corrective action, is a serious drawback. In contrast, IDL has exceptions that can be used to detect and then overcome faults in blocking operations. This said, the RPC approach prevents the use of timers to guard transactions, one of the key benefits of SDL compared to other implementation languages.

Handling exceptions in IDL operations. Support of IDL exceptions is essential to make SDL attractive to the CORBA developers, it also an essential pre-requisite to build fault-tolerant applications. The introduction of exceptions to the SDL language is a medium term possibility. Consequently, even if this concept is standardised, one must wait for the appearance of suitable tool support. Therefore SCREEN is considering the adoption of alternative short term solutions based on existing SDL96 concepts. Figure 7 presents a IDL operation *op(v)* that raises exception *e1*. The conceptual SDL implementation is no more than a simple expansion of the underlying SDL RPC semantics with the addition of branches to raise and handle exceptions.

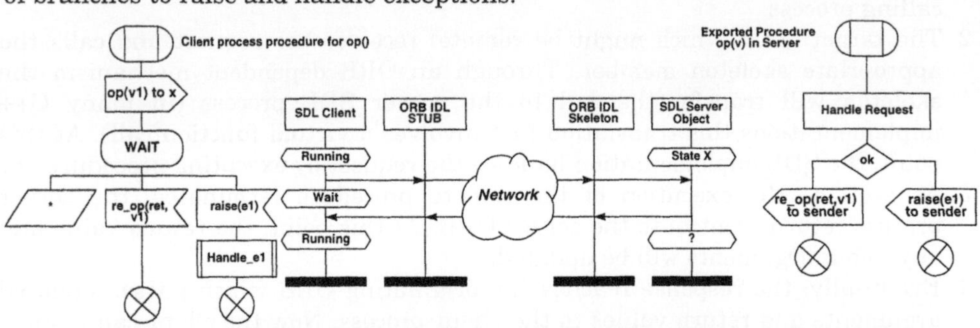

Figure 7: Conceptual support of IDL exception with basic SDL constructs.

To be practical this method requires full automation on the client side and at least partial automation on the server side. This can be achieved by generating an SDL process(es) that acts as an IDL stub and/or skeleton. By inheritance the application developer implements Client and Server process types that specialise the SDL process types that were automatically generated from the IDL specifications. On the client side the base process type contains:

- One SDL procedure for each IDL operation. The signature is the same as the IDL operation plus one extra parameter for the remote object reference.
- One SDL procedure for each IDL *oneway* operation and two SDL procedures for each IDL attribute (*get_xxx* and *set_xxx*).
- One virtual procedure to handle each IDL exception.
- Optionally, timers and time-out handling virtual procedures to supervise the duration of the IDL transactions.
- SDL signal declarations and gates to allow simulation, in SDL, of IDL operations (these are optional and not used by the application).

And on the server side:

- One variable for each IDL attribute.
- One virtual exported procedure for each operation.
- One local procedure to raise each IDL exception (for simplicity this is show as a signal output in Figure 7).

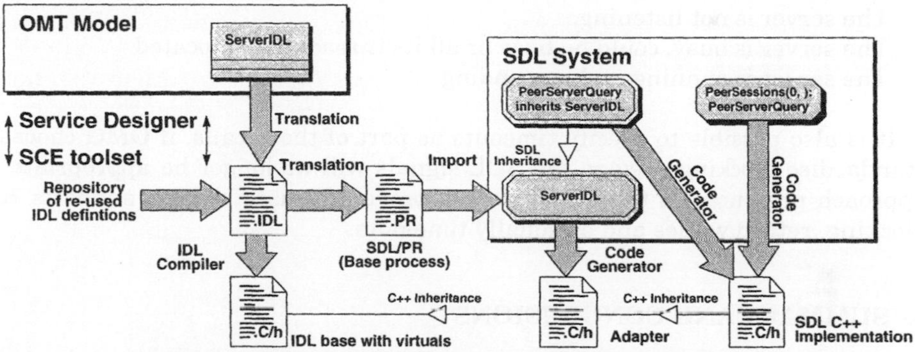

Figure 8: Conversion flow for SDL targeting.

The use of inheritance clearly separates the SDL part generated from the IDL description from the hand-coded SDL application, thus maintainability is improved and the consistency problem is reduced[4]. The main reason for generating the SDL bases is to ensure the semantic correctness of the SDL description and to allow simulation with standard SDL tools.

Figure 8 illustrates application code generation. The service designer defines the IDL specification in the OMT editor, or alternatively the user may reuse an existing IDL specification. The IDL model is then used to generate a PR file with

[4] However, the designer must still ensure the coherence between base and derived process types.

the description of the base SDL process type which will be specialised by the service creator. The specialised process is translated to a C++ implementation class; the base process is translated to an adapter C++ class that redefines the virtual functions of a "IDL base". This base is simply the output of the IDL compiler supplied by the ORB vendor.

3.3 Blocking CORBA oneway operations

Section 3.1 presented the use of SDL asynchronous signals to implement CORBA *oneway* operations, since these return no results and are meant to return immediately. However *oneway* operations are somewhat controversial since, for reliable operation and proper flow control, they usually require explicit backward confirmation. CORBA users are well aware of this; some have simply abandoned the asynchronous *oneway* in favour of synchronous requests. The OMG issued a Messaging Request for Proposal early in 1996 with a deadline for the end of 1996. Proposals received may well address the problem of blocking *oneway* operations.

Currently, this support is not provided. A possible solution might be to adopt the mechanisms similar to those used by DCE (Distributed Computing Environment)[14]. A DCE asynchronous operation returns a result which tells the client one of three things:

1. The server is not listening.
2. The server is busy, could be busy or all its threads are allocated.
3. The server is running and responding.

It is also possible to specify timeouts as part of these calls, if OMG chooses to standardise blocking *oneway* the SDL signals will no longer be appropriate, the approach presented in the previous may prove adequate since it supports caller blocking, return values and optionally time-outs.

4. SUMMARY AND CONCLUSIONS

This paper has presented an approach to advanced telematics service creation which combines the flexibility and traceability of OMT object analysis and design with the power and applicability of SDL specifications of communicating entities, and which also provides specific guidance for targeting these services to CORBA-based distributed processing environments.

Section 2 discussed the advantages of using OMT as a primary basis for both analysis and object design, with SDL extended finite state machines providing the power and precision required to define communicating service components. It also provided a detailed presentation of OMT as a basis for specifying architectural design, public and implementation interfaces, and targeting information. The object model provides a graphical view of the service data structures, along with object instance relationships, some of which are described by IDL definitions. This "data oriented" view is complemented by a more or less orthogonal static signal flow view furnished by the SDL structure. Hence the method provides graphical notation for both aspects of the design process, along with automatic code generation and targeting - something that OMT or SDL alone can not provide.

Section 3 then addressed a specific problem caused by semantic mismatch between SDL and IDL. The problem is that exceptions are supported by CORBA IDL, but not by SDL. A mechanism to solve this problem by translating from OMT to IDL was described. This complements the translations from OMT concepts to SDL concepts discussed in Section 2.

The overall approach is currently being evaluated by means of service creation trials, both within and outside the SCREEN project. These trials will provide important feedback regarding the practical use of the approach.

Meanwhile, initial evaluation indicates that using OMT as a primary source of analysis and design notation, which is then used to assist automatic generation SDL and IDL, as well as targeting to a CORBA-based DPE, results in a highly manageable, traceable, flexible and practical approach to service creation.

5. ACKNOWLEDGEMENTS

The authors would like to thank our SCREEN partners for their comments and input to this paper: Munir Tag, Philippe Francoise, Xavier Crespel (FT Telis); Kathleen Milsted, Pierre Combes (FT CNET); Anders Olsen, Mikael Jorgensen (Tele Danmark); Didoe Prevedourou, Sofoklis Efremidis (Intracom); Panagiotis Demestiches, Anagnostou Miltos (Intrasoft); Laurence Demounem, Pierre Quentin (Alcatel Alsthom Recherche); Han Zuidweg, Westerhuis Frank (Alcatel Bell); Maria Marques, Elsa Cardoso, José Oliveira (INESC); Emlyn Phillips (University of Wales Aberystwyth); Rossitza Goleva (Technical University of Sofia).

6. REFERENCES

1. Telelogic SDT3.1, Methodology Guidelines Part 1, the SOMT Method. Telelogic, Sweden, 1996.
2. Rumbaugh, M. Blaha, W. Premerlani, F. Eddy and W. Lorensen. Object-Oriented Modeling and Design. Prentice Hall, 1991.
3. ITU-T Recommendation Z.100. Specification and Description Language (SDL). Geneva, 1993.
4. [Z.100AppI] ITU-T Recommendation Z.100 - Appendix I. SDL Methodology Guidelines. Geneva, 1992.
5. [Z.100Supp1] ITU-T Recommendation Z.100 - Supplement 1. SDL+ Methodology: Use of MSC and SDL (with ASN.1). Geneva, 1993.
6. Seigel. CORBA Fundamentals and Programming. Wiley, 1996. See also

http://www.omg.org/corfun/corfunhp.htm
7. ObjectGEODE Method Guidelines. Verilog, France, 1995.
8. Telelogic Tau 3.1 SDT3.1 user's manual, Telelogic, Sweden, 1996.
9. Dorota Witaszek, et. al., A Development Method for SDL-92 Specification Based on OMT, SDL'95 with MSC and CASE, Rolv Bræk and A. Sarma (eds.), Elsevier Science Publ. (1995) pp. 103-113.
10. Fuyin Guo, Thomas W. Mackenzie, Translation of OMT to SDL-92, SDL'95 with MSC and CASE, Rolv Bræk A. Sarma (eds.), Elsevier Science Publ. (1995) pp. 115-125.
11. Booch and J. Rumbaugh. Unified Method for Object-Oriented Development. Documentation set version 0.8.
12. Booch, I. Jacobson and J. Rumbaugh. Unified Method Language for Object-Oriented Development. Documentation set version 0.91 Addendum, September 96.
13. Project AC227: Service Creation Engineering Environment SCREEN - Basic Object-Oriented Technology for Service Creation. Deliverable D21.
14. Open Software Foundation. Introduction to DCE. OSF, 11 Cambridge Center, Cambridge MA 02142.
15. Telelogic Tau 3.1 User's manual, Chapter 71 the CORBA integration, Telelogic, Sweden, 1996.

SDL '97: TIME FOR TESTING - SDL, MSC and Trends
A. Cavalli and A. Sarma (Editors)

Combining Object-Oriented and Real-Time programming from an OMT and SDL design

Vincent Perrier[a] and Nicolas Dervaux[b]

[a]Customer Service and [b]*Object*GEODE development team, VERILOG,
150 rue Nicolas Vauquelin, B.P. 1310, 31106 Toulouse Cedex, France
Tel: +33 5 61 19 29 39
E-mail: info@verilog.fr
http://www.verilog.fr

ABSTRACT

Real-time software engineering does not cope with time constraints only. More and more embedded and distributed systems include large parts of data management, user interfaces or algorithms. A solution consists of combining SDL with object-oriented techniques like OMT. If SDL-OMT co-modeling is mastered enough at design level and is supported by usual commercial tools, co-targeting at code level is still an open issue.
This study investigates the possible integration strategies of OMT and SDL designs. Afterwards, it presents usual independent implementation solutions from OMT and SDL. At last, it shows how the code produced from OMT can be integrated into the SDL application. The first difficulty is to deal with the SDL language limitations and map at the design level the OMT constructs onto the SDL constructs. Actually, no class concept exists in SDL. The second problem comes from the programming languages usually selected to implement the designs: C code is preferred for implementing the reactive and real-time parts of the system, whereas C++ code is preferred for data processing. The last issue is to provide extra code in order to interface the C++ and C codes.
This paper details how SDL and OMT designs and their implementations can be integrated. The presented solution is illustrated by an example.

Keywords: OMT design, SDL design, OO programming, real-time programming, C, C++, concurrent objects, passive objects, abstract data type.

1. MOTIVATION

Real-time systems can be roughly classified in two categories. The first one corresponds to systems with *hard* real-time constraints. Requirements are such that early or late results are worthless or false results. Communication protocols or software control units embedded on aircraft, missiles or cars are typical examples. SDL (Specification and Description Language) [ITUa96] has proven its suitability to solve such hard real-time constraints for reactive and

discrete systems (as opposed to periodic systems). This design formalism becomes more and more used for this purpose.
The second category represents systems for which real-time constraints are *soft* constraints. Requirements are such that slightly late or early results have a greater value than no result at all. Billing systems, network management applications, some new telecommunications services or applications for air traffic management are typical examples. As data management and GUI's (Graphical User Interface) are major parts of such systems, project managers hesitate to use real-time techniques like SDL exclusively, or object-oriented techniques like OMT (Object Modeling Technique) [Rum91] exclusively.

SDL is clearly not sufficient to help designers to develop data management and GUI's. Traditional OO (Object-Oriented) techniques are not suitable to cope with complex behaviors and time constraints. So more and more project managers decide to use both techniques, and as far as OO techniques are concerned, OMT is the most selected. To help developers to put SDL into practice for such projects, the ITU-T group for SDL has defined in complement to the SDL recommendation released in 1996, a complete methodology proposing a joint use of SDL and OO techniques for the analysis phase [ITUb96]. Similar works can be found in [Leb96], with a greater development on the joint use of OMT for software design. These co-modeling methods can be applied on projects by using commercial tools. The return of investment is generally positive.

However, if co-modeling with SDL and OMT is mastered enough, OMT and SDL integration at the coding stage still requires some attention.

The usual SDL implementation strategy is C code using Real-Time Operating System (RTOS) primitives. SDL dynamic concepts such as finite state machines, instances, signals or viewed/revealed variables are managed directly in C or using RTOS primitives. Even if most of the cross-development tools compile C and C++, C is preferred for portability and performance reasons.
To support OO concepts in OMT such as inheritance, encapsulation or reuse, C++ coding is more suitable than C.

The work presented hereafter aims at proposing a solution regarding code generation and targeting, which describes how C and C++ code can be integrated.

2. CO-MODELING OF THE APPLICATION WITH SDL AND OMT

SDL focuses on system behavior modeling: inter-process communication and synchronization, time controlling, etc. SDL designers build the system architecture by successive refinements as a hierarchy of inter-communicating architectural components such as blocks and processes. A process instance is the elementary dynamic entity. Its behavior is described by a finite state machine.
At execution time, an application can be viewed as a network of process instances, also called *concurrent objects*, exchanging signals through routes and channels. Each instance receives signals through an unbounded individual queue.

Block and process types, genericity and inheritance facilitate the reuse of components (blocks and processes). See [Ols94] to get information on the SDL notation and the related engineering method.

As far as data processing is concerned, SDL supports basic data types like `boolean`, `integer`, `real`, `string`, and generators of list, array and set of types. Complex types are defined in the form of abstract data types (ADT), also called *passive classes*. ADT's are well-suited to integrate data processing or external resources. The ADT public interface is given as a data structure definition and operators declarations.
The definitions of ADT operators can be given in axiomatic or algorithmic forms. The ASN.1 notation can also be used jointly with SDL to describe ADT's [ITUc96]. However, implementation details can be hidden and described externally from the SDL design. Usually, an ADT is translated into C language in a procedure-oriented way, the data structure becomes a C `struct` data record and the operators become C functions. This is fair for a certain usage, but this approach is limited for data-intensive systems. Therefore, using OMT to describe passive objects classes ([Leb96]) is much more convenient. With OMT, designers can benefit from graphical notations and support OO concepts, especially for reuse.

SDL is the main model. It implements the expected real-time behavior of the system by means of communicating concurrent objects (process instances). The OMT model corresponds to the design of the passive classes which are integrated in the SDL model through ADT's. At run-time, SDL concurrent objects instantiate OMT passives classes.

From now and on the following paragraphs, the discussion will be illustrated by the example of a magnetic card reader device. The `MagneticCardManager` SDL process-type shown in figure 1 is a class of concurrent objects managing a magnetic card reader.

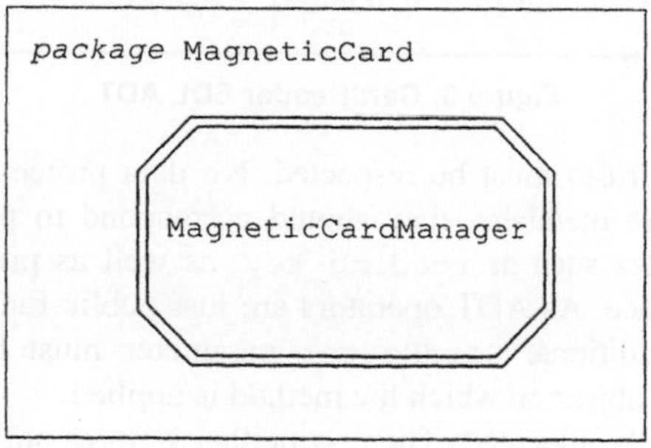

Figure 1: MagneticCardManager SDL process type

`MagneticCardManager` can be informed when a card is inserted into the reader, it can be requested to read the card data using a given decoding key, and to spit-out or swallow the card. It also indicates when a card is inserted.
It uses the `CardReader` OMT passive class shown in figure 2.

```
CardReader
-----------------------------------------------
reading_key: integer
cardInserted: boolean
data: CardData
-----------------------------------------------
CardReader(key: integer): CardReader
getCardData(key: integer): readStatus
swallowCard(): boolean
spitOutCard(): boolean
```

Figure 2: CardReader OMT passive class

The `CardReader` constructor takes as input the value of the `reading_key` attribute used to decode the card data. The `getCardData` operation reads the card data, decodes the data using `key` which should match with `reading_key`, then updates the `data` attribute and returns the reading status.

Since SDL and OMT are two separate "worlds", it's impossible for an SDL process to directly use an OMT class. The OMT class must be translated first into an SDL ADT as shown in figure 3.

```
NEWTYPE CardReader
  STRUCT
    cardInserted BOOLEAN;
    CardData data;
  OPERATORS
    newCardReader: INTEGER -> CardReader;
    getCardData: CardReader, INTEGER -> readStatus;
    swallowCard: CardReader -> BOOLEAN;
    spitOutCard: CardReader -> BOOLEAN;
    deleteCardReader: CardReader -> BOOLEAN;
ENDNEWTYPE;
```

Figure 3: CardReader SDL ADT

OMT to SDL translation rules must be respected. No data protection is available for ADT operators or data structure members, they should correspond to public operations or class attributes. Private attributes such as `reading_key` as well as private operations must not appear in the ADT interface. As ADT operators are just public functions and not operations related to a class, an additional `CardReader` parameter must be added for each ADT operator. It represents the object on which the method is applied.

SDL variables are statically allocated. There is neither pointer notion nor dynamic memory management in SDL. It can be a problem for passive objects which are created with constructors and deleted with destructors. SDL cannot accept a C++-like declaration such as `DCL cr(4721) CardReader;` where `4721` is the `key` value. So, memory must be dynamically allocated and released for `CardReader` objects:

- `DCL cr CardReader;` is used to declare an object,
- `TASK cr := newCardReader(4721);` to allocate memory for the object,
- `TASK result := deleteCardReader(cr);` to free the memory space used by the object with `DCL result BOOLEAN;`.

From an implementation point of view, it means that passive objects are managed using pointers. This point is discussed further in this paper. Furthermore, as many memory allocation and free ADT operators must be declared as constructors and destructor are given in the OMT class. Since it's possible in SDL to overload an ADT operator with several signatures, constructors can be given the same name in the ADT interface. The default constructor and destructor (with no parameters) provided by C++ compilers don't need to appear in the OMT class, but must be declared in the ADT interface.

Unfortunately, restrictions can also occur. OMT class operations returning `void` cannot be handled in SDL since ADT operators must return a value. As well, SDL ADT operators parameters are read only parameters. They are passed by value and not by address to insure complete determinism in the operators behavior, and allow axiomatic definitions of operators. That means OMT class operations with read/write parameters should not be allowed. They can be anyway using implementation mechanisms (see further).

Figure 4 shows the `MagneticCardManager` finite state machine and the `CardReader` ADT usage.

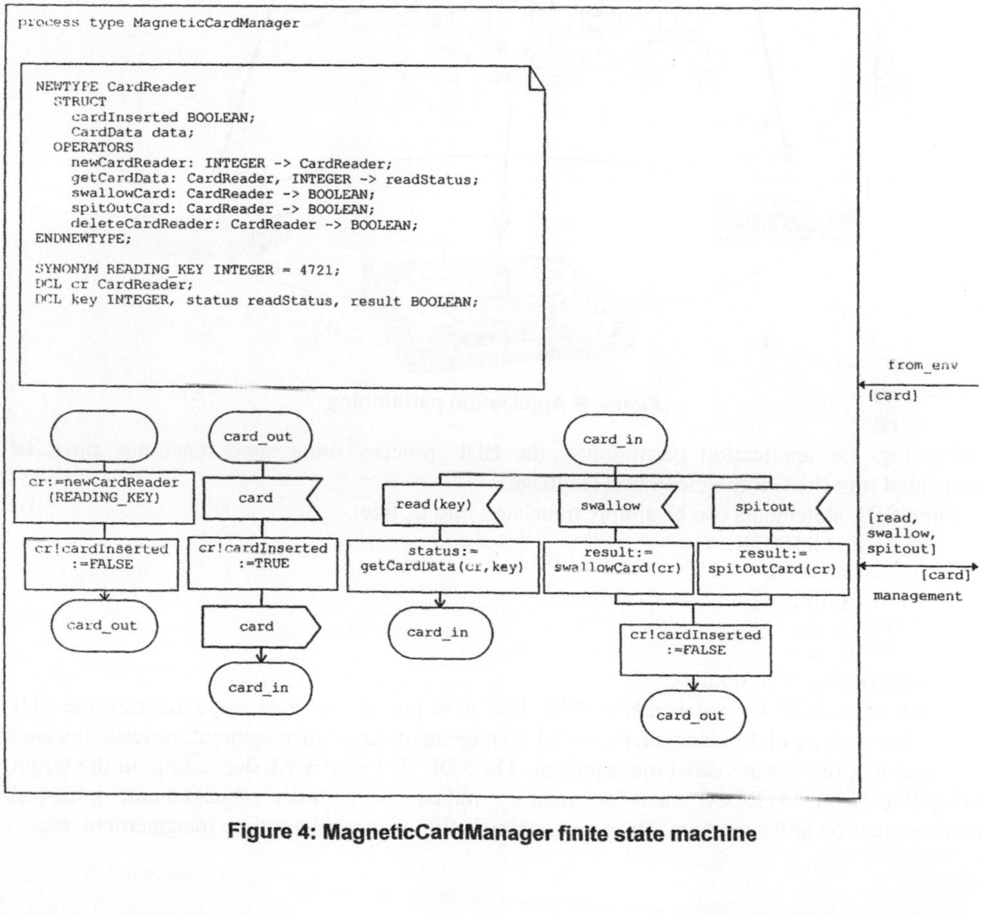

Figure 4: MagneticCardManager finite state machine

3. USUAL GENERATION OF C CODE FROM AN SDL DESIGN

3.1 Target Implementation

The SDL static and dynamic semantics as defined by the ITU-T recommendation is totally independent of any implementation consideration. SDL simulation offers a "virtual world" in which the SDL description can run according to these standard rules.

On the other hand, a real target environment cannot apply the same rules. A software application cannot possess unlimited resources such as CPU's or OS tasks, it must obey to communication and synchronization means provided by the selected RTOS and hardware composing the target platform.

The *application partitioning* is the definition of the dynamic architecture of the target as shown in figure 5. The SDL logical hierarchy, made of blocks and processes, must be mapped onto the logical and physical target architecture, made of tasks and coupled nodes [Enc93].

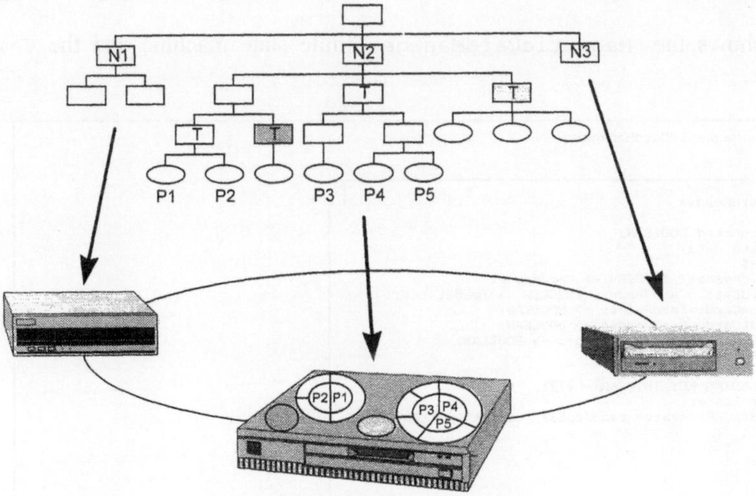

Figure 5: Application partitioning

Following the application partitioning, the SDL process finite state machines must be translated into the C implementation language.

If some SDL statements can be simply translated into C, like:

```
DCL i INTEGER;          ⇨    int i;
TASK i := i + 1;        ⇨    i = i + 1;
```

some of them, like:

```
SIGNAL s;
OUTPUT s;
```

need a particular development.

The aim of an *SDL Virtual Machine (SDL VM)* is to provide services implementing the SDL dynamics such as PID management, signal management, timer management, process instance management or view/revealed management. The SDL VM may need, depending on the target, primitives from a RTOS such as memory management, tasks management, inter-task communication and synchronization, mutual exclusion management, time management, etc.

Figure 6 shows an implementation strategy of the `MagneticCardManager` process where each process of the system corresponds to a RTOS task and associated message queue.
The body of a process is implemented as a double-nested switch on the state of the receiving process instance and the received signal. A process instance is just a part of the task memory context. A process transition is a C code sequence called by the double switch.
Extra code is also needed to manage the target-specific implementations (state machine, task management, message queue management, etc.).

```
K_GLOBAL_INIT(magneticcardmanager);     /* process global declarations      */

SDL_PROCESS(magneticcardmanager)        /* process/task entry point         */
{
int current_signo;                      /* current signal number            */
int CURRENT_STATE;                      /* current process instance state   */
K_LOCAL_INIT(magneticcardmanager);      /* process specific initialization */

  while (SDL_TRUE)       /* infinite loop                                    */
  {
    S_READ_QUEUE()       /* read the input queue and update current_signo */
    I_SWITCH_CTX()       /* receiving instance context switching            */

    /*  double nested state/event switch */
    switch (CURRENT_STATE) {
      SDL_STATE(start):
        switch (current_signo) {
          SDL_START:
            transition_START();
          default:
            break;
        } break;
      SDL_STATE(card_out):
        switch (current_signo) {
          SDL_INPUT(card):
            transition_CARD_OUT_card();
          default:
            break;
        } break;
      SDL_STATE(card_in):
        switch (current_signo) {
          SDL_INPUT(read):
            transition_CARD_IN_read();
          SDL_INPUT(swallow):
            transition_CARD_IN_swallow();
          SDL_INPUT(spitout):
            transition_CARD_IN_spitout();
          default:
            break;
        } break;
      default:
        break;
    } /* end switch */

    S_RELEASE();         /* release the signal that has been consumed       */

  } /* end while */
} /* SDL_ENDPROCESS */
```

Figure 6: C implementation of the MagneticCardManager state machine

The C code of the `transition_CARD_IN_read()` transition shown in figure 7 looks like a *meta-SDL/PR* where SDL statements have been replaced by macros prefixed by "`SDL_`".

```
/*
 * transition STATE card_in INPUT read(key)
 */
#define transition_CARD_IN_read() \
  SDL_INPUT_read(key); \
  SDL_TASK status = CardReader_getCardData(cr, key); \
  SDL_NEXTSTATE(card_in); \
  break;
```

Figure 7: C translation of the MagneticCardManager transition on state card_in and input read

Some SDL statements can be easily defined:

```
#define SDL_PROCESS(process) main()
#define SDL_TASK
#define SDL_NEXTSTATE(state) CURRENT_STATE = state
#define SDL_JOIN(label) goto SDL_LABEL_label
```

Whereas some other statements need to be defined using primitives of the SDL Virtual Machine:

```
#define SDL_INPUT_signal(...) ...
#define SDL_OUTPUT_signal(...) ...
```

Some SDL VM primitives are also directly included:

```
K_LOCAL_INIT(process)
S_READ_QUEUE()
I_SWITCH_CTX()
S_RELEASE()
```

Figure 8 shows the translation of the `MagneticCardManager` PR declaration.
The definition of `CardReader` is given in a separate file `CardReader.h`.

```
#include "CardReader.h"

#define SDL_SYNONYM_READING_KEY 4721
CardReader *cr;
SDL_INTEGER key; readStatus status; SDL_BOOLEAN result;
```

Figure 8: C translation of the MagneticCardManager PR declaration

3.2 Transformation of an ADT

An ADT can be easily translated into C.
The data structure is translated into a C record, and the operators are translated into C functions.

Figures 9 and 10 present a C code implementation of the `CardReader` ADT.

```
#ifndef CardReader_h
#define CardReader_h

typedef struct {
  SDL_BOOLEAN cardInserted;
  CardData data;
} CardReader;

CardReader *CardReader_newCardReader(SDL_INTEGER);
readStatus  CardReader_getCardData(CardReader *, SDL_INTEGER);
SDL_BOOLEAN CardReader_swallowCard(CardReader *);
SDL_BOOLEAN CardReader_spitOutCard(CardReader *);
SDL_BOOLEAN CardReader_deleteCardReader(CardReader *);

#endif
```

Figure 9: C header file "CardReader.h"
CardReader ADT data structure definition and functions declarations

```
#include "CardReader.h"

CardReader *CardReader_newCardReader(SDL_INTEGER key) {
  /* operator body to be hand-written */
}

readStatus  CardReader_getCardData(CardReader *cr, SDL_INTEGER key) {
  /* operator body to be hand-written */
}

SDL_BOOLEAN CardReader_swallowCard(CardReader *cr) {
  /* operator body to be hand-written */
}

SDL_BOOLEAN CardReader_spitOutCard(CardReader *cr) {
  /* operator body to be hand-written */
}

SDL_BOOLEAN CardReader_deleteCardReader(CardReader *cr) {
  /* operator body to be hand-written */
}
```

Figure 10: C Source File "CardReader.c"
CardReader ADT functions definitions

3.3 Software Architecture Implemented from the SDL Design

A typical software architecture generated from an SDL design is described in figure 11. In this picture, we assume that the hardware platform is made of two CPU's connected together through a UDP/IP link.

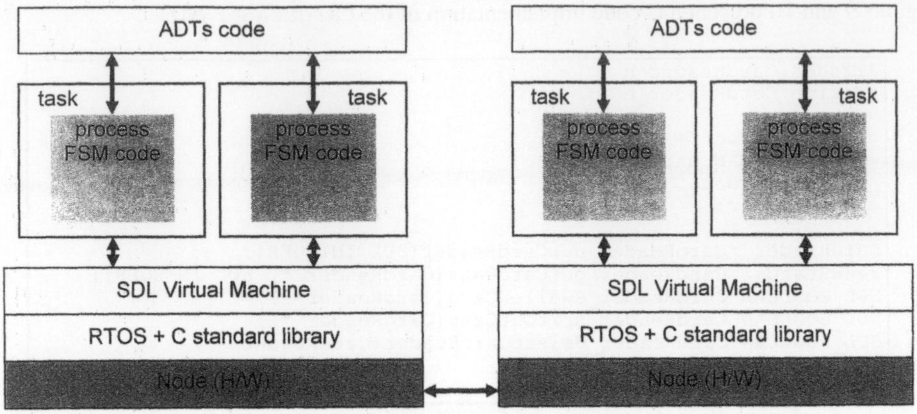

Figure 11: Typical target architecture implemented from an SDL Design

4. USUAL TRANSLATION OF C++ CODE FROM AN OMT DESIGN

4.1 Code Generation Strategy

An OMT class diagram can be easily translated into C++.

An OMT class becomes a C++ class. Information must be added on attributes and methods such as the access rights, instance or class member, virtual, etc. The associations and aggregations can be implemented in different ways: transformation into object pointers, linked lists, etc. Inheritance is directly supported in C++.

4.2 Details on the Generated C++ Code

Figures 12 and 13 show a C++ code implementation of the `CardReader` class.

```
#ifndef CardReader_h
#define CardReader_h

class CardReader {
private:
  int reading_key;
public:
  int cardInserted;
  CardData data;
  CardReader(int);
  readStatus getCardData(int);
  int swallowCard(void);
  int spitOutCard(void);
};

#endif
```

Figure 12: CardReader class C++ interface "CardReader.h"

```
#include "CardReader.h"

CardReader::CardReader(int key) {
  /* method body to be hand-written */
}

readStatus CardReader::getCardData(int key) {
  /* method body to be hand-written */
}

int CardReader::swallowCard(void) {
  /* method body to be hand-written */
}

int CardReader::spitOutCard(void) {
  /* method body to be hand-written */
}
```

Figure 13: CardReader class C++ implementation "CardReader.C"

5. INTEGRATION OF C++ CODE INTO C CODE

5.1 Current Issues

An SDL ADT is not strictly speaking an OMT class as discussed in paragraph 2. The operators of an ADT are functions, not methods applied on objects. An ADT operator must return a value. ADT parameters are passed by value, no pointers or references are available. There is no data protection and no object constructor/destructor.

These differences can lead to some restrictions on the use of OMT to describe passive objects. Some of them can be overpassed using SDL to C/C++ translation board effects.

5.2 Details on the Code Interfacing the C and the C++ Parts

Here is the situation we have to face to:

- OMT design of a passive object interface (class),
- translation of the OMT class into an SDL ADT,
- C++ class implementation of an OMT class,
- C data structure & functions implementation of an SDL ADT.

Two solutions can be envisaged to support the two last points in a consistent way:

- implementing an OMT class into C,
- implementing an SDL ADT into C++.

The second solution seems to be the best in order to benefit from the OO and C++ programming advantages: inheritance, reuse, genericity, encapsulation, etc.

In the case of automatic code generation, we first have to cancel the C definition and declarations translated from the SDL design of the ADT. Otherwise, the definitions given figure 9 and 12 for the same `CardReader` will lead to a compilation conflict.

This requires one to be able to indicate that the `CardReader` ADT definition is external from the SDL design, which means that no C definition is needed.

A notation solution can be the following:

```
NEWTYPE CardReader
  ...
ENDNEWTYPE COMMENT 'imported';
```

Then, the `CardReader.h` file included in the figure 8 corresponds to the C++ `CardReader` class interface given figure 12.

Note that this *import* mechanism of externally defined C or C++ constants, data types or functions into the SDL design (which only requires declarations) can be very useful to manage pointers in SDL.

Then, we have to map each ADT operator call onto its corresponding C++ class method call. The figures below describe this solution for the `CardReader` class.

```
CardReader *cr; int key; readStatus status;
   cr = new CardReader(4721);
status = cr->getCardData(key);
         delete cr;
```

Figure 14: Usage of the getCardData method in a C++ code fragment

```
DCL cr CardReader, key BOOLEAN, status readStatus, result BOOLEAN;
TASK      cr := newCardReader(4721);
TASK status := getCardData(cr, key);
TASK result := deleteCardReader(cr);
```

Figure 15: Usage of the getCardData ADT operator in an SDL process FSM code fragment

```
CardReader *cr; SDL_BOOLEAN key; readStatus status; SDL_BOOLEAN result;
SDL_TASK     cr = CardReader_newCardReader(4721);
SDL_TASK status = CardReader_getCardData(cr, key);
SDL_TASK result = CardReader_deleteCardReader(cr);
```

Figure 16: Meta-SDL translated from the SDL/PR given figure 15

```
CardReader *cr; int key; readStatus status; int result;
    cr = CardReader_newCardReader(4721);
status = CardReader_getCardData(cr, key);
result = CardReader_deleteCardReader(cr);
```

Figure 17: C code expanded from the meta-SDL given figure 16 (pre-processing)

At this stage, the codes given figures 14 and 17 should be the same ones.

The obtained code figure 17 is not consistent with the definition of the C++ `CardReader` class. Unresolved symbols `CardReader_newCardReader`, `CardReader_getCardData` and `CardReader_deleteCardReader` will be warned by the C++ linker.

To solve this problem, we need to introduce other definitions:

```
#define CardReader_newCardReader(key) \
  new CardReader(key)
#define CardReader_getCardData(object, key) \
  (object)->getCardData(key)
#define CardReader_deleteCardReader(object) \
  1; delete object
```

If we expand the meta-SDL figure 16 with this new definitions, we match the usage of the C++ `CardReader` class figure 14. Everything is now consistent.

The solution is very simple and allows the co-targeting in C and C++ of an SDL and OMT design.

This integration has, of course, to be generalized to all the ADT operators:

```
#define CardReader_swallowCard(object) \
  (object)->swallowCard()
#define CardReader_spitOutCard(object) \
  (object)->spitOutCard()
```

6. CONCLUSION

The C/C++ code generation strategy proposed in this paper is applicable for systems designed jointly with SDL for the real-time parts and with OMT for data management, GUI's and algorithms.
The solution described for a coherent co-targeting makes the deployment of complex and data-intensive systems easier, even on distributed platforms with hard real-time constraints.

The expected benefits are various.

- **Portability**: application portability is a major issue for right-sizing. With the proposed solution, the generated application can be deployed on any platform on which runs the SDL Virtual Machine (it requires also a C++ compiler). As a consequence, porting applications on a specific platform consists in porting the SDL Virtual Machine once on the selected RTOS (which should not exceed 2 months, independently of the complexity of the ported application).
- **Reuse and extendibility**: reuse of components, whether they belong to the real-time domain or to the data processing domain, is easy thanks to the high modularity of the generated application. Reusable components can be integrated at the design level, either in the OMT model or in the SDL model. The implementation strategy investigated here allows also to directly integrate C or C++ code into the generated structure. Coupling the generated application with legacy systems is also easy, at the OMT/C++ level as well as at the SDL/C level.
- **Project mastered**: by automating this solution with SDL and OMT tools, the developer can work at design level with modeling techniques more abstract than programming languages, with the efficiency of the final application being still preserved. The project progress is more visible and the software quality is easier to evaluate: graphical models are more understandable than thousands of lines of C or C++ code!
- **Performances**: the actual application performances mainly depend on the basic mechanisms implementing the real-time features: creation and deletion of tasks, inter-task communication, etc. This is why the proposed solution is based on the direct use of a RTOS instead of having redeveloped a (non-efficient) OS layer on top of the hardware target.

This study has been conducted and validated with the *Object*GEODE toolset [VER96]. In particular the OMT C++ Generator and the SDL C Code Generator, parts of this toolset, have been exercised in this way.

I would like to thank the VERILOG team in charge of the *Object*GEODE toolset and especially Philippe Leblanc and Nicolas Dervaux for their support in this work.

BIBLIOGRAPHY

[Enc93] V. Encontre et al., "Building Real-time Distributed Software with the New Generation of GEODE", 6th SDL Forum, 1993

[ITUa96] ITU-T, Recommendation Z.100, "Specification and Description Language (SDL) ", Geneva, 1996

[ITUb96] ITU-T, "SDL+ Methodology", Geneva, 1996

[ITUc96] ITU-T, Recommendation Z.105, "SDL Combined with ASN.1", Geneva, 1996

[Leb96] Ph. Leblanc, "Object-Oriented and Real-Time Techniques: Combined Use of OMT, SDL and MSC", Current Issues in Electronic Modeling Series, Issue # 7, Kluwer Academic Publishers, 1996

[Ols94] A. Olsen, O. Faergemand, B. Moller-Pedersen, R. Reed, J.R.W. Smith, "System Engineering Using SDL-92", North-Holland, 1994

[Rum91] J. Rumbaugh et al., "Object-Oriented Modeling and Design", Prentice-Hall, 1991

[VER96] VERILOG, *Object*GEODE Toolset Documentation, 1996

XI

Verification and Validation II

SDL '97: TIME FOR TESTING - SDL, MSC and Trends
A. Cavalli and A. Sarma (Editors)

Interconnecting the *Object*GEODE and CÆSAR-ALDÉBARAN toolsets

Alain Kerbrat, Carlos Rodriguez-Salazar[a*] and Yves Lejeune[b]

[a]Verimag, centre Equation, 2 rue de Vignate, 38610 Gières, France
e-mail: {Alain.Kerbrat, Carlos.Rodriguez}@imag.fr
www: http://www.imag.fr/VERIMAG

[b]Verilog, 150 rue Nicolas Vauquelin, BP1310, 31106 Toulouse cedex, France
e-mail: lejeune@verilog.fr
www: http://www.verilog.fr

Most of SDL tools, either commercial or academic, propose functionalities related to the code generation and test suites generation or application; this is sometimes combined with some formal analysis capabilities, based on a more or less exhaustive and controlled simulation. But no SDL tools propose more advanced formal verification activities, like the evaluation of temporal logic formula or the use of bisimulation relations to compare SDL specifications or minimize SDL models. This paper presents the interconnection of the formal verification toolbox CÆSAR-ALDÉBARAN with the commercial toolbox *Object*GEODE. This interconnection allows to extend the formal analysis capabilities of the *Object*GEODE simulator. One part of this connection is done through an API to the internal functions of the simulator, thus allowing to apply the 'on the fly' verification methods of CÆSAR-ALDÉBARAN.

1. Introduction

Most of SDL tools, either commercial or academic, propose functionalities related to the generation of executable code, often completed with the generation of test; this is sometimes combined with some formal analysis capabilities, based on a more or less exhaustive and controlled simulation. The more advanced in this respect are probably the commercial tools *Object*GEODE and SDT as they both propose exhaustive state space exploration, with optionally Holzmann's bit-state hashing [9]. They also include the use of deterministic observers to allow for some behavioral verification.

On the other hand, there exist many academic tools offering more advanced verification capabilities. Many tools propose the evaluation of temporal logic formulae, like μ-calculus or CTL. Others allow to use various equivalence or preorder relations like bisimulation equivalences to compare two behavioral specifications at different levels of abstraction. However, most of these tools are designed to work with more academic FDTs like ESTELLE and LOTOS.

*Verimag is a joint laboratory of Université Joseph Fourier, CNRS and INPG

The CADP(CÆSAR-ALDÉBARAN Distribution Package) [7] toolset corresponds to this description. It allows to describe, compile, simulate and verify programs using either the LOTOS language or a more basic description language based on extended communicating automata. It is composed of several verification tools, either for μ-calculus checking, behavioral comparison using various bisimulation equivalences and reduction and visualization of the behavior graph built from the program's description.

However, the principle of a connection of CADP with SDL compilers was not explored until one year ago, when VERILOG provided us with an Application Programming Interface to the *Object*GEODE simulator. In this paper, we present such a connection, how it is performed and what are the benefits of this combination.

This paper is organized as follow. In section 2, we present the model checking principle and how it is applied in the validation and verification functionalities of each toolset. In section 3, we explain how the connection of the toolsets is performed. In section 4, we present what are the additional Validation & Verification functionalities that CADP brings.

2. Model based Validation and Verification techniques

Model checking [5,15] consists in building a finite model of the system under analysis and to check the desired requirements on this model. The check itself amounts to a partial or complete exploration of the model.

The main advantages of this technique are that it can be automated and it is fast. Furthermore, model checking allows the easy production of counterexamples, when a property happens to be false. The main problem of model checking is the potential size of the model, which depends on the system complexity and can be huge. This problem is the *state explosion problem*.

Given this model, it is then possible to simulate step by step, or randomly the system. Furthermore, if the model is finite, we can also explore it exhaustively, thus providing the basis for formal verification.

The model considered in the case of the two toolsets presented below is a Labelled Transition System (LTS). A LTS is a state graph with anonymous states (no information except a distinguishing number) and transitions labelled with an identification of the actions performed during the states change.

We first give a general presentation of the ALDÉBARAN part of the CADP toolset, as ALDÉBARAN is a good illustration of model based verification techniques.

2.1. ALDÉBARAN presentation

ALDÉBARAN is a formal verification tool. It has been developed for 8 years and integrates state-of-the-art techniques as well as less recent, but intensively tested and applied techniques. It is a part of the CÆSAR-ALDÉBARAN [7] toolbox.

The architecture of this toolset is centered on the model. More precisely, three main issues are addressed (see figure 1):

Model Generation: Use or design compilers from high level languages to generate the functions needed for the model exploration.

Model Representation: How to store efficiently this model.

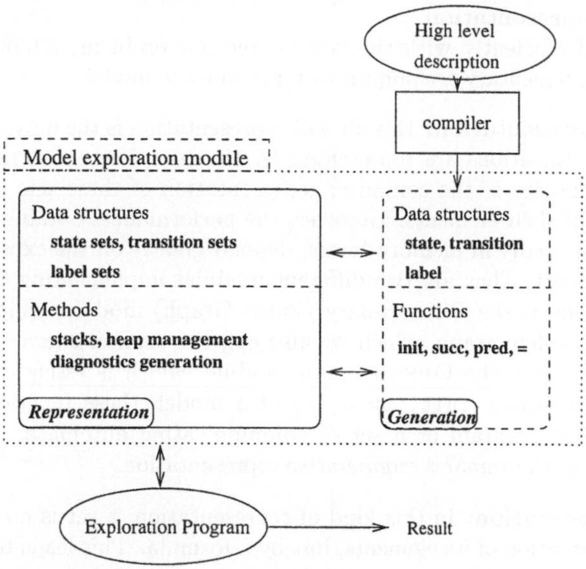

Figure 1. CADP principles

Exploration Program: Use or design algorithms and tools to explore this model for simulation and verification purposes.

So the *model exploration module* presented in figure 1 is a generic box providing what is necessary for the exploration of the model. Once completed by a compiler with the generation functions, this module can be coupled to an exploration program. We detail each of these issues, and present the available exploration programs in the next paragraphs.

2.1.1. Model generation

ALDÉBARAN is independent of any language, as the model it works with is low level and sufficiently general. However, to ease the description of complex systems, we usually use compilers from high-level languages to produce the functions needed for the model exploration. Generally, the functions `init` (returning the initial state), `succ` (computing the firable transitions from any state) and = (comparing two states) are needed. Depending on the exploration to do, it is sometimes necessary to have the function `pred` (computing the transitions leading to a state). The compiler usually also indicates the exact structure of a state, a transition and a label.

ALDÉBARAN works with several different compilers. The main is CÆSAR , which is an efficient compiler of LOTOS description. Another ad-hoc compiler allows the generation of the model from Communicating Extended Automata. It is internal to ALDÉBARAN and serves for experimentation purposes.

2.1.2. Model Representation

In order to deal efficiently with the state explosion problem, ALDÉBARAN uses two different, but complementary techniques to represent the model.

Enumerative representation: this kind of representation is the most classical one; sets of states or transitions are represented by the complete enumeration of their elements. So the size of the computer representation of these sets is proportional to the number of their elements. However, the performances obtained with this representation, especially in memory terms, depend greatly on the exploration technique used (see below). They are two different modules implementing this kind of representation. One is the BCG (Binary Coded Graph) module, which allows to store efficiently complete graph, which we also call the *explicit enumerative* representation. The other is the OPEN-CÆSAR module, which is essentially an API to the generation functions (`init, succ, =`) of a model, these functions coming either from a LOTOS program or a set of communicating automata. We call this last representation the *implicit enumerative* representation.

Symbolic representation: in this kind of representation, a set is no more represented by the enumeration of its elements, but by a formula. This leads to a representation of a set which is no more proportional to its number of elements. In ALDÉBARAN, this representation is based on Binary Decision Diagrams (BDD) [4], which is a very efficient technique for the manipulation of boolean formulae. The module implementing this is the SMI [3] (Symbolic Model Interface) module.

Enumerative and symbolic representations are complementary. Depending on the system from which the model is built, one of the representation can be more efficient than the other. So it is important to be able to work with both.

2.1.3. Model Exploration

All the validation and verification activities are performed with a more or less exhaustive exploration of the model. This exploration necessitates the use of data structures to keep record of explored states, of fired transitions and other useful information. These data structures usually depend on the kind of representation chosen for the model. For enumerative representation, CADP provides everything needed to represent sets of states or transitions (for example hash-tables), to manage efficiently stacks and the heap (for depth-first or breadth-first exploration) and provides means to easily built diagnostics (i.e. execution sequences leading to faulty states). For symbolic representation, less data structures are necessary, as the representation of sets is the basis of symbolic representation, and the exploration does not need stacks.

2.1.4. Exploration Programs

The exploration program is the algorithm which pilots the exploration of the model to check some properties, compute some information or allow the user to simulate the system. It is coupled more or less tightly with the exploration module, depending on the kind of representation chosen. When we leave aside any interaction of the user, the efficiency of the exploration becomes a crucial factor for successful verification. This efficiency depends in part on the representation of the model and the data structures used for its exploration, which is discussed in the previous paragraph. It depend also on the quality of the algorithm and on the optimizations one can bring to the model's size.

When we consider an enumerative representation of the model, we can choose two different approaches:

Working with the explicit representation: this consists in using the exploration module to fully compute the reachable parts of the model and store all the transitions on the way, then to apply the exploration program. In that case, the exploration program can be implemented rather independently of the exploration module, and have its own way of retrieving and storing the model. This is obviously limited to models of "reasonable" size, however it is sometimes necessary for algorithms needing a global knowledge of a model to work on it, like some minimization algorithms.

Working with the implicit representation: this consists in designing exploration algorithms which directly interact with the exploration module, to pilot the exploration of the model according to their own strategies. This allows to implement so-called "on the fly" verification. One of the benefits of this approach is in terms of memory, as it is not usually necessary to record the transitions of the graph. For some algorithms, it is even not necessary to keep an exact idea of the explored states, keeping either partial information (like in Holzmann's bitstate hashing) or only some states (at least the stack in a depth-first search). So the savings in memory can be considerable.

Finally, working with the symbolic representation requires the exploration algorithm to be implemented with respect to the API of the exploration module. The algorithms working with this representation tend to be very different, as they operate directly on sets of states, so in a breadth-first like mode. Algorithms working on enumerative representations work with individual states, generally depth-first.

2.2. Available exploration programs

The available exploration programs of CADP include an interactive simulator, tools for locating deadlocks, livelocks, or some execution sequences specified by a regular expression.

On the verification side, ALDÉBARAN capabilities belong to two main categories, behavioral verification and logical verification.

Behavioral verification

Behavioral verification consists in comparing two different descriptions of the behavior of a system. One should be the SDL description, the other can be a set of execution sequences, MSCs, or another Labelled Transition System. This LTS can itself be produced from another SDL description, possibly more abstract or from another point of view.

A crucial point with behavioral verification is the definition of an adequate comparison relation. As we want to compare behaviors, a good candidate for a comparison relation should satisfy most or all of the following criteria:

preservation of execution sequences : this is the basis of behavioral comparison, it ensures that two LTSs said equals represent the same sets of execution sequences (equivalence of language or `trace` equivalence).

abstraction : we would like to compare two different descriptions of a same system, at different levels of abstraction. This means for example that a given event can be present in the more detailed description, and absent from the more abstract one, or an event of the most abstract can be refined into a sequence of events in the more detailed description. So the comparison relation should take into account some abstraction/observation criteria to allow the comparison of the descriptions at the same abstraction level. This is usually done by defining a set of *observable* events, and by considering other events as internal, thus anonymous or invisible.

preservation of the branching structure : two LTSs can represent the same language, yet be different in their structure. This structure reflects the internal choices made in the corresponding system. These internal choices can often influence the interactions one system has with another. So it is important to take them into account when verifying some properties.

The relations considered in ALDÉBARAN belong to the class of the *simulation* and *bisimulation* [14] relations. These relations respect all the criteria defined above. By variation of the abstraction criteria, and of how internal actions are considered, we obtain a lattice of relations, from the weakest, *safety equivalence*, to the strongest, *strong bisimulation*, an interesting compromise being the *branching bisimulation*. Strongest here means the relation which distinguishes more LTSs. The strength of one relation is directly related to the kind of properties it preserves. For example, the strong bisimulation preserves every properties (safety or liveness), where the safety equivalence preserves only safety properties. So choosing the right relation depends on what is to be verified.

Minimization

If we have two LTSs equivalent for one of these bisimulation relations, obviously it is better to work with the smallest one (in term of number of transitions), as verifying properties on it is equivalent to verifying properties on the other. As these equivalence relations define equivalence classes for LTSs, we would like to be able to pick one of the smallest in this class, and to continue to work with it. Some of the algorithms for behavioral comparison does in fact compute this minimal equivalent LTS. Two of these algorithms [13,2] are implemented in ALDÉBARAN, and are in effect used also to produce this minimal LTS.

Logical verification

Logical verification consists in checking if the system verifies a property expressed as a temporal logic formula.These are classical logics extended with *modal* operators, i.e. operators allowing references to the past or the future. Classical temporal logics include CTL [5] and its variants, the μ-calculus [12], ... ALDÉBARAN integrates an up-to-date tool for logical verification. This tool, called EVALUATOR, allows to check μ-calculus formulae. EVALUATOR works "on the fly" with the enumerative representation of a model. It is also implemented with the symbolic representation, using a different algorithm.

2.3. *Object*GEODE presentation

*Object*GEODE is a real time systems development toolset, devoted to the use of the SDL and MSC languages. It includes graphical editors, compilers, a code generator and a simulator which allows the debugging and some verification of SDL programs. As we are interested mainly in validation and verification, we will focus on the SIMULATOR tool.

The SIMULATOR tool

The SIMULATOR allows to simulate the execution of the program, without having to actually execute it in a real environment. It can be seen as a sort of abstract debugger, as it allows to simulate the description step by step, to undo execution steps, to set break points and to watch the contents of variables and queues. Finally, it also allows to record, visualize as MSCs or replay some simulation sequences.

It is also more than a debugger, as it allows to perform automatic simulation, either randomly or exhaustively, with systematic comparison of the behavior with special state machines called observers. The simulator working principle is based on the model checking principle (see section 2). Its architecture correspond to the figure 1. The GSMCOMP SDL compiler produces the needed functions for the graph generation and some of the data structures for the model's representation. The SIMULATOR itself provides the data structures for the model exploration (hash-tables, stacks and heap management). It integrates exploration programs such as deadlock and livelock search, assertion checking and comparison with observers.

Observers

The core of the verification methods of *Object*GEODE is based on the observers [1]. They can be directly written using the GOAL language or compiled from MSCs. Observers are state machines which are executed side by side with the SDL description. Every time an event occurs (for example the firing of the whole transition, or the input of a signal, or an informal decision), the observer checks if it is an event he is able to recognize (there is a transition from its current state which matches the system's transition). If it is the case, it executes its corresponding transition, otherwise he ignores the event. The states of observers can be qualified either as success or error states. During the comparison of a description with an observer, sequences leading to error states can be saved as diagnostics.

This synchronous-like execution mode is similar to the technique used for behavioral comparison (see previous section). More precisely, given a system S and an observer O, it allows to check if the language (set of execution sequences) of S is contained in the language of O. As *Object*GEODE imposes that observers are deterministic (by applying a determinization algorithm if necessary), then this computation reduces to check if there is a *safety simulation* of S by O, so it allows to check safety properties.

However, observers are more, they can be considered as a substitute to the user for exhaustive and random simulation modes. An observer uses a set of *probes*, given as access paths to the entities (blocks, processes, queues, variables) to be observed. These probes allow to observe events like transition firing, communications of signals, creation or stopping of processes, time progression or procedure calls. They also give the possibility to change the program behavior, by changing the value of variables, so they can be used for example for fault-injection in the system.

3. From *Object*GEODE to ALDÉBARAN

As *Object*GEODE and ALDÉBARAN both work on the model checking principle, they interconnect naturally at the model's level. Both toolsets use a LTS for the model, however, the LTS of *Object*GEODE presents some particularities.

3.1. *Object*GEODE LTS

The LTS of *Object*GEODE can be obtained using the command `define edges_dump 'filename'` of the SIMULATOR during an exhaustive simulation.

One transition of this LTS correspond generally to one full SDL transition. which can contain several events, like I/O events, tasks, procedure calls, timers setting, process instances creation and stop ... Among them, we usually want only to observe communication events (I/O events plus optionally timer expiration signal).

The label which decorates a transition t is built from the names of the different events performed during the execution of the corresponding SDL transition or part of a transition. A label is a string, whose structure is given by the following (very abstract) grammar :

`geode_label` :: `event interaction*`

`event` :: `process_id` : `reference`

`interaction` :: `I/O_event` | `timer_event` | `procedure_call` | `create_stop_event`

where `process_id` is an identification of the process which fires the transition, `reference` indicates the input state, input signal and input parameters (if any) which were at the origin of this transition.

Structure of an I/O event

An SDL I/O event is composed of the following information:

- the name of the signal
- the type (input or output) of the event
- the parameters values
- the process identification of the sender (from) and receiver (to)
- the communication link used (via)

For example, here is the label of a randomly chosen transition of the ISUP LTS [11]:

"trans cpci(1) : from_wait_for_acm_input_rlc with rlc
input rlc from env to cpci(1)
output call_failure from cpci(1) via cpci to cc!cc(1)
  p1 = ind
output rel from cpci(1) via chan2 to env
set t1(15) from cpci(1)
set t5(60) from cpci(1)"

This transition corresponds to the execution by the first instance of the process `cpci` (`cpci(1)`) of a transition from the SDL state named `wait_for_acm`. The transition fired from this state is enabled by the input of the signal `rlc`. All this information is summarized in the transition *reference*, on the first line. The rest of the label indicates all the events taking place during the firing of the transition, with the concrete values for signals parameters ("p1 = ind") and timers setting. The references are built such that they allow to identify uniquely the SDL transition which has been fired. In fact, only references are used to build *Object*GEODE 's diagnostics, which allow to replay a given execution sequence with the SIMULATOR.

Now that we know the information available for each transition of *Object*GEODE LTS, we have to decide what is to be kept in ALDÉBARAN labels and how they are built.

3.2. ALDÉBARAN LTS

We present in this section how the LTS in ALDÉBARAN format is produced. The main concern is in fact how a label of a given transition of *Object*GEODE LTS is translated into ALDÉBARAN format. We first explain why there should not always be a one to one correspondence, then we explain how ALDÉBARAN labels are built.

Transformation into a IOLTS

One transition of the *Object*GEODE graph correspond generally to one full SDL transition (except for variable imports, informal decisions and blocking outputs due to bounded queues or rendez-vous). However, properties are usually defined in terms of single I/O events. So it is often interesting to slice the *Object*GEODE transitions in order to have exactly one I/O event on one transition. The resulting LTS is an Input/Output LTS (IOLTS). This transformation is generally straightforward, except when we consider a SDL transition where several `outputs` are performed to the environment, using different channels. As an SDL transition is considered to be atomic and instantaneous, all the output signals should be simultaneously present on the channels used. It is usually modeled by the interleaving of the corresponding inputs. However, these inputs are not modeled in the LTS generated by the SIMULATOR, as there is no process for the environment. To model this, we choose to generate all the needed interleaving between the output events going to different channels, as illustrated in figure 2. However, even if the transformation of the LTS into an IOLTS is often useful or necessary, it is not always needed and is left as an option.

Abstraction

Some of the information provided in the *Object*GEODE LTS are of no use for ALDÉBARAN. In fact, most of ALDÉBARAN 's algorithms consider as significant events only interactions between the system entities. So procedure calls, timers events and transition references should not appear in the LTS used by ALDÉBARAN.

Furthermore, not all information concerning a given I/O event are to be kept. Very often, properties are defined with only the names of the signals exchanged, but no reference to the sending or receiving process instances, or to the communication link chosen. Abstraction consists also in hiding away some irrelevant information for the property we want to check.

This abstraction is performed during the generation of the ALDÉBARAN labels. To

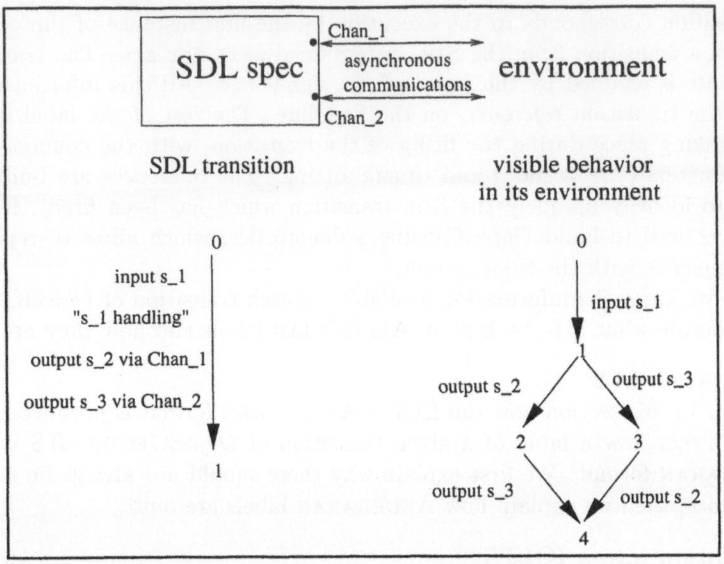

Figure 2. Interleaving of simultaneous outputs

allow for flexibility, we provide two complementary techniques for the user to build labels suitable for its verification tasks :

Providing one's own labeling function Once all information about an SDL transition are available, it is easy to provide a function writing a label in one's desired format. So in addition to default functions, a user can specify its own function.

Applying hiding and renaming rules A functionality which proved very useful in ALDÉBARAN is the possibility to apply hiding or renaming rules to the labels, depending on the property under check. These rules are given as regular expressions. Any label matching a rule is either hidden or renamed, the other labels being left untouched.

Both techniques can be used together. One can provide its default labeling function to write a specific default format, then for each property, or each analysis activity, apply a set of renaming rules on the output of the labeling function.

Example of abstraction by hiding and renaming
Hiding and renaming can be used to select a partial view on the model. For example, if we only want to observe interactions with the `cpci`, we can use the following file of hiding rules:

```
hide all but
".* from cpci(1) .*"
".* to cpci(1) .*"
```

If we want to observe only the input of a failure, and the output of a `release` to the env, map these signals to a new name and hide everything else, we can use the following file of renaming rules:

```
rename
"input call_failure.*" -> call_failure
"output rel .* to env" -> external_release
".*" -> i
```

All rules are applied in their appearing order. The first matching rule is applied. In this example, the last rule will be applied on all remaining labels, thus hiding them.

3.3. Interconnection

Interconnecting *Object*GEODE simulator and ALDÉBARAN can be done at two different levels :

- We can use the simulator to produce the full model exhaustively in a file, then convert this file to be used as an input to ALDÉBARAN. This is explained in section 3.3.
- or we can integrate some of ALDÉBARAN 's verification modules into the simulator, so they can be used during the SIMULATOR work. This is explained in section 3.3.

Connection of the explicit representations

This connection is the most straightforward one. It basically consists in translating the syntax of the graph descriptor and of each transition from the *Object*GEODE format to the ALDÉBARAN format. Practically, this translation works in several phases :

Syntactic analysis This is done using a YACC parser. Its YACC grammar's first version was written accordingly to the GÉODE SIMULATOR manual, where the syntactic form of labels is given. It was later improved for taking into account *Object*GEODE's output.

(optional) Slicing If the user wants the result to be an IOLTS, then each transition containing several I/O events are sliced into as many labelled transitions as necessary.

Abstraction The rules for abstraction are specified in a separate file, as a set of regular expressions in the UNIX `regex` format. Each label matching one of the regular expression is changed according to the corresponding rule.

Graph generation The last phase consists in the re-generation of the graph in the ALDÉBARAN 's format.

Connection of the implicit representations

Connecting the two toolsets at the implicit level allows to apply most of the "on the fly" algorithms of ALDÉBARAN. As this often avoids the complete graph generation, it is generally a more interesting alternative than the explicit kind of connection. This connection is performed through an Application Programming Interface to the SIMULATOR. This API was developed in agreement with VERILOG. This interface is written in C and makes available the functions needed to generate the graph (`init, succ, =`) as well as the storage of states and the management of stacks. It also provides access to the scenario generation functions. So the diagnostics computed in case of a failed verification can be played back by the SIMULATOR even when generated from ALDÉBARAN algorithms.

Last but not least, all the filtering, signal feeding, assertions and observers checking can still be enabled through this API. So one can combine these checks with a verification done with ALDÉBARAN. We did not investigate much this possibility, except for the use of filters and feeds during the exploration. However, this API does not provide yet an interface to the state internal information (what is the value of a variable, the content of a queue), so we did not exploit this possibility (but we intend to).

Most of the work at this level is essentially to interpose our own API for the CADP tools. This API is responsible for the graph translation. It works "on the fly", with optional transition slicing, optional user defined labeling function and the application of renaming rules.

4. Added functionalities

In this part, we describe what we have found to be useful in the conjoined use of *Object*GEODE with ALDÉBARAN. We have experimented this combination of two different case studies. One was a small part of a communication protocol, and was meant to illustrate the interests of this connection. The results of this experiment are described in [11]. The other was a much larger case study, concerning a embedded system for satellite control [16]. Due to lack of space, we are not able to describe the example which served as a support to these experimentations. So we draw here only the conclusions.

*Object*GEODE and ALDÉBARAN share a number of functionalities, like deadlock and livelock detection, interactive or random simulation. On the verification side, both allow exhaustive exploration of the state space, possibly with Holzmann's bitstate hashing. Both allow the checking of trace inclusion by observers.

As *Object*GEODE has a more user friendly interface, it is better to apply it for all the functionalities in common. In particular, the SIMULATOR allows to replay diagnostics with references to the source languages(SDL and MSC). ALDÉBARAN, being independent of the source language, does not offer by itself this possibility.

So the added value of ALDÉBARAN is essentially in the new functionalities it brings. Among them, we distinguish what we think are the most useful ones, namely comparison of LTSs for bisimulation equivalences, minimization and visualization of the LTS, checking of temporal logic formulae. All of these work with the explicit connection, i.e. on the fully generated LTS, translated into ALDÉBARAN format. With the implicit ("on the fly") API, we have connected the tool EVALUATOR for μ-calculus evaluation, we have developed a prototype connection for a part of the behavioral comparison algorithm (so far, it allows only to check inclusion for strong and safety simulation, but no equivalence), and we have tested the connection with the tool TGV , which is presented later. The minimization algorithms don't work "on the fly", as they need the pred function which is not provided by the SIMULATOR.

4.1. Behavioural comparison

ALDÉBARAN extends the possibilities of the *Object*GEODE observers, as it proposes a choice of equivalence relations as well as simulation relations. The choice of the equivalence applied is done according to the kind of property checked (is it a safety property ? a liveness property ? ...). Furthermore it allows the use of non deterministic observers. Finally, it allows to compare the LTSs of two SDL descriptions of the same system. This can be seen as a sort of "non-regression verification" if these two descriptions are two different versions of the same description.

4.2. Minimization

The minimization of the *Object*GEODE LTS yelds interesting results. Even when using the strong bisimulation (i.e. the least reducing), it usually reduces the size of the *Object*GEODE LTS by a 2 to 10 factor, with very good performances : for example, the LTS of a satellite control protocol was reduced from 147007 states and 555877 transitions to 66695 states and 254030 transitions in 6 min on a SPARC 20 with 128MB of memory. When we combine this with abstraction, we reduce the LTS much further, as we can take profit of weaker, more reducing bisimulations like the branching bisimulation. When the number of observable labels is small enough, the resulting LTS usually ends up with only a handful of states.

Minimization is useful especially for two purposes, first the possibility of visualizing the resulting minimal model, second the possibility of speeding-up the verification process.

Visualization of the minimal model

During the design of a SDL specification, it becomes rapidly difficult to understand how the different interactions occur. Trying to understand the behaviours of the system by replaying scenarios with the SIMULATOR or by visualizing MSCs does not always help. Too often the key events are bogged down in too many insignificant events. However, once the LTS has been minimized, it is possible to draw it to grasp its structure, and sometimes discover and understand some behaviours which were hidden in the description's complexity. It is particularly effective when choosing a handful (usually 2 or 3) of key events and hiding everything else. The resulting minimized model if usually very small, yet often more complex than one expects.

The CADP toolbox integrates a tool for the automatic drawing and interactive edition of LTSs. It allows to picture rapidly and easily the structure of these small LTSs (at most 10 to 20 states). Even if this LTS remains too big to be drawn, the CÆSAR-ALDÉBARAN simulator still allows to explore it interactively. So combining the abstraction, minimization and visualization allows to do what is sometimes called "visual verification", that is verify "on sight" on a small enough model that a property is correct.

Speeding-up the verification process

Another aspect of minimization is purely a performances aspect. Usually, the verification process includes many various properties, so it involves many model's explorations. Some of the properties will need only a simple exploration (e.g. for deadlocks), others the checks of liveness conditions (e.g. for livelocks), some other the use of elaborate algorithms involving the computation of bisimulations. So if before performing all these checks, it is possible to generate a minimized model with respect to a suitable equivalence, the whole verification process will be sped up by at least the reduction factor (and usually much more, as many of the verification algorithms involved are not linear). Furthermore, ALDÉBARAN offers a efficient storage for the model, through the BCG (Binary-Coded Graphs) file format. The BCG format is a binary encoding of the model, on which is applied a specific compression algorithm. This results in much more compact files for model's storage than textual formats. Typical compression rates can go as high as 20x, and are usually better than those obtained with the UNIX tool `gzip` .

4.3. Logical verification

Temporal logic is a supplementary formalism to express properties. It allows to express global properties of a system in a concise way. It can be particularly useful, as often informal requirements are rather easily translated as a logical formula, and less easily as a set of MSCs or a LTS. For example, the ISUP requirement " Releasing the line should always be possible" is expressed by the EVALUATOR formula `ALL (POT<"input rel">T)` which means that from all (`ALL`) states, there exists (`POT`) an execution sequence where the release signal `rel` is treated.

Furthermore, it is often better to describe a system using two different formalisms : in our case behaviorally (SDL, MSCs, observers) and logically (temporal logic), as it can avoid to repeat the same kind of errors through the same kind of description.

4.4. Test sequence generation

An important tool connected to the CADP toolset is the tool TGV [8] . Given a SDL description, and a test purpose, this tool is able to *automatically* generate *correct* conformance test suites in the TTCN language. This is a major gain as many testing processes involve writing test scenarios by hand, which is tedious and error-prone.

TGV uses algorithms usually applied for formal verification, but adapted here to the specific problem of automatic test cases generation. Provided that the SDL description is correct, then the test cases are also correct. This allows to test an implementation derived from an SDL description, but not necessarily compiled from it.

We have developed a prototype connection of TGV to *Object*GEODE , through the implicit level connection. It allowed to confirm the possibility of this connection, but still lacks the "on the fly" consideration of the testing architecture. However, this prototype connection can serve as a basis for the already planned transfer of TGV in a next distribution of *Object*GEODE.

5. Conclusion

We have presented the interconnection of *Object*GEODE and ALDÉBARAN and what are the benefits of this interconnection. We have experimented this combination for one year, on two different case studies. Using ALDÉBARAN with *Object*GEODE allowed to facilitate the verification and deepen the understanding of these protocols, especially when using minimization. It allowed also to discover some shortcomings of MSCs for the description of properties.

We plan to extend the interconnection of the toolsets, especially to allow the use of the symbolic methods available in ALDÉBARAN for the representation of the model. We are currently working on such a connection for our BDD based methods, as VERILOG offers in its commercial distribution an interface to the syntactic tree built by its SDL analyzer.

Other possibilities would be to have an extended API to the SIMULATOR, allowing the access to the states information. This should allow to perform analysis using convex polyhedra like in [10], or to evaluate temporal formulae with reference to the values of variables as predicates. Another direction of interest is the connection of *Object*GEODE to the KRONOS tool [6], to allow for efficient verification of timing constraints.

The tool `Geodeparse`, for the connection of the explicit representation, is available as ftp://ftp.imag.fr/pub/VERIMAG/ALDEBARAN/geodeparse.tar.gz. The libraries for implicit interconnection will be available soon, pending some improvements and the agreement of VERILOG.

Acknowledgments We would like to thank Laurent Mounier, for the proof-reading of this paper, and Marius Bozga, for his help in the connection of the EVALUATOR tool to the SIMULATOR.

REFERENCES

1. B.Algayres, Y.Lejeune, and F.Hugonnet. Goal: Observing sdl behaviors with geode. In *SDL forum'95*. Elsevier Science (North Holland), 1995.
2. Ahmed Bouajjani, Jean-Claude Fernandez, and Nicolas Halbwachs. Minimal model generation. In R. P. Kurshan and E. M. Clarke, editors, *Proceedings of the 2nd Workshop on Computer-Aided Verification (Rutgers, New Jersey, USA)*, volume 3 of *DIMACS Series in Discrete Mathematics and Theoretical Computer Science*, pages 85–92. AMS-ACM, June 1990.
3. Dorel Marius Bozga. Vérification formelle de systèmes distribués : diagrammes de décision multivalués. Master's thesis, Université Joseph Fourier, 1996.
4. Randal E. Bryant. Symbolic boolean manipulation with ordered binary decision diagrams. Technical report, School of Computer Science, Carnegie Mellon University, Pittsburgh, PA 15213, 1992.
5. E. Clarke, E. A. Emerson, and A. P. Sistla. Automatic verification of finite-state concurrent systems using temporal logic. In *10th Annual Symposium on Principles of Programming Languages*. ACM, 1983.
6. C. Daws, A. Olivero, S. Tripakis, and S. Yovine. The tool KRONOS. In *Hybrid Systems III, Verification and Control*, pages 208–219. Lecture Notes in Computer Science 1066, 1996.
7. J.C. Fernandez, H. Garavel, A. Kerbrat, R. Mateescu, L. Mounier, and M. Sighireanu. Cadp: A protocol validation and verification toolbox. In Rajeev Alur and Thomas A. Henzinger, editors, *Proceedings of the 8th Conference on Computer-Aided Verification (New Brunswick,*

New Jersey, USA), August 1996.

8. Jean-Claude Fernandez, Claude Jard, Thierry Jéron, Laurence Nedelka, and César Viho. Using on-the-fly verification techniques for the generation of test suites. In R. Alur and T. A. Henzinger, editors, *Proceedings of the 8th International Conference on Computer-Aided Verification (Rutgers University, New Brunswick, NJ, USA)*, volume 1102 of *LNCS*. Springer Verlag, 1996. Also available as INRIA Research Report RR-2987.
9. Gerard J. Holzmann. An analysis of bitstate hashing. In Piotr Dembinski and Marek Sredniawa, editors, *Proceedings of the 15th IFIP International Workshop on Protocol Specification, Testing and Verification (Warsaw, Poland)*. IFIP, Chapman & Hall, June 1995.
10. A. Kerbrat. Reachable states space analysis of lotos programs. *7th international Conference on Formal Description Techniques for Distributed Systems and Communication Protocols*, October 1994.
11. Alain Kerbrat, Dave Penkler, and Nicolas Raguideau. Using aldébaran and object-géode for the development of telecommunications services. Technical report, Hewlett Packard / Verimag, 1996.
12. D. Kozen. Results on the propositional μ-calculus. In *Theoretical Computer Science*. North-Holland, 1983.
13. Robert Paige and Robert E. Tarjan. Three partition refinement algorithms. *SIAM Journal of Computing*, 16(6):973–989, December 1987.
14. David Park. Concurrency and automata on infinite sequences. In Peter Deussen, editor, *Theoretical Computer Science*, volume 104 of *LNCS*, pages 167–183. Springer Verlag, March 1981.
15. Jean-Pierre Queille and Joseph Sifakis. Fairness and related properties in transition systems — a temporal logic to deal with fairness. *Acta Informatica*, 19:195–220, 1983.
16. VERIMAG. Dms design validation (ddv) verification report : Verification using aldébaran. Technical report, VERIMAG, 1996.

SDL '97: TIME FOR TESTING - SDL, MSC and Trends
A. Cavalli and A. Sarma (Editors)

Specifying the Steam-Boiler Case Study with SDL

F. Ammar Boudjelal, J.-Y. Lafaye, G. Louis*
L3i, Université de La Rochelle,
15 Rue de Vaux de Foletier, 17026 La Rochelle Cedex 01, France

ABSTRACT

This work is devoted to relating and discussing an experience in specifying a benchmark case in formal specification, namely the Steam-Boiler. Several such specifications have been published, that use various methods and languages, but none used SDL. We present the outlines of our approach intending to show how the basic features of SDL were either guidelines or constraints. We conclude by putting forward some propositions to enforce the former and diminish the latter.

1. INTRODUCTION

The Steam-Boiler specification problem has recently been proposed as a challenge to the Formal Specification community by J.R Abrial [1]. It was asked to propose a full study of the problem, from analysis and formal specification to executable code, the resulting program being tested against a common set of pre-established but unknown test cases [5]. A collection of the first 21 specifications has just been published [2].

It appears that the Steam Boiler problem is quite stimulating, since it presents several features which either are or are not within the natural scope of SDL. In Section II, we first present the problem, and then discuss the points in which SDL appears or not appropriate. The structural decomposition of the system is a basis for the dynamic SDL specification. The Boiler System structure and main justifications are evoked in Section III, whilst Section IV treats the dynamic aspects. As a conclusion, we point out the major difficulties we encountered in working out the SDL specification, and propose some additional facilities that could, in our point of view, make the specification process easier and improve the readability of the SDL documents, with little disruption of the original SDL syntax or semantics.

We completed the whole analysis, specification, design, coding and simulation process with the SDT Tool from Telelogic [4]. This results in a 40 pages document of SDL diagrams (comments excluded), and 1700 lines of C code. The specification can be obtained on request to the authors.

---

* fammar@iut-lr.univ-lr.fr, jylafaye@iut-lr.univ-lr.fr, glouis@iut-lr.univ-lr.fr

2. THE STEAM-BOILER SPECIFICATION PROBLEM

2.1. Some History

An original text by J.C. Bauer [3] was first presented at the Institute of Risk Research during a symposium at Waterloo University, Ontario (Canada). The problem was proposed as a challenge for the audience. The challenge was to design a system that could achieve automated control of the water level in a steam-boiler which is part of a nuclear station. Obviously, the system presents critical safety aspects, so any abnormal behaviour must lead to an emergency stop. On the other hand, a false alarm is also extremely damaging. The system's components are liable to failure. Under some conditions, the whole system can go on, operating in a degraded mode, when a recoverable failure occur.

In 1994, one year after J.C. Bauer's challenge, J.R Abrial proposed a simplified version of the Steam Boiler Case, focussing upon main safety and real time control process and leaving aside some secondary details. A Tcl-Tk animation program was created, that implemented a battery of significant test cases to be confronted to actual Steam-Boiler control programs. These programs should be generated from Formal Specification of the problem, so as to confront them to one another for evaluation.

2.2. Informal Specification

In the following, we of course only retain from the informal specification by J.R. Abrial, the main features which prove to be useful to understand the problem and its solution, or that are directly related to SDL concepts.

2.2.1. Equipment and devices

The system consists of the boiler itself, and of various pieces of equipment and measurement devices. The boiler can be viewed as a reservoir which is filled by means of a water pump, and emptied by opening a valve. Steam goes out the boiler and activates an engine which is external to the system. Several devices allow measurement of raw values for water level, steam rate and water flow through the pump. The valve or pump is either open or closed, and the water flow (either in or out) is supposed to equal either zero or a specified positive constant. The system includes a message transmission sub-system, and a computer to transform raw measurements into adjusted ones.

An external operator stands to start or stop the boiler, and to react to failures and to report repairs to the system.

2.2.2. Behaviour

There are two distinct phases to be taken into account when sketching out the boiler behaviour, namely the initialisation phase, and the permanent cyclic behaviour.

The operator begins initialisation, and starts the various pieces of equipment. The matter is to ensure that the conditions are nominal before allowing to start the boiler. The outgoing steam rate must be equal to zero, otherwise, the system has to be shut down. The water level unit starts a control process of the pump and the valve, so that the water level in the boiler is set within a nominal range. Only once this process is complete and the steam output is correct, can the second phase begin. Once initialisation is complete, the valve can no longer be activated, only pump and steam unit can regulate the water level.

Unlike the asynchronous initialisation phase, the next phase is synchronous. Execution is cyclic and refers to a timer that synchronises the whole system. In order to preserve safety conditions, three operating modes are defined : *normal mode*, *degraded mode* and *rescue mode*. Under some conditions, an extra *emergency stop mode* immediately leads to a system shut down. The system automatically switches from one mode to another when detecting equipment failure, i.e. when actual raw values appear inconsistent with the values having been estimated at the previous cycle.

<table>
<tr><th>LEVEL</th><th>STEAM</th><th>PUMP</th><th>OPERATING MODE</th></tr>
<tr><td rowspan="4">OK</td><td rowspan="2">OK</td><td>OK</td><td>Normal Mode</td></tr>
<tr><td>Broken</td><td rowspan="3">Degraded Mode</td></tr>
<tr><td rowspan="2">Broken</td><td>OK</td></tr>
<tr><td>Broken</td></tr>
<tr><td rowspan="4">Broken</td><td rowspan="2">OK</td><td>OK</td><td>Rescue Mode</td></tr>
<tr><td>Broken</td><td rowspan="3">Emergency Stop Mode</td></tr>
<tr><td rowspan="2">Broken</td><td>OK</td></tr>
<tr><td>Broken</td></tr>
</table>

Diagram 1 : Operating mode's switching rules

The degraded mode allows to go on controlling the boiler, waiting for repair, in case the steam and/or pump are broken. Under degraded mode, estimates of steam rate and/or water flow are computed and replace dubious raw values. Under rescue mode, the level measurement device is broken but both steam and pump must be correct, otherwise, a shut down is required. In this case, water level is estimated.

At each cycle, the program that controls the boiler, schematically repeats the following tasks :

- Receive and record raw measures from devices.
- Collate the raw measures and the limits that were computed at the previous cycle.
  Take convenient safety decisions so as to eventually correct the water level in the boiler.
  Update the operating mode.
- On the basis of the current values and some physical and technical rules about steam and water in the boiler, compute new confidence intervals for next cycle values.

2.3. Choosing SDL for specifying the Steam-Boiler

The Steam-Boiler clearly is a reactive system in which complexity is mainly related to real-time control. Hence, use of SDL is quite natural.

With regard to abstract structure, the boiler splits into cooperating sub-systems, each of them providing specific services. Such a decomposition is naturally well supported by SDL. On another hand, as far as dynamic aspects are concerned, it is of no doubt that all the control operations, can be directly translated in terms of signal exchange. Among the specifications proposed to answer J.R. Abrial challenge, many devote much work to the specification of the sole communication process. This is because the specification languages they use are not particularly suited for that. Conversely, all of communication management for the boiler problem can be simply handed over to SDL. This is mostly true within the initialisation phase, which is asynchronous; but SDL specification of the synchronous current execution is more complicated. As a matter of fact, using SDL to specify synchronous systems makes it mandatory to achieve a very precise scheduling of message exchange so as to be either independent on the order in which signals are sent and received or to fully control message sequencing.

3. SDL STRUCTURE OF THE STEAM-BOILER

We decided that the system should include a Supervisor and three controllers (one for each of steam, water level and water flow) which together form the so called Equipment block.

3.1. Equipment

Controllers have local knowledge of their state (i.e. OK v. Broken), and of both estimated and raw values of the physical parameter they deal with. During current cyclic operation, the operating mode (normal, degraded, rescue, emergency stop) is also known.

Some devices are cited in the informal specification, such as the valve, the pump and a message transmission system. We assumed that both pump and valve device were external to the system. The reason for this is related to failure detection. For instance, in case of a water flow failure, it is impossible to decide whether the pump itself or the pump controller is at fault. It goes similarly with the valve. So it is of no use to include such devices within the system. Anyway, the informal specification is quite vague about the relationship between the pump and its controller.

We already pointed out that we relied upon SDL for message management. So, there is no message transmission sub-system.

3.2. Supervisor

The Supervisor is necessary, because updating the operating mode requires instantaneous knowledge of all steam, level and water flow values. Without a Supervisor, concurrency between processes, and communication routes network, should be uselessly intricate, especially during the synchronous phase.

3.3. System and Block Diagrams

Each of the Diagrams below, shows a communication graph between blocks during the initialisation phase. In Diagram 2.1, the operator sends a start message to the equipment units. Diagram 2.2 accounts for relationship between level and pump controller for adjusting the water level in the boiler according to the initial conditions. In Diagram 2.3, the Supervisor waits for ready messages from the equipment units and then returns a program ready message before entering the cyclic operational phase.

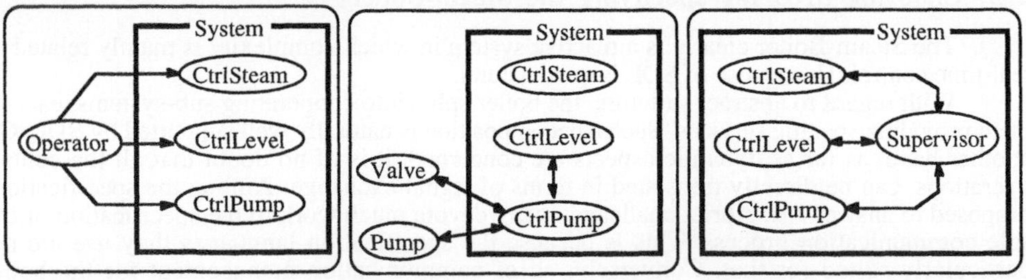

Diagrams 2.1, 2.2, 2.3 : Communication graphs - Initialisation phase

With respect to the previous relationship between system components, we derive the following SDL System Diagram restricted to the initialisation phase.

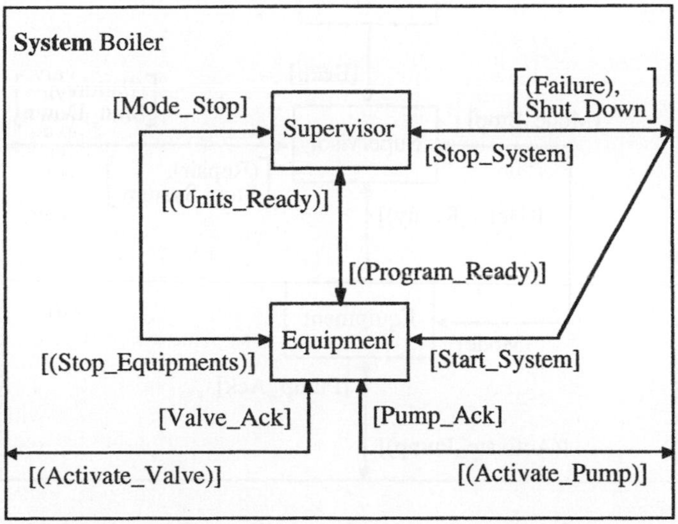

Diagram 3 : SDL system description - Initialisation phase

Once the operational phase is entered, the interactions between components repeat themselves from one cycle to another. Specific roles concerning water level, steam and water flow are distributed among corresponding units, while the Supervisor collects information from all of them and schedules the entire system in a synchronous execution. This strong connection is shown in Diagram 4, and Diagram 5 presents the corresponding SDL structure, including a clock to allow synchronous implementation.

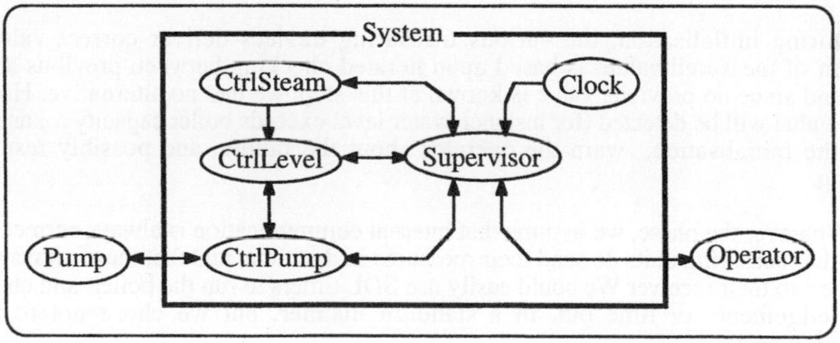

Diagram 4 : Communication graph - Operational phase

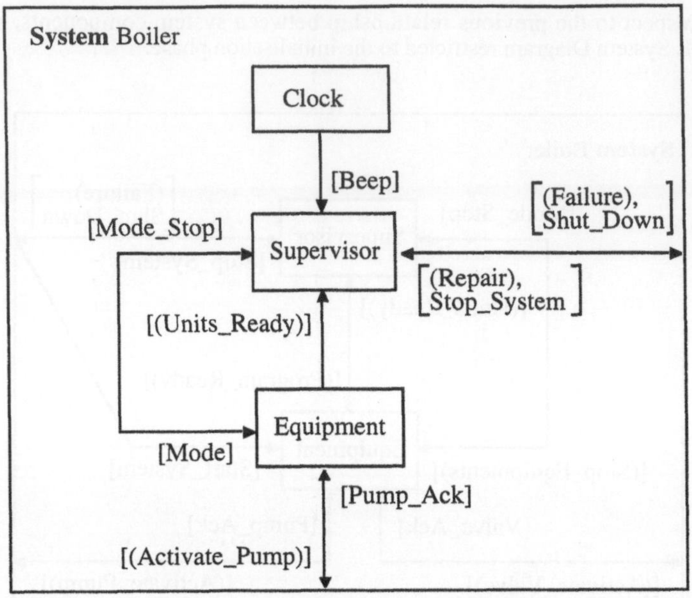

Diagram 5 : SDL system description - Operational phase

4. DYNAMIC ASPECTS

4.1. Decision and assumptions

The informal specification is not very precise about the initialisation phase, and some points in the current operation cycle are not completely deterministic (among responses to J.R. Abrial, many specifications skip the initialisation). Assumptions are to be made. So, we suppose the following, that is a set of necessary assumptions, in order to ensure safety.

During initialisation, the various measuring devices deliver correct values. Since validation of measured values is based upon iterated checking between previous and current values, and since no previous value is known at this step, we had no alternative. However, an aberrant value will be detected (for instance water level exceeds boiler capacity ...) and will lead to stop the initialisation, warn the operator about the failure, and possibly resume at the beginning.

Whatever the phase, we assume that internal communication is always correct. That is to say that the measuring units do send their measures in due time, and that these message are well transmitted to their receiver.We could easily use SDL timers to run the boiler and check receipt acknowledgement or time out, in a standard manner, but we chose not to make our specification heavy.

On the contrary, time out procedures are activated any time a communication with the environment (pump and valve) is attempted. Moreover, receiving a repair message when no failure has been detected leads to declare a transmission system failure.

It might be understood from the informal specification that a repair message from the operator, stands as a proof of good working order. We decided to be more drastic. Receiving a repair message is not enough, and a unit is not assumed to be repaired yet, unless the values it delivers are judged consistent with the limits estimated under degraded or rescue mode. This is to protect from possibly erroneous repair messages.

Apart from that, our SDL specification is in strict accordance with the deterministic rules of the informal specification.

4.2. SDL processes

It can be seen from Diagram 6, that except BlockPump, every sub-block in BlockEquipment is built in the same manner, i.e. it includes two processes, one for measuring, the other for controlling and computing. BlockPump only performs control, and we already discussed why the pump physical unit is external. The Supervisor has only one process. This dynamic structure allows each item to fulfil its specified contract as described in the next paragraph.

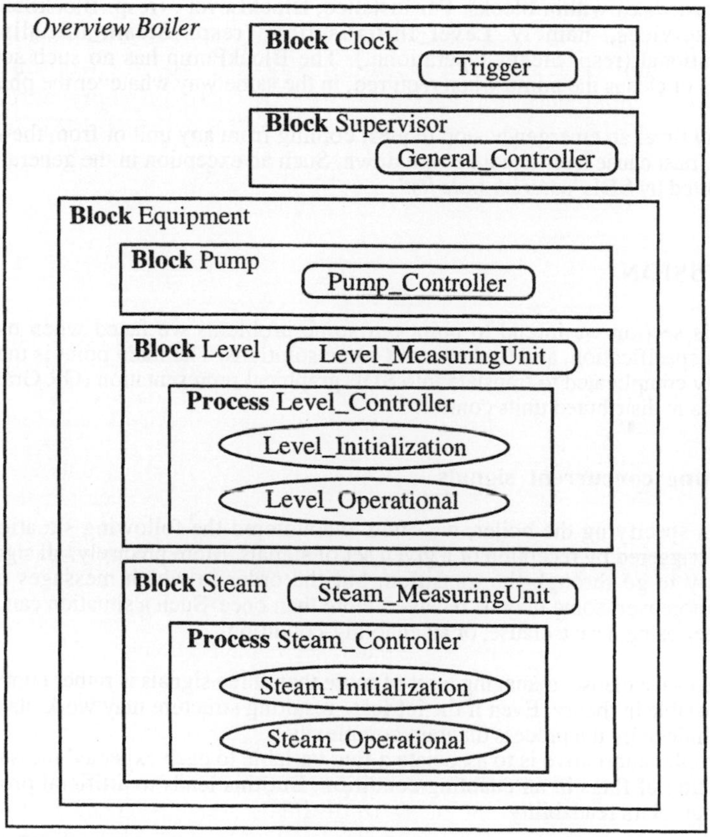

Diagram 6 : System structure overview

The Supervisor is in charge of scheduling operations. During initialisation it waits for ready messages from the equipment, and starts current execution. Then it regularly echoes the timer's tick signal for synchronisation, receives the status (OK / Broken) from all equipment units, selects the current mode (normal, degraded, rescue, emergency stop), and multicasts it to the Equipment.

On tick reception, BlockLevel accepts a raw value from the level measurement unit, checks it is within an estimated nominal range, sends a message to the Supervisor about correctness of the level, and computes new limit estimates for the next cycle. In case the level, while remaining between safety limits, shows a significant drift, BlockLevel sends a request to the PumpController Process for opening or closing the pump and doing so, corrects the deviation. BlockSteam behaves in the same way as BlockLevel except it has no pump control duty. It only updates confidence limits and warns when steam output is drifting. BlockPump waits for a request from BlockLevel. The PumpController Process controls the external pump device and manages the time out for response. It informs the Supervisor with messages for good working or failure.

We used SDL Service structure so as to make explicit the two operating phases by structuring processes within blocks. For instance, BlockLevel , (resp. BlockSteam) contains two SDL services, namely Level_Initialisation (resp. Steam_Initialisation), and Level_Operational (resp. Steam_Operational). The BlockPump has no such services, for it simply opens or closes the pump when required, in the same way whatever the phase.

At any time, an emergency stop request coming from any unit or from the supervisor or the operator must cause an immediate shut down. Such an exception in the general procedure is easily supported by SDL '*asterisk state list*'.

5. DISCUSSION

In this section we intend to point out some problems we faced when using SDL for analysis and specification, and to sketch out some solutions. The main point is that we found it unnecessarily complicated to translate into SDL graphical representation (GR Grammar), some usual patterns in distributed units control.

5.1. Treating concurrent signals

When specifying the boiler, we often encountered the following situation. A process transition is triggered by reception of a given set of signals. More precisely, all signals in the set are necessary to go through the transition, but the order in which messages may arrive is irrelevant ; moreover, some may be received more than once. Such a situation can be handled in SDL by either using a save clause, or an enabling-condition.

With a save clause, managing a set of more than three signals is rather cumbersome even if always possible in theory. Even if the intricate resulting structure may work, its semantics are completely hidden by the process diagram complexity.

A simpler alternative is to associate a flag variable to each expected message and to test the conjunction of flags in an enabling condition. But this leads to artificial process diagram expanses, that blurs readability.

Examples of such treatments for concurrent signals are given below. (see Diagram 7 : Solution (1) is for the *enabling condition*, and Solution (2) for the *save clause*).

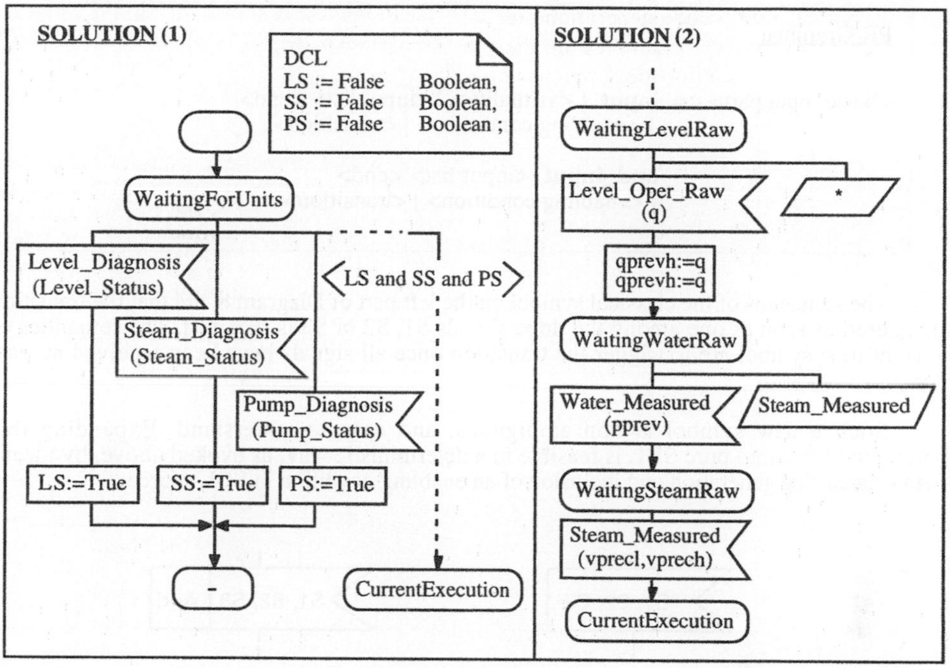

Diagram 7 : Treatments for concurrent signals

We suggest to define a new symbol *(and_input symbol)* specific for this case. We derive it from the existing SDL input symbol. The syntactic extensions we propose, are expressed hereunder, in terms of PR and GR SDL grammar.

GR Grammar

<basic input area> ::= <input symbol> ***contains*** { [<virtuality>] <input list> }
is followed by
{ [<enabling condition area>] <transition area> }

| <and_input symbol> ***contains*** <input list>
is followed by
{ [<enabling condition area>] <transition area> }

<and_input symbol> ::=

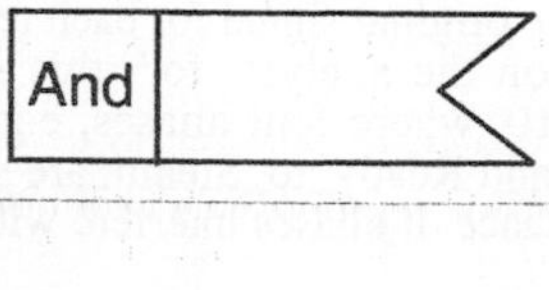

PR Grammar

<basic input part> ::= **input** [<virtuality>] <input list> <end>
[<enabling condition >] <transition>

| **and_input** <input list> <end>
[<enabling condition>] <transition>

The semantics of the classical symbol on the left part of Diagram 8, are that the transition is triggered as soon as one among the three signals S1, S2 or S3 is received. The semantics of the right new symbol are to trigger the transition once all signals have been received at least once.

Such a new symbol is non ambiguous, and easy to understand. Expanding this abbreviated form into pure SDL is feasible in a deterministic way, as evoked above, by means of automated flag generation and inclusion of an enabling condition in SDL source.

Diagram 8 : Standard SDL input symbol and extended *and_input symbol*

5.2. Multicast

Another frequent situation is that of a process in charge of multicasting one message to a set of receiver processes. This is here the case when the supervisor sends the current mode to all equipment units. The communication protocol for SDL processes is that a message must be sent to a unique precise receiver : either a Pid is specified, or a path (otherwise, any possible receiver may be selected). Explicit specification of a path may be necessary, and achieved by using a 'via' clause, when a message is declared on several routes. This does not allow multicasting, nor does the 'via all' clause. Moreover, the use of Pid is not straightforward in a synchronous system. In fact, messages are generally not sent by a process on request from another, but are triggered by a timer. So any potential receiver should first declare its Pid to the sender before a signal could be multicast. This not a natural behaviour in the present case.

In the absence of separate compilation, the compiler can have an entire knowledge of all possible paths by checking the 'connect' clauses (i.e. of the whole system network). Nevertheless the via clause only accesses the routes that actually appear in the process where the signal to be multicast is declared.

The only solution we found to simulate the multicast, is to create aliases, defining a special renamed copy of the original signal for each receiver, and draw as many output symbols as necessary. Relying upon the analyst for this systematic task is not satisfactory (see Diagram 9 and Diagram 10, where four aliases, e.g. Ready_to_Pump, Ready_to_LevelCtrl, Ready_to_LevelMesUnit and Ready_to_Steam, are structured as the (Program_Ready) signal list). Moreover, overabundance of aliases interfere with readability.

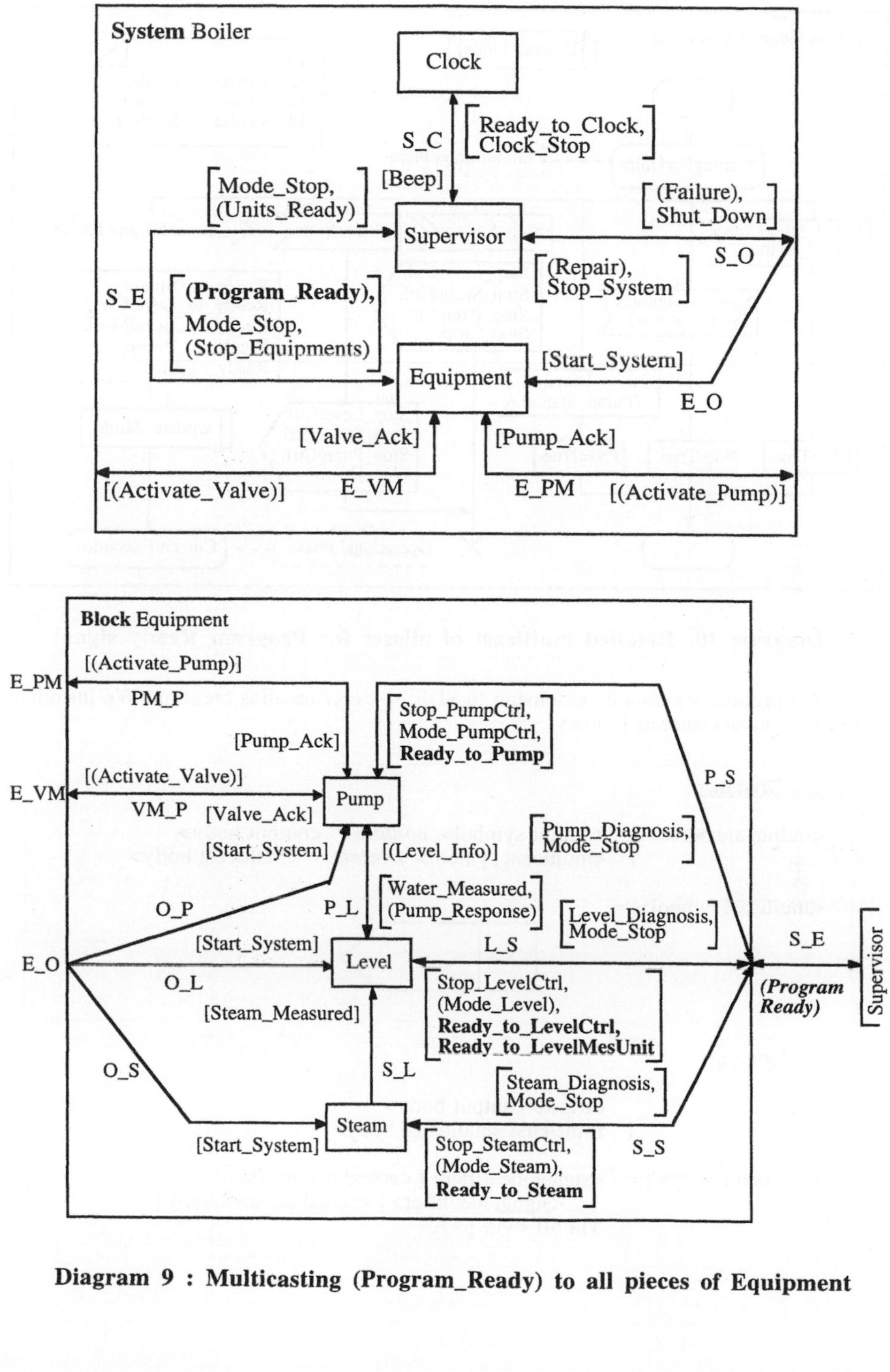

Diagram 9 : Multicasting (Program_Ready) to all pieces of Equipment

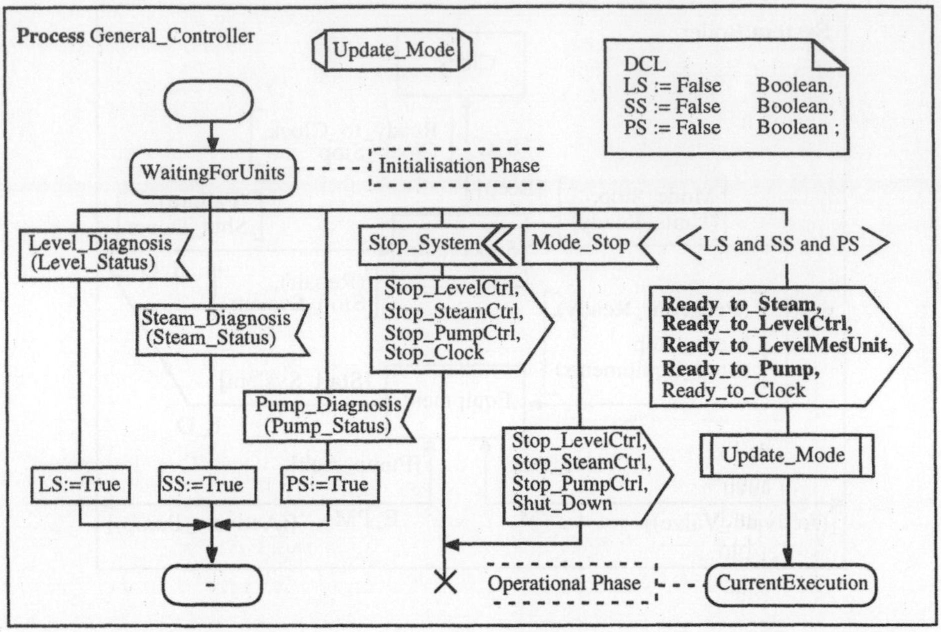

Diagram 10: Detailed multicast of aliases for Program_Ready signal

We propose a syntactic extension to SDL, to describe alias creation. We introduce a 'multicast' output clause as follows :

GR Grammar :

<output area> ::= <output symbol> ***contains*** <output body>
| <multicast symbol> ***contains*** <multicast body>

<multicast symbol>::=

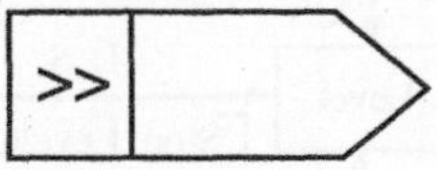

PR Grammar :

<output> ::= **output** <output body>
| **multicast** <multicast body>

<multicast body> ::= <signal identifier> [<actual parameters>]
{, <signal identifier> [<actual parameters>] }*
via all <via path>

A signal identifier occurring in a multicast clause is a 'collective signal', and can only occur in such a clause.

For collective signals, which in fact indicate a collection of aliases, a constraint has to be relaxed : in standard SDL, a channel C conveying a signal S cannot split into several communication paths C1, ..., Cn conveying the same signal S. This does no longer stand when S appears in a multicast clause.

For instance, the upper block diagram in diagram 11 is legal, provided process P contains a clause such as : 'multicast S via all R1'. The system lists all possible receivers, namely process Q and R, declares to new aliases for S, e.g. S1 and S2, and automatically generates the lower block diagram which is standard SDL.The multicast clause in process P is translated into the sequence : 'output S1 via R1; output S2 via R1'.

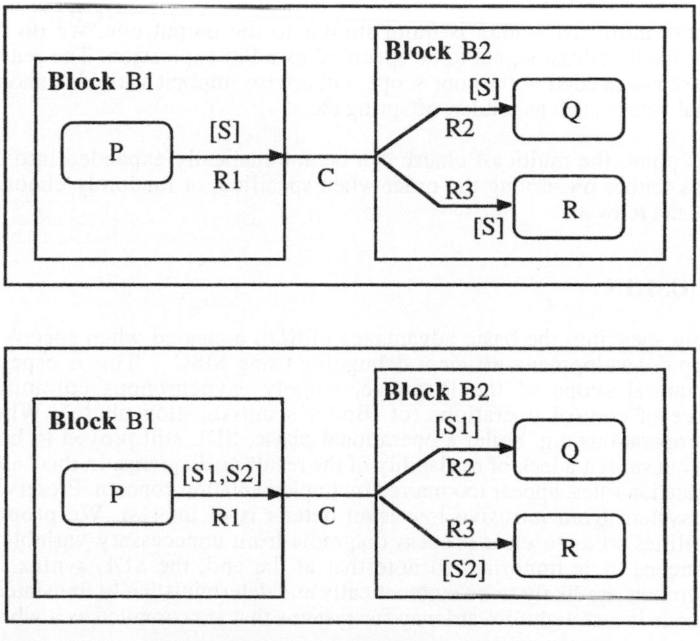

Diagram 11 : Example of multicast

A problem with such a multicast clause is obviously related to signal sequencing. If more than one item appear in the signal identifier list, the order in which signals are considered, is given by the list. For one given signal in the signal identifier list, there may be several path elements in the via path which may convey the signal. The path element are ordered as they appear in the via path. For one signal, and one path element, there is no simple way to specify the order in which the aliases are to be sent to all possible receivers. Hence, the output sequencing is unspecified by the analyst and depends on the implementation.

Either the analyst is responsible for verifying that any implementation will perform a correct execution, in accordance with the abstract view, or this task is discharged upon a syntactic and semantic analyser that must prove that execution does not depend on the output sequencing. To make such an automated analysis possible, receiver and sender process bodies have to be constrained.

A rough solution is to ensure that when the aliases are sent, all possible receivers are in such a state that only the multicast signal may be received (This is the case with the supervisor). In several typical cases, this proof is straightforward (e.g. : there is only one input symbol in the receiver's transition, or all acceptable signals in the transition are sent by the author of the multicast ...). Weaker pre-conditions are under investigation.

Another point of discussion is related with dynamic aspects. Some among the multicast signals, may cause new process instance creation. This brings ambiguity, since the connection with the multicasting process might be modified. We assume that multicast does not apply to set of instances. In case a receiver of a multicast signal is a set of instances, then, according to the usual interpretation for the via all clause, one particular instance is selected and receives the signal.

Although multicast syntax is quite similar to the output one, we do not allow the destination of the broadcast signal to be specified as a Pid expression. The reason is that Pid expressions are not needed within our scope. Otherwise implicit variables should be used to store the initial values such as sender, offspring etc...

At this point, the multicast clause can be automatically expanded into standard SDL output clauses (either preserving the order when specified, or randomly choosing any order when order is not relevant).

6. CONCLUSION

Broadly speaking, the basic advantages of SDL appeared when specifying the steam boiler. i.e. rapid development, efficient debugging using MSC ... This is especially the case within the natural scope of the language, namely asynchronous communication with preponderance of control operations (cf. Boiler's initialisation phase). When specifying synchronous operations e.g. boiler's operational phase, SDL still proved to be adequate for development but we felt a lack of readability of the resulting diagrams. In this case, SDL syntax and communication rules, appear too marred by implementation concern. Preserving an abstract view of the system from intrusive low level details is of interest. We propose additional syntactic facilities so as to clear process diagrams from unnecessary variables, signals and decision branches. It is important to note that at the end, the SDL syntax is not altered. Additional symbols are likely to be automatically and deterministically translated into genuine SDL source code in a straightforward way for systems that are compiled as a whole.

Split compilation and other questions such as multicast to Pid Expression, dynamic aspects, multicast to all instances in a set, present with problems we do not address here. Solutions are under investigation but we preferred to limit our concern to proposal that do not significantly alter SDL spirit.

The extensions we propose take place at an upper layer and should tend to make the transition easier from semi abstract specifications (e.g. : OMT classes and state charts) towards SDL process diagrams.

7. REFERENCES

[1] J.-R. Abrial. *Steam-boiler control specification problem.* Material for The Dagstuhl Meeting Methods for Semantics and Specification , 4-9 June 1995, August 1994, 6p.

[2] J.-R. Abrial, E. Boerger, H. Langmaack. *Formal methods for industrial applications : specifying and programming the steam boiler control.* Lectures Notes in Computer Science, Vol. 1165. Springer-Verlag, 1996. 519p.

[3] J.C. Bauer. *Specification for a software Program for a Boiler Water Content Monitor and Control System.* Institute of Risk Research, University of Waterloo, Ontario, Canada 1993.

[4] Combitech Group Telelogic (Saab-Scania). *SDT Tool 3.02.* 1995.

[5] A. Lötzbeyer. *A Tcl/Tk-based steam boiler simulator.* Forschungszentrum Informatik, Karslruhe, Germany, 1995. (published in [2]).

SDL '97: TIME FOR TESTING - SDL, MSC and Trends
A. Cavalli and A. Sarma (Editors)

The SDL Specification of the Sliding Window Protocol Revisited

Christian Facchi[a], Markus Haubner, Ursula Hinkel[b]

[a]Siemens AG, PN KE CPT 51, D-81359 München, Christian.Facchi@pn.siemens.de

[b]Institut für Informatik, Technische Universität München, D-80290 München, {haubnerm,hinkel}@informatik.tu-muenchen.de

This paper is a corrigendum to the SDL specification of the sliding window protocol which was first published by the ISO/IEC as a technical report. We present some results of a tool supported simulation of the SDL specification of the sliding window protocol. We found out that the specification contains significant errors and does not meet the informal description of the protocol. In this paper we describe these errors and give a correct version of the SDL specification.

1. INTRODUCTION

CCITT[1] and ISO have standardized the formal description techniques (*FDT*) Estelle, LOTOS, SDL and MSC for introducing formal methods in the area of distributed systems. The specification and description language SDL is one of them. SDL is a widespread specification language, which, in our opinion due to its graphical notation and structuring concepts, is well-suited for the formulation of large and complicated specifications of distributed systems.

We will present some results of a case study [3], in which we examined the tool supported development of protocols. Because of its practical relevance and simplicity we chose the SDL specification of the sliding window protocol as an example for this examination. An SDL description of the sliding window protocol is given in [7,11]. Working with the tools we did not follow any method for the testing of SDL systems but did just use the various facilities of the tools like the graphical editor and the simulator. When editing and simulating the SDL specification of the sliding window protocol, we found some incorrect parts within this specification. The specification does not meet the informal description of the protocol which is also given in [7,11]. We will explain these discrepancies by examples which we drew of the simulation. Then we will present a corrected specification with respect to the previously found errors. Therefore, this paper can be regarded as a corrigendum to some parts of [7,11].

Based on our experience we propose the use of formal methods with tool assistance. Although a formal specification may contain errors (which of course should be avoided), it

[1]In 1993 the CCITT became the Telecommunication Standards Sector of the International Telecommunication Union (ITU-T). If a document is published by CCITT, this organization name will be used instead of ITU-T in the sequel.

helps the designer to achieve a better understanding of the system to be built. Tools are extremely useful in achieving a correct specification. Design inconsistencies, ambiguities and incompleteness are detected in an early stage of software development.

This paper is organized as follows. In Section 2 we will give an informal introduction to the sliding window protocol. The main part of this paper, Section 3, describes the errors that we found and their correction. Moreover, we will explain how we discovered the errors using SDL tools. Section 4 summarizes the results and draws a conclusion.

2. THE SLIDING WINDOW PROTOCOL

The sliding window protocol is a widespread protocol describing one possibility of the reliable information exchange between components. The sliding window protocol can be used within the data link layer of the ISO/OSI basic reference model [6]. Due to its purpose it describes a point to point connection of two communication partners (a transmitter and a receiver) without an intermediate relay station. The latter aspect is dealt with in higher layers of the ISO/OSI basic reference model. Note that the connection establishment and disconnection phase are not part of the sliding window protocol. It serves only to establish a bidirectional reliable and order preserving data transfer within an existing connection.

The basic principle of the sliding window protocol is the usage of a sending and receiving buffer. For the transmitter it is possible to transmit more than one message while awaiting an acknowledgement for messages which have been transmitted before. In hardware description an equivalent property is called *pipelining*.

According to [9], the protocol can be described as follows: The transmitter and the receiver communicate via channels that are lossy in the sense that messages may disappear. Messages may also be corrupted which has to be detectable by the protocol entity. Each message is tagged with a sequence number. The transmitter is permitted to dispatch a bounded number of messages with consecutive tags while awaiting their acknowledgements. The messages are said to fall within the transmitter's window. At the other end, the receiver maintains a receiver's window, which contains messages that have been received but which to this point in time cannot be output because some message with a lower sequence number is still to be received. The receiver repeatedly acknowledges the last message it has successfully transferred to the receiving user by sending the corresponding sequence number back to the transmitter.

We demonstrate the advantages of the sliding window protocol by an example: Station A wants to transmit 3 frames to its peer station B. Station A sends the frames 1, 2 and 3 without waiting for an acknowledgement between the frames. Having received the three frames, station B responds by sending an acknowledgement for frame 3 to station A.

The SDL specification of the sliding window protocol [7,11] is based on a *sliding window protocol using "go back n"* according to [10]. For simplicity only a unidirectional flow of data is described. Thus, it is possible to distinguish two components: *transmitter* and *receiver*. Note that the flow of acknowledgements is in the opposite direction to the data flow. Each frame is identified by a unique sequence number. As an abstraction of real protocols, in which a wrap around may occur, an unbounded range of sequence numbers is used in [7,11]. The sequence number is attached to each data frame by the transmitter and it is later used for the acknowledgement and for the determination of the frame's sequential order. The transmitter increments the sequence number for each new data element.

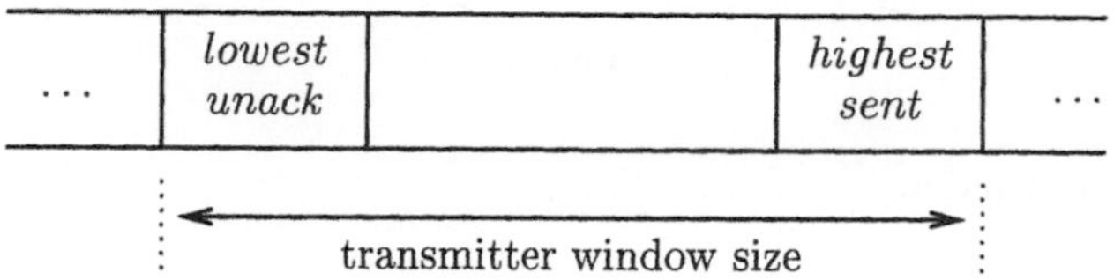

Figure 1. Transmitter window

The transmitter window shown in Figure 1 is used for buffering the unacknowledged frames. The variable *lowestunack* is used as an indicator for the lowest sequence number of an unacknowledged frame which has not necessarily been sent. Initially it is set to 1. The variable *highestsent* indicates the sequence number of the last sent frame and is initialized by 0. Both values determine the size of the transmitting window bounded by the constant *tws*.

If the transmitter wants to send a data frame, then it has to check first whether the actual window size (*highestsent* − *lowestunack*) is less than *tws*. If this condition is not fulfilled, the data frame is not sent until it is possible. In the other case the transmitter increments *highestsent* by one, emits the data combined with *highestsent* as sequence number and starts a timer for that sequence number. Whenever a correct acknowledgement (not corrupted and with a sequence number greater or equal than *lowestunack*) is received, all timers for frames with lower sequence numbers beginning by the received one down to *lowestunack* are cancelled. Then *lowestunack* is set to the received sequence number incremented by one. When a timeout occurs, all timers according to the sequence number of the message for which the timeout has occurred up to *highestsent* are reset and the corresponding frames are retransmitted in a sequential order starting with the message for which the timeout occurred. This includes also the repeated starting of the timers.

In Figure 2 the second window, which is located at the receiver, is presented. The receiver window is used to buffer the received frames which can not yet be handed out to the user because some frame with a lower sequence number has not been received. The variable *nextrequired*, whose initial value is 1, is used to indicate the sequence number of the next expected frame. The maximum size of the receiver window is described by the constant *rws*. If a noncorrupted frame is received with a sequence number in the range of [*nextrequired*..*nextrequired* + *rws* − 1] all messages starting by *nextrequired* up to the first not received message are delivered to the user. Then *nextrequired* is set to the number of the first not received message and *nextrequired* − 1 is sent as an acknowledgement to the transmitter.

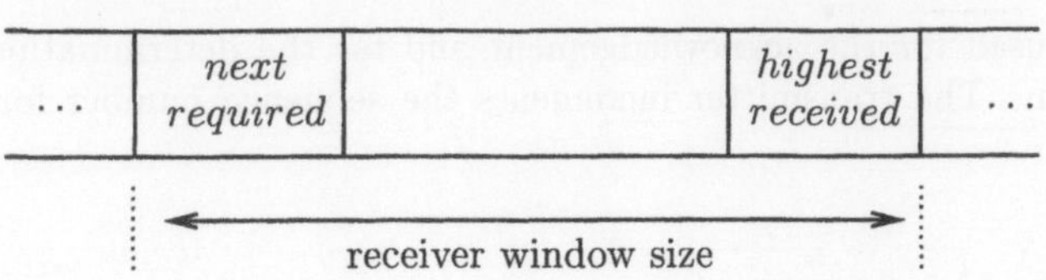

Figure 2. Receiver window

3. AN ANALYSIS OF THE SLIDING WINDOW PROTOCOL

In this section we present the errors that we found in the SDL specification of the sliding window protocol ([7,11]). We will first describe each error in an abstract way and then show a scenario in which it occurs followed by a corrected specification.

3.1. Tracing the errors

For our case study, in which we evaluated the facilities of SDL tools, we chose the sliding window protocol as an example, because it is a well known, simple protocol. We did not follow any systematic testing method (like e.g. using TTCN or a test case generation) but concentrated on the evaluation of the various facilities of SDL tools.

One way to check the behaviour of the protocol is to use the simulation as it is offered by some SDL tools. By simulating the SDL specification the behaviour of the specified system can be debugged. We started with executing a single step simulation. We sent signals from the environment to the system and observed the reaction of the SDL processes. The exchange of signals as well as the internal status of the system like the values of variables and the input ports are displayed and can be observed during the simulation. We immediately recognized that there was something wrong with the behaviour of the protocol.

Thinking that the problem might have its cause in our specification of the protocol which we used as input to the tools, or that we might have made some mistakes during the simulation, we generated Message Sequence Charts of the simulation. We analysed the MSCs and checked the corresponding parts of the SDL specification with paper and pencil. Thus, we found the errors described further below.

The advantage of using tools is the visualization of the dynamic behaviour of the system specified by SDL. The interaction of the processes and the exchange of signals as well as the changing of the data values within the processes are difficult to imagine without tool support. Especially the display of the values of the variables of the processes and the message flow with the values of parameters transmitted by the signals were very helpful for the detection of the errors.

3.2. A short overview of the SDL specification

We give only a short description of the structure of the SDL specification which is presented in full details in [11]. The specification is based on SDL 88. Figure 3 gives an overview of the structure of the specification but omits signals, channel identifiers and data declarations.

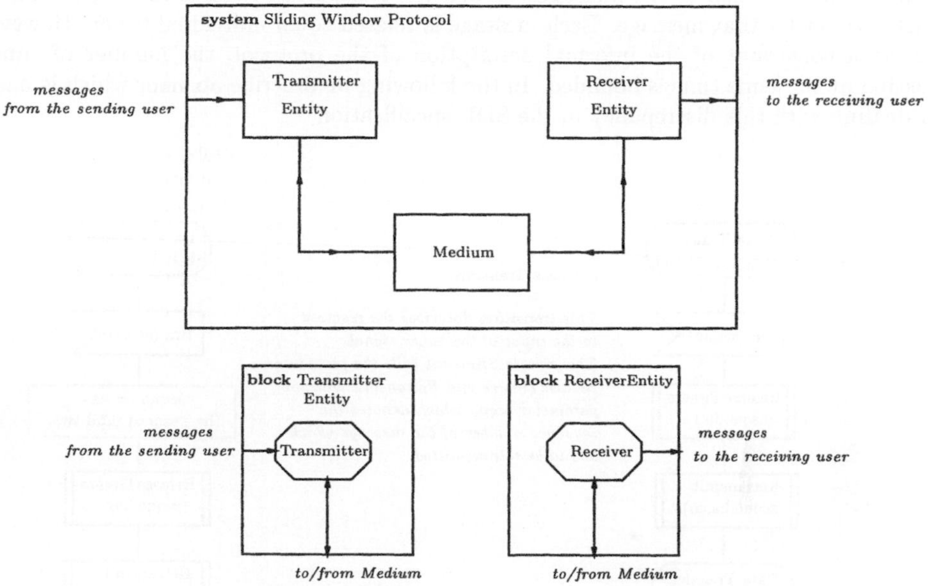

Figure 3. The structure of the SDL specification

The SDL specification of the protocol is composed of three blocks: TransmitterEntity, ReceiverEntity and Medium. The sending and the receiving users are part of the environment and interact with the corresponding protocol entities by signals. The two blocks TransmitterEntity and ReceiverEntity communicate via channels with the block Medium. The block Medium models an unreliable medium, which can nondeterministically lose, corrupt, duplicate or re-order messages. Its behaviour is described in Section 3.6. The behaviour of the block Medium is not part of the SDL specification of the sliding window protocol itself. However, there is an SDL specification of an unreliable medium in another chapter of [7,11]. Thus, we took this specification for the medium of the Sliding Window Protocol.

The TransmitterEntity sends data, which it gets as input from the sending user, via the medium. The ReceiverEntity gets data from the medium and sends acknowledgements over the medium to the TransmitterEntity. Data, which have been correctly transmitted, are given to the receiving user.

The block TransmitterEntity consists of the process Transmitter which includes two procedures: ReleaseTimers and Retransmit. The block ReceiverEntity consists of the process

Receiver which includes the procedure DeliverMessages.

3.3. Errors Concerning the Sequence Number

In the formal description of the sliding window protocol ([7,11]) unbounded sequence numbers are attached to the messages. When the transmitter sends a message, it has to start a timer for that message. Each message is related to an individual timer. However, due to a constraint of the informal description of the protocol, the number of timers existing at the same time is bounded. In the following we describe an error which is based on dealing with this discrepancy in the SDL specification.

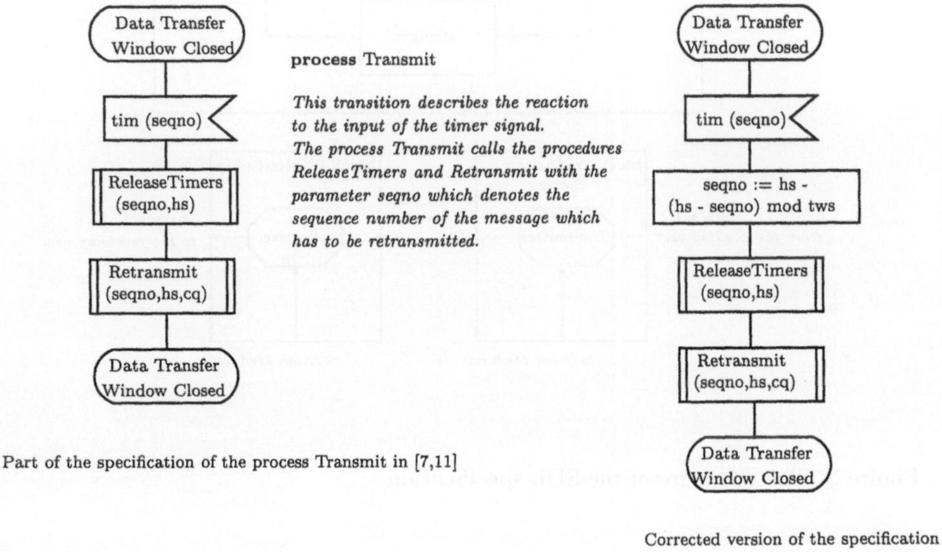
Data Transfer Window Closed
tim (seqno)
ReleaseTimers (seqno,hs)
Retransmit (seqno,hs,cq)
Data Transfer Window Closed
process Transmit
This transition describes the reaction to the input of the timer signal. The process Transmit calls the procedures ReleaseTimers and Retransmit with the parameter seqno which denotes the sequence number of the message which has to be retransmitted.
Part of the specification of the process Transmit in [7,11]
Data Transfer Window Closed
tim (seqno)
seqno := hs - (hs - seqno) mod tws
ReleaseTimers (seqno,hs)
Retransmit (seqno,hs,cq)
Data Transfer Window Closed
Corrected version of the specification

Figure 4. The use of sequence numbers in Process Transmitter

3.3.1. Description of the Error

In the process Transmitter, after a new message was sent, the timer is set to the sequence number of the message modulo *tws* by the statement "$set(now+delta, tim(hs \bmod tws))$" (*highestsent* is abbreviated by *hs*). However, after a timeout, the parameter of the timer is treated as if it contained the sequence number itself and not the modulo number (see left diagram in Figure 4).

In the procedure Retransmit the same error occurs. Instead of the sequence number of the retransmitted message the sequence number modulo *tws* is sent and used to set the timer (see left diagram in Figure 5).

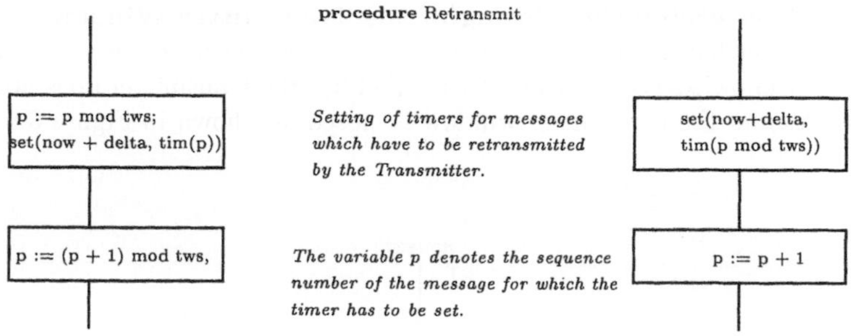
procedure Retransmit
p := p mod tws;
set(now + delta, tim(p))
Setting of timers for messages which have to be retransmitted by the Transmitter.
set(now+delta, tim(p mod tws))
p := (p + 1) mod tws,
The variable p denotes the sequence number of the message for which the timer has to be set.
p := p + 1

Part of the specification of the procedure Retransmit in [7,11]

Corrected version of the specification

Figure 5. The setting of timers in the procedure Retransmit

The procedure Retransmit calculates the sequence numbers of the messages to retransmit modulo tws, so the receiver will not accept retransmitted messages that have sequence numbers which differ from the modulo sequence number.

3.3.2. Erroneous Scenario

Suppose the transmitter window size is 5 and the value of *highestsent* (abbreviated by hs) is 12. Suppose further the receiver is waiting for a retransmission of message 11, because message 11 was corrupted. Having received the timer signal, the transmitter will retransmit the messages 11 and 12 with the sequence numbers $11 \bmod tws = 1$ and $12 \bmod tws = 2$. The receiver already got the messages 1 and 2 , so it will ignore the newly transmitted messages and will still be waiting for message 11. Now the sliding window protocol is in a livelock, where the transmitter will retransmit messages 11 and 12 with sequence numbers 1 and 2 forever and the receiver will never accept them, because their sequence numbers are lower than *nextrequired*.

3.3.3. Correction of the Specification

In order to solve this problem and to keep the changes to the specification minimal, concerning the process Transmitter we insert the assignment $seqno := hs - (hs - seqno) \bmod tws$ in a task after the input symbol of the timeout signal (see right diagram in Figure 4). It calculates the correct sequence number from the modulo sequence number and *highestsent*, so the correct sequence number will be passed to the procedures ReleaseTimers and Retransmit. In the procedure Retransmit the line "$p := (p + 1) \bmod tws$" is changed into "$p := p + 1$" and in the task "$p := p \bmod tws$; $set(now + delta, tim(p))$" the assignment is removed and the set statement is changed into "$set(now + delta, tim(p \bmod tws))$" (see right diagram in Figure 5).

3.4. Errors Concerning the Closing of the Transmitter Window

The transmitter has a limited buffer for messages which have been received but have not yet been acknowledged. If this buffer is filled up, the transmitter does not accept any more messages and the transmitter window is closed, as shown in Figure 6.

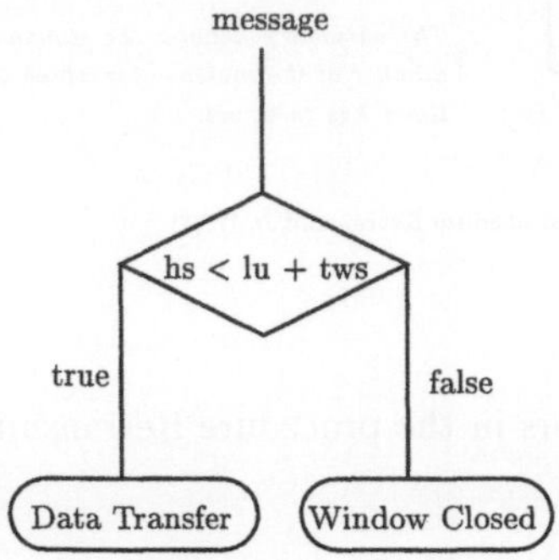

Figure 6. Closing the transmitter window

3.4.1. Description of the Error

In the process Transmitter the transmitter window is closed too late. Even if there are *tws* unacknowledged messages, *lowestunack* + *tws* is greater than *highestsent* and the window is still open. As a consequence, the next message, that is sent, will also use the timer of the lowest unacknowledged message, although it is still in use. Therefore, one timer is used for two different messages. If the lowest unacknowledged message is not received correctly by the receiver, the transmitter will not get a timeout for this message. The transmitter will not retransmit the message and the receiver will not pass on any messages until it will have received the missing message. Thus, the sliding window protocol is in a livelock.

3.4.2. Erroneous Scenario

Suppose $tws = 5$, $highestsent(hs) = 5$, $lowestunack(lu) = 1$ and the queue is set to $< 1, 2, 3, 4, 5 >$ (five messages have been sent, they are all still unacknowledged)[2]. The transmitter window is full and should have been closed after message 5 had been sent. However, the evaluation of the condition $hs < lu + tws$ $(5 < 1 + 5)$ in the decision symbol returns true, so the window is not closed. Suppose the transmitter sends message 6. Now the queue $< 1, 2, 3, 4, 5, 6 >$ keeps more than *tws* elements. As a consequence, the timer for message 1 is overwritten with the timer for message 6, because in the set statement

[2]Note that the messages are represented only by their sequence numbers. For simplicity we have omitted their content.

set (*now* + *delta*, *tim* (*hs* mod *tws*)) the timer instance 1 is attached to both messages. One message later than expected the condition $hs < lu + tws$ $(6 < 1 + 5)$ evaluates to false and the transmitter window is closed.

3.4.3. Correction of the Specification

The condition $hs < lu + tws$ is changed into $hs < lu + tws - 1$, so the transmitter window will be closed one message earlier, just in time.

3.5. Errors Concerning the Spooling of the Transmitter Queue in the Retransmit Process

During the retransmission of messages, a rotation of the messages stored in the transmitter queue is necessary, because the message that has got the timeout has to be retransmitted first. In the following we describe an error which occurs during this rotation process (see Figure 7).

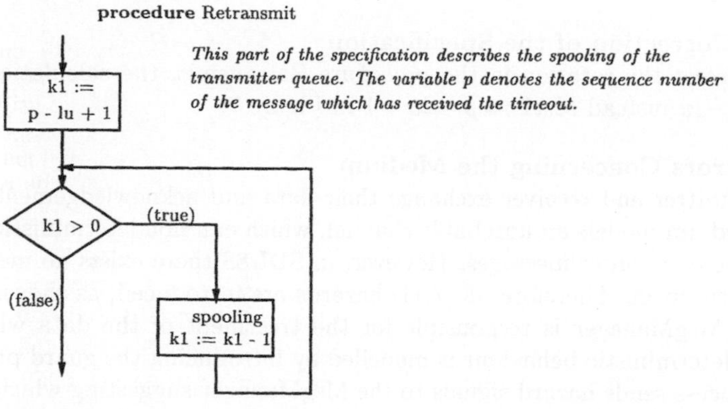
procedure Retransmit
This part of the specification describes the spooling of the transmitter queue. The variable p denotes the sequence number of the message which has received the timeout.
k1 :=
p - lu + 1
k1 > 0
(true)
(false)
spooling
k1 := k1 - 1

Figure 7. The spooling of the transmitter queue

3.5.1. Description of the Error

In the procedure Retransmit the message queue should be rotated until the first message to be retransmitted is at the beginning of the queue. However, the calculation of the messages that have to be rotated is incorrect, because the queue is always rotated one message further than it should be. As a result, when the messages are retransmitted the message bodies will not fit to their sequence numbers.

3.5.2. Erroneous Scenario

Suppose a scenario in which four messages are in the transmitter window, $queue = <1, 2, 3, 4>$, $lu = 1$.
Now message 2 receives a timeout, so $p = 2$.

The rotation of the messages in the queue starts:
$k1 := p - lu + 1 = 2 - 1 + 1 = 2$
$k1 = 2 > 0$
The queue is rotated once: $queue =< 2, 3, 4, 1 >$
Despite the fact that the messages are in the correct order the rotation of the messages continues.
$k1 := k1 - 1 = 1$
$k1 = 1 > 0 :$
The queue is rotated a second time: $queue =< 3, 4, 1, 2 >$
$k1 := k1 - 1 = 0$
Now the value of $k1 \;\; > 0$ is false, the rotation is finished and the retransmission starts. Message 2 is retransmitted with the first element in the queue as content. Thus, the new message has the sequence number 2, but the body of message 3. Sequence number 3 will be combined with message body 4 and sequence number 4 will be sent with the message body 1. As the checksums are calculated after the new combinations, the receiver will not notice the altered sequence of the message bodies and the message is corrupted.

3.5.3. Correction of the Specification

To correct the rotation in the procedure Retransmit, the calculation of $k1$ has to be $k1 := p - lu$ instead of $k1 := p - lu + 1$ in Figure 7.

3.6. Errors Concerning the Medium

Transmitter and receiver exchange their data and acknowledgements over a medium. This medium models an unreliable channel, which can nondeterministically lose, corrupt, duplicate or re-order messages. However, in SDL 88 there exists no means for expressing nondeterminism. Therefore, in [7,11] hazards are introduced, as shown in Figure 8. The process MsgManager is responsible for the treatment of the data within the medium. Its nondeterministic behaviour is modelled by introducing the guard process MsgHazard. This process sends hazard signals to the MsgManager suggesting which operations are to be carried out by the MsgManager on the data: normal delivery (MNormal), loss (MLose), duplication (MDup), corruption (MCorrupt) or reordering (MReord) of messages. The data within the medium are stored in a queue called Medium Message Queue mq, which is a local variable of the SDL process MsgManager.
The treatment of acknowledgements within the medium is handled by the process AckManager. For modelling its nondeterministic behaviour the process AckHazard is introduced and specified similar to MsgHazard.

3.6.1. Description of the Error

A hazard may send signals to its manager, although its manager's message queue mq is empty. Some operations performed by the manager on the queue mq after having received a signal produce an error if the queue mq is empty.

3.6.2. Erroneous Scenario

Suppose message 3 waits in the queue mq to be transmitted:
$MediumMessageQueue : mq =< 3 >$
Suppose that the hazard signal $MNormal$ appears:

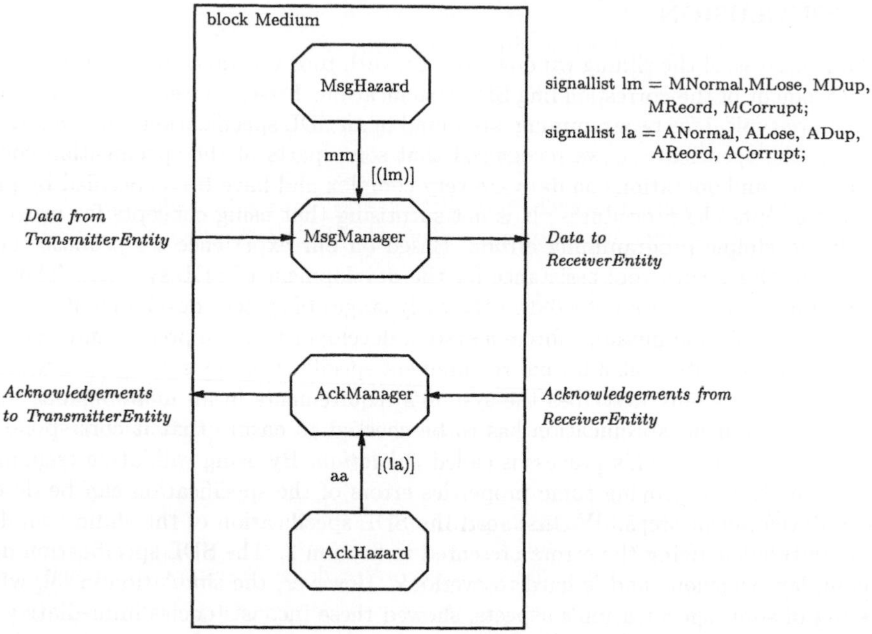

Figure 8. Structure of the block Medium

$qitem := qfirst(mq) = 3$
Now the queue is empty:
$mq := qrest(mq) = qnew$
Message 3 is sent to the receiver.
Suppose the hazard signal $MNormal$ appears again:
Then $qitem$ is set to $qfirst(mq) = qfirst(qnew)$
According to the axiom $qfirst(qnew) == error!$ the execution of the SDL system will stop and an error message will be displayed.

3.6.3. Correction of the Specification

To prevent these errors the manager always checks if its message queue mq is empty when it gets a signal from its hazard. Only if the message queue mq is not empty, the hazard signal will be processed, otherwise the manager will not do anything.

Note that this error would not have occurred if SDL 92 was used which includes explicit language constructs for nondeterminism, because the usage of the SDL processes *MsgManager* and *AckHazard* is not necessary.

4. CONCLUSION

Our analysis of the sliding window protocol with tool assistance resulted in a significant improvement of the corresponding SDL specification. First, we were suprised that errors, which are typical for programming, are found in an SDL specification. But taking a closer look at the specification, we recognized that some parts of the specification concerning data types and operations on data are very complex and have been specified by programming concepts like procedures. It is not surprising that using concepts for programming results in simple programming errors. Based on our experience we propose the use of formal methods with tool assistance for the development of SDL systems. Thus, typical programming errors are detected in the early stages of system development.

The use of formal methods forces a system developer to write precise and unambiguous specifications. Note that a formal requirement specification does not guarantee a correct specification. It only describes the system's requirements in an unambiguous way. The formal requirement specification has to be checked to ensure that it corresponds to the specifier's intuition. This process is called *validation*. By using validation techniques like e.g. simulation or proving some properties errors of the specification can be detected in early development steps. We first read the SDL specification of the sliding window protocol without noticing the errors presented in Section 3. The SDL specification describes a complex behaviour and is hard to overlook. However, the simulation in [3], which is a testing of some specification's aspects, showed these inconsistencies immediately. Indeed we found these errors during the simulation without using any systematic methodology. We think that a systematic approach for the simulation might yield even more errors. Moreover, writing a specification without a later simulation is quite similar to programming without testing the program. A programmer would not rely on an untested program, except the program had been formally verified. However, even a formally verified program should be tested in order to check whether it meets the requirements. The validation of a specification should be tool supported, because in most cases a manual approach is very time consuming so that the validation will be omitted or be done only for some parts of the specifications. We think that in practice a simulation should be chosen rather than a formal verification. A simulation can be carried out without having mathematical knowledge which is essential for formal proofs. There exists a variety of tools for SDL which are of great assistance in editing and checking syntactically and semantically SDL specifications. During the tutorials of the last SDL Forum ([1]) methods for the testing and the validation of SDL systems were presented (see [5,2]).

The importance of simulating SDL specifications is demonstrated by the fact that, although the authors of the specification of the sliding window protocol are SDL experts and did a detailed analysis of the informal description of the protocol, they did not succeed in giving a correct SDL specification.

Although large programs and specifications or text are likely to contain some errors, we have been surprised that these fundamental errors of the specification of the sliding window protocol have not been noticed before. If an implementation of the protocol had been based on the SDL specification, the errors should have been discovered immediately.

In another case study we found some errors in the specification of the Abracadabra protocol, too [8,4]. Therefore, we suggest that all SDL specifications which are part of

ITU-T standards or ISO technical reports, like [7,11], should be checked by tools and if necessary be corrected. This could result in a corrigendum to [7,11]. It might also be interesting to have a closer look at the Estelle and LOTOS specifications included in [7,11] and to analyse whether these specifications are correct or include some errors not yet known.

ACKNOWLEDGEMENTS

We thank Manfred Broy, Øystein Haugen, Stephan Merz, Franz Regensburger and Ekkart Rudolph who read earlier drafts of this paper and provided valuable feedback. For analysing and simulating the SDL specification of the sliding window protocol we used the SDL tools ObjectGeode by Verilog and SICAT by Siemens AG.

REFERENCES

1. R. Bræk and A. Sarma. *SDL '95: with MSC in CASE.* North-Holland, 1995.
2. A.R. Cavalli, B.-M. Chin, and K. Chon. Testing Methods for SDL Systems. *Computer Networks and ISDN Systems*, 28(12):1669 – 1683, 1996.
3. M. Haubner. Vergleich zweier SDL-Werkzeuge anhand des Sliding Window Protokolls. Fortgeschrittenenpraktikum, Technische Universität München, 1995. in German.
4. U. Hinkel. An Analysis of the Abracadabra-Protocol, 1996. Internal report, in German.
5. D. Hogrefe. Validation of SDL Systems. *Computer Networks and ISDN Systems*, 28(12):1659 – 1667, 1996.
6. ISO. ISO 7498: Information Processing Systems - Open Systems Interconnection - Basic Reference Model, 1984.
7. ISO/IEC. Information Technology - Open System Interconection - guidelines for the application of Estelle, LOTOS and SDL. Technical Report ISO/IEC/TR 10167, 1991.
8. C. Klein. Spezifikation eines Dienstes und Protokolls in FOCUS – Die Abracadabra Fallstudie, 1995. in German.
9. K. Stølen. Development of SDL Specifications in FOCUS. In R. Bræk and A. Sarma, editors, *SDL '95: with MSC in CASE*, pages 269–278. North-Holland, 1995.
10. A. S. Tanenbaum. *Computer Networks.* Prentice Hall, 1988.
11. K. J. Turner. *Using Formal Description Techniques - An Introduction to Estelle, Lotos and SDL.* John Wiley & Sons, 1993.

XII
Applications II

SDL '97: TIME FOR TESTING - SDL, MSC and Trends
A. Cavalli and A. Sarma (Editors)

Configuring Communication Protocols Using SDL Patterns*

Birgit Geppert, Reinhard Gotzhein, and Frank Rößler

Computer Networks Group, Computer Science Department, University of Kaiserslautern
P.O. Box 3049, D-67653 Kaiserslautern, Germany
{geppert, gotzhein, roessler}@informatik.uni-kl.de

Due to the large variety of modern applications and evolving network technologies, a small number of general-purpose protocol stacks will no longer be sufficient. Rather, customization of communication protocols will play a major role. In this paper, we present an approach that has the potential to substantially reduce the effort for designing customized protocols. Our approach is based on the concept of *design patterns*, which is well-established in object oriented software development. We specialize this concept to communication protocols, and - in addition - use formal description techniques (FDTs) to specify protocol design patterns as well as rules for their instantiation and composition. The FDTs of our choice are SDL-92 and MSC, which offer suitable language support. We propose an advanced SDL pattern description template, present a particular SDL pattern in detail, and summarize the configuring of a resource reservation protocol.

1. INTRODUCTION

Today's communication systems are typically structured into several layers, where each layer realizes a defined set of protocol functionalities. These functionalities have been carefully chosen such that a wide range of applications can be supported, which has led to the development of a small number of general-purpose protocol stacks. However, due to increasing communication demands as found in many modern applications, the communication services provided by these protocol stacks are not always adequate. In particular, varying demands on throughput and delay as well as on delay jitter, synchronization and multicasting are not well supported by existing protocol stacks. Also, classical protocols are not designed to exploit the advantages of advanced transmission technologies (e.g., fiber optics) and high-speed networks (e.g., ATM), which combine high bandwidth with low error rates. Rather, they enforce the use of mechanisms that may actually not be needed by a given application, for instance, the use of error control mechanisms, which leads to reduced performance.

To improve this situation, different communication architectures as well as a new generation of general-purpose protocols are currently being developed. It is expected that in order to increase flexibility and to support applications in the best possible way, also customization of special-purpose communication protocols will play a major role. Here, the configuring of protocols from reusable components (called *protocol building blocks* in this paper) seems to be a promising way to reduce the additional development effort.

---

*. This work has been supported by the German Science Foundation (DFG) as part of the Sonderforschungsbereich 501 "Development of Large Systems with Generic Methods" under grant SFB 501-B4.

Several approaches to the configuring of protocols have been reported in the literature. Early research focused on the identification and collection of suitable protocol components by reverse engineering of existing transport and network protocols. A protocol implementation was then automatically configured from a subset of these components. Well-known projects in this area are F-CCS [22] [19], Da CaPo [8] [9], and ADAPTIVE [13] [14] [15] (see [6] for an overview). These approaches have in common that protocol *implementations* are configured. As a major drawback, the use of implementation languages prevents the resulting communication system from being verified, which is further complicated by the configuring of protocols during connection establishment. Here, the use of formal description techniques allowing an abstract, unique specification of protocol components and component interactions seems to be mandatory. Also, the extension of the component pool appears to be difficult in these approaches because of missing flexibility in describing reusable design decisions.

The reuse of predesigned solutions for recurring design problems is of major concern in object oriented software development in general. During the past few years, *design patterns* have emerged as an especially fruitful concept from other well-known approaches such as *frameworks,* or *toolkits* (in the sense of object oriented libraries) [5] [1] [10]. Early experience in reuse of protocol specifications with SDL has been reported in [17], where a protocol building block was designed as a reusable library class, however, according to the authors, with limited success.

In this paper, we present a new approach for designing customized protocols. Our approach is based on the concept of *design patterns*, which we specialize to communication protocols. In addition, we use SDL-92 and MSC to formally specify protocol design patterns and rules for their instantiation and composition. An important advantage of our approach is that the configuring leads to formal specifications of communication protocols, which may then be used for validation and implementation purposes.

The remainder of the paper is organized as follows: In Section 2, we propose an advanced SDL pattern description template and present a specific SDL pattern in detail. The process of pattern employment is discussed subsequently. In Section 3, the pattern-based configuring of a resource reservation protocol, which is part of the realization of a real-time communication service based on a conventional token ring network, is summarized (see [7] for details). We conclude with experiences and an outlook in Section 4.

2. SDL PATTERNS

An *SDL pattern* describes a generic solution for a context-specific design problem from the domain of communication protocols. It is assumed that the target language for pattern instantiations is SDL-92. Thus the pattern description comprises syntactical rules for pattern application as well as semantic properties defining the patterns intent more precisely. This definition of SDL pattern is similar to those of conventional design patterns used in object oriented software development:

- "*Design Patterns are descriptions of communicating objects and classes that are customized to solve a general design problem in a particular context.*" *[5]*
- "*A pattern for software architecture describes a particular recurring design problem that arises in specific design contexts, and presents a well-proven generic scheme for its solution. The solution scheme is specified by describing its constituent components, their responsibilities and relationships, and the ways in which they collaborate.*" *[1]*

The differences between design patterns and SDL patterns are that we choose a particular application domain (communication protocols), and that we combine the advantages of the formal description technique (FDT) SDL with the patterns' concept. Instead of specifying and applying the patterns rather informally, SDL offers the possibility to specify what the application of a specific pattern precisely means, under which assumptions this will be allowed, and what the consequences are. Here we are in line with the advocates of design pattern formalization inside the design patterns community, though we are even more rigorous by demanding the use of an FDT for this purpose. As a consequence, the description of SDL patterns differs in some ways from design patterns in [5] and [1].

In Section 2.1., a description template for SDL patterns is presented and related to existing description templates. A detailed description of a particular SDL pattern is given in Section 2.2. Finally, Section 2.3. describes the design steps for the application of SDL patterns.

2.1. SDL pattern description template

To describe SDL patterns, a proper format is needed. We propose an SDL pattern description template with the items listed below and relate it to the existing pattern description templates of [5] and [1]. As already mentioned, instantiations of this template are called SDL patterns which, itself instantiated, form the constituent parts of an SDL protocol specification.

SDL pattern description template	
Name	The name of the pattern, which should intuitively describe its purpose.
Intent	A short informal description of the particular design problem and its solution.
Motivation	An example from the area of communication systems, where the design problem arises. This is appropriate for illustrating the relevance and need of the pattern.
Structure	A graphical representation of the structural aspects of the design solution using an OMT object model. This defines the involved components and their relations.
Message scenario	Typical scenarios describing the interactions between the involved objects are specified by using MSC diagrams.
SDL-fragment	The mere syntactical part of the design solution is defined by a generic SDL-fragment, which is adapted and syntactically embedded when applying the pattern. If more than one SDL *versions* of the design solution are possible (realization as SDL service or procedure, interaction by message passing or shared variables, etc.), fragments for the most frequent versions are included. We plan to substitute versioning by a special kind of pattern parameterization. For each fragment, corresponding *syntactical embedding* rules are defined: • Rules for *renaming* of the abstract identifiers of the SDL-fragment. • Rules for *specialization* of embedding SDL superclasses in order to integrate the instantiated pattern. Here, "specialization" is meant in the sense of specialization of SDL types as defined in [23]. This could, for instance, result in the *addition* of new transitions or SDL services as well as the *redefinition* of existing virtual types or transitions.

SDL pattern description template	
Semantic properties	Properties of the resulting specification that are introduced by the embedded pattern. This also includes a description of assumptions under which the properties hold. The semantic properties define the patterns intent more precisely.
Redefinition	An embedded pattern instance can be further redefined, e.g., by the embedding of another SDL-fragment in subsequent development steps. Redefinitions compatible with the patterns intent and semantic properties are specified.
Cooperative usage	Possible usage with other patterns of the pool is described. This is feasible and especially useful for a specific application domain as in our case.

Table 1
Comparison of the description templates of [5] and [1].

Gamma et al.	Buschmann et al.	
Pattern Name and Classification, Intent	Name	Name and short description of intent
Also Known As	Also Known As	Other well-known names
Motivation	Example	Real-world example illustrating the design problem
Applicability	Context	Situations in which the pattern should/should not be applied
	Problem, Solution	General description of the design problem and the offered solution (detailed intent)
Structure, Participants, Collaborations	Structure, Dynamics	Graphical Graphical representation of participating objects (OMT) and their interactions
Implementation, Sample Code	Implementation	Guidelines for implementation, including code fragments in C++, Smalltalk, ...
	Example Resolved, Variants	Description of other important aspects of the given example not addressed so far and other possible variants or specializations of the pattern
Known Uses	Known Uses	Systems in which the pattern has been applied
Consequences	Consequences	Benefits and results of using the pattern.
Related Patterns	See Also	List of similar patterns

The description template for SDL patterns and existing templates for design patterns (see Table 1) have some items in common: *name, intent, motivation, structure*, and *message scenario*. For SDL patterns, these items are specialized to the communication systems domain. Thus participating objects typically include protocol entities, protocol functions, service users or service providers. Interactions between them can be described by Message Sequence Charts (MSC), with the additional advantage to perform MSC based validation.

Different from [5] and [1], SDL patterns are part of a dedicated pool of protocol building blocks and have a formal foundation. Thus an SDL pattern can be related to other pool components by specifying their *cooperative usage*. This is strongly supported by restriction to design problems of a certain domain. The formal foundation results from the use of the standardized FDT SDL, where, for instance, the *syntactical embedding* of the pattern, i.e. its integration into a given SDL specification, can be specified uniquely in terms of the SDL syntax. Furthermore, the formal semantics of SDL supports the formalization of a pattern's intent by *semantic properties*. This includes both desired properties and necessary assumptions, which have to be satisfied to ensure the intended use of the pattern. This is important for validation of the resulting communication protocol. The possibility to simulate the design specification between consecutive development steps or before implementation is another advantage of the SDL based approach. Undetected design errors can therefore be identified in early stages of the development process.

Items not already incorporated into the SDL pattern template, for instance "Also Known As", "Known Uses" or "Related Patterns", may be added in future versions. However, it seems more important to further improve the template as far as pattern interactions or system validation are concerned.

2.2. The SDL pattern *BlockingRequestReply*

Below, the SDL pattern BlockingRequestReply is listed. We assume that the reader is already familiar with OMT [12], MSC [24], and SDL-92 [23].

Name: BlockingRequestReply

Intent: The BlockingRequestReply pattern introduces a two-way handshake between two given automata Automaton_A and Automaton_B. Being triggered, Automaton_A will send a request and is blocked until receiving a reply. After reception of a request, Automaton_B sends a reply. To assure finite response time and proper connection, certain assumptions about the embedding environment (including the superclasses Automaton_A and Automaton_B) are in place.

Motivation: After initiating a connection setup, a service user waits for a reply from the service provider ("accepted", "refused by callee", "refused due to lack of resources",...). In case of refusal, the user may try again with lower quality of service requirements.

Structure:

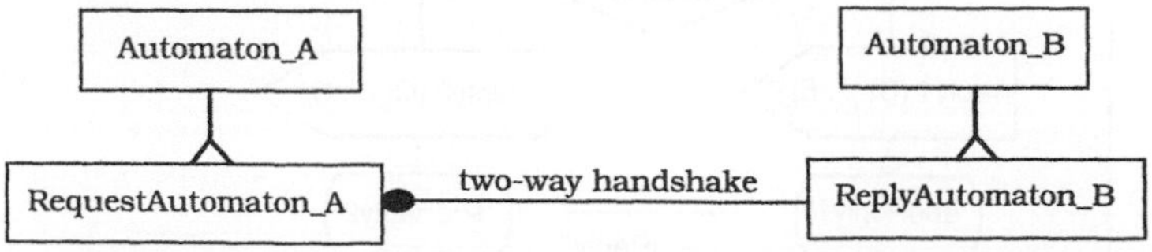

Message scenario:

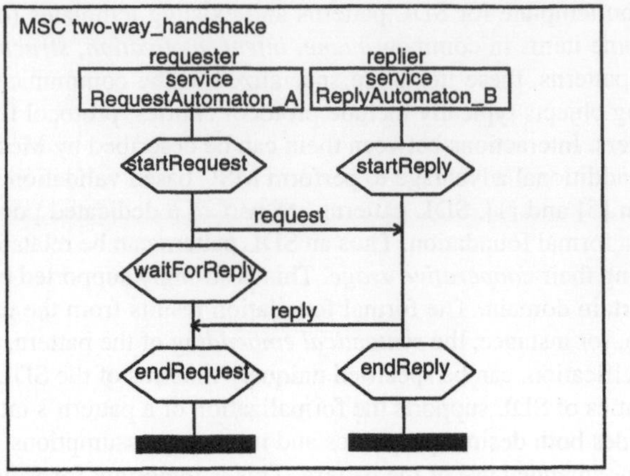

SDL-fragment (Version 1):

RequestAutomaton_A

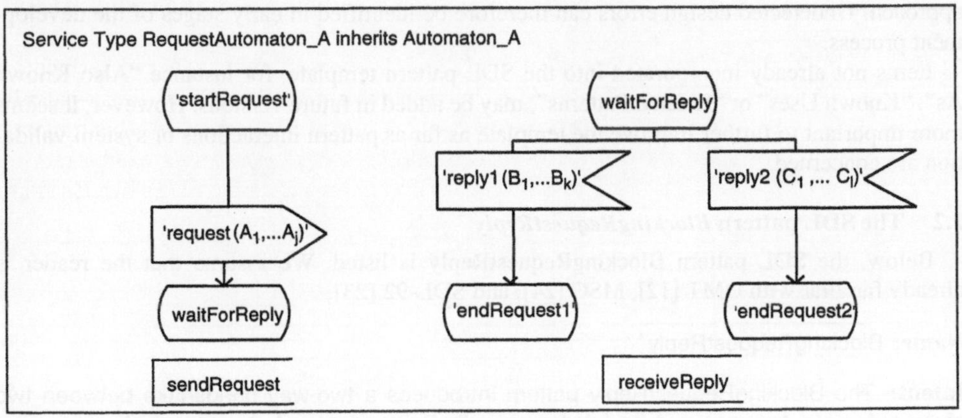

ReplyAutomaton_B

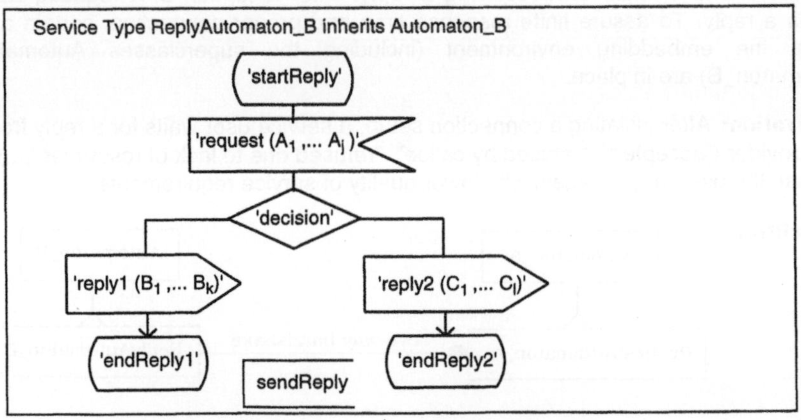

Syntactical Embedding

- Automaton_A:

Specialization: Add transitions *sendRequest* and *receiveReply* to the given SDL service *Automaton_A*.
Renaming: The signals *request, reply1*, and *reply2* and the state *waitForReply* may be renamed but are required to be locally unique. The states *startRequest, endRequest1*, and *endRequest2* may be identified with each other or any state in the given SDL service *Automaton_A*.

- Automaton_B:

Specialization: Add transition *sendReply* to the given SDL service *Automaton_B*, which must be different to *Automaton_A*.
Renaming: The signals *request, reply1*, and *reply2* may be renamed but are required to be locally unique and of the same name as the corresponding signals in *RequestAutomaton_A*. The states *startReply, endReply1 and endReply2* may be identified with each other or any state in the given SDL service.

SDL-fragment (Version 2):
RequestAutomaton_A

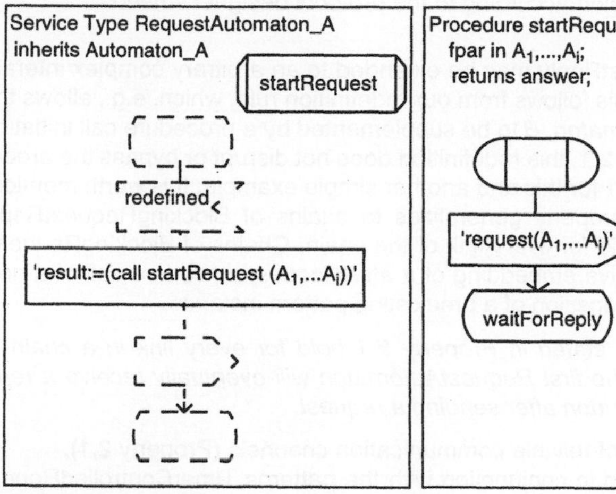

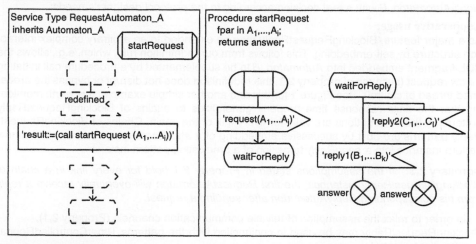

ReplyAutomaton_B
same as in Version 1

Syntactical Embedding

- Automaton_A:

Specialization: redefine a proper transition by mere supplementation of the procedure call *startRequest*.
Renaming: The signals *request, reply1*, and *reply2* and the state *waitForReply* may be renamed but are required to be locally unique.

- Automaton_B:

same as in Version 1

Semantic properties:

Property 2.1: *If the assumptions stated below hold,* RequestAutomaton_A *will eventually receive a reply from* ReplyAutomaton_B *after sending a request. The assumptions are:*

- *The request and reply signals are not implicitly consumed by the respective superclass.*
- *Communication between RequestAutomaton_A and ReplyAutomaton_B for transmission of the request and reply signals is reliable.*
- *The state startReply of ReplyAutomaton_B will always eventually be reached.*

Redefinition:

Normally, the embedded SDL-fragment will be supplemented by additional statements, e.g., to prepare signal parameters. The following property determines the allowed redefinitions of the BlockingRequestReply pattern.

Property 2.2: *Property 2.1 still holds, if the BlockingRequestReply pattern is redefined by the introduction of additional statements, which do not disrupt or bypass the thread of control from predefined input to predefined output statements.*

There is one mandatory redefinition, namely the replacement of the comment 'decision' in *ReplyAutomaton_B* with a real decision according to the protocol designer's needs.

Cooperative usage:

As a major feature, BlockingRequestReply may be extended to an arbitrary complex interaction structure by self-embedding. This follows from our redefinition rule, which, e.g., allows the SDL-fragment embedded into *Automaton_B* to be supplemented by a procedure call initiating a new request (because of property 2.1, this redefinition does not disrupt or bypass the predefined thread of control). See Figure 1 for this and another simple example. It is worth mentioning that the finite response time property generalizes to chains of BlockingRequestReply patterns, if the assumptions are valid for every link of the chain. Chains of BlockingRequestReply patterns are built by successive embedding of a *startRequest* procedure call of a new pattern instance into a *sendReply* transition of a preexisting pattern instance.

Corollary 2.3: *If the assumptions stated in Property 2.1 hold for every link in a chain of BlockingRequestReply instances, the first RequestAutomaton will eventually receive a reply from his corresponding ReplyAutomaton after sending a request.*

In order to relax the assumption of reliable communication channels (Property 2.1), BlockingRequestReply may be used in conjunction with the patterns TimerControlledRepeat and DuplicateControl.

2.3. Selection, adaptation, and composition of SDL patterns

Protocol configuration is a promising way to cope with the enormous number of possible customized protocols. Actually we suggest to provide a pool of reusable and formally specified protocol building blocks (which are represented by SDL patterns) from which the protocol designer may select components according to the specific communication requirements. After suitable adaptation, these building blocks are ready for composition to build part of the customized communication protocol (Figure 2).

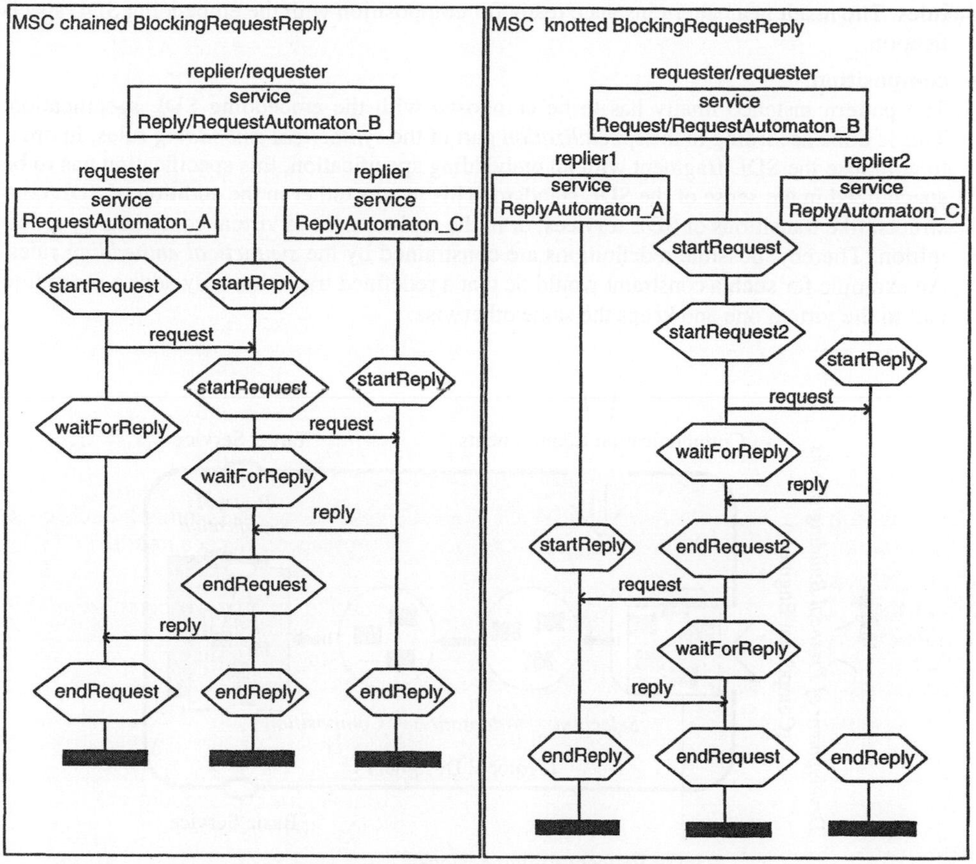

Figure 1. Multiple employment of BlockingRequestReply

Based on the information provided by SDL patterns, these design steps can be explained in more detail:

- **selection**:
  Several SDL methodologies suggest to use OMT and MSC for analysis [11] [18] [20]. To fit with these methodologies, we reduce the semantic gap between analysis and design models by employing OMT and MSC for pattern descriptions as well. By comparing OMT and MSC analysis diagrams with the *structure* and *message scenario* descriptions of the SDL patterns and by further examination of the patterns' *intent*, *semantic properties,* and *motivation,* protocol building blocks are to be selected.
- **adaptation**:
  Depending on the given SDL specification into which the pattern shall be embedded, a suitable *version* of the pattern has to be identified. The chosen version additionally must be adapted by *renaming* the abstract identifiers (e.g., signals, parameters, variables) in order to seamlessly fit the SDL specification at hand. This is guided by the *syntactical embedding*

rules. The result is a pattern instance ready for composition with the embedding SDL specification.

- **composition**:
The pattern instance finally has to be composed with the embedding SDL specification. This is done according to the *specialization* part of the *syntactical embedding* rules. In order to compose the SDL fragment with an embedding specification, this specification has to be specialized in the sense of the SDL standard. This results either in the addition of SDL constructs, like transitions or SDL services, or in the replacement of virtual constructs by redefinition. Thereby, possible redefinitions are constrained by the *syntactical embedding* rules. An example for such a constraint would be that a redefined transition only adds a procedure call to the virtual one and keeps the same otherwise.

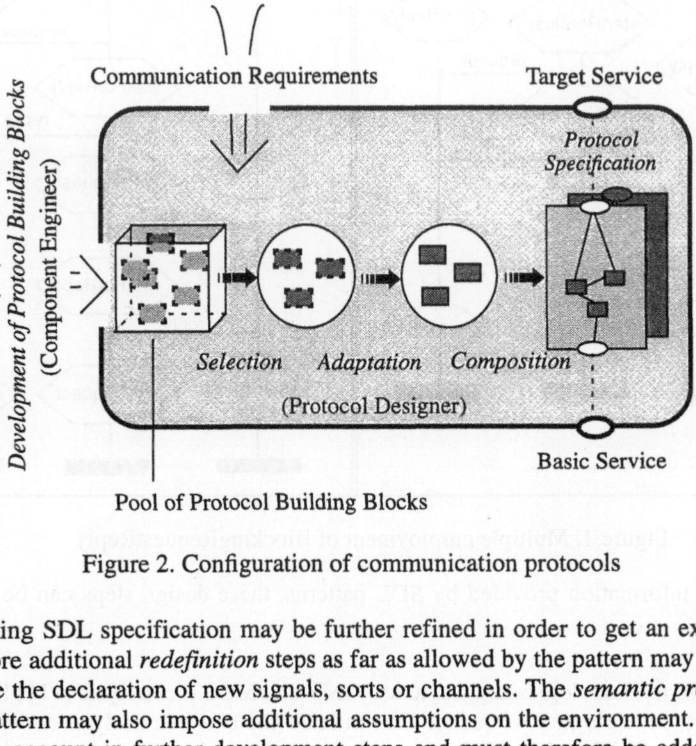

Figure 2. Configuration of communication protocols

The resulting SDL specification may be further refined in order to get an executable version. Therefore additional *redefinition* steps as far as allowed by the pattern may be necessary. Examples are the declaration of new signals, sorts or channels. The *semantic properties* of an embedded pattern may also impose additional assumptions on the environment. They have to be taken into account in further development steps and must therefore be added to a list of assumptions.

3. CONFIGURING OF A RESOURCE RESERVATION PROTOCOL

In this section, we summarize the configuring of a resource reservation protocol. Roughly speaking, this protocol supports connection setup in conjunction with the reservation of sufficient network resources to guarantee a specified quality of service during data transfer. Together with adequate mechanisms for traffic policing, scheduling, connection admission control, and user interfacing, it provides a real-time communication service that we have realized on the basis of a conventional token ring network.

3.1. Resource reservation service

The resource reservation service (also called *target service*) allows to establish and close unidirectional real-time connections between two communicating peers. For establishing a real-time connection, the calling user has to specify the required quality of service, including the expected amount of traffic load. Only the calling user is allowed to close a connection. More than one connection per node may be active at the same time. Therefore unique local connection identifiers (CIds) are employed. The service users are informed of their CIds through the service primitives *ConnectConf* and *ConnectInd.* Additionally, several service users per node may exist, which are distinguished by local, user provided identifiers (userId) passed at the service interface (*ConnectReq, ConnectInd*). The communicating peers can therefore be globally identified by a combination of node address and userId. The calling user provides both with the connection setup request.

3.2. Overview of the protocol configuration process

The protocol implementing the resource reservation service was configured in an incremental way, where each step consisted of selecting, adapting, and composing predesigned protocol building blocks represented as SDL patterns. We started by configuring a protocol providing a subset of the target service based on a reliable underlying service. By incorporating further service requirements and/or relaxing the assumptions w.r.t. the underlying service, we finally obtained a complete solution in four development steps. In our target platform, the underlying service is provided by a conventional token ring network (5 Pentium-PCs running under QNX and connected with IBM 16/4 Token Ring Network Adapter II). In the remainder of this section, we sketch the configuring of the resource reservation protocol. For details including the specification of the applied SDL patterns and the SDL specification of the configured protocol, the reader is referred to [7].

The initial subset of the target service supports a single connection between two nodes. Furthermore, the underlying service is assumed to be reliable. With these simplifications, we have configured a first version of the reservation protocol. The protocol consists of two entities establishing a connection and a resource manager. The behaviour of these entities is determined by applying the BlockingRequestReply pattern (see Section 2.2) two times. Essentially, the calling protocol entity requests a connection from the called protocol entity, which itself requests necessary resources from the resource manager. The interaction between calling user and calling protocol entity as well as the interaction between called user and called protocol entity are further instances of the BlockingRequestReply pattern. The resulting reservation protocol is formally specified in SDL, the underlying service is represented by two SDL channels connecting the two protocol entities and the called entity with the resource manager.

In the second step, we have replaced these SDL channels by an SDL block with channels connecting the protocol entities and the resource manager. This step can be seen as a structural refinement, as we still assume a reliable underlying service. The interfacing of the entities with the underlying service represented by this SDL block is configured by applying the Codex pattern to the first version of the reservation protocol. Codex allows two or more entities to interact through an underlying service represented by an SDL block/process by means of service primitives, i.e. Codex essentially provides a translation from protocol data units to service primitives. Again, the resulting reservation protocol is formally specified in SDL.

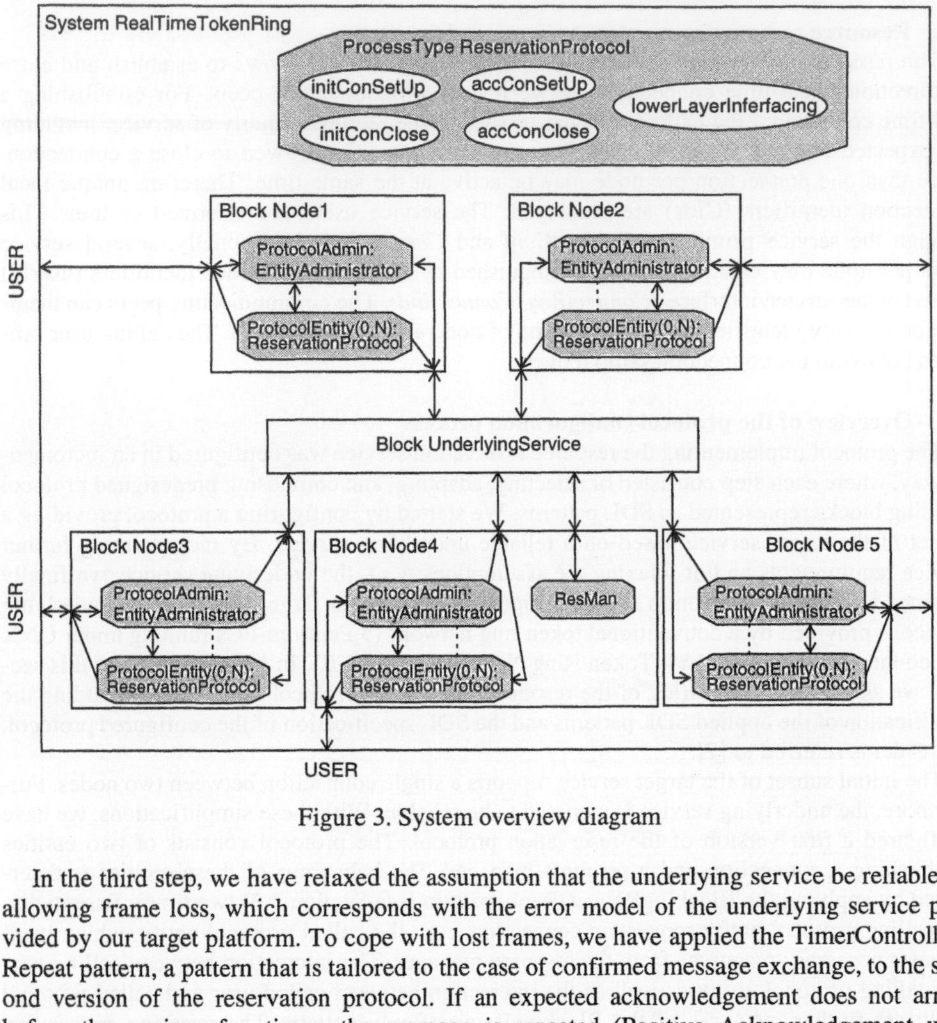

Figure 3. System overview diagram

In the third step, we have relaxed the assumption that the underlying service be reliable by allowing frame loss, which corresponds with the error model of the underlying service provided by our target platform. To cope with lost frames, we have applied the TimerControlledRepeat pattern, a pattern that is tailored to the case of confirmed message exchange, to the second version of the reservation protocol. If an expected acknowledgement does not arrive before the expiry of a timer, the message is repeated (Positive Acknowledgement with Retransmission). Since retransmission may lead to duplication of messages (not treated by TimerControlledRepeat), another pattern named DuplicateControl has been applied. Duplicate messages are detected by an unique message identifier and discarded.

In the fourth and last step, we have considered the full target service supporting several nodes as well as several connections per node and user. Each connection is managed by a separate set of protocol entities, which are created and released dynamically. The required mechanisms including the forwarding of incoming messages to protocol entities are incorporated by applying the DynamicEntitySet pattern.

The structure of the final SDL specification is shown in Figure 3. For each node, one SDL process *ProtocolAdmin* is instantiated, which creates and releases protocol entities as connections are requested and closed (see step 4 of the protocol configuring). The number of SDL processes *ProtocolEntity* varies with the number of connections. Additionally, an SDL process *ResMan* assuming the role of the resource manager is instantiated. Different from other reservation protocols such as RSVP [21] or ST2+ [4], our solution uses a centralized resource manager, which was configured (from a patterns point of view) similar to normal protocol instances.

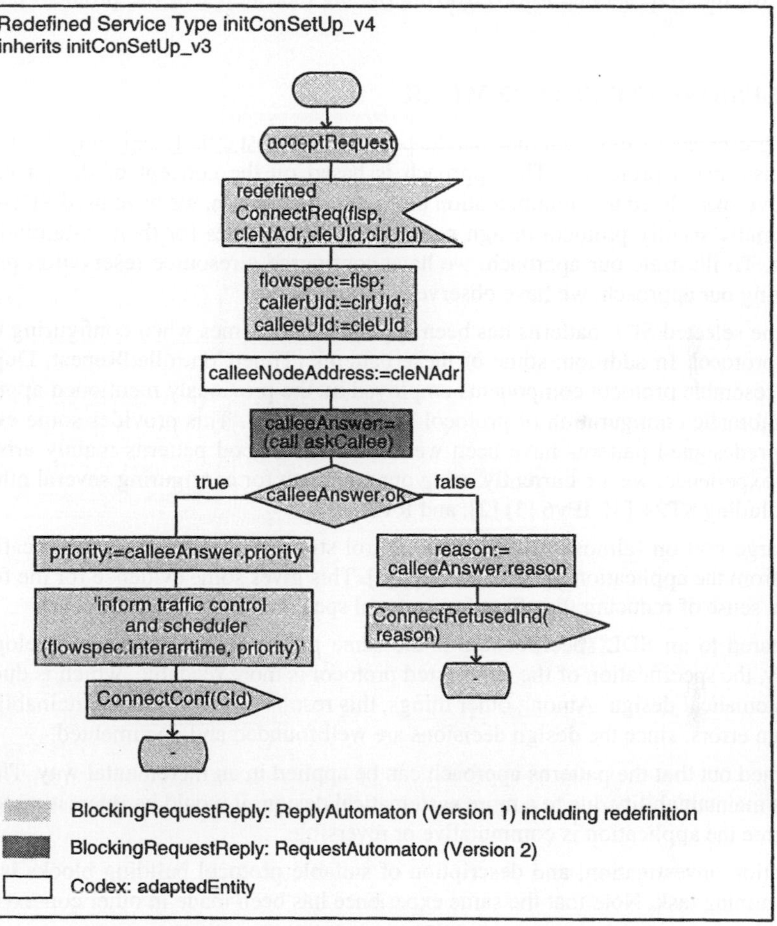

Figure 4. Behaviour definition of SDL service initConSetUp

Protocol entities are internally structured using the concept of SDL services (see *Process Type ReservationProtocol* in Figure 3). These SDL services are the result of applying SDL patterns as described before. *LowerLayerInterfacing*, for instance, has resulted from the application of the Codex pattern during the second development step. As another example, consider the SDL service *initConSetUp* shown in Figure 4. The differently shaded parts indicate where SDL patterns have been applied. The region shaded represents a redefined Blocking-RequestReply instance responsible for the interaction with the calling user (see step 1 of the protocol configuring). Additionally, the procedure call shaded requests a connection from the called protocol entity (see also development step 1). Note that the procedure reference *askCallee* is not shown in Figure 4, because it is part of the corresponding superclass definition. The same applies for missing declarations of variables. Finally, the statement that is shaded results from applying the Codex pattern and provides necessary interface control information for the SDL service *lowerLayerInterfacing* (see step 2 of the protocol configuring).

4. CONCLUSIONS AND FUTURE WORK

We have presented an approach that has the potential of substantially reducing the effort for designing customized protocols. The approach is based on the concept of design patterns, which we have specialized to communication protocols. In addition, we have used SDL-92 and MSC to formally specify protocol design patterns as well as rules for their instantiation and composition. To illustrate our approach, we have configured a resource reservation protocol. When applying our approach, we have observed the following:

- Each of the selected SDL patterns has been applied several times when configuring the reservation protocol. In addition, some of these patterns (TimerControlledRepeat, Duplicate-Control) resemble protocol components employed by the previously mentioned approaches [6] for automatic configuration of protocol implementations. This provides some evidence that the predesigned patterns have been well chosen. As good patterns mainly arise from practical experience, we are currently using our approach for configuring several other protocols including ST2+ [4], IPv6 [3] [2], and RTP [16].
- A very large portion (almost 100% of the control structure) of the final specification has resulted from the application of SDL patterns [7]. This gives some evidence for the feasibility (in the sense of reducing the effort for protocol specification) of our approach.
- As compared to an SDL specification of the same protocol that has been developed the usual way, the specification of the configured protocol is more readable, which is due to the more systematical design. Among other things, this results in improved maintainability and less design errors, since the design decisions are well founded and documented.
- It has turned out that the patterns approach can be applied in an incremental way. This, too, improves maintainability due to a more systematical design. It would be interesting to see to what degree the application is commutative or reversible.
- Identification, investigation, and description of suitable protocol building blocks is a very time consuming task. Note that the same experience has been made in other contexts where design patterns are used.
- The SDL patterns applied to the configuring of the resource reservation protocol have been of rather fine granularity. Coarser patterns may have the advantage of reducing the overall development effort, since less patterns need to be applied to configure a protocol. However, this is merely a question of identifying suitable protocol building blocks and does not affect our approach itself.

From these observations, we infer that our approach has the potential of substantially reducing the effort for customizing and maintaining communication protocols, which seems to be a prerequisite for developing protocols that support applications in the best possible way. However, in order to draw a final conclusion, further experience with this approach will be needed. In particular, we plan an experiment-based evaluation of the cost-effectiveness of our approach.

The configuring of protocols classifies as a synthesis approach, meaning that systems are constructed from predesigned components such that by following certain rules, required system properties such as freedom of deadlocks, freedom of unspecified receptions, or conformance to a service specification can be guaranteed a priori. We see this as a fertile field for future research.

REFERENCES

[1] F. Buschmann, R. Meunier, H. Rohnert, P. Sommerlad, and M. Stal, *Pattern-Oriented Software Architecture - A System of Patterns*, John Wiley & Sons, 1996

[2] A. Conta and S. Deering, *Internet Control Message Protocol (ICMPv6) for the Internet Protocol Version 6 (IPv6) Specification*, RFC 1885, 1995

[3] S. Deering and R. Hinden, *Internet Protocol, Version 6 (IPv6) Specification*, RFC 1883, 1995

[4] L. Delgrossi and L. Berger (Ed.), *Internet Stream Protocol Version 2 (ST2), Protocol Specification - Version ST2+*, RFC 1819, 1995

[5] E. Gamma, R. Helm, R. Johnson, and J. Vlissides, *Design Patterns - Elements of Reusable Object-Oriented Software*, Addison-Wesley, 1995

[6] B. Geppert and F. Rößler, *Automatic Configuration of Communication Subsystems - A Survey*, SFB 501 Report 17/96, University of Kaiserslautern, Germany

[7] B. Geppert and F. Rößler, *Pattern-based Configuring of a Customized Resource Reservation Protocol with SDL*, SFB 501 Report 19/96, University of Kaiserslautern, Germany

[8] T. Plagemann, B. Plattner, M. Vogt, and T. Walter, *Modules as Building Blocks for Protocol Configuration*, Proceedings of ICNP'93, International Conference on Network Protocols, San Francisco, 1993

[9] T. Plagemann, J. Waclawczyk, and B. Plattner, *Management of Configurable Protocols for Multimedia Applications*, Proceedings of ISMM International Conference on Distributed Multimedia Systems and Applications, Honolulu, USA, 1994

[10] W. Pree, *Design Patterns for Object-Oriented Software Development*, Addison-Wesley, 1995

[11] R. Reed, *Methodology for Real Time Systems*, Computer Networks and ISDN Systems 28 (1996), 1685-1701

[12] J. Rumbaugh, M. Blaha, W. Premerlani, F. Eddy, and W. Lorensen, *Object-Oriented Modeling and Design*, Prentice Hall, 1991

[13] D.C. Schmidt, *An Object-Oriented Framework for Dynamically Configuring Extensible Distributed Systems*, IEE Distributed Systems Engineering Journal (Special Issue on Configurable Distributed Systems), Volume 2, No 4, Dec. 1994

[14] D.C. Schmidt, D.F. Box, and T. Suda, *ADAPTIVE: A Dynamically Assembled Protocol Transformation, Integration, and eValuation Environment,* Concurrency Practice and Experience, Vol. 5, No. 4, 1993

[15] D.C. Schmidt, B. Stiller, T. Suda, and M. Zitterbart, *Configuring Function-based Communication Protocols for Multimedia Applications*, Proceedings of the 8th International Working Conference on Upper Layer Protocols, Architectures, and Applications, Barcelona, Spain, 1994

[16] H. Schulzrinne, S. Casner, R. Frederick, and V. Jacobson, *RTP: A Transport Protocol for Real-Time Applications*, RFC 1889, 1996

[17] A. Sinton and M. Crowther, *SDL-92 support for re-use in protocol system specifications - some early experience*, SDL'95 with MSC in CASE, Proceedings of the 7th SDL Forum, Oslo, Norway, 1995

[18] SDT 3.1 Methodology Guidelines: *The SOMT Method*, Telelogic, 1996

[19] B. Stiller, *Flexible Protokollkonfiguration zur Unterstützung eines diensteintegrierenden Kommunikationssubsystems*, PhD thesis (in german), VDI-Verlag, Reihe 10, Nr. 306, 1994

[20] D. Witaszek, E. Holz, M. Wasowski, S. Lau, and J. Fischer, *A Development Method for SDL-92 Specifications Based on OMT*, SDL'95 with MSC in CASE, Proceedings of the 7th SDL Forum, Oslo, Norway, 1995

[21] L. Zhang, S. Deering, D. Estrin, S. Shenker, and D. Zappala, *RSVP: A new Resource ReSerVation Protocol*, IEEE Network, Sep. 1993

[22] M. Zitterbart, *Funktionsbezogene Parallelität in transportorientierten Kommunikationsprotokollen*, PhD thesis (in german), VDI-Verlag, Reihe 10, Nr. 183, 1991

[23] Z.100 (03/93) *CCITT Specification and Description Language (SDL)*, ITU-T, 1994

[24] Z.120 (10/96) *Message Sequence Chart (MSC)*, ITU-T, 1996

Code Generation Using GEODE : A CASE Study.

Ranjit "Raj" Singh
Lead Software Engineer

Jerry Serviss
Principal Staff Engineer

EMX Software Development
Cellular Infrastructure Group
Motorola, Inc.

Abstract

Reduction of the overall product development cycle time while maintaining quality is one of the key initiatives and challenges facing today's software development community. While generation of code using CASE tools is not new to the software industry, the need for incorporation of such tools into our software development community has never been as imperative as it is today due to the pressures of cycle time reduction. Generating code using CASE tools needs to be re–evaluated and given serious consideration in terms of reducing cycle time. This paper discusses how code generation is possible using SDL and GEODE. SDL (Specification and Description Language) is a standard developed by ITU–T for the development of real–time and message–based telecommunications software. The GEODE toolset includes SDL, MSC, and OMT editors, a simulator, a code generator that can be customized for different target platforms and a TTCN test–case generator. Also discussed are evaluation criteria for code generation tools, some of the pros and cons of code generation, and some hurdles to overcome.

1. INTRODUCTION

Poised as we are to greet the next millennium with all of its challenges, it is important that we renew our dedication to the continued development of quality software that exceeds the needs and wants of our customers. We must recognize and adapt to the new face that software development presents to us now and even more so in the new millennium : increasing complexity, cycle time reduction, demand for uncompromising quality and global competition.

Challenges exist in the key areas of : extensive software research; global development and testing; improved estimating and planning; accurate effort measurement and the iterative refinement of estimation formulae; process and quality improvements; organised and cohesive reuse strategies; and most importantly overall cycle time rcduction.

Reduction of product development cycle time is without a doubt the key concern of the software industry today. The specter of losing customers to competitors that promise and deliver products to customers earlier than they can shadows every supplier in the industry. The importance of overall cycle time reduction is reinforced by the financial success of vendors that are first to market with new products and services.

Further we must recognize that our customers are operating in highly competitive markets as well. If they are to be successful, we need to deliver new products and features to them before any of their competitors can obtain them. It should go without saying that they expect zero–defect quality built into these new products. Automatic code generation helps greatly in reducing cycle time as well as improving quality as discussed here.

2. ACHIEVING CYCLE TIME REDUCTION

To meet the expectations of the corporation and more importantly our customers we need an optimal blend of processes, methodologies, and tools that yields short cycle time and outstanding quality. There is, therefore, a great need to re–evaluate and optimize the processes, methods and tools used by our engineers to enable them to be faster and better than any other.

CASE tools can help satisfy the need to reduce cycle time and improve quality by automating or replacing activities that are repeatable and mechanical. We recognize that CASE tools are by no means necessary for the development of quality software. However, the dedicated application of CASE tools are essential and indispensable in making a software engineer more productive and thus reducing cycle time.

The class of application programs we have targeted for our first application of code generation are termed HMIs. They are used to provide the Human Machine Interface to our cellular telephone switch. HMIs do not have very stringent real–time performance requirements although the response times must be satisfactory. In addition, these HMI programs tend to be totally new development work so there is little if any issues with legacy code. These two attributes made them an excellent target for the application of code generation.

3. WHY PICK SDL ?

Given the need for 10X cycle time improvements and six sigma quality we in the EMX2500 product development group selected the ITU–T developed notation called Specification and Description Language (SDL), for our design methodology. The reasons that we selected SDL are based on an evaluation of the state of development processes and CASE tools applicable to our product. In that evaluation we identified our unique process and product related requirements. These requirements are over and above the previously identified needs to improve cycle time and reduce escape defects. The needs identified are:

- **Large Software Project**:
We have several million lines of source code under our control. The selected method must work in this environment.
- **Telephony Application**:
Many specifications are provided by outside organizations. These come in many forms but SDL is most common. In addition our specification group uses a tool that produces a message sequence chart notation that is very similar to the one which is a part of SDL.
- **Mature Product, Constantly Being Evolved**:
We are doing maintenance as well as a significant amount of new development on our product. The method selected had to fit both reverse engineering and new development.
- **Processes Based On Finite State Machine Model:** We needed something that fitted our state–event model and supports the way most of our engineers think about problems.

In addition to these requirements we wanted to find a method and tool set that supported the evolution of our product and anticipated future process needs. The issues that are identified here are more anticipated process needs then actual product requirements. These desires are:

- **Support Of Full Development Life Cycle**:
The SDL and MSC notations provide the

ability to support development activities from requirements to testing.

- **Evolution to an Object Oriented Paradigm:** SDL provides this with the 1992 version of the language and this is further supported by integration of the OMT method into the specification phase by the SDL tools vendors.

- **Capability to Simulate at Design Level**: We felt it was necessary to have the capability to simulate the processes that would be developed prior to creating executable code. SDL's formal semantics support this goal very well.

- **Capability to Generate Full Programs**: With the evolution of technology it was apparent that it would be possible to generate full applications. We wanted to be able to take advantage of that technology. Again the formal semantics of SDL support this very well.

- **Automation of Testing :** It is possible to combine SDL with the ITU notation called Tree and Tabular Combined Notation (TTCN). TTCN can be used to describe test cases in a format that enables machine execution on commercial tools. These TTCN test cases can be generated from Message Sequence Charts which are a part of the SDL specification.

We selected SDL as it was the best fit for our needs at that time that we made our selection in early 1994. In retrospect it was a very good choice even though there has been a significant amount of advancement in the CASE tool arena. SDL has allowed us to improve our product development process as well as to provide our engineers with a state of the art tool set. The deployment of full application code generation is a significant step forward towards our goal of a complete tool.

4. GEODE

GEODE is a toolset whose latest release, known as ObjectGEODE, addresses all phases of software development, from requirements analysis to testing. It is developed by Verilog S.A. in France.

The analysis phase of a project is addressed by the construction of the Object Modeling Technique (OMT) model of the system. This includes a description of the objects of the system and a description of the environment of the system. This is done using the OMT Class Diagram editor. Then OMT Instance Diagrams are created. These diagrams illustrate the relations between the instances of objects in the system.

Use–cases and process interaction are described by MSCs created using the MSC editor, and grouped together in scenario diagrams. While these are not currently translated into an SDL skeleton, the data dictionary from the MSC editor as well as the OMT editor is shared with the SDL editor to avoid rework.

Test cases are described in parallel with the design by the successive iterative refinement of the use–cases according to the system architecture, thus ensuring traceability.

The creation of the system architecture is done using the SDL/FSM editor. The SDL editor is used to create the block level description of the system and the channels that connect those blocks. The SDL editor is also used to define the processes that make up the system's blocks. Finally, the FSMs that describe the behaviors of the processes are also constructed using the SDL editor. The design is completed by the description of SDL procedures which contain functionality that does not involve state transitions.

Simulation can then be done using the ObjectGEODE Simulator for verification or rapid prototyping purposes. Incomplete models may also be simulated. Verification is achieved by the developer viewing the behaviors of the system and values of the data variables. Errors such as deadlock, live locks, or dead code are highlighted. The use–cases defined using MSCs are now used as test inputs to the simulator to validate the system.

Simulation may be done in 3 modes : random, interactive, or exhaustive. The mode can be picked depending on the phase the development is in. Random simulation can be used to detect errors quickly. The exhaustive mode can be used to detect all errors. Each error scenario is saved as an MSC to be used to recreate the problem. The simulator also has undo/redo capabilities.

Performance evaluation is done by adding an execution delay to the FSM symbols. Thus simulation can be used to ensure that all possible error scenarios have been detected.

The implementation phase is basically code generation. C code is generated from the SDL part and C++ from the OMT part. The generated code is independent of the target environment at this point. It is integrated into the target by using run–time libraries relevant to the operating system being used. These libraries may be customized for unique operating systems needs or constraints.

The physical architecture of the system on which the application will execute is described with the help of the concept of nodes (or processors) and tasks. The logical SDL structure is mapped into the physical architecture so that the generated code can be optimised. This allows the SDL architecture to remain static while the physical architecture is changed by a modification of the mapping.

The execution of the application on the target generates traces that can be transformed into MSCs. These MSCs may be compared to the MSCs created during analysis and design phases, or be transformed into test programs that can execute on the target environment.

The design can be traced using the Object-GEODE Design Tracer which offers a graphical view of the execution of the system on the target, which can also be saved and replayed later. All these execution scenarios can be transformed into MSCs and can be viewed from the MSC editor to verify consistency with the SDL design.

Tree and Tabular Combined Notation (TTCN) tests can be automatically generated using the TTCgeN tool. The test objectives can be described using MSCs. All of the generated tests can be integrated with any TTCN test environment that is commercially available today.

Another tool is the ProjectOrganizer which facilitates the management of components of the system. These could be requirements, design, or source code. Properties such as ownership and status are highlighted. All the other tools within the toolset may be invoked from the ProjectOrganizer. Compilers and other such third–party tools can also be integrated in by adding them to customized buttons.

5. CODE GENERATION AND COMPILATION USING GEODE

A GEODE application is comprised of :

- a run–time library dedicated to the target OS.
- code generated from GEODE.
- code written by the user for constructs.

Generating a target application could involve upto 3 platforms : the platform for the GEODE tool set, the cross development host to compile and link, and the target platform or executive on which the application will execute.

Through both the generation and compilation phases a mapping from an SDL process to an OS process needs to be specified. An SDL process is a unit of parallelism in the SDL sense, whereas the OS process or task is the unit of parallelism in the target OS. GEODE supports 3 mappings of an OS task : task to SDL process (T/P) mapping, task to SDL process instance (T/I) mapping, task to SDL block or system (T/B) mapping. A block is a collection of parallelisms in SDL, but could be a single parallelism if the target OS does not support T/P mapping.

Code generation requires that a complete SDL design be created, and that the verification for code generation is successful. The steps taken to generate code using GEODE are outlined in Figure 1 [8]. The GEODE C Application Generators can provide fully executable code from the SDL description and generated makefiles to automate the build process. The code generated is independent of individual target systems but can be easily mapped onto such a system via a run–time library provided in source code.

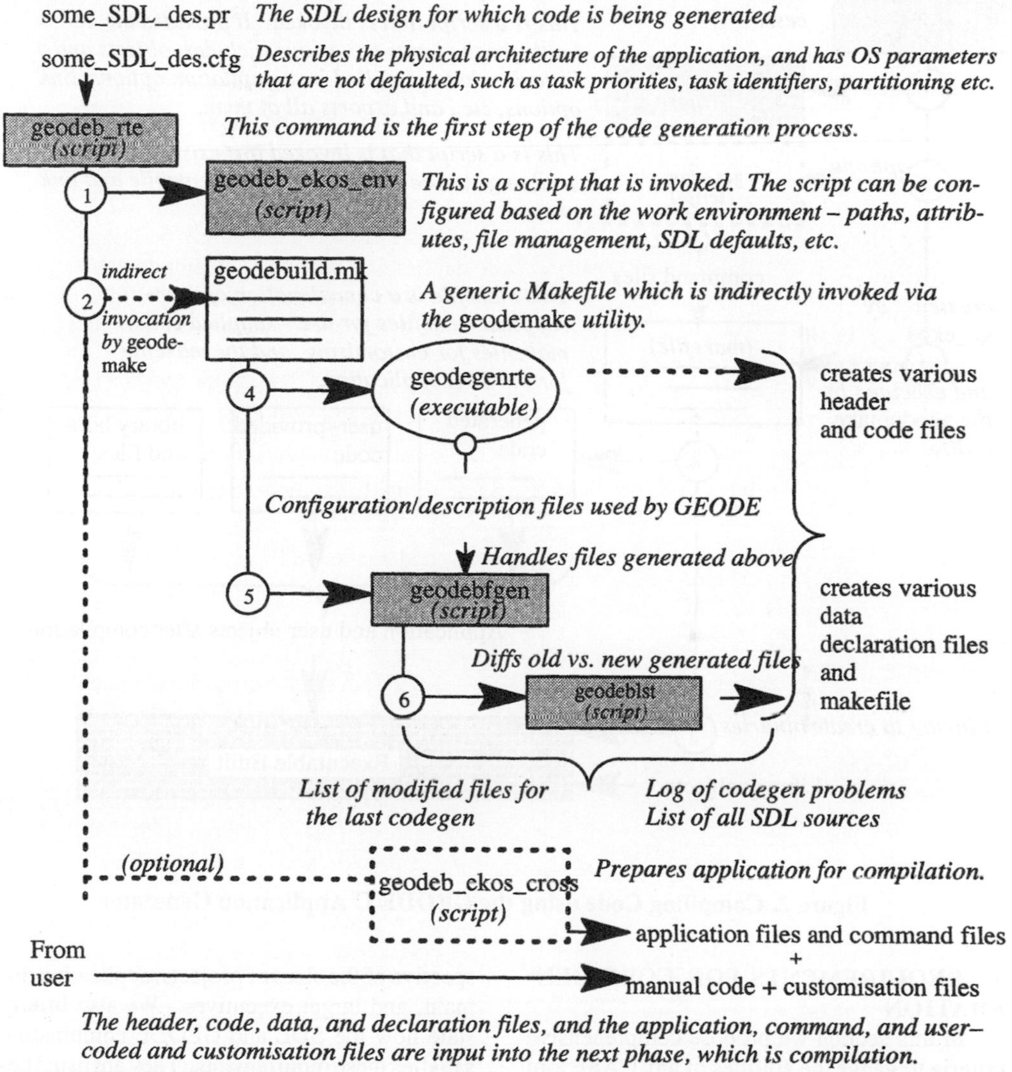
some_SDL_des.pr
The SDL design for which code is being generated
some_SDL_des.cfg
Describes the physical architecture of the application, and has OS parameters that are not defaulted, such as task priorities, task identifiers, partitioning etc.
geodeb_rte (script)
This command is the first step of the code generation process.
1
geodeb_ekos_env (script)
This is a script that is invoked. The script can be configured based on the work environment – paths, attributes, file management, SDL defaults, etc.
indirect
2
invocation by geodemake
geodebuild.mk
A generic Makefile which is indirectly invoked via the geodemake utility.
4
geodegenrte (executable)
creates various header and code files
Configuration/description files used by GEODE
Handles files generated above
5
geodebfgen (script)
creates various data declaration files and makefile
Diffs old vs. new generated files
6
geodeblst (script)
List of modified files for the last codegen
Log of codegen problems
List of all SDL sources
(optional)
geodeb_ekos_cross (script)
Prepares application for compilation.
application files and command files
+
From user
manual code + customisation files
The header, code, data, and declaration files, and the application, command, and user–coded and customisation files are input into the next phase, which is compilation.

Figure 1. Generating Code using the GEODE C Application Generator.

Prior to the actual generation, any custom configuration parameters must be specified using a configuration file specific to the application being generated. This is not required if all parameters are to be defaulted.

The customisation files, generated files, user–provided code and makefiles are all passed into the compilation phase which produces an executable. Figure 2 [8] illustrates the compilation process.

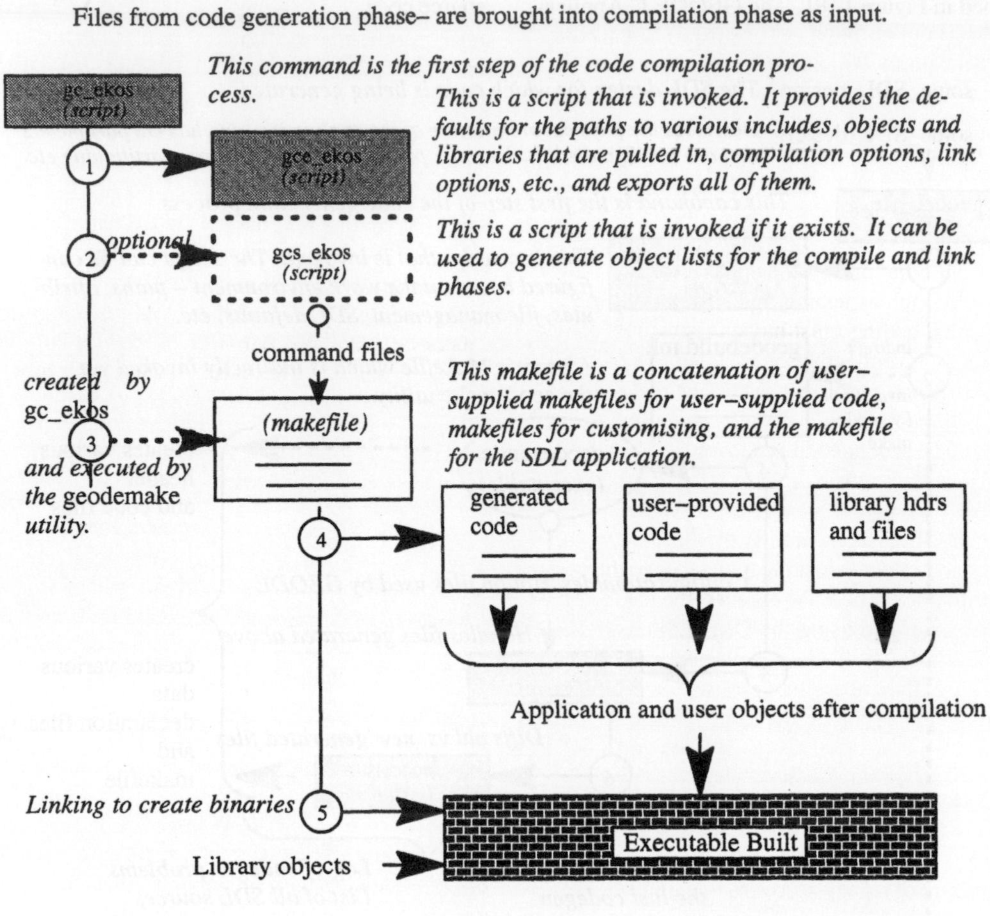
Files from code generation phase– are brought into compilation phase as input.
This command is the first step of the code compilation process.
gc_ekos (script)
1
gce_ekos (script)
This is a script that is invoked. It provides the defaults for the paths to various includes, objects and libraries that are pulled in, compilation options, link options, etc., and exports all of them.
2
optional
gcs_ekos (script)
This is a script that is invoked if it exists. It can be used to generate object lists for the compile and link phases.
command files
created by gc_ekos
3
and executed by the geodemake utility.
(makefile)
This makefile is a concatenation of user–supplied makefiles for user–supplied code, makefiles for customising, and the makefile for the SDL application.
4
generated code
user–provided code
library hdrs and files
Application and user objects after compilation
Linking to create binaries
5
Executable Built
Library objects

Figure 2. Compiling Code using the GEODE C Application Generator.

6. REQUIREMENTS FOR CODE GENERATION

In this section we propose comprehensive criteria to gauge the abilities of any CASE tool that professes to generate code. These are irrespective of the sizes of projects, application domain, and target executives. We also briefly state how the SDL and GEODE combination satisfies these requirements. They are listed below in the approximate order of importance and criticality.

- **Generation of Complete Executables :**
It is essential that the ability to generate code for complete executables exists. Generation of just the header files or a skeleton architecture is not of much use. Partially generated applications which have to be mixed with manual coding will invariably lead to problems unless there is interface–coupling combined with physical segregation of files between the two. The problems will be with the integrity of the software interfaces, configuration management, and lack of support for automation in other phases of the life–cycle, such as testing and simulation. Any manual coding must have an interface coupling with either the source language or with the method / tool that generates the code to avoid these problems. Also, generated code should never need to be corrected or manipulated manually in order to obtain an executable.

GEODE has the ability to generate full applications and not just the interfaces or the skeleton thereof. The FSM is generated in C and the objects defined using the OMTEditor are generated in C++. If there is no external / legacy code involved then the application is immediately ready to run on the target executive.

- **Interfacing with Legacy / External Code :**
This is extremely important for development organizations that have a significant amount of legacy software that can't be discarded. Also, it is sometimes necessary to interface with external routines that are more optimal or less cumbersome than the source constructs for implementing certain functionalities. Facilities and constructs that allow this must exist or else the tool is doomed to limited usage or none at all.

Most methodologies and CASE tools fail in satisfying this critical requirement, as they assume or require involvement from the initial stages of the project. This is what prevents projects from adopting most CASE tools in mid–stream even if these tools are suitable to other needs.

The SDL ADT construct interfacing with external routines that could be legacy or new external code. The interface to these routines must be defined in SDL in order to be visible to the generated code that calls it and GEODE generates the C function prototypes based on the SDL description of the interface, thus maintaining integrity.

- **Customisation :**
It is imperative that the ability to customise is provided by the tool. Customisation is needed for the target executive parameters, configuration management and development environment parameters, source language / method constructs, generation and compilation parameters, and pre– and post–processing when mapping source constructs into target OS equivalents.

- **Isolation of Generated Files :**
All of the above must be achieved without any manipulation of the generated code or any ancillary entities such as generated scripts or makefiles. Any manual updating of generated files is counter–productive. This is important for maintaining the integrity of the application. All customisation must be completely segregated from the generated files and achieved without manipulation of the same.

GEODE provides facilities for both of the above needs, and all of this is done external to the generated files. Generated files are not changed manually, and all external code is maintained in separate files that are segregated physically but integrated by interface. Only the interface for the ADT routines is in generated files. The implementation is physically separated. Also, all customisation is achieved without changing any generated file.

- **De–coupling of Source Language / Constructs from Target Executive :**
This is very important for portability from

one platform to another, although such migration is rare for large systems.

Code generated using GEODE is completely independent and de–coupled from the target executive. It is generated in C++ and C using generic constructs. Only during compilation does the translation occur from these constructs into those supported by the target executive.

- **Readability / Structure / Organization :**

  At first glance this does not seem to be an issue since the generated code is not reviewed or inspected. However, readability of the generated code is important for debugging and maintenance. The code should be reasonably decipherable so that problem investigations are not hindered. The generated code should be structured in a modular and logical manner, along the organization and the structure of the design. This criterion is not important if the target platform supports source level debugging for the source language/method being used.

Code generated from GEODE is well organised. Separate header files are generated for the different levels in the architectural hierarchy, and separate C files are generated for the tasks, procedures, and ADTs. The generated code is adequately readable and structured.

- **Efficiency / Performance / Size Tradeoffs :**

  There should not be significant tradeoffs in terms of execution time or size of the executable, especially in real–time and/or embedded platforms. This may not be as relevant depending on the efficiency and intelligence of the compiler used. In the generated code, constructs provided by the target language that are more efficient than others should be used as applicable.

The code generated from GEODE seems quite efficient using constructs that aid in performance. There's a slight increase in the size of the executable. Performance and executable sizes have not been benchmarked at this point in time, however. We found that generation of some SDL constructs could detract from optimal performance which we are correcting with Verilog's help.

- **Source–level Trace Facilities :**

  Trace facilities that can trace through the source language/method constructs while executing should exist to aid in recreation of problems and in testing.

There is an option to turn on such a facility in GEODE and it displays the lines of source SDL as they're executed. There is also the DesignTracer tool that allows for SDL–level traces.

- **Debugging :**

  Constructs should be available that support debugging needs of the target platform. For instance it may be necessary to make symbols visible to the debugger using special compiler directives.

GEODE provides some hooks to support such debugger needs on a limited basis.

- **Speed of Code Generation :**

  The time taken to generate a particular application should not be more than a few minutes. Large builds of whole subsystems should not be more than a matter of a few hours.

GEODE takes only a few seconds to generate small applications. While benchmarking has not been done yet, we are confident that it will be within acceptable standards for large applications.

- **Automated Testing :**

  It would be very desirable to have facilities to test the generated applications. This would involve both generation of test cases and execution of test cases.

GEODE provides a simulator as detailed earlier which test the SDL state machines. It also provides a TTCN test case generator which generates tests for sub–system and system level testing.

- **Selective Generation :**

  It will probably be necessary for large systems to have the ability to selectively generate code, since generation of whole systems for a single minor change is logistically challenging and prohibitive.

GEODE generates all files necessary and then discards any files that have not changed. Generation of the files is necessary to maintain SDL integrity and for visibility into data structures and SDL data entities at different levels in the hierarchy

- **Standards :**
The generated code does not necessarily have to conform to the coding standards of the organization or some standards set by industry. Facilities for adaptation of the generated code to conform to such standards are not necessary, but if provided by the tool then they should be used.

There is no provision in GEODE to generate code conforming to organizational coding standards. However GEODE generates C code per ANSI standards.

7. BENEFITS OF CODE GENERATION

- **Cycle Time Reduction :**
Generation of code using CASE tools can be a significant contributor to the reduction of cycle time. Note that some of the coding effort will shift into the design phase since more detailed designs may be required to generate code and some into the testing phase since more intensive testing may be required.

- **Quality :**
Since manual coding is mostly eliminated, the probability of human error is restricted to that of the non–generated code. There are 3 categories which non– generated code may fall into : code from libraries, code in common objects that are linked into the image, and new code that is manually created to perform functions that could not be modelled in the source design and thus could not be generated. The last 2 categories could be a significant element of risk due to human intervention. However it is hoped that entities in a depository or library are tested thoroughly and are as defect–free as possible. This leaves the last category as the primary source of potential errors.

The use of manual coding will tend to be limited to a small percentage of the total in any application once a library for interfaces into legacy code and useful routines is built up. It is estimated based on the experience of other institutions [7] that for those subsystems that use code generation 90% of the total code can be generated or reused. Therefore this will result in a proportionately small amount of errors.

An improvement in quality of designs may also be seen since the use of the graphical form of SDL results in designs that are easier to understand and review. Also, simulation of designs can help reduce the number of defects in the designs. significantly.

- **Customer Satisfaction :**
This increases because the number of defects that are found post–release is reduced as shown above.

- **Cost Reduction :**
Since the cycle–time to develop the software is reduced, significant savings in cost reduction can be expected. This is especially true for large telecom products where software usually represents about 70% of development costs of communications networks [3].

Another form of cost reduction is the savings of maintenance resources. Since there are fewer defects from coding there is less maintenance.

Another source of cost savings can be the reduction in the number of code reviews or inspections since generated code will not be subject to the same.

- **Pattern / Code Reuse :**
Reuse has many forms and takes place on an informal basis every day. It does not need to be institutionalized in order to happen, although that makes it efficient, easier, prevalent, and possible to quantify accurately. It is

our contention based on experience that for efficient reuse of code, the code being reused has to be well tested, well documented, isolated, and needs to provide atomic functionality. Reuse of routines that are large and have a lot of functionality is dangerous unless all of the functionality is understood well in order to determine what parts to use and not to use. Also, the more functionality there is, the higher the chances that some of the functionality of the routine may not be generic enough which leads to multiple versions of these "reusable" generic routines. Reuse of large, complex and cumbersome routines that provide major functionality will often lead to unnecessary or dead code, be harder to maintain, introduce unnecessary complexity and problems, and be poorly understood.

Code generation will lead to the reuse of smaller routines that provide atomic functionality since the major functionality will be modelled in the source language / method such as SDL and therefore be generated. This will create a need for the creation and reuse of small and atomic routines.

A more natural and daily occurrence in real–world software development than code reuse is pattern reuse. Pattern reuse will also occur by creating a library of source language algorithmic constructs that can be integrated and modified as necessary. These will result in more productive reuse than code reuse since a source language construct will probably result in more than a single SLOC when generated.

- **Productivity :**
Increased productivity can be achieved through code generation and code and pattern reuse.

8. COSTS OF CODE GENERATION

Costs associated with code generation are mostly initial startup costs. Examples are the purchase of the code generation tools, purchase of other supporting tools, training costs, and the cost of building up an environment that facilitates it. The environmental needs are that of processes, procedures, standards, templates, and configuration management, and can be substantive.

9. ASSOCIATED ISSUES OF CODE GENERATION

- **Longer Design Phase :**
Any tool or method that leads to code generation will require a certain level of detail for completeness and preciseness. This may be more detailed than the norm for some organizations, thus leading to a longer design phase than expected. If simulation is incorporated into the design phase then it will be further lengthened.

- **Testing :**
This is one of the first issues brought up by developers – how to test generated code? Does unit testing apply? Does integration testing apply?

Most of the errors found in unit testing usually are introduced in coding. These would be not be present in generated code. Therefore unit testing is really not applicable. The balance of errors should be caught by intensive functional testing at the program level and by simulation. Testing should focus on mapping to the designs and ensuring that the functionality of the design is represented by the code.

- **Debugging :**
Another one of the first questions is : how is debugging done? If the code is readable and easy to follow, then debugging is made easier. Also, there may be tools in the toolset that provide an integrated source–level debugging facility or some trace facility to allow recreating a problem. If this is not available, then one may need to be developed. Also, people will need to get used to debugging at a higher level than the source code. There may be a need for tools that provide design level debugging.

- **Configuration Management :**
The issues here are with configuration man-

agement of both the source level files that comprise the design, and the files that contain the generated code. Integration with existing configuration management tools/environments may be required. Sometimes these efforts are prohibitive for a small organization, and it may be necessary to buy additional off–the–shelf products.

- **Mindset Change :**
A big hurdle to overcome is mindset. The mindset of engineers who justifiably pride themselves on their ability to stay up several nights in a row and debug the minutest code problem, the mindset of engineers who have spent countless hours cleaning up problem code and so mistrust anyone else's code, and the traditional and understandable mistrust and resistance of any tool taking over part of their jobs. There is also the perceived loss of complete control of the code in the applications they develop.

Any mindset change can be initiated by pointing out the benefits to everyone and then letting the inevitable happen. Software engineers are quick to adapt and try out new concepts and tools, and when some of the drudgery of the job is reduced, then it will be welcomed.

- **The Pipe–Dream Syndrome :**
There are those who question that it is even possible to generate whole applications, or question the efficiency and quality of any generated code. Any such code, they argue, is only as good as the developer of the tool, and aspersions are cast on the abilities or quite often the ancestry of said developer. To counter this argument we remind these protagonists of the commonplace usage of compilers, design tools upon whom we may depend on to verify the design, simulators to test our application and debuggers to investigate or patch them. Also, convincing proof of the fact that complete applications can be generated needs to be shown.

- **Not Always Applicable :**
There will be certain applications which are not suited to the source language being used and these will still be coded as before.

- **Process Compatibility / Impacts :**
There will be impacts to the development process. Inspections for generated code will be eliminated, the intensity and logical level of testing has to be decided upon, estimation formulae revised, potentially new metrics may need to be collected, the content and structure of the designs, standards for designs, training / documentation for the toolset, where simulation fits into the life–cycle, standards, reuse, and many other issues will arise and have to be resolved in order to make this successful.

- **Impacts to Environment and Other Tools :**
Project management tools such as any change control tools may need to be adapted to a new process with different steps for coding. Some build tools may be impacted by the need to invoke necessary pre–processors or unique needs of the code generator. Other tools such as code count tools may need to be adapted to generated code.

- **Metrics / Measurement / Benchmarking :**
This is is very important to prove or disprove the benefits of using any CASE tool, especially those for code generation. Metrics that provide measurements of developer productivity, cycle time reduction, image sizes, software performance measurements, and software quality improvements need to be identified, benchmarked and collected.

10. CONCLUSION

Using SDL and GEODE to design and develop real–time applications has the potential to significantly impact the coding phase and with the ability to generate whole applications. Although there will be startup costs, these are to be expected and the benefits and savings will far outweigh the initial outlay.

Even without automation of other phases the generation of code will be a significant contribution to the reduction of cycle time.

While code generation may not be the proverbial silver bullet, it is definitely one of the steps necessary for cycle time reduction. Experiences have shown [6] that a 4:1 reduction in cycle time can be achieved by using SDL and GEODE for code generation.

It is also a key step to deliver on our promise to our customers that we will provide them with just what they demand and need: world–class software delivered yesterday. It is one of the many changes we need to make in order to propel us into the next millennium ahead of the competition.

11. REFERENCES

[1] Ferenc Belina, Dieter Hogrefe and Amardeo Sarma, *"SDL with Applications from Protocol Specification"*, Prentic Hall, 1991.

[2] A. Olsen, O. Faergemand, B. Moller–Pedersen, R. Reed, J.R.W. Smith, *"Systems Engineering Using SDL–92"*, North–Holland, 1994.

[3] Vincent Encontre, *"Software Development for Cellular Systems"*, TELECOMMUNICATIONS, May 1995.

[4] Magnus W. Froburg, *"Automatic code generation from SDL to a declarative programming language"*, Proceedings of the SDL '93 Forum.

[5] Matthew Englehart, *"High Quality Automatic Code Generation for Control Applications"*, IEEE, May 1994.

[6] Steven F. Mazure, *"Increased Productivity using GEODE in the Development of the ORBCOMM System"*, Verilog Communication, Summer 1993.

[7] Milenko Alain, Mathaz Dolenc, Ana Robnik, *"Industrial Experience on using SDL in Iskratel"*, Proceedings of the SDL '95 Forum.

[8] Verilog, Inc., *"GEODE C Application Generators – Reference Manual"*, 1995.

AUTHOR INDEX

Printed and bound by CPI Group (UK) Ltd, Croydon, CR0 4YY
03/10/2024
01040430-0015